Liferay Portal 6 Enterprise Intranets

Build and maintain impressive corporate intranets with Liferay

Jonas X. Yuan

[PACKT] open source
community experience distilled
PUBLISHING

BIRMINGHAM - MUMBAI

Liferay Portal 6 Enterprise Intranets

First published: April 2010

Production Reference: 1230410

Published by Packt Publishing Ltd.
32 Lincoln Road
Olton
Birmingham, B27 6PA, UK.

ISBN 978-1-849510-38-7

www.packtpub.com

Cover Image by Karl Swedberg (karl@englishrules.com)

Credits

Author
Jonas X. Yuan

Reviewer
Amine Bousta

Acquisition Editor
Dilip Venkatesh

Development Editor
Mehul Shetty

Technical Editors
Aditya Belpathak

Alfred John

Charumathi Sankaran

Copy Editors
Leonard D'Silva

Sanchari Mukherjee

Indexers
Hemangini Bari

Rekha Nair

Editorial Team Leader
Aanchal Kumar

Project Team Leader
Lata Basantani

Project Coordinator
Shubhanjan Chatterjee

Proofreaders
Aaron Nash

Lesley Harrison

Graphics
Geetanjali Sawant

Nilesh Mohite

Production Coordinators
Avinish Kumar

Aparna Bhagat

Nilesh Mohite

Cover Work
Aparna Bhagat

About the Author

Dr. Jonas X. Yuan is a Senior Technical Analyst at CIGNEX. He holds a Ph. D. in Computer Science from the University of Zurich, specializing in Integrity Control in Federated Database Systems. He earned his M.S. and B.S. degrees from China, where he conducted research on expert systems for predicting landslides. Jonas is experienced in Systems Development Life Cycle (SDLC). Previously, he worked as a Project Manager and a Technical Architect in Web GIS (Geographic Information System). He has hands-on skills in J2EE technologies. Most importantly, he has developed a BPEL (Business Process Execution Language) Engine called BPELPower from scratch in the NASA data center. He has a lot of experience with content management and publishing such as Media/Games/Publishing. He is also an expert on Liferay Portal, Content Management Systems (CMS) Alfresco, Ad Server OpenX, BPM Intalio, Business Intelligence Pentaho, LDAP, and SSO.

Acknowledgement

I would like to thank all my team members at Liferay, specially Raymond Auge, Brian Chan, Bryan Cheung, Jorge Ferrer, Michael Young, Jerry Niu, Ed Shin, Craig Kaneko, Brian Kim, Bruno Farache, Thiago Moreira, Amos Fong, Scott Lee, David Truong, Alexander Chow, Mika Koivisto, Julio Camarero, Douglas Wong, Ryan Park, Eric Min, John Langkusch, Marco Abamonga, Ryan Park, Eric Min, John Langkusch, Marco Abamonga, Michael Han, Samuel Kong, Nate Cavanaugh, Arcko Duan, Richard Sezov, Joshua Asbury, Shuyang Zhou of Liferay for providing all the support and valuable information.

A special thanks to all my team members at CIGNEX for making this book a reality. I would like to thank Paul Anthony, Munwar Shariff, and Rajesh Devidasani for their encouragement and great support; our sales and presales team, Amit Babaria, Harish Ramachandran, helped me understand what customers are looking at. Our consulting team Robert Chen, Mike Walker, Venkata Challagulla, Michael Venford and Frank Yu presented me the various flavors of Liferay implementations with real-life examples. I am thankful to them.

I sincerely thank and appreciate Dilip Venkatesh and Mehul Shetty, Senior Acquisition Editor and Development Editor respectively at Packt Publishing for criticizing and fixing my writing style. Thanks to Aditya Belpathak, Alfred John, Charumathi Sankaran, Shubhanjan Chatterjee and entire team at Packt Publishing; it is really joyful to work with them.

Last but not least, I would like to thank my parents and my wife, Linda, for their love, understanding and encouragement. My special thanks to my wonderful and understanding kid Joshua.

About the Reviewer

Amine Bousta is a French Senior Technical Analyst in Groupe Open. He holds a French diploma of Computer Engineering (equivalent to master's degree) and a Technology Research Diploma in Artificial Intelligence (neural networks applied to e-commerce). Specialized in JEE, he monitors and studies most of the related technologies and open source products in order to apply them as solutions for various companies' needs. From 2007, his technology watch on open source Java Portal Engines led to Liferay Portal as the most flexible and complete free portlets engine. The Liferay Community Site gave him the opportunity to meet Dr Jonas X. Yuan and read his previous publications, then become the technical reviewer of this book.

I would like to warmly thank my family, my dear co-workers, and my friends for not spamming me with their usual pointless technical questions while I was reviewing this book!

So... my special thanks to the following List of Nominees in Java Harassment Category: Julien Nicolet, Laurent Witt, Jacques Scius, Nicolas Burg, Olivier Spieser, Angelo Zerr, Olivier Dub, Diana Garzon, Hadrien Beaufils, Mohamadou Kane, and Mohamed Cherroud.

And in the Microsoft-Software-Time-Wasting-Questions Category: my beloved mom and sister. ;-)

Table of Contents

Preface

When you plan to build an amazing website based on a portal, you may commonly consider a lot of questions. Some of them might be:

- Are you planning to build a website with an open source enterprise portal solution using SOA framework, ESB, and Web 2.0 technologies?

- Do you want to add collaborative tools, like Wikis, Blogs, Discussion Forums, Shared Calendar, RSS, mail, folksonomy and taxonomy, instant messaging, knowledge base, and tools for building social networking and Social Office in the same website?

- Do you want to manage, publish (both locally and remotely), maintain and audit web content, documents, and many other assets in the same website?

- Are you eager to integrate with LDAP, SSO, and third-party systems such as JBoss jBPM, Drools, Solr, Alfresco, OpenX, Terracotta, Orbeon Forms, and Pentaho BI/Reporting in the same website?

Liferay would be the best choice in terms of answering the above questions. Liferay Portal is one of the most mature portal frameworks in the market and offers the above basic benefits. Liferay is backed by a comprehensive professional services network, and it offers custom development, training, and support across the world.

As the world's leading open source portal platform, Liferay provides a unified web interface to data and tools scattered across many sources. Within Liferay Portal, a portal interface is composed of a number of portlets — self-contained interactive elements that are written to a particular standard. Since portlets are developed independently of the portal itself, and loosely coupled with the portal, they are apparently **SOA (Service-Oriented Architecture)**.

Liferay has a wide range of portlets freely available for things such as Blogs, Calendar, Document Library, Image Gallery, Mail, Message Boards, Polls, RSS feeds, Wiki, folksonomies and taxonomies, Auditing, Reporting, Rule base, Knowledge base, and many others. Liferay Portal also ships with Liferay **CMS (Content Management Systems)** and **WCM (Web Content Management)**, which provides a lot of ECMS (Enterprise Content Management Systems) features. If you need a robust enterprise content management system then you can integrate it with Alfresco. Liferay is a good portal on top for small team collaboration. The data for events can be specific to a small group within a company. In any organization, some data will be relevant at a team level—and other data, across the whole business. Liferay has very good support for such things.

As the world's leading open source enterprise portal solution, Liferay portal uses the latest in Java, J2EE, and Web 2.0 technologies in order to deliver solutions to enterprises across both the public and private sectors. Meanwhile, Liferay CMS and WCM publish, manage, maintain and audit web content, documents, and other assets. In addition, Collaboration Suite takes advantage of the benefits of the virtualized work environment for collaboration; Social Office provides a social collaboration solution for the enterprise—full virtual workstation streamlines communication, saving you time, building group cohesion, and raising productivity. The best part of Social Office is that you don't need any IT intervention—all you have to do is install and log in.

This book is your complete guide to build an intranet with Liferay—assess your needs, install the software, start using it, deploy portlets, customize as per your requirements, and train users. The book focuses on leveraging the Liferay framework by configuring the XML files and the properties files without changing the underlying Java code.

What this book covers

Chapter 1: Introducing Liferay for Your Intranet introduces Liferay portal, CMS and WCM, collaboration, social networking, and Social Office.

Chapter 2: Setting Up a Home Page and Navigation Structure for the Intranet discusses how to implement a portal page with portlets. It also shows how to customize the look and feel of pages and portlets through themes and look and feel preferences. It helps us understand the portal, portlet container, and portlet according to the JSR-286 specification—how to set up the portal, including installation options and deployment matrix, how to configure the home page and all the other pages of the intranet website. Then it introduces us to building basic pages, as well as setting up the portal pages. Going further, it discusses how to navigate the structure of the intranet via portlets, for example, Site Map, Breadcrumb, and Navigation. It also shows how to configure the portal, how to customize the Dock bar menu, and how to configure database and mail. Finally, it provides guidance to bring pages together in action, to share any portlet within a portal page, and to customize the Control Panel.

Chapter 3: Bringing in Users first introduces how to create and manage organizations and locations and teams; how to add users and manage (for example, view, search, update, deactivate, restore, delete, and impersonate) users; how to add user groups and manage (for example, view, search, update, delete, and assign) user groups. Then it introduces how to integrate with different authentication servers: LDAP, LDAP, CAS, NTLM, OpenID, OpenSSO (renamed as OpenAM), SiteMinder. Further, it introduces how to manage permissions, and how to add roles and manage (for example, view, search, update, delete, and assign) roles.

Chapter 4: Forums, Categorization, and Asset Publishing describes how we can add categories and subcategories in Message Boards. Then it discusses how to add a tag and manage (add, delete, and update) categories and vocabulary, as well as how to tag assets and display tags. Finally, it addresses how to publish assets through the Asset Publisher portlet and how to configure and customize the Asset Publisher portlet.

Chapter 5: Wikis, Web Forms, and Polls introduces how to add and manage (view, update, and delete) nodes of Wikis, to add pages at the nodes in Wikis, to manage (view, update, delete, and search) pages for a given node in Wikis, to use permissions of Wikis portlet and permissions on nodes, and to publish Wiki articles in the intranet first. Then it introduces how to set up Web Form in order to collect users' suggestions, to configure polls and to display the survey in order to assess public opinions. In addition, it introduces how to integrate OpenOffice, Orbeon forms, and Alloy UI forms briefly.

Chapter 6: Blogs, WYSIWYG Editors, and RSS introduces how to add entries of Blogs; how to manage (for example, view, update, and delete) entries of Blogs; and how to add comments for a given entry of Blogs first. Then it discusses how to assign permissions on the Blogs portlet and entries of Blogs. It also introduces the ways to publish Blogs by Recent Bloggers portlet and Blogs Aggregator portlet and to build Blogs with the WYSIWYG editor CKEditor. Finally, it discusses RSS and related portlets the RSS portlet, Weather portlet, Announcements portlet, and Alerts portlet.

Chapter 7: Roll Out to Other Teams introduces the communities portlet, discussed how to add a community; first how to manage (edit, delete, search, join, leave) communities and teams. Then it discusses how to add and manage the pages and users within a community; to assign permissions on communities, and to show what's different between organization and community. How to employ community virtual hosting is also introduced. Further, it discusses how to use stage, preview, and publish websites, and manage staging workflow. Scheduling and remote publishing are also addressed in detail. Finally, it introduces how to use community tools, for example, my communities, bookmarks, invitation, directory, and so on.

Chapter 8:CMS and WCM introduces how to add folders and sub folders for images; to manage folders and sub folders; to add images in folders and manage images; to set up permission on folders and images first. Then it discusses how to add folders and sub folders for documents; to manage documents, to add comments, to give your rating, to view versions; to set up permission on folders and documents; and to publish documents. Moreover, it introduces structures management, templates management and articles management. It emphasizes how to build articles based on structures and templates, and how to set up permissions on Web Content Management, articles, templates, structures, and Feeds. Finally, it introduces how to publish articles and to employ other WCM tools. In a word, WCM doesn't only provide high availability to publish, manage, and maintain web contents and documents, but it also separates content from the layout.

Chapter 9: Social Office, Hooks, and Custom Fields introduces how to add a participant for chatting; to manage (view and delete) participants in a chat portlet; to start chatting; and to set up a chat portlet first. Then it discusses how to manage (check, delete, add, reply, forward, search) emails and further, to set up a mail portlet properly. It states how to manage a SMS Text Messenger portlet and to send SMS text messages. Then it mainly discusses how to build social office with so-theme, so-portlet together with hooks and other portlets. Finally it states how to apply custom fields on any assets.

Chapter 10: Search, WAP, CRM, Widgets, Reporting, and Auditing introduces how to employ federated search and how to integrate search against content from plugins first. Then it discusses how to use CSZ search and map search portlets. In particular, it discusses the OpenSearch concept. It also introduces Web Content search and how to configure sitemap and pluggable enterprise search. Finally, it discusses plugins management, WAP sites, reporting, auditing, CRM, and Widgets.

Chapter 11: Ongoing Admin Tasks introduces system administration which provides the ability to view sever information, to create and manage instances. Moreover, it discusses monitoring portal and portlets operations, dynamic data source (database read-writer), and database sharding. Then it introduces portal administration, which doesn't just allow users with permissions to manage users, organizations, user groups, and roles; but also shows portal settings information, password policies, and monitors users' activities. It also addresses how to build a clustering environment, how to back up data and migrate data, and how to speed up the portal. In addition, it discusses full integration with Alfresco by web services, RESTful services such as OpenSearch, and moreover, CMIS. Further, it introduces full integration of LDAP, SSO CAS, Liferay, and Alfresco. Finally, it discusses Ad Server OpenX integration.

What you need for this book

This book uses Liferay portal version 6.0.2 with the following settings:

- MySQL database 5.1
- Java SE 6.0
- Liferay portal bundled with Tomcat 6.0

Optionally, you can also work in both Windows and Linux with the following settings:

- Liferay portal 6 or higher, either CE Community Edition or EE Enterprise Edition
- Java SE 5.x
- Liferay portal bundled with JBoss + Tomcat 5.x
- MySQL database 5.x

You can use one of following bundles with any database in almost any OS. Geronimo + Tomcat, Glassfish 3, Glassfish 2 for AIX, Glassfish 2 for Linux, Glassfish 2 for OS X, Glassfish 2 for Solaris, Glassfish 2 for Solaris (x86), Glassfish 2 for Windows, JBoss + Tomcat 4.2, JBoss + Tomcat 5.x, Jetty, JOnAS + Jetty, JOnAS + Tomcat, Resin, Tomcat 5.5, Tomcat 6.x.

Who this book is for

This book is for beginners to Liferay and "Do-It-Yourselfers" who want to develop a simple but powerful corporate Intranet. The book assumes technical confidence but does not require specialist administrator or developer skills.

Conventions

In this book, you will find a number of styles of text that distinguish between different kinds of information. Here are some examples of these styles, and an explanation of their meaning.

Code words in text are shown as follows: " You can override these properties in `portal-ext.properties`."

A block of code will be set as follows:

```
<swimlane name="user_admin">
<assignment class="com.liferay.jbpm.handler.IdentityAssignmentHandler"
config-type="field">
<type>role</type>
<companyId>liferay.com</companyId>
<id>1001</id>
```

New terms and important words are introduced in a bold-type font. Words that you see on the screen, in menus or dialog boxes for example, appear in our text like this: "**Permission** is an action on a resource."

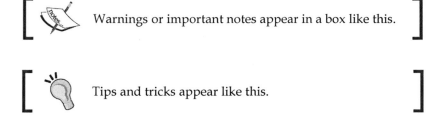

> Warnings or important notes appear in a box like this.

> Tips and tricks appear like this.

Reader feedback

Feedback from our readers is always welcome. Let us know what you think about this book, what you liked or may have disliked. Reader feedback is important for us to develop titles that you really get the most out of.

To send us general feedback, simply drop an email to feedback@packtpub.com, making sure to mention the book title in the subject of your message.

If there is a book that you need and would like to see us publish, please send us a note in the SUGGEST A TITLE form on www.packtpub.com or email suggest@packtpub.com.

If there is a topic that you have expertise in and you are interested in either writing or contributing to a book, see our author guide on www.packtpub.com/authors.

Customer support

Now that you are the proud owner of a Packt book, we have a number of things to help you to get the most from your purchase.

Downloading the example code for the book

Visit http://www.packtpub.com/files/code/0387_Code.zip to directly download the example code.

The downloadable files contain instructions on how to use them.

Errata

Although we have taken every care to ensure the accuracy of our contents, mistakes do happen. If you find a mistake in one of our books—maybe a mistake in text or code—we would be grateful if you would report this to us. By doing this you can save other readers from frustration, and help to improve subsequent versions of this book. If you find any errata, report them by visiting http://www.packtpub. com/support, selecting your book, clicking on the Submit Errata link, and entering the details of your errata. Once your errata are verified, your submission will be accepted and the errata are added to the list of existing errata. The existing errata can be viewed by selecting your title from http://www.packtpub.com/support.

Questions

You can contact us at questions@packtpub.com if you are having a problem with some aspect of the book, and we will do our best to address it.

1
Introducing Liferay for your Intranet

This book will show you how to create a company Intranet with Liferay. In this chapter, we will look at:

- The features your intranet will have by the time you reach the end of this book
- How Liferay is an excellent choice for building your intranet
- Some other things people are using Liferay for, besides intranets
- Finding more technical information about what Liferay is and how it works

So let's begin by looking at exactly what kind of site we're going to build in this book.

What are we going to build?

Over the course of this book, we're going to build a complete corporate Intranet using Liferay. Let's discuss some of the features your intranet will have.

Hosted discussions

Are you still using e-mail for group discussions? Then it's time you found a better way! Running group discussions over e-mail clogs up the team's inbox—this means you have to choose your distribution list in advance, and that makes it hard for team members to 'opt in and out' of the discussion.

Using Liferay, we will build a range of discussion boards for discussion within and between teams. The discussions are archived in one place, meaning that it's always possible to go back and refer to them later.

On one level, it's just more convenient to move e-mail discussions to a discussion forum designed for the purpose. But once the forum is in place, you will find that a more productive group discussion takes place here than ever did over e-mail.

Collaborative documents using wikis

Your company probably has guideline documents that should be updated regularly, but swiftly lose their relevance as practices and procedures change. Even worse, each of your staff will know useful, productive tricks and techniques—but there's probably no easy way to record that knowledge in a way that is easy for others to find and use.

We will see how to host 'wikis' within Liferay. A wiki enables anybody to create and edit web pages, and link all of those web pages together without requiring any HTML or programming skills. You can put your 'guideline' documents into a wiki, and as practices change, your frontline staff can quickly and effortlessly update the guideline documentation.

Wikis can also act as a shared notebook, enabling team members to collaborate and share ideas and findings, and work together on documents.

Team and individual blogs

Your company probably needs frequent, chronological publications of personal thoughts and web links in the intranet. Your company probably has teams and individuals working on specific projects in order to share files and blogs about a project process and more. You can use HTML text editors to create or update files and blogs and to provide RSS feeds.

We will see how teams and individuals share files and blogs within Liferay. Blogs provide a straightforward blogging solution with features such as RSS support, user and guest comments, *browsable* categories, tags and labels, and an entry rating system. Liferay's RSS with subscription feature provides the ability to frequently read RSS feeds from within the portal framework.

At the same time, **What You See Is What You Get (WYSIWYG)** editors provide the ability to edit web content, including the blogs' content. Less technical people can use the WYSIWYGs editor instead of sifting through complex code.

Shared calendars

Your company may be required to provide calendar information and share the calendar among users from different departments. At the same time, it is required to provide workflow ability, such that normal users can submit requests and the manager can make a decision on the requests. Moreover, it is required to publish third-party content on the intranet website.

We will see how to share a calendar within Liferay. The shared calendar can satisfy the basic business requirements incorporated in a featured business intranet such as scheduling meetings, sending meeting invitations, checking for attendees' availability, and so on. Therefore, you can provide an environment for users to manage events and share calendar.

Furthermore, you can employ a **Web Services** for **Remote Portlets (WSRP)** proxy effectively, as well as other portlets smoothly such as the web proxy portlet, the IFrame portlet, and the flash portlet—to share portlets, also known as applications.

Document stores—CMS

Within Image Gallery, you can add folders and subfolders for images, manage folders and subfolders, add images to folders, manage those images, and set up permissions on folders and images. Within Document Library, you can add folders and subfolders for documents to manage and publish documents. The Image Gallery and Document Library make **Content Management Systems** (**CMS**) available for intranets. Both of them are equipped with customizable folders and act as a web-based shared drive for all your team members, no matter where they are. As content is accessible only by those authorized by administrators, each individual file (either a document or an image) is as open or as secure as you would need it to be.

Web Content Management—WCM

Your company may have a lot of images and documents, and you may need to manage all these images and documents as well. Therefore, you require the ability to manage a lot of web content, and then publish web content in intranets.

We will see how to manage web content and how to publish web content within Liferay. Liferay Journal (Web Content) not only provides high availability to publish, manage, and maintain web content and documents, but it also separates content from layout. WCM allows us to create, edit, and publish web content (articles) as well as article templates for one-click changes in layout. It has built-in workflow, article versioning, search, and metadata.

Personalization and internalization

All users can get a personal space that can be either made public (published as a website with a unique, friendly URL) or kept private. You can also customize how the space looks, what tools and applications are included, what goes into the Document Library and Image Gallery, and who can view and access all of this content.

In addition, you can use your own language. Multilingual organizations get out-of-the-box support for up to 22 languages. Users can toggle among different language settings with just one click and produce/publish multilingual documents and web content. You can also easily add other languages in your public, and private pages, or other organizations.

Workflow, staging, scheduling, and publishing

You can use a workflow to manage definitions, instances, and tasks. You can also use the Web Content article two-step workflow, **Staging Working**, jBPM workflow, and Intalio | BPMS. In addition, Liferay portal allows you to define publishing workflow that tracks changes to web content as well as the pages of the site in which they live.

Generally speaking, the Web Content article two-step workflow is a step-fixed article-creation and article-approval workflow, which means that you can't configure this workflow. Moreover, this workflow must be applied on Web Content articles only. On the other hand, staging workflow is role-based multiple-step workflow. That is, you can configure this workflow for page creation, page review, and page publishing. In particular, this workflow would be applied on pages of staging environments.

As a content creator, you may update what you've created and publish it in a staging workflow. Other users can then review and modify it. Moreover, content editors could make a decision on whether to publish web content from staging to live. That is, you could easily create and manage everything from a simple article of text and images to fully-functional websites in staging, and then publish them live.

Before going live, you may schedule web content as well. For instance, you may publish web content immediately or schedule it for publishing on a specific date. Furthermore, you may schedule a specific portlet for specific web content. For publishing features, you may choose either local publishing or remote publishing; you may publish either the entire website or just a subset of all the pages. Liferay portal not only provides the capability to stage web content of the website and publish web content either locally or remotely, but it also provides a flexible framework to make the customization and extension of "staging and publishing" easy to use.

Social network and Social Office

Liferay portal supports social networks—you can easily manage your Facebook, MySpace, Twitter, and other social network accounts in Liferay. In addition, you can manage your instant messenger accounts such as AIM, ICQ, Jabber, MSN, Skype, YM, and so on smoothly from inside Liferay.

Social Office gives us a social collaboration on top of the portal—a full virtual workspace that streamlines communication and builds up group cohesion. All components in Social Office are tied together seamlessly, getting everyone on the same page by sharing the same look and feel. More importantly, the dynamic activity tracking gives us a bird's-eye view of who has been doing what and when within each individual site.

And more...

The intranet will also arrange staff members into teams and communities, provide a way of real-time IM and chatting, and give each user an appropriate level of 'access'. This means that they can get all the information they need; edit and add content as necessary, but won't be able to mess with sensitive information that they have no reason to see.

In particular, the portal provides an integrating framework so that you can integrate external applications easily. For example, you could integrate external applications with the portal such as Alfresco, OpenX, LDAP, SSO CAS, Orbeon Forms, Konakart, PayPal, Solr, and so on.

In a word, the portal offers compelling benefits to today's enterprises—reduced operational costs, improved customer satisfaction, and streamlined business processes.

Everything in one place

All of these features are useful on their own. However, it gets better when you consider that all of these features will be combined in one easy-to-use searchable portal.

A user of the intranet, for example, can search for a topic—let's say 'financial report', and find the following in one go:

- Any group discussions about financial reports
- Blog entries within the intranet concerning financial reports
- Documents and files—perhaps the financial reports themselves

- Wiki entries with guidelines on preparing financial reports
- Calendar entries for meetings to discuss the financial report

Of course, users can also restrict their search to just one area if they already know exactly what they are looking for.

Liferay provides other features such as tagging, in order to make it even easier to organize information across the whole intranet. We will do all of this and more over the course of the book.

Introducing Palm Tree Publications

In this book, we are going to build an intranet for a fictional company as an example; focusing on how to install, configure, and integrate it with other applications and also implement portals and plugins (portlets, themes, layout templates, hooks, and webs) within Liferay. By applying the instructions to your own business, you will be able to build an intranet to meet your own company's needs.

"Palm Tree Publications" needs an intranet of its own, which we will call bookpub.com.

The enterprise's global headquarters are in the United States. It has several departments—editorial, website, engineering, marketing, executive, and human resources.

Each department has staff in United States, in Germany, or both.

The intranet site provides a community called "Book Lovers" consisting of users who have an interest in reading books. The enterprise needs to integrate collaboration tools such as wikis, blogs, discussion forums, instant messaging, mail, RSS, shared calendars, tagging, and so on.

Palm Tree Publications has some more advanced needs too: a workflow to edit, approve, and publish books. Furthermore, the enterprise has a lot of content such as books stored and managed in Alfresco currently. Now, it wants to publish the contents of Alfresco on the intranet website.

In order to build the intranet site, the following functionality should be considered:

- Installing the portal, experiencing the portal and portlets, and customizing the portal and personal web pages.
- Bringing the features of enabling document sharing, calendar sharing, and other collaboration within a business to the users of the portal.

- Discussion forums—employees should be able to discuss book ideas and proposals.
- Wikis—keeping track of information about editorial guidance and other resources that require frequent editing.
- Distribution of knowledge via blogs—small teams working on specific projects share files and blogs about a project process.
- Sharing a calendar among employees and using workflow to manage (edit, approve, and publish) pages within web content among employees.
- Document repository—using effective Content Management Systems (CMS), a natural fit for a portal for secure access, permissions, and distinct roles (such as writers, editors, designers, administrators, and so on).
- Collaborative chat and Instant Messaging, social network and Social Office, and knowledge management tools.
- Managing a community named "Book Lovers" that consists of users who have the same interest in reading books; staging, scheduling, and publishing web content related to books.
- Federated search for discussion forum entries, blog posts, wiki articles, users in Directory, and content in both Document Library and Alfresco; search by tags.
- Integrating back-of-the-house software applications such as Alfresco, Orbeon Forms, Drools rule server, Jasper Server, and BI/Reporting Pentaho. Strong authentication and authorization with LDAP. Single authentication to access various company sites besides the intranet site.

The enterprise may have the following groups of people:

- **Admin**: Installs systems, manages membership, users, user groups, organizations, roles and permissions, security on resources, workflow, servers and instances, and integrates with third-party systems
- **Executives**: Executive management handles approvals
- **Marketing**: Handles websites, company brochures, marketing campaigns, projects, and digital assets
- **Sales**: Presentations, contracts, documents, and reports
- **Website Editors**: Manage pages of the intranet; write articles, review articles, design the layout of articles, and publish articles
- **Book Editors**: Write, review, and publish books, approve and reject publishing of books
- **Human Resources**: Manages corporate policy documents
- **Finance**: Manages account documents, scanned invoices and checks, and notifications

- **Corporate Communications**: Manages external public relations, internal news releases, and syndication
- **Engineering**: Sets up the development environment and collaborates on engineering projects and presentation templates

Liferay portal framework

The Liferay portal architecture supports high availability for mission-critical applications using clustering and the fully–distributed cache and replication support across multiple servers. The following figure depicts the various architectural layers and functionalities of portlets:

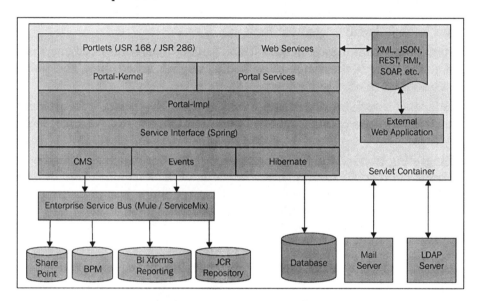

Service Oriented Architecture

Liferay portal uses **Service Oriented Architecture (SOA)** design principles throughout and provides the tools and framework to extend SOA to other enterprise applications. Under Liferay enterprise architecture, not only can the users access the portal from traditional and wireless devices, but the developers can also access it from the exposed APIs via REST, SOAP, RMI, XML-RPC, XML, JSON, Hessian, Burlap, and custom-tunnel classes.

Liferay portal is designed to deploy portlets that adhere to the portlet API compliant with both JSR-168 and JSR-286. A set of useful portlets are bundled with the portal including Image Gallery, Document Library, Calendar, Message Boards, Blogs, Wikis, and so on. They can be used as examples for adding custom portlets.

In a word, the key features of Liferay include using SOA design principles throughout such as reliable security, integrating the portal with SSO and LDAP, multitier and limitless clustering, high availability, caching pages, dynamic virtual hosting, and so on.

Enterprise Service Bus

The **Enterprise Service Bus** (ESB) is a central connection manager that allows applications and services to be added quickly to an enterprise infrastructure. When an application needs to be replaced, it can easily be disconnected from the bus at a single point. Liferay portal uses Mule or ServiceMix as ESB.

Through ESB, the portal could integrate with SharePoint, BPM (such as jBPM workflow engine, Intalio | BPMS engine), BI Xforms reporting, JCR repository, and so on. It supports JSR 170 for Content Management Systems with the integration of JCR repositories such as Jackrabbit. It also uses Hibernate and JDBC to connect to any database. Furthermore, it supports an events system with asynchronous messaging and lightweight message bus.

Liferay portal uses the Spring framework for its business and data services layers. It also uses the Spring framework for its transaction management. Based on service interfaces, `portal-impl` is implemented and exposed only for internal usage—for example, they are used for the extension environment. `portal-kernel` and `portal-service` are provided for external usage (or for internal usage)—for example, they are used for the Plugins SDK environment. Custom portlets, both JSR-168 and JSR-286, and web services can be built based on `portal-kernel` and `portal-service`.

In addition, the Web 2.0 Mail portlet and Chat portlet are supported as well. More interestingly, scheduled staging and remote staging and publishing serve as a foundation through tunnel web for web content management and publishing.

Liferay portal supports web services to make it easy for different applications in an enterprise to communicate with each other. Java, .NET, and proprietary applications can work together easily because web services use XML standards. It also supports REST-style JSON web services for lightweight, maintainable code, and supports AJAX-based user interfaces.

Liferay portal uses industry-standard, government-grade encryption technologies, including advanced algorithms such as DES, MD5, and RSA. Liferay was benchmarked as one of the most secure portal platforms using LogicLibrary's Logiscan suite. Liferay offers customizable single sign-on with Yale CAS, JAAS, LDAP, NTLM, Netegrity, Microsoft Exchange, and more. Open ID, OpenAuth, Yale CAS, Siteminder, and OpenAM integration are offered by it out of the box.

In short, Liferay portal uses the ESB in general, in order to provide an abstraction layer on top of an implementation of an enterprise messaging system. It allows integration architects to exploit the value of messaging without writing code.

Why use Liferay to build an intranet?

Of course, there are lots of ways to build a company intranet. What makes Liferay such a good choice?

It has got the features we need

All of the features we outlined for our intranet come built into Liferay: discussions, wikis, calendars, blogs, and so on are part of what Liferay is designed to do.

It is also designed to tie all of these features together into one searchable 'portal', so we won't be dealing with lots of separate components when we build and use our intranet. Every part will work together.

It's easy to set up and use

Liferay has an intuitive interface that uses icons, clear labels, and drag-and-drop to make it easy to configure and use the intranet.

Setting up the intranet will require a bit more work than using it, of course. However, you will be pleasantly surprised by how simple it is — no programming is required to get your intranet up and running.

It's free and open source

How much does Liferay cost? Nothing! It's a free, open source tool.

Here "being free" means that you can go to Liferay's website and download it without paying anything. You can then go ahead and install it and use it.

Liferay makes its money by providing additional services, including training. However, standard use of Liferay is completely free. Now that you've bought this book, you probably won't have to pay another penny to get your intranet working.

Being open source means that the program code that makes Liferay work is available for anybody to look at and change. Even if you're not a programmer, this is still good for you:

- If you need Liferay to do something new, then you can hire a programmer to modify Liferay to do it.

- There are lots of developers studying the source code, looking for ways to make it better. Lots of improvements get incorporated into Liferay's main code.

- Developers are always working to create 'plugins'—programs that work together with Liferay to add new features.

Probably, for now, the big deal here is that it doesn't cost any money. But as you use Liferay more, you will come to understand the other benefits of open source software for you.

It will grow with you

Liferay is designed in a way that means it can work with thousands and thousands of users at once. No matter how big your business is, or how much it grows, Liferay will still work and handle all of the information you throw at it.

It also has features especially suited for large international businesses. Opening offices up in non-English speaking countries? No problem! Liferay has internationalization features tailored to many of the world's popular languages.

It works with other tools

Liferay is designed to work with other software tools—the ones that you're already using and ones that you might use in the future. For example:

- You can hook Liferay up to your LDAP directory server and SSO so that users' details and login credentials are added to Liferay automatically

- Liferay can work with Alfresco—a popular and powerful Enterprise CMS (used to provide extremely advanced document management capabilities, which are far beyond what Liferay does on its own)

It is based on "standards"

This is a more technical benefit, however, it is a very useful one if you ever want to use Liferay in a more specialized way.

Liferay is based on standard technologies that are popular with developers and other IT experts. These include:

- **Built using Java**: Java is a popular programming language that can run on just about any computer. There are millions of Java programmers in the world, so it won't be too hard to find developers who can customize Liferay.

- **Based on tried and tested components**: With any tool, there's a danger of bugs. Liferay uses lots of well known, widely tested components to minimize the likelihood of bugs creeping in. If you are interested, here are some of the well known components and technologies Liferay uses—Apache ServiceMix, Mule, ehcache, Hibernate, ICEfaces, Java J2EE/JEE, jBPM, Intalio | BPMS, JGroups, Alloy UI, Lucene, PHP, Ruby, Seam, Spring and AOP, Struts and Tiles, Tapestry, Velocity, and FreeMarker.

- **Uses standard ways to communicate with other software**: There are various standards established for sharing data between pieces of software. Liferay uses these so that you can easily get information from Liferay into other systems. The standards implemented by Liferay include AJAX, iCalendar, and Microformat, JSR-168, JSR-127, JSR-170, JSR-286 (Portlet 2.0), JSR-314 (JSF 2.0), OpenSearch, Open platform with support for web services (including JSON, Hessian, Burlap, REST, RMI, and WSRP), WebDAV, and CalDAV.

- **Makes publication and collaboration tools WCAG 2.0 (Web Content Accessibility Guidelines) compliant**: The new W3C Recommendation to make web content accessible to a wide range of people with disabilities, including blindness and low vision, deafness and hearing loss, learning disabilities, cognitive limitations, limited movement, speech disabilities, photosensitivity, and combinations of these. For example, the portal integrates CKEditor - standards support such as W3C (WAI-AA and WCAG), 508 (Section 508).

- **Alloy UI** : Supports HTML 5, CSS 3, and YUI 3 (Yahoo! User Interface Library).

- **Supports Apache Ant 1.8 and Maven 2**: Liferay portal could be built through Apache Ant by default, where you can build services, clean, compile, build JavaScript CMD, build language native to ASCII, deploy, fast deploy, and so on. Moreover, Liferay supports Maven 2 SDK, providing **Community Edition** (CE) releases through public maven repositories as well as **Enterprise Edition** (EE) customers to install maven artifacts in their local maven repository.

Many of these standards are things that you will never need to know much about, so don't worry if you've never heard of them. Liferay is better for using them, but mostly, you won't even know they are there.

What else can Liferay do?

Liferay isn't just for intranets! Users and developers are building all kinds of different websites and systems based on Liferay.

Corporate extranets

An intranet is great for collaboration and information sharing within a company. An extranet extends this facility to suppliers and customers, who usually log in over the Internet.

In many ways, this is similar to an intranet—however, there are few technical differences. The main difference is that you create user accounts for people who are not part of your company.

Collaborative websites

Collaborative websites not only provide a secure and administrated framework, but they also empower users with collaborative tools such as blogs, instant e-mail, message boards, instant messaging, shared calendars, and so on. Moreover, they encourage users to use other tools, such as tags' administration, fine-grained permissions, *delegable* administrator privileges, enterprise taxonomy, and ad-hoc user groups. By means of these tools, as an administrator, you can ultimately control what people can and cannot do in Liferay.

In many ways, this is similar to an intranet too— however, there are a few technical differences. The main difference is that you use collaborative tools simply; such as blogs, instant e-mail, message boards, instant messaging, shared calendar, and so on.

Content management and web publishing

You can also use Liferay to run your public company website with content management and web publishing.

Content management and web publishing are useful features in websites. It is a fact that the volume of digital content for any organization is increasing on a daily basis. Therefore, an effective CMS is vital part of any organization. Meanwhile, document management is also useful and more effective when repositories have to be assigned to different departments and groups within the organization.

Content management and document management are effective in Liferay. Moreover, when managing and publishing content, we may have to answer many questions, such as "who should be able to update and delete a document from the system?". Fortunately, Liferay's security and permissions model can satisfy the needs for secure access and permissions, and distinct roles (for example, writer, editor, designer, and administrator). Furthermore, Liferay integrates with the workflow engine. Thus, users can follow a flow to edit, approve, and publish content in the website.

Content management and web publishing are similar to an intranet— however, there are few technical differences. The main difference is that you can manage content and publish web content smoothly.

Infrastructure portals

Infrastructure portals integrate all possible functions, as we stated previously. This covers collaboration and information sharing within a company, collaborative tools, content management, and web publishing. In the infrastructure portals, users can create a unified interface to work with content, regardless of source via content interaction APIs. Furthermore, by the same API and the same interface as that of the built-in CMS, users can also manage content and publish web contents from third-party systems such as Alfresco, Vignette, Magnolia, FatWire, or Microsoft Share-Point, and so on.

Infrastructure portals also are similar to an intranet— there are a few technical differences. The main difference is that you can use collaborative tools, manage content, publish web contents, and integrate other systems in one place.

Why do you need a portal? The main reason is that a portal can serve as a framework to aggregate content and applications. A portal normally provides a secure and manageable framework where users can easily make new and existing enterprise applications available. In order to build an infrastructure portal smoothly, Liferay portal provides an SOA-based framework to integrate third-party systems.

Finding more information

In this chapter, we have looked at what Liferay can do for your corporate intranet, and briefly seen why it's a good choice.

If you want more background information on Liferay, the best place to start is the Liferay corporate website (`http://www.liferay.com`) itself. You can find the latest news and events, various training programs offered world wide, presentations, demonstrations, and hosted trails. More interestingly, Liferay eats its own dog food; corporate websites within forums (called message boards), blogs, and wikis are built by Liferay using its own products. It is a real demo for the Liferay portal software.

Liferay is 100 percent open source and all downloads are available from Liferay portal website (`http://www.liferay.com/web/guest/downloads/portal`) and the SourceForge website at `http://sourceforge.net/projects/lportal/files`. The source code repository is available at `svn://svn.liferay.com/repos/public` (for the credentials—enter the username `Guest` and no password) and source code can be explored at `http://svn.liferay.com`.

The Liferay website's wiki (`http://www.liferay.com/web/guest/community/wiki`) contains documentation including a tutorial, user guide, developer guide, administrator guide, roadmap, and so on.

The Liferay website's discussion forums can be accessed at `http://www.liferay.com/web/guest/community/forums` and the blogs at `http://www.liferay.com/web/guest/community/blogs`. The road map can be found at `http://www.liferay.com/web/guest/community/wiki/-/wiki/Main/RoadMap`. The official plugins are available at `http://www.liferay.com/web/guest/downloads/official_plugins`.

The community plugins available at `http://www.liferay.com/web/guest/downloads/community_plugins` are the best place to share your thoughts, to get tips and tricks about Liferay implementation, to know about the road map, and to use and contribute community plugins.

If you would like to file a bug or know more about the fixes in a specific release, then you must visit the bug tracking system at `http://issues.liferay.com/`.

Summary

In this chapter, we looked at what Liferay can offer your intranet. Particularly, we saw:

- That our final intranet will provide shared documents, discussions, collaborative wikis, and more in a single, searchable portal
- That Liferay is a great choice for the intranet because it provides so many features, it's easy to use, it's free and open source, extensible, and well integrated with other tools and standards
- What other kinds of sites Liferay is good for—such as extranets, collaborative websites, content management and web publishing, and infrastructure portals
- The various pages on `Liferay.com` that can provide us with more background information

In the next chapter, we're going to install Liferay and start the hands-on task of building the intranet.

2

Setting Up a Home Page and Navigation Structure for the Intranet

This chapter will first assist administrators and normal users in the enterprise "Palm-Tree Publications" with implementing a portal page with portlets. It will then guide us through setting up the portal, building pages, setting up portal pages, and customizing portlets. It will also address how to navigate the structure of intranet websites. Finally, it will provide guidance on configuring the portals, as well as bringing pages together in action. In addition, it will show us how to share portlets within a portal page and how to configure the Control Panel.

By the end of this chapter, you will have learned how to:

- Use a portal page with portlets, get basic knowledge about a portlet, and how the portal works
- Set up the portal
- Build pages
- Set up portal pages
- Customize portlets
- Navigate the structure of the intranet
- Configure the portal
- Bring pages together in action
- Share portlets within a portal page
- Configure the Control Panel

Experiencing the portal

When an administrator at the enterprise **Palm-Tree Publications** say "Palm Tree", you can first experience the portal locally. After starting up the portal, you will see a portal page interface similar to following screenshot, by typing URL `http://localhost:8080` in a browser. Generally speaking, a portal page is made up of a set of portlets — for example, **Sign In**, **Hello World**, plus the company logo, the **Sign In** icon and link, the navigation bar, and the breadcrumb bar. Note that a context path — **/web/guest** and a string **;jsessionid=...** are automatically added after the URL **http://localhost:8080**.

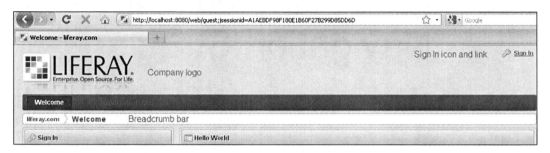

Getting portal pages

Suppose we have a set of variables, where `$PORTAL_VERSION` represents the current portal version, `$LIFERAY_PORTAL` represents the working folder containing the portal that we are planning to install. Logically, you can have a different folder name. But for simplicity, we will use a folder named `Liferay-Portal`. More specifically, you will have a value for `$LIFERAY_PORTAL` — that is, `C\:/Liferay-Portal` in Windows, and `/Liferay-Portal` in Linux, Unix, and Mac OS. In addition, we use a variable `$LIFERAY_HOME` to represent the current folder where the portal is installed. Therefore, we would have the following expression.

```
$LIFERAY_HOME=$LIFERAY_PORTAL/liferay-portal-$PORTAL_VERSION
```

In order to get the preceding portal page with portlets, let's install the portal in your local machine using the following steps:

1. Download the latest Liferay Portal Standard Edition bundled with Tomcat 6.x from the website `http://www.liferay.com/web/guest/downloads/portal`. It is a large file of about 140 MB. You have to wait for a while to download it.

2. Unzip the downloaded file into `$LIFERAY_PORTAL`

3. Remove these folders: $TOMCAT_AS_DIR/webapps/sevencogs-hook and $TOMCAT_AS_DIR/webapps/sevencogs-theme. The variable $TOMCAT_AS_DIR refers to the Tomcat folder under $LIFERAY_HOME. Why? sevencogs is just some sample data that will override the default admin user and the default home page.

4. Run $TOMCAT_AS_DIR/bin/startup.bat for Windows; or $TOMCAT_AS_DIR/bin/startup.sh for Linux. Note that you may need to wait for about 60 seconds for it to start up.

5. Open your browser, and type http://localhost:8080 if it doesn't open automatically.

6. Log in with the e-mail address test@liferay.com and password **test**.

7. Select the I **Agree** option under Terms of **Use**, and answer Test for the reminder question.

Consequently, you can see a portal interface like the one shown in the following screenshot. The portal page shows different content after you have logged in. It consists of portlets; for example, **Sign In, Hello World,** plus a dock bar menu, company logo, navigation bar, and breadcrumb bar. In the **dock bar menu**, there are a few drop-down menus (such as **Add, Manage,** and **Go To**), links (the current logged-in user's display name, that is, **Test Test, Sign Out**), and a checkbox named **Toggle Edit Controls**.

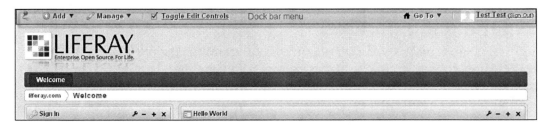

Congratulations! You now have a running copy of the portal. The remainder of this section will explain what a portal is, what a portlet is, and how to implement a portal page with a set of portlets.

Does it work well? Make sure that you have downloaded the latest version of JDK. It is available at `http://java.sun.com` for every OS. You need to install JDK in your local machine and set the `JAVA_HOME` variable as well. This is the only thing you need in order to run the portal properly. Especially in the Windows environment, the bundle will use embedded JRE. You can remove the embedded JRE in the file `$TOMCAT_AS_DIR/bin/setenv.bat` by removing the lines: `if not "%JAVA_HOME%" == "" ( set JAVA_HOME= ) set` and `JRE_HOME=%CATALINA_HOME%/jre1.5.0_22/win`. However, you could use the default version of the JDK that you have just installed instead.

What's happening?

What you have previously seen is a portal page with the name **Welcome**. The portal page **Welcome** has a dock bar menu, a logo, a navigation bar (that is, a list of page names), a breadcrumb bar, a set of portlets, and a footer. When you have logged in, the portal will generate this page automatically. If you select another page name, then the portal will generate another page at runtime.

An intranet website is made up of a set of pages such as **Welcome**. The portal can be used to build and manage these pages smoothly.

Experiencing portlets

A portal page is made up of a set of portlets. For example, the portal page, such as **Welcome**, contains portlets. In this example, they are **Sign In**, **Hello World**, and others. Moreover, the portlet **Sign In** has icons (such as **Look and Feel**, **Configuration**, **Export / Import**, **Minimize**, **Maximize**, and **Remove**), title icon and title (that is **Sign In**), and a window which may contain contents. It's also possible to display a contextual help icon.

Normally, a **portlet** is an application that provides a specific piece of content (such as information or a service) to be included as part of a portal page. It is managed by a portlet container that processes requests and generates dynamic content. Actually, portlets are used by portals as pluggable user interface components that provide a presentation layer to information systems.

Loosely speaking, portlets are fragments of an HTML page—pieces of markup (such as HTML, XHTML, WML, and so on). The content of a portlet is normally aggregated with the content of other portlets to form the portal page. The lifecycle of a portlet is managed by the portlet container. The content generated by a portlet may vary from one user to another, depending on the user's configuration for the portlet.

The portal comes with several useful bundled portlets and also supports JSR-168 / JSR-286 standards 100 percent, which allow the portal to deploy third-party portlets.

What's JSR-168 and JSR-286?

JSR-168 means Portlet Specification 1.0/1.1 and JSR-286 means Portlet Specification 2.0. Refer to `http://jcp.org/en/jsr/detail?id=168` and `http://jcp.org/en/jsr/detail?id=286` for more details.

Using the portlet container

The portlet **Hello World** is running in the portal page. It requires a runtime environment, that is, a portlet container.

Generally, a portlet container provides portlets with persistent storage for preferences and the required runtime environment. A portlet container manages a portlet's lifecycle and receives requests from the portal to execute requests on the portlets. A portlet container is mostly the responsibility of the portal to handle the aggregation.

How does the portal work?

The following is a typical sequence of events, initiated when you access a portal page, for example, the **Welcome** page.

1. A client (for example, "Palm Tree") after being authenticated makes an HTTP request to the portal.

2. The request is received by the portal (for example, the Liferay portal).

3. The portal determines if the request contains an action targeted to the portlets. For example, **Sign In** is associated with the portal page such as **Welcome**.

4. If there is an action targeted to a portlet, for example, **Sign In**, then the portal requests the portlet container to invoke the portlet to process the action

5. The portal invokes portlets such as **Hello World**, **Sign In**, and so on, through the portlet container.

6. The portal aggregates the output of portlets in the portal page and sends it to the client (for example, "Palm Tree").

Working of portlets

Before going deeper, let's add the portlet **Language** to the page **Welcome**. Move your mouse on the **Add** drop-down menu of the dock bar menu, as shown in the following screenshot, and click on the link **More...**. Then drag the portlet **Language** to place it on the page, close the **Search applications** page, and drag the portlet **Language** to the top of the portlet **Hello World**.

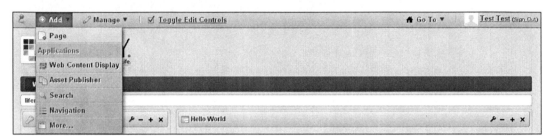

How does the portlet **Language** work? Let's focus on the portlet **Language**, and click on the language icon for Deutsch (Deutschland). You will see that the portal page's language has been changed to German, as shown in the next screenshot.

Furthermore, let's perform one more action on the portlet **Language**. Simply click on the remove icon on the right-hand side corner of the portlet **Language**. You will see a message, "**Are you sure you want to remove this component ?**"—reply to it by clicking on the US flag to see this message page with an **OK** button. Then you can click on the **OK** button. You will see that the portlet **Language** has disappeared.

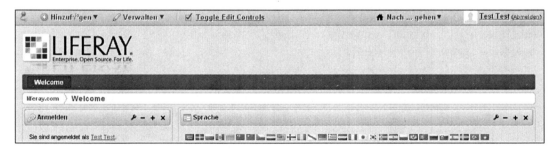

What the portal did, as stated above, is related to the portlet lifecycle. The understanding of the next part isn't necessary if you just want to use and configure a Liferay intranet.

Portlet lifecycle

A portlet has a lifecycle defining how it is loaded, instantiated, and initialized, as well as how it handles requests from clients, and how it's taken out of service. The lifecycle of a portlet includes the `Init`, `processAction`, `render`, and `destroy` of the portlet interface, as shown in the following figure:

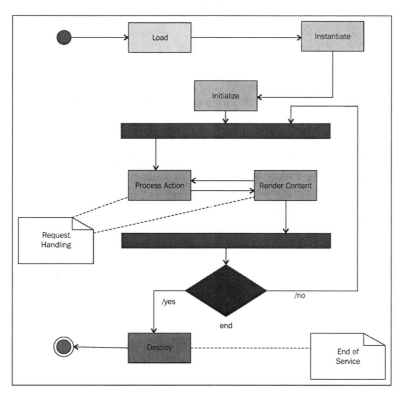

- **Loading** and **instantiation**: The loading and instantiation can occur when the portlet container starts the portlet application, or it can be delayed until the portlet container determines that the portlet needs to service a request.

- **Initialization**: Portlets can initialize resources and perform other one-time activities.

- **Request handling**: The portlet container may invoke the portlet to handle client requests. The portlet interface defines two methods for handling requests — the `processAction` method and the `render` method, as shown in the next figure.

  Generally speaking, during a render request, portlets such as **Language**, **Sign In**, and **Hello World** generate content based on their current state.

- **End of Service**: When the portlet container determines that a portlet should be removed from service, it calls the `destroy` method of the portlet interface, in order to allow the portlet to release any resource it is using and save any persistent state.

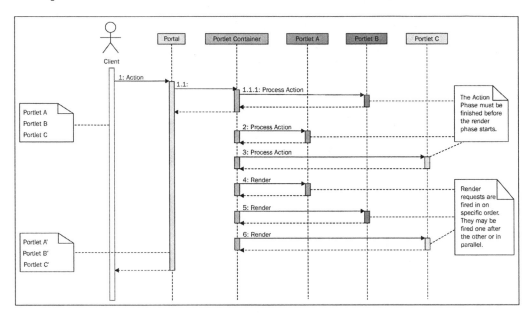

Terminologies, scope, and hierarchy

We have discussed portal, pages, and the portlets. What are the relationships between them? Let's look at a high-level overview of the terminologies, scope, and hierarchy within the portal. As shown in next figure, the portal is implemented by portal instances. The portal can manage multiple portal instances in one installation. Of course, you can install multiple portal instances in multiple installations, separately.

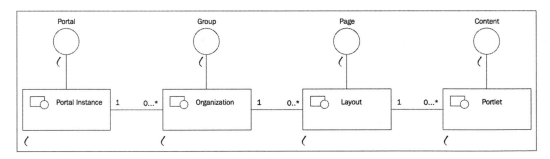

Each **portal instance** can have many groups which may be implemented as organizations, communities, user groups, and users. Note that each user can be represented as a group by itself. For example, if a user is a power user, then the user will get access to public pages and private pages like any other group. Here we can use the term **organization** to represent organizations (or locations), communities, user groups, and users (only one user in a group). Each portal instance has a complete isolation of the users, organizations, locations, and user groups. There is a hierarchy in organizations; for example: the parent organization, child organizations, and locations.

Each group has two sets of pages (that is public and private, called portal pages) implemented as layouts. There is a hierarchy in layouts, for example, parent pages and child pages.

Each page may contain different content implemented as portlets. Therefore, the content will have different scopes. For example, the content would be *scoped* into a page, group, portal instance, or portal. This pattern is called **Portal-Group-Page-Content**. We will address the scope and hierarchy terminologies in detail later in this book.

Setting up the portal

As an administrator at the enterprise "Palm-Tree Publications", you will need to undertake many administrative tasks such as installing the portal, installing and setting up databases, and so on.

You can install the portal in different ways based on your needs. Normally, there are three main installation options:

1. Using an open source bundle: It is the easiest and fastest installation method in order to install the portal as a bundle. By using a Java SE runtime environment with an embedded database, you can simply unzip and run the bundle just as we had done in the beginning.

2. Detailed installation procedure: You can install the portal in an existing application server. This option is available for all the supported application servers.

3. Using the extension environment: You can use a full development environment to extend the functionality.

We will consider the second installation option, "the detailed installation procedure", later. We will leave the third installation option, that is "using the extension environment" in another book. In the previous section, we have used the first installation option. Let's look at the other details in the coming sections.

Using the Liferay portal bundled with JBoss 5.x in Windows

Firstly, let's consider one scenario—you, as an administrator, need to install the portal in Windows with a MySQL database and your local Java version is Java SE 6.0. Let us install the portal bundled with JBoss 5.x in Windows through the following steps:

1. Download the latest Liferay Portal Standard Edition bundled with JBoss 5.x from the website `http://www.liferay.com/web/guest/downloads/portal`

2. Unzip the downloaded file into `$LIFERAY_PORTAL`.

3. Remove the folders `$JBOSS_AS_DIR/server/default/deploy/sevencogs-hook.war` and `$JBOSS_AS_DIR/server/default/deploy/sevencogs-theme.war`. The variable `$JBOSS_AS_DIR` refers to the JBoss AS folder under `$LIFERAY_HOME`.

4. Create a database named `lportal` and an account called `lportal/lportal` in MySQL as follows:

   ```
   drop database if exists lportal;
   create database lportal character set utf8;
   grant all on lportal.* to 'lportal'@'localhost' identified by 'lportal' with grant option;
   grant all on lportal.* to 'lportal'@'localhost.localdomain' identified by 'lportal' with grant option;
   ```

5. Create a file named `portal-ext.properties` at `$JBOSS_AS_DIR/server/default/deploy/ROOT.war/WEB-INF/classes`, and add the following lines at the end of `portal-ext.properties`:

   ```
   ## MySQL
   jdbc.default.driverClassName=com.mysql.jdbc.Driver
   jdbc.default.url=jdbc:mysql://localhost:3306/lportal?useUnicode=true&characterEncoding=UTF-8&useFastDateParsing=false
   jdbc.default.username=lportal
   jdbc.default.password=lportal
   ```

6. Run `$JBOSS_AS_DIR/bin/run.bat`, and note that it will take a long time to complete because it creates tables and data in MySQL automatically, at this very first launch.

7. Open your browser and type the URL `http://localhost:8080` if it doesn't open automatically.

8. Log in as an administrator with the e-mail address `test@liferay.com` and password `test`.

Note that the bundle comes with an embedded HSQL database loaded with sample data from the public website of Liferay portal. Don't use the Hypersonic databases in production.

Using Liferay portal bundled with Tomcat 6.x in Linux

Let's consider another scenario in which you, as an administrator, need to install the portal in Linux with a MySQL database, and your local Java version is JDK 6.0. Let's install the portal bundled with Tomcat 6.x in Linux as follows:

1. Download latest Liferay Portal Standard Edition bundled with Tomcat 6.x from the website `http://www.liferay.com/web/guest/downloads/portal`.

2. Unzip the downloaded file into `$LIFERAY_PORTAL`.

3. Remove folders `$TOMCAT_AS_DIR/webapps/sevencogs-hook` and `$TOMCAT_AS_DIR/webapps/sevencogs-theme`. The variable `$TOMCAT_AS_DIR` refers to the Tomcat folder under `$LIFERAY_HOME`.

4. Create a database `lportal` and an account `lportal`/`lportal` in MySQL as follows:

    ```
    drop database if exists lportal;
    create database lportal character set utf8;
    grant all on lportal.* to 'lportal'@'localhost' identified by 'lportal' with grant option;
    grant all on lportal.* to 'lportal'@'localhost.localdomain' identified by 'lportal' with grant option;
    ```

5. Create a file named `portal-ext.properties` at `$TOMCAT_AS_DIR/webapps/ROOT/WEB-INF/classes`, and add following lines at the end of `portal-ext.properties`.

    ```
    ## MySQL
    jdbc.default.driverClassName=com.mysql.jdbc.Driver
    jdbc.default.url=jdbc:mysql://localhost:3306/lportal?useUnicode=true&characterEncoding=UTF-8&useFastDateParsing=false
    jdbc.default.username=lportal
    jdbc.default.password=lportal
    ```

6. Run `$TOMCAT_AS_DIR/bin/startup.sh`.

7. Open your browser, and type URL `http://localhost:8080`
   (or `http://www.bookpub.com:8080`, supposing that the current
   Linux box has the domain name `www.bookpub.com`)

8. Log in as an administrator with the e-mail address **test@liferay.com** and the
   password **test**.

Once Tomcat starts, the portal will create tables and populate the previously
mentioned MySQL database `lportal` with default data. From now on, we will
use the default data from the MySQL database `lportal`.

> Note that the portal will create the tables it needs along with example
> data the first time it starts. Furthermore, it is necessary to make the script
> executable by running `chmod +x filename.sh`. It is often necessary to
> run the executable from the directory where it resides.
>
> On Linux, table names are case sensitive in MySQL, whereas this is
> not the case in Windows. If you want to copy tables from your local
> Windows machine to a Linux server you should take this into account.

Clean and restart

For some reason, you may clean and restart the portal. When doing so, you should
the following procedure into account:

- Run `$TOMCAT_AS_DIR/bin/shutdown.sh`
- Remove all files and folders in `$TOMCAT_AS_DIR/temp`
- Remove all files and folders in `$TOMCAT_AS_DIR/work`
- Delete all files in `$TOMCAT_AS_DIR/conf/Catalina/localhost`,
  except `ROOT.xml`.
- Run `$TOMCAT_AS_DIR/bin/startup.sh`

Setting up production servers

If the portal was used for production, then you may need to reset the JVM
parameters as follows:

- Locate the `setenv.sh` file in `$TOMCAT_AS_DIR/bin`.
- Remove all current lines, and add the following lines in the `setenv.sh` file:

```
JAVA_OPTS="$JAVA_OPTS -Xms2048m -Xmx2048m -XX:MaxPermSize=1024m
-Dfile.encoding=UTF8 -Duser.timezone=GMT -Djava.security.auth.
login.config=$CATALINA_HOME/conf/jaas.config -Dorg.apache.
catalina.loader.WebappClassLoader.ENABLE_CLEAR_REFERENCES=false"
```

The previous code shows the JVM parameters and reasonable values for a production environment.

Setting up domains

Additionally, if the portal was used for production, you may need to test the domain (a real domain or a virtual domain) instead of `localhost`. As mentioned earlier, we can type the URL `http://www.bookpub.com:8080` into a browser. How to make it happen?

- Locate the `hosts` file in the `etc` folder and open it. Note that in a Windows environment, the `etc` folder would be something like `C:/Windows/System32/drivers/etc`

- Add the following line at the end of the `hosts` file and save it:

  `127.0.0.1 www.bookpub.com`

The preceding code maps the IP address `127.0.0.1` to the domain `www.bookpub.com`. Note that you should use the real IP address of your production system and the real domain. Therefore, a portal with a real domain name in this box will be available on the Internet.

Shortening the URL

As you can see, there is a port number `8080` in the URL. You may want to remove the port number and make the URL shorter, to something like `http://www.bookpub.com`. You can do this by following these steps:

- Locate `server.xml` at `$TOMCAT_AS_DIR/conf` and open it.

- Replace port number `8080` with `80` and save it. Make sure you don't have any other process running on port `80` such as the Apache server.

  The preceding code resets the port number. Normally, the number `80` gets hidden in the URL. This is an option we can use to shorten the URL. There are other options that we can use to make the URL even shorter such as **Friendly URL Mapping** and **Virtual Hosting**. These options will be addressed in the coming chapters.

More options for portal installation

You can use one of following options for servlet containers and full Java EE application servers in order to install the Liferay portal:

- Bundled with Geronimo + Tomcat
- Bundled with Glassfish 3
- Bundled with Glassfish 2 for AIX
- Bundled with Glassfish 2 for Linux
- Bundled with Glassfish 2 for OS X
- Bundled with Glassfish 2 for Solaris
- Bundled with Glassfish 2 for Solaris (x86)
- Bundled with Glassfish 2 for Windows
- Bundled with JBoss + Tomcat 4.2
- Bundled with JBoss + Tomcat 5.x
- Bundled with Jetty
- Bundled with JOnAS+Jetty
- Bundled with JOnAS+Tomcat
- Bundled with Resin
- Bundled with Tomcat 5.5
- Bundled with Tomcat 6.x

You can choose the preferred bundle according to your requirements and directly download it from the official download page (refer to `http://www.liferay.com/ web/guest/downloads/portal`). The examples in this book are based on the Liferay portal bundled with Tomcat 6.x and JBoss + Tomcat 5.x.

Flexible deployment matrix

As an administrator, you can install Liferay portals on all major application servers, databases, and operating systems. There are over 700 ways to deploy Liferay portal. Therefore, you can reuse your existing resources, stick with your budget, and get an immediate return on investment that everyone will be happy with.

In general, you can install the portal on Linux, UNIX, or Windows with any one of the following application servers (or servlet containers) and by selecting any one of the following database systems.

Application server	Borland ES, Apache Geronimo, Sun GlassFish 2 UR1, JBoss, JOnAS, JRun 4 Updater, Oracle AS, Orion, Pramati, RexIP, SUN JSAS, WebLogic, WebSphere, Jetty, Resin, Tomcat
Database	Apache Derby, IBM DB2, Firebird, Hypersonic, H2 (Hypersonic 2), Informix, InterBase, JDataStore, MySQL, Oracle, PostgresSQL, SAP, SQL Server, Sybase
Operating system	LINUX (Debian, RedHat, SUSE, Ubuntu, and so on.), UNIX (AIX, FreeBSD, HP-UX, OS X, Solaris, and so on.), Windows, and Mac OS X

Building pages

As a "Palm Tree" administrator of the enterprise "Palm Tree Publications", you may be expected to build pages like the home page that you see when you are signed in by default. Generally, the pages could be public pages or private pages of different communities. Before doing it, you may have a look at the dock bar menu. As shown in following screenshot, you can see some items in the dock bar menu.

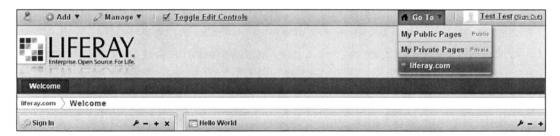

- A red pin that makes the dock bar always visible, even if you scroll down the browser window.

- The **Add** drop-down menu, where you can add pages or portlets (also known as applications) such as Web Content Display, Asset Publisher, Search, Navigation, and many more.

- The **Manage** drop-down menu, where you can find links to the **Control Panel**, manage pages (including **Page**, **Sitemap**, and **Setting**), and **Page Layout** option. Note that **Page Layout** would be hidden if the current page doesn't need layout templates.

- The **Staging** drop-down menu (it is only available in a staging group), where you will see these links: **View Live Page**, **Propose Publication**, **View Proposals**, and **Publish to Live** if you have activated only staging but not workflow.

- The **Toggle Edit Controls** checkbox, using which you can either display or hide editing controls (such as **Preferences**, **Minimize**, **Maximize**, **Remove**, and so on) of your portlets.

- The **Go To** drop-down menu, where you will see these links: **My Public Pages Public**, **My Private Page Private**, and **Guest**. Note that there is no private page in Guest at the moment, thus the Guest isn't distinguished with the display text Public or Private. If you add one private page in Guest, then you will see both **Guest Public** and **Guest Private**, respectively.

- A link with text like **Test Test** to **My Account** with current user's first name and last name as display text.

- A link with the text **Sign Out** that allows you to sign out.

As you can see, every user will have their own public pages and private pages. Furthermore, you will see a page named Welcome with a set of portlets in both public pages and private pages:

- **private page**: A private page is a page in a community that can only be accessed by users who've logged in and are part of the community. If a user isn't logged in (that is, the user is a guest) or if a user does not belong to your community, then the user cannot access the private pages.

- **public page**: A public page is a page in a community that can be accessed by guests. As long as the guest has the appropriate URL, the guest can access any public page.

After logging in successfully, you are ready to build pages in the default community "Guest" for carrying out the following tasks:

- Add or remove or update pages
- Add or remove portlets in newly created pages
- Change layout templates for newly added pages.

In general, registered users who have the appropriate permissions will have access to their own public pages and private pages, and then they may have the ability to build pages in the Guest community.

Adding pages

You are ready to add two pages—**Home** and **Books** to your personal area. Let's add a page **Home** as follows:

- Click on the **Add** | **Page** link under the dock bar menu
- Simply enter a page name such as **Home**, and then click on the gray-colored OK icon next to the page name

Repeat the above process to add another page, called Books.

> Note that the possibility of adding pages depends on a specific theme by default. With the theme **Classic**, you can add pages to the navigation bar. However, this function may not be available for other themes. In the theme Classic, it states `class="sort-pages modify-pages"` at `$TOMCAT_AS_DIR/webapps/ROOT/html/themes/classic/templates/navigation.vm`. What's a theme? You can refer to the coming sections to learn more about them.

Of course, you can add as many pages as you want. After adding a set of pages, we can view the pages.

You may want to change the page name **Home** to **My Home**. It is simple to do so. Simply double-click on the page name and change it to **My Home**, and then press the gray-colored OK icon next to the page name.

Removing pages

If you decide you do not need the Home page, and want to remove it, we can do this by following these steps:

- Move the mouse to the page named **Home**. If the page isn't the current page, then the delete icon will appear.
- Click on the delete icon next to the page name. A message, "Are you sure you want to delete this page?", with the **OK** and **Cancel** buttons will appear.
- Click the **OK** button if you want to remove the page.

As you can see, you can remove others pages as well. Removing a page is a simple but dynamic process.

> Note that there is no delete icon for the current page. If you want to delete the current page, then you need to click on another page and make that page a normal page first. Then you can delete it, as previously stated. Furthermore, any instance of portlets of the page would be removed if the page has been deleted.

Adding portlets

It is now time to add portlets to newly created pages. Let's say, we need to add the portlet **Sign In** to the page **Books**. Let's do it in the following way:

- Click on the **Books** link in the menu in order to go to the **Books** page you've just created.
- Click on the link **Add | More...** under the dock bar menu. This will bring up the **Add Application** panel on your screen.
- Enter the portlet name **Sign In**, and locate the portlet "Sign In" from the menu.
- Click on the **Add** button next to the right of the portlet named **Sign In**.
- Click on the close icon of **Add Application** panel to close it.

You will see that the portlet **Sign In** has been added to the top of your page. Now, you are ready to change the portlet placement. Click on the title bar of the portlet, and drag it to where you like. You can add many portlets, just as you expected to pages.

Removing portlets

If we decide that we no longer need the **Sign In** functionality on the **Books** page, we can remove the portlet by following these steps:

- Locate the portlet **Sign In**.
- Click on remove icon at the upper-right of the portlet.
- A message "**Are you sure you want to remove this component?**" with the **OK** and **Cancel** buttons will appear.
- Click on the **OK** button.

Of course, you can remove any portlet from any page if you have the proper permissions.

 Note that portlet preferences related to the portlet in the page would be removed if the portlet was removed from the page. You cannot recover these after deletion. By the way, if you remove a portlet, such as web content display from a page, it will not remove portlet content such as the web content itself.

Changing layout templates

You can also change layout templates for pages. A layout template allows us to arrange portlets in one, two-two, or one-two-one columns as well as designate the width of the columns. You can add and arrange all portlets that you would like on pages using the layout templates.

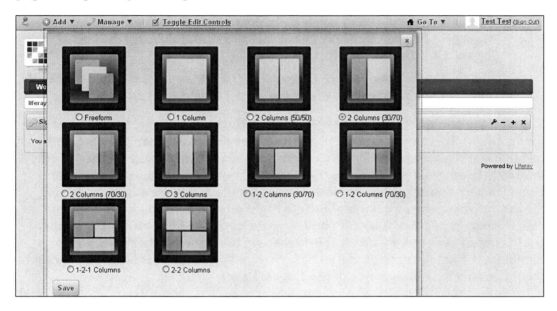

Generally speaking, layout templates define areas where you can place portlets on a page. By default, the portal comes with several different layout templates, as shown in the previous screenshot. Normal users or administrators can choose different layout templates for each portal page.

In most cases, default layout templates would be suitable. But you may need a very specific portlet window organization such as website games/videos/playlist landing pages. The portal provides maximum flexibility to deploy extra layout templates.

Note that if preloaded layout templates are insufficient for your needs, you can create your own deployable layouts—use a sample layout template or use a community-submitted one from http://www.liferay.com/web/guest/downloads/official_plugins and http://www.liferay.com/web/guest/downloads/community_plugins respectively.

Setting up portal pages

We have discussed how to build a home page. Now, let's see how to set up normal pages with layouts hierarchy. As an administrator or website editor, you are required to set up pages of any community. Let's say that you're expected to set up **Public Pages** of the community **Guest** with the following tasks:

- Edit pages and add child pages to the current page. You can use the link **Manage | Page** under the dock bar menu first, and then use the tab **Pages-_Children** under the portlet **Manage Pages**.

- Change the look and feel for Guest public pages. You can use the link **Pages** and the **Look and Feel** tab under the portlet **Manage Pages**.

Through the portlet **Manage Pages** (portlet ID 88), you can change the look and feel with a single click, manage portal pages, insert JavaScript, sitemap protocol, and metadata, and also set friendly URLs. Note that the portlet **Manage Pages** will only be able to manage pages of groups (or logged-in user's public pages and private pages), where you are currently located. For example, if you are currently visiting the group **Guest**, then the portlet **Manage Pages** (also known as a link) would be able to manage pages of Guest. If you are currently visiting **My Public Pages**, then the **Manage Pages** link would be able to manage the pages of **My Public Pages**. Similarly, if you are currently visiting **My Private Pages**, then the **Manage Pages** link would be able to manage pages of **My Private Pages**.

Managing pages

Let's say that you are currently visiting the pages of Guest by clicking on **Go To | Liferay.com**. Now, you can manage pages by clicking on **Manage | Page**, as shown in following screenshot. As you can see, you can manage **Page**, **Page Layout**, **Sitemap**, **Settings**, and **Control Panel** under the drop-down menu **Manage**.

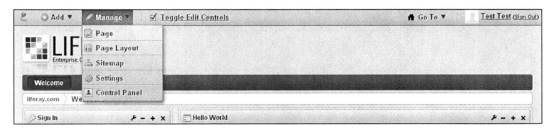

Adding a child page

Suppose you need to add a child page called **Awards** under the **Guest** community, you can add this page in the following way:

- Click on the root **Guest**.
- Select the tab **New Page** after selecting the **Children** tab.
- Enter the child page name **Awards**.
- Select a type **Portlet**.
- Select the checkbox **Hidden** if you want to hide the page in the navigation bar.
- Click on the **Add Page** button when you are ready to add a page.

Of course, you add more child pages as you had expected. The root, pages, and all child pages form a hierarchical tree, as shown in following screenshot:

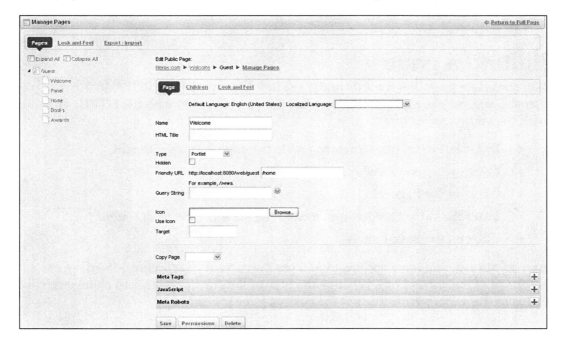

Changing the display order

You can change the display order of child pages under **Manage** | **Page** in the dock bar menu as follows:

- Select the tab **Display Order**.
- Click on a child page like **Books**, and then click on the **Move Up** button to move the selected page up—or click on the **Move Down** button to move the selected page down—or click on the **Remove** button to delete the selected page.
- Click on the **Update Display Order** button when you are ready.

 Note that the resulting first page, either public pages or private pages of a given group, must not have one of these types: **URL** and **Link to Page**. The resulting first page must not be hidden—it should not have the value **Hidden**.

Editing a page

You can edit a page like **Awards** under the link **Manage** | **Page** in the dock bar menu. For example, if you want to replace the page **Awards** with the **HTML Title** with the value **Our Awards**:

- In the left-hand tree structure, locate the page you want to edit.
- Click on the page **Awards**.
- Click on the **Page** tab.
- Enter the value **Our Awards** next to the **HTML Title** of the page.
- Click on the **Save** button.

As you can see, you have options to rename the current page, change the display language of the current page, change the type of the current page, and change the status of the page, whether or not the current page is hidden.

Multiple languages

The portal is designed to handle as many languages as you want to support. By default, it supports up to 22 languages. When a page is loading, the portal will detect the language it should use, pull up the corresponding language file, and display the text in the correct language.

For the page **Awards**, the default language is English (United States). If you select a localized language—German (Germany), then you have the capability to enter the **Name** and **HTML Title** in German.

In addition, you may type the value for **Query String**. Optionally, the portal will use this query string when there isn't any other present. This behaves as the default parameter for the page.

Friendly URL

You can eventually provide a **Friendly URL** for a page. For example, you could have the URL for the **Awards** page be `http://localhost:8080/web/guest/awards`.

As many parameters are passed in through the URL, the portal URL is very long and difficult to read. However, you can give your page a **Friendly URL** to make it easier to read and access.

The portal provides a **Friendly URL** for each group (including community, organization, and user). Therefore, you just type in a **Friendly URL** for a page (it must also start with "/") **/awards**. If there is no duplication, you can now access your page using the following URL pattern:

`http://${server-name}/${group-friendly-url}/${page-friendly-url}`

Page icon

You can upload an icon for the current page and change whether the icon is used or not. For instance, you can upload an image as the icon of the page **Awards**. Moreover, you have the ability to use the icon by selecting the checkbox **Use Icon**.

Target controls where the page will be displayed when the user follows a link. You can enter the following values for `target`: `_blank`, `_parent`, `_self`, and `_top`.

Copying pages

You already have a page named **Awards** in the Guest community. On the other hand, you want to set up a page named **Others**, which is just like the page **Awards**. In such a case, you can use the **Copy Page** function. Just select the page (like `Awards`) that you want to copy from the drop-down next to **Copy Page** link, and then click on the **Save** button when editing the page **Others**. Your current page **Others** will be an exact copy of the page **Awards** that you selected, except for the page's name.

Furthermore, you can specify meta tags, JavaScript, and meta robots for a given page. For example, if you need to add a function to redirect to an external website on a page, you could directly add JavaScript code in the JavaScript part of that page as shown in the following line:

```
window.location="http://liferay.cignex.com";
```

Deleting a page

For some reason, say the page similar to **Awards** doesn't exist anymore, and you need to delete it. You can delete pages under the link **Manage Pages**.

- In the left-hand tree structure, locate the page you want to delete.
- Click on the page **Awards**.
- Click on the **Page** tab.
- Click on the **Delete** button.
- A screen will appear asking if you want to delete the selected page. Click on the **OK** button to confirm the action.

 Note that deleting a page will delete all child pages related to that page and remove all portlet instances that the page owns.

Changing the look and feel: themes

At this point, you may have all the portlets you expected on pages. You can now change the look and feel of pages. The portal contributes pre-bundled with different themes that you may apply to pages. As an administrator in the portal, you may want to configure some additional themes.

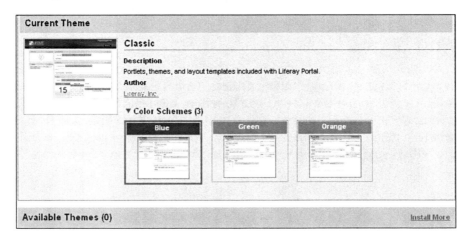

In order to change the theme, you can refer to the following instructions:

- Click on the link **Manage | Page**.
- Select the page you would like to change the theme for from the left-hand side. Note that, by default, all child pages will inherit a theme from their parent. If you want to inherit the look and feel from the root node, first click on the **Look and Feel** tab for that page, then choose **Yes** for the box **Inherit look and feel from the private root node?** Otherwise, choose **No**.
- Choose the **Look and Feel** tab for that page.
- You will see a number of bundled themes that are available. Choose your theme and color scheme. You can experiment with it as much as you like until you find a theme that pleases you.

Themes customize the overall look and feel of websites. The portal groups themes into two categories—Regular Browser and Mobile Devices. By default, Regular Browser's themes are further divided into three sub groups—themes, color schemes, and **Cascading Style Sheets** (**CSS**). As shown in previous screenshot, there is a theme named **Classic**, it is the default theme, and it covers three color schemes: **Blue**, **Green**, and **Orange**.

You can insert custom CSS that will be loaded after the theme. In addition, the portal provides **Wireless Application Protocol** (**WAP**) theme that is designed to run on mobile devices. If you had WAP clients, then the WAP theme would be an ideal choice for the look and feel.

You can easily switch among different presentational layers through themes. As a designer or developer, you can deliver an integrated package of HTML with Velocity templates, JavaScript, image and configuration files (that is, a WAR file) that will control all presentation logic and design attributes for a portal community.

How do you get additional themes?
Refer to http://www.liferay.com/web/guest/downloads/ official_plugins and http://www.liferay.com/web/ guest/downloads/community_plugins.

Customizing portlets

As an administrator or a normal user from website editorial department at the enterprise "Palm-Tree Publications", you have added a set of portlets in pages. Now, it is time to customize the portlets in a portal page.

As mentioned earlier, the portlet **Sign In** has tabs—**More**, **Minimize**, **Maximize**, and **Remove**. These icons are standard links for all portlets. The icon **More** mostly contains subset options: **Look and Feel**, **Configuration**, and **Export/Import**. Note that some portlets, like Hello World, don't have the icon **Export/Import**, as there is no real content inside portlet.

The function of the link Look and Feel is the same for all portlets. The icon **Configuration** mostly contains tabs such as **setup**, **permissions**, **sharing**, **communication**, **supported- clients**, and **scope**. The functions of permissions and sharing are the same for all portlets. For example, the **Sign In** portlet doesn't have the tabs scope, communication, and supported-clients. On the other hand, the Hello World portlet doesn't have the tabs setup, communication, supported-clients, and scope. We will discuss in detail about permissions and scope in coming chapters, and we will address sharing in the next section. In particular, we will address communication and supported-clients in coming chapters.

This section focuses on the Look and Feel and setup portlets. Let's say that you are using the portlet Sign In and you want to customize it in the following way:

- Change portlet look and feel: The background color, the font, and text size, change the title, and hide the border of portlet
- Change portlet configuration setup

Portlet Look and Feel

In order to change the background color, font, and text size of the portlet, you can simply click on the **More | Look and Feel** tab that appears in the portlet **Sign In** first. The portlet customization screen will appear. Then, by selecting the tab **Background Style**, you can change the background color, and by selecting the tab **Text Style**, you can change the font and text size. Click the **Save** button when you are ready, or click on the **Reset** button if you want to reset your changes.

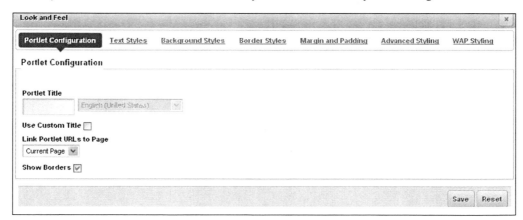

In order to change the title and hiding border of the portlet, you can simply click on the **More | Look and Feel** link that appears in the portlet **Sign In** first. Then, you simply enter a title, select a language, select the checkbox **Use Custom Title**, and uncheck the checkbox **Show Borders**. Click on the **Save** button when you are ready.

The portal provides us with the ability to change the look and feel of portlets dynamically with the following possibilities. Eventually, these functions of the portlet CSS are specified by the portlet **CSS** (with the portlet ID 113).

- **Portlet configuration**: Using a custom title, showing borders, selecting languages for the title, and so on
- **Text Style**: Font, size, color, alignment, text decoration, word spacing, line height, letter spacing, and so on
- **Background Style**: Background color
- **Border Style**: Border width, border style, border color, and so on
- **Margin and Padding**: Padding, margin, and so on
- **Advanced Styling**: Entering in your custom CSS
- **WAP Styling**: Entering in your custom CSS for WAP

Setting up portlet configuration

As shown in next screenshot, you can carry out the following steps for Portlet configuration setup:

- Click on the link **More | Configuration | Setup**
- Under the tab **Setup**, you can either change the current setup, for example, **Current | Authentication Type** (which can be **Default**, **By Email Address**, **By Screen Name**, and **By User ID**)
- Or change **Current | Email Notification | General** and **Current | Email Notification | Password Changed Notification**.

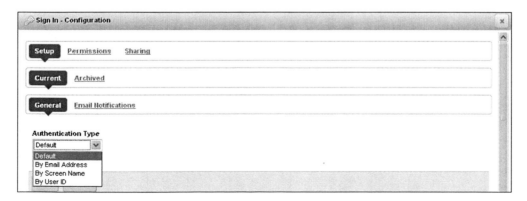

Eventually, the previously mentioned functions of the portlet configuration are specified by the portlet Configuration (portlet ID 86).

Navigating the structure of an intranet site

As an administrator or a normal user from the website editorial department at the enterprise "Palm-Tree Publications", you have customized pages in the portal. Now, it is time to navigate the structure of the website. Let's say that your current page is **Home** and you want to provide the following functions:

- Show the structured directory of links to all the pages in the portal. You simply add **Site Map** portlet (portlet ID 85) in a page if the portlet isn't there
- Display a directory of links reflecting page structure, with drill down into current page. You can add a **Navigation** portlet (portlet ID 71) in a page
- Displays a trail of parent pages for the current page. You just add the **Breadcrumb** portlet (portlet ID 73) in a page

The **Breadcrumb** portlet displays a trail of parent pages for the current page. It can be placed on public portal pages as a navigational aid to publish websites. It helps the user visualize the structure of a website and quickly move from a page to a broader grouping of information.

A Navigation portlet provides a directory of links to reflect page structure, with drill down into current page. Style and appearance are adjustable. The Navigation portlet displays links for other pages outside the current page's trail of parent pages. It helps users visualize the structure of a website and provides links to quickly move from one page to another. Moreover, it displays more information about the current page.

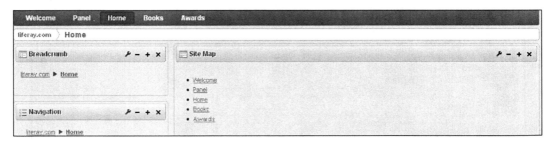

The **Site Map** portlet provides us with the ability to display a structured directory of links to all pages of a website. It is used to navigate directly to any page on a website. Furthermore, it can be configured to display the entire site or a sub-section of pages.

When do you use these portlets? In order to display a trail of parent pages, for example, for books for the current page like **Home**, you can use the **Breadcrumb** portlet. In order to display a trail of parent pages, for example, books for the current page like **Home** and page structure of current page, you can use the **Navigation** portlet. In order to display a structured directory of links to all the pages in the portal, use the **Site Map** portlet.

On the other hand, you can change the **Display Style** of the **Breadcrumb** portlet by clicking on the link **More | Configuration | Setup | Current**. Similarly, you can change **Display Style** and Bullet Style of the portlet **Navigation** by clicking on the link **More | Configuration | Setup | Current** — and also you can configure **Root Layout, Display Depth, Include Root in Tree, Show Current Page, Use HTML Title**, and **Show Hidden Pages** of the portlet **Site Map** by clicking on the link **More | Configuration | Setup | Current**.

Configuring portal

As an administrator at the enterprise "Palm-Tree Publications", you may need to customize the portal through configuration files in order to satisfy your own requirements.

Let's see an example of how to customize the Portal's configuration. As you can see, the default language is English (United States) and the default time zone is **UTC** (Coordinated Universal Time) when the portal starts. Now, we plan to set the default language as German (Germany) and the default time zone as **CET** (Central European Time) when the portal starts. We can implement it as follows:

1. Shut the portal down, if the portal is still running, by running `$TOMCAT_AS_DIR/bin/shutdown.sh`.

2. Clean Tomcat, as mentioned earlier.

3. Create the properties file `system-ext.properties` in `$TOMCAT_AS_DIR/webapps/ROOT/WEB-INF/classes` and open it.

4. Add the following line to the beginning of the properties file `system-ext.properties` and save it:

   ```
   user.country=DE
   user.language=de
   user.timezone=Europe/Paris
   ```

5. Restart the portal by running `$TOMCAT_AS_DIR/bin/startup.sh`.

After clicking on the link **Manage | Page**, you will see that the Default Language is **Deutsch** (Deutschland). The previous code set default locale used by the portal to **de_DE** (German/ Germany). This locale is no longer set at the VM level. It also sets the default time zone used by the portal to **CET** (Europe/Paris). This time zone is no longer set at the VM level. Of course, you can set a different country, language, and time zone.

The portal provides high customizability through website (Administration UI) and configuration files. Let's see how we can customize and configure the portal.

Configuring portal paths

Before customizing the configuration files, it is better to review and adjust the values of the following properties, shown with their default values at the time of writing.

- `auto.deploy.deploy.dir=${liferay.home}/deploy` for auto-deploy
- `jdbc.default.url=jdbc:hsqldb:${liferay.home}/data/hsql/lportal` for Hypersonic SQL scripts
- `lucene.dir=${liferay.home}/data/lucene` for search and indexing
- `jcr.jackrabbit.repository.root=${liferay.home}/data/jackrabbit` for JCR jackrabbit
- `image.hook.file.system.root.dir=${liferay.home}/data/images` for Image Gallery
- `dl.hook.file.system.root.dir=${liferay.home}/data/document_library` for Document Library

What's the variable `liferay.home`? What are the folders `/data` and `/deploy` used for? By default, the portal has the following settings:

```
liferay.home=$LIFERAY_HOME
```

For this reason, after installing the portal, you will see following folders under `$LIFERAY_HOME`:

- `deploy`: A folder for hot deploy
- `data`: A folder for runtime data
- `ee`: A folder for license information, used only for **Enterprise Edition** (**EE**)
- `license`: A folder for license information, used only for **Community Edition** (**CE**)
- `$APPLICATION_SERVER_DIR`: A folder for the application server directory

As shown in the previous code, you will have the default folders `/deploy` and `/data` for the properties such as `auto.deploy.deploy.dir`, `lucene.dir`, and so on. Of course, you can set the `liferay.home` variable to any folder you desire.

Customizing portal configuration

The portal can be configured through two properties files—`portal.properties` and `system.properties`. You should not directly modify `portal.properties` and `system.properties`, but you can create two files named `portal-ext.properties` and `system-ext.properties` respectively, and write in only the properties whose values you want to override.

The portal uses EasyConf to read `portal.properties` and `system.properties`. The main configuration file is `portal.properties`, which contains a detailed explanation about the properties that it defines. If you want to change the value of any of its properties, do it through the properties file called `portal-ext.properties`. When the server starts, the portal will first load `portal.properties` and then `portal-ext.properties`.

The `system.properties` file is provided as a convenient way to set all properties for the JVM machine and related system settings. When the server starts, the portal will first load `system.properties` and then `system-ext.properties`.

What's EasyConf?

EasyConf is a library to access the configurations of software components and applications. It defines simple conventions to make it easier to use.

In order to know every possible configuration value, get the original `system.properties` and `portal.properties` files from the Liferay portal source code or from `portal-impl.jar` into your application server installation `$PORTAL_ROOT_HOME/WEB-INF/lib`

Adding extended properties files

We can override the settings through properties files and determinately configure the portal through the properties files `portal-ext.properties` and `system-ext.properties`. These properties files are stored in the global classpath of application servers, presented as a variable `$PORTAL_EXT_PROPERTIES_HOME`. That is, you can create these properties files and store them at `$PORTAL_EXT_PROPERTIES_HOME`. Moreover, let's introduce another variable `$PORTAL_ROOT_HOME`, presenting the global portal ROOT path. Therefore, you will have the following expression:

```
$PORTAL_EXT_PROPERTIES_HOME=$PORTAL_ROOT_HOME/WEB-INF/classes
```

Obviously, the value of $PORTAL_ROOT_HOME is different from the application server as compared to the application server. Moreover, the variable $AS_WEB_APP_ HOME presents the global web apps folder of the application servers. For example:

- Tomcat: $AS_WEB_APP_HOME=`$TOMCAT_AS_DIR/webapps`; `$PORTAL_ ROOT_HOME=$TOMCAT_AS_DIR/webapps/ROOT`

- JBoss: $AS_WEB_APP_HOME=`$JBOSS_AS_DIR/server/default/deploy` `$PORTAL_ROOT_HOME=$JBOSS_AS_DIR/server/default/deploy/ROOT.war`

- Geronimo: $AS_WEB_APP_HOME=`$GERONIMO_AS_DIR/deploy` `$PORTAL_ ROOT_HOME=$GERONIMO_AS_DIR/deploy/liferay-portal.war`

- Glassfish: $AS_WEB_APP_HOME=`$GLASSFISH_AS_DIR/domains/domain1/ applications $PORTAL_ROOT_HOME=$GLASSFISH_AS_DIR/domains/ domain1/applications/liferay-portal`

- JOnAS: $AS_WEB_APP_HOME=`$JONAS_AS_DIR/webapps/autoload` `$PORTAL_ROOT_HOME=$JONAS_AS_DIR/webapps/autoload/liferay- portal.war`

- Resin: $AS_WEB_APP_HOME=`$RESIN_AS_DIR/webapps $PORTAL_ROOT_ HOME=$RESIN_AS_DIR/webapps/ROOT`

- Jetty: $AS_WEB_APP_HOME=`$JETTY_AS_DIR/webapps $PORTAL_ROOT_ HOME=$JETTY_AS_DIR/webapps/root`

- Other application servers: Check the documentation provided with them

As shown in the previous example, `$TOMCAT_AS_DIR` represents the Tomcat folder under `$LIFERAY_HOME`, `$JBOSS_AS_DIR` represents the JBoss folder under `$LIFERAY_ HOME`, `$GERONIMO_AS_DIR` represents the Geronimo folder under `$LIFERAY_HOME`, and `$JONAS_AS_DIR` represents the JOnAS folder under `$LIFERAY_HOME`. Similarly, `$RESIN_AS_DIR` represents the Resin folder under `$LIFERAY_HOME` and `$JETTY_ AS_DIR` represents the Jetty folder under `$LIFERAY_HOME`. Therefore, we could use `$APPLICATION_SERVER_DIR` to present previously mentioned values — `$TOMCAT_AS_ DIR`, `$JBOSS_AS_DIR`, and so on.

Portal structure

The portal has the following structure or called folders under `$PORTAL_ROOT_HOME`.

- `dtd`: XML Document Type Definitions such as data types, display, hook, layout templates, look and feel, portlet application, and ext.

- `errors`: Error page `404.jsp`

- `html`: Main folder for the website

- `layouttpl`: Standard or custom layout templates

- `wap`: Main folder for WAP site — including common themes, portal layout, themes mobile, and so on
- `WEB-INF`: Web specification such as `web.xml`, including the folders `classes`, `lib`, and `tld`.

The folder `html` has the following subfolders:

- `common`: Common themes
- `icons`: A set of icon images
- `js`: JavaScript for both portal and portlets
- `portal`: Portal layout and enterprise edition pages
- `portlets`: Default portlet views, including activities, admin, and so on
- `sound`: Sound files — for example, sound files for mail
- `taglib`: `taglib` for portlet, theme, and UI
- `themes`: Default themes folders such as `_style`, `_unstyle`, `classic`, and `control_panel`

One of the biggest aspects of implementing the portal is, of course, customization of the user experience — this mostly involves modifying portal JSP files. As shown in the previous portal structure, you would be able to modify portal JSP files under folders like `/html/portlet`, `/html/taglib` via hooks in plugins. For more details, refer to the section on hooks in Chapter 10.

Portal context

As you have noticed, the portal started from the path `ROOT` under `$TOMCAT_AS_DIR/webapps`. What's happening? The property `portal.ctx` has been set by default in `portal.properties` as follows:

```
portal.ctx=\
```

The previous code specifies the path of the portal Servlet context. You can set this property at the end of the properties file `portal-ext.properties` if you deploy the portal to another path besides `ROOT`.

As you have seen, a browser was automatically launched to a URL `http://localhost:8080` when the portal was fully initialized. Why like this? How can you customize this? The property `browser.launcher.url` has been set by default in `portal.properties` as follows:

```
browser.launcher.url=http://localhost:8080
```

The previous code specifies a URL to automatically launch a browser to that URL when the portal is fully initialized. You can set this property at the end of the `portal-ext.properties` properties file as a blank URL if you want to disable this feature.

Besides the URL (that is `http://localhost:8080`), it also adds the context path `/web/guest`. This behavior is related to the property `company.default.home.url`. The property `company.default.home.url` has been set by default in `portal.properties` as:

```
company.default.home.url=/web/guest
```

The previous code sets the default home URL of the portal. Similarly, you can customize this feature in the properties file `portal-ext.properties`.

You may have noticed that the portal remembered your last visited path upon a successful login. How does it work? The property `auth.forward.by.last.path` has been set by default in `portal.properties` as follows.

```
auth.forward.by.last.path=true
```

The previous code shows that users are forwarded to the last visited path upon successful login. If you set it to false in the properties file `portal-ext.properties`, then users will be forwarded to their default layout page.

Terms of Use

The portal provides the ability to force all users to accept some "terms of use" text before using the portal for the first time. For example, before using the portal for the first time, the portal forces the user `test@liferay.com/test` to accept the **Terms of Use**. The reason is that the property `terms.of.use.required` has been set by default in `portal.properties` as follows:

```
terms.of.use.required=true
```

The previous code shows that all users are required to agree to the Terms of Use before using the portal for the first time. If you set the property to `false` in the properties file `portal-ext.properties`, then every user is not required to accept some terms of use text before using the portal for the first time.

Default text is included within the portal. However, in most of the installations where this feature is used, this text will need to be customized. Fortunately, you can use a Web Content article to change the text of Terms of Use with the following settings
in the properties file `portal-ext.properties`.

```
terms.of.use.journal.article.group.id=$ARTICLE_GROUP_ID
terms.of.use.journal.article.id=$ARTICLE_ID
```

The previous code shows the group ID ($ARTICLE_GROUP_ID) and the article ID ($ARTICLE_ID) of the Journal (Web Content) article that will be displayed as the Terms of Use. The default text will be used if no Journal article is specified. Therefore, all administrators can manage the terms of use instead of the developers. Note that the group ID ($ARTICLE_GROUP_ID) should be the identifier of a community where the article was created. For more details about Web Content, refer to Chapter 8.

Reminder queries

The portal provides the ability to enable reminder queries before using the portal for the first time. For instance, after accepting using the portal for the first time and after accepting **Terms of Use**, the portal forces the user test@liferay.com/test to select a reminder query question, and more importantly, to input a textual answer to the selected question. The reason is that the property users.reminder.queries. enabled has been set to true by default in portal.properties. In short, you can set the property users.reminder.queries.enabled to true in order to enable reminder queries that are used to help reset a user's password.

```
users.reminder.queries.enabled=true
users.reminder.queries.custom.question.enabled=true
```

As shown in previous code, the property users.reminder.queries.enabled enables the mechanism of reminder queries and makes them essential to obtain a new password, the property users.reminder.queries.custom.question.enabled allows users to write their own questions so that they can choose one of their own ones in addition to the ones offered to them by default.

The list of questions used for reminder queries is specified using the property users.reminder.queries.questions by default in portal.properties as follows:

```
users.reminder.queries.questions=what-is-your-primary-frequent-flyer-
number,what-is-your-library-card-number,what-was-your-first-phone-
number,what-was-your-first-teacher's-name,what-is-your-father's-
middle-name
```

As shown in the previous code, the property users.reminder.queries.questions allows us to write the previously set reminder queries. That is, you can input a list of questions used for reminder queries. Note that you need to separate questions by commas, and there is no capital letter and hyphen between words. You can write them in the same format in different languages in the properties file portal-ext.properties.

In addition, any organization can define its own reminder queries instead of the default ones. For more details, refer to the next chapter.

Additionally, you can set the following property to `false` in order to enable users without a reminder query to reset their password. In other words, you can set it to `true` to enable users to reset their password with a reminder query.

```
users.reminder.queries.required=false
```

In brief, the portal allows users to obtain a new password by e-mail if they forget their passwords. This feature will allow a second security mechanism based on reminder queries. When this feature is enabled, the portal will go to **Forgot Password** and then introduce a user's e-mail address/login. After that, the portal will show some text verification and the question, and then the user will have to provide the answer so that the new password is sent to his/her e-mail address, as shown in following screenshot.

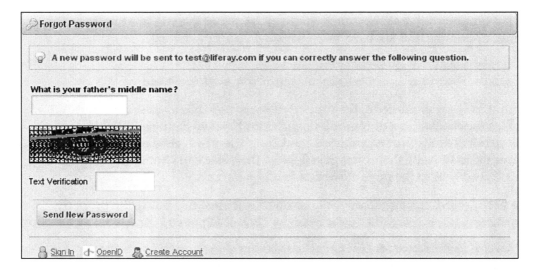

Session settings

As you can see, the default browser was automatically launched to a URL `http://localhost:8080`, when the portal was fully initialized, with a context path `/web/guest` and a string like `;jsessionid=48CFD42598E445CD083193C156F54F 6F`. The string is made up of a parameter key like `;jsessionid=` and a session ID `48CFD42598E445CD083193C156F54F6F`. More interestingly, the session ID value will be different from time to time. What's the string? How can we remove it? The reason is that the property `session.enable.url.with.session.id` has been set to `true` by default in the `portal.properties` file as follows.

```
session.enable.url.with.session.id=true
```

The previous code sets the property `session.enable.url.with.session.id` to `true` in order to enable sessions when cookies are disabled. To disable it, you can set the property `session.enable.url.with.session.id` to `false` in the properties file `portal-ext.properties`.

Eventually, you may receive either of the following warning messages, as shown in following screenshot:

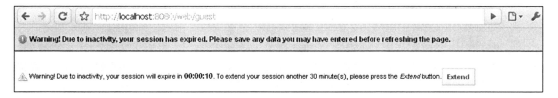

Of course, you can configure session-related features as well. For instance, you may override the following properties in the properties file `portal-ext.properties`:

```
session.timeout=30
session.timeout.warning=1
session.timeout.auto.extend=false
session.timeout.redirect.on.expire=false
session.enable.persistent.cookies=true
```

As shown in the previous code, the property `session.timeout` specifies the number of minutes before a session expires. This value is always overridden by the value set in `web.xml` under the folder `$PORTAL_WEB_INF_HOME`. The property `session.timeout.warning` specifies the number of minutes before a warning is sent to the user informing the user of the session expiration. You can specify `0` to disable any warning.

For the property `session.timeout.auto.extend`, you can set auto-extend mode to true in order to avoid having to ask the user whether to extend the session or not. Instead, it will be automatically extended. The purpose of this mode is to keep the session open as long as the user's browser is open, with a portal page loaded. It is recommended to use this setting along with a smaller `session.timeout`, such as 5 minutes for better performance.

For the property `session.timeout.redirect.on.expire`, you can set it to `true` if the user is redirected to the default page when the session expires. By default, the user isn't redirected to the default page. Furthermore, you may set the property `session.enable.persistent.cookies` to `false` to disable all persistent cookies, so that features like automatically logging in don't work.

In this case, you may get annoyed with session timeout. Fortunately, the session can be automatically extended. How can you achieve this? The following is an option:

- First, comment out the following lines in `$PORTAL_ROOT_HOME/WEB-INF/web.xml`. The default session timeout was set at 30 minutes.

```
<session-config>
  <session-timeout>30</session-timeout>
</session-config>
```

- Then add the following lines at the end of `portal-ext.properties`. The default value of the property `session.timeout.auto.extend` — auto-extend mode was set as `false`.

```
session.timeout=5
session.timeout.warning=1
session.timeout.auto.extend=true
```

As shown in the previous code, the property `session.timeout` was set with a smaller value like 5 minutes for better performance. Note that the property `session.timeout.warning` must be set to 1 minute. Why? As shown in following code from `$PORTAL_ROOT_HOME/html/common/themes/session_timeout.jspf`, only if the property `session.timeout.warning` is set as 1, then the property `session.timeout.auto.extend` would be checked.

```
<c:if test="<%= sessionTimeoutWarning > 0 %>">
  AUI().use(
    'liferay-session',
    function(A) {
      Liferay.Session.init( {
        autoExtend: <%= PropsValues.SESSION_TIMEOUT_AUTO_EXTEND %>,
        timeout: <%= sessionTimeout %>,
        timeoutWarning: <%= sessionTimeoutWarning %>,
        redirectOnExpire: <%= PropsValues.
        SESSION_TIMEOUT_REDIRECT_ON_EXPIRE %>
      } );
    } );
</c:if>
```

Layout types

We have built a set of pages with the type **Portlet**. We also experienced other layout types like (display text) **Panel, Embedded, Web Content, URL**, and **Link to Page**. What's happening? The property `layout.types` has been set to a list by default in `portal.properties` as follows.

```
layout.types=portlet,panel,embedded,article,url,link_to_layout
```

The previous code sets a list of layout types. You can create new layout types and specify custom settings for each layout type. The following list details the default types and their main features.

- `portlet`: Allows users to put portlets in certain areas determined by a layout template.
- `panel`: Allows users to create pages with panel-like look and feel.
- `embedded`: Shows an external website or application as a page of a website through an IFrame.
- `article`: Shows a single article (web content) created with the Web Content portlet.
- `url`: Adds a link to an external resource to the website menu.
- `link_to_page`: Makes links to other pages of the same website.

As shown in the following screenshot, the page **Welcome** has the `panel` layout type. Two applications (**SMS Text Messenger** under the category **Collaboration** and **Reports** under the category **Sample**) have been selected, which are available in the panel now. Of course, you can configure the pages with different applications under the layout type `panel` as well.

Default user public layouts and private layouts

When you're logged in using the default Admin account, public pages and private pages will be created automatically. How does this happen? The portal has the following properties set by default.

```
layout.user.private.layouts.enabled=true
layout.user.private.layouts.modifiable=true
layout.user.private.layouts.auto.create=true
```

The previous code sets whether or not private layouts are enabled, whether or not private layouts are modifiable, whether or not private layouts should be automatically created if a user has no private layouts. If private layouts are not enabled, then the other two properties are assumed to be false. In addition, you could set the property layout.remember.maximized.window.state to true to remember maximized window states across different pages.

```
layout.user.public.layouts.enabled=true
layout.user.public.layouts.modifiable=true
layout.user.public.layouts.auto.create=true
layout.remember.maximized.window.state=false
```

Similarly, the preceding code sets whether or not public layouts are enabled, whether or not they are modifiable, and whether or not public layouts should be automatically created if a user does not have any public layouts. If public layouts are not enabled, then the other two properties are assumed to be false. In addition, you could set the property layout.remember.maximized.window.state to true to maintain maximized window states across different pages.

If both properties — layout.user.public.layouts.enabled and layout.user.public.layouts.auto.create are set to true, then users will have public layouts and they will automatically be created. The following settings are used for the creation of initial public pages.

```
default.user.public.layout.name=Welcome
default.user.public.layout.template.id=2_columns_ii
default.user.public.layout.column-1=82,23
default.user.public.layout.column-2=8,19
default.user.public.layout.column-3=
default.user.public.layout.column-4=
default.user.public.layout.friendly.url=/home
```

The previous code sets the name of the public layout, the default layout template ID, the portlet IDs for columns specified in the layout template, and the friendly URL of the public layout. This is the reason that the default public page of the user test has the name Welcome, layout template ID as 2_columns_ii, portlet IDs 82 (Language portlet), 23 (Dictionary portlet), 8 (Calendar), and 19 (Message Boards portlet) along with friendly URL as /home. Additionally, you may refer to portlet IDs and names at $PORTAL_ROOT_HOME/WEB-INF/portlet-custom.xml.

In the same way, if both layout.user.private.layouts.enabled and layout.user.private.layouts.auto.create properties are set to true, then users will have private layouts and they will be automatically created.

The following settings are used for the creation of initial private pages:

```
default.user.private.layout.name=Welcome
default.user.private.layout.template.id=2_columns_ii
default.user.private.layout.column-1=71_INSTANCE_OY0d,82,23,61
default.user.private.layout.column-2=11,29,8,19.
default.user.private.layout.column-3=
default.user.private.layout.column-4=
default.user.private.layout.friendly.url=/home
```

The previous code shows a message listing the user's private pages—the same as that of public pages, except for the portlet IDs in columns. The portlet IDs include an instance of 71 (Navigation), 82 (Language portlet), 23 (Dictionary portlet), 61 (Loan Calculator portlet), 11 (Directory portlet), 29 (My Communities portlet), 23 (Dictionary portlet), and 19 (Message Boards portlet).

Default admin

As you have seen, the default admin account is test@liferay.com/test. The screen name of the default account is test, its default first name is Test, and its default last name is Test too. This default account has been specified in portal.properties as follows:

```
default.admin.password=test
default.admin.screen.name=test
default.admin.email.address.prefix=test
default.admin.first.name=Test
default.admin.middle.name=
default.admin.last.name=Test
```

The previous code sets the default admin account password, screen name prefix, e-mail address prefix, first name, middle name, and last name. Of course, you can override these properties in the properties file portal-ext.properties.

Guest layouts

The Guest group must have at least one public page. The settings for the initial public page are specified in following properties:

```
default.guest.public.layout.name=Welcome
default.guest.public.layout.template.id=2_columns_ii
default.guest.public.layout.column-1=58
default.guest.public.layout.column-2=47
default.guest.public.layout.column-3=
default.guest.public.layout.column-4=
default.guest.public.layout.friendly.url=/home
```

The previous code sets the name of the public layout, the default layout template ID, the portlet IDs for the columns specified in the layout template, and the friendly URL of the public layout. This is the reason that the default public page of Guest has the name `Welcome`, layout template ID `2_columns_ii`, portlet IDs `58` (Sign In portlet) and `47` (Hello World portlet), and the friendly URL `/home`.

Friendly URL

As you can see, private pages for the user `test@liferay.com/test` have friendly URLs like `/user/test`, and public pages for the user `test@liferay.com/test` have friendly URLs like `/group/test`. The public pages of Guest have friendly URLs such as `/web/guest` and the private pages of Guest have friendly URLs such as `/group/guest`. Why like this? This is because the `layout.friendly.url.private.group.servlet.mapping` property is set as `/group`, the `layout.friendly.url.private.user.servlet.mapping` property is set as `/user`, and the `layout.friendly.url.public.servlet.mapping` property is set as `/web` in `portal.properties`.

```
layout.friendly.url.private.group.servlet.mapping=/group
layout.friendly.url.private.user.servlet.mapping=/user
layout.friendly.url.public.servlet.mapping=/web
```

The previous code shows that the friendly URLs for users and groups can be set at runtime.

When typing keywords for a friendly URL, you should not use reserved keywords. The property `layout.friendly.url.keywords` specifies a set of reserved keywords in the properties file `portal.properties`.

```
layout.friendly.url.keywords=c,group,web,image,wsrp,
                        page,public,private,rss,tags
```

The preceding code sets reserved keywords that cannot be used in friendly URLs. You can reset the value of the `layout.friendly.url.keywords` property in the properties file `portal-ext.properties`.

Look and Feel

As mentioned earlier, users who have proper permissions will have the ability to modify the look and feel of pages. Why? How can you disable this? The feature is set by the property `look.and.feel.modifiable` in `portal.properties`.

```
look.and.feel.modifiable=true
```

The preceding code sets the property `look.and.feel.modifiable` to `true`. You can set this to false if the system should not allow users to modify the look and feel.

As you have noticed, a default layout template `2_columns_ii` (2 Columns (30/70)) has been applied to the newly created pages. What's happening? The reason is that the value of property `default.layout.template.id` has been specified as `2_columns_ii` in `portal.properties`.

```
default.layout.template.id=2_columns_ii
```

The preceding code sets the default layout template ID as `2_columns_ii`. Of course, you can set the template ID to something other than `2_columns_ii` in the properties file `portal-ext.properties`. The following is a list of default layout template IDs:

- `freeform`: Free form
- `1_column`: 1 Column
- `2_columns_i`: 2 Columns(50/50)
- `2_columns_ii`: 2 Columns(30/70)
- `2_columns_iii`: 2 Columns(70/30)
- `3_columns`: 3 Columns
- `1_2_columns_i`: 1-2 Columns(30/70)
- `1_2_columns_ii`: 1-2 Columns(70/30)
- `1_2_1_columns`: 1-2-1 Columns
- `2_2_columns`: 2-2 Columns

Additionally, you can find details about the preceding default layout templates at `$PORTAL_WEB_INF_HOME/liferay-layout-templates.xml`.

As you have experienced, there are default and color themes for both regular browsers, for example, Current Theme **Classic**, Color Theme **Blue**, and also for Mobile Devices, like Current Theme **Mobile**. These properties are specified in `portal.properties` as follows:

```
default.regular.theme.id=classic
default.regular.color.scheme.id=01
default.wap.theme.id=mobile
default.wap.color.scheme.id=01
```

The previous code sets the default theme ID for regular themes, the default color scheme ID for regular themes, the default theme ID for WAP themes, and the default color scheme ID for WAP themes.

You may want one change in the theme selection of public or private pages to be automatically be applied to the other. The `theme.sync.on.group` property has been specified in `portal.properties` as follows:

```
theme.sync.on.group=false
```

The preceding code sets `theme.sync.on.group` to `false`. You can set it to true if you want a change—for example, in the cases where public theme selection of public or private pages needs to applied automatically to the other. In most cases, private page themes should always be the same.

Dock bar menu

As mentioned earlier, the portal introduced a new dock bar menu called **dockbar**. In the dock bar menu, you would see a red pin, a set of drop-down menus such as **Add**, **Manage**, **Staging**, and **Go To** (or called **My Places**), a checkbox **Toggle Edit Controls**, an icon and the full name of the current user with a link to **My Account**, and a link to **Sign Out**. Depending on who signed in, the dock bar menu will show different items—each drop-down menu would contain different items too. What's happening?

At the same time, the current look and feel of the dock bar menu may not satisfy your requirements. This seems like a limitation of using the dock bar menu in different scenarios. Fortunately, you can customize it according to your expectations.

What's happening?

The portal has defined the dock bar menu as a portlet called Dockbar (portlet ID `145`). The portlet Dockbar has been specified, as follows, in `$PORTAL_ROOT_HOME/WEB-INF/liferay-portlet.xml`.

```
<use-default-template>false</use-default-template>
<show-portlet-access-denied>false</show-portlet-access-denied>
<show-portlet-inactive>false</show-portlet-inactive>
<restore-current-view>false</restore-current-view>
<add-default-resource>true</add-default-resource>
<system>true</system>
```

As shown in the preceding code, the portal sets the `use-default-template` value to `false`, allowing the developer to own and maintain the portlet's entire output content. It can be set to `true` if the portlet uses the default template to decorate and wrap content. The portal sets the `show-portlet-access-denied` value to `false`, so that users are never shown the portlet if they don't have access to the portlet. It can be set to true if users are shown the portlet with an "access denied" message, when they don't have access to the portlet. The portal sets the `show-portlet-inactive` value to `false`, so users are never shown the portlet if it is inactive. It can be set to true if users are shown the portlet with an inactive message, when the portlet is inactive.

The portal sets the `restore-current-view` value to `true`—therefore, the portlet will reset the current view when toggling between maximized and normal states. The default value is true. If the `restore-current-view` value is set to true, the portlet will restore the current view when toggling between maximized and normal states. The `add-default-resource value` is set to `false`, so the portlet doesn't belong to a page that has been dynamically added, and then the user will see that he/she doesn't have permissions to view the portlet. If the `add-default-resource` value is set to true, then the default portlet resources and permissions are added to the page. The user can then view the portlet. Most portlets are harmless, and one can benefit from this flexibility. However, in order to prevent security loopholes, the default value is set to false.

Last but not least, the portal sets the `system` value to `true`. Therefore, the portlet is a system portlet that a user can't manually add to their page. The default value is false.

You can get details about the dock bar menu at `$PORTAL_ROOT_HOME/html/portlet/dockbar/view.jsp`. The following is a piece of code showing you how to display predefined portlets, which will be shown directly in the "Add Application" menu.

```
List<Portlet> portlets = new ArrayList<Portlet>();
for (String portletId : PropsValues.DOCKBAR_ADD_PORTLETS) {
    Portlet portlet = PortletLocalServiceUtil.
                    getPortletById(portletId);
  if (portlet.isInclude() && portlet.isActive() &&
      portlet.hasAddPortletPermission(user.getUserId())) {
      portlets.add(portlet);
  }
}
```

In addition, the portal has specified the following property to set the portlet IDs that will be shown directly in the "Add Application" menu in `portal.properties`.

```
dockbar.add.portlets=56,101,3,71
```

As shown in the preceding code, the portal allows specifying the quick add application links through the property `dockbar.add.portlets` where `56` stands for the portlet Web Content Display, `101` stands for the portlet Asset Publisher, `3` stands for the portlet Search, and `71` stands for the portlet Navigation.

Of course, you would be able to customize the portlet IDs that will be shown directly in the "Add Application" menu in `portal-ext.properties`.

Dock bar menu in themes

You can add/remove the dock bar menu in themes. By default, the portal has the dock bar menu specified in the **classic** theme at `$PORTAL_ROOT_HOME/html/themes/classic/templates/portal_normal.vm`, as follows.

```
#if($is_signed_in)
  #dockbar()
#end
```

If you're going to add the dock bar menu to your themes, then you can simply add the preceding code in `portal_normal.vm`. If you want to hide the dock bar menu to your themes, then you should simply comment out the preceding code in `portal_normal.vm`.

In fact, the portal has defined **Alloy UI** (short for AUI) for the dock bar menu at `$PORTAL_ROOT_HOME/html/js/liferay/dockbar.js`. The following is a piece of code to do it:

```
AUI().use(
  'context-overlay',
  'io-plugin',
  'overlay-manager',
  'tool-item',
  function(A) {
    Liferay.Dockbar = {
      init: function() {
        var instance = this;
        var body = A.getBody();
        var dockBar = A.one('#dockbar');
        // Ignore details
```

My Places

As you can see, the portlet Dockbar has provided a drop-down menu **Go To**, which is the portlet My Places (portlet ID 49). Actually, you will be able to find the following code at `$PORTAL_ROOT_HOME/html/portlet/dockbar/view.jsp`.

```
<c:if test="<%= user.hasMyPlaces() %>">
  <li class="my-places has-submenu"
      id="<portlet:namespace />myPlaces">
    <a class="menu-button" href="javascript:;">
      <span>
        <liferay-ui:message key="go-to" />
      </span>
    </a>
```

```
       <div class="aui-menu my-places-menu aui-contextoverlay-hidden"
          id="<portlet:namespace />myPlacesContainer">
         <div class="aui-menu-content">
           <liferay-ui:my-places />
         </div>
       </div>
     </li>
   </c:if>
```

As shown in the preceding code, it first checks whether the current user has My Places or not. If yes, then it will show My Places with the taglib UI `<liferay-ui:my-places />`. You will certainly be able to find details about this in `<liferay-ui:my-places>` within `$PORTAL_ROOT_HOME/html/taglib/ui/my_places/page.jsp`. If you want, you can customize this via hooks in Plugins SDK.

By default, the portal has specified the following properties for the portlet My Places in `portal.properties`.

```
       my.places.display.style=simple
       my.places.show.user.public.sites.with.no.layouts=true
       my.places.show.user.private.sites.with.no.layouts=true
       my.places.show.organization.public.sites.with.no.layouts=true
       my.places.show.organization.private.sites.with.no.layouts=true
       my.places.show.community.public.sites.with.no.layouts=true
       my.places.show.community.private.sites.with.no.layouts=true
       my.places.max.elements=10
```

As shown in the previous code, the portal allows My Places to be configured in order to be displayed in either a simple way like `simple`, or a classic way like `classic` through the property `my.places.display.style`. Moreover, public sites and private sites of users, organization, and communities will be displayed in My Places without page layouts through propertyvia property `my.places.show.*`. The property `my.places.max.elements` sets the maximum number of elements that will be shown in the My Places navigation menu. For instance, if the maximum is set to 10, then, at most, 1 personal community, 10 organizations, and 10 communities will be shown.

Database connections

The portal supports two approaches for database connections: the JNDI name used to look up the JDBC data source, and the properties used to create the JDBC data source.

JNDI name

The portal can again use the connection pools provided by application servers, by specifying the JNDI name. First, you would be able to set the JNDI name to look up the JDBC data source in `portal-ext.properties` using the following property:

```
jdbc.default.jndi.name=jdbc/LiferayPool
```

Then, you need to configure database connections in different application servers, by updating the respective files for the application servers, as shown in the following table:

Application server	File
Tomcat	`$TOMCAT_AS_DIR/conf/Catalina/localhost/ROOT.xml`
Glassfish	`$GLASSFISH_AS_DIR/domains/domain1/config/domain.xml`
JBoss	`$JBOSS_AS_DIR/server/default/deploy/liferay-ds.xml`
Jetty	`$JETTY_AS_DIR/etc/jetty.xml`

Properties

The portal unifies the configuration of the database in a properties file for all application servers such as JBoss, Glassfish, Geronimo, JOnAS, Resin, Jetty, Tomcat, and so on. Therefore, you can set the properties used to create the JDBC data source. Note that these properties will only be read if the property `jdbc.default.jndi.name` isn't set.

The portal allows us to choose whether to use **C3PO, DBCP,** or Primrose for database connection pooling. The default provider is set as `c3po` in `portal.properties`.

```
jdbc.default.liferay.pool.provider=c3po
```

Of course, you can set the property `jdbc.default.liferay.pool.provider` to `dbcp` or `primrose` in `portal-ext.properties`.

The following properties will be read by C3PO if the portal is configured to use C3PO in the `jdbc.default.liferayPoolProvider` property.

```
jdbc.default.acquireIncrement=5
jdbc.default.idleConnectionTestPeriod=100
jdbc.default.maxIdleTime=3600
jdbc.default.maxPoolSize=100
jdbc.default.minPoolSize=10
jdbc.default.numHelperThreads=3
```

The following properties will be read by DBCP if the portal is configured to use DBCP in the `jdbc.default.liferayPoolProvider` property.

```
jdbc.default.maxActive=100
jdbc.default.minIdle=10
```

The following properties will be read by Primrose if the portal is configured to use Primrose in the property `jdbc.default.liferayPoolProvider`.

```
jdbc.default.base=100
jdbc.default.idleTime=1800000
jdbc.default.numberOfConnectionsToInitializeWith=10
```

The default settings are configured for an in-memory database called Hypersonic that isn't recommended for production use.

```
jdbc.default.driverClassName=org.hsqldb.jdbcDriver
jdbc.default.url=jdbc:hsqldb:${liferay.home}/data/hsql/lportal
jdbc.default.username=sa
jdbc.default.password=
```

In general, you need to change the properties to use another database such as DB2, Derby, Ingres, MySQL, Oracle, P6Spy, PostgresSQL, SQL Server, Sybase, and so on.

Populating with default data

The portal has specified the following settings to create the tables and populate them with default data in `portal.properties`.

```
schema.run.enabled=true
schema.run.minimal=true
```

The preceding code sets the property `schema.run.enabled` to `true` in order to automatically create tables and populate them with default data if the database is empty. It also sets the property `schema.run.minimal` to `true` in order to populate the database with minimal amount of data. You can set this to false to populate it with a larger amount of sample data in `portal-ext.properties`.

In addition, you may have your custom tables, and moreover, you're going to update the schema of custom tables regularly. Therefore, you could set the following line in `portal-ext.properties`:

```
hibernate.hbm2ddl.auto=update
```

Transaction isolation

The portal has specified the following settings for transaction isolation in `portal.properties`:

```
transaction.isolation.portal=2
```

As shown in the previous code, the property `transaction.isolation.portal` sets the definition of the portal transaction isolation level. Note that the portal transaction isolation level isn't a real isolation level. It is just a pointer to a real isolation level. You can set the value to -1 in order to use the database's default isolation level, to 2 in order to use "read committed", to 1 to use "read uncommitted"—set the value to 4 in order to use "repeatable read", and to 8 to use "serialize-able".

Custom SQL

The portal has specified the following custom SQL configurations in `portal.properties`:

```
custom.sql.configs=custom-sql/default.xml
```

As shown in the previous code, you could provide input of a list of comma-delimited custom SQL configurations in `portal-ext.properties`.

Some databases don't recognize a "NULL IS NULL" check. Therefore, you need to set the properties `custom.sql.function.isnull` and `custom.sql.function.isnotnull` for a specific database.

For DB2, you may set the following in `portal-ext.properties`.

```
custom.sql.function.isnull=CAST(? AS VARCHAR(32672)) IS NULL
custom.sql.function.isnotnull=CAST(? AS VARCHAR(32672)) IS NOT NULL
```

For Sybase, you may set the following in `portal-ext.properties`:

```
custom.sql.function.isnull=ISNULL(CONVERT(VARCHAR,?), '1') = '1'
custom.sql.function.isnotnull=ISNULL(CONVERT(VARCHAR,?), '1') = '0'
```

In addition, you need to specify any database vendor specific settings. For example, for MySQL, the following specific settings are provided in `portal.properties`.

```
database.mysql.engine=InnoDB
database.mysql.function.lower.enabled=false
```

Mail configuration

In general, there are three parts involved in configuring a mail system integrated with the portal.

1. Installing the mail systems
2. Configuring the portal to read and to send e-mails
3. Integrating the portal and the mail system for the creation of new accounts

Usually, installing mail systems involves installing an SMTP server and an IMAP server. This is not related to the portal, so for that, you should check the documentation provided with the mail server software.

The portlet Mail allows us to visualize all our e-mails from several e-mail accounts. It can be used to integrate the portal and the mail system for the creation of new accounts. This will be addressed in Chapter 10.

This section will introduce you to configuring the portal in order to read and send e-mails. Normally, there are two options: by JNDI name `mail/MailSession` and by Java mail.

Mail session

The property `mail.session.jndi.name` sets the JNDI name to look up the Java Mail session. In order to enable the JNDI name, you need to add the following line at the end of `portal-ext.properties` first.

```
mail.session.jndi.name=mail/MailSession
```

If no name is set, then the portal will attempt to create the Java Mail session based on the properties prefixed with `mail.session.*`.

Then, you need to set Global JNDI Lookup. This process differs from application server to application server. For Tomcat, add the following lines after the line `<Context path="" crossContext="true">` in `$TOMCAT_AS_DIR/conf/Catalina/localhost/ROOT.xml` (or `domain.xml` for Glassfish)

```
<Resource name="mail/MailSession"
        auth="Container"
        type="javax.mail.Session"
        mail.imap.host="imap.gmail.com"
        mail.imap.port="993"
        mail.pop.host="pop.gmail.com"
        mail.store.protocol="imap"
        mail.transport.protocol="smtp"
        mail.smtp.host="smtp.gmail.com"
```

```
            mail.smtp.port="465"
            mail.smtp.auth="true"
            mail.smtp.starttls.enable="true"
            mail.smtp.user="${username}"
            password="${password}"
            mail.smtp.socketFactory.
            class="javax.net.ssl.SSLSocketFactory"
    />
```

Note that the preceding code is sample code that uses Gmail as an example. You need to replace mail servers (IMAP, SMTP, and POP), domain names, port numbers, and user accounts.

For JBoss 5.x.GA, replace `$JBOSS_AS_DIR/server/default/deploy/mail-service.xml` with the following lines:

```
<?xml version="1.0" encoding="UTF-8"?>
<server>
    <mbean code="org.jboss.mail.MailService"
        name="jboss:service=MailSession">
      <attribute name="JNDIName">mail/MailSession</attribute>
      <attribute name="User">${username}</attribute>
      <attribute name="Password">${password}</attribute>
      <attribute name="Configuration">
        <configuration>
          <property name="mail.store.protocol" value="imap" />
          <property name="mail.transport.protocol" value="smtp" />
          <property name="mail.imap.host" value="imap.gmail.com" />
          <property name="mail.pop.host" value="pop.gmail.com" />
          <property name="mail.smtp.host" value="smtp.gmail.com" />
          <property name="mail.smtp.socketFactory.class"
                    value="javax.net.ssl.SSLSocketFactory" />
          <property name="mail.smtp.port" value="465" />
          <property name="auth" value="Container" />
          <property name="mail.smtp.auth" value="true" />
          <property name="type" value="javax.mail.Session" />
          <property name="mail.smtp.starttls.enable" value="true" />
        </configuration>
      </attribute>
    </mbean>
</server>
```

Again, the preceding code is sample code—using Gmail as an example. In the same pattern, you will be able to replace mail servers (like IMAP, SMTP, and POP) domain names, port numbers, and user account with real mail servers.

In the same pattern, you could configure Mail Session in other application servers, like Geronimo, JOnAS, Resin, Jetty, and so on. For example, in Glassfish, update the file $GLASSFISH_AS_DIR/domains/domain1/config/domain.xml, or in Jetty, update the file $JETTY_AS_DIR/etc/jetty.xml.

Java-mail

The portal has unified the configuration of Java-mail in a properties file so that it's the same for all application servers, that is, Geronimo, JOnAS, Resin, Jetty, Glassfish, JBoss, Tomcat, and so on. You would be able to add the following lines at the end of portal-ext.properties.

```
mail.session.mail.pop3.host=pop.gmail.com
mail.session.mail.pop3.password=
mail.session.mail.pop3.port=110
mail.session.mail.pop3.user=
mail.session.mail.imap.host=imap.gmail.com
mail.session.mail.imap.port=993
mail.session.mail.store.protocol=imap
mail.session.mail.transport.protocol=smtp
mail.session.mail.smtp.host=smtp.gmail.com
mail.session.mail.smtp.password=${password}
mail.session.mail.smtp.user=${username}
mail.session.mail.smtp.port=465
mail.session.mail.smtp.auth=true
mail.session.mail.smtp.starttls.enable=true
mail.session.mail.smtp.socketFactory.class=
                javax.net.ssl.SSLSocketFactory
```

The previous code sets the properties used to create the Java mail session. The property prefix 'mail.session.' will be removed before it is used to create the session object. These properties will only be read if the property mail.session.jndi.name isn't set.

Note that the preceding code is just sample code that uses Gmail as an example. In the same pattern, you will be able to replace mail servers (IMAP, SMTP, and POP), domain names, port numbers, and user accounts with real mail servers.

By default, the portal has Java Mail specified in portal.properties in this way:

```
mail.session.mail.pop3.host=localhost
mail.session.mail.pop3.password=
mail.session.mail.pop3.port=110
mail.session.mail.pop3.user=
mail.session.mail.smtp.auth=false
mail.session.mail.smtp.host=localhost
mail.session.mail.smtp.password=
```

```
mail.session.mail.smtp.port=25
mail.session.mail.smtp.user=
mail.session.mail.store.protocol=pop3
mail.session.mail.transport.protocol=smtp
```

According to properties in the previous code, the same features are provided in the Web UI in the Control Panel. You could use the Web UI by going to **Server | Server Administration | Mail** under the Control Panel, and also by configuring the mail server settings such as POP and SMTP. It seems as limitation on mail setting through the Web UI. Fortunately, the Web UI provides us with the ability to set up **Advanced Properties**, where you would be able to manually specify additional Java-mail properties to override the preceding configuration. Therefore, you could configure the same main configuration through the Web UI, in a similar way to the mail configuration that you performed earlier in `portal-ext.properties`.

Mail hook

Besides the previously discussed settings, you could override the following properties in `portal-ext.properties`.

```
mail.mx.update=true
mail.audit.trail=
mail.hook.impl=com.liferay.mail.util.DummyHook
```

The preceding code sets the property `mail.mx.update` to `true`. You could set it to false if the administrator shouldn't be allowed to change the mail domain via **Server | Server Administration | Mail** or via **Portal | Settings|General** in the Control Panel. Through the property `mail.audit.trail`, you could enter a list of comma-delimited e-mail addresses that will receive a BCC of every e-mail sent through the mail server.

Moreover, using the property, you could set the name of a class that implements `com.liferay.mail.util.Hook` such as `CyrusHook`, `DummyHook`, `FuseMailHook`, `GoogleHook`, `SendmailHook`, and `ShellHook`. Note that the mail server will use this class to ensure that the mail and portal servers are synchronized with user information. The portal will know how to add, update, or delete users from the mail server only through this hook.

In addition, you would be able to configure following properties in `portal-ext.properties`:

```
google.apps.username=
google.apps.password=
```

As shown in the preceding code, you will be able to set the default username and password for Google Apps integration. The domain used by Google Apps is retrieved from the portal's mail domain. Note that Google Apps integration isn't used unless the property `mail.hook.impl` is set with the value `com.liferay.mail.util.GoogleHook`.

Bring pages together in action

Toggle Edit Controls provides us with the ability to toggle the edit controls of portlets in pages. By default, toggling the edit controls affects all pages of the user's desktop. You can turn on/off **Toggle Edit Controls**.

By the way, it would be better if **Toggle Edit Controls** only affects the controls on the current page after a toggle and not all the pages of the user's desktop. A user might want one of the public pages to show up with borders and controls, where edit controls are required in his/her other public pages. That is, the functionality of toggling edit controls should be scoped into a page **Current Page**. This feature should come out in the coming version.

Page Comments

The Page Comments portlet (portlet ID `107`) allows users to easily add comments to a page. By using this portlet, you can easily add or edit or delete comments. Let's do it as follows:

1. Add the **Page Comments** portlet to a page that says **Home** of the Guest community, where you want to add comments, if the portlet isn't there.

2. Click on the **Add Comment** link if you want to add comments.

3. Input your comments—click on the **Reply** button to save the comments or the **Cancel** button to cancel them.

4. You can edit comments by clicking on the **Edit** button first. Then update the comments. Click on the **Update** button to save the changes, or **Cancel** button to cancel the changes, as shown in the next screenshot.

5. You can delete page comments by clicking on the **Delete** button. A screen will appear asking you if you want to delete this. Click on the **OK** button to confirm deletion, or the **Cancel** button to cancel deletion.

6. Or you can go to the top of the Page Comments portlet, by clicking on the **Top** button, if there are a lot of page comments and you are not at the top of the list.

The Page Comments portlet is scoped into the current page. As the Page Comments portlet isn't *instance-able*, one page can have only one Page Comments portlet.

 How do you add a UI tag to incorporate comments to a portlet?
You can simply use a taglib `<liferay-ui: discussion>`, which allows users to discuss any type of content or pages in any portlet.

Page Ratings

The portlet Page Ratings (portlet ID `108`) allows users to rate a page with 1 to 5 stars. You can add the Page Ratings portlet to a page to receive page ratings.

The Page Ratings portlet can be placed in any portal page to allow users to rate contents available on that page as a whole. It can be used in a user profile page too, as a way to allow end users to rate the user. As shown in the following screenshot, the Page Ratings portlet uses AJAX-based ratings that avoid a full page reload—the rating belongs to an authenticated user and it doesn't allow the same user to rate a page more than once. However, the rating can be changed at any time and it has a nice appearance based on graphical stars.

Similar to the Page Comments portlet, the Page Ratings portlet is scoped into the current page. The Page Ratings portlet isn't *instance-able*, one page can have only one Page Ratings portlet.

How can I add a UI tag to incorporate rating to a portlet?
You can simply use a UI taglib `<liferay-ui: ratings>` that allows users to rate any type of content or pages in any portlet.

Page Templates

As you have seen, for each newly created page, we have added portlets and changed the layout template and theme. So how do we create one page with the required portlets, layout template and theme as a layout prototype, and then apply it to newly created pages automatically? The answer is the portlet Page Templates (portlet ID `146`). The Page Templates portlet provides us with the ability to create a set of layout prototypes; later, newly created pages will have an option to apply these layout prototypes, as shown in the following screenshot:

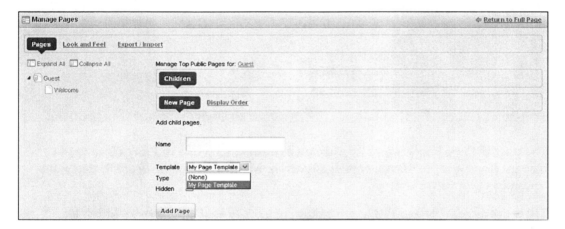

The following are sample steps you should take create a layout prototype.

1. First, go to **Manage** | **Control Panel** under the dock bar menu, and then go to **Control Panel Portal** | **Page Templates**.

2. Create a page template with the name **My Page Template** and description **My Page Template**.

3. Click on the **Save** button.

4. Locate the page template **My Page Template**, and click on it.

5. Click on the link **Open Page Template** under **More** | **Configuration**, add portlets, and change the layout template and theme.

That's it! When you create a new page, the preceding page template will be available for application in the portlet Manage Pages (portlet ID 88) or in the Navigation bar. Note that page templates are scoped into portal instances by default. Therefore, the page templates will be available in the current portal instance. Fortunately, you can set the scope of the portlet Page Templates as a page **Current Page** through **More-Configuration | Scope**.

Page Flags

The portlet Page Flags (portlet ID 142) can be placed in any portal page to allow users to flag content in the current page as inappropriate. It will enable a user to flag some content as inappropriate for a reason and warn the administrator about it. As shown in following figure, the flags are AJAX based that avoid a full page reloading; it will send an e-mail to the administrators so that they can take appropriate action.

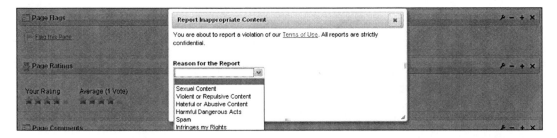

The portlet Page Flags normally appears as a small icon of a red flag close to the content (for example, blogs, message boards), which will enable users to flag some content as inappropriate.

There are several properties in `portal.properties` that can be overridden in `portal-ext.properties`:

```
flags.reasons=sexual-content,violent-or-repulsive-content,hateful-or-
abusive-content,harmful-dangerous-acts,spam,infringes-my-rights
flags.email.from.name=Joe Bloggs
flags.email.from.address=test@liferay.com
flags.guest.users.enabled=false
```

As shown in the previous code, you can enter a list of questions used for flag reasons, override e-mail notification settings, and set `flags.guest.users.enabled` to `true` in order to enable guest users to flag content.

Programmatically, you can use a UI taglib `<liferay-ui:flags>` that allows you to flag any type of content or page in any portlet. How does it work? You can refer to the JSP file `$PORTAL_ROOT_HOME/html/portlet/flags/edit_entry.jsp`.

How do you share portlets within a portal page?

Within the portal, especially the portlet **Sharing** with the portlet ID `133`, you can share as many portlets as you want. All portlets will have the tab **Sharing** at **More | Configuration**. As shown in the following screenshot, you can share any portlet (for example, Sign In) with any website: **Facebook**, **Google Gadget**, **Netvibes**, and **Friends**.

It's possible to use any portlet in any website, including these built-in scripts with static HTML pages. For example, to share the application **Sign In** with any website, just copy the following code, paste it into your web page, and this application will show up.

```
<script src="http://www.bookpub.com:8080/html/js/liferay/widget.js"
        type="text/javascript">
</script>
<script type="text/javascript">
  Liferay.Widget({ url:'http://www.bookpub.com:
             8080/widget/web/guest/home/-/58'});
</script>
```

The preceding code uses a **Widget** to display the portlet **Sign In** of the page **Home**.

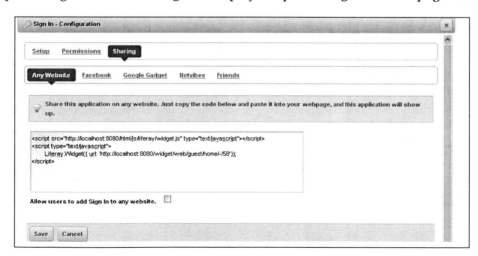

By the way, if you select the checkbox **Allow users to add Sign In to any website**, you will see an icon plus a link **Add to any Website** under **Configuration**.

It's also possible to use any portlet as a Facebook application. The Facebook integration is implemented through an IFrame (It is also possible to use FBML.). Each portlet in the portal is automatically exposable to Facebook. Simply go to **More | Configuration | Sharing | Facebook**, first set your **Facebook API key** (for example, **136be69d497ed2688fc853a651c81f17**) and **Canvas Page URL** (for example, **test**). Then copy the following **callback URL** and specify it in Facebook. This application will be exposed to Facebook via an IFrame:

```
http://www.bookpub.com:8080/widget/web/guest/home/-/58
```

In addition, if you select the checkbox **Allow users to add Sign In to Facebook**, you will see an icon plus a link **Add to Facebook** under **Configuration**.

Similarly, you can use the following Google Gadget URL to create a Google Gadget:

```
http://www.bookpub.com:8080/google_gadget/web/guest/home/-/58
```

And you can also use the following Netvibes Widget URL to create a Netvibes Widget:

```
http://www.bookpub.com:8080/netvibes/web/guest/home/-/58
```

Note that the preceding URLs are generated automatically in the portal. You have to use the real URLs of servers in order to make them work properly.

How does it work? You can refer to the JavaScript details in `$PORTAL_ROOT_HOME/html/js/liferay/portlet_sharing.js`.

Configuring Control Panel

As mentioned earlier, we have managed a logged-in user's private pages and public pages through **Manage | Page**. Now, let's go further and see how to manage a logged-in user's private pages and public pages through **Control Panel**.

Generally speaking, the Control Panel is a feature of the portal that allows us to modify portal settings and controls. As shown in following screenshot, Control Panel provides a centralized administration for all content, users, organizations, communities, roles, server resources, and more. Additionally, it provides full customizability with the ability to hide different parts of the form as desired, or to add custom parts with portlets.

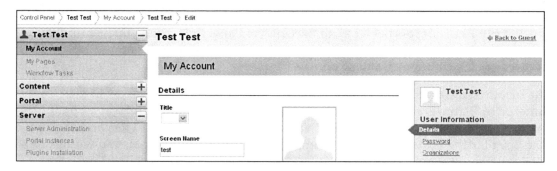

Administration

The Control Panel is a unified way to access all portal administration tools within the portal. It provides access to four categories: **My**, **Content**, **Portal**, and **Server**, as shown in the preceding screenshot.

- My administration (with the keyword **my**) of the logged-in user's account, for example, My account, My Pages, and Workflow Tasks.

- Content administration (with the keyword **content**): Web content, Document Library, Image Gallery, and so on.

- Portal administration (with the keyword **portal**): User administration, organization administration, role administration, and so on.

- Server administration (with the keyword **server**): Memory used, cache, log levels, plugins, and so on.

Each of the preceding tools is organized into corresponding categories (that is, **my**, **content**, **portal**, and **server**) and will be accessible through a link in the left menu of Control Panel. All registered users have access to the Control Panel through a link in the dock bar menu **Manage | Control Panel**.

Once inside Control Panel, the logged-in user will only be able to see the tools in the left menu for which he/she has permissions. A regular user with no administration permissions will only see the option to administer his/her own account.

My Account

As an administrator, you are now running the portal and you see a set of portlets in the default page. It is ready for you to update your profile anytime, to update screen name, e-mail address, first name, last name, icon, language, display settings, and so on.

In order to update the profile, you simply use the **My Account** link, that is, the portlet My Account (portlet ID 2), in the Control Panel first. Then you just update name, e-mail address, language, time zone, greetings, password, phone, SMS messenger ID, comments, and so on.

As mentioned earlier, the portal administrator is named as "Palm Tree" in the enterprise "Palm-Tree Publications". Now it is time to change the admin account name. You can simply enter the First Name **Palm** and Last Name **Tree**, and click on the **Save** button under the default Admin **My Account**. Afterwards, you would see that the default admin account name has been changed from "Test Test" to "Palm Tree" in both Control Panel and the My Account link of the dock bar menu.

For example, if you want to display your icon in other portlets, let's say, discussion forums and blogs, you need to upload your own image by clicking on the **Change** link. Then upload image file `PalmTree_logo_small.png` and click on the **Save** button to save the changes. If you do not want to change anything, then simply click on the **Cancel** button. After updating the icon, you would see your own icon in the **My Account** link of the dock bar menu too.

 Note that if you changed your e-mail address and password, then you would need to memorize your update because you have to use the updated e-mail address and password for your next login.

In a word, **My Account** link is useful for a logged-in user in the enterprise "Palm Tree Publications" to update their profile.

My Pages

The portal, especially the portlet My Pages (portlet ID 140), provides us with the ability to update the user's personal pages, for example, public pages and private pages dynamically, by using the **My Pages** link in Control Panel. As shown in following screenshot, you can manage both your public pages and your private pages in the Control Panel via the link **My Pages**. As mentioned earlier, the link **Manage | Pages** can only manage either public pages or private pages at a time. Therefore, we can say that the link **My Pages** in the Control Panel can manage a logged-in user's public pages and private pages all in one place.

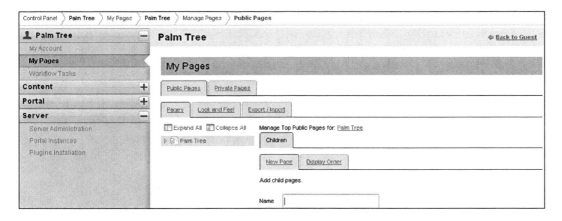

In addition, the portal provides us with the ability to manage My Tasks, that is, the Workflow Tasks portlet (portlet ID 150) in the Control Panel. By using the link **Workflow Tasks**, you would be able to manage your pending tasks and completed tasks.

Configuration and settings

As you can see, the layout of the Control Panel comes with a title like **Control Panel** and a friendly URL like /manage. The properties control.panel.layout.name and control.panel.layout.friendly.url were specified by default in portal.properties as follows:

```
control.panel.layout.name=Control Panel
control.panel.layout.friendly.url=/manage
```

The preceding code sets the name of the layout as Control Panel and it sets the friendly URL of the layout as /manage. Of course, you can override these properties in portal-ext.properties.

The Control Panel comes with a default theme, controlpanel, as shown in portal.properties.

```
control.panel.layout.regular.theme.id=controlpanel
```

The preceding code sets the theme of the layout to Control Panel. It's possible to configure it to use any custom theme. To that end, the property control.panel. layout.regular.theme.id can be overridden in portal-ext.properties.

```
control.panel.navigation.max.communities=50
```

The preceding code sets the maximum number of communities that will be shown in the navigation menus. A large value might cause performance problems if the number of communities that the user can administer is very large.

```
control.panel.navigation.max.organizations=50
```

The preceding code sets the maximum number of organizations that will be shown in the navigation menus. A large value might cause performance problems if the number of organizations that the user can administer is very large.

Adding custom portlets

It's possible to configure Control Panel to remove certain portlets, even if they are enabled, and also to add custom portlets. This can be done individually for each portlet through the portlet configuration file. For each portlet, only one parameter has to be provided and the category of Control Panel where it will appear. There are four values allowed for categories: **my**, **content**, **portal**, and **server**.

For example, we plan to *hot-deploy* the portlet WSRP producer and consumer. Although the WSRP portlet can be deployed in several different ways, we just use the
hot-deploy approach as follows:

1. Download `${wsrp.portlet.war}` from `http://liferay.cignex.com/ palm_tree/book/0387/chapter02/wsrp-portlet-6.0.0.1.war`.

2. Copy `${wsrp.portlet.war}` to `$LIFERAY_HOME/deploy`

If the portal is running, the WSRP portlet will be deployed automatically. After deploying it completely, you will see **WSRP** under the category **Portal** in the Control Panel, as shown in following screenshot. As you can see, WSRP was added at the end of the Category portal.

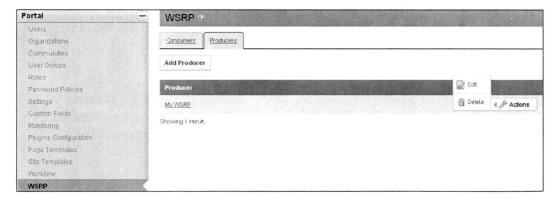

What's happening?

You will find the following code in $AS_WEB_APP_HOME/wsrp-portlet/WEB-INF/liferay-portlet.xml.

```
<control-panel-entry-category>portal</control-panel-entry-category>
<control-panel-entry-weight>14.0</control-panel-entry-weight>
```

The preceding code sets the Control Panel Entry Category as portal. In this example, the WSRP portlet has been added at the end of the category portal, that is, position 14.0.

Note that the portlet added in the Control Panel cannot be *instance-able*, that is, the property in liferay-portlet.xml must be false, for example <instanceable>false</instanceable>. By default, the property <instanceable> was specified as false. If the property <instanceable> was not specified in liferay-portlet.xml manifestly, it means that the property <instanceable> has the value false.

Summary

This chapter discussed how to implement a portal page with portlets. It also showed how to customize the look and feel of pages and portlets through themes and look and feel preferences. It helped us to understand the portal, portlet container, and portlets according to the JSR-286 specification—how to set up the portal, including installation options and deployment matrix, how to configure the home page and all the other pages of the intranet website. Then it introduced us to building basic pages, as well as setting up the portal pages. It also discussed how to navigate the structure of the intranet via portlets, for example, **Site Map**, **Breadcrumb**, and **Navigation**. It also showed us how to configure the portal, how to customize the dock bar menu, and how to configure the database and mail options. Finally, it provided guidance to bring pages together in action, to share any portlet within a portal page, and to customize the Control Panel.

In the next chapter, we're going to bring in users, user groups, organizations, roles, and permissions.

3
Bringing in Users

In the previous chapter, we discussed the box page in the details of the pattern: **Portal-Group-Page-Content**. In this chapter, we're going to open the box group and take a deeper look at it. The portal provides a powerful and yet highly configurable full security model for controlling resources, permissions, roles, users, organizations, locations, communities, and user groups. This full security model incorporates fine-grained permissions and role-based access control to give administrators full control over access and privileges to portlets, layouts, groups, and content within the portal. By role-based access control, users can assign permissions to other users, communities, organizations, locations, and user groups via roles. Moreover, users can control permissions scoped up to the portal or down to the page or the content.

This chapter begins with enterprise, departments and locations, and hierarchy and role-based access control model. Then it proceeds on to how to bring in users, organizations, locations, user groups, roles. Furthermore, it will discuss all the ways to assign users to organizations, communities, user groups, and roles. In addition, it introduces authentications related to manage accounts, LDAP (Lightweight Directory Access Protocol), SSO (Single Sign-on) CAS, NTLM, OpenID, OpenSSO, and SiteMinder. Finally, it gives details about how to manage permissions, how to use permission algorithms and how to assign permissions to different resources via roles.

In this chapter, you will learn how to:

- Build a hierarchy of enterprises, departments, and locations
- Set up organizations and locations
- Build user groups
- Bring in users
- Establish authentication
- Manage roles
- Assemble authorization

Enterprise, departments, and locations

The enterprise **Palm-Tree Publications** has a global headquarters in the US with several departments (such as **Editorial**, **Engineering**, **Marketing**, **Website**, and so on). Each department has staff in the United States, or in Germany, or both. As shown in following figure, the enterprise, departments, and locations form a hierarchy. In this chapter, we will build this hierarchy with a model called **role-based access control (RBAC)**.

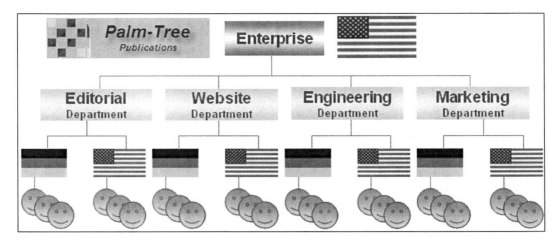

Before starting, assume that we have a set of users in the enterprise **Palm-Tree Publications**. We will plan to bring the following users into the portal. Briefly, a **user** is an individual who performs tasks using the portal.

Full Name	Screen Name	Email	Organization	Location
Palm Tree	**admin**	admin@bookpub.com	Enterprise	US
David Berger	**david**	david@bookpub.com	Editorial	US
Lotti Stein	**lotti**	lotti@bookpub.com	Editorial	US
Rolf Hess	**rolf**	rolf@bookpub.com	Editorial	US
Julia Maurer	**julia**	julia@bookpub.com	Editorial	Germany
Martin Gall	**martin**	martin@bookpub.com	Editorial	Germany
James Masse	**james**	james@bookpub.com	Website	US
Raja Fuchs	**raja**	raja@bookpub.com	Engineering	Germany
John Stucki	**john**	john@boobpub.com	Marketing	Germany

Suppose that as an administrator of the enterprise **Palm-Tree Publications**, you are planning to create a set of users as listed above, a set of organizations and locations to represent the preceding hierarchy. Moreover, you are planning to set up authentication and authorization, and you are also planning to do more with the user administration and organization administration as well.

Role-based access control

Traditional membership security models address two basic criteria: **authentication** (who has access) and **authorization** (what they can do).

- Authentication is a process of determining whether someone or something is, in fact, who or what it is declared to be.
- Authorization is a process of finding out if the person, once identified, is permitted to have access to a resource.

The portal extends the preceding security model by terminologies: resources, users, organizations, locations, user groups, communities, roles, permissions, and so on. The portal provides a role-based, fine-grained permission security model—a full access control security model. At the same time, it also provides a set of administrative tools (which we will discuss later) which can be used to configure and control membership.

The remainder of this section will explore these concepts and relationships among these terminologies, as shown in the following figure. Without a doubt, it would be useful to provide a big picture on how to bring in users. For example, as a user in the engineering department, you may plan to develop a number of portlets to satisfy the enterprise **Palm-Tree Publications** current requirements or even plan for future requirements. The following figure gives a view of the big picture of the security model.

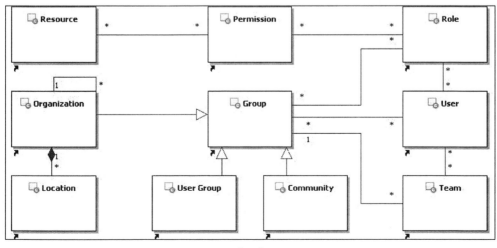

Role and permission

As shown in the previous figure, a **Resource** is a base object. It can be a portlet (for example, Message Boards, Calendar, Document Library, and so on), an entity (for example, Message Board Topics, Calendar Event, Document Library Folder, and so on), and a file (for example, documents, images, applications, and so on). Resources are scoped into portal, group, page, and content—model-resource and application (or portlet) types.

A **Permission** is an action on a resource. Portal-level permissions can be assigned to the portal (for example, users, user groups, communities, and organizations) through roles. Group-level permissions can be assigned to groups (for example, organization and communities). Page-level permissions can be assigned to page layouts. Model permissions can be assigned to model resources, (for example, blogs entries, web content, and so on). Portlet permission can be assigned to portlets (for example, view, configuration, and so on).

A **Role** is a collection of permissions. Roles can be assigned to a user, user group, community, location, or organization. If a role is assigned to a user group, community, organization, or location, then all users who are members of that entity receive permissions of the role.

User

A **User** is an individual who performs tasks using the portal. Depending on the permissions that have been assigned via roles, the user either has permission or doesn't have permission to perform certain tasks.

Additionally, each user can have public pages and private pages. More interestingly, user's private pages and public pages do have the ability to use page templates that can be used to customize a set of pages.

Organization and Location

An **Organization** represents the enterprise-department-location hierarchy. Organizations can contain other organizations as sub-organizations. Moreover, an organization acting as a child organization of a top-level organization can also represent departments of a parent corporation.

A **Location** is a special organization, having one and only one parent organization associated and having no child organization associated. Organizations can have any number of locations and sub organizations. Both roles and users can be assigned to organizations (locations or sub organizations). By default, locations and sub organizations inherit permissions from their parent organization via roles.

UserGroup and Community

A **Community** is a special group with a flat structure. It may hold a number of users who share common interests. Thus we can say that a community is a collection of users who have a common interest. Both roles and users can be assigned to a community.

Actually, communities are special groups that have a set of users. That is, a community may have a set of users associated. Normally a community is used to represent a set of users who share common interests. More details about communities can be found in *Chapter 7, Roll Out to Other Teams*.

How is a community different from an organization? Communities give us the ability to join and invite members, whereas organizations don't have this kind of capability. However, organizations are hierarchical in nature while communities are flat. Most importantly, both organizations and communities will have their own private pages and public pages. They also have the ability to apply site templates to easily customize websites.

Last but not least, a **UserGroup** is a special group with no context, which may hold a number of users. In other words, users can be gathered into user groups. Users can be assigned to user groups, and permissions can be assigned to user groups via roles too. Therefore, every user that belongs to that user group will receive role-based permissions.

In addition, each user group can have public pages and private pages. Thus users in a user group can share private pages and public pages. More interestingly, a user group's private pages and public pages do have the ability to apply page templates in order to quickly customize a set of pages.

Organizations

As mentioned earlier, we can use organizations to represent the enterprise Palm-Tree Publications and its department's hierarchy.

Adding a top-level Organization

First of all, we need to create a 'top-level' organization (that is, the enterprise) for the whole company—in this case, Palm Tree Publications. Carry out the following steps in order to add a top-level organization:

Log in to the portal as an administrator **admin,** using the user e-mail and password that you had updated through My Account in the previous chapter.

1. Go to **Manage | Control Panel** under the **Dock bar menu.**
2. Click on **Organizations** under the **Portal** category.
3. Click on the **Add** link under **Organizations.**
4. Enter enterprise information in the **Name** input field, **Palm Tree Enterprise.**
5. Select a value for **Type**—using the default value **Regular Organization.**
6. Select a value for **Parent Organization** using a default value.
7. Click on the **Save** button to save the inputs.

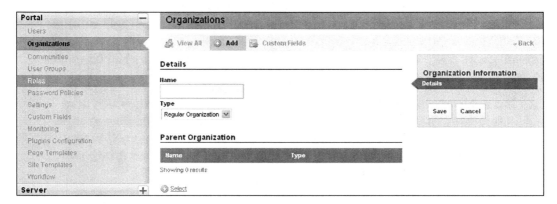

Note that the Enterprise is the top-level organization. It has no parent organization. At the same time, it is an organization that will have a set of sub organizations. Therefore, the Enterprise can be represented as a regular organization with the type value **Regular Organization.**

As you can see, there is a toolbar used for top-level navigation. This toolbar is located at the top of the organizations section just below the title **Organizations,** providing a quick access to the most used functions when working with organizations:

- **View All**: Shows a list of all the organizations
- **Add**: Shows adding organization forms; only the users with the proper permissions will be able to see this in the toolbar.
- **Custom Fields**: Manages custom attributes (also know as custom fields) of organizations. Similar to **Add,** it is available only to users with the Administrator role.

So we've created a top-level organization. Now we need to create organizations for the main departments in the Enterprise.

Managing organizations

Organizations can contain other organizations as sub organizations. This is useful in large companies where each department might almost be a separate company, with little interaction among them.

Adding child organizations

Let us create two departments within 'Palm Tree Publications' Enterprise, **Editorial**, and **Marketing** by following these steps:

1. Click on **Organizations** under the **Portal** category of **Control Panel**.
2. Click on the **Add** link under **Organizations**;
3. Enter the enterprise information in the **Name** input field, say **Editorial Department**.
4. Select a value for **Type** — using default value **Regular Organization**.
5. Click on the **Select** button to select the **Parent Organization**. In the organization selection page, choose **Palm Tree Enterprise**.
6. Click on the **Save** button to save the inputs.

Similarly, you can add a child organization, **Marketing Department**. Optionally, you can add the child organization **Marketing Department** from the parent organization **Palm Tree Enterprise** by following these steps:

1. Click on **Organizations** under the category **Portal** category of **Control Panel**.
2. Locate the desired parent organization, for example, **Palm Tree Enterprise**.
3. Click on the **Add Regular Organization** icon from **Actions** next to the right of the organization.
4. Enter the enterprise information in the **Name** input field, say **Marketing Department**.
5. Leave **Regular Organization** as the default value of Type.
6. Leave **Palm Tree Enterprise** as the default value of the **Parent Organization**.
7. Click on the **Save** button to save the inputs, or click on the **Cancel** button to discard the inputs.

Of course, you can create other departments in most organizations similarly. After adding child organizations—for example, Engineering Department and Website Department—you can view organizations.

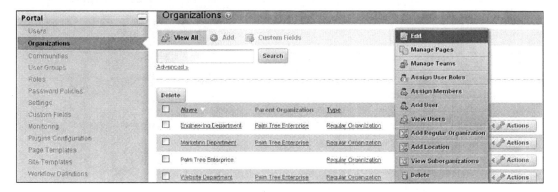

Viewing organizations

As compared to adding child organizations, viewing organizations is much simpler. This is explained as follows:

- Click on **Organizations** under the category **Portal** of **Control Panel**. It displays a set of organizations with name, parent organization, type, city, region, and country.

- Locate an organization, for example, Palm Tree Enterprise, which you want to view first and then click on the organization from the link, for example, Palm Tree Enterprise.

- In addition, click on the **View Suborganizations** icon from the **Actions** next to the organization if you want to view sub organizations, for example, **Editorial Department**.

Searching organizations

You can find organizations by using either a basic search or an advanced search. To search for organizations, click on **Organizations** under the category **Portal** of **Control Panel** and then input some search criterion for basic search. Or you can input organization information in input fields (for example name, street, city, zip, country, and region), and select Type value **Regular Organization** for advanced search and click on the **Search** button. A list of organizations matching the search criterion appears on the bottom of organizations screen.

For a basic search, it will search both organizations and locations. Using the advanced search, you may search organizations with the **Type** value **Regular Organization**, and locations with the **Type** value **Location**, or both with **Type** value **Any**.

Editing an organization

After adding organizations, we are ready to manage them. For example, we want to update the organization **Website department** information (for example, changing name, parent organization, and logo). Let us do it by following these steps:

1. Click on **Organizations** under the **Portal** category of **Control Panel** first and then locate organization, (for example, Website department with the **Type** value **Regular Organization**, which you want to edit).

2. Click on the **Edit** icon from **Actions** next to the right of the organization; or click on any links of the organization, for example, Website department.

3. Type the changes in the **Name** input field.

4. Remove the current parent organization through the **Remove** link, or select an organization as the parent organization through the **Select** link.

5. Click on the **Change** link and upload a logo, for example, **Organization-logo.png**.

6. Click on the **Save** button to save the changes.

Note that one organization can have one and only one parent organization. When you select an organization as the parent organization of an organization that already has a parent, the current parent organization will get overridden by the selected one. Of course, an organization should not select itself as its parent organization.

As you can see, the portal provides a menu at the right-hand side of the screen which shows all sections of forms, thereby allowing faster navigation through them in a way that doesn't require a page reload. Forms for adding and editing organizations are different, which allows a fast and easy way to create organizations and a deeper personalization afterwards. Items in the menu are grouped into three sections: **Organization Information**, **Identification**, and **Miscellaneous**. By default, when creating an organization, only the organization's details are visible. When editing an organization, you would be able to see the rest of the enabled sections by following these steps:

1. **Pages**: manages an organization's private pages and public pages. If site templates are available, then you would be able to apply existing site templates on both private pages and public pages.

2. **Categorization**: adds tags; each organization can have multiple tags.

3. **Addresses**: holds mail address information; each organization can have multiple addresses.

4. **Phone Numbers**: manages phone numbers; each organization can have multiple phone numbers.

5. **Additional Email Addresses**: manages e-mail addresses; each organization can have multiple e-mail address.

6. **Websites**: manages websites; each organization can have multiple websites, either intranets or public.

7. **Services**: manages services; each organization can have multiple services.

8. **Comments**: manages comments; each organization can have one comment boxes

9. **Reminder Queries**: manages reminder queries in different languages.

10. **Custom Fields**: manages values of custom attributes, if custom attributes have been added to the current organization.

 Note that no changes are applied until the **Save** button is clicked.

Deleting an organization

For some reason a department (for example, the Website Department) does not exist anymore. We need to delete this organization in the portal. We will do it by following these steps:

1. Click on **Organizations** under the **Portal** category of **Control Panel**.

2. Locate the organization which you want to delete (for example, the Website Department).

3. Click on the **Delete** icon from the **Actions** to the right of the organization, or select the checkbox to the left of the organization and press the **Delete** button.

4. A screen will appear asking if you want to delete the selected organizations. Click on the **OK** button to confirm, or click on the **Cancel** button to cancel.

 Note that you can't delete an organization which has child organizations, locations, or users associated with it. In order to delete this organization, you need to remove sub organizations, locations, or users from this organization first, and only then will you be able to delete it.

Assigning users to an organization

Users can be assigned to an organization by following these steps:

1. Click on **Organizations** under the **Portal** category of **Control Panel**.

2. Locate an organization (for example, the Website Department).

3. Then click on the **Assign Members** icon from **Actions** to the right of the organization.

4. Click on the **Available** tab to display a list of all available users in the portal. Search for the desired users using the search form (by either basic search or advanced search). Tick the checkboxes to the left of the desired users. If you would like to select all of the users on the current page, then check the checkbox next to the **Name** column.

5. Click on the **Update Associations** button to assign users to an organization. Optionally, to confirm that desired users were successfully associated with the organization, click on the **Current** tab.

Additionally, you can view users by clicking on the **View Users** icon from **Actions** to the right of the organization. Moreover, each organization has its own public pages and private pages. You can manage these pages by clicking on the **Manage Pages** icon from **Actions** to the right of the organization. Else, you can assign user roles by clicking on the **Assign User Roles** icon from **Actions** to the right of the location. In addition, you can have many teams for a given organization. You can then manage these teams by clicking on the **Manage Teams** icon from **Actions** to the right of the organization and assign members to teams.

Using organizations in an effective way

Organizations represent the enterprise and departments hierarchy. Each organization has a set of basic properties such as name, parent organization (not for top-level organizations), status, country, and so on. It may also have a set of optional properties such as, e-mail addresses, mail addresses, websites, phone numbers, services, comments, custom fields, and so on.

An organization can represent a parent corporation. An example would be the Enterprise 'Palm Tree Publications'.

An organization which acts as a child organization of a top-level organization can also represent departments of a parent corporation. Examples would be Editorial Department, Marketing Department, and so on.

Logically, users can be members of more than one organization. For best practice, it is better to make a user belong to only one organization. So make sure your organizations don't overlap. For example, if you have a department called Marketing Department and another department called Engineering Department, then the marketing manager can be in one department or the other, but not in both.

This might seem limiting, but there is an answer — user groups. A user can be a member of any number of user groups, and 'mangers' is a common user group. We'll see how to work with them later.

Locations

A company might have several locations, just like it has many departments. Palm Tree Publications has one location in San Jose, United States, and one in Berlin, Germany. Let us go ahead and create them.

Adding a location for the enterprise

First of all, we need to add a location for the enterprise 'Palm Tree Publications', that is the organization "Palm Tree US". Let's do that now:

1. Click on **Organizations** under the **Portal** category of **Control Panel** first.
2. Then click the **Add** button.
3. Enter the enterprise information in the **Name** input field (for example, Palm Tree US), select a country from the **Country** menu (for example, United States), and a region from the **Region** (for example, California).
4. Click on the **Select** button to select the **Parent Organization**. In the organization selection page, choose **Palm Tree Enterprise**.

5. Select **Type** with the value **Location**.

6. Click on the **Save** button to save the inputs.

So we've added a location for a top-level organization. Now we need to create locations for the Editorial Department.

Generally speaking, a location is a special organization which associates with a parent organization. Most importantly, locations can't have any child organizations associated with them. Locations may be distinguished by their geographic position mostly. An organization may have any number of sub organizations and locations. Obviously, locations are the leaves of organizations.

Adding locations for main organizations

Let us create a location called Editorial US for the department "Editorial" by following these steps:

1. Click on **Organizations** under the **Portal** category of **Control Panel**.

2. Then click on the button **Add**.

3. Enter the enterprise information in the **Name** input field (for example, Editorial US and select country from **Country** menu, for example, United States, and region from **Region** menu, for example, "California".

4. Click on the **Select** button to select a value for **Parent Organization**. In the organization selection page, choose Editorial department.

5. Select **Type** with the value "Location"; Note that you should select **Type** in the first step in order to see the country and region options.

6. Click on the **Save** button to save the inputs.

7. Similarly, we can add another location called Editorial Germany for the Editorial Department or we can add it directly as follows:

8. Click on **Organizations** under the **Portal** category of **Control Panel**.

9. Locate a parent organization.

10. Click on the **Add Location** icon from the **Actions** to the right of the organization.

11. Enter enterprise information in the **Name** input field (Editorial Germany), select country from the **Country** menu (Germany), and region from **Region** menu (Berlin).

12. Keep the **Type** default value **Location**;

13. Keep the default value of **Parent Organization**.

14. Click on the **Save** button to save the inputs.

You can create other locations for most organizations in the same way, after which, you can view them.

Viewing locations

Compared to adding locations, viewing them is much simpler. It is done by following these steps:

1. Click on **Organizations** under the **Portal** category of **Control Panel**; a list of locations appears on the bottom of the organizations screen.

2. Locate an organization with the **Type** value **Location** , which you want to view first, and then click on this organization.

Optionally, you can view locations for a given organization. To view locations that belong to a specific organization is simple and done by following these steps:

1. Click on **Organizations** under the **Portal** category of **Control Panel**.

2. Then click on **View Suborganizations** icon from the **Actions** to the right of an organization. A screen will appear showing organizations including the locations that belong to the specific organization.

3. Locate an organization with the **Type** value **Location**, which you want to view first and then click on the organization by links (for example, name).

Searching locations

Locations are searchable either by advanced search or by basic search. To search for locations, simply click on **Organizations** under the category **Portal** of **Control Panel** first; then input organization information in the input fields and select **Type** value **Location** in advanced search, and click the **Search** button.

You can find both regular organizations and locations in one place using the basic search.

Editing a location

After adding locations, we are ready to manage them. Consider that we want to update the location information of Website US (For example, changing name and parent organizations, and adding e-mail addresses and comments). We can do it by following these steps:

1. Click on **Organizations** under the **Portal** category of **Control Panel**.
2. Find the location, (for example, **Website US**) with the **Type** value **Location** that you want to edit.
3. Click on the **Edit** icon from the **Actions** to the right of the location; or click on links of the location (for example, name **Website US**.
4. Then in the editing page, type the changes in the **Name** input field and select values from the **Country** and **Region** menus to make changes. Or click on links on the right side such as: **Email Addresses**, **Addresses**, **Websites**, **Phone Numbers**, **Services**, **Comments**, **custom fields**, and so on.
5. Click on the **Save** button to save the changes.

Deleting a location

For some reason, a location like **Website US** doesn't exist anymore. Therefore, we need to delete this location in the portal. We can do it by following these steps:

1. Click on **Organizations** under the **Portal** category of **Control Panel**.
2. Locate the location you want to delete, for example **Website US**.
3. Click on the **Delete** icon from the **Actions** to the right of the location; or select checkbox to the left of the location and press the **Delete** button.
4. A screen will appear asking if you want to delete the selected locations. Click the **OK** button to confirm.

 Note that you can't delete a location which has users associated with it. In order to delete this location, you need remove all users from it first.

Assigning users to a location

Users can be assigned to a location as follows:

Click on **Organizations** under the **Portal** category of **Control Panel**.

1. Locate a particular location (for example, **Editorial US**).
2. Then click on the **Assign Members** icon from **Actions** to the right of the location.
3. Click on the **Available** tab to display a list of all available users in the portal.
4. Click on the **Update Associations** button to assign users to the current location. Optionally, to confirm that the desired users were successfully associated with the current location, click on the **Current** tab.

In addition, you can view a location's users by clicking on the **View Users** icon from **Actions** next to the right of the location. As you can see, each location has its own public pages and private pages. Fortunately, you can manage these pages by clicking on the **Manage Pages** icon from **Actions** to the right of the location. Last, but not least, you may be interested in assigning user roles in a location, clicking on the **Assign User Roles** icon from **Actions** to the right of the location. And moreover, you can have many teams associated to a location. Then you can manage the teams by clicking on the Manage Teams icon from Actions to the right of the location and assign members to teams.

Using locations in an effective way

Locations are special organizations associated with a parent organization and have no child organizations. A location can be used to represent a child corporation of an organization and is mostly distinguished by its geographic location. An organization can have any number of sub organizations and locations, while a location must belong to one and only one organization. Some examples would be Editorial US, Editorial Germany, and so on.

Each location has a set of basic properties, (for example, name, parent organization, country, and so on). As a special organization, each location may also have a set of optional properties as well as the properties of a regular organization, for example, e-mail addresses, addresses, websites, phone numbers, services, comments, custom fields, and so on.

Organization settings

As you have seen, there are two types for adding and editing organization: regular organization and location. When adding an organization or adding a regular organization, the default value of type would be **Regular Organization**; when adding a location for a regular organization, the default value of type would be Location.

When you choose the type **Regular Organization**, the drop-down menus **Country** and **Region** are invisible. But when you choose the type **Location**, the drop-down menus **Country** and **Region** are visible again. How does it work?

As you can see, there is a difference between forms for adding or editing organizations. When adding an organization or a location, you will see only one section **Organization Information with Details**. When editing an organization or location, you will be able to see all the rest of the enabled sections such as **Identification, Miscellaneous,** as well as the section **Organization Information**. Under the **Organization Information** section, **Details, Pages,** and **Categorization** are visible. Under the section **Identification**, you would see **Addresses, Phone Numbers, Additional Email Addresses, Websites,** and **Services**. Under the section **Miscellaneous**, you will have **Comments, Reminder Queries,** and **Custom Fields**. How can we customize it?

The portal provides the organization administration tool with the following design patterns to achieve better usability and more flexibility. You can customize the preceding features using the overriding properties.

Organization types

Organization types are configurable. By default, the following properties are set in portal.properties.

```
organizations.types=regular-organization,location
organizations.rootable[regular-organization]=true
organizations.children.types[regular-organization]=regular-
organization,location
organizations.country.enabled[regular-organization]=false
organizations.country.required[regular-organization]=false
organizations.rootable[location]=false
organizations.country.enabled[location]=true
organizations.country.required[location]=true
```

The preceding code shows configuration of organization types. The property `organizations.types` specifies two organization types: `regular-organization` and `location`. This configuration mandates that `regular-organization` can be a root at the top level with no parents, and it can have `regular-organization` and `location` as children. The `location` must always have a `regular-organization` as a parent, and it can't have any children.

The `country` is disabled for `regular-organization`, and it isn't required for `regular-organization` too. However, it is enabled and required for `location`. This is the reason that when you choose the type **Regular Organization**, the drop-down menus **Country** and **Region** are invisible. When you choose the type **Location**, the drop-down menus **Country** and **Region** are visible.

You can override these properties in `portal-ext.properties`.

Organization forms

Just like organization types, organization forms are configurable too. There are two kinds of forms: `add` form and `update` form. The following properties have been set for the `add` form by default in `portal.properties`.

```
organizations.form.add.main=details
organizations.form.add.identification=
organizations.form.add.miscellaneous=
```

As shown in the above code, you can input a list of sections that will be included as part of the organization form, when adding an organization. For the `add` form, only the `main` section has one item, `details`. Thus when adding an organization or location, you will see only one section, **Organization Information with Details**.

The following properties have been set for the `update` form, by default, in `portal.properties`.

```
organizations.form.update.main=details,pages,categorization
organizations.form.update.identification=addresses,phone-
numbers,additional-email-addresses,websites,services
organizations.form.update.miscellaneous=comments,reminder-
queries,custom-attributes
```

As shown in the preceding code, you can input a list of sections that will be included as part of the organization form when updating an organization. For the `update` form, three sections (`main`, `identification`, and `miscellaneous`) are available. Therefore, when editing an organization or location, you will be able to see all sections; including **Identification**, **Miscellaneous**, and **Organization Information** (that is, `main`).

These properties can be overridden in `portal-ext.properties`. For example, you can hide some items in any sections or add new items to a given section.

Overriding assignment and membership

In addition, you can override properties related to assignment and membership. By default, the following properties have been set in `portal.properties`.

```
organizations.assignment.auto=false
organizations.assignment.strict=true
organizations.membership.strict=false
organizations.user.group.membership.enabled=false
```

As shown in the preceding code, you can set the property `organizations.assignment.auto` to `true`, so that any organization that an administrator creates can be automatically assigned to that organization. Similarly, you can set the property `organizations.assignment.strict` to `false` if you want any administrator of an organization to be able to assign any user to that organization. By default, the administrator will only be able to assign the users of organizations and sub organizations that he/she can manage.

In the same way, you can set the property `organizations.membership.strict` to `true` if you want users to only be members of the organizations to which they are assigned explicitly. By default, they will also become implicit members of the ancestors of those organizations. For example if a user belongs to Editorial US, then he/she will implicitly be a member of the ancestors Editorial Department and Palm-Tree Enterprise, and he/she will be able to access their private pages.

Again, you can set the property `organizations.user.group.membership.enabled` to `true` to allow user groups to be a member of organizations. These properties can be overridden in `portal-ext.properties` instead.

Hierarchy, tree, and Shared Global

As mentioned earlier, organizations and locations are the mechanisms to organize the users and websites just as the portal following a hierarchical structure. Each attached website can have a team and a dedicated workflow. That is the only way to have a hierarchical structure of websites. Organization represents the logical structure of the company or institution where the portal is going to be used. It has a hierarchical structure with as many levels as required. A location represents a physical location where the company or the institution users may work. Each location belongs to an organization.

Organization hierarchy

Regular organization can be a root, having no parent organization; or regular organization can have a parent organization and many child organizations or locations. Location must have a regular organization as parent, and have no child organizations. Therefore, organizations and locations form a hierarchical structure: regular organizations form root and trunk; while locations form leaves.

What can you benefit from organization hierarchy? The first benefit you can get is inherited permissions. Each user can be assigned to at most one organization inheriting the permissions and associations of that organization. The user will also inherit all permissions and associations of parent organizations of that organization that have been marked as inherited. Each user can be assigned to at most one location. That location must belong to an organization which the user is assigned or to one of the inherited parent organizations of that organization.

The second benefit you can get is content sharing in organization hierarchy. As mentioned in the previous chapter, content could be scoped into page and group. Organizations and locations have their own content. Through a hierarchical structure, content in parent organization could be shared in child organizations. For example, content in "Palm Tree Enterprise" would be accessible in the department "Editorial Department". And furthermore content in both "Palm Tree Enterprise" and "Editorial Department" would be accessible in the location "Editorial US".

Organization tree

It would be nice that parent organization can have multiple child organizations or locations. This parent-child relationship forms a hierarchical structure. But regular organization doesn't have siblings, for example, left-side regular organization (or location) and right-side organization (or location). Parent-child relationship plus left-side regular organization and right-side organization form a tree, called organization tree. This feature will come out soon.

Shared Global

The portal provides a global space called **Shared Global** that only the administrator can manage. Any content in the global space will be publishable in any community or organization pages. In addition, web content structures and templates will be reusable all across the portal. It's very useful to share a Dictionary (categories/tags) as well. Vocabularies are often shared between organizations for normalization purposes.

Note that Shared Global is not portal-wide. It is limited to the portal instance in which it resides, that is, Shared Global is associated to a portal instance. You would have one unique shared global scope for each portal instance.

User groups

Like many departments, a company might have several user groups. Palm Tree Publications has Raja Fuchs, an engineering manager in the Germany office and John Stucki, a marketing manager also in the Germany office. Both are managers but belong to different departments, thanks to the user group called **Managers** that contains a number of users belonging to different departments. Let us go ahead and create them.

Adding a user group

First of all, we will create a user group **Managers**, which contains users Raja Fuchs and John Stucki as follows.

1. Click on **User Groups** under the **Portal** category of **Control Panel**.
2. Then click on the **Add** button.
3. Enter a name for the user group in the **Name** input field (for example, **Managers**).
4. Click on the **Save** button to save the inputs.
5. Then click on the **Assign Members** icon from the **Actions** next to the right of the user group **Managers**.
6. Click on the **Available** tab to display a list of all the available users in the portal. Check the checkboxes to the left of the desired users. Note that these users don't exist at the moment. We'll learn about adding users in the next section.
7. Click on the **Update Associations** button to assign users to a user group. Optionally, to confirm the desired users were successfully associated with the user group, click on the **Current** tab.

Other user groups can be created in a similar fashion. After adding one more user group **Developers**, we can view user groups, as shown in following screenshot:

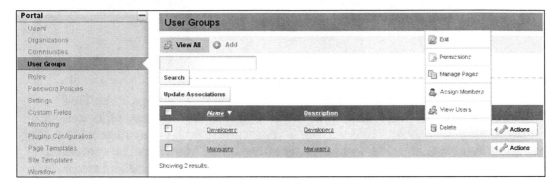

As you can see, there is a toolbar for top-level navigation. The toolbar is located at the top of the user groups section just below the title **User Groups**. It provides a quick access to the most used functions when working with user groups.

8. **View All** shows a list of all the user groups.

9. **Add** shows the adding user groups form (only the users with proper permissions will be able to see this in the toolbar).

Comparing this with the organization's top-level navigation, there is no **Custom Attributes** in the user group's top-level navigation. The pattern **View-All-Add** of the top-level navigation is reused by **Site Templates**, **Page Templates**, **Password Policies**, **Roles**, **Communities**, and so on.

Managing user groups

As mentioned earlier, a user group can hold any number of users. In fact, a user group is also a special group which may have a set of users and permissions by virtue of the roles they are associated with. User groups are different from both organizations and communities because they have no context associated with them.

Viewing user groups

To view user groups, click on **User Groups** under the **Portal** category of **Control Panel**. A list of user groups appears on the bottom of the screen. Click on the user group that you want to view (for example, **Managers**). The portal will display the **Name** and **Description** of that user group.

Searching user groups

User groups are searchable. To search user groups, click on **User Groups** under the **Portal** category of **Control Panel**. Then type a user group name as search keywords, and click on the **Search** button.

Editing a user group

You may need to edit a user group. Click on **User Groups** under the category **Portal** of **Control Panel**, and then locate the user group that you want to edit. Click on the **Edit** icon from the **Actions** button to the right of the user group, or click on any links of the user group. In the **Edit** page, type the changes in the **New Name** input field and the **Description** input field. Then click on the **Save** button to save the changes.

Deleting user groups

For some reason the **Developers** user group does not exist anymore. We need to delete this user group in the portal. We will delete the user group **Developers** as follows:

1. Click on **User Groups** under the **Portal** category of **Control Panel**.
2. Locate a user group that you want to delete.
3. Then click on the **Delete** icon from the **Actions** button to the right of the user group, or check the box on the left of the user group, and click on the **Delete** button.
4. A screen will appear asking if you want to permanently delete the selected user groups.
5. Click on the **OK** button to delete the selected user group.

Similarly, you can delete multiple user groups by checking the checkboxes located to the left of the user groups that you want to delete first, and then click on the **Delete** button. All user groups can be deleted at one go by checking the checkbox located next to the **Name** column, and then clicking on the **Delete** button. A screen will appear asking if you want to permanently delete the selected user groups. Click on the **OK** button to delete or the **Cancel** button if you do not want to delete the selected user groups.

Assigning users to a user group

Users can be assigned to a user group by following these steps:

1. Click on **User Groups** under the **Portal** category of **Control Panel**.
2. Locate the user group to which you want to assign members, and click on the **Assign Members** icon from the **Actions** button to the right of the user group.

3. Click on the **Available** tab to display a list of all available users in the portal. To assign users to the current user group, click on the **Update Associations** button. Optionally, to confirm that desired users were successfully associated with the current user group, click on the **Current** tab.

In addition, you can view users by clicking on the **View Users** icon from the **Actions** button to the right of the user group. As you can see, each user group has its own public pages and private pages. Of course, you can manage these pages by clicking on the **Manage Pages** icon from the **Actions** button next to the right of the user group. Note that users who belong to current user group will have these pages copied to their user pages when the user is first associated with the current user group.

Users

Finally, with the company, departments, organizations, locations, and user groups in one place, we can add some users.

Adding users

As stated earlier, a user is an individual who performs tasks using the portal. Users can belong to a regular organization, a special organization, a location, or a user group. Before adding new users, let's suppose that the admin account **Palm Tree** changed its e-mail address to admin@bookpub.com under **My Account**. Let's also say the admin **Palm Tree** changed **Main Configuration Name** and **Mail Domain** to **bookpub.com** and updated the company logo to PalmTree_logo.png under **Settings** of the category **Portal**, as shown in following screenshot:

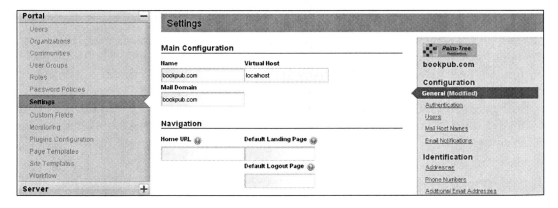

First of all, we will add Martin Gall, who works in the editorial department in the Germany office.

1. Click on **Users** under the **Portal** category of **Control Panel**.
2. Then click on **Add** button.
3. Enter the user's information in the input field, and select the values from the drop-down menus. Most importantly, **Screen Name**, (for example, **Martin**) and **Email Address**, (for example, martin@bookpub.com) are required, along with the **First Name** and the **Last Name**, since both act as unique identifiers for this user. When this user logs in, the **Screen Name, Email Address,** or **User Id** will be used as the login ID.
4. A location can be selected by clicking on **Organizations** in the menu to the right (like **Editorial Germany** that the new user belongs to).
5. Click on the **Save** button to save the inputs, as shown in following screenshot:

As shown in previous screenshot, there is a toolbar used for top-level navigation. This toolbar is located at the top of the **Users** section, below the title **Users**, which provides a quick access to the most used functions, when working with users.

1. **View All** shows a list of all the users.
2. **Add** shows the adding user form; only the users with proper permissions will be able to see this in the toolbar.
3. **Custom Fields** manages custom attributes of users. It is available only to users with the Administrator role.
4. **Export** is a very simple export functionality to download a CSV file that contains the **User ID** and **Email Address** of all the users. Just like Custom Attributes, it is available only to users with the Administrator role.

What's happening?

We added our first user to the portal. When we created the new account, the portal will send an e-mail to the specified e-mail address notifying the user that they can log in and start using the portal.

Note that the e-mail will only be sent successfully if you have specified an SMTP server in the mail portlet for the portal to use. Refer to *Chapter 10, Social Office, Hooks, and Custom Fields*.

Here's an example of the e-mail that Martin will receive:

```
Dear Martin,

    Welcome! You recently created an account at http://bookpub.com/. Your
    password is your ********. Enjoy!
    Sincerely,
    Palm Tree
    admin@bookpub.com
    http://bookpub.com
```

When the user clicks the link, he will be taken to a page that displays signing in as regular account. After inputting his e-mail address and password and clicking on the **Sign in** button, he will be taken to a page that displays terms and conditions, **Terms of Use**.

 Note that you would be able to change the e-mail notification (for example, Account created notification and password changed notification). Refer to Chapter 13 for detailed instructions.

Adding more users

We will add a few more users. We can add two more users; David Berger and Lotti Stein in the way we just mentioned. Both belong to the editorial department in the US offices.

Fortunately, there are two more options for adding users: to add a user for a given organization and to add a user from scratch, as mentioned.

We will add David Berger from scratch by following these steps:

1. Click on **Users** under the **Portal** category of **Control Panel**.
2. Click on the **Add** button.

3. Enter the user's information in the input fields, then select values from drop-down menus, and then select a location (**Editorial US**).

4. Click on the **Save** button to save the inputs.

Let us add **Lotti Stein** through a given organization by following these steps:

1. Click on **Organizations** under the **Portal** category of **Control Panel**.

2. Select a location (**Editorial US**) to which you want to add a new user.

3. Click on the **Add User** icon from the **Actions** located to the right of the organization to which you want to add a user. You will see that the selected organization has been selected by default.

4. Enter the user's information in the input fields, and select values from drop-down menus.

5. Click on the **Save** button to save the inputs.

Adding users in bulk

It won't be long before you're bored of manually adding users. Fortunately, you don't need to type them all in one at a time. There are several options for adding users in bulk:

- **LDAP** — Lightweight Directory Access Protocol (for example, Apache Directory Server, Fedora Directory Server, Microsoft Active Directory Server, Novell eDirectory, OpenLDAP, and so on).

- **Single Sign-On (SSO)** — A method of access control that enables a user to authenticate once, and gain access to the resources of multiple software systems (for example, CAS, NTLM, OpenSSO, SiteMinder, and so on).

- **OpenID** — A decentralized single sign-on system.

Creating an account on the fly

As an administrator at Palm Tree Publications, you can set up the portal allowing users to create an account on the fly. For example, Rolf Hess accesses the portal login page, and clicks on the **Create Account** tab. He inputs the user information and text verification, and then presses the **Save** button. How do we do this? Go to **Control Panel | Settings | Authentication**, and check the box **allow users to create accounts**.

The portal will create an account for the user **Rolf Hess** and send an e-mail to him with a new password.

Note that there is no organization or location selected for the new account created on the fly. In order to set proper organization and location to the new account, administrators have to update this account in the portal.

Fortunately, as an administrator, you can set up default user associations on communities, roles, and user groups. You can find this feature at **Settings | Users | Default User Associations** under the **Portal** category of **Control Panel**.

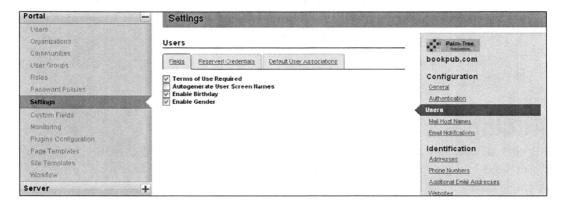

What to do when a user forgets the password?

If a user forgot his/her password, then he/she can access the portal login page and can click on the tab **Forgot Password**. He/she needs to input their e-mail address and text verification and then press the **Send New Password** button. The portal will create a new password for the user and mail it to him/her. As mentioned in the previous chapter, you can configure this feature.

Managing users

You can add users of others departments in most organizations in a similar fashion. After adding more users, we can view the users.

Viewing users

Users could either be active or inactive in the portal. It is simple to view active users. Click on **Users** under the category **Portal** of **Control Panel**. A list of users appears on the bottom of the user's screen. Locate the user that you want to view first, and click on the user's name (for example, Rolf Hess).

To view deactivated users, click on the **Active** menu from the advanced search, and select the **No** item. Click on the **Search** button to display a list of deactivated users.

Optionally, we can view users for a specific organization or location. To view users that belong to a specific organization, simply click on the **Organizations** section. Then click on the **View Users** icon from the **Actions** button next to the right of an organization or location. You may view a user by locating it and then clicking on it.

Similarly, you may view users that belong to a specific user group by clicking on the **User Groups** section and then by clicking on **View Users** icon from the **Actions** button to the right of a user group. Most interestingly, you may view users associated with a specific role by clicking on **Roles section** and then by clicking on **View Users** icon from the **Actions** button to the right of the role.

Searching for users

Users are searchable. First you can search users by clicking on **Users** under the category **Portal** of **Control Panel**. After that, input the search criterion for basic search or input the user's information in the input fields and select a value (**Yes** or **No**) from the **Active** menu options for an advanced search. Finally click on the **Search** button. A list of users matching the search criteria appears at the bottom of the user's screen.

Note that basic search is only useful for active users. You cannot find inactive users by basic search. To find inactive users, you have to use the advanced search option and select **No** from the **Active** menu options.

Editing a user profile

After adding users, we are ready to manage them. For example, we want to update the profile of Lotti Stein, (such as changing the name, parent organizations, and adding e-mail addresses and comments). Let's do it by following these steps:

1. Click on **Users** under the **Portal** category of **Control Panel** first.

2. Then locate the user whose record you want to update, and click on the user.

3. Click on the **Edit** icon from the **Actions** button next to the right of the user, click any links of the user, or select the checkbox to the left of the user.

4. A screen will appear displaying the user's information. Type the changes in the **First Name**, **Middle Name**, **Last Name**, **Email Address**, **Screen Name**, and **Job Title** input fields, and select from **Title**, **Suffix**, **Birthday**, and **Gender** menus to make the changes.

5. Optionally, you can change the icon, **Display Settings** (including **Display Language**, **Time Zone**, and **Greeting**), **Password**, **Role**, **Organization**, **Additional Emails Address**, **Addresses**, **Comments**, **Custom Attributes**, and so on.

6. Click on the **Save** button to save the changes.

 Note that the functions for editing a user are the same as that of updating the profile in **My Account**. In **My Account**, you can only update your own information. You can update any user's information if you have the proper permissions to do so.

As you can see, the portal provides a right menu for users, showing sections of forms which allow navigating through them in a fast way that doesn't require page reload. Forms for adding and editing users are different, allowing an easy and fast way to create users and a deeper personalization afterwards. Similar to forms of organizations, items in the right menu are grouped into three sections: **User Information**, **Identification**, and **Miscellaneous**. By default, when creating a user, only **Details**, **Organizations**, and **Pages** are visible.

When editing the organization, you would be able to see the rest of the enabled sections in the following screenshot:

- **Password**: changes the user's password.

- **Organizations**: changes membership in organizations (or locations) association. Each user can be a member of multiple organizations (or locations).

- **Communities**: changes membership in communities. Each user can be a member of multiple communities.

- **User Groups**: changes membership in user groups. Each user can be a member of multiple user groups.

- **Roles**: changes associations of roles. Each user can be associated with multiple roles.

- **Pages**: manages a user's private pages and public pages. If site templates are available, then you would be able to apply existing site templates on both private pages and public pages. Note that this is only available for users who have the role Power User.

- **Categorization**: adds tags. Each user can have multiple tags.

- **Addresses**: holds mail address information. Each user can have multiple addresses.

- **Phone Numbers**: manages phone numbers. Each user can have multiple phone numbers.

- **Additional Email Addresses**: manages e-mail addresses. Each user can have multiple e-mail address.
- **Websites**: manages personal websites. Each user can have multiple websites, either intranets or public.
- **Instant Messenger**: manages Instant Messenger.
- **Social Network**: manages Social Network.
- **SMS**: manages SMS.
- **OpenID**: manages OpenID.
- **Announcement**: manages announcements.
- **Display Settings**: manages display settings.
- **Comments**: manages comments.
- **Custom Fields**: manages values of custom attributes, if custom attributes have been added to the current user.

Note that no changes are applied until the **Save** button is clicked. Obviously, the right menu shows at all times which sections have been modified and if a save is pending. It allows us to making changes to different sections and to save everything at once. The **Save** and **Cancel** buttons have been placed right below the menu, so that they are always in the same place, independent of how large the form section is. It's easier for users to find the **Save** and **Cancel** buttons. Therefore, clicking the **Save** button will save all the changes to any of the sections of the form.

Deactivating a user

Imagine that "Lotti Stein" has become inactive, and we need to deactivate their user account. To deactivate a user just follow these steps:

1. Click on **Users** under the **Portal** category of the **Control Panel**.
2. Locate the user that you want to deactivate.
3. Then click on the checkbox next to the user you want to deactivate, and click on the **Deactivate** button. Alternatively, you can also deactivate a user by clicking on the **Deactivate** icon from the **Actions** tab next to a user.

To deactivate all users listed on a page, click on the checkbox next to the **Name** column, and click on the **Deactivate** button. A screen will appear asking if you want to deactivate the selected users. Click on **OK** to deactivate them or **Cancel** if you don't want to deactivate the selected users.

Activating a user

If we want to make an inactive user active again in the portal, we need to restore or activate that user account. Restoring a user is simple. Just follow these steps:

1. Click on **Users** under the **Portal** category of **Control Panel**.

2. Click on **Activate** menu in advanced search, and select **No** first. Then click on the **Search** button to display a listing of deactivated users.

3. Click on the checkbox located next to the user you want to reactivate and then click the **Restore** button. Alternatively, you can also reactivate a user by clicking on the **Activate** icon from the **Actions** tab to the right of the user.

To restore all users listed on a page, click the checkbox next to the **Name** column, and click on the **Restore** button.

Deleting a user

If a user doesn't exist anymore, we need to delete him/her from the portal as follows. User accounts must be deactivated before they can be deleted.

1. Click on **Users** under the **Portal** category of **Control Panel**.

2. Click on the **Active** menu in advanced search, and select **No item**. Click on the **Search** button to display a list of deactivated users.

3. Click on the checkbox located next to the user you want to delete, and click on the **Delete** button. Another way to delete a user is by clicking on the **Delete** icon from the **Actions** tab to the right of the user.

To delete all users listed on a page, click the checkbox located next to him/her in the **Name** column. Then, click the **Delete** button. A screen will appear asking if you want to permanently delete the selected users. Click the **OK** button to delete, or click the **Cancel** button if you don't want to delete the selected users.

Impersonating a user

Administrators and normal users with the **Impersonate User** function can conveniently review updates performed to other users. For example, the administrator gives permissions to the user 'Lotti Stein' to edit all users in the 'Palm Tree Publications' US location. To verify that the edit permission has been correctly given to a user, the administrator can sign in as that user. Alternatively, the administrator can search for the user in **Users** under the category **Portal** of **Control Panel** and click the **Impersonate User** icon from the **Actions** tab to the right of the user. By using the Impersonate function, the administrator can impersonate the user to review updates, without having to sign in as the user.

Using the Actions tab

As mentioned earlier, each user has his/her own public pages and private pages (only if he/she is a power user). These pages can be managed by clicking on the **Manage Pages** icon from the **Actions** tab to the right of the user. In addition, you can set up permissions for a specific user by clicking on the **Permissions** icon from the **Actions** tab to the right of the user.

User settings

As you can see, forms for adding or editing users are different. When adding a user, you will see the sections **User Information**, **Details**, **Organizations**, and **Pages**, whereas, when editing a user profile, you will be able to see the rest of the enabled sections such as **Identification**, **Miscellaneous**, as well as **User Information**.

For example, while editing the user profile, you could be able to assign roles, organizations, and communities to the user without leaving the form. Any change will be saved, along with the rest of the form, when the **Save** button is clicked.

The portal provides user administration tool following design patterns to achieve better usability and more flexibility. You can customize the preceding features by overriding properties.

User forms

User forms can be configured easily. Two kinds of forms are identified: add form and update form.

- The following properties are set for the add form by default in portal.properties.

  users.form.add.main=details,organizations,pages

  users.form.add.identification=

  users.form.add.miscellaneous=

  As shown in the previous code, you can input a list of sections that will be included as part of the user form when adding a user. For the add form, the main section has item **Details**, **Organizations**, and **Pages**. This is the reason that when adding a user, you will see only one section **User Information** with **Details**, **Organizations**, and **Pages**.

- The following properties have been set for the update form by default in portal.properties.

  users.form.update.main=details,password,organizations,communities, user-groups,roles,pages,categorization

  users.form.update.identification=addresses,phone-numbers,additional-email-addresses,websites,instant-messenger,social-network,sms,open-id

  users.form.update.miscellaneous=announcements,display-settings,comments,custom-attributes

  As shown in the previous code, you can input a list of sections that will be included as part of the user form when updating a user. For the update form, three sections (**Main**, **Identification**, and **Miscellaneous**) are available. For this reason, you'll see these sections when editing a user profile.

These properties can be overridden in portal-ext.properties. For example, you can hide or add new items to a given section.

Overriding user-related properties

User-related properties can be overridden. By default, the following properties have been set in portal.properties.

```
users.delete=true
users.screen.name.always.autogenerate=false
users.email.address.required=true
users.image.max.size=307200
users.update.last.login=true
users.search.with.index=true
```

As shown in the previous code, you can set the property `users.delete` to `false`, if the users cannot be deleted. Similarly, you can set the property `users.screen. name.always.autogenerate` to `true` to always auto-generate user screen names, even if the user gives a specific user screen name.

In the same way, you can set the property `users.email.address.required` to `false` if you want to be able to create users without an e-mail address. Note that not requiring an e-mail address would disable some features that depend on an e-mail address being provided.

Again, you can set the maximum file size for user portraits using the property `users.image.max.size`. You can use a value of `0` for the maximum file size to indicate unlimited file size. The property `users.update.last.login` is set to `true` by default to record the last login information for a user. The property `users. search.with.index` is set to `true` by default to search users from the index. Set this to `false` to search users from the database. Note that setting this to `false` will disable the ability to search users based on **Custom Attributes**.

Alternatively, you can override these properties in `portal-ext.properties`.

Authentications

As mentioned earlier, you don't need to type users all in one at a time. You can add users in bulk via LDAP and SSO. At the same time, you may require the facility for strangers to create accounts and for the users to then request their password via the Forgot Password function. How can you customize these features? Let's take a deeper look at authentications.

General configuration

Generally speaking, user login functions are configurable in the portal. By default, authentication is based on the portal database. But as an administrator, you would be able to set up authentication based on LDAP and SSO, other than that on the portal database.

As shown in the following screenshot, you could set up the portal so that users can authenticate by e-mail address, screen name, or user ID. You could allow users to automatically login, to request forgotten passwords, allow strangers to create accounts, allow strangers to create accounts with a company e-mail address, and require strangers to verify their e-mail address.

For example, imagine that you are planning to set authentication by screen name. You can do it as follows:

- Go to **Settings | Authentication** under **Portal** category of **Control Panel**.
- Select **By Screen Name** from the drop-down menu **How do users authenticate**.
- Click on the **Save** button.

What's happening?

As you can see, following items are set to true:
Allow users to automatically login? Allow users to request forgotten passwords? Allow strangers to create accounts? Allow strangers to create accounts with a company email address? Only the item, that is, **Require strangers to verify their email address?** is set to `false` by default.

The portal has the following settings by default in `portal.properties`.

```
basic.auth.password.required=true company.security.auth.
type=emailAddress
company.security.auth.requires.https=false
company.security.auto.login=true
company.security.send.password=true
company.security.strangers=true
company.security.strangers.verify=false
```

As shown in the previous code, the portal sets the property `basic.auth.password.required` to `true` to require a password when using basic authentication. Moreover, the portal can authenticate users based on their e-mail address, screen name, or user ID. By default, the property `company.security.auth.type` is set as `emailAddress`. You can set the property `company.security.auth.requires.https` to `true` to ensure that users login with HTTPS. The portal sets the property `company.security.auto.login` to `true` to allow users to select the "remember me" feature to automatically log in to the portal, sets the property `company.security.send.password` to `true` to allow users to ask the portal to send them their password, and sets the property `company.security.strangers` to `true` to allow strangers to create accounts and register themselves on the portal. In addition, you can set the property `company.security.strangers.verify` to `true` if strangers who create accounts need to be verified via e-mail.

Basic authentication

The portal has specified basic authentication as follows in `portal.properties`.

```
basic.auth.password.required=true
```

The previous property is set to `true` to require a password when using basic authentication. Note that you should only set this to `false` if additional security measures are in place to ensure that users have been properly authenticated.

Auto login

The portal has specified auto login as follows in `portal.properties`.

```
auto.login.hooks=com.liferay.portal.security.auth.CASAutoLogin,com.
liferay.portal.security.auth.NtlmAutoLogin,com.liferay.
portal.security.auth.OpenIdAutoLogin,com.liferay.portal.
security.auth.OpenSSOAutoLogin,com.liferay.portal.security.
auth.RememberMeAutoLogin,com.liferay.portal.security.auth.
SiteMinderAutoLogin
auto.login.ignore.hosts=
auto.login.ignore.paths=
```

As shown in the previous code, the property `auto.login.hooks` inputs a list of comma delimited class names such as CAS, OpenId, OpenSSO, NTLM, SiteMinder, and so on that implement `com.liferay.portal.security.auth.AutoLogin`. These classes will run in consecutive order for all unauthenticated users until one of them returns a valid user ID and password combination. If no valid combination is returned, then the request continues to process normally. If a valid combination is returned, then the portal will automatically login that user with the returned user ID and password combination.

In addition, the property `auto.login.ignore.hosts` sets the hosts that will be ignored for auto login and the property `auto.login.ignore.paths` sets the paths that will be ignored for auto login.

LDAP authentication

The portal supports LDAP authentication. The portal provides support, by default, for Apache Directory Server, Fedora Directory Server, Microsoft Active Directory Server, Novell eDirectory, OpenLDAP, OpenDS, and so on.

This section will show you how to set up LDAP authentication by examples. For instance, the enterprise 'Palm Tree Publications' is planning to store and manage all users in an LDAP server (that is, Apache Directory Server). The LDAP server, in this example, has the following information.

```
Base Provider URL: ldap://docs.cignex.com:10389
Base DN: ou=book,ou=system
Principal: uid=admin,ou=system
Credentials: secret
```

Thus, you can set authentication through the previous LDAP server. Let's do it by following these steps:

1. Click on **Settings | Authentication** under the **Portal** category of **Control Panel**.

2. Click on the **LDAP** tab.

3. In connection settings, check **Enabled** and **Required**. Note that when the checkbox **Required** was selected, the authentication will be done only on LDAP servers.

4. Click on the button **Add** under the section **LDAP Servers**.

5. Input LDAP-DOCS as the server name.

6. Select default value **Apache Directory Server**.

7. Under **Connection** section, enter Base Provider URL: ldap://docs. cignex.com:10389; Base DN: ou=book, ou=system; Principal: uid=admin,ou=system; Credentials: secret.

8. Use default values on **Users**, **Groups**, and **Import/Export** sections.

9. Select the checkbox **Import Enabled** under the section **Import/Export** if you want to import users in bulk.

10. Select the checkbox **Export Enabled** under the section **Import/Export** if you want to synchronize LDAP servers with the portal database.

11. Select the checkbox **Use LDAP Password Policy** under the section **Password Policy** if you are going to use LDAP password policy.

12. Click on the **Save** button when you are ready.

LDAP (Lightweight Directory Access Protocol) is an application protocol for querying and modifying directory services running over TCP/IP. A **Directory Information Tree (DIT)** is data represented in a hierarchical tree-like structure consisting of the distinguished names (DNs) of the directory entries.

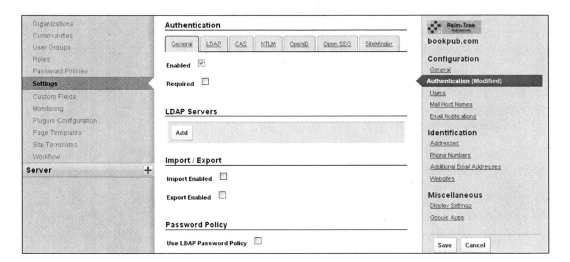

What's happening?

We have integrated the portal with an LDAP server. Next time, when a user logs into the portal, it will authenticate them with the LDAP server. Once a user is logged in successfully, the portal will import current user information into the system.

As you can see, there are default values for users and values. Why? The portal has the following settings for LDAP by default.

```
ldap.auth.search.filter=(mail=@email_address@)
ldap.user.default.object.classes=top,person,inetOrgPerson,organizatio
nalPerson
ldap.user.mappings=screenName=cn\npassword=userPassword\
nemailAddress=mail\nfirstName=givenName\nlastName=sn\njobTitle=title\
ngroup=groupMembership
ldap.group.mappings=groupName=cn\ndescription=description\
nuser=uniqueMember
ldap.import.method=user
ldap.export.enabled=true
ldap.users.dn=ou=users,dc=example,dc=com
ldap.groups.dn=ou=groups,dc=example,dc=com
ldap.password.policy.enabled=false
```

The preceding code sets default values for LDAP settings. The value of the Authentication Search Filter depends on authentication styles: either `By Email Address` or `By Screen Name`. If it is `By Email Address` in any LDAP server (including `Apache Directory Server` and `Microsoft Active Directory Server`), the value of Authentication Search Filter should be `(mail=@email_address@)`; otherwise, it must be `(cn=@screen_name@)`.

The value of Import Search Filter depends on LDAP servers. For `Apache Directory Server`, `OpenLDAP`, and `OpenDS`, it is `(objectClass=inetOrgPerson)`, and for `Microsoft Active Directory Server`, it is `(objectClass=organizationalPerson)`.

The value of **Screen Name** must be `cn` for both `Apache Directory Server` (including `OpenLDAP` and `OpenDS`) and `Microsoft Active Directory Server`. The value of **Email Address** is `mail` for `Apache Directory Server` (similar to `OpenLDAP` and `OpenDS`) and `userPrincipalName` for `Microsoft Active Directory Server`. Similarly, the value of **Group** is `groupMembership` for `Apache Directory Server` (similar to `OpenLDAP` and `OpenDS`) and `memberOf` for `Microsoft Active Directory Server`.

The admin is allowed to log in, even if the integration with LDAP is broken. This allows the administrator account to fix the problem.

Using LDAP effectively

It is very important to choose a suitable security model in the beginning of the portal implementation. The authentication mechanism, the storage for user data, the security settings, and the business rules are based on the security model that you choose.

The portal imposes authentication through the login ID of the user (e-mail address or user ID) and password. This is where you choose a security model (for example, database-based managed accounts, **SSO (Single Sign-on)**, or LDAP).

The portal imposes authorization by assigning a role to a specific user on a specific group. This is going to be the same, irrespective of which model you choose.

The security model that you choose (either database-based managed account or external systems such as LDAP or SSO) will be based on the requirements of your enterprise.

In any case, you can't authenticate the portal against SSO and/or LDAP. Therefore, you will have to remove LDAP and SSO settings from the portal. Fortunately, you could run the following query:

1. Shut down the portal.
2. Run the following SQL script:
   ```
   Delete from PortletPreferences where portletId = 'LIFERAY_PORTAL';
   ```
3. Restart the portal.

The previous query removed all settings related to the portlet ID LIFERAY_PORTAL.

LDAP authentication chain

There are two kinds of authentication chains supported in the portal: LDAP with portal database and multiple LDAP servers.

When configuring an LDAP server, you would have the ability to enable the LDAP server and make it required. If the LDAP server was marked as required, then authentication only goes through the LDAP server. If the LDAP server wasn't marked as required, then authentication goes through the LDAP server first and then goes through the portal database. Suppose that you have a lot of users in an LDAP server, and a set of users existing in the portal database, then you could mark the LDAP server as non-required—building authentication chain: authentication first goes through the LDAP server and then through the portal database. In this example, you integrated two-pool users both in LDAP and in the portal database.

The portal allows authentication from multiple LDAP servers. Multiple LDAP servers can be specified in the **Control Panel** under **Settings | Authentication | LDAP**. The portal will try to authenticate them from top to bottom in order.

CAPTCHA

A **CAPTCHA** is a program that can generate and grade tests that humans can pass but current computer programs cannot. CAPTCHA have several applications for practical security, including, but not limited to: preventing comment spam in blogs, protecting website registration, online polls, preventing dictionary attacks, search engine bots, worms, and spam. Refer to http://recaptcha.net/captcha.html.

The portal has specified a set of properties for CAPTCHA in portal.properties.

```
captcha.max.challenges=1
captcha.check.portal.create_account=true
captcha.check.portal.send_password=true
captcha.check.portlet.message_boards.edit_category=false
captcha.check.portlet.message_boards.edit_message=false
```

As shown in the previous code, the property `captcha.max.challenges` sets the maximum number of CAPTCHA checks per portlet session. Set this value to 0 to always check. Set this value to a number less than 0 to never check. Unauthenticated users will always be checked on every request if CAPTCHA checks are enabled.

By default, the portal sets whether or not to use CAPTCHA checks for portal actions: creating an account via the property `captcha.check.portal.create_account`; sending a password via the property `captcha.check.portal.send_password`. In addition, the portal sets whether or not to use CAPTCHA checks for portlet actions, editing a category in the portlet Message Boards via the property `captcha.check.portlet.message_boards.edit_category`, editing a message in the portlet Message Boards via the property `captcha.check.portlet.message_boards.edit_message`.

You would be able to override the mentioned properties in `portal-ext.properties`. By the way, Liferay 6 provides a lot of LDAP enhancements, but not limited, like: being able to synchronize user custom attributes between Liferay and LDAP, to implemented LDAP pagination via Page-Results-Controls, to configure the portal to create a role for each LDAP group, and to override LDAP import and export processes via Spring.

SSO authentication

The portal also supports SSO integration. The portal provides integration with CAS, NTLM, OpenID, OpenSSO, and SiteMinder, by default.

This section will show you how to set up SSO authentication with the help of examples. Suppose that the enterprise 'Palm Tree Publications' has CAS server with URL `http://docs.cignex.com/cas-web`, it is planning to set authentication through the SSO CAS server directly, as shown in following screenshot. Let's do it by following these steps.

1. Go to **Settings | Authentication** under the **Portal** category of **Control Panel**.
2. Click on the **CAS** tab.
3. Select the **Enabled** checkbox.
4. Select the **Import from LDAP** checkbox. If this is checked, then users authenticated from CAS, who do not exist in the portal, will be imported from LDAP. Note that LDAP must be enabled.
5. Input the following values as an example:

   ```
   Login URL: http://docs.cignex.com/cas-web/login;
   Logout URL: http://docs.cignex.com/cas-web/logout;
   Server URL: http://docs.cignex.com/cas-web ;
   Server Name: www.bookpub.com:8080.
   ```
6. Click the **Save** button.

Now you are ready to use SSO CAS. Similarly, you can integrate OpenID, NTLM, OpenSSO, and SiteMinder with the portal.

What's happening?

Next time a user logs in to the portal, they will be redirected to the CAS server's login screen, if everything is set up correctly. The portal integrates CAS Server to set up single sign on (SSO).

As you have seen, the CAS server integrated with LDAP. How do we implement this? The previous example updated LDAP URL in $TOMCAT_AS_DIR/webapps/cas-web/WEB-INF/deployerConfigContext.xml as follows.

```xml
<bean id="contextSource" class="org.springframework.ldap.core.support.
LdapContextSource">
  <property name="pooled" value="true"/>
  <property name="urls">
    <list>
      <value>ldap://docs.cignex.com:10389/</value>
    </list>
  </property>
  <property name="userDn" value="uid=admin,ou=system"/>
  <property name="password" value="secret"/>
  <property name="baseEnvironmentProperties">
    <map>
      <entry>
        <key>
          <value>java.naming.security.authentication</value>
        </key>
        <value>simple</value>
```

```
        </entry>
      </map>
    </property>
  </bean>
```

As you can see, you can define multiple LDAP server URLs and connection credentials. That is, the LDAP authentication chain got supported in CAS SSO in nature. Note that you can update the preceding LDAP URL other than `ldap:docs.cignex.com:10389`. Moreover, the CAS server should be installed with ports 80 and 443.

 The JA-SIG Central Authentication Service (CAS) is an open single sign-on service `http://www.ja-sig.org`.

In general, the portal has specified the following properties for CAS SSO in `portal.properties`.

```
cas.auth.enabled=false
cas.import.from.ldap=false
cas.login.url=https://localhost:8443/cas-web/login
cas.logout.url=https://localhost:8443/cas-web/logout
cas.server.name=localhost:8080
cas.server.url=https://localhost:8443/cas-web
cas.service.url=
```

As shown in the preceding code, CAS SSO is set as disabled by default. You can set the property `cas.auth.enabled` to `true` to enable CAS single sign on. If it is set to true, then the property `auto.login.hooks` must contain a reference to the class `com.liferay.portal.security.auth.CASAutoLogin` and the filter `com.liferay.portal.servlet.filters.sso.cas.CASFilter` must be referenced in `$PORTAL_ROOT_HOME/WEB-INF/web.xml`.

A user may be authenticated from CAS and not yet exist in the portal. You should set the property `cas.import.from.ldap` to `true` to automatically import users from LDAP, if they don't exist in the portal. In addition, you need to set the default values for the required CAS URLs like `cas.login.url`, `cas.logout.url`, and `cas.server.url`. Setting `cas.server.name` allows deep linking.

OpenID authentication

We can also use **OpenID** as authentication. Let's enable OpenID authentication by following these steps:

1. Click on **Settings | Authentication** under the **Portal** category of **Control Panel**.
2. Click on the **OpenID** tab.
3. Select the checkbox to enable OpenID.
4. Click the **Save** button to save the changes.

Now it is ready for users to log in through OpenID. OpenID is a decentralized single sign-on system. Refer to http://openid.net.

By default, the portal has the following configuration in portal.properties.

```
open.id.auth.enabled=true
```

As shown in the preceding code, the portal sets the property open.id.auth. enabled to true to enable OpenId authentication. If this property is set to true, then the property auto.login.hooks must contain a reference to the class com. liferay.portal.security.auth.OpenIdAutoLogin. OpenId authentication can be disabled by setting the following property in portal-ext.properties, instead of the preceding Web UI.

```
open.id.auth.enabled=false
```

Once we set open.id.auth.enabled to false, either by property or by Web UI, OpenID authentication gets disabled, and the OpenID sign-in link will get hidden in the portlet Sign In.

NTLM authentication

NTLM (NT LAN Manager) is a Microsoft authentication protocol used with the **SMB (Server Message Block)** protocol. Refer to http://jcifs.samba.org/src/ docs/ntlmhttpauth.html.

```
ntlm.auth.enabled=false
ntlm.auth.domain.controller=127.0.0.1
ntlm.auth.domain=EXAMPLE
jcifs.netbios.cachePolicy=30
jcifs.smb.client.soTimeout=35000
```

By default, NTLM got disabled in the portal via the property `ntlm.auth.enabled`. You can set the property `ntlm.auth.enabled` to true to enable NTLM single sign on. Note that NTLM will work only if LDAP authentication is also enabled and the authentication is made by screen name. If it is set to true, then the property `auto.login.hooks` must contain a reference to the class `com.liferay.portal.security.auth.NtlmAutoLogin` and the filter `com.liferay.portal.servlet.filters.sso.ntlm.NtlmFilter` must be referenced in `$PORTAL_ROOT_HOME/WEB-INF/web.xml`.

In addition, you can configure the domain controller and domain according to your NTLM server. And especially, you can set `jcifs.netbios.cachePolicy` to reduce redundant name queries, and set `jcifs.smb.client.soTimeout` to prevent the client from holding server resources unnecessarily.

Open SSO authentication

Sun OpenSSO Enterprise (short for **Open SSO** — renamed as **OpenAM**) is the single solution for Web access management, federation, and web services security. Refer to `http://www.sun.com/software/products/opensso_enterprise/index.xml`.

The portal has specified the following properties to integrate Open SSO in `portal.properties` and the corresponding Web UI.

```
open.sso.auth.enabled=false
open.sso.login.url=http://openssohost.example.com:8080/opensso/UI/
Login?goto=http://portalhost.example.com:8080/c/portal/login
open.sso.logout.url=http://openssohost.example.com:8080/opensso/UI/
Logout?goto=http://portalhost.example.com:8080/web/guest/home
open.sso.service.url=http://openssohost.example.com:8080/opensso
open.sso.screen.name.attr=uid
open.sso.email.address.attr=mail
open.sso.first.name.attr=cn
open.sso.last.name.attr=sn
```

As shown in the preceding code, Open SSO is disabled by default, since the property `open.sso.auth.enabled` is set to `false`. You could set this to `true` to enable Open SSO. If the property is set to `true`, then the property `auto.login.hooks` must contain a reference to the class `com.liferay.portal.security.auth.OpenSSOAutoLogin`.

When enabling Open SSO, you need specify the properties login URL `open.sso.login.url`, logout URL `open.sso.logout.url`, and service URL `open.sso.service.url`. You need override these properties in `portal-ext.properties`.

For example, let's say that an Open SSO has been installed at a service URL `http://liferay.cignex.com:8090/opensso`, and the Liferay portal is installed at `http://liferay.cignex.com:8080`. If so, then you would have the following values:

```
Login URL open.sso.login.url=http://liferay.cignex.com:8090/
opensso/UI/Login?goto=http://liferay.cignex.com:8080/c/portal/
login
Logout URL open.sso.logout.url=http://liferay.cignex.com:8090/
opensso/UI/Logout?goto=http://liferay.cignex.com:8080/web/guest/
home
```

In addition, the following attributes are configurable: `firstName=cn`, `lastName=sn`, `screenName=givenName`, and `emailAddress=mail` via properties `open.sso.screen.name.attr`, `open.sso.email.address.attr`, `open.sso.first.name.attr`, and `open.sso.last.name.attr`.

> Note that if Open SSO and Liferay are installed in the same domain with a default configuration like `Encode Cookie Value = True`, then it works fine. If Open SSO and the portal are installed in different domains with the same settings, then it will get redirect loop. But anyway, Open SSO and the portal should work well across domains. This issue is still open at the time of writing.

SiteMinder authentication

Computer Associates (CA) **SiteMinder** is a centralized web access management system that enables user authentication and single sign-on, policy-based authorization, identity federation, and auditing of access to web applications and portals. Refer to `http://www.ca.com/us/internet-access-control.aspx`.

The portal has specified following properties to integrate SiteMinder in `portal.properties` and the corresponding web UI:

```
siteminder.auth.enabled=false
siteminder.import.from.ldap=false
siteminder.user.header=SM_USER
```

As shown in the preceding code, the CA SiteMinder single sign on is disabled by default, since the property `siteminder.auth.enabled` is set to `false`. You could set this to `true` to enable CA SiteMinder single sign on. If set to `true`, then the property `auto.login.hooks` must contain a reference to the class `com.liferay.portal.security.auth.SiteMinderAutoLogin` and the `logout.events.post` must have a reference to `com.liferay.portal.events.SiteMinderLogoutAction` for logout to work.

When the property `siteminder.import.from.ldap` is set to `false`, a user may be authenticated from SiteMinder and may not yet exist in the portal. You should set this to `true` to automatically import users from LDAP if they don't exist in the portal. If this is checked (that is, `siteminder.import.from.ldap` is set to `true`), then users authenticated from SiteMinder that don't exist in the portal will be imported from LDAP. Note that, in this case, LDAP must be enabled.

The property `siteminder.user.header` sets the name of the user header that SiteMinder passes to the portal.

Authentication token

Liferay 6 provides capabilities to allow individual portlet to disable authentication token checks and to add authentication token to prevent **CSRF (Cross-Site Request Forgery)** attacks; an attack which forces an end user to execute unwanted actions on a web application in which he/she is currently authenticated. Authentication token is configurable as follows in `portal.properties`.

```
auth.token.check.enabled=true
auth.token.ignore.actions=/asset/rss,/blogs/rss,\
/document_library/edit_file_entry,\
/journal/rss,/image_gallery/edit_image,\
/login/login,/message_boards/rss,\
/wiki/edit_page_attachment,/wiki/rss
```

As shown in above code, you can set the property `auth.token.check.enabled` to `true`/`false` to enable / to disable authentication token security checks in `portal-ext.properties`. The checks can be disabled for specific actions via the property `auth.token.ignore.actions` or for specific portlets via the init parameter `check-auth-token` in `portlet.xml`. Of course, you can input a list of comma delimited struts actions, with the property `auth.token.ignore.actions` in `portal-ext.properties`, which will not be checked for an authentication token.

Roles

Before playing with roles, we need to create roles. 'Palm Tree Publications' needs roles for users to handle the **Message Board** portlet in their page. Let us name these roles as **MB Topic Admin** and **MB Category Admin**.

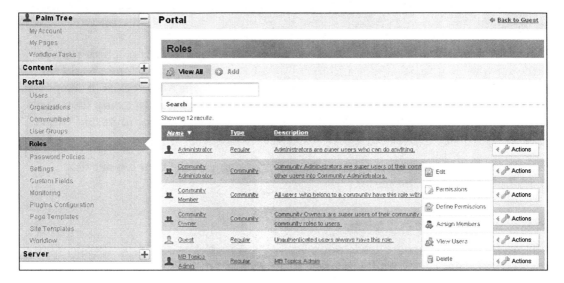

Adding a role

First of all, we need to create a role called **MB Topic Admin**. Let's do that now:

1. Click on **Roles** under the **Portal** category of **Control Panel**.

2. Click on the **Add** button.

3. Enter a value **MB Topic Admin** in the **Name** input field, as well as that of the **Title** input field and the **Description** input field.

4. Select a type with values: **Regular**, **Organization**, and **Community**.

5. Click on the **Save** button if you are ready.

Other roles can be created in a similar way. After adding roles, we can view them.

What's happening?

There are three kinds of roles: Regular, Organization, and Community.

A community role would grant access only within a community, while an organization role would grant access only within an organization or location. The main difference between community roles and regular roles is that while the latter is assigned to the whole portal, whereas, the former is assigned to a community. And the main difference between organization roles and regular roles is that while the latter is assigned to the whole portal, the former is assigned to an organization or a location.

Considering the pattern 'portal-group-page-content' again, roles are used to define permissions across scope: across the portal, across a group—an organization, a location, or a community.

Managing roles

As mentioned earlier, a role is a collection of permissions. There are system roles, system community roles, system organization roles, and customized roles. The standard system roles are Administrator, Guest, Power User, and User. These roles cannot be removed or renamed.

The standard system community roles are: Community Administrator, Community Member, and Community Owner. These roles cannot be removed or renamed. The standard system organization roles are: Organization Administrator, Organization Member, and Organization Owner. Similar to the standard system community roles, these roles cannot be removed or renamed.

You cannot edit or delete system roles at the UI level. Optionally, system roles could be renamed at the system level. Customized roles are built by users, which can be edited and deleted.

Viewing roles

Roles can be viewed by following these steps:

1. Click on **Roles** under **Portal** of **Control Panel**. A list of roles appears on the bottom of the roles screen.

2. Locate the role you want to view first.

3. Then click on the role by the links.

Searching roles

Roles are searchable. Click on **Roles** under **Portal** of **Control Panel**. Then type a role name in the search keywords field. Click on the **Search** button.

Editing a role

To edit a role, click on **Roles** under **Portal** of **Control Panel** first. Then locate the role you want to edit. Click on the **Edit** icon from the **Actions** tab to the right of the role or click any links of the role. In the edit page, type changes in the **Name** input field, **Title** input field, and **Description** input field. Then click on the **Save** button to save the changes. Note that you can update customized roles only, and you cannot edit or delete system roles.

Deleting roles

For some reasons, a role does not exist anymore. We can delete this role from the portal by following these steps:

1. Click on **Roles** under **Portal** category of **Control Panel** first.
2. Locate the role (for example, 'MB Category Admin') that you want to delete.
3. Then click on the **Delete** icon from the **Actions** tab to the right of the role. A screen will appear asking if you want to permanently delete the selected roles.
4. Click the **OK** button.

Note that you can delete a customized role whether it has members associated or not. When a customized role gets deleted, membership and permission definitions would get removed permanently.

Assigning members

We can assign a particular role to a specific user. This can be done by following these steps:

1. Click on **Roles** under the **Portal** category of **Control Panel**.
2. Click on the **Assign Members** icon from the **Actions** tab next to the role that you want to assign members to.
3. Since the **Current** tab is selected by default, there are no users associated with this role. Therefore, click on the **Available** tab in order to search for the user of your choice.
4. Check the checkbox next to the user.

5. Click on the **Update Associations** button. If you need to verify this, it can be done by clicking on the **Current** tab to confirm that the association was set successful.

6. If you as an administrator decided that this association should be discarded, then you can uncheck the checkbox next to the user's name, and click on the **Update Associations** button again.

Similarly, we can assign other entities, (such as community, organization, location, or user group), to a regular customized role or system roles (such as Administrator, Power User, and so on). To do so, we just need to repeat the preceding steps. In fact, an identical result would have been achieved by associating the previously selected role with an appropriate entity, instead of directly to the user, if he/she was a member of an entity.

Using roles in an effective way

There are three types of roles: regular, organization, and community, as described below. Community roles allow administration of roles to be scoped to a specific community. The objective is to create a new type of role that is associated with a community when it is assigned to a user.

1. **Community Owner**: This role is automatically given to the creator of a community and gives him/her total control over the community management, including website configuration and content management.

2. **Community Administrator**: Users with this role can administer the community but cannot assign new users or edit existing one. They can create new content in the community portlets, but they cannot manage the content created by others.

3. **Community Member**: This role is automatically given to users when they are assigned to a community. It does not give any special rights by default but can be edited by the portal administrator to add privileges that might be desirable in certain scenarios.

Organization roles are administrative roles scoped to a specific organization. An organization role is a role associated with an organization or location when it is assigned to a user.

1. **Organization Owner**: Organization Owners are super users of their organization and can assign organization roles to users.

2. **Organization Administrator**: Organization Administrators are super users of their organization but can't bring other users into this role.

3. **Organization Member**: All users who belong to an organization have this role within that organization.

Name	Type	Permission Actions on Roles					
		Edit	Permissions	Define Permissions	Assign Members	View Users	Delete
Administrator	Regular		☐		☐	☐	
Community Administrator	Community		☐			☐	
Community Member	Community		☐	☐		☐	
Community Owner	Community		☐			☐	
Organization Administrator	Organization		☐			☐	
Organization Member	Organization		☐	☐		☐	
Organization Owner	Organization		☐			☐	
Guest	Regular		☐	☐	☐	☐	
Power User	Regular		☐	☐	☐	☐	
User	Regular		☐	☐	☐	☐	
Customized regular role	Regular	☐	☐	☐	☐	☐	☐
Customized community role	Community	☐	☐	☐			☐
Customized organization role	Organization	☐	☐	☐			☐

What's happening?

As mentioned earlier, there are a set of system roles, system organization roles, and system community roles. You cannot edit or delete system roles at the UI level. Optionally, system roles could be renamed at the system level.

The portal has been specified the following properties, by default, in `portal.properties`.

```
system.role.Administrator.description=Administrators are super users
who can do anything.
system.role.Guest.description=Unauthenticated users always have this
role.
```

```
system.role.Owner.description=This is an implied role with respect to
the objects users create.
system.role.Power.User.description=Power Users have their own public
and private pages.
system.community.role.Community.Administrator.description=Community
Administrators are super users of their community but cannot make
other users into Community Administrators.
system.community.role.Community.Member.description=All users who
belong to a community have this role within that community.
system.community.role.Community.Owner.description=Community Owners
are super users of their community and can assign community roles to
users.
system.organization.role.Organization.Administrator.
description=Organization Administrators are super users of their
organization but cannot make other users into Organization
Administrators.
system.organization.role.Organization.Member.description=All users who
belong to an organization have this role within that organization.
system.organization.role.Organization.Owner.description=Organization
Owners are super users of their organization and can assign
organization roles to users.
```

This code sets the description of system roles. Of course, you can override the description of system roles in `portal-ext.properties`.

Authorization

As mentioned earlier, authorization is a process of finding out if the user, once identified, is permitted to access a resource. This process is implemented by assigning and checking permissions (using roles).

Permission

A permission is an action on a resource. The portal provides a full security model incorporated with fine-grained permissions and role-based access control. It will give administrators full control over access and privileges to portlets, layouts, and groups within the portal. This means that there are two main features on permissions. First of all, permissions are fine-grained in the portal. For example, for a given page, permissions would be **Add Discussion, Delete Discussion, Update, Update Discussion, Permissions, Delete**, and **View**.

Permission Actions on Pages

Permission Name	Permission functional description
Add Discussion	Ability to add discussions (comments) on a page
Delete Discussion	Ability to delete discussions (comments) on a page
Update	Ability to update the current page
Update Discussion	Ability to update discussions (comments) on a page
View	Ability to view the current page
Permissions	Ability to assign permissions on a page
Delete	Ability to delete a page

Secondly, permissions are always assigned through roles in the portal. For example, the user 'Rolf Hess' is a member of the role 'MB Topic Admin'. As mentioned in the previous chapter, we have the **Welcome** page in the **Guest** community. Now we are going to assign permission **View** on that page for 'Rolf Hess', as shown in the following screenshot:

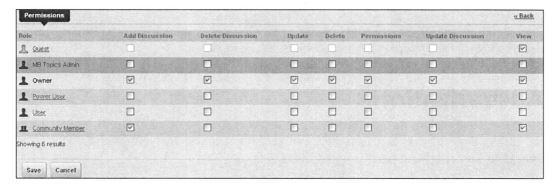

It can be implemented as follows:

- Log in as an admin (for example, **Palm Tree**), go to the **Welcome** page of the **Guest** community under **Go To**, and click on **Manage | Page** under the dock bar menu.

- Click on **Permissions** and check the checkbox **View** on the role 'MB Topic Admin'. This is a role-based access control. Permissions are always assigned through roles only.

- Click on the **Save** button when you are ready.

Then log in as Rolf Hess in another browser. You will see that you can only view the **Welcome** page, but you can't update the page—there is no edit control on portlets, and there is no **Layout** option under **Manage**.

Permissions in scope

Considering the pattern `Portal-Group-Cage-Content`, permissions can be managed across scope: across the portal, across a group (an organization or a location, or a community), across the page, and across the content. That is, permissions are in scope: portal-level permissions, organization-level or community-level permissions, page-level permissions, model-resource permissions, and portlet permissions.

In the following figure, portal-level permissions (grouped as category `Portal`), model-resource permissions (grouped as category `Content`), and portlet permissions (grouped as category `Application`) can be seen.

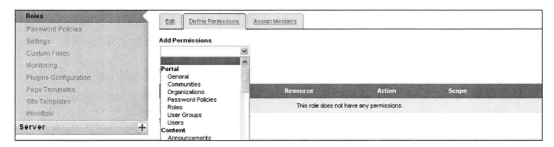

To get this permission list, click on **Portal** in the **Control Panel**. Then locate a custom regular role, and click on the **Define Permissions** icon from the **Actions** tab to the right of the role. That's it!

In the same way, clicking on the **Define Permissions** icon from the **Actions** tab to the right of a community role, you would see community-level permissions (grouped as category `Administration`), model-resource permissions (grouped as category `Content`), and portlet permissions (group as category `Application`). Similarly, clicking on the **Define Permissions** icon from the **Actions** tab next to the right of an organization role, you would see organization-level permissions (grouped as category `Administration`), model-resource permissions (grouped as category `Content`), and portlet permissions (group as category `Application`).

The community-level permissions would be discussed in *Chapter 7*, while model-resource permissions would be introduced in the coming chapters. The following section will talk about portal-level permissions and portlet permissions in general.

Assigning portal-level permissions

The portal-level permissions include general, communities, organizations, password policies, roles, users, and user groups. As mentioned in the previous sections, we have specified permission actions on roles. Now, let us take a look at general, users, and user groups, while leaving permission actions on communities, organizations, password policies to the coming chapters. The following table depicts portal-general permissions.

Permission actions on Portal General

Action	Description	Action	Description
Add Community	Ability to add communities	Add Password Policy	Ability to add password policies
Add Layout Prototype	Ability to add page and site templates	Add Role	Ability to add roles
Add License	Ability to add licenses	Add User	Ability to add users
Add Organization	Ability to add organizations	Add User Group	Ability to add user groups

As shown in the preceding table, you can assign permissions (**Add Community, Add Layout Prototype, Add License, Add Organization, Add Password Policy, Add Role, Add User, Add User Group**) on regular roles.

Similarly, you could find permission actions on users as follows:

Permission actions on Portal Users

Action	Description	Action	Description
Delete	Ability to delete users	Update	Ability to update users' profiles
Impersonate	Ability to impersonate users	View	Ability to view users
Permissions	Ability to assign permissions to users		

As shown in above table, you can assign permissions (**Delete, Impersonate, Permissions, Update, View**) on users.

In the same way, you could find permission actions on user groups as follows.

Permission actions on Portal User Groups

Action	Description	Action	Description
Assign Members	Ability to assign members	Manage pages	Ability to manage user groups' pages
Delete	Ability to delete user groups	Update	Ability to update user groups
Manage Announcements	Ability to manage announcements of a user group	View	Ability to view user groups
Permissions	Ability to assign permissions on user groups		

As shown in this table, you can assign permissions (Delete, Permissions, Update, view, Assign Members, Manage Announcements, and Manage Pages) on user groups.

Based on the mentioned permissions, let's consider a scenario where as an **Palm Tree** administrator, you are planning to assign permissions to the user "Rolf Hess"—he can view roles, users, user groups in the control panel. He can also add users, roles, and groups. How to implement it? Let's do it by following these steps.

- Click on **Roles** under the **Portal** category of **Control Panel**.

- Locate a role and then click on the **Define Permissions** icon from the **Actions** tab next to the right of the role.

- Click on the **Portal | General** link and check the checkboxes: Add Role, Add User, and Add User Group. Click on the **Save** button when you are ready.

- Click on the **Portal | Roles** link, check the checkbox **View**, and click on the **Save** button when you are ready.

- Click on the **Portal | Users** link, check the checkbox **View**, and then click on the **Save** button when you are ready.

- Click on the **Portal | User Groups** link, check the checkbox **View**, and then click on the **Save** button when you are ready.

As shown in these steps, you have assigned the permissions (Add Role, Add User, Add User Group, and View) to the user 'Rolf Hess' on the role 'MB Topic Admin'. As he is a member of this role, he inherits the same permissions. Therefore, he should be able to see the **Add** icon for users, roles, and user groups. Currently, portlets (**Users, Roles,** and **User Groups**) under the category **Portal** of **Control Panel** are invisible. This is because you haven't assigned proper portlet permissions to the user. We'll learn how to do so in the next section.

Assigning individual portlet permissions

Portlet permissions include **View**, **Configuration**, and **Access in Control Panel**. Normally, all portlets have **View** and **Configuration** permissions. Only a few of them (**Users**, **Roles**, and **User Groups**) have the additional permissions action **Access in Control Panel**.

Permission Actions on Portlets Users, Roles, and User Groups

Permission Name	Permission functional description
Access in Control Panel	Ability to access the portlet in the Control panel
Configuration	Ability to configure the portlet
View	Ability to view the portlet

Considering the preceding example, the user should have permission actions (**View** and **Access in Control Panel**) on portlets **Users**, **Roles**, and **User Groups**. Let's do it by following these steps:

1. Click on **Roles** under the **Portal** category of **Control Panel**.

2. Then locate a role, and click on the **Define Permissions** icon from the **Actions** tab to the right of the role.

3. Click on the **Applications | Users** link, check the checkboxes **Access in Control Panel** and **View**, and then click on the **Save** button when you are ready.

4. Click on the **Applications | Roles** link, check the checkboxes **Access in Control Panel** and **View**, and click on the **Save** button when you are ready.

5. Click on the **Portal | User Groups** link, check the checkboxes **Access in Control Panel** and **View**, and then click on the **Save** button when you are ready.

That's it. From now on, the user should be able to see **Users**, **Roles**, and **User Groups** under the category **Portal** of **Control Panel**.

Using permissions in an effective way

In short, a permission is an action on a resource. Permissions in the portal are fine-grained and assigned through roles only. The portal provides inclusive permission mechanism. If a user has a permission action on a resource, then the user will own the permission, no matter when the permission got assigned or which role the permission got defined.

Let's say that "Rolf Hess" was a member of regular roles "MB Category Admin" and "MB Topic Admin". At one time, we assigned permissions (**Update** and **View**) on the **Welcome** page of the **Guest** community via the role 'MB Category Admin', thinking that the user "Rolf Hess" has the permissions **View** and **Update** on the page. For a while, we forgot what we had done before and we're going to assign the permission **View** only to the page "Welcome" via the role "MB Topic Admin", while imagining that the user "Rolf Hess" should have the permission **View** only on the page **Welcome**.

What do we get at the end of a permission assignment? As shown in the preceding screenshot, the user would have both the permissions **View** and **Update** on the page. And the same thing happens for permissions given to user groups and communities assigned to him. If a user is a member of several groups that have different permissions, then he inherits all of the permissions without restriction.

Permission algorithms

The portal includes a pretty flexible permission system based on the concepts of roles, permissions, and resources, which provide several different implementations for the algorithm used to check whether a given user has permissions to perform certain actions or not.

RBAC stands for **Role Based Access Control**. It is a permission system in which permissions are always assigned through roles. RBAC implementation was started in the portal 5.1 as a way to improve the existing system, especially in terms of ease of use and performance. There are two algorithms for RBAC implementation at the time of writing.

- Algorithm 5 was introduced in the portal 5.1 or above. It uses a regular normalized implementation
- Algorithm 6 was introduced in the portal 5.3 or above. Algorithm 6 is an improved version of Algorithm 5. It provides the exact same functionality as that of Algorithm 5, but it uses bitwise operations for even faster speed

The legacy algorithms were used in the portal 5.0 or below. All of them offer the same functionality and more flexibility to assign permissions to users. In particular, it's possible to assign permissions, not only through roles, but also directly to organizations, communities, and individual users. However, this flexibility has a cost in performance and UI complexity. There are four different legacy algorithms, and they are as follows:

```
Algorithm 1
Algorithm 2
Algorithm 3
Algorithm 4
```

These algorithms are essentially the same but make calls in different orders depending on how the database is optimized and how the portal permissions are used. There is no golden rule for choosing one or the other. By the way, algorithms 1-4 are changeable, and so are algorithms 5-6. Data migration of algorithms 1-4 to 5-6 (RBAC) is available, but the data migration of algorithms 5-6 (RBAC) to 1-4 is unavailable. Thus, if you want to change algorithms 6 into algorithms 1-4 in the properties file in order to assign permissions directly to a user, both the portal and the web UI won't allow you to do this.

What's happening?

The portal has set a default permission algorithm in `portal.properties`. The default value of the permission algorithm for version 5.0 or below is 2. The default value of the permission algorithm for versions 5.1 and 5.2 is 5. Starting from the version 5.3, the default value of the permission algorithm is 6. This is as follows.

```
permissions.user.check.algorithm=6
```

This code sets the algorithm used to check permissions for a user. This is useful, so that you can optimize the search for different databases. Of course, depending on data, you can use different algorithms. To do so, just override the property `permissions.user.check.algorithm` in `portal-ext.properties`. For example, if you are using the portal version 5.0 or an earlier release with the algorithm 2, and now you want to upgrade to the current portal version, then you can set the following in `portal-ext.properties`.

```
permissions.user.check.algorithm=2
```

As compared to `Algorithm 5`, `Algorithm 6` reduces the database size by 66%. Let's say that a database is 60 GB when using `Algorithm 5`. It will now be just 20 GB when using `Algorithm 6`. A query to check if many actions can be performed on a resource used to take many SQL query calls. Now it takes only one. The portal consolidates the permission `Algorithm 6` to just one table.

In fact, there are two new tables involved for permissions in `Algorithm 6`: `ResourceAction` and `ResourcePermission`. `ResourceAction` maps the permission names (such as **View** and **Update**) to a long number. This is done automatically on startup, and it is cached for better efficiency. Hot deployed portlets are given unique numbers — this can only be initialized serially before the portal or portlets are available — so that the retrieval is thread safe and very fast. How can we achieve this? Use bit-wise masks. The portal would map to 0 to mean no permissions and 1 to mean **View** and others. In addition, the most logical as **View** is a common `ResourceAction` among all resources. `ResourcePermission` stores the permission in one big number, and the portal will do bit-wise operations to check if a user has proper permission actions.

By the way, **View** permission on an object must get checked if the user has the view permission on the parent container. Fortunately the portal has specified the following property in `portal.properties`.

```
permissions.view.dynamic.inheritance=true
```

As shown in the preceding code, the portal sets the property `permissions.view. dynamic.inheritance` to `true` to automatically check the view permission on parent categories or folders when checking the permission on a specific item. For example, if the property was set to `true` to be able to have access to a document, a user must have the **View** permission on the document's folder and all its parent folders.

Data migration

In addition, you may plan to move data from `Algorithms 1-4` to `5-6` (RBAC). You can do it by following these steps:

1. Click on **Server Administration** under the category **Server of Control Panel**.
2. Click on the tab **Data Migration**.
3. Click on the **Execute** button to convert the legacy permission algorithm, as shown in the following screenshot:

Note that automatic conversion will create all necessary roles to support all existing permission assignments, and it will let you merge them manually, if so desired (for example, merging redundant roles, reassigning system roles, and so on). When moving `Algorithms 1-4` to `5-6` (RBAC), you would lose functionality in exchange for speed and maintainability. A golden rule is "if you don't want that, then don't migrate!"

Summary

This chapter first introduced us to creating and managing organizations and locations. We saw how to add and manage (for example, view, search, update, deactivate, restore, delete, and impersonate) users and how to add and manage (for example, view, search, update, delete, and assign) user groups. Then it introduced integration with different authentication servers such as LDAP, CAS, NTLM, OpenID, Open SSO, and SiteMinder. Furthermore, it introduced how to manage permissions, and how to add roles and manage (for example, view, search, update, delete, and assign) roles. We learned that:

- A resource is a base object
- A permission is an action on a resource
- A role is a collection of permissions. Roles can be assigned to a user, user group, community, location, organization
- A user is an individual who perform tasks using the portal
- Organizations represent the enterprise-department-location hierarchy
- A location is a special organization, having one and only one parent organization associated and having no child organization associated
- A community is a special group with a flat structure
- A user group is a special group with no context, which may hold a number of users

In the next chapter, we're going to learn about tagging Assets, and using Message Boards and Asset Publisher.

4
Forums, Categorization, and Asset Publishing

In the intranet website bookpub.com of the enterprise "Palm Tree Publications", it would be nice to provide an environment for employees to discuss book ideas and proposals. It would also be nice to share important and interesting content with other users inside or outside of the intranet website, content tagging, and publishing. The Message Boards portlet (also called discussion forums) provides a full-featured discussion forums solution. Tags and taxonomies provide a way of organizing and aggregating content. The Asset Publisher portlet allows us to publish any type of content, including message board messages, as if it were web content—filtering either through a set of publishing rules dynamically or by manual selections.

In the preceding chapters, we revealed the page and group boxes in the portal-group-page-content pattern. In this chapter, we're going to open the content box and first introduce us to the item "Message Boards" in the content box. This chapter will introduce us to Message Boards first and focus on how to use message boards, how to configure the portlet, and how to implement the above requirements within message boards. Then, we will address taxonomies and tags as well as organizing and aggregating content—for example, message board threads and posts. Finally, it will introduce us to the Asset Publisher portlet for publishing any type of content including Message Boards messages through categories or tags.

By the end of this chapter, you will have learned how to:

- Manage categories, threads, and posts of message boards
- Set permissions on Message Boards categories, threads, and posts
- Manage tags, tag content, and display tags
- Set permissions on tags
- Manage categories, tag content, and display categories
- Set permissions on categories
- Publish assets via tags and categories

Message Boards

In brief, Message Boards (portlet ID 19) is a full-featured forum solution with threaded views, categories, RSS capability, avatars, file attachments, previews, dynamic list of recent posts, and forum statistics. Message Boards work with the fine-grained permissions and role-based access control model to give detailed levels of control to administrators and users. This section will give examples of how to use, configure, and implement Message Boards.

In order to provide an environment for employees to discuss book ideas and proposals, we could use the Message Boards portlet of the Guest public pages as an example. In this section, suppose that we're using the Message Boards portlet for the page of Guest public pages. A category called **Book Category** will be created. The category contains four categories — **Book Category A**, **Book Category B**, **Book Category C**, and **Book Category D**.

As an administrator of the enterprise "Palm Tree Publications", you would create a page called **Forums** in the Guest public pages and then add the Message Boards portlet to the page **Forums**. Then you are ready to create a category called Book Category. After doing that, add four subcategories to the category "Book Category" — they are "Book Category A," "Book Category B", "Book Category C", and "Book Category D".

Of course, you can customize Message Boards in the Control Panel, instead of doing the same on a specific page. You may refer to the scope of Message Boards in the coming section. Message boards are one of the most widely used collaboration features and are called discussion forums. They allow us to post messages (threads and posts) on a website for others to read. These messages are sorted within categories.

Managing categories

As an administrator of the enterprise "Palm Tree Publications", you are going to create the category "Book Category" and subcategories "Book Category A," "Book Category B", "Book Category C", and "Book Category D". These subcategories will hold messages related to book ideas and proposals.

Adding categories

First of all, we are going to create a category called "Book Category":

1. Go to the Guest public pages by clicking on **Go To | liferay.com** under the dock bar menu.

2. Add a page called **Forums** to the Guest public pages if the page isn't there, and change **Layout Template** to **1 Column** by clicking on **Manage | Page Layout** under the dock bar menu.

3. Add the **Message Boards** portlet to the Forums, if the Message Boards portlet isn't already there.

4. Click on the **Add Category** button.

5. Enter the name **Book Category** and the description **Books**.

6. Set permissions by clicking on the **Configure** link. In order to configure additional permissions, click on the **More** link—here we just use the default settings, as shown in next screenshot.

7. Configure the **Mailing List**. We just use the default settings at this time.

8. Click on the **Save** button to save the inputs.

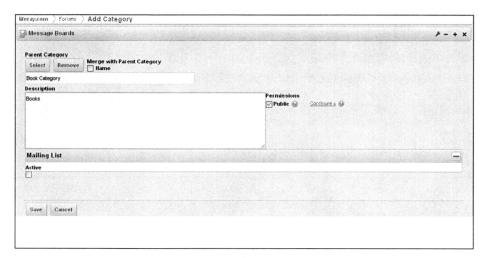

You can definitely add other categories. Generally speaking, message boards may have many categories, and each category may have many categories called subcategories within itself. That is, a category has a hierarchical structure. For example, the category "Book Category" contains four categories—"Book Category A", "Book Category B", "Book Category C", and "Book Category D". Let's create the category "Book Category A" by following these steps:

1. Locate the newly created category "Book Category", and then click on its name.

2. Click on the **Add Subcategory** button.

3. Enter the name "Book Category A" and the description "Liferay books".

4. Set permissions by clicking on the **Configure** link. To configure additional permissions, click on the **More** link. Here again, we just use the default settings.

5. Configure **Mailing List**—leave it at its default value.

6. Click on the **Save** button to save the inputs.

Of course, you can add as many other categories or subcategories as you want. After creating subcategories such as "Book Category B", "Book Category C", and "Book Category D", we can view the category and its subcategories, as shown in the following screenshot. In particular, "Book Category B" and "Book Category C" categories use the default permission setting, whereas category "Book Category D" uses only the "View" permission in the role Community Member column.

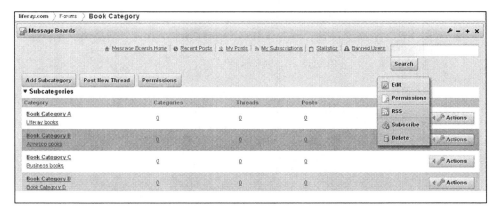

Editing categories

Categories or subcategories are editable. For example, you may need to change the description of the "Book Category" category from "Books" to "Books discussion category". Let's do it this way:

1. Locate a category, for example, "Book Category", which you want to edit.

2. Click on the **Edit** icon from the **Actions** button next to the category.

3. Keep the name value as is and update the description of the selected category, that is, "Book Category" with a value "Books discussion category".

4. Click on the **Save** button to save the changes.

Also, you can update the name. For example, we can update the name "Book Category" with a value "Books". Similarly, we can edit subcategory, for example, "Book Category C", by updating the name with the value "Liferay books".

Optionally, you can change the parent category of a specific category or subcategory by selecting a particular category as its parent category. You can also merge the current category with its parent category or remove its parent category. If you remove the parent category, the current category will become a category at the root level.

Deleting categories

Categories and subcategories are removable. For instance, as the subcategory "Book Category B" doesn't exist anymore, you should remove it. Let's do it by following these steps:

1. Locate the "Books" category in order to list its subcategories.

2. Locate a subcategory, say "Book Category B", which you want to delete.

3. Then click on the **Delete** icon from the **Actions** next to the category.

4. A screen will appear asking you if you want to delete this category. Click on **OK** to confirm deletion.

 Note that deleting the category will delete all related subcategories, threads, and posts which belong to this category.

View RSS feeds

You can view the RSS feeds of all message boards, categories, or subcategories. Suppose that you need to view RSS feeds of the "Books" category, you can do this as follows:

1. Select a category, for example, "Books"

2. Click on the **RSS** icon from the **Actions** next to the category.

Refer to the instructions in *Chapter 6, Blogs, WYSIWYG Editors and RSS* to know about RSS.

Managing threads

After adding categories and subcategories, we are ready to post new threads. Generally speaking, a forum may have many categories, and each category may have many subcategories and threads.

Adding threads

Let's say we're going to post new thread "**Let's discuss book Liferay**" under the category **Liferay books**. We'll do it by following these steps:

1. Select the category **Books** where you want to find subcategory **Liferay books**.

2. Select the subcategory **Liferay books** where you want to add a thread by clicking on the subcategory name.

3. Click on the **Post New Thread** button.

4. Enter the subject **Let's discuss the Liferay book** and a body "**It is time now to discuss the Liferay book**" through the default editor.

5. Deselect the checkbox **Mark as a Question**—if this is selected, then subsequent replies to this message can be marked as answers.

6. Deselect the checkbox **Anonymous**—if this is selected, then this message will be posted anonymously.

7. Select one of priorities (choose from **none, urgent, sticky,** and **announcement**). For example, **urgent**.

8. Input tags **book** and **liferay**, or select tags from existing tags.

9. Set permissions by clicking on the **Configure** link. To configure additional permissions, click on the **More...** link. We just use the default settings, as shown in following screenshot.

10. Click on the **Save** button to save the inputs.

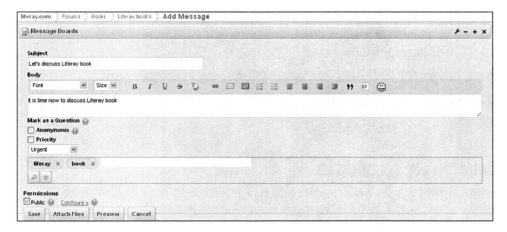

1. In addition, you can attach files by clicking on the **Attach Files** button and upload files afterwards.

2. Similarly, you can preview the thread by clicking on the **Preview** button.

3. In particular, adding a new thread with a subject, for example, "**Let's discuss the Liferay book**", will add a post automatically with the subject same as that of the thread.

Refer to tags instructions in the next section for information on tags.

Likewise, you can add other threads. Note that there's a breadcrumb at the top of the page that eases navigation. After adding the thread "**Where is the outline of the Liferay book?**", you can view threads as shown in following screenshot:

Editing threads

Threads are editable too. You may need to change the subject of the thread "Where is the outline of the Liferay book?" to "Did you find the outline of the Liferay book?". Let's do this by following these steps:

1. Locate the thread "**Where is the outline of the Liferay book?**", which you want to edit.

2. Click on the **Edit** icon from the **Actions** next to the thread.

3. Update the subject of the selected category "**Where is the outline of the Liferay book?**" with the value "**Did you find the outline of the Liferay book?**".

4. Click on the **Save** button to save the changes.

Of course, you can update the body, tags, and select the checkbox **Mark as a Question** as well. Updating the subject of the thread, that is "**Let's discuss the book Liferay?**", will automatically update the subject of the top-level post with the same subject as that of the thread.

Alternatively, you can change the category by clicking on the **Move Thread** icon next to the thread and then selecting a category as a parent category of the thread. In addition, you will be able to lock the thread by clicking on the **Lock Thread** icon next to the thread if the thread is unlocked. Conversely, you can unlock the thread by clicking on the **Unlock Thread** icon next to the thread if the thread is locked.

Deleting threads

Threads are removable too. For example, if the thread "Where is the outline of the Liferay book?" doesn't exist anymore, and you are required to remove it, do it by following these steps:

1. Locate the thread "**Where is the outline of the Liferay book?**", which you want to delete.

2. Then click on the **Delete** icon from **Actions** next to the thread.

3. A screen will appear asking you if you want to delete this thread. Click on the **OK** button to confirm deletion.

 Note that deleting a thread will delete all related posts that belong to that thread.

Viewing RSS feeds

You can view RSS feeds of threads as well as categories. Suppose that you need to view RSS feeds of the thread "**Let's discuss the book Liferay**". Let's do it by following these steps:

1. Navigate the category **Books** and the subcategory **Liferay books**.
2. Locate the thread **Let's discuss the book Liferay**.
3. Click on the **RSS** icon under **Actions** located next to the thread.

Managing posts

Finally we are ready to add more posts. As you can see, a forum may have many categories. Each category may have many subcategories and threads, and each thread may have a lot of posts associated with it. Fortunately, you are able to manage posts easily by editing posts, replying to posts, deleting posts, viewing posts, and so on. For instance, if the user **Rolf Hess** is a member of the Guest community, then he can easily reply to posts and edit posts.

Adding posts

The user "Rolf Hess" wants to reply to the thread "Let's discuss the book Liferay" with the message "OK". Let's do it as follows:

1. Log in as **Rolf Hess** and go to the page **forums** under the Guest public pages.

2. Locate the category **Books** and the subcategory **Liferay books**.

3. Click on the thread with the name "**Let's discuss the book Liferay**".

4. Locate the post—for example, "**Let's discuss the book Liferay**", to which you want to reply first.

5. Then click on the **Reply** icon at the top-right of the post.

6. Keep the default subject "**Re: Let's discuss the Liferay book**". Input the value of the body "OK" via an editor and also the `select` tags or `input` tags.

7. Set permissions by clicking on the **Configure** link. In order to configure additional permissions, click on the **More...** link—here we will use the default settings.

8. Deselect the checkbox **anonymous**.

9. Click on the **Save** button to save the inputs.

In addition, you can attach a file by clicking on the **Attach Files** button and preview the post by clicking on the **Preview** button. Moreover, you can reply with a quote by clicking on the **Reply with Quote** icon at the top-right of the post.

You can reply to other posts in order to contribute your ideas or proposals.

Editing posts

Posts are editable. To edit a post, click on the **Edit** icon at the bottom-right of the post. You can change the subject and body via an editor and tags. Then you simply have to click on the **Save** button to save the changes or click on the **Cancel** button to cancel those changes. Optionally, you can attach a file by clicking on the **Attach Files** button or preview the post by clicking on the **Preview** button.

In particular, updating the subject of the top-level post, for example, "Let's discuss the book Liferay" will automatically update the subject of the thread (that the top-level post belongs to) with the same subject as that of the top-level post.

In addition, you would be able to split the current post into a new thread as well as add an explanation post to the source thread. To do this, first log out and then log in as an administrator to get the permission to split threads and ban users. Then locate a post, click on the **Split Thread** icon, followed by selecting the checkbox **Add explanation post to the source thread**. Add a subject and a body for the explanation, and then click on the **OK** button. Optionally, you will be able to reply to the current post with a quote by clicking on the **Reply with Quote** icon.

Ban users

In addition, you can ban a user if you have proper permissions. As previously stated, **Rolf Hess** has a post called **OK** under the category **Book Category A**. As an administrator, you will see icon **Ban this User** under the logo of the user **Rolf Hess**. If you need to ban this user, then simply click on the icon **Ban this User**. Then you will see that the icon **Ban this User** becomes **Un-ban this User**.

When the user **Rolf Hess** is logged in, he will see the message at the Message Board: "**You have been banned by the moderator**".

As an administrator, you can un-ban the user "Rolf Hess" simply by clicking on **Un-ban this User**. Then you will see that **Un-ban this User** becomes **Ban this User**.

Deleting posts

Posts are removable too. For example, as the post "Re: Let's discuss the Liferay book" doesn't exist anymore, you can remove it. Let's do it by following these steps:

1. Locate the post "**Re: Let's discuss the Liferay book**", which you want to delete.
2. Click on **Delete** icon at the bottom-right of the post.
3. A screen will appear asking you if you want to delete this. Click **OK** to confirm the deletion or **Cancel** to cancel the deletion.

More interestingly, if the top-level post—for instance, "**Let's discuss the Liferay book**", was deleted, the thread that the top-level post belongs to will be linked to the low-level post such as "**Re: Let's discuss the Liferay book**". If the top-level post, for example "**Let's discuss the Liferay book**" is the only post in the thread, and if it is deleted, then the thread which the top-level post belongs to will also be deleted.

 Note that only the current post will be deleted when deleting a post inside a thread. The lower-level posts related to the current post will have a link to the top-level post of the current thread.

Viewing posts

All posts of a given thread may have different views such as the combination view, flat view, or tree view. For example, the default view mode is **Combination View**. In order to change the current view mode to flat view, simply click on the **Flat View** button next to the navigation. Without a doubt, you can use **Tree View**.

You can also change the thread by clicking on **Previous** or **Next**, next to **Threads**. Moreover, you can change the categories by clicking on the category name on the breadcrumb bar.

Searching posts

You can easily find messages by searching. For instance, in order to search for posts which contain "book" in the Message Boards, simply input that text as your search criterion. For example, enter "book" and then click on the **Search Categories / Search this category** button. A list of categories that contain the keywords as messages appears with the following columns: categories, messages (thread subject), thread posts, thread views and score.

Search is scoped by category. For example, if you just need to search for messages which contain the word "book" in the category **Categories | Books | Liferay books**, simply navigate to the category "Liferay books" first. Then input the message keyword, for example, "book", and click on the **Search Categories / Search this category** button.

What are 'messages' in search?
Messages here refer to content of threads and posts. The content contains the subject and body of threads and posts.

Viewing My Posts

You can view your own posts by clicking on the **My Posts** tab in the Message Boards. A list of your posts will appear with **Thread, Started by, Posts, Views, Last Post**, and **Actions** menu with a set of options (such as edit, permissions, RSS, subscribe/unsubscribe, delete, and so on.).

Viewing Recent Posts

Similarly, you can view recent posts by clicking on the **Recent Posts** tab of the Message Boards. A list of recent posts will appear with thread, started by, posts, views, last post, and actions with **Thread, Started by, Posts, Views, Last Post**, and **Actions** menu with a set of options (such as edit, permissions, RSS, subscribe/unsubscribe, delete, and so on.).

Viewing Statistics

Furthermore, you can view general statistics by clicking on the **Statistics** tab of the message boards. On doing so, statistical data such as the number of categories, the number of posts and the number of participants will appear. In addition, click on the **Top Posters** sub-tab to display a list of the most active users.

Viewing Banned Users

You can view a list of banned users if you have proper permissions. To do this, simply click on the **Banned Users** tab in the message boards. A list of banned users will appear with their name, ban date, un-ban date, and the **Un-ban this User** icon. In order to un-ban this user, you just click on the icon **Un-ban this User** next to the un-ban date.

Subscribing categories and threads

As users of Message Boards, you may be interested in the changes to messages in specific categories and threads. For example, as the "Palm Tree" administrator, you may be interested in the messages in the "Book Category A" category. You want to watch out for any changes of the messages in this category. You can certainly use the subscription function on the "Book Category A" category. Let's do it by following these steps:

1. Locate the category "Book Category A".
2. Click on the **Subscribe** icon from the **Actions** menu next to the category. The **Subscribe** icon will become an **Unsubscribe** icon for this category.
3. Of course, you can subscribe to other categories. You may be interested in the message of the thread "Let's discuss the Liferay book". Therefore, you can subscribe to it as follows:

    1. Locate the category "Liferay books" and locate the thread "Let's discuss the book Liferay"
    2. Click on the **Subscribe** icon from the **Actions** next to the thread. The **Subscribe** icon will become **Unsubscribe**.

Obviously, you can subscribe to other threads. In addition, you can view your subscriptions by clicking on the **My Subscriptions** tab. You will find lists of subscribed categories and threads.

Unsubscribing from categories and threads

In addition, you can unsubscribe from categories, subcategories, or threads that you are currently subscribed to. For example, you may need to unsubscribe from the thread "**Let's discuss the Liferay book**". Let's do it by following these steps.

1. Click on the **My Subscriptions** tab in Message Boards.

2. Locate the thread "Let's discuss the Liferay book".

3. Click on the **Unsubscribe** icon from the **Actions** located next to the thread. The thread "Let's discuss the Liferay book" will disappear from the view of **My Subscriptions**.

You can also unsubscribe from the thread "Let's discuss the Liferay book" from the Categories view by following these steps:

1. Locate the category "Liferay books" and then locate the thread "Let's discuss the book Liferay".

2. Click on the **Unsubscribe** icon from the **Actions** menu next to the thread. The **Unsubscribe** icon will become **Subscribe**.

In brief, there are two options for subscribing to and unsubscribing from Message Boards:

1. subscribe / unsubscribe through categories or subcategories

2. subscribe / unsubscribe through threads

That is, Message Boards portlet supports e-mail both as a means of sending new posts to users and as a way for those users answer to posts or create new threads.

What's happening?

If you have subscribed to some categories or threads, and the messages of subscribed categories or threads have changed, then you will receive notification of those changes.

Subscription is, generally speaking, an agreement to receive electronic text or services, especially over the Internet. Thread subscription provides a useful function, that is, to be notified by e-mail when a new message has been posted or updated. On one hand, you can subscribe to a thread for a given category or subcategory. Whenever a message has been posted or updated, you will be notified by e-mail. On the other hand, you can unsubscribe from a thread of a given category or subcategory if it has been subscribed to already. On doing this, you wouldn't be notified by e-mail, even if a message has been posted or updated.

Moreover, category subscription provides a useful function for notification by e-mail when a category has been updated. As with thread subscription, you can subscribe to a category or subcategory. Whenever a category or subcategory has been updated, you will be notified by e-mail. To learn how to set up mail notifications, refer to the next section.

Customizing Message Boards

As an administrator of the "Palm Tree Publications" enterprise, you can set up message boards. For example, you can configure subscription e-mails.

Setup

To configure Message Boards, for including the subscription function, click on **More | Configuration** on Message Boards. When the **Setup | Current** tab is selected, it shows a set of sub-tabs: **General, Email From, Message Added Email, Message Updated Email, Thread Priorities, User Ranks**, and **RSS**.

As shown in following screenshot, the **Allow Anonymous Posting, Enable Flags**, and **Enable Ratings** checkboxes are checked by default. This means that, by default, the portal allows anonymous posting and enabling of flags and ratings.

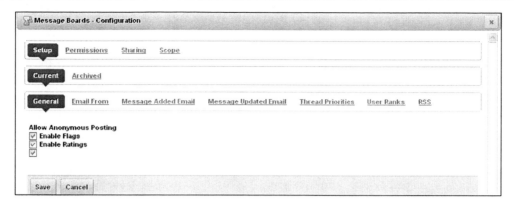

What's happening? The portal sets the following property in `portal.properties` by default.

```
message.boards.anonymous.posting.enabled=true
```

The preceding code snippet sets the property `message.boards.anonymous. posting.enabled` to `true` in order to allow anonymous posting. Of course, you could override the value of the property in `portal-ext.properties` if you want. In addition, you would like to see the UI taglibs. You can find `<liferay-ui:ratings>` and `<liferay-ui:flags>` UI taglibs in `$PORTAL_ROOT_HOME/html/portlet/ message_boards/view/view_thread_message.jspf`.

With the **Email From** tab selected, you can change the name and address of the e-mails being sent.

The **Message Added Email** tab allows us to edit the e-mail that is sent whenever a post is added. For disabling e-mail alerts, deselect the **Enabled** box first and then click on the **Save** button after making changes.

Similarly, the **Message Updated Email** tab allows us to edit the e-mail that is sent whenever a post is updated. As mentioned in the previous paragraph, you can disable e-mail alerts by deselecting the **Enabled** box first and then clicking on the **Save** button after making changes.

As you can see, there are default values for **Email From**, **Message Added Email**, and **Message Updated Email**. How? The portal sets the following properties in `portal.properties`.

```
message.boards.email.from.name=Joe Bloggs
message.boards.email.from.address=test@liferay.com
message.boards.email.html.format=true
message.boards.email.message.added.enabled=true
message.boards.email.message.updated.enabled=true
```

The preceding code configures e-mail notification settings. Obviously, you could override these properties in `portal-ext.properties` if necessary.

With the **Thread Priories** tab selected, you can manage the thread priorities profiles. The following table depicts default settings. By the way, as an administrator, you can change the name, image, and priority requirements by making changes directly and clicking on the **Save** button.

Name	Image	Priority	Description
Urgent	`/message_boards/` `priority_urgent.png`	3.0	Enter the name, image, and priority level in descending order. Threads with a higher priority are displayed before threads with a lower priority.
Sticky	`/message_boards/` `priority_sticky.png`	2.0	
Announcement	`/message_boards/` `priority_` `announcement.png`	1.0	The name is the display name of the priority.
			The image is the display image of the priority and can be a complete URL or a path relative to the theme.

Note that you need to enter the name, image, and priority level in descending order. Threads with a higher priority are displayed before threads with a lower priority. The name is the display name of the priority, while the image is the display image of that priority and can be a complete URL or a path relative to the theme. More interestingly, localized languages are supported as well.

With the **User Ranks** tab selected, as an administrator, you can manage the ranking profiles. The following table shows the default settings. Of course, you can change the ranking names and posting number requirements by making changes directly and then clicking on the **Save** button.

Rank	Minimum posts	Description
Youngling	0	Enter rank and minimum post pairs per line. Users will be displayed with a rank based on their number of posts.
Padawan	25	
Jedi Knight	100	
Jedi Master	250	
Jedi Council Member	500	
Yoda	1000	

Note that you can enter rank and minimum post pairs per line, while users will be displayed with a rank based on the number of posts. You can definitely use a language other than English.

With the **RSS** tab selected, you can manage the RSS settings. Of course, as an administrator, you can change "Maximum Items to Display", "Display Style", and "Format". Having done that, click on the **Save** button. As you might have noticed, the RSS abstract is limited to 200 characters. Why? This is because the portal sets the following property in `portal.properties`.

```
message.boards.rss.abstract.length=200
```

The preceding code sets the `message.boards.rss.abstract.length` property's value to `200`. You can override the value of the property in `portal-ext.properties`.

 Note that it is also possible to activate SMTP events to allow users to respond to mails sent by the message boards. In order to avoid HTML problems when posting through replies, the mails are now sent in plain text.

In addition, the portal allows messages to post pingbacks to any blogs or any other pingback consumer. The portal has defined following property to `true` in `portal.properties`

```
message.boards.pingback.enabled=true
```

As you can see, the portal sets this property to `true` by default to enable pingbacks. Of course, you could disable pingbacks by setting this property to `false` in `portal-ext.properties`

What's happening?

As you can see, you would be able to configure the portlet Message Boards with Threads Priorities and User Ranks as portlet preferences. What's happening? The portal has specified the portlet preferences Threads Priorities and User Ranks after the line `<portlet-name>19</portlet-name>` in `$PORTAL_ROOT_HOME/WEB-INF/portlet-custom.xml`.

```xml
<portlet-preferences>
  <preference>
    <name>priorities</name>
    <value>Urgent,/message_boards/priority_urgent.png,3.0</value>
    <!-- ignore details -->
  </preference>
```

```
<preference>
  <name>ranks</name>
  <value>Youngling=0</value> <!-- ignore details -->
</preference>
</portlet-preferences>
```

As shown in the preceding code, the portal specifies portlet preferences `priorities` and `ranks`. Of course, you can override the values of the portlet preferences for `priorities` and `ranks` if you need to.

Ban and unban users

As mentioned earlier, the portal provides the capability to ban and un-ban users. In the case of banning users, you may ask questions such as "How often is this job run?" "What time in days should be set for automatically expiring bans on users?"

The portal has the following default settings in `portal.properties`:

```
message.boards.expire.ban.job.interval=120
message.boards.expire.ban.interval=10
```

The preceding code sets time in minutes for how often this job is run with the property `message.boards.expire.ban.job.interval`. For example, if a user's ban is set to expire at 12:05 PM and the job runs at 2 PM, then the expiration will occur during the 2 PM run. The code also sets time in days to automatically expire bans on users. You can set the property `message.boards.expire.ban.interval` to `0` to disable auto-expiration in `portal-ext.properties`.

Thread views

As stated earlier, a thread may have different views—combination view, flat view, or tree view. The default view is combination view. Thread view and default view are set through the following properties in `portal.properties`.

```
message.boards.thread.views=combination,flat,tree
message.boards.thread.views.default=combination
```

The preceding code sets thread views to allowed and sets the default thread view. Of course, you can override these properties in `portal-ext.properties`.

Using Message Boards as a mailing list

You may have noticed that you can activate mailing lists when creating a new category or subcategory. In this scenario, you are able to input a default e-mail address, an incoming mail configuration, and an outgoing mail configuration. Once a mailing list gets activated, users are allowed to subscribe to threads of that category or subcategory, and the portal will store a list of all users that have subscribed in the database. When a new post is added to the Message Boards, the portal will query the database asynchronously in order to retrieve the users that have subscribed to the thread where the post is attached, and also retrieve the hierarchy of categories to which it belongs. Moreover, it sends each of them an e-mail with the contents of the post.

Going deeper, the portal allows users to answer to these e-mails or even write their own new threads using e-mail. How to achieve it? As stated above, the portal assigns an e-mail address to each category / subcategory in Message Boards. Such an e-mail address is automatically added to the reply-to headers of the e-mail sent to subscribers, so that a reply to e-mails received from Message Board will result in a new post in the appropriate category / sub category and thread.

Message Boards in scope

One of the most powerful characteristics of Message Boards is the fact that when they are added to different groups, they act as completely independent portlets, each with its own data. By default, any portlet, like Message Boards, is scoped into a group. That is, when portlets are added to a group, either public pages or private pages, they act as same portlets.

For instance, when the portlet Message Boards is added to a page, for example "Forums" of the Guest community, it will use the default scope. If you add the portlet Message Boards to a second page, say "Welcome", it will show the same data as that of the first page. When the portlet Message Boards is added to a page, it will immediately get scoped into the group to which the current page belongs.

As you can see, the portlet Message Boards was scoped into the group Guest when it was added to a page of the group Guest. You don't have flexibility of switching groups in this case. But this limitation can be solved through the Control Panel. In the Control Panel, you are able to switch the content of the portlet Message Boards to different groups. You can implement this by following these steps.

1. Go to **Manage | Control Panel**

2. Locate **Message Boards** under the category **Content**, and click on **Message Boards**. You would see the same categories and threads as that of the page "Forums", because by default, the content of the portlet Message Boards is scoped into the group **Guest**.

3. Switch groups by selecting different groups from the **Content for** drop-down menu.

A portlet like Message Boards could get scoped into a page. How to scope the Message Boards portlet into a page? To make the portlet Message Boards use a different data scope, you would follow these simple steps:

1. Locate a page such as "Forums" and the portlet Message Boards on the current page.

2. Go to **More | Configuration** of the portlet Message Boards.

3. Click on the tab **Scope**.

4. Choose "Current page (Forums)" from the selection menu **Scope** and click on the **Save** button.

If you previously entered data in the default scope and then switched to page scope, don't be afraid if you see all of your categories vanish. They will still remain in the group scope and can be retrieved using the Control Panel or by switching back to the default scope. Note that you shouldn't implement the steps we discussed in the Control Panel, otherwise you will scope the portlet message. However, scoping the content of the portlet Message Boards into the page "Current Page (Control Panel)" will be of no use.

Considering the pattern Portal-Group-Page-Content, the content of the portlet Message Boards could be scoped into a group, for example, by default, content such as all pages including both private pages and public pages. Moreover, it could be scoped into an individual page — this means that a set of data, for example, forum categories and threads, is isolated from other data of the same portlet.

The portal has default settings for the portlet Message Boards in $PORTAL_ROOT_HOME/ WEB-INF/liferay-portlet.xml as follows:

```
<control-panel-entry-category>content</control-panel-entry-category>
<control-panel-entry-weight>6.0</control-panel-entry-weight>
<scopeable>true</scopeable>
```

The preceding code shows that the portlet message boards will appear in the Category content and at position 6, and it is *scope-able*, that is, you are able to use the tab **Scope** and change the scope from default to current page.

In addition, you may be interested in the **Edit Scope** page. You can find more information about scope editing at `$PORTAL_ROOT_HOME/html/portlet/portlet_configuration/edit_scope.jsp`.

Friendly URL

When you view categories or subcategories, you will see a URL like `/web/guest/forums/-/message_boards/category/10322`. Similarly, when you view messages (thread and posts), you would see a URL like `/web/guest/forums/-/message_boards/message/10333`. This is a short and friendly URL. In fact, the portlet Message Boards supports friendly URL mapping as follows in `$PORTAL_ROOT_HOME/WEB-INF/liferay-portlet.xml`.

```
<friendly-url-mapper-class>
   com.liferay.portlet.messageboards.MBFriendlyURLMapper
</friendly-url-mapper-class>
```

The preceding code shows that the content inside a portlet needs a friendly URL via the `friendly-url-mapper-class` tag.

Archive, Export, and Import

As stated above, you have set up the portlet Message Boards, displaying general information, E-mail notification, user ranking, RSS, and so on. It would be nice if you could save these settings, and moreover, revert these changes later. This feature can be achieved through **Archive Setup**. You can set up archives using the following steps.

1. Locate the portlet Message Boards in a page.
2. Go to **More | Configuration | Setup | Archived**.
3. Input the archive name for the current setup, for example, "My MB", and click on the **Save** button.

After creating an archive, you will be able to see archives with the columns Name, User, Modified Date, and the icon **Actions** with **Restore** and **Delete** sub-icons. Obviously, you can restore the setup via an archive or delete an archive.

Note that this feature is available for portlets for which the **Setup** tab is visible because the portal specifies this function in the portlet configuration file `archived_setup_action.jsp` and `edit_archived_setups.jsp` under `$PORTAL_ROOT_HOME/html/portlet/portlet_configuration`. More details and archives are stored in portlet preferences of the portal instance. Therefore, you shouldn't use this feature for backing up data from one portal instance to another portal instance.

Fortunately, you can use the **Export / Import** feature for backup functions. The portal provides capability to export and import portlet specific data to a **Liferay Archive (LAR)** file. As shown in following screenshot, you can export portlet Message Boards-specific data to a LAR file.

1.   Locate the portlet Message Boards in a page.
2.   Go to **More | Export / Import**, and select the tab **Export**.
3.   Specify the LAR filename in order to export the selected data.
4.   Set what you would like to export.
5.   Click on the **Export** button.

Similarly, you may import LAR in the following steps:

1.   Go to **More | Export / Import**, and select the tab **Import**.
2.   Choose the LAR file in order to import the data.
3.   Set what you would like to import.
4.   Click on the **Import** button when you are ready.

Note that the selection of what you would like to import should be the same as that of what you would like to export.

Why does a portlet like **Message Boards** have Export / Import capability, whereas others portlets like Hello World don't have such a capability? The reason is that the portlet Message Boards has the following setting that the portlet Hello World doesn't have.

```
<portlet-data-handler-class>
   com.liferay.portlet.messageboards
   .lar.MBPortletDataHandlerImpl
</portlet-data-handler-class>
```

The preceding code shows that the content could be backed up as a LAR file via the tag `portlet-data-handler-class`.

Note that in order to export / import data properly, versions of source portal instance and target portal instance should be completely identical. Otherwise, you may meet migration issues.

What're the differences between archives and Export / Import? Using the feature of Export / Import, you could export LAR from one portal server and import it into another portal server. as long as the two portal servers are running the same version. On the other hand, when you use the feature Archive, only one portal instance is involved. The main difference is that archives back up setup configuration, whereas LAR contains data.

Portlet configuration

As you can see, there is a **Setup** tab under **More | Configuration** of the portlet
Message Boards, similar to that of the portlet **Sign In**. However, the portlet Hello
World doesn't have this tab. A portlet will have the **Setup** tab under **More |
Configuration** if the tag `configuration-action-class` is specified as follows
in `$PORTAL_ROOT_HOME/WEB-INF/liferay-portlet.xml`.

```
<configuration-action-class>
   com.liferay.portlet.messageboards.action.ConfigurationActionImpl
</configuration-action-class>
```

The preceding code shows that the tag `configuration-action-class` allows users
to configure the portlet at runtime. If the tag `configuration-action-class` isn't
specified in the portlet configuration, then there will be no **Setup** tab under **More
| Configuration**. As mentioned in *Chapter 2, Setting Up a Home Page and Navigation
Structure for the Intranet*, all portlets have tabs **Permissions** and **Sharing** under **More
| Configuration**. Therefore, you may ask: how many tabs are available for a specific
portlet? The following are the possible tabs for portlet configuration (portlet ID `86`).

- **Setup**: Specified through the tag `configuration-action-class`. Refer
  to `$PORTAL_ROOT_HOME/html/portlet/portlet_configuration/edit_
  configuration.jsp` to see how it works.

- **Supported Clients**: Specified by the tag `supports` and multiple sub-tags
  such as `mime-type` in `$PORTAL_ROOT_HOME/WEB-INF/portlet-custom.xml`.
  Refer to `$PORTAL_ROOT_HOME/html/portlet/portlet_configuration/
  edit_supported_clients.jsp` to see how it works.

- **Permissions**: This tab is available for all portlets. Refer to `$PORTAL_ROOT_
  HOME/html/portlet/portlet_configuration/edit_permissions.jsp` to
  see how it works.

- **Communication**: Specified via the tag `supported-public-render-
  parameter` in `$PORTAL_ROOT_HOME/WEB-INF/portlet-custom.xml`. Refer
  to `$PORTAL_ROOT_HOME/html/portlet/portlet_configuration/edit_
  public_render_parameters.jsp` to see how it works.

- **Sharing**: This tab is available for all portlets. Refer to `$PORTAL_ROOT_HOME/
  html/portlet/portlet_configuration/edit_sharing.jsp` to see how
  it works.

- **Scope**: Specified by the tag `scopeable` in `$PORTAL_ROOT_HOME/WEB-INF/
  portlet-custom.xml`. Refer to `$PORTAL_ROOT_HOME/html/portlet/
  portlet_configuration/edit_scope.jsp` to see how it works.

As shown in the tabs discussed previously, all portlets have the tabs **Permissions** and **Sharing** by default. You can find detailed specification in `$PORTAL_ROOT_HOME/html/portlet/portlet_configuration/tab1.jsp`.

Assigning permissions

We have used default settings for the Message Boards portlet in the page "Forums" under the Guest public pages. As shown previously, when the administrator "Palm Tree" logged in, he/she will see the "Add Category" button in Message Boards. As mentioned earlier, the user "Lotti Stein" is also a member of the Guest community. While trying to log in as "Lotti Stein", you would see Message Boards in the page "Forums", but you will find out that there is no button "Add Category" in Message Boards.

What's happening? This is something related to permissions. In general, there are three levels of permissions—permissions on Message Boards, permissions on categories, and permissions on messages.

The permissions on Message Boards portlet

The following table shows the permissions on the Message Boards portlet. The role Community Member may set up all permissions (marked as 'X') namely **Access in Control Panel**, **Add to Page**, **Configuration**, and **View**. However, the role Guest only has the possibility to set up **View** and **Add to Page** (marked as 'X'). By default, a community user has the (marked as '*') View action permissions of his own as well as that of a guest.

Action	Description	Community	Guest
Access in Control Panel	Ability to access the portlet Message Boards in Control Panel	X	
Add to Page	Ability to add the portlet Message Boards in a page	X	X
Configuration	Ability to configure portlet	X	
View	Ability to view the content of the portlet	X, *	X, *

Obviously, as a member of the Guest community, "Lotti Stein" only has the permission **View** on the portlet Message Boards by default. As the role Community Member doesn't have the **Configuration** and **Access in Control Panel** permissions, "Lotti Stein" wouldn't have the **Configuration** and **Access in Control Panel** permissions too. That is, "Lotti Stein" doesn't have the ability to configure the portlet Message Boards in the page "Forums" or to access the portlet Message Boards in Control Panel.

What's the permission action **Access in Control Panel**? The permission action **Access in Control Panel** represents the ability to access the portlet Message Boards in the Control Panel. By default, the user "Lotti Stein" doesn't have the ability to access the portlet Message Boards in the Control Panel. But the requirement is that the user "Lotti Stein" should have ability to access the portlet Message Boards in the Control Panel. How to implement? The following is an example — assigning permission action **Access in Control Panel**.

1. Log in as an admin, say "Palm Tree".

2. First click on **Roles** under the category **Portal** of **Control Panel**.

3. Then locate a role, say "MB Topic Admin".

4. Click on the **Assign Members** icon and update association — assigning the user "Lotti Stein" as a member of the role "MB Topic Admin".

5. Then click on the **Define Permissions** icon from the **Actions** next to the right of the role. Note that you should click on the **Define Permissions** tab directly after saving members assignment.

6. Click on the **Applications | Message Boards** link, check checkboxes — **Access in Control Panel** and **View**.

7. Click on the **Save** button when you are ready.

As shown in the preceding steps, the user "Lotti Stein" has the permission actions **Access in Control Panel** and **View** via the role "MB Topic Admin". This means that the user "Lotti Stein" does have the ability to access the portlet Message Boards in the Control Panel. Trying to log in as "Lotti Stein", you would see **Message Boards** under the category **Content of Control Panel**.

Permissions on Message Boards content

Likewise, the following table shows permissions on Message Boards content. The role Community Member may have the ability to set up all permissions (marked as 'X'): **Add Category, Add File, Move Thread, Reply to Message, Subscribe,** and **Ban User**, while the role Guest doesn't have these capabilities.

Action	Description	Community	Guest
Add Category	Ability to add top-level category	X	
Add File	Ability to add a file as attachment at the root category		
Ban User	Ability to ban or unban users	X	
Move Thread	Ability to move thread at the root category	X	
Reply to Message	Ability to reply to message at the root category	X	
Subscribe	Ability to subscribe at the root category	X	

As you can see, as a member of the Guest community, "Lotti Stein" doesn't have the **Add Category** and **Ban User** permissions on the Message Boards content by default. Of course, "Lotti Stein" could get these permissions by assigning permissions via roles. Take a look at the following. It is an example to show how permission actions **Add Category** and **Ban User** are assigned.

1. Log in as an admin, says "Palm Tree".
2. First click on **Roles** under the category **Portal** of the Control Panel.
3. Then locate a role, say "MB Topic Admin".
4. Then click on the **Define Permissions** icon from the **Actions** next to the right of the role.
5. Click on the **Content | Message Boards** link and check checkboxes **Add Category** and **Ban User**.
6. Finally, click on the **Save** button when you are ready.

That's it! From now on, the user "Lotti Stein" has the **Add Category** and **Ban User** permissions on Message Boards content via the role "MB Topic Admin".

Permissions on category

The following table shows permissions on categories and subcategories. The role Community Member is able to set up all permissions (marked as 'X'): **Add File, Add Message, Add Subcategory, Delete, Move Thread, Permissions, Reply to Message, Subscribe, Update, Update Thread Priority,** and **View**. However, the role Guest only has the possibility to set up Add Message, Delete, Permissions, and View (marked as 'X'). By default, the role Community Member has permission actions (marked as '*'), namely, Add File, Add Message, Subscribe, and View, whereas the role Guest only has a single permission action (marked as '*'): View. Note that these permissions can be scoped to a particular community or to the entire portal thanks to the **limit scope** link, located to the right of each permission action's name.

Action	Description	Community	Guest
Add File	Ability to add a file as attachment to the category	X, *	
Add Messages	Ability to add message to the category	X, *	X
Add Subcategory	Ability to add subcategory	X	
Delete	Ability to delete the sub category and its threads	X	X
Move Thread	Ability to move thread	X	
Permissions	Ability to assign permissions	X	X
Reply to Messages	Ability to reply to messages	X, *	X
Subscribe	Ability to subscribe to the category	X, *	
Update	Ability to update the category	X	
Update Thread Priority	Ability to update the thread priority of the category	X	
View	Ability to view categories	X, *	X, *

Obviously, as a member of the Guest community, "Lotti Stein" has only **View, Add File, Add Message, Reply to Message,** and **Subscribe** permissions for the subcategories "Book Category A", "Book Category B", and "Book Category C". This is because we have added them by the role Community Member with the default settings. "Lotti Stein" has **View** permissions only on "Book Category D" because we have added it with view permission for the role Community Member.

As an administrator, you may need to set up users of the role Community Member having the default permissions setting (**View, Add File, Add Message, Reply to Messages**, and **Subscribe**) for the category "Book Category D". That is, you need to add permission actions **Add File, Add Message, Reply to Messages**, and **Subscribe** on the category **Book Category D** via the role Community Member. Let's do it by following these steps:

1. Click on the parent category **Books** in order to list its subcategories.

2. Locate the subcategory **Book Category D** where you want to change permissions.

3. Then click on the **Permissions** icon from the **Actions** next to the category.

4. Select permissions: **Add File, Add message, Reply to Message**, and **Subscribe** for the role Community Member.

5. Click on the **Submit** button.

From now on, as a member of the Guest community, **Lotti Stein** has the permission actions **View, Add File, Add Message, Reply to Messages**, and **Subscribe** on the subcategory "Book Category D".

The preceding steps provide a way to update permissions for an individual resource, for example, "Book Category D". How about permissions on categories—existing ones or newly created ones? Let's consider a use case: the user "Lotti Stein" should have the permission **Update** on categories, including subcategories—both existing ones and newly created ones. How to implement this use case? The following is the answer, as an example: by assigning permissions via roles in Control Panel.

1. Log in as an admin, says **Palm Tree**.

2. First click on **Roles** under the category **Portal** of **Control Panel**.

3. Then locate a role, say **MB Topic Admin**.

4. Then click on the **Define Permissions** icon from the **Actions** next to the right of the role.

5. Click on the **Content | Message Boards** link, select the **Update** checkbox under the **Message Boards** category.

6. Finally, click on the **Save** button.

As shown in preceding steps, the user is assigned the **Update** permission on Message Boards category across all groups in the current portal instance via the role "MB Topic Admin". The user "Lotti Stein" is a member of the role "MB Topic Admin". Therefore, the user "Lotti Stein" got the Update permission on the Message Boards category across all groups in the current portal instance.

Permissions on message

The following table shows the default permissions on messages, either threads or posts. The role Community Member is able to set up all permissions (marked as 'X'): **Delete**, **Permissions**, **Subscribe**, **Update**, and **View**. However, the role Guest is able to set up **Delete**, **Permissions**, and **View** (marked as 'X'). By default, the role Community Member has the actions (marked as '*') Subscribe and View, whereas the role Guest only has the **View** action (marked as '*').

Action	Description	Community	Guest
Delete	Ability to delete messages	X	X
Permissions	Ability to assign permissions	X	X
Subscribe	Ability to subscribe to the thread	X, *	
Update	Ability to update messages	X	
View	Ability to view the details of messages	X, *	X, *

Note that the role Owner is able to set up all permissions and, by default, has all permission actions. Of course, as an administrator, you can create a new role and assign any permission, based on the role, to different users.

As you can see, as a member of the Guest community, "Lotti Stein" only has the permission actions **View** and **Subscribe** on messages (threads and posts). That's because we have added them through the role Community Member as the default settings. Now suppose that we're going to add the permission Update on message (both thread and post) in following scopes:

- Individual thread or post
- A set of threads and posts belonging to a category like "Book Category D"
- All threads and posts in a group like Guest community
- All threads and posts in a portal instance like current portal instance

How to implement the above use cases? For individual threads or posts, you can assign permissions in the portlet Message Boards through custom regular roles or a custom community role (or Community Member) for community pages or a custom organization role (or Organization Member) for organization pages.

For all threads and posts in a group, you can assign permissions in the Control Panel through a custom community role (or Community Member) for community pages or a custom organization role (or Organization Member) for organization pages.

For all threads and posts in a portal instance, you can assign permissions in the Control Panel through custom regular roles. For a set of threads and posts belonging to a category, you could use a category hierarchy structure.

In practice, when you assign any permission on a message to a role, make sure that you assign the related permissions, at least `View`, on both the portlet Message Boards and the message's subcategories and category. Otherwise, you wouldn't be able to view the portlet and the related categories. Moreover, the message would be invisible to people with the role.

Using Message Boards effectively

The following figure depicts a forum structure overview of Message Boards. A forum is made up of a set of categories. Each category may have many subcategories and threads. Furthermore, each thread may have many posts (in the form of replies). The thread refers to the collection of messages.

A thread itself is a post too. The posts may be displayed in flat chronological order by date of posting or in a question-answer order. The figure shows a thread of one question followed by all the answers in a hierarchy. Actually, threads can be regarded as the root level posts. Sub-posts are also supported, which enable comments in one of the replies to start another thread that remains linked to the original. Moreover, you can enable flags, thereby allowing users to flag content as inappropriate. In addition, you can subscribe to categories / subcategories and threads.

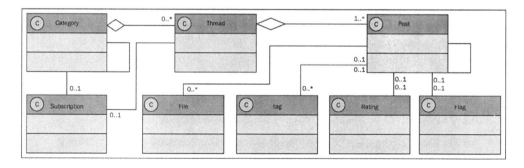

As shown in the preceding figure, you are able to attach a set of files to posts (and threads because a thread itself is a post). In addition, you are able to select existing tags or add new tags to posts.

Category hierarchy

As you can see, there are top-level categories with the permission action **Add Category**. A top-level category forms a root, that is, a message container. Each category can have many subcategories with the permission action **Add Subcategory**. Therefore, categories and subcategories form a hierarchical structure—categories form the root, while subcategories form the trunk and leaves.

How can you benefit from category hierarchy? The main benefit you can get is inherited permissions. Another benefit you can get is content sharing within a category hierarchy. As mentioned earlier, when you assign any permission on message to a role, you must make sure that you assign related permissions—at least, **View**, on the message's subcategories and categories. Therefore, we could use category hierarchy to assign permissions for a set of threads and posts belonging to a category or a subcategory.

Semantics and Ontology

When a message has been created, the portal will check for the spelling. That is, the message does have a specific syntax, but it doesn't involve semantics. **Semantics** is the study of the meanings of linguistic expressions (as opposed to their sound, spelling, and so on.). Moreover, it would be useful if messages could be managed through semantics.

As previously mentioned, you can tag messages through folksonomy. Later, you would be able to apply taxonomy on messages. A folksonomy is a user-generated taxonomy used to categorize and retrieve web content, using open-ended labels called tags. On the other hand, taxonomy is the practice and science of classification—hierarchical in structure and commonly displaying parent-child relationships.

This is a good way to approach a semantic classification of content like messages. Moreover, it would be possible to build a complete ontology based on the concepts of folksonomy and taxonomy. In this way, content could be classified as instances, and properties of content can be used to navigate through concepts declared in the ontology, which isn't ready yet but is highly awaited.

Categorization

Sooner or later, you will have a lot of posts on the Message Boards. Therefore, it is useful to allow users to generate content post and classify that content post in their own unique way. Let's first experience tagging assets.

Tagging assets

As an administrator at the enterprise "Palm Tree Publications", you may need to add tags "liferay" and "book" in the post "**RE: Let's discuss book Liferay**". Let's do it by following these steps:

1. In a post updating page, locate the **Tag** box.

2. In the **Tag** text box, simply start typing the tag name and a list of tags will appear. For example, when "li" is typed into the textbox and a list of the available tags is populated. Select the tag you want, say "liferay", and that tag should show up on the top of the box.

3. Similarly, when "bo" is typed into the textbox and a list of the available tags is populated. Select the tag you want, say "book", and the tag should show up on the top of the box too.

4. Click on the **Save** button when you are ready.

5. For some reason, let's say, you need to remove a tag "Book" from the tag list. To remove a tag "Book", simply click on the mark "[x]" located next to the tag first, and then click on the **Save** button when you are ready.

6. Similarly, you can tag content including Bookmark entries, Blog entries, Document Library documents, Image Gallery images, Wiki articles, Web Content articles, Message Board messages, and so on.

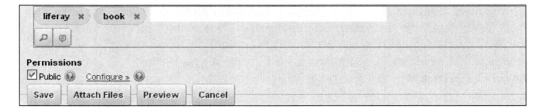

Folksonomies

As you can see, there is an open set of tags that could be extended by end users called `Folksonomies`. In general, as a user, you are able to carry out the following tasks based on the tags:

- Extend tags by entering a tag, and press *Enter*

- Select tags by clicking on the **Selected Tags** button, where it displays a set of existing tags for you to select multiple tags

- Find tags by clicking on the **Suggestions** button, where it uses advanced search techniques to find out tags

In short, the portal provides meta tag `Folksonomies`, which is a tagging system that allows us to tag web content, documents, message board messages, and more. It also dynamically publishes content by tags. The meta tags can later be used to classify assets as well as search and aggregate them.

Taxonomies

Besides the meta tag `Folksonomies`, you could use another kind of tag called `Taxonomies`. In general, taxonomies are a way of organizing and aggregating content—a closed set of categories (that is, tags in a different name) of the vocabulary, which are created and organized in a hierarchical structure.

Before going deeper, let's see an example. Consider that we have to build the vocabulary **Book**, along with the categories **Chapter** and **Section** in a hierarchy. We're going to build them in the next section. Now we're going to apply these tags—categories on Web Content—by following these steps:

1. Login as an admin, say, **Palm Tree**.

2. Click on **Web Content** under the category **Content** of the Control Panel first.

3. Then select the tab **Web Content**.

4. Click on the **Add Web Content** button.

5. In the **Web Content** editing page, click on **Select Categories** under **Categorization**. This would give you the ability to apply categories on the current web content, as shown in following screenshot:

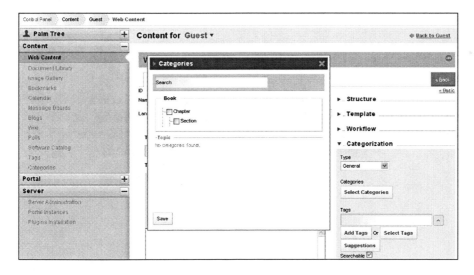

As you can see, categories are displayed in a hierarchical structure. You are able to choose as many categories as you expected. You could search and find your favorite categories in a quick way when the number of categories is huge. Let's see how to build the categories hierarchy in the next section.

Tags administration

The following is a summary of tags and their related portlets in the portal.

Administration:

- **Tags**: This manages folksonomies — tags and their properties
- **Categories**: This manages taxonomies — vocabulary, categories, and their properties

Tag different types of assets in the portal:
These include Bookmarks' entries, Blogs' entries, Wiki articles, Document Library documents, Image Gallery images, Web Content articles, and Message Board messages.

Aggregate assets in the portal: Asset Publisher

Display tags:

- Tag Cloud — a visual depiction of user-generated tags.
- Tags Navigation — used to display user-generated tags in multiple styles
- Categories Navigation — used to display predefined tags in a hierarchy structure

Tags portlet

To manage tags, you should go to **Tags** under the category Content of **Control Panel**. Using the Tags portlet (portlet ID 99), you can add tags and manage their properties. As shown in following screenshot, the Tags portlet provides the capabilities to manage tags with the options **Search**, **Add Tag**, and **Permissions**.

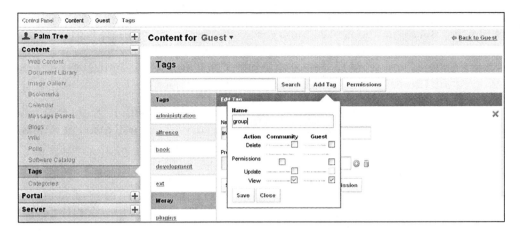

To search for tags, you could simply input a search criterion say "ext" first, and then click on the **Search** button. Search results will appear dynamically.

To add a tag, simply click on the button **Add Tag**, input the tag name, say "ext", and change the default permission settings first. Then click on the **Save** button to save inputs or the **Cancel** button in order to discard inputs. If the tag doesn't exist in the current group, then the tag will be added by associating it to the current group and it will bring us to the **Edit Tag** view. Otherwise, it will display a message stating "**That tag already exists**".

Suppose that you want to change the tag "ext" to "extension", how would you do this? The process is simple, just click on the tag "ext" using edit links. In **Edit Tag** view, the tag name and properties are displayed. In the tag name "ext", you could type "extension", and click on the **Save** button. Optionally, you can click on the **Close** button or close icon to cancel the current process.

To delete a property of a given tag, say "extension", locate the property first and then click on the Delete icon next to the property. In order to add one more property of a given tag, say "extension", just click on add icon first. Then simply input the name and value. You could click Click on the **Save** button to save the inputs or the **Cancel** button to cancel the inputs.

Don't forget that you can merge tags with drag-and-drop. For example, you can drag the tag "book" and drop it to the tag "liferay", and you would see a pop-up message that says: **Are you sure you want to merge "book" into "liferay"?**
This will change all items tagged with "book" to be tagged with "liferay".

Properties are a way to add more detailed information to a specific tag. They are separated into key-value pairs that allow us to associate detailed information with a tag.

To delete a tag, locate the tag, for example, "book", and then click on the tag using the edit links like the name "book" Follow it up by clicking on the **Delete** button in the **Edit Tag** view, as shown in the preceding screenshot. A pop up will appear asking you "**Are you sure you want to delete this tag**". Click on the **OK** button to confirm deletion, or the **Cancel** button to the cancel deletion process.

As you can see, a tag could have many properties associated with it. Note that when a tag gets deleted, the properties that belong to the current tag will also get removed.

Categories portlet

In order to manage vocabularies and categories, you could go to **Categories** under the category **Content** of **Control Panel**. Using Categories portlet (portlet ID 147), you can add vocabularies and categories and also manage categories' properties. As shown in the following screenshot, the Categories portlet provides capabilities to manage tags including **Search**, **Add Vocabulary**, **Add Category**, and **Permissions**.

As you may have noticed, the vocabulary **Topic** was created by default, and it was shown under the column **Vocabularies**. Of course, you can search vocabularies and categories in a convenient way. In order to do so, you could simply input a search criterion, say "book", first, then select types—either Categories or Vocabularies, and then click on the **Search** button. Search results will appear dynamically.

To add a vocabulary, simply click on the **Add Vocabulary** button, input the vocabulary name, for example, "Book", and change the default permission settings first. Then click on the **Save** button to save inputs or the **Cancel** button to discard inputs. If the vocabulary doesn't exist in the current group, then the vocabulary will be added associated to the current group. Otherwise, it will show "**That vocabulary already exists**". That is, the vocabulary names must be unique in the current group.

Suppose that you want to change the vocabulary "Portal" to "Portals". In order to implement it, double-click on the vocabulary "Portal" using edit links. In the Edit view, the vocabulary name would be editable. Where the vocabulary name is "Portal", you could type "Portals", and click on the **Save** button. Again, the updated vocabulary name must be unique in the current group.

If needed, you can delete a vocabulary. You could first locate a vocabulary say "Book", and click on the **Delete Vocabulary** button at the bottom of the title categories. As you can see, a vocabulary could have many categories associated with it. Therefore, when a vocabulary gets deleted, the categories which belong to the current vocabulary will get removed too.

After adding vocabularies, you are ready to add categories, as shown in the following screenshot:

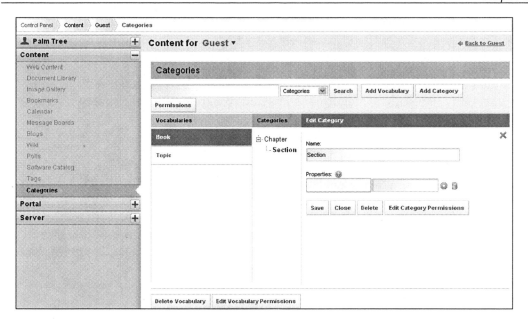

In order to add a category, simply locate a vocabulary, for example "Book", and click on the button **Add Category**, input a tag name, say "Chapter", and change the default permission settings. Optionally, you are able to select different vocabularies from the drop-down list. Then click on the **Save** button to save inputs, or the **Cancel** button to discard inputs. If a category doesn't exist in the current vocabulary, then the category will be added to the current vocabulary, and it will bring us to the Edit Category view. Otherwise, it will throw an error message "**That category already exists**".

In cases where you want to change the category "Chapter" to "Main Chapter", click on the category using the edit links, say "Chapter". In the Edit Category view, the category name and properties are displayed. In the category name "Chapter", you could type "Main Chapter", and click on the **Save** button. Optionally, you can press the **Close** button or close icon to cancel the current process. Again, the updated category name must be unique in the current vocabulary.

A category can have another category as its parent category. That is, categories support hierarchical structure. In order to build the hierarchy, you could add categories such as "Chapter" and "Section" first, and then you can drag-and-drop a category called "Section" to a correct parent category, say "Chapter". That's it!

To delete a property of a given category called "Chapter", locate the property first. After locating it, click on the delete icon next to the property. In order to add one more property of a given category, say "Chapter", just click on the add icon first. Then simply input the name and value. Finally, click on the **Save** button to save inputs or the **Cancel** button to cancel inputs.

As you can see, a category could have many properties associated with it. Note that when a category gets deleted, the properties which belong to the current category will get removed too.

As stated above, a vocabulary may have many categories associated with it, each category may have other categories as its child categories, and each category may in turn have many properties.

Tags configuration

As you have noticed, when you click on **Categories** under the category **Content** of **Control Panel**, a vocabulary **Topic** is created by default. However, when you add categories, there is no default property for a newly created category. Moreover, when you click on **Tags** under the category **Content** of **Control Panel** and add tags, you will see that there is no default tag property for newly created tags. The portal has the following settings by default in `portal.properties`.

```
asset.categories.properties.default=
asset.tag.properties.default=
asset.vocabulary.default=Topic
```

As shown in the preceding code, you could input a list of comma-delimited default properties for newly created categories via the property `asset.categories.properties.default`. Note that each item of the list should have the format `key:value`. You could also input a list of comma-delimited default tag properties for newly created tags via the property `asset.tag.properties.default`. Again, each item on the list should have the format `key:value`. Moreover, you could set a name, other than **Topic**, as the default vocabulary. Of course, you could override these properties in `portal-ext.properties` if required.

In addition, the portal has the following settings by default in `portal.properties`:

```
asset.categories.search.hierarchical=true
```

The preceding code shows that the property `asset.categories.search.hierarchical` is set to `true`, thus the child categories are also included in the search. Of course, you can set it to `false` in order to specify that searching and browsing using categories should only show assets that have been assigned the selected category explicitly.

Tags publishing

There are several portlets available for publishing tags. These portlets include Tag Cloud (portlet ID `148`), Tags Navigation (portlet ID `141`), and Categories Navigation (portlet ID `122`). How to get these portlets in one place? As an example, you can simply create a page called "Tags" in the Guest public pages and add these three portlets using **Add | Application** under the dock bar menu.

The Tag Cloud portlet provides a visual depiction of user-generated tags, shown with varying font size. Note that there is a tab **Communication** under **More... | Configuration** and the shared parameter tag could be mapped into `categoryId` because the portlet has the following configuration in `$PORTAL_ROOT_HOME/WEB-INF/portlet-custom.xml`.

```
<supported-public-render-parameter>tag</supported-public-render-parameter>
```

The Tags Navigation portlet gives us the capability to navigate user-generated tags in different ways. Like the Tag Cloud portlet, there is a tab **Communication** under **More... | Configuration**, and the shared parameter `tag` could be mapped into `categoryId` using it. Additionally, the portlet has a tab **Setup** under **More... | Configuration**. Therefore, you can configure views of user-generated tags via the tab **Setup**. As shown in the preceding screenshot, tags could be viewed in the default view. By using Setup, you would be able to show the asset count, select the asset type (for example, **Any, Blogs Entry, Bookmarks Entry, Document Library Document, Image Gallery Image, Web Content, Message Boards Message, Wiki Page**, and so on), select the display type (for example, **Number, Cloud**), and show tags with no assets.

What happens when we map `tag` to `categoryId` or vice versa? `tag` and `categoryId` are defined as **Public Render Parameters**. With the Public Render Parameters feature, the render parameters set in the `processAction` of one portlet will be available in the `render` parameter of other portlets as well. Using public render parameters instead of **Events** avoids the additional process event call. In the portlet section, each portlet can specify the public render parameters it would like to share via the `supported-public-render-parameter` element. For more details about **Inter-Portlet Communication (IPC)**, you can refer to *Chapter 2, Working with JSR-286 Portlets* of the book *Liferay Portal 5.2 Systems Development, Packt Publishing*.

When mapping `tag` to `categoryId`, the render parameters set `categoryId` instead of `tag` in one portlet, which will be available in other portlets. Similarly, when mapping `categoryId` to `tag`, the render parameters set `tag` rather than `categoryId` in one portlet, which will be available in other portlets.

The Categories Navigation portlet provides capability to navigate categories in a hierarchical structure. Like the Tag Cloud portlet, but in reverse order, there is a tab **Communication** under **More... | Configuration**. The shared parameter `categoryId` can be mapped to `tag` because the portlet has the following configuration in `$PORTAL_ROOT_HOME/WEB-INF/portlet-custom.xml`.

```
<supported-public-render-parameter>categoryId</supported-public-
render-parameter>
```

Assigning permissions

As stated above, we have discussed how to manage tags, vocabularies, and categories. Now you may ask questions such as "How do I assign permissions?", and "Do Asset Tags have restriction on scope?". This section is going to answer these questions.

Permissions on portlet

The following table shows the permissions on portlets Tags, Categories, Tag Cloud, Tags Navigation, and Categories Navigation. The role Community Member may set up all permissions (marked as 'X'), namely, **Access in Control Panel, Configuration**, and **View**. However, the role Guest only has the possibility to set up **View** (marked as 'X'). By default, a community user has (marked as '*') a View action of his/her own as well as that of a guest.

Action	Description	Community	Guest
Access in Control Panel	Ability to access portlets in the Control Panel	X	
Configuration	Ability to configure the portlet	X	
View	Ability to view the content of the portlet	X, *	X, *

Note that only the Tags portlet and Categories portlet come with the permission **Access in Control Panel**. This is the reason that the Tags and Categories portlets are available in the Control Panel. On the other hand, portlets such as Tag Cloud, Tags Navigation, and Categories Navigation, don't have the permission action **Access in Control Panel**.

Permissions on tags

The following table shows permissions on Tags. The role Community Member has the ability to set up all permissions (marked as 'X') including **Add Vocabulary**, **Add Category**, and **Add Tag**. By default, only the role Owner has permission actions **Add Vocabulary**, **Add Category**, and **Add Tag**.

Action	Description	Community	Guest
Add Vocabulary	Ability to add vocabulary	X	
Add Category	Ability to add category	X	
Add Tag	Ability to add tag	X	

How can you assign these permissions? You simply go to **Categories** under the category **Content** of **Control Panel** first, and then click on the **Permissions** button. Alternatively, you will get the same if you go to **Tags** under the category **Content** of **Control Panel** first, and then click on the **Permissions** button.

Note that these permissions are scoped into a group, say "Guest", by default.

Permissions on tag, vocabulary, and category

The following table shows the default permissions on tag, vocabulary, and category. The role Community Member is able to set up all permissions (marked as 'X'), namely, **Delete**, **Permissions**, **Update**, and **View**. However, a role Guest is able to set up the Delete, Permissions, and View (marked as 'X') actions. By default, both the role Community Member and the role Guest have (marked as '*') the View action.

Action	Description	Community	Guest
Add Category	Ability to add category for a give category	X, *	
Delete	Ability to delete tag, vocabulary, or category	X	X
Permissions	Ability to assign permissions	X	X
Update	Ability to update tag, vocabulary, or category	X	
View	Ability to view tag, vocabulary, or category	X, *	X, *

The permission **Add Category** is available only for categories. By default, the role of Community Member has the ability to set up this permission, whereas the role Guest doesn't have this ability. On the other hand, the role Community Member has this permission by default.

How to assign permissions on an individual to a given group? For individual vocabulary, you can do it by following these steps:

1. Go to **Categories** under the category **Content** of **Control Panel**.

2. Select a group under **Content** for, say "Guest".

3. Locate a vocabulary, say "Topic", and click on it.

4. Click on the **Edit Vocabulary Permissions** button and assign permissions on the current vocabulary via roles.

In the same way, you can assign permissions on individual tags and categories.

How can you assign permissions on vocabularies, categories, and tags in the current portal instance or a group? For these elements in the current portal instance, you will be able to assign permission in the Control Panel through regular custom roles by following these steps:

1. Go to **Roles** under the category **Content** of **Control Panel**.

2. Locate a custom regular role, say "MB Topic Admin", and click on **Define Permissions** of the **Actions** icon next to the role.

3. Under **Add Permission**, select **Content | Tags**.

4. Assign desired permissions to the role.

For all the vocabularies, categories, and tags in a group, you will be able to assign permissions in the Control Panel through the custom community role (or Community Member) for community groups, or the custom organization role (or Organization Member) for organization groups.

Tags in scope

As you can see, tags and categories are scoped into a group by default. For example, we have added a set of tags and categories under **Content for Guest**. This means that these tags and categories are only visible in the group Guest community for both private pages and public pages. However, they are invisible in the "Palm Tree Enterprise" organization or other groups.

This sounds like a limitation. But thanks to the group **Shared Global**, we could scope tags and categories into the portal instance. If we add a set of tags and categories under **Content for Global**, then these tags and categories are widely visible in the portal instance. This means that these tags and categories would be globally visible in any of the groups of the current portal instance.

Using tags effectively

The portal tagging system allows us to tag web content, documents, message board threads, and more and dynamically publish assets by tags. Tags provide a way of organizing and aggregating content. Basically, the tag administration determines which tags are available for use. The users use these tags on their content. Any content that is tagged can be grouped or aggregated.

The following figure depicts an overview of tags, categories, and assets:

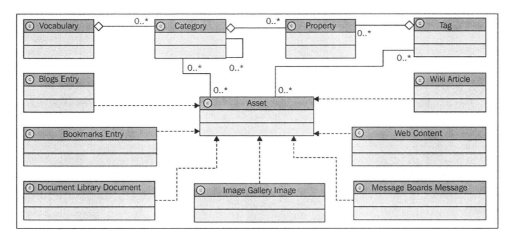

Folksonomies

Folksonomies are a user-driven approach to organizing content through tags, cooperative classification, and communication through shared metadata. The portal implements folksonomies through tags. A tag may be associated with many assets, whereas an asset may have many tags associated with it. This is what we called tagging content. Also, a tag may have many properties. Each property is made up of name-value pair.

A tag may be associated with content. Using tags, you can tag almost anything: Bookmarks' entries, Blogs' entries, Wiki articles, Document Library documents, Image Gallery images, Journal articles and Message Board threads, and so on. You can also use these tags to pull content within the Asset Publisher portlet.

Taxonomies

Taxonomies are a hierarchical structure used in scientific classification schemes. Although taxonomies are common, it can be difficult to implement them. The portal implements taxonomies as "vocabularies and category tree vocabularies" in order to tag contents and classify them.

You can have more than one vocabulary, which forms a top-level item of the hierarchy. Each vocabulary may have many categories. That is, a category cannot be a top-level item of the hierarchy. However, a category can have other categories as its child or siblings. Therefore, vocabulary and categories form a hierarchical tree structure.

In the same way, a category may have many properties. Each property is made up of a name and a value.

In addition, a predefined category will be applied to any asset. In a word, assets could be managed and grouped by categories.

> Do Meta Tags work for educating purpose? The answer is clearly no. Meta Tags allow users to generate content and classify that content in their own unique way. If educating tags was the need, then you could use taxonomies.

What makes tags interesting?

Tags are important so that users can generate content and classify that content in their own unique way.

For example, suppose that you have a photo-sharing site where users can tag their humorous pictures from a vacation. They tag some pictures only as "hawaii", others are tagged as "funny". Surely, they tag a number of pictures as both "funny" and "hawaii". Later, when they want to view their pictures from Hawaii, they will simply select "hawaii". If they want to view all their funny pictures, then they would select "funny". If they want to view only their funny pictures from Hawaii, then they would simply select both "hawaii" and "funny".

Let's consider another example. Suppose that you have a website about hobbies and you have lots of users that like fishing. Thus, when users input data, photos, reviews or anything you might dream up, they will invariably tag their posts with "fishing". Some of users will tag their posts with "angling", and others may use two or more tags such as "fishing vacation" or "holiday fishing".

Then you can generate website with the following data:

- Fishing—100 posts
- Angling—200 posts
- Fishing Vacation—300 posts
- Holiday Fishing—400 posts

Furthermore, imagine creating menus and pages based on these categories. Besides classification, the aim of tagging is to improve the relevancy of search engines. In particular, taxonomies give us a way for indirect searches. For example, **California** is under the category **USA**. If a contributor tags a document with the **California** category, and people search a document with the keyword **USA**, then the search engine would be able to retrieve this document because **California** is a child of **USA**. This approach is called **top-down** hierarchy — the child categories are also included in the search. Fortunately, this approach is also supported in the portal.

There is another approach called **bottom-up** hierarchy — the parent categories are also included in the search. For instance, if people search a document with the keyword **California**, search engine should be able to retrieve the document with the keyword **USA** because **USA** is the parent of **California**. Moreover, a strong taxonomy system should be able to deal with synonyms as well. These features weren't supported at the time of writing, but are expected to be present in the coming version.

Category Tree

It is useful that parent categories can have multiple child categories. This parent-child relationship forms a hierarchical structure. However, categories don't have siblings, for example, left-side category and right-side category. Parent-child relationship plus left-side category and right-side category form a tree called **Category Tree**. This feature will be available soon.

Why it doesn't merge both kinds of tags using ontology

As you can see, there are two kinds of tags: taxonomies and folksonomies. Both of them can be used as a way of organizing and aggregating content. Folksonomy is a way of classification, creating, and managing tags to annotate and categorize content, whereas taxonomy is a hierarchical structure only for classification.

In fact, taxonomies and folksonomies are different. Taxonomies are a closed set of categories (also called tags) and the vocabulary, created and organized in a hierarchical structure. It helps standardization, especially when you store it in the Shared Global group to standardize categorization through all of the organizations. In a word, folksonomies are an open set of tags, which are extended by the end user.

Can't we merge both of them through ontology? **Ontology** — the study of entities and their relations — is less concerned with what "is" than with what is possible. The answer would be "yes".

Asset Publisher

As stated above, we have discussed how to build assets, for example, message board messages. We have also introduced how to add tags and categories on assets like message board messages. Now it is time to investigate how to publish assets with tags and categories. Asset Publisher is a flexible tool to publish many types of assets within the portal. It allows for the showing of lists of web content, blog entries, images, documents, bookmarks, wiki pages, and so on. Each element on the list could be displayed as a title, a summary (that is, abstract), in full details, and much more.

Main features

Let's say you have a page named "Asset Publishing" in the Guest public pages and you are going to publish any assets including a Message Boards message in this page. How will you publish any assets on a page? Obviously, the Asset Publisher portlet is the key! First you could create a page named "Asset Publishing" under the Guest public pages via **Add | Page** of the dock bar menu. Then you can add Asset Publisher via **Add | Application**.

After adding Asset Publisher, you would see that assets, especially Message Board's messages in this example, get published as shown in following screenshot.

What are the main features of the Asset Publisher portlet? The following are the main features. However, the Asset Publisher has many other features too:

- The ability to add new assets, including Image Gallery image, Web Content, Document Library Document, Blogs Entry, and Bookmarks Entry, all in one place
- The capability to publish many types of assets within the portal
- The ability to edit different types of assets in one place

- Showing lists of web content, blog entries, images, documents, bookmarks, wiki pages, and Message boards messages as a title, a summary, or even in full detail through publishing rules. Note that this summary doesn't support multiple languages.

- Supporting pagination in different styles.

- Allowing users to click an asset in order to see it in full detail.

- Supporting both manual and dynamic selection of asset types.

In a word, Asset Publisher portlet allows users to publish any type of asset in the portal as if it were Web Content, filtering either through a set of publishing rules or by manual selection.

The Asset publisher portlet provides a way to display tagged assets: Bookmarks entries, Blogs entries, Document Library documents, Image Gallery images, Wiki articles, Web Content articles, and Message Board messages. Given a set of tags or categories, assets "tagged" with specific tags or categories will be displayed in the Asset Publisher portlet.

In addition, you can easily add assets (such as Bookmarks entries, Blogs entries, Document Library documents, Image Gallery images, and Web Content articles) within the portlet.

 For Bookmarks entries, Blogs entries, Document Library documents, Image Gallery images, Wiki articles, and Web Content articles, refer to instructions given in the coming chapters.

Configuration

Generally speaking, the Asset Publisher portlet is highly configurable. You can select assets manually or dynamically. Using **More | Configuration | Setup | Current**, you will be able to set up publishing rules: Asset Selection Manual and Asset Selection Dynamic. By the way, you are able to save the current setup in the archives under **More | Configuration | Setup | Archived**. This process is the same as that of the Message Boards archives' setup.

Selecting assets manually

Once you've chosen Asset Selection **Manual**, as shown in following screenshot, you will be able to select assets manually. In general, there are two sections for manual asset publishing: Selection and Display Settings. In the section **Selection**, you are able to choose what will be published in Asset Publisher, whereas in the section **Display Settings**, you are able to set up how to display assets in Asset Publisher.

In the section **Selection**, there are two options: creating a new asset and selecting it as default and selecting an existing asset. The assets that you would be able to create as new are Image Gallery Image, Web Content, Document Library Document, Blogs Entry, and Bookmark Entry. Obviously, at one time, you are able to create one asset and mark it as selected automatically. Similarly, the assets that you would be able to select are Blogs Entry, Bookmark Entry, Document Library Document, Image Gallery Image, and Web Content. As you can see, you are able to select only one asset at a time. But you could repeat the processes mentioned above and select many existing or newly created assets.

Once you've selected multiple assets, you are able to view the selected assets with columns **Type** and **Title** plus the icons **Move Up** / **Move Down** and **Delete**. If needed, you can change the order of assets by clicking on the icon **Move Up** / **Move Down** next to the asset, or remove an asset from the list by clicking on the icon **Delete** next to the asset.

As shown in the next screenshot, Display Settings specifies the style in which selected assets will be displayed. For assets in Asset Publisher, you could specify the following styles:

- **Display Style**: It has Table, Title List, Abstracts, and Full Content as options
- **Abstract Length**: This specifies the number of characters to display for abstracts
- **Asset Link Behavior**: This can either be set to **Show Full Content** or **View** in a specific portlet and gives you options to decide what happens when a user clicks on an asset—showing the content right where you are or by taking you to the page where the content was originally published.
- **Maximum Items to Display**: A number used for dynamic selection only
- **Pagination Type**: None, Simple, or Regular; for dynamic selecting only
- **Exclude Assets with 0 View**: A checkbox for dynamic selecting only
- **Show Available Locales**: Enables the display of available locales
- **Convert To**: Enabling OpenOffice integration provides documents' conversion functionality. The possible formats involved are DOC, ODT, PDF, RTF, SXW, TXT, but this list is not limited.
- **Enable Print**: This checkbox enables print capability on assets
- **Enable Ratings**: This checkbox enables ratings capability on assets
- **Enable Comments**: This checkbox to enable comments capability on assets
- **Enable Comments Ratings**: A checkbox enables ratings capabilities on comments of assets
- **Enable Tag Based Navigation**: This checkbox only for manual selection. If this is checked and a tag is selected when displaying the page, then assets with that tag will be shown instead of the assets that were manually selected.

How do you use this? Imagine that there there is a page called "Home" containing the Tags Navigation portlet and the Categories Navigation portlet on the left, and the Asset Publisher portlet on the right. If you have created a few Message Boards messages with the tag "book" and you have checked the checkbox **Enable Tag Based Navigation** in the Asset Publisher portlet, then you would see the tag "book" with a link behind in the portlet Tags Navigation. Clicking on the tag "book" when displaying the page, assets Message Board's messages with that tag "book" will be shown instead of the assets that were manually selected in the Asset Publisher portlet. Similarly, you could apply the same on categories of assets.

- **Show Metadata**: This shows metadata of assets and available metadata include Author, Categories, Create Date, Expiration Date, Modified Date, Priority, Publish Date, Tags, and View Count. You could also add metadata by clicking on the Add icon from Available to Current, remove metadata by clicking on the **Remove** icon from Current to Available, or change order of metadata in Current by clicking on the **Move Up** or **Move Down** icons for a selected metadata in Current.

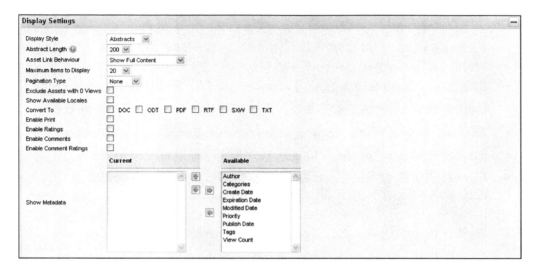

Selecting assets dynamically

Once you've chosen **Asset Selection Dynamic**, as shown in the next screenshot, you are able to select assets dynamically. In general, there are four sections for dynamic asset publishing: Source, Filter, Ordering and Grouping, and Display Settings.

In the **Source** section, there are two options, selecting **Scope** and **Asset Type**.

The default scope is current group. As Asset Publisher was added to the page "Asset Publisher" of the Guest public pages, the default scope is the group Guest. If Asset Publisher was added to the page "Asset Publishing" of the "Palm Tree Enterprise" organization's public pages, the default scope would've been the group organization "Palm Tree Enterprise".

Besides the default scope, there is another group called Shared Global available in the portal. Therefore, you would have three options for scope: default scope only, Shared Global only, or both default scope and Shared Global. By using any of these options, you would be able to add a scope by clicking on the **Add** icon from Available to Current, or remove a scope by clicking on the **Remove** icon from Current to Available. Moreover, you could change the order of scopes in Current by clicking on the **Move Up** or **Move Down** icon for a selected scope in Current.

The default asset type would be "any". That is, the assets that you would be able to include are Image Gallery Image, Web Content, Document Library Document, Blogs Entry, Wiki Pages, Message Board Messages, and Bookmarks Entry. Of course, you could choose some asset types. You will be able to add an asset type by clicking on the **Add** icon from Available to Current, or remove an asset type by clicking on the **Remove** icon from Current to Available; or even change orders of asset types in Current by clicking on the **Move Up** or **Move Down** icon for a selected asset type in Current.

In the Filter section, there are two options, that is, selecting display rules and a checkbox "Include Tags specified in the URL". The displayed assets must follow these rules. The display rule has an expression: find assets which "contain / don't contain" "any / all" "tags / categories". Moreover, you can have as many of these expressions as you want.

By default, "tags" was selected, and not "categories". In order to input tags which displayed the content must "contain / not contain" "any / all", simply start typing the tag and a list of tags will appear. Pick up a tag where displayed content must **contain / not contain**, and click on the button Add Tags. The selected tags will appear on top of the input box. Optionally, simply click on the button **Select Tags** and then pick up one or more tags. To remove a tag, click on the **[x]** mark located next to the tag.

To use categories instead of tags, select "categories" first, and then click on the button **Select Categories**. Pick up one or more categories. To remove a category, click on the **[x]** mark located next to the category.

The checkbox "Include tags specified in the URL" shows whether the portal includes tags specified in the URL or not. By default, this checkbox is selected, which means that the portal will include tags specified in the URL. Of course, you can deselect this checkbox to disable this functionality if you want.

In the section **Ordering and Grouping**, there are three options, namely, **Order by Column 1**, **Order by Column 2**, and **Group by**. The metadata for **Order by Column 1** and **Order by Column 2** would be **Title**, **Create Date**, **Modified Date**, **Published Date**, **Expiration Date**, **Priority**, and **View Count** — the order would be ascending or descending.

The metadata of **Group by** would be Asset Type or Vocabulary. That is, you would be able to group assets by asset types (for example, Image Gallery, Web Content, Document Library, Blogs, Wiki, Message Boards, and Bookmarks) or vocabulary (for example, "Book", and "Topic").

In the section Display Settings, you could specify the style in which selected assets will be displayed. The processes would be the same, or tightly speaking, similar to those of Asset Selection Manual.

Finally, you could click on the **Save** button to save the changes if you are ready, or click the **Cancel** button to cancel the changes.

Flexible operators support

As you noticed, the Asset Publisher portlet supports assets' advanced search based on multiple operators and tags (by using tags in general in order to represent both tags and categories). For search criteria, the tags would be like "contain / does not contain" "any / all". This is powerful for most use cases. For example, if there are four tags—T1, T2, T3, and T4, we use three operators—and, or, and not. By default, Asset Publisher supports four use cases (as basic expressions in general).

1. Contain any of these tags: T1, T2, T3, or T4
2. Contain all tags: T1, T2, T3, and T4
3. Does not Contain any tag: not (T1, T2, T3, or T4)
4. Does not Contain all tags: not (T1, T2, T3, T4)

At the same time, the Asset Publisher portlet allows the preceding basic expressions to appear as many times as possible with an AND operator.

Let's go ahead and consider one more use case, for instance, building a search criterion—find assets which contain any of the tags T1, T2, and T3, but don't contain the tag T4. We could express this condition as follows:

```
(T1 or T2) and T3 and (not T4)
```

The previous use case is just one example. It could be represented through three basic expressions through the current UI.

1. Exp_1: (T1 or T2)
2. Exp_2: T3
3. Exp_1: (not T4)

Thus we would have the following final expression. Obviously, the UI is a little bit complicated.

```
Exp_1 and Exp_2 and Exp_3
```

You may have many use cases which require flexible operators' support. As shown in the following screenshot, it is good that the Asset Publisher supports flexible operators through web UI simply, without being complex.

Customization

As you can see, there are four display styles—Tables, Title List, Abstracts, and Full Content. The portal has the following setting by default in `portal.properties`:

```
asset.publisher.display.styles=table,title-list,abstracts,full-content
```

As shown in the preceding code, you may input a list of comma-separated display styles that will be available in the configuration screen of the Asset Publisher portlet. Of course, you can override this property in `portal-ext.properties`.

In addition, there is one more property related to the tag, that is, "Include tags specified in the URL" as follows.

```
tags.compiler.enabled=true
```

The preceding code sets the property `tags.compiler.enabled` to true in order to provide the ability to compile tags from the URL. This is the reason that the checkbox "Include tags specified in the URL" was selected by default. Note that disabling this feature can speed up performance.

What's happening?

As you can see, Asset Publisher can publish any of the assets from the portal core part like Message Boards messages, Wiki articles, Blogs entries, Bookmark entries, Document Library documents, Image Gallery images, and Web Content articles. In addition, Asset Publisher can publish any assets from plugins like the Knowledge Base portlet.

What's happening? The portal provides a framework called **Asset Renderer Framework** with the tag `asset-renderer-factory` at `$PORTAL_ROOT_HOME/definitions/liferay-portlet-app_6_0_0.dtd`. This framework will allow registering custom asset types so that generic portlets like Asset Publisher can be used to publish them. Note that the `asset-renderer-factory` value in the custom asset types must be a class that implements `com.liferay.portlet.asset.model.AssetRendererFactory` and is called by the Asset Publisher.

Enhancement

As stated above, Asset Publisher is a flexible and robust tool to publish many types of assets within the portal. Although it covers many use cases of asset publishing, some use cases are still pending. Here we list some of them. Of course, you would have more complex requirements on the Asset Publisher portlet.

Configurable look and feel

Currently, views (assets' display styles) of the Asset Publisher portlet are fixed in JSP files. This means if you need to change the view (look and feel) of the Asset Publisher portlet, you will need a developer's help to make changes to the JSP files. Can we allow end users, and not developers, to update the views without touching code? The answer is "yes".

That is, we can implement the views through templates. CSS and JavaScript should be available as templates as well. It would be easy for end users, not developers, to customize velocity templates (including CSS and JavaScript) directly.

It would be a good idea to add velocity templates for views in the Asset Publisher portlet. The following is brief proposal:

1. Define a set of templates (for different views: table, title list, abstracts, full content) in the folder /vm (or in some other folder) in Asset Publisher.

2. In the Render action, pick up a proper template to generate the view. In addition, variables of velocity templates should consider fields of web structures in order to make summaries localizable.

Share assets across groups

As mentioned earlier, the Asset Publisher portlet could publish assets of the current group plus those of shared Global. For example, if the Asset Publisher portlet was added in the page of Guest—pubic pages or private pages, then the Asset Publisher portlet could publish assets of the group Guest plus shared Global. If Asset Publisher was added in the page of "Palm Tree Enterprise" organization—pubic pages or private pages, then the Asset Publisher portlet could publish assets of the group "Palm Tree Enterprise" plus those of shared Global. Obviously, Asset Publisher can't publish assets across groups Guest and "Palm Tree Enterprise" at the same time.

It would be very useful if the Asset Publisher portlet could publish assets for any group other than current group plus those for shared Global. For instance, the Asset Publisher portlet could publish assets of both the Guest community and the organization "Palm Tree Enterprise" groups, plus shared Global at the same time. Name and abstracts should also be localizable in web content. This feature isn't ready yet, but it is expected to be released soon.

Summary

This chapter first introduced us to how we can add categories and subcategories in Message Boards. Then it discussed how to add a tag and manage (add, delete, and update) categories and vocabulary, as well as how to tag assets and display tags. Finally, it addressed how to publish assets through the Asset Publisher portlet and how to configure and customize the Asset Publisher portlet.

In this chapter, we have learned how to:

- Manage the categories, threads, and posts of message boards
- Set permissions on Message Boards' categories, threads, and posts
- Manage tags, tag content, and display tags
- Set permissions on tags
- Manage categories, tag content, and display categories
- Set permissions on categories
- Publish assets through tags and categories

In the next chapter, we're going to introduce other important content such as Wiki, Web Forms, and Polls.

5
Wikis, Web Forms, and Polls

On the intranet website "bookpub.com" of the enterprise "Palm Tree Publications", it would be useful to keep track of information about editorial guidance and other resources that require frequent editing. For example, to keep track of votes on the topic "Is this book on Liferay a proper book?" and to collect suggestions on subjects such as "Liferay books". The Wiki portlets provide a straightforward wiki solution; the Web Form portlet provides a way to collect users' suggestions, while the Polls portlets provides surveys to assess public opinions.

This chapter is going to introduce us to Wikis, Web Forms, Alloy UI, and the Polls portlet, how to configure them, and how to implement requirements based on them.

By the end of this chapter, you will have learned how to:

- Manage (view, update, and delete) nodes of wikis
- Manage (view, update, delete, and search) pages of a given node in a wiki
- Assign permissions on wiki nodes and pages
- Publish wiki pages
- Convert documents
- Set up Web Forms
- Integrate the portal with Orbeon forms
- Work with Alloy UI forms
- Configure the Polls portlet
- Display polls

Wikis

In order to provide an environment for employees at the enterprise "Palm Tree Publications", which keeps track of information about editorial guidance and other resources that require frequent editing, we can use the Wikis portlet (portlet ID 36) in the Guest community (public pages).

As an administrator of the enterprise "Palm Tree Publications", you need to create a page called **Wikis** in the Guest community and add the Wikis portlet in the page **Wikis**. Then you are ready to create the "Liferay" and "Alfresco" nodes.

Managing nodes

As an administrator of the enterprise "Palm Tree Publications", we're going to create nodes called "Liferay" and "Alfresco". As shown in the next screenshot, when the portal was set up, a node called "Main" was created for default groups, for example, Guest and Shared Global; and a default page for the node "Main" called "FrontPage" was also created with empty content. First navigate to **Go To | liferay.com** under the dock bar menu, then go to **Manage | Control Panel** under the dock bar menu, and you would see something similar to the following screenshot. How does the portal implement these? This is answered in the next section.

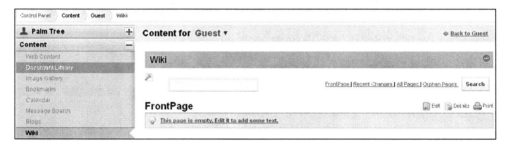

Adding nodes

First of all, we need to create a node called "Liferay". Let's create a node as follows:

1. Log in as an administrator, for example, "Palm Tree".
2. Select **Go To | liferay.com** under the dock bar menu, and then go to **Manage | Control Panel** under the dock bar menu.
3. Click on **Wiki** under the category **Content** of **Control Panel**.
4. By default, the node "Main" is created—click on the **Manage Wiki** icon on the top-left of the FrontPage.

5. Click on the **Add Wiki** button on the top of the nodes list.

6. Enter the name "Liferay" and the description "Liferay root".

7. Set **Permissions** by clicking on the **Configure** link. To configure additional permissions, click on the **More** link. Here we just use the default settings.

8. Click on the **Save** button to save the inputs.

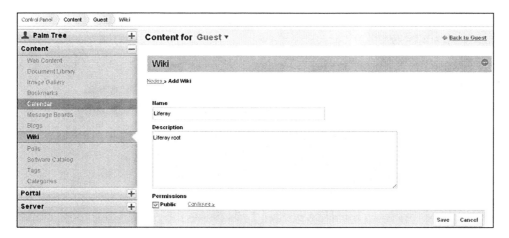

Of course, you can add other nodes, as expected. After creating the node called "Alfresco", we can view Wikis' nodes. Nodes are displayed via node names, number of pages, last post date, and the **Actions** menu next to the node with a set of icons (that is, **Edit, Permissions, Import Pages, RSS, Subscribe**, and **Delete**).

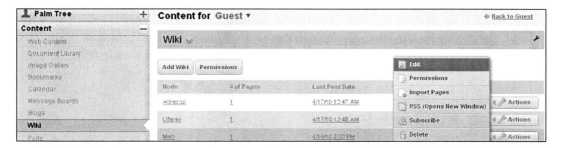

In short, we can create a node by clicking on the **Add Wiki** button and filling the name and optionally the description. An initial page called **FrontPage** (called a wiki article or a wiki page) is created automatically when the node is created.

Generally speaking, a set of pages in groups is called **nodes**. Each node acts as a whole wiki. Nodes may have their own set of permissions, recent changes list, and a listing of all pages. After creating nodes, we can manage wiki nodes easily.

Editing a node

Nodes are editable. For example, we plan to change the description of the node "Liferay" from the value "Liferay root" to the value "Liferay Wikis Root". Let's do it by following these steps:

1. Locate the "Liferay" node.
2. Click on the **Edit** icon from the **Actions** menu next to the node.
3. Update the description with the value "Liferay Wikis Root" only.
4. Click on the **Save** button to save the changes.

Deleting a node

Nodes are removable. For instance, the node "Alfresco" doesn't exist anymore. We have to remove this from the Wiki portlet. Let's delete it by following these steps:

1. Locate the "Alfresco" node that you want to delete.
2. Click on the **Delete** icon from the **Actions** menu located next to the node.
3. A screen will appear asking if you want to delete this. Click on the **OK** button to confirm deletion, or click on the **Cancel** button to cancel the processes.

 Note that deleting a node will delete all related pages that belong to this node. Moreover, any comments related to the pages of this node will also get deleted.

Viewing RSS feeds

You can view RSS feeds of nodes. Let's say that you need to view RSS feeds of the node "Liferay". You can do it by following these steps.

1. Locate the "Liferay" node.
2. Click on the **RSS** icon from the **Actions** menu next to the node.

Importing pages

In addition, the portal provides the capability to import pages from MediaWiki. **MediaWiki** is a free software Wiki package written in PHP, originally for use on Wikipedia (refer to www.mediaWiki.org for more detail).

Suppose that you are going to import pages from MediaWiki to the "Liferay" node, you can do it by following these steps:

1. Locate the "Liferay" node.

2. Click on the **Import Pages** icon from the **Actions** menu next to the node.

3. In the page of **Import Pages**, specify the required or optional items, as shown in the following code and the next screenshot:

   ```
   Pages File: submit an XML file exported by MediaWiki through the
   "Special:Export" page;
   Users File (Optional): submit a CSV file with the email addresses
   of the users to match with those in the portal. The file should
   have two columns: the user name and the email address. This file
   can be obtained using SQL directly from MediaWiki's database.
   Images File (Optional): submit a ZIP file of the images to
   import. You can zip the images folder of MediaWiki directly,
   sometimes it's called "upload", removing the directories called
   "archive", "temp" and "thumbs" to reduce the ZIP size since they
   will be ignored.
   FrontPage (Optional): default name is "Main Page";
   Import only the latest version and not the full history:
   a checkbox.
   ```

4. Click on the **Import** button to import, or click on the **Cancel** button to cancel the importing process.

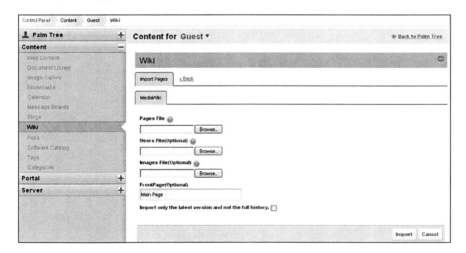

Managing pages

As you can see, the default page FrontPage has been created. This is an entry point. Through the page FrontPage, you can add and manage as many pages as you can imagine.

Adding pages

As an administrator of the enterprise "Palm Tree Publications", you would like to add more pages under the "Liferay"node, namely, "Liferay and Alfresco Integration" and "Liferay Book". Let's do it by following these steps.

1. Click on **Wiki** under the category **Content** of **Control Panel**.
2. Click on the name of the "Liferay" node.
3. Click on the **Edit** icon next to the page "FrontPage".
4. Select the format "Creole".
5. In editing mode, input "[[Liferay and Alfresco Integration]]" and "[[Liferay Book]]".
6. Click on the **Select Categories** button to add categories.
7. Click on the **Select Tags** button or input tag, and click on the **Add Tags** button if you need to add tags.
8. Type a summary for the current edit if required. Check the checkbox **This is a minor edit**, if it is a minor edit—note that there is no configuration link, as it is an action to an edit.
9. Click on the **Save** button when you are ready.

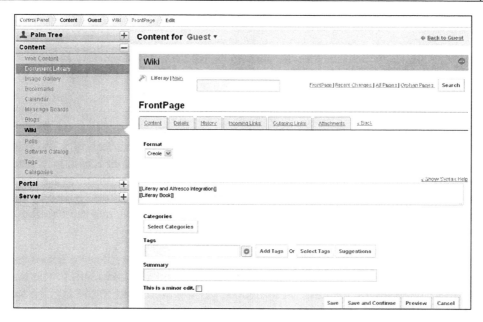

In brief, the most common way of creating wiki pages (wiki articles) is usually by creating a link from another article, for example, [[my new page]]. Then when you click on the red link, it will generate a page with that name. The benefit of doing it this way is that we'll interconnect related pages so that it's easier for users to navigate through them.

Of course, you can add pages directly. Let's say that you want to add a page "My Page" under the node "Liferay". Let's add this page by following these steps:

1. Click on **Wiki** under the category **Content** of **Control Panel**.
2. Click on the name of the "Liferay" node.
3. Click on the icon **Add Child Page** under the page "FrontPage".
4. Enter the page title "My Page" — note that there is a configuration link here because we add a page instead of editing it.
5. Set Permissions by clicking on the **Configure** link. To configure additional permissions, click on the **More** link. Here we just use the default settings.
6. Click on the **OK** button to save the changes.

As mentioned earlier, there are two editing modes in the current version, that is, formats to edit wiki pages — wiki Creole, short for Creole and HTML. Select one of the editing modes. By default, the Creole editing mode is selected. Of course, you can have more, for example, Classic and Plain Text. How to configure it? Refer to the coming section.

Creole is a common wiki markup language to be used across different wikis, which enables wiki users to transfer content seamlessly across wikis and novice users to contribute more easily. Refer to http://www.Wikicreole.org for more details.

You can definitely follow the wiki Creole mode syntax to edit wiki pages. For example, represent internal links by beginning with double brackets ([[), the page display name, and ending with double brackets (]]). On the other hand, you can represent external links by beginning with double brackets ([[), then the URL, a vertical bar (|), the display name, and ending with double brackets (]]), or by using the URL directly. For more details about wiki Creole syntax, please refer to the coming section.

You can simply start typing a tag in the tag text box, and you will see a list of tags. Just select the tags you want. You will see the tag showing up adjacent to the box. You can remove a tag by clicking on the mark "[x]" located next to the tag. To save the inputs, just click the **Save** button. To cancel all actions, just click on the **Cancel** button.

Of course, you can create others pages that you need. Let's say that we need to add a page called "Book Wiki" under the "Liferay Book" page. Let's do it by following these steps:

1. Locate the "Liferay" node.
2. Click on the name of the "Liferay" node.
3. Find the "Liferay Book" link, and click on the name "Liferay Book ".
4. Click on the **Edit** icon next to the page "Liferay Book".
5. Select the format, for example, "Creole".
6. In the editing page, input "[[Book Wiki]]" or other content.
7. Click on the **Select Categories** button to input categories.
8. Click on the **Select Tags** button to input tags, and click on the **Add Tags** button if you need to add tags, or search tags by clicking on the **Suggestions** button.
9. Type the summary of the current edit if required. Check the checkbox **This is a minor edit**, if it is a minor edit indeed.
10. Set **Permissions** by clicking on the **Configure** link. To configure additional permissions, click on the **More** link. Here we just use the default settings.
11. Click on the **Save** button when you are ready.

Viewing pages

As shown in the following screenshot, the Wiki portlet provides rich messages about wiki pages. This message is grouped into different sections: Content, Details, History, Incoming Links, Outgoing Links, and Attachment. As you have noticed, when editing a wiki page, it will bring you to the **Details | Content** tab, where "Details" is an icon next to the **Edit** icon.

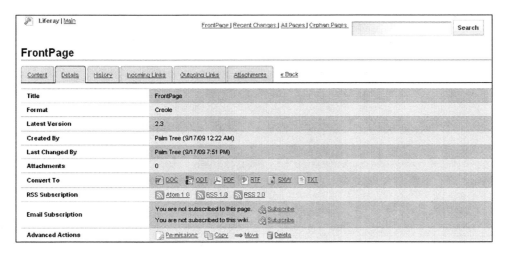

In a word, in order to create new pages (Wiki Article), you have to edit an existing page and use the syntax to create a link to the new page. When the page is created instead of being converted to a link, the name of the new page is identified by the link. When you click on the name, the portlet will create the page automatically. Furthermore, you can edit it regularly, once the page is created. At the same time, the name of the page on the original page will be converted to a link.

You may need to view Page Links—either outgoing links or incoming links for the page "Liferay Book". You can do it by following these steps:

1. Locate the "Liferay" node.
2. Click on the name of the node "Liferay".
3. Locate the "Liferay Book" link, and click on the name "Liferay Book".
4. Click on **Details | Incoming Links** or **Details | Outgoing Links**. A list of pages with the current page as incoming links or outgoing links will appear.

A wiki page can have many attachments. You can manage attachments by clicking on **Details | Attachments**. The functionality related to attachments' management includes, but isn't limited to, adding attachments, downloading attachments, and removing a specific attachment.

You may need to view the page history of the "Liferay Book" page. You can do it, as shown in preceding screenshot, as folloby following these steps:

1. Locate the "Liferay" node.
2. Click on the name of the "Liferay" node.
3. Find and click on the name "Liferay Book".
4. Click on **Details | History**. A list of pages with their histories (different versions with minor edits or major edits) will appear.

As you can see, you can compare versions by selecting different pages and clicking on the **Compare Versions** button. Alternatively, you can bring the content of a page back to a specific version by clicking on the **Revert** icon.

Last but not least, you are able to print the current page by clicking on the **Print** icon next to the page.

Searching pages

As shown in the following screenshot, you are able to search pages for a specific node. The node here could represent an entire wiki. To search wiki pages, first locate a node, say "Liferay", then input a search criterion, say "book", and click on the **Search** button next to the **Manage Wiki** icon. A list page with number, wiki name (Node name), page title, and score will appear below the **Search** button. Additionally, you would have the ability to create a new page on this topic as well.

Just in front of the **Search** button, you can see a few useful links: **FrontPage**, **Recent Changes**, **All Pages**, and **Orphan Pages**. When a node is created, a page called "FrontPage" would be created for this node automatically. This page is the entry point of the node, and contains the message "**This page is empty. Edit it to add some text.**".

As an administrator, you may be interested in the recent changes of all the pages in a given node. For doing so, you can use **Recent Changes**. When you click on the link **Recent Changes** (like one week period), a list of pages with columns (**Page**, **Revision**, **User**, **Date**, **Summary**, and a set of actions — **Edit**, **Permissions**, **Copy**, **Move**, **Subscribe**, and **Delete**) will appear at the bottom of the link **Recent Changes** and ordered by their modified dates. As you can see, you can manage these pages in order to edit a page, to assign permissions on the page, to copy a page, to move a page, to subscribe or unsubscribe a page, and even to delete a page. Moreover, you may be interested in RSS feeds such as Atom 1.0, RSS 1.0, and RSS 2.0. Note that RSS feeds are used for pages with recent changes to a given node.

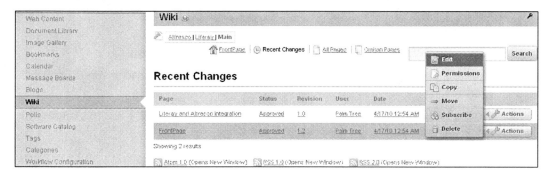

Similarly, you can view all of the pages of a given node. Simply click on the link **All Pages**. When all of the pages of a given node are displayed, you would be able to add a page by clicking on the **Add Page** button. To view orphan pages (the pages don't have parent pages associated with them), simply click on the link **Orphan Pages**.

Adding comments

As stated above, the administrator has created a page called "Liferay Book". As a user of the enterprise "Palm Tree Publications", say "Lotti Stein", if you want to review this page and add comments like "This is a good book", you can just do it by following these steps:

1. Log in as "Lotti Stein".
2. Navigate to **Go To | liferay.com** under the dock bar menu.
3. Create a page named "Wiki" by clicking on **Add | Page** under the dock bar menu.
4. Add a Wiki portlet in the page "Wiki" by clicking on **Add | More...** under the dock bar menu.
5. Navigate to the "Wiki's" page.
6. Locate the "Liferay" node.
7. Click on the name of the node "Liferay".
8. Locate the "Liferay Book" link and click on the name "Liferay Book".
9. Locate **Add Comments** tab, at the bottom of the page.
10. Input comments "This is a good book".
11. Finally, click on the **Reply** button to save the inputs.

As an administrator, you can view comments from "Lotti Stein" for the page "Liferay Book" by following these steps:

1. Locate the "Liferay" node.
2. Click on the name of the node "Liferay".
3. Locate the "Liferay Book" link, and click on the name "Liferay Book".

As you can see, you can add as many comments as possible and manage comments (perform update, delete, and add vote on comments) if you have the proper permissions. Note that users can only vote once on a specific comment.

To reply to a comment, first locate the comment that you want to reply to. Then click on the **Post Reply** icon at the bottom-left of the comment. Input comments, and then click on the **Reply** button to save the inputs or the **Cancel** button to cancel.

To edit a comment, click on the **Edit** icon at the bottom-left of the comment if you have the proper permissions. You could log in as an administrator, like "Palm Tree", to test this feature. You can change the subject and body. Then click on the **Update** button to save the changes or the **Cancel** button to cancel the changes.

To delete a comment, click on the **Delete** icon at the bottom-left of the comment. A screen will appear, asking you if you want to delete this. Click on **OK** to confirm deletion, or **Cancel** to cancel deletion.

 Note that only the current comment has been deleted on action. The low-level comments related to the current comment will have a link to the parent comment of the current comment.

To go to the top of the comments, simply click on **Top** button at the left-bottom of any comment.

Generally, to add discussion for the current page, simply click on **Add Comments** at the bottom of page first. Then simply input comments. Finally, click on **Reply** button to save the comments or **Cancel** button to cancel the comments.

Additionally, to edit a comment, simply click on **Edit** icon at the bottom of the post first. Then change the comments of the post. Furthermore, click on **Update** button to save the changes or **Cancel** button to cancel the changes.

Adding ratings

In addition, users can add ratings for wiki pages. As an end user, you may have different options on pages, thus you can rate the content of a specific page. The Wiki portlet provides the ability to allow the end user to rate the contents of wiki pages—rating a wiki page from 1 to 5 stars. Note that users can only vote once on a specific page. A user can vote several times on the same page. However, it will be counted as one vote in the statistics. This allows users to change their vote.

Subscribing nodes and Wiki pages

Being users of wiki pages, you would be interested in the wiki pages' changes in a specific node. For example, as a member of the Guest group, you may be interested in the pages in the "Liferay" node. You expect to watch out for any changes of the pages in this node. Therefore, you can use a subscription function on the "Liferay" node. Let's do it by following these steps.

1. Click on the **Manage Wiki** icon, you would see a list of nodes.
2. Locate the "Liferay" node.
3. Click on the **Subscribe** icon from the **Actions** menu next to the node. The **Subscribe** icon will become the **Unsubscribe** icon for this node.

Of course, you can subscribe to other nodes. You may be interested in any changes to the "Liferay and Alfresco Integration" page. Thus, you can subscribe to it by following these steps:

1. Click on the "Liferay" node—you would see the page "FrontPage".
2. Click on the **All Pages** link.
3. Locate the page "Liferay and Alfresco Integration".
4. Click on the **Subscribe** icon from the **Actions** menu next to the page. The **Subscribe** icon will become **Unsubscribe**.

Obviously, you can subscribe to other pages. Optionally, you can go to **Details | Email | Subscription** in order to either subscribe to or unsubscribe from the current page or even current node.

What's happening?

If you have some nodes or pages you've subscribed to and the content of the subscribed node or page gets changed, then you will receive notifications for these changes. Moreover, node subscription provides the useful function of being notified by e-mail when node and its pages have been updated. Page subscription provides the useful function of being notified by e-mail when the content of the page has been updated.

Assigning permissions

We have used the default settings for the Wikis portlet in the page "Wikis" of the page. When you're logged in as a "Palm Tree" administrator, you will see the "manage Wiki" icon in the Wikis. As you know, the user "Lotti Stein" is a member of the Guest community. Try to log in as "Lotti Stein", and you will see that there is no "Manage Wiki" icon in the Wikis. Furthermore, you see the node "Liferay" and "Main", but you don't have the ability to add new nodes or update existing nodes.

What's happening? This is something related to permissions. There are four levels of permissions: permissions on the Wiki portlet, permissions on wiki, permissions on the wiki node, and permissions on wiki page.

Permissions on the Wiki portlet

The following table shows permissions on the Wiki portlet. The role Community Member is able to set up all permissions (marked as 'X'): **View**, **Add to Page**, **Configuration**, and **Access in Control Panel**; whereas the role Guest may set up the permissions **View**, **Add to Page**, and **Configuration**. By default, the role Community Member as well as the role Guest have permission action **View** (marked as '*').

Action	Description	Community	Guest
View	Ability to view the portlet	X, *	X, *
Configuration	Ability to configure the portlet	X	X
Add to Page	Ability to add the portlet to a page	X	X
Access in Control Panel	Ability to access the Control Panel	X	

Obviously, as a member of the Guest community, "Lotti Stein" only has the permission View on the portlet Wiki by default. Of course, as an administrator, you can assign permissions **Configuration** and **Access in Control Panel** to a user "Lotti Stein" through roles.

What's permission action **Access in Control Panel**? The permission action Access in Control Panel represents the ability to access the portlet Wiki in the Control Panel. By default, the user "Lotti Stein" doesn't have the ability to access the portlet Wiki in the Control Panel. Suppose you want the user "Lotti Stein" to have the ability to access the portlet Wiki in Control Panel, how would you implement it? The following is an example — assigning the permission action **Access in Control Panel**.

1. Log in as an administrator, say "Palm Tree".
2. Click on **Roles** under the category **Portal** of the **Control Panel** first.
3. Then locate a role, say "MB Topic Admin".
4. Click on the **Assign Members** icon and update association — by assigning the user "Lotti Stein" as a member of the role "MB Topic Admin".
5. Then click on the **Define Permissions** icon from the **Actions** menu next to the right of the role.
6. Click on the **Applications | Wiki** link, check checkboxes **Access in Control Panel** and **View**.
7. Click on the **Save** button.

As shown in the preceding steps, the user "Lotti Stein" will get access rights for **Access in Control Panel** and **View** via the role "MB Topic Admin". When you try to log in as "Lotti Stein", you'll be able to access **Wiki** under the category **Content** of **Control Panel**.

Permissions on Wiki

The following table shows permissions on Wiki. The role Community Member is able to set up all permissions (marked as 'X'), that is, **Add Node and Permissions**, whereas the role Guest doesn't have this capability.

Action	Description	Community	Guest
Add Node	Ability to add node	X	
Permissions	Ability to assign permissions		X

Obviously, as a member of Guest community, "Lotti Stein" doesn't have the permission **Add Node** on Wikis by default. Note that the permission **Add Node** is scoped to a group or portal instance. If you want the user "Lotti Stein" to have the ability to add nodes for all groups in the current portal instance, how will you implement it? The following is an example—assigning permission action **Add Node**.

1. Log in as an admin, say "Palm Tree"
2. Click on **Roles** under the category **Portal** of the **Control Panel** first.
3. Then locate a role, says "MB Topic Admin".
4. Then click on the **Define Permissions** icon from the **Actions** menu next to the right of the role.
5. Click on the **Content | Wiki** link, and check the checkbox **Add Node**.
6. Click on the **Save** button.

As shown in preceding steps, the user "Lotti Stein" will get access rights for **Add Node** via the role "MB Topic Admin". As the role "MB Topic Admin" is a regular role, the user "Lotti Stein" will get access rights for **Add Node** scoped to the current portal instance. If the role is organization or community role, then the user "Lotti Stein" gets access rights on **Add Node** scoped to the group: either organization or community.

Permissions on Wiki nodes

The subsequent screenshot shows permissions on a node in the Wiki portlet. The role Community Member is able set up permissions (marked as 'X') namely **View**, **Delete**, **Permissions**, **Update**, **Add Attachments**, **Add Page**, **Import**, and **Subscribe**. On the other hand, role Guest could set up permissions with **View**, **Delete**, **Permissions**, and **Import**. By default, the role Community Member has permission actions (marked as '*') including **View**, **Subscribe**, **Add Attachment**, and **Add page**, whereas the role Guest only has the **View** permission.

Obviously, as a member of Guest, "Lotti Stein" only has permissions (**View** and **Add page**) on the node "Liferay" because we have added them using default settings. She doesn't have permissions such as **Delete**, **Permissions**, and **Update**. Thus she will not see the icon **Actions** menu next the node "Liferay".

As an administrator, you may need to set up the role Community Member having permissions **Update** as well as **View** and **Add Page** permissions on the node "Liferay". That is, you need to add permission **Update** on the node "Liferay" for the group Guest. Let's do this by following these steps:

1. Click on the icon "Manage Wiki" in the upper-left of the portlet Wiki in the page "Wiki".
2. Locate the node "Liferay" for which you want to change permissions.
3. Then click on the **Permissions** button from the **Actions** menu located next to the node.
4. Select permission **Update** under the role Community Member.
5. Click on the **Submit** button.

Now "Lotti Stein" has the permissions **View**, **Add Page**, and **Update** on the node "Liferay" finally. Try to log in as "Lotti Stein", and you will see the Actions menu next to the node "Liferay" with an **Edit** icon.

As you can see, we assign permissions individual nodes. How can you assign permissions on all nodes scoped into either a group or portal instance? You can do this by using roles in **Control Panel**. If the role is regular role, you assign permissions on all nodes scoped into the current portal instance. On the other hand, if the role is either an organization role or a community role, you will assign permissions on all nodes scoped into a group either organization or community.

Permissions on Wiki pages

The subsequent screenshot shows permissions on a page of a given node. The role Community Member could set up permissions (marked as 'X'), such as **View, Delete, Permissions, Update, Subscribe, Add Discussion, Delete Discussion, Update Discussion**, whereas the role Guest may set up permissions including **View, Delete, Add Discussion**, and **Subscribe**. By default, the role Community member has permission actions (marked as '*'), such as **View, Update**, and **Add Discussion**, whereas the role Guest only has permission **View**.

As you can see, as a member of the Guest community, "Lotti Stein" only has permissions **View, Update, Add discussion**, and **Subscribe** on the pages. This is because the pages under the node "Liferay" have been added by default settings. She doesn't have permissions such as **Delete, Permissions**, and others.

In general, you are able to assign permissions on pages on two levels: individual or in groups. As shown in the preceding screenshot, you can locate a page first, and then go to **Details | Permission**, and assign permission on individual pages via the roles. Furthermore, you can assign permissions in pages through roles in the Control Panel. If the role is a regular role, you can assign permissions on pages scoped into the current portal instance. On the other hand, if the role is either an organization role or a community role, you can assign permissions on pages scoped into a group: either organization or community.

Using the Wiki portlet effectively

Wiki was originally described as a simple online database. Actually, a Wiki is a web-based collaboration platform that lets any user write, place pictures, and post links anywhere on any page. That is, anyone can edit anything on any page. You can do it through the web interface without the need for any additional software. Surely, you don't need to learn HTML or wait for a designated webmaster to upload your files.

Characteristics

You can write Wiki documents collaboratively in a simple markup language using a web browser. Here, a single page in Wiki is called a Wiki page. While the entire body of pages, which are usually highly interconnected via hyperlinks, is the Wiki. Loosely speaking, a wiki is a database to create, browse, and search information.

A Wiki page can be created and updated simply. But there is no review before modifications are accepted for a Wiki page. On one hand, some Wikis may be open to the general public without the need for registering any user account. In order to acquire a Wiki-signature cookie for auto-signing edits, you need to log in for a session. However, many edits on a Wiki page can be made in real time and appear online almost instantaneously. This may lead to abuse of the system. On the other hand, private Wiki pages require users' authentication to edit pages, add new pages, and even read pages.

Pros and cons

Wikis have their own advantages and disadvantages. The advantages include:

- No need of installation of HTML authoring tools
- Minimal amount of training is required
- It can help develop a culture of sharing and working together
- It's useful for joint working when there are shared goals you have agreed upon

Disadvantages of Wikis include:

- The success of one wiki (such as Wikipedia) may not necessarily be replicated by another.
- There is not yet a standard lightweight Wiki markup language.
- A collaborative Wiki may suffer from lack of a strong vision.
- There may be copyright and other legal issues regarding collaborative content.
- It can be ineffective when there is a lack of consensus. And navigation is less efficient than in a real collaborative website. This is because there are no real pages tree views, menus, or breadcrumbs. When using a wiki, we often use the search engine instead of navigating naturally in a tree. That gives the feeling that pages are not organized.

 Wikipedia (http://www.Wikipedia.org/) is the biggest multi-lingual free-content encyclopedia on the Internet.

What can Wikis be used for?

Wikis are useful for a number of purposes. We just list some of them as follows:

- Enabling users to contribute information on public websites easily.
- Providing an opportunity to learn about team work and trust for teaching.

- Making it easier to develop collaborative documents for researchers.
- Providing the ability to manage departmental content on intranets, useful for departmental administrators with minimum HTML experience.
- Wikis can also be used as knowledge centers.
- They are useful at events for note-taking in discussion groups.

Using Liferay wikis

Liferay wikis allow creation of contents in the collaboration style. It is based on Friki with the features discussed here, as well as those which are commonly found in good wikis, including content parsing, **Access Control List (ACL)** security style, easy-to-use macros, easy-to-adapt security, and versioning, and managing all content and security by console tools.

>
> What's Friki?
> **Friki** (`http://sourceforge.net/projects/friki/`) is a Wiki engine developed in Java.

Pages are designed in groups called nodes in Liferay. Each node can act as a whole wiki. It has its own set of permissions, recent changes list, and listing of all pages like Wiki articles. The wiki in Liferay has a very powerful functionality with its robust security model. For example, users can use the wiki in the traditional way (open to public) or as a tool to organize private information for certain organizations or user groups of people.

The following diagram depicts the Liferay wiki structure overview. Liferay Wiki is made up of a set of nodes. Each node may have many pages. Each node has at least one page called "Front Page" by default. Each page may have many comments. In addition, each wiki page can have many versions, ratings, and attachments. Moreover, each page can have subscriptions, tags, and categories associated with it.

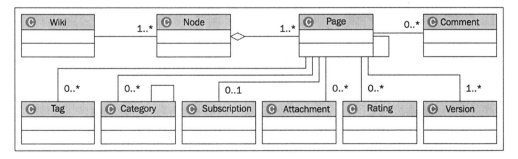

In general, Wiki comes with four editing modes: classic, HTML, Creole, and plain text.

Classic mode

The classic editing mode uses text conventions to format the text. The text is later converted to HTML, which will be presented by the Friki engine.

Liferay Wiki uses the following syntax:

- Text styles: At the beginning and at the end of the text.
- Single quote (') for a quote.
- Two single-quotes (' ') for emphasis, usually italics.
- Three single-quotes (' ' ') for strong emphasis, usually bold.
- Four single-quotes (' ' ' ') for strong emphasis, usually bold and italics.
- Lists.
- Tab * (or 8 spaces and *) for first level, tab-tab * for second level, and so on.
- * for bullet lists, '1.' for numbered lists (mix at will) — always use '1.' because it will be renumbered automatically.
- Headers.
- Single equals sign (=) for header 1.
- Doubled equal-sign (==) for header 2.
- Tripled equal-sign (===) for header 3.
- Embedded and formatted RAW HTML as well as HTML table tags.
- Horizontal rule: Four or more hyphens (----) at the beginning of a line make a horizontal rule.
- Mono-spaced indent: A blank or more spaces (not 8 spaces) at the beginning of the line.
- Internal links: Two or more words together without spaces between them and uppercasing the first letter of each of the words.
- External links: Beginning with a bracket ([ ), then URL, space, display name, and ending with a bracket ( ]) and beginning with a two quotation marks ("), then display name, and double quotation marks ("), followed by URL.
- Definitions: Starting with tab, then term, followed by colon and tab, and finally the definition.
- Indented paragraphs: Tab plus space at the beginning of the paragraph.

Creole mode

As shown in Syntax help, you could get the following details on the Creole mode:

- Text Styles: Italics—should begin with double slashes (//), followed by text, and end with double slash, bold—begin with two asterisks (**), followed by text, and end with two asterisks.
- Headers: Large headings should begin with double equal sign(==), followed by text, and end with double equal-sign and medium heading should begin with three equal signs, followed by text, and end with tripled equal-signs (===). On the other hand, small headings should begin with quadruple equal-signs (====), followed by text, and end with quadruple equal-signs.
- Links: Internal links should begin with double brackets ([[), page title, and end with double brackets (]]). External links should begin with double brackets ([[), followed by URL, optionally vertical bar (|), followed by display name and end with double brackets (]]).
- Lists: Item should begin with an asterisk (*) and end with text, sub items should begin with double asterisks (**) and end with text, ordered items should begin with a number-sign (#) and end with text, whereas ordered sub-items should begin with double number-sign (##) and end with text.
- Images: Attached image should begin with double brackets ({{), an attached image filename, and end with double brackets (}}). The page image should begin with double brackets ({{), page name, slash (/), page image filename, optionally vertical bar (|) followed by label, and end with double brackets (}}).
- Table of contents: It should begin with double brackets (<<), the keyword TableOfContents, and end with double brackets (>>).
- Preformatted: It should begin with triple brackets ({{{), the keyword Preformatted, and end with triple brackets (}}}).

HTML mode

The text area incorporates an embedded HTML text editor in the HTML mode. The HTML mode allows the user to write the document in a WYSIWYG editor, which is similar to how users work in MS Word or Open Office. What's HTML text editor? How to use the WYSIWYG editor? Refer to the instructions given in *Chapter 6, Blogs, WYSIWYG Editors, and RSS*.

Plain text mode

The text area incorporates pure plain text in plain text mode as well as in classic mode without rules or syntax. It is the same as editing the source in an HTML text editor.

Configuration

As an administrator of the enterprise "Palm Tree Publications", you can set up the Wiki portlet as well. For example, you can configure subscription e-mails. Let's say that the Wiki portlet was added to the page "Wiki" of the group Guest, and you are going to configure the portlet in this way.

To configure the Wiki portlet, include the subscription function in the following way: click on the **More | Configuration** icon on the upper-right of the Wiki portlet. With the **Setup | Current** tab selected, there are a set of sub-tabs namely **Email From, Page Added Email, Page Updated Email, Display Settings**, and **RSS**.

The **Email From** name is **Joe Bloggs** and the **From-Address** is test@liferay.com by default. This means that the portal will use the name and address as e-mail **From-Name** and **From-Address**.

In addition, under the tab **Display Settings**, you would see following settings:

- **Enable Page Ratings**: A checkbox, checked by default
- **Enable Comments**: A checkbox, checked by default
- **Enable Comment Ratings**: A checkbox, checked by default
- **Visible Wikis**: Multiple selection of Wiki nodes

What's happening?

As you can see, when the portal started, the default node "Main" and page "FrontPage" were created for the group Guest. "What's happening?", you may ask. The portal has the following default settings in portal.properties.

```
Wiki.front.page.name=FrontPage
Wiki.initial.node.name=Main
```

As shown in the preceding code, it sets the name of the default page for a Wiki node as FrontPage. Note that the name for the default page must be a valid Wiki word, that is, the first letter should be in uppercase. A Wiki word follows the format of having an uppercase letter followed by a series of lowercase letters, in turn followed by another uppercase letter and another series of lowercase letters. It also sets the name of the default node as Main that will be automatically created when the Wiki portlet is first used in a group like organization and community. Of course, you can override these properties in portal-ext.properties.

Moreover, when you input a value for Wiki page title, the portal will validate the title. Similarly, when viewing the Wiki page, you would be able to add ratings and comments. In fact, the portal has the following settings in portal.properties.

```
Wiki.page.titles.regexp=([^/\\[\\]%&?@]+)
Wiki.page.titles.remove.regexp=([/\\[\\]%&?@]+)
Wiki.page.ratings.enabled=true
Wiki.page.comments.enabled=true
Wiki.formats=creole,html
Wiki.formats.default=creole
```

As shown in the preceding code, it specifies validation for the names of Wiki pages via the property `Wiki.page.titles.regexp`. By default, only a few characters are forbidden. You can uncomment the preceding regular expression to allow only CamelCase titles. It also specifies the characters that will be automatically removed from the titles when importing Wiki pages using the property `Wiki.page.titles. remove.regexp`. This should remove any characters that are forbidden in the `regexp` specified in the property `Wiki.page.titles.regexp`.

In addition, it sets the property `Wiki.page.ratings.enabled` to `true` to enable ratings for Wiki pages and the property `Wiki.page.comments.enabled` to `true` to enable comments for Wiki pages. It sets the list of supported Wiki formats via the property `Wiki.formats` and the default wiki format via the property `Wiki. formats.default`. Note that supported wiki formats would be `creole`, `html`, `classic_Wiki` (called Classic Wiki), `plain_text` (called Plain text). You can definitely customize these properties in `portal-ext.properties`.

More interestingly, Wiki importers, e-mail notification, and RSS abstract are configurable. The portal has specified the following properties in `portal.properties`.

```
Wiki.importers=MediaWiki
Wiki.email.from.name=Joe Bloggs
Wiki.email.from.address=test@liferay.com
Wiki.email.page.added.enabled=true
Wiki.email.page.updated.enabled=true
Wiki.rss.abstract.length=200
```

As shown in the preceding code, the portal sets the list of supported wiki importers via the property `Wiki.importers`. By default, `MediaWiki` is supported. It configures e-mail notification settings via properties `Wiki.email.from.name`, `Wiki.email. from.address`, `Wiki.email.page.added.enabled`, and `Wiki.email.page. updated.enabled`. Finally, the portal sets the maximum length of RSS abstract to `200` via the property `Wiki.rss.abstract.length`.

In addition, the Wiki page would be locked for `20` minutes by default. Why? The portal has specified the following setting in `portal.properties`.

```
lock.expiration.time.com.liferay.portlet.wiki.model.WikiPage=1200000
```

Of course, you can override this property in `portal-ext.properties` depending on your requirements.

Wiki in scope

More interestingly, one of the most powerful characteristics of the Wiki portlet is the fact that when wikis are added to different groups, they act as completely independent portlets, each with its own data. By default, the portlet Wiki is scoped into a group—when portlets are added to a group, either public or private pages, they act as the same portlets.

For instance, when the portlet Wiki is added to a page—for example, "Wikis", of the group Guest, the default scope will be used for the group Guest. If you add the portlet Wiki to a second page, say "Welcome", it will show the same data as that of the first page. As you can see, the portlet Wiki is scoped into the group Guest when it is added to any pages of the group Guest. It seems that you don't have the flexibility to switch groups in this case. Fortunately, this limitation could be overcome through the Control Panel. In the Control Panel, you are able to switch the content of the portlet Wiki to different groups. You can do this by following these simple steps.

1. Go to **Settings | Control Panel**.
2. Locate **Wiki** under the category **Content** of **Control Panel**, and click on **Wiki**. You would then see same nodes and pages as that of the page "Wiki" because, by default, the content of the portlet Wiki is scoped to the group **Guest**.
3. Switch groups by selecting different groups from the drop-down menu **Content for**.

The portlet Wiki could get scoped into a page. How to scope a Wiki portlet into a page? The following is just a sample:

1. Locate a page, say "Wiki", and the portlet Wiki in the current page.
2. Go to **More | Configuration** of the portlet Wiki.
3. Click on the tab **Scope**.
4. Choose **Current page (Wiki)** from the select menu **Scope**, and click on the **Save** button.

Considering the pattern Portal-Group-Page-Content, the content of portlet Wiki could be scoped into a group—for example, all pages, including both private and public pages, by default. It could also be scoped into an individual page—this means that a set of data, for example, nodes and pages, is isolated from other data of the same portlet.

How can we customize the scope feature? The portal has default settings for the portlet Wiki in $PORTAL_ROOT_HOME/WEB-INF/liferay-portlet.xml.

```
<control-panel-entry-category>content</control-panel-entry-category>
<control-panel-entry-weight>8.0</control-panel-entry-
weight><scopeable>true</scopeable>
```

As shown in the preceding code, the portlet Wiki will appear in the category **Content** of the Control Panel position 8, and it is *scope*-able. This means that you are able to use the tab **More | Configuration | Scope** and change the scope from default to the current page.

Wikis in communication

Note that there is a tab **Communication** under **more | configuration**, and the shared parameters could be mapped into categoryId, nodeId, tag, and title because the portlet has the following configuration in $PORTAL_ROOT_HOME/WEB-INF/portlet-custom.xml:

```
<supported-public-render-parameter>categoryId</supported-public-
render-parameter>
<supported-public-render-parameter>nodeId</supported-public-render-
parameter>
<supported-public-render-parameter>tag</supported-public-render-
parameter>
<supported-public-render-parameter>title</supported-public-render-
parameter>
```

As shown in the preceding code, there are four parameters, namely, categoryId, nodeId, tag, and title. You can set mapping among these parameters or even ignore some or all of them in the tab **more | configuration | Communication**. You can add Tags and Category Navigation portlets in the wiki page, so that you can see for yourselves all of the benefits to using this configuration.

Enhancement

As you can see, the portal provides the capability to display recent changes on pages. It would be nice if the time period would be configurable like a day, a week, a month, and so on. Of course, you may have other expectations from the Wiki portlet.

Publishing wiki pages

As stated above, we have discussed how to create nodes and how to add pages in order to keep track of information about editorial guidance and other resources that require frequent editing. As an administrator at the enterprise "Palm Tree Publication", you have created the node "Liferay". Now you can publish Wiki articles for the node "Liferay", as shown in the following screenshot.

Carry out the following steps to publish Wiki articles for the Liferay node:

1. Create a page "Wiki" in the Guest public pages by clicking on the link **Add | Page** under the dock bar menu.

2. Add the portlet **Wiki Display** in the page "Wiki" by clicking on **Add | More...** under the dock bar menu.

3. Click on the **More | Configuration** icon | **Setup | Current** on the upper-right of the Wiki display portlet.

4. Select a node name "Liferay" that you want to publish as a Wiki in your page and the page "FrontPage".

5. Click on the **Save** button to save the changes. If required, click on the **Return to Full Page** icon to return.

Obviously, the Wiki Display portlet (portlet ID 54) provides a way to publish Wiki articles in a page of a group. The following screenshot depicts the Wiki display portlet in a Wiki page.

As a member of the group Guest "Lotti Stein", you may have the proper permission to edit the current Wiki page by clicking on the link **Edit** next to the Wiki page title, add comments on the current Wiki page, and add ratings to the current Wiki page. Note that users can only rate once on a specific page. The vote will be counted once, but users can change their rating later.

Additionally, you will also be able to change permissions on wiki pages if you have proper access rights to do so. By clicking on the link **Details**, you would have the capability to view **Content, Details, History, Incoming Links, Outgoing Links,** and **Attachments**, and the same functions as that of the Wiki portlet. Last but not least, you can print the current wiki page by clicking on the icon **Print** next to the wiki page title.

Why the Wiki Display portlet?

The Wiki Display portlet allows publishing specific Wiki nodes, while hiding a lot of administration options.

Firstly, the Wiki Display portlet is configurable—you can configure a specific node and Wiki page to be published. Secondly, the portlet Wiki Display is *instance*-able. Therefore, you could add more than one Wiki Display portlet to a given page. Thirdly, it hides a lot of administration options like managing Wiki nodes.

Assigning permissions

As a user at the "Palm Tree Publications" enterprise, say "Lotti Stein", you have the permission to edit the current Wiki page and to add comments on the current Wiki page. However, you can't change page permissions because you don't have proper access rights to do so. This is something related to permissions.

The subsequent table shows permissions on a page, for example, "FrontPage" of a given node, say "Liferay" in the Wiki Display portlet. The role Community Member is able to set up permissions (marked as 'X') including **View, Delete, Permissions, Update, Add Discussion, Delete Discussion, Update Discussion,** and **Subscribe**. On the other hand, the role Guest is able to set up permissions with **View, Delete,** and **Permissions**. By default, the role Community Member has the permission actions (marked as '*'): **View, Update, Add Discussion,** and **Subscribe**, while the role guest only has the permission **View**.

Action	Description	Community	Guest
View	Ability to view the pages	X, *	X, *
Delete	Ability to delete the page	X	X
Permissions	Ability to assign permissions on the page	X	X
Update	Ability to update pages	X, *	
Add Discussion	Ability to add comments on the page	X, *	
Delete Discussion	Ability to delete comments on the page	X	
Update Discussion	Ability to update comments on the page	X	
Subscribe	Ability to subscribe to / unsubscribe from the page	X, *	

Obviously, as a member of Guest community, "Lotti Stein" only has the permissions **View**, **Update**, **Add Discussion**, and **Subscribe** on the pages because the pages under "Liferay" have been added by default settings. Thus she doesn't have the permissions such as **Delete**, **Permissions**, **Delete Discussion**, and **Update Discussion**.

As an administrator, you may need to set up the role Community Member having the permissions **View** and **Update** only on the page "FrontPage" of the node "Liferay". That is, you need to remove the permissions **Add Discussion** and **Subscribe** on the page "FrontPage" of the node "Liferay" for the group Guest. Let's do it by following these steps:

1. Click on the **Details | Permissions** icon next to the page "FrontPage".
2. Uncheck the permissions **Add Discussion** and **Subscribe** under the role "Community Member".
3. Click on the **Submit** button if you are ready.

Now, as a member of the group Guest, "Lotti Stein" has the permissions **View** and **Update** on the page "FrontPage" of the node "Liferay". If you try to log in as "Lotti Stein", you will see the page "FrontPage" of the node "Liferay" without the "Add Comments" icon. You can go to **Details | Details**, but you wouldn't see the icon "Subscribe" for the current page.

Note that you can only assign permissions on individual pages using the portlet Wiki Display. If you want to assign permissions at the group level or at the portal instance level, you need to define permissions of roles under the Control Panel.

In addition, there are **View** and **Configuration** permissions on the portlet. By default, the role Community Member and Guest have the **View** permission on the portlet Wiki Display.

What's happening?

As you can see, you can add more than one Wiki Display portlet in a given page, while there is only one Wiki portlet in the page. Why are they different? The portlet Wiki Display was specified as being *instance*-able in $PORTAL_ROOT_HOME/WEB-INF/ liferay-portlet.xml. This is as follows:

```
<configuration-action-class>
com.liferay.portlet.Wikidisplay.action.ConfigurationActionImpl
</configuration-action-class>
<portlet-url-class>com.liferay.portal.struts.StrutsActionPortletURL
</portlet-url-class>
<instanceable>true</instanceable>
<scopeable>true</scopeable>
```

As shown in the preceding code, the portlet Wiki Display has specified the tag instanceable with the value true. This is the reason why you can add more than one Wiki Display portlet to a given page. Moreover, the portlet Wiki Display has specified the tag configuration-action-class with a value com.liferay. portlet.Wikidisplay.action.ConfigurationActionImpl. Therefore, after clicking on **More | Configuration** on the upper-right of the portlet, you would see **Setup | Current** and **Setup | Archived**, that is, the portlet Wiki Display is configurable.

As you can see, the portlet Wiki Display is scope-able. The portlet Wiki Display is scoped into the group Guest when it is added in any pages of the group Guest. Moreover, the portlet Wiki Display could get scoped into a page. How can we customize this? To make the portlet Wiki Display using a different data scope, you would follow these simple steps.

1. Locate a page, say "Wiki", and the portlet Wiki Display in the current page
2. Go to **More | Configuration** of the portlet Wiki Display
3. Click on the tab **Scope**
4. Choose "Current page (Wiki)" from the select menu **Scope**, and click on the **Save** button.

Considering the pattern Portal-Group-Page-Content, the content of the portlet Wiki Display could be scoped into a group—for example, all pages including both private and public pages, by default. Furthermore, it could be scoped into an individual page—this means that a set of data, for example, Wiki pages, is isolated from other data of the same portlet.

Converting documents with OpenOffice

It would be useful to convert documents of different office formats. For example, in the Display Settings of the Asset Publisher portlet, we have the ability to convert current documents to different documents formats, for example, DOC, ODT, PDF, RTF, SXW, and TXT. Likewise, we are able to convert Wiki articles to different documents formats—for example, DOC, ODT, PDF, RTF, SXW, and TXT. When clicking on the link, for example, PDF, the portal will convert the current Wiki article to that format—for example, PDF. How to achieve this? Let's integrate OpenOffice with our portal.

How to integrate OpenOffice

OpenOffice.org is a multi-platform and multi-lingual office suite and an open-source project. First of all, you need to download the latest version of OpenOffice. It is available at http://www.openoffice.org for every OS. The installation instructions can also be found here. When you install it, make a note of the location because you will need it when setting your OPENOFFICE_HOME variable.

To start OpenOffice as a service, go to $OPENOFFICE_HOME/program, and run the following command:

```
soffice -headless -accept="socket,host=127.0.0.1,port=8100;urp;"
```

As shown in the preceding code, we start OpenOffice as a service with the host 127.0.0.1 and the port 8100.

Configuration

Then we need to enable OpenOffice integration by providing document conversion functionality. How do we do this? We could implement this using Server Administration, as shown in the following screenshot:

1. Log in as an admin, for example, "Palm Tree" and go to **Manage | Control Panel** under the dock bar menu.

2. Go to **Server Administration | OpenOffice** under the category **Server** of **Control Panel**.

3. Check the checkbox **Enabled**.

4. Finally, click on the **Save** button.

 Note that if OpenOffice was installed on a remote machine, we would have to change the host and port accordingly. How to implement it?

What's happening?

The portal provides the capability to enable OpenOffice integration and allows the Document Library portlet and the Wiki portlet to provide conversion functionality. The following are the default settings in `portal.properties`.

```
openoffice.server.enabled=false
openoffice.server.host=127.0.0.1
openoffice.server.port=8100
openoffice.cache.enabled=true
```

The preceding code sets the OpenOffice server by default. As you can see, the property `openoffice.server.enabled` has the value `false`, and the property `openoffice.cache.enabled` has the value `true`. pTherefore, by default, the OpenOffice server is disabled and the cache is enabled. The host was specified via the property `openoffice.server.host`, while the port was specified via the property `openoffice.server.port`. By default, OpenOffice was installed in the same machine (`127.0.0.1`) as that of the portal with port `8100`. If OpenOffice was installed on a remote machine, then you could override the host using the property `openoffice.server.host` and also the port using the property `openoffice.server.port` in `portal-ext.properties`.

Convert documents

Through OpenOffice, documents could be converted automatically to multiple formats. For example, the document "Full RESTful integration of Liferay and Alfresco" is originally provided in plain text format. Thus we can download it as a text file. At the same time, it would be converted into DOC, ODT, PDF, RTF, SXW, and so on. How does it happen? The following table shows the possible formats for automatic conversion through OpenOffice. Obviously, the plain text of a described document could be converted into Portable Document Format (PDF), OpenDocument Text (ODT), OpenOffice.org 1.0 Text (SXW), Rich Text Format (RTF), Microsoft Word (DOC), and so on.

Category	From	To
Text formats	OpenDocument Text (*.odt)	Portable Document Format (*.pdf)
	OpenOffice.org 1.0 Text (*.sxw)	OpenDocument Text (*.odt)
	Rich Text Format (*.rtf)	OpenOffice.org 1.0 Text (*.sxw)
	Microsoft Word (*.doc)	Rich Text Format (*.rtf)
	WordPerfect (*.wpd)	Microsoft Word (*.doc)
	Plain Text (*.txt)	Plain Text (*.txt)
Spreadsheet formats	OpenDocument Spreadsheet (*.ods)	Portable Document Format (*.pdf)
	OpenOffice.org 1.0 Spreadsheet (*.sxc)	OpenDocument Spreadsheet (*.ods)
	Microsoft Excel (*.xls)	OpenOffice.org 1.0 Spreadsheet (*.sxc)
	Comma-Separated Values (*.csv)	Microsoft Excel (*.xls)
	Tab-Separated Values (*.tsv)	Comma-Separated Values (*.csv)
		Tab-Separated Values (*.tsv)
Presentation formats	OpenDocument Presentation (*.odp)	Portable Document Format (*.pdf)
	OpenOffice.org 1.0 Presentation (*.sxi)	Macromedia Flash (*.swf)
	Microsoft PowerPoint (*.ppt)	OpenDocument Presentation (*.odp)
		OpenOffice.org 1.0 Presentation (*.sxi)
		Microsoft PowerPoint (*.ppt)
Drawing formats	OpenDocument Drawing (*.odg)	Scalable Vector Graphics (*.svg)
		Macromedia Flash (*.swf)

Web forms

A web form on a web page allows a user to enter data that is sent to a server for processing. The portal provides the Web Form portlet, a tool allowing a web administrator to define a form to be published on the website—users visiting the website can then fill the form. It is then sent to a configured e-mail address.

The Web Form portlet

Do you want to collect suggestions about "Liferay book"? Do you want to collect comments on other topics? The Web Form portlet would be a useful tool.

Generally speaking, the Web Form portlet allows a web administrator to define a form to be published in the website. Users who visit the website can then fill the form, which is then sent to a configured e-mail address. There are two modes for the Web Form portlet: view mode and edit mode.

How does it work?

In case the Web Form portlet isn't shipped with the portal, then you will need to first download and install it. How does it work? The following is a sample that could bring the portlet Web Form into the portal.

1. Download the WAR file `${web.form.portlet.war}` from `http://liferay.cignex.com/palm_tree/book/0387/chapter05/web-form-portlet-6.0.0.1.war`

2. Drop the WAR file `${web.form.portlet.war}` into the folder `$LIFERAY_HOME/deploy` when the portal is running.

View mode

The following screenshot depicts the view mode of the Web Form portlet. As an administrator, you may need to add the Web Form portlet on the page "Forms" of the Guest public pages.

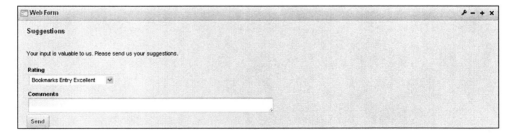

You can add the portlet for using the **View** mode by following these steps:

1. Go to **Add | Page** under the dock bar menu and type "Forms".
2. Go to **Add | More...** under the dock bar menu.
3. Type "Web Form" under "Search applications" (it searches as you type).
4. Click on the **Add** link next to "Web Form".

As a normal user, for example, "Lotti Stein", you may plan to submit your comments on "Liferay Book". You can do it by following these steps:

1. Log in as "Lotti Stein", and go to the page "Forms".
2. Input name, for example, "Liferay Book" for suggestions under the message, "**Your input is valuable to us. Please send us your suggestions.**".
3. Select a rating from a checkbox (such as, **Excellent**, **Good**, **Satisfactory**, and **Poor**) — for example, **Good**.
4. Input your comments, if possible.
5. Click on the **Send** button when you are ready to send the form.

The portal will send e-mails according to the configuration that you have set up.

As you have noticed, as a normal user, for example, "Lotti Stein", you can view the portlet Web Form, but the configuration **More | Configuration** is hidden, that is, you don't have the permission to configure the Web Form portlet.

Edit mode

As an administrator, you can view the edit mode of the Web Form portlet. You have to simply click on **More | Configuration** at the upper-right of the Web Form portlet. The following screenshot depicts the edit mode of the Web Form portlet. You can set up a form to be published in the website and configure permissions if you have proper access rights.

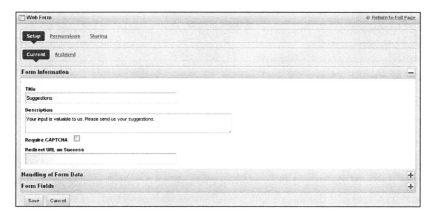

In general, the Web Form portlet in the edit mode has the following features:

- Form information: The title and introductory description of the form shown to the users are configurable—**Require CAPTCHA** and **Redirect URL on Success** are also configurable.

- Handling of form data: E-mail—send as e-mail, the e-mail address, and subject of the e-mail are configurable in every form. Database—**Save to Database** is configurable. In addition, file items **Save to File**, **Path**, and **File Name** are also configurable.

- Instance-able: Having as many different forms per website and page as desired.

- Supporting many types of fields: These include text, textbox, options (separated by commas), radio button, paragraph, and checkbox.

- Form fields: You can have as many form fields as you want. In order to add a new form field, simply click on the icon **Add**. On the other hand, to remove a form field, simply click on the icon **Delete** next to the form field. Click on **Save** to save the changes or **Cancel** to cancel the changes.

What's happening?

As stated above, there is a lot of default data when configuring Web Form such as the title **Suggestions**, the description "**Your input is valuable to us. Please send us your suggestions**", and so on. When modifying these default values, the updates would be saved per portlet instance, and not in the database. How? The portlet Web Form has a set of portlet preferences, which is specified as follows in $AS_WEB_APP_HOME/web-form-portlet/WEB-INF/portlet.xml.

```
<portlet-preferences>
  <preference>
    <name>title</name>
    <value>Suggestions</value>
  </preference>
  <preference>
    <name>description</name>
    <value>Your input is valuable to us.
          Please send us your suggestions.
    </value>
  </preference> <!-- ignore details -->
</portlet-preferences>
```

The preceding code shows portlet preferences, allowing the portlet to store configuration data. Note that it is not done to replace general purpose databases. Of course, you can override these portlet preferences as expected.

As you can see, you can add more than one Web Form portlet in a given page. The portlet Web Form was specified as being instance-able as follows in `$AS_WEB_APP_HOME/web-form-portlet/WEB-INF/liferay-portlet.xml`.

```
<configuration-action-class>
    com.liferay.webform.action.ConfigurationActionImpl
</configuration-action-class>
<instanceable>rue</instanceable>
```

The preceding code sets the instance-able value to true, that is, the portlet Web Form can appear multiple times in a page. Of course, you can set the tag `instanceable` to false, so that the portlet can only appear once on a page.

In addition, the preceding code shows that the tag `configuration-action-class` allows users to configure the portlet at runtime. This is the reason that the portlet Web Form has the capabilities to be configured at runtime.

Moreover, the portlet Web Form uses a lot of JavaScript. By default, the portlet has the following setting in `$AS_WEB_APP_HOME/web-form-portlet/WEB-INF/classes/portlet.properties`.

```
validation.script.enabled=false
```

The preceding code sets the property `validation.script.enabled` to `false`. It means that validation of JavaScript is disabled. Of course, you can enable JavaScript validation by setting the property `validation.script.enabled` to `true`.

By the way, you may want to customize the view of the portlet Web Form. You can go to the JSP file `$AS_WEB_APP_HOME/web-form-portlet/view.jsp` and modify it to your liking. You may want to customize the configuration of the portlet Web Form as well. Definitely, you can go to the JSP file `$AS_WEB_APP_HOME/web-form-portlet/configuration.jsp` and modify it as well.

Assign permissions

There are only two permission actions for the portlet: view and configuration.

- **View** permission — users can view and fill the form, which is then sent to a configured e-mail address
- **Configuration** permission — users can set up a form to be published on the website and configure permissions, for example, reassign permissions and delegate permissions for users, user groups, organizations, community, and guests via roles.

The following table shows the permissions on the Web Form portlet. The role Community Member may set up all permissions (marked as 'X'), namely, **Configuration** and **View**. On the other hand, the role Guest only has the possibility to set up views (marked as 'X'). By default, a community user has the action **View** (marked as '*') as that of a guest.

Action	Description	Community	Guest
Configuration	Ability to configure the portlet	X	
View	Ability to view the content of the portlet	X, *	X, *
Add to Page	Ability to add the portlet to a page	X	

As you can see, as a member of the Guest community, "Lotti Stein" only has the permission **View** on the portlet Web Form by default. These are the standard settings for most of portlets. Of course, as an administrator, you can assign the permission **Configuration** to users via roles.

Enhancement

The Web Form portlet is a powerful tool to build forms and save the data. But there is still space to improve functionalities. Although you may have your own requirements on the Web Form portlet, here we just list some features that are highly expected.

- Ability to support more field types, for example, multiple selections
- Capability to store the answers in a database
- Ability to show statistics of the answers
- Ability to store localizable field names like that of the Polls portlet
- Capability to send e-mails to multiple contacts, for example, comma-separated lists

Alloy UI Forms

In this section, we are going to introduce Alloy UI. Note that Alloy Forms is an API for development purpose, whereas Web Form and Orbeon Form are portlets. You may skip this section if you have nothing related to the development or customization of a portlet's UI.

From version 6, UI forms called Alloy have been introduced. Alloy (`aui`) is UI meta-framework, providing a consistent and simple API for building web applications across all three levels of the browser: structure, style, and behavior. It provides unified styling—all the forms look the same and are controlled in one place. Alloy UI is based on HTML 5, CSS 3, and YUI 3, working with Ajax, elements and events, animation, drag and drop, plugins, widgets, and so on.

Moreover, it supports dynamic attributes, that is, any attribute that can be used for a tag `html` can be used for a tag `aui`. For example, you can use `onClick`, `onChange`, `onSubmit`, `title` in any `aui:form`, `aui:select`, `aui:input`, just as you use them in a plain form, `select` or `input`.

The tags of Alloy UI forms include form, field set, button, button row, model context, input, select, option, link, field wrapper, legend, layout, and column. These tags are specified as `aui:form`, `aui:fieldset`, `aui:button`, `aui:button-row`, `aui:model-context`, `aui:input`, `aui:select`, `aui:option`, `aui:a`, `aui:field-wrapper`, `aui:legend`, `aui:layout`, and `aui:column` respectively.

For instance, the tags `aui:form`, `aui:button` and `aui:button-row` have been specified as follows in `$AS_WEB_APP_HOME/web-form-portlet/configuration.jsp`.

```
<aui:form action="<%= configurationURL %>"
        cssClass="portlet-web-form" method="post"
        name="fm" onSubmit="submitForm(this);
        return false;">
<aui:input name="<%= Constants.CMD %>"
        type="hidden" value="<%= Constants.UPDATE %>" />
<aui:input name="redirect" type="hidden" value="<%= redirect %>" />
<!-- ignore details -->
  <aui:button-row>
    <aui:button type="submit" value="save" />
    <aui:button onclick="<%= redirect %>" value="cancel"/>
  </aui:button-row>
</aui:form>
```

Text-area elements can be specified using `aui:input`, whereas radio elements can be specified using `aui:field-wrapper` and `aui:input`. For example, a radio element has been specified as follows in `$AS_WEB_APP_HOME/web-form-portlet/view.jsp`.

```
<c:when test='<%= fieldType.equals("radio") %>'>
  <aui:field-wrapper cssClass='<%= fieldOptional ? "optional":
    StringPool.BLANK %>'
      label="<%= HtmlUtil.escape(fieldLabel) %>"
      name="<%= fieldName %>">
  <% // ignore details %>
  </aui:field-wrapper>
</c:when>
```

If you are interested in `aui` **Tag Library Descriptor (TLD)**, then you can refer to the file `$PORTAL_ROOT_HOME/WEB-INF/tld/liferay-aui.tld`. You can also have a look at the definitions of these tags in the folder `$PORTAL_ROOT_HOME/html/taglib/aui`.

Orbeon Forms

As you can see, the Web Forms portlet is a powerful tool to build forms and save the data. In some use cases, the Web Forms portlet may not satisfy all your requirements. No worries, you can integrate other forms, such as Orbeon Forms, in the portal. **Orbeon Forms** is an open source forms solution that handles the complexity of forms typical of the enterprise or government. The great thing about Orbeon Forms is that Orbeon Forms hide the complexity of the portlet API in order to allow most Orbeon Forms applications to work unmodified within the portal. Moreover, it supports a standard **XForm**: XForms is an XML format for the specification of a data-processing model for XML data and user interface(s) for the XML data.

First of all, you need to download the latest version of Orbeon Forms. It is available at `http://www.orbeon.com`. The installation instructions can also be found here. When you install it, make a note of the location, as you will need it when setting your `ORBEON_FORMS_HOME` variable.

Then, we need to deploy Orbeon Forms in the portal. Locate `orbeon.war` at `$ORBEON_FORMS_HOME/../`, and drop `orbeon.war` into the deploy directory `$LIFERAY_HOME/deploy` when the portal is running. You have to wait for a few seconds, and the portal will deploy Orbeon Forms.

Once Orbeon Forms has been deployed completely, you can use it in the portal, as shown in following screenshot. The following steps are samples to using Orbeon Forms in a page.

1. Go to the **Add | More...** link from the dock bar menu.
2. Type "Orbeon", and you should see the Orbeon Form portlet appear in the menu.
3. Select **Add** to add the portlet to the page.
4. The portlet displays a welcome page with links to Orbeon Forms examples.
5. Here is the Flickr Resize example running in the portlet, as shown in the following screenshot.
6. Enter one or more Flickr tags, for example, "yellow stone".
7. Click on the **Find** button. You can then use the slider to resize the images returned.

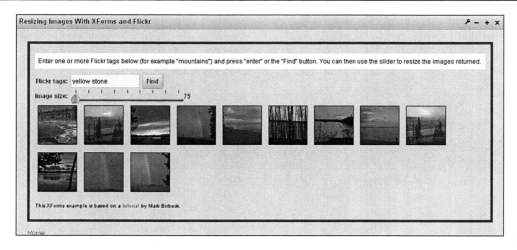

How does it work?

The following is a sample that could bring the portlet Orbeon Forms into the portal.

1. Download the WAR file ${orbeon.forms.portlet.war} from http://liferay.cignex.com/palm_tree/book/0387/chapter05/orbeon.war

2. Drop the WAR file ${orbeon.forms.portlet.war} in the folder $LIFERAY_HOME/deploy when the portal is running.

Create forms

As you can see, once the portlet gets deployed properly, you would see the welcome message about the Orbeon Forms example portlet with a few links like viewing and editing portlet preferences and the following examples.

```
Calculator: an example for calculator;
Flickr Resize: an example for Flickr
Google Suggests: sample of Google suggestions function;
Translate: sample of Google translation;
Wizard with Switch: sample of Wizard with Switch
Wizard with PFC: sample of Wizard with PFC (PowerBuilder Foundation
Class)
Bookshelf form - Summary (FR): an XForm example with summary;
Bookshelf form - New (FR):  a New XForm example
```

As shown in the following screenshot, you would be able to update the sample XForm **Bookshelf form - Summary (FR)**. Of course, you can find the sample XForm at the folder `$AS_WEB_APP_HOME/orbeon/WEB-INF/resources/forms/orbeon/bookshelf/form` and the XForm file `form.xhtml` as well.

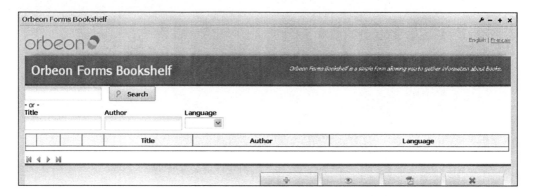

 Note that results of forms won't be stored in the portal but in Orbeon Forms.

Polls

Do you want to keep track of votes on "Is Liferay Book a proper book"? The Polls portlet (portlet ID 25) and the Polls Display portlet (portlet ID 59) are useful tools. The Polls portlet allows us to create multiple choice polls that keep track of votes and display results on a page where a lot of separate polls could be managed, and it is configurable to display a specific poll's results; while the Polls Display portlet allows us to vote for a specific poll's question and view the results.

The Polls portlet

First of all, we plan to add questions. As an administrator, you may need to create a lot of questions for polls, like "Is Liferay Book a proper book?", "Do you plan to buy Liferay book next month?", and then manage these questions as well as the votes on these questions. Let's do it using the following steps:

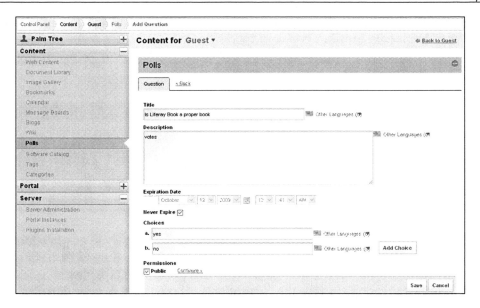

1. Log in as an admin, say "Palm Tree".

2. Go to **Manage | Control Panel** under the dock bar menu.

3. Go to Polls under the category Content of Control Panel.

4. Select a group, using default value like Content for Guest, since you are coming from the Guest public pages.

5. Click on the button "Add Question" under the portlet Polls.

6. Input the name "Is Liferay Book a proper book", description "votes"; by the way, you have options to input the name and the description in different languages.

7. Type values for choices a. and b., for example "yes" and "no"; there must be at least two choices — these can't be deleted.

8. Add more choices by clicking on the **Add Choice** button. After clicking on the Add Choice button, you can delete a choice by clicking on the Delete button located next to the choice name input box.

9. Check the checkbox Never Expire, using default settings; but you can uncheck the checkbox and also set an expiration date.

10. Set Permissions by clicking on the link Configure. To configure additional permissions, click on the link More; here we use default settings like checking the checkbox Public.

11. Click on the Save button to save the inputs.

Of course, you can add other questions. After adding the question "Do you plan to buy Liferay book next month", you could view the questions.

As shown in the preceding screenshot, poll questions are displayed as question name, numbers of votes, last vote date, expiration date, and actions with a set of icons: edit, permissions, and delete. By default, this portlet will display all questions scoped into the current group for the current user who has the proper permissions.

Note that the Polls portlet is visible in the Control Panel under the category Content only.

Editing a question

All questions are editable. Supposed that we want to change the description of the questions "Do you plan to buy Liferay book next month" from "Liferay book" to "votes for Liferay book", we need to update it. Let's do it by following these steps:

1. Locate the question, say "Do you plan to buy Liferay book next month" in Polls portlet, and click on the icon Edit from the Actions next to the question.
2. Type the value of the description like "votes for Liferay book".
3. Click on the Save button to save the inputs.

Deleting a question

All questions are removable. Let's say that the question "Do you plan to buy Liferay book next month" does not exist anymore, then we need to delete it. Let's delete it by following these steps:

4. Locate the question "Do you plan to buy Liferay book next month" that you want to delete.
5. Click on the **Delete** icon from the **Actions** located next to the question.
6. A screen will appear asking if you want to delete this. Click on the **OK** button to confirm deletion.

Note that deleting a question will delete all related votes which belong to this question.

Viewing votes

Suppose that you want to view votes for the question "Do you plan to buy Liferay book next month" in different ways. You can simply click on the name of the question and then click on View Results. You will see votes in percentage or other charts such as Area, Horizontal Bar, Line, Pie, and Vertical Bar. Furthermore, you can view actual voters if you have proper permissions.

There are three votes on the question "Do you plan to buy Liferay book next month". You could see votes in percentage, actual voters displayed together with choice and vote date, and a Pie chart as an example.

What's happening?

As you can see, the portlet Polls is located at position 9 under the category **Content** of the Control Panel. At the same time, you would have the capability to export / import polls under the **More | Export/Import**. Why, you may ask?

The portal has some default settings for the portlet Polls, as follows, in `$PORTAL_ROOT_HOME/WEB-INF/liferay-portlet.xml`.

```
<portlet-data-handler-class>com.liferay.portlet.polls.lar.
PollsPortletDataHandlerImpl</portlet-data-handler-class>
<control-panel-entry-category>content</control-panel-entry-category>
<control-panel-entry-weight>9.0</control-panel-entry-weight>
```

The preceding code shows that the portlet Polls will appear in the category **Content** via the tag `control-panel-entry-category` and position 9 via the tag `control-panel-entry-weight`. Meanwhile, the content polls could be backed up as a LAR file via the tag `portlet-data-handler-class`.

Features

As you can see, we can summarize the following features of the Polls portlet.

- Manages (add, delete, and update) questions with multiple choices
- Creates a graph showing the votes automatically
- Expires the poll automatically
- Fine grained permissions and role-based access control for polls

- Each user can vote on a specific question only once
- Export and import data, for example, questions, votes, and permissions, for a given group
- Scope polls into different groups (communities and organizations) and portal instances

The Polls Display portlet

Do you want to display a specific poll's results in the Intranet? The Polls Display portlet would be a useful tool. The Polls Display portlet allows users to vote for a specific poll's questions and see the results of votes. Note that questions must be created from the Polls portlet in the **Control Panel** under the category **Content**.

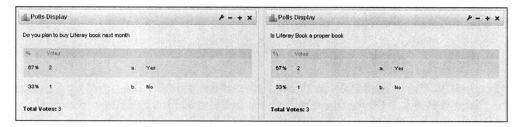

As shown in above image, we're going to put votes on the question "Do you plan to buy Liferay book next month" in a page of Guest public pages. Afterwards, users can vote on this question and view the vote results. At the same time, you would see one more portlet instances in the following screenshot – this is called instance-able.

As you can see in the Polls Display portlet, polls votes for a given question, for example, "Do you plan to buy Liferay book next month", are displayed as percentages, numbers of votes, and choice names. The selected question name is shown at the upper-left and the total votes are shown at the bottom-left. By default, this portlet will display all votes of a given poll question for the current users who have proper permissions.

How to achieve it?

As an administrator, you can create a page "Polls" in the Guest public pages first, and then add the portlet Polls Display by clicking on **Add | More...** under the dock bar menu. Afterwards, you can select different poll questions by simply clicking on the **More | Configuration** icon at the upper-right of the Polls Display portlet. Then you can select a question from a list of poll questions to be published in the website by selecting **Setup | Current** tab.

Of course, you could archive current settings by selecting **Setup | Archive** tab. Furthermore, you can configure permissions if you have the proper access right by selecting the Permissions tab and set up sharing by selecting the Sharing tab.

In this example, you can select a question, for example, "Do you plan to buy Liferay book next month" under **More | Configuration | Setup | Current | Question**. Then you can click on the **Save** button when you are ready.

From now on, when guests view the page "Polls", they can view vote results. When a user like "Lotti Stein" as a member of Guest signs in and views the page "Polls", she would see the vote page with a button "Vote" and a set of selections with the radio button such as "yes" and "no" first. After choosing an answer and clicking on the Vote button, she would be able to see vote results.

What's happening?

As you have noticed, you can add more than one Polls Display portlet in a given page, while there is only one Polls portlet at the category Content of the Control Panel. Why are they different? The portlet Polls Display was specified as being instance-able as follows in $PORTAL_ROOT_HOME/WEB-INF/liferay-portlet.xml.

```
<configuration-action-class>com.liferay.portlet.pollsdisplay.action.
ConfigurationActionImpl</configuration-action-class>
<instanceable>true</instanceable>
```

The preceding code sets the instance-able value to true, that is, the portlet Polls Display can appear multiple times on a page. Of course, you can set it to false so that the portlet can only appear once on a page. The default value is false. The portlet Polls doesn't have the above settings, thus it uses the default value — the portlet Polls can only appear once on a page.

In addition, the preceding code shows that the tag configuration-action-class allows users to configure the portlet at runtime. This is the reason that the portlet Polls Display has the capabilities to be configured at runtime. If the tag configuration-action-class isn't specified in portlet configuration, then there would be no tab **Setup** under **More | Configuration**. As you can see, the portlet Polls doesn't have this setting. Therefore, it uses the default value — the portlet Polls doesn't have tab **Setup** under **More | Configuration**.

Features

As you can see, the portlet Polls Display has the following features:

- Easily configure the questions and change the question to be displayed
- Instance-able: the portlet can appear multiple times on a page. Therefore, you can publish more and more questions in a page with multiple portlet instances
- Publish questions across groups—for example, default group and shared global
- One user can vote once only for a given question

Assigning permissions

As stated above, trying to log in as an administrator "Palm Tree" and going to **Manage | Control Panel**, you will see Polls under the category **Content** of **Control Panel**. As mentioned earlier, the user "Lotti Stein" is also a member of the Guest community. Try to log in as "Lotti Stein", and go to **Manage | Control Panel**. You will see that Polls under the category **Content** of **Control Panel** is invisible.

What's happening? This is something related to permissions. In general, there are three levels of permissions: permissions on portlets, permissions on polls, and permissions on poll questions.

The Permissions on Polls portlet

The following table shows the permissions on Polls portlet. The role Community Member may set up all permissions (marked as 'X'): Access in Control Panel, Configuration, and View. While the role Guest only has the possibility to set up View (marked as 'X'). By default, a community user has the action View (marked as '*') as well as that of a guest.

Action	Description	Community	Guest
Access in Control Panel	Ability to access the portlet Wiki in Control Panel	X	
Configuration	Ability to configure portlet	X	
View	Ability to view the content of the portlet	X, *	X, *

Obviously, as a member of the Guest community, "Lotti Stein" only has the permission **View** on the portlet Polls by default. As the role Community Member doesn't have permission **Configuration** and **Access in Control Panel**, "Lotti Stein" also wouldn't have these permissions. That is, "Lotti Stein" doesn't have ability to configure the portlet Polls and access the portlet Polls in the Control Panel.

As you can see, even though the user "Lotti Stein" has the permission **View**, she wouldn't access the portlet in the Control Panel. The reason is that she doesn't have the permission **Access in Control Panel**. Let's say that you want the user "Lotti Stein" to be able to see the portlet Polls in the Control Panel. How would you implement it? You can assign permissions via the Roles. The following is an example — the user "Lotti Stein" is a member of the role "MB Topic Admin".

1. Log in as an admin, for example "Palm Tree".
2. First click on **Roles** under the category **Portal** of **Control Panel**.
3. Then locate a role, say "MB Topic Admin".
4. Then click on the **Define Permissions** icon from the **Actions** next to the right of the role.
5. Click on the **Applications | Polls** link, select checkboxes **Access in Control Panel** and **View**.
6. Click on the **Save** button.

As shown in the preceding steps, the user "Lotti Stein" has permission actions **Access in Control Panel** and **View** through the role "MB Topic Admin". That is, the user "Lotti Stein" has the ability to access the portlet Rolls in the Control Panel. Try to log in as "Lotti Stein", you would see **Polls** under the category **Content** of **Control Panel**.

Permissions on the Polls Display portlet

The following table shows permissions on the Polls Display portlet. The role Community Member may set up all permissions (marked as 'X') including **Configuration** and **View**. While the role Guest only has the possibility to set up permission **View** (marked as 'X'). By default, a community user has the action **View** (marked as '*') similar to that of a guest.

Action	Description	Community	Guest
Configuration	Ability to configure the portlet	X	
View	Ability to view the content of the portlet	X, *	X, *

Obviously, as a member of the Guest community, "Lotti Stein", only has the permission **View** on the portlet Wiki by default. As the role Community Member doesn't have permission **Configuration**, "Lotti Stein" also wouldn't have this permission. That is, "Lotti Stein" doesn't have the ability to configure the portlet Polls Display in the page "Polls".

Permissions on Polls

As you can see, if logged in as "Lotti Stein", you would see **Polls** under the category **Content** of the **Control Panel**. You would see a set of questions displayed with Question, Number of Votes, Last Vote Date, and Expiration Date when you click on **Polls**, but you wouldn't see the button "Add Question". That is, the user "Lotti Stein" doesn't have the ability to add questions. Why?

The following table shows permissions on Polls. Both the Community Member and the Guest roles don't have the permission Add Question by default.

Action	Description	Community	Guest
Add Question	Ability to add questions		

As you can see, as a member of the Guest community, "Lotti Stein" doesn't have the permission **Add Question**. If we want the user "Lotti Stein" to have the permission **Add Question**, how do we implement this requirement? The following is an example.

1. Log in as an admin, say "Palm Tree".
2. Click on **Roles** under the category **Portal** of the **Control Panel** first.
3. Then locate a role, say "MB Topic Admin".
4. Then click on the **Define Permissions** icon from the **Actions** next to the right of the role.
5. Click on the **Content | Polls** link, select **Add Question** checkbox under Polls.
6. Click on the **Save** button.

As shown in the preceding steps, the user "Lotti Stein" has the permission action **Add Question** using the role "MB Topic Admin". That is, the user "Lotti Stein" has the ability to add questions in the portlet Polls. When you try to log in as "Lotti Stein", you would see the button **Add Question** under the portlet **Polls** under the category **Content** of the Control Panel.

Note that the permission **Add Question** was used for all content poll questions in a group, not for individual poll questions. Therefore, you couldn't assign this permission to any individual content.

Permissions on Polls Questions

As a user at the "Palm Tree Publications" enterprise, like "Lotti Stein", you have the proper permissions **View** and **Add Vote** on the question "Is Liferay Book a proper book?". However, you do not have permissions such as **Update** and **Delete**.

What's happening? The subsequent table shows permissions for **Polls Questions**. The role Community Member may have permissions (marked as 'X'), namely, **View**, **Delete**, **Permissions**, **Update**, and **Add Vote**. On the other hand, the role Guest may have permissions with **View**, **Add Vote**, **Delete**, and **Permissions**. By default, the role Community Member has the permission actions (marked as '*'): **View** and **Add Vote**, while the role Guest only has the permission **View**.

Action	Description	Community	Guest
View	View polls questions	X, *	X, *
Delete	Delete polls questions	X	X
Permissions	Configure permissions of polls questions	X	X
Update	Update polls questions	X	
Add Vote	Add vote for the question	X, *	X

As you can see, as a member of the Guest community, "Lotti Stein" only has the permissions **View** and **Add Vote** on the question.

As an administrator, you may need to set up the user "Lotti Stein" to have the permissions **View**, **Add Vote**, **Delete**, and **Update** on the question "Is Liferay Book a proper book". Let's do it by following these steps.

1. Log in as an administrator, say "Palm Tree".
2. Locate the question "**Is Liferay Book a proper book**".
3. Click on the **Permissions** button from the **Actions** menu next to the question "**Is Liferay Book a proper book**".
4. Select permissions **Delete** and **Update** under the role "MB Topic Admin".
5. Click on the **Save** button.

From now on, as a member of Guest, "Lotti Stein" finally has permissions **View**, **Add Vote**, **Update**, and **Delete** on the question "Is Liferay Book a proper book". Try to log in as "Lotti Stein", you will see the **Actions** menu with the icons **Edit** and **Delete** next to the question "**Is Liferay Book a proper book**".

As stated above, we have added the permissions **Delete** and **Update** on an individual question. Now we're going add the permission **Delete** and **Update** on questions in the following scopes:

- All questions in a group like the Guest community
- All questions in a portal instance like the current portal instance

How to implement these use cases you ask? For all questions in a group, you will be able to assign permissions in the Control Panel through the custom community role (or Community Member) for community pages, or custom organization role (or Organization Member) for organization pages. For all questions in a portal instance, you will be able to assign permission in the Control Panel through custom regular roles. The following is a sample process—assigning permissions **Delete** and **Update** on questions in the current portal instance.

1. Log in as an admin, let's say "Palm Tree".
2. Click on **Roles** under the category **Portal** of **Control Panel** first.
3. Then locate a role, say "MB Topic Admin".
4. Then click on the **Define Permissions** icon from the **Actions** next to the right of the role.
5. Click on the **Content | Polls** link under the **Add Permissions**, select **Delete** and **Update** checkboxes under **Polls Questions**
6. Click on the **Save** button.

Using polls effectively

Generally speaking, users (who have proper permissions) or administrators can create multiple-choice polls that keep track of votes and display results on the page in the Polls portlet. On one hand, the polls portlet manages many separate polls. On the other hand, a separate portlet, like the Polls Display portlet, can be configured to display a specific poll's results.

Actually, the Polls portlet acts as a voting application in order to take public opinions. It provides users with scientifically sampled surveys to assess public opinions. Meanwhile, it effectively uses portal's customization and personalization features. Furthermore, it also provides an end user to customize the results that will be displayed.

As poll administrators, you can easily add and delete the poll topics. You can customize portlet by changing the result title, reordering the poll options, and specifying whether the user can select multiple options.

As shown in following figure, polls are made up of questions. That is, polls will have many questions associated with them. Each question must have two or more choices. In other words, a question would have at least two or more choices associated with it. In turn, each choice may have many votes associated with it. Note that a given user on a specific question can have at most one vote.

Polls versus surveys

In theory, polls are scheduled to open and close at a given time. As poll administrators, you may view previous poll results if you want to make use of this information for your statistical analysis. At the same time, you may configure the portlet instance to determine what poll is to be shown in the portlet.

In a word, there are differences between surveys and polls. A **survey** is a multiple-page survey questionnaire. Whereas a poll is a one-page questionnaire, and is replaced by poll results after voting. Either by way of multiple choices or by text, polls consist of straightforward lists related to questions and potential responses. When information-gathering requirements are simple and you don't require the identification of the respondents, then you could use polls. Otherwise, you should use surveys.

Polls in scope

Considering the pattern `Portal-Group-Page-Content`, the content questions of portlet polls could be scoped into a group, for example, all pages including both private pages and public pages, by default. The content questions of the portlet Polls in the group Shared Global would be scoped into the portal instance. This would be the current portal instance—the content questions of the portlet Polls in the group Shared Global would be visible across all groups in the current portal instance.

As you can see, one of the most powerful characteristics of the Polls Display portlets is the fact that when they are added to different groups, they act as completely independent portlets, each with their own default group. By default, the portlet Polls Display is scoped into a group. That is, when one or more Polls Display portlets are added to a group of either public or private pages, they act as completely identical portlets, but with their own portlet preferences, for example, **More | Configuration | Setup**.

For instance, when the portlet Polls Display is added to a page for example, "Polls", of the Guest community, it will use the default scope–the group Guest. If you add the portlet Polls Display to a second page, let's say "Welcome", it will show same questions as those shown in the first page of the group Guest. When the portlet Polls Display is added to a page, it will immediately get scoped into the group to which the current page belongs.

Obviously, the portlet Polls Display is scoped into the group Guest when it is added to any of pages of this group. You don't have the flexibility to switch groups in this case. However, you can solve this limitation through the Control Panel. In the Control Panel, you are able to switch the content of the portlet Polls between different groups. How to implement it? You will be able to do it by following these steps:

1. Go to **Manage | Control Panel** under the dock bar menu.

2. Locate **Polls** under the category **Content**, and click on **Polls**. You would see the same questions because, by default, the content of the portlet Polls is scoped to the group **Guest**.

3. Switch groups by selecting different groups from the drop-down menu **Content for**.

Use Polls through JSON services

The portal provides services that allow invoking its methods directly through HTTP using **JavaScript Object Notation (JSON)** as a data serialization mechanism. The JSON API is automatically generated by the Service Builder from a remote service interface. Of course, you can use polls through JSON services.

In general, you can use any HTTP client and JSON services to access the service. Alternatively, you can use JavaScript plus Velocity templates to access JSON Service API. As shown in the following lines of code, we show an example of using JavaScript plus Velocity templates.

```
<script type="text/javascript">
  Liferay.Service.Polls = {
  servicePackage: "com.liferay.portlet.polls.service."
  };
// ignore details
</script>
```

As shown in the preceding code, it uses JSON API (for example, `com.liferay.portlet.polls.service.`) and Velocity templates (for example, `$poll`) to form JavaScript functions: vote and addVote. You may refer to JavaScript `service.js` in `$PORTAL_ROOT_HOME/html/js/liferay`. Of course, you can use the preceding code with article templates for different purposes.

In addition, you may need to add polls as a type of Web Content Structure, just as that of Image Gallery images and Document Library documents. Moreover, you can build dynamic articles with polls. For more details, you can refer to *Chapter 7, Customizing CMS and WCM, Liferay Portal 5.2 Systems Development*.

Enhancement

At the time of writing of this book, only those questions that get scoped to the group of the page, where the portlet Polls Display was added, are available. It would be nice to provide the capability to select groups in the Polls Display portlet. For example, the default group Guest, shared Global, and so on. This feature is not available yet, but highly expected.

Summary

This chapter introduced us to adding and managing (view, update and delete) nodes of wikis, adding pages at the nodes in wikis, managing (view, update, delete, and search) the pages for a given node in wikis. We also saw how to use permissions of the Wikis portlet and permissions on nodes, and how to publish wiki articles in the intranet first. Then it introduced us to how we can set up Web Forms in order to collect users' suggestions and how to configure polls and display surveys in order to assess public opinions. In addition, it briefly introduced us to how we can integrate OpenOffice, Orbeon forms, and Alloy UI forms.

In this chapter, we have learned how to:

- Manage (view, update, and delete) nodes of wikis
- Manage (view, update, delete, and search) the pages of a given node in wikis
- Assign permissions on wiki nodes and pages
- Publish wiki pages
- Convert documents
- Set up Web Forms
- Integrate portal with Orbeon forms
- How to work with Alloy UI forms
- Configure the Polls portlet
- Display polls

In the next chapter, we're going to introduce blogs, RSS, and the WYSIWYG editor.

6
Blogs, WYSIWYG Editors, and RSS

In the intranet website "bookpub.com" of the enterprise "Palm Tree Publications", it would be nice to let small teams work together on specific projects, share files and Blogs about project processes—use WYSIWYG editors to create or update files and Blogs, and also employ RSS feeds. The Blogs portlet provide a straightforward Blogs solution with features such as RSS support, user and guest comments, browseable categories, tags and labels, and an entry rating system. The RSS portlet with subscription provides the ability to frequently read RSS feeds from within the portal framework. At the same time, **What You See Is What You Get (WYSIWYG)** editors provide the ability to edit web content, including Blog content. Less technical people can use WYSIWYG editors without sifting through complex code.

This chapter will first introduce us to working with Blogs; that is, how to customize and publish Blogs. Then it will address how to build Blog content with WYSIWYG editors and how to configure different WYSIWYG editors. Finally, it will discuss how to work with RSS and related portlets, as well as how to implement them for different requirements.

By the end of this chapter, you will have learned how to:

- Add entries to blogs
- Manage (view, update, and delete) entries on blogs
- Add comments and ratings on entries of blog entries
- Assign permissions on the Blogs portlet and blog entries
- Publish blogs using the Recent Bloggers portlet and the Blogs Aggregator portlet
- Build blogs with WYSIWYG editors

- Configure WYSIWYG editors
- Use RSS including the RSS portlet, the Alert portlet, the Announcement portlet, and the Weather portlet.

Blogs

The Blogs portlet includes full WYSIWYG editing capability and publication date, RSS support, threaded user and guest comments, tags and labels, social bookmarking links, e-mail notifications of blog replies, and an entry rating system. In order to let small teams work on specific projects—share files and Blogs about project processes, we should use the Blogs portlet at the Guest community public pages.

As an administrator of the enterprise "Palm Tree Publications", you may want to create a page called **Blogs** at the Guest community and then add the Blogs portlet (portlet ID 33) in the page "Blogs". Then you are ready to create Blogs entries named "How to write a computer book" and "Is your book sellable?".

Adding entries

First of all, we need to create an entry called "How to write a computer book". Let's create the entry, as shown in the following screenshot.

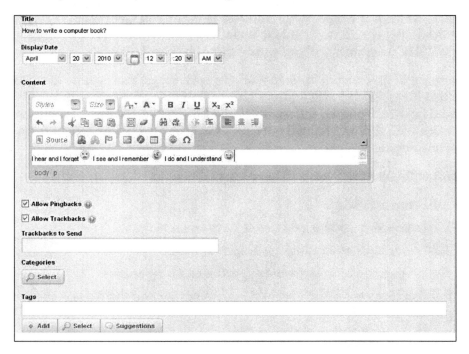

1. First of all, log in as an administrator, say Palm Tree, and locate **Go To |
   liferay.com** under the dock bar menu.

2. Add a page called "Blogs" in the Guest community public pages by clicking
   on **Add Page** under the dock bar menu.

3. Add the **Blogs** portlet in the page "Blogs" of the Guest community where you
   want to manage Blogs entries by clicking on **Add | More...** under the dock
   bar menu.

4. Click on the **Add Blog Entry** button.

5. Input a title, say "How to write a computer book", which could be duplicated.

6. Input a display date—default date and time are the current date and time
   respectively.

7. Input content—text, graphics, and any links using the WYSIWYG editor.

8. Check the checkbox "Allow Incoming Trackbacks"—note that in order
   to allow track backs, you must also ensure that the entry's guest view
   permission is enabled.

9. Input an e-mail address for "Trackbacks to Send"—here we use the default
   settings.

10. Select proper categories by clicking on the **Select Categories** button.

11. Press the **Select Tags** button or input a tag and press *Enter* if you need to add
    tags—or search tags by clicking on the **Suggestions** button.

12. Set **Permissions** by clicking on the **Configure** link. In order to configure
    additional permissions, click on the **More** link. Here we just use the default
    settings. By the way, the checkbox **Public** is selected by default.

13. Save inputs by clicking on the **Publish** button or the **Save Draft** button. Only
    published blogs would be visible to users.

Of course, you can create other entries as desired. After creating the entry called "Is
your book sellable?", we can view entries, as shown in the following screenshot.

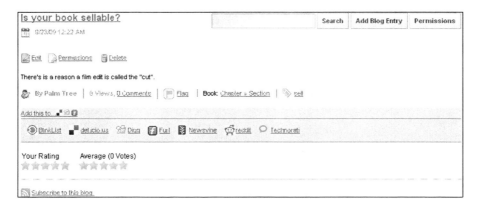

Managing entries

After adding entries, we can manage them smoothly via the portlet Blogs. Blog entry management would involve, but is not limited to, editing, deleting, searching, rating, commenting, RSS feeds, bringing entries into third-party blog systems, and so on.

Editing entries

Entries are editable. For example, we are planning to change the title of entry "Is your book sellable?" from the value "Is your book sellable?" to the value "How to write sellable book". Let's do it by following these steps:

1. Locate the entry, say "Is your book sellable?", that you want to edit.
2. Click on the **Edit** icon below the title "Is your book sellable?".
3. Update the title, say "Is your book sellable?" with new value "How to write sellable book?".
4. Retain the values of the display date, content, categories, tags, and so on. If required, you can update them.
5. Save inputs by clicking on the **Save** button.

 Note that in the edit page, you can update title, display date, track backs, categories, and tags, everything except assigning permissions. In order to change permissions, you have to use functions of permissions' assignment.

Deleting entries

Entries are removable. For instance, the entry "How to write a sellable book?" is not needed anymore. We should remove this from the Blogs portlet. Let's delete it by following these steps:

1. Locate the entry, say "How to write sellable book?", that you want to delete.
2. Click on the **Delete** icon below the title "How to write sellable book?".
3. A screen will now appear, asking you if you want to delete this. Click on the **OK** button to confirm deletion, or click on the **Cancel** button to discard changes.

Note that deleting an entry will delete all related comments that belong to this entry.

Searching entries

The content of entries is searchable. Let's say that, as an administrator, you want to search entries by the keyword "book". Let's perform a search as follows:

1. Locate the input box next to the button **Search Entries** in the Blogs portlet.
2. Input the search criterion (that is, keyword), for example, "book".
3. Click on the **Search** button.

A list of entries appears at the bottom of the Blogs portlet. Entries are listed by number, category, entry, and score. Obviously, entries are displayed in a descending order based on their score.

You can search for entries using any keyword. In short, there is only one condition — that is, you need to have the proper **View** permission for the entries. This means that if you don't have the proper **View** permissions on the entries, you won't be able to view them using search.

For example, as an administrator, you simply need to change permissions on the entry "How to write sellable book?". The roles Community Member and Guest don't have the **View** permission on this entry. First, after approaching the page "Blogs" as a guest user, you just input the search criterion "book", and click on the button **Search**. You wouldn't see the entry "How to write sellable book?" because the role Guest doesn't have the **View** permission on this entry.

Then try to log in as "Lotti Stein". You just input the search criterion, "book", and click on the button **Search**. You will see the entry "How to write sellable book?". However, when you click on its title, you will receive a message that says "You do not have the required permissions".

 What's happening? This is something related to permissions on the entries. Refer to the section *Assigning permissions*.

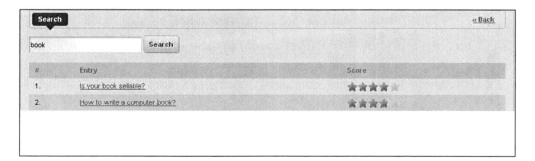

Giving your rating

You can give your own rating for any entries if you are logged in and if you have proper permissions to view them. For instance, as an administrator, you have read the entry "How to write a computer book" and want to give your rating, for example, two stars. You simply have to click on the second star under "Your Rating" of the entry "How to write a computer book".

Try to log in as "Lotti Stein", and you can also read the entry "How to write a computer book" and give your rating—that is, three stars. You simply have to click on the third star under "Your Rating" of the entry "How to write a computer book". Now you will find the average is two and a half stars, with the message "2.5 stars".

Note that a guest can view the rating, but can't vote—users can vote only once on a given Blogs entry. More interestingly, you, as a user with proper permissions, could change your vote on a specific Blogs entry anytime.

Why does each entry have ranks? There is a taglib called `<liferay-ui:ratings>`, allowing you to rate any type of content or pages in any portlet. Meanwhile, you could find UI taglib `<liferay-ui:ratings>` at `$PORTAL_ROOT_HOME/html/portlet/blogs/view_entry_content.jspf`. To associate any object with ranks, all you need is its `Class-Name` and `Primary-Key`. Note that `$PORTAL_ROOT_HOME` represents the root folder of the portal (refer to *Chapter 2, Setting Up a Home Page and Navigation Structure for the Intranet* for details).

Employing RSS feeds

You can export Blogs entries as RSS feeds. Let's do it by following these steps:

1. Click on the **RSS Feed** icon, say "Subscribe to this blog" at the bottom of the entries.

2. The RSS feeds page appears. All entries are displayed with brief content.

3. You can subscribe to the feed using different applications.

4. Locate the entry (by title) that you want to view, and click on the link.

5. You would be able to return to the entry view page.

Flagging inappropriate content

As you can see, you can flag the content of Blogs entry as inappropriate. For each entry, you would see a small icon of a red flag, which will enable a user to flag the content of a blog entry as inappropriate for a reason and warn the administrator about it.

Why does each entry have a flag? There is a taglib called `<liferay-ui:flags>` allowing you to flag any type of content or pages in any portlet. If you are interested in details, you could also find implementation of flags `<liferay-ui:flags>` at `$PORTAL_ROOT_HOME/html/taglib/ui/flags/page.jsp`. On the other hand, you could find UI taglib `<liferay-ui:flags>` at `$PORTAL_ROOT_HOME/html/portlet/blogs/view_entry_content.jspf`.

Social bookmarks

The feature of social bookmarking on blog entries is very cool because it allows for the posting of entries to various popular social bookmarking sites such as `blinklist`, `delicious`, `digg`, `furl`, `newsvine`, `reddit`, and `technorati`. Why does each entry have social bookmarks? There is a taglib called `<liferay-ui:social-bookmarks>` that allows for the posting of entries to various popular social bookmarking sites. You could find the UI taglib `<liferay-ui:social-bookmarks>` at `$PORTAL_ROOT_HOME/html/portlet/blogs/view_entry_content.jspf`.

If you are interested in more details, you could also find the implementation of the social bookmarks `<liferay-ui:social-bookmarks>` at `$PORTAL_ROOT_HOME/html/taglib/ui/social_bookmarks/page.jsp` and the implementation of the social bookmark `<liferay-ui:social-bookmark>` at `$PORTAL_ROOT_HOME/html/taglib/ui/social_bookmark/page.jsp`.

What's happening? How can we configure social bookmarks for Blogs entries? The portal has the following settings by default in `portal.properties`.

```
social.bookmark.types=blinklist,delicious,digg,furl,newsvine,reddit,t
echnorati
social.bookmark.post.url[blinklist]=http://blinklist.com/index.
php?Action=Blink/addblink.php&url=${liferay:social-bookmark:url}&Title
=${liferay:social-bookmark:title}
social.bookmark.post.url[delicious]=http://del.icio.us/
post?url=${liferay:social-bookmark:url}&title=${liferay:social-
bookmark:title}
social.bookmark.post.url[digg]=http://digg.com/submit?phase=2&url=${li
feray:social-bookmark:url}
social.bookmark.post.url[furl]=http://furl.net/storeIt.
jsp?u=${liferay:social-bookmark:url}&t=${liferay:social-
bookmark:title}
```

```
social.bookmark.post.url[newsvine]=http://www.newsvine.com/_tools/
seed&save?u=${liferay:social-bookmark:url}&h=${liferay:social-
bookmark:title}
social.bookmark.post.url[reddit]=http://reddit.com/
submit?url=${liferay:social-bookmark:url}&title=${liferay:social-
bookmark:title}
social.bookmark.post.url[technorati]=http://technorati.com/cosmos/sea
rch.html?url=${liferay:social-bookmark:url}
```

As shown in the preceding code, the property `social.bookmark.types` specifies the types of social bookmarks, whereas the property `social.bookmark.post.url` specifies URL and title for a given bookmark, using type as a parameter. You can override these properties in `portal-ext.properties`.

Adding comments

As stated, as an administrator, you have created an entry called "How to write a computer book". Being a user of the enterprise "Palm Tree Publications", "Lotti Stein" wants to review the entry and add a comment to say "Cool!". Let's do it by following the next set of steps, as depicted in the following screenshot:

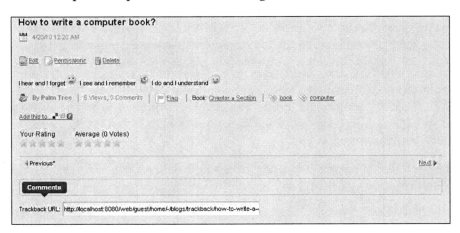

1. Log in as "Lotti Stein".
2. Navigate to the Guest community by clicking on **Go To | Guest** under the dock bar menu.
3. Navigate to the Blog's page.
4. Locate an entry by clicking on the link of the previous page or the next page you want to view, and click on the entry by title, for example, "How to write a computer book".

5. Click on the link "Comments" under the content of the Blogs entry.

6. Under the **Comments** tab, click on the **Add Comment** link, if you want to add new topic or subject.

7. Or under a subject, click on the **Post Reply** link if you want to add new sub topic or subject.

8. Input some text, for example, "Cool!".

9. Click on the **Reply** button to save the input.

10. As a normal user or a guest user, you can view comments from "Lotti Stein" for the entry "How to write a computer book" if you have proper permissions, as shown in the following screenshot.

11. Locate the entry **How to write a computer book**.

12. Click on the title of this entry.

13. Click on the link **Comments** under the content of the Blogs entry.

14. Under the **Comments** tab, click on the **Add Comment** link if you want to add a new topic or subject.

15. You could also do it by clicking on the **Post Reply** link below a subject, if you want to add a new sub topic or subject.

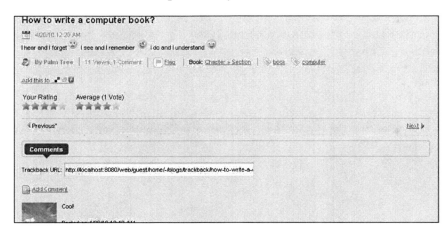

In addition, you can reply to a comment. You could locate the comment that you want to reply to first. Then click on the **Post Reply** icon at the bottom-left side of the comment. Enter comments, and then click on the **Reply** button to save the inputs, or click on the **Cancel** button to cancel the changes.

Furthermore, you could edit a comment. You simply click on the **Edit** icon at the bottom-left side of the comment. You will be able to change the subject and body. Then click on the **Update** button to save the changes or the **Cancel** button to cancel the changes.

Moreover, you can delete a comment if you have the proper permissions. You click on the **Delete** icon at the bottom-left side of the comment. A message will appear asking if you want to delete this. Click on **OK** to confirm deletion or **Cancel** to cancel deletion.

 Note that only the current comment has been deleted following the action. The low-level comments related to the current comment will have a link to the parent comment of the current comment.

Finally, in order to go to the top of the comments, simply click on the **Top** button at the bottom-left side of any comment.

What's happening?

Why does each entry have comments? There is a taglib called `<liferay-ui:discussion>` that allows us to comment any type of content or pages in any portlet. If you are interested in more details, then you could also find implementation of comments `<liferay-ui:discussion>` at `$PORTAL_ROOT_HOME/html/taglib/ui/discussion/page.jsp`.

Meanwhile, you could find UI taglib `<liferay-ui:discussion>` at `$PORTAL_ROOT_HOME/html/portlet/blogs/view_entry.jspf`. All you need is `Class-Name`, `Primary-Key`, `user-Id`, and `subject`, and other keywords of any object to associate it with comments.

Assigning permissions

We have used default settings for the Blogs portlet in the page "Blogs" of the Guest community. As shown previously , when the administrator "Palm Tree" logs in, he/she will see the button "Add Entry" in the Blogs portlet. As we already know, the user "Lotti Stein" is also a member of the Guest community. Try to log in as "Lotti Stein", you will see that there is no "Add Entry" button in the Blogs portlet. Furthermore, you would see the entry "How to write a computer book" without any action icons (such as edit, permissions, and delete).

What's happening? This is something related to permissions. There are three levels of permissions: permissions on portlet, permissions on Blogs entries, and permissions on entry.

Permissions on portlet

Someone with the Community Member role may set up all permissions (marked as 'X') such as **View**, **Configuration**, and **Access in Control Panel**. On the other hand, someone with the Guest role may set up the permissions: **View** and **Configuration**. By default, the role Community Member has the permission action **View** (marked as '*') just like the role Guest.

Action	Description	Community	Guest
View	Ability to view the portlet	X, *	X, *
Configuration	Ability to configure the portlet	X	X
Access in Control panel	Ability to access the portlet in the Control Panel	X	

Obviously, as a member of the Guest community, "Lotti Stein" only has the permission **View** on the portlet Blogs, by default. "Lotti Stein" can't access the portlet Blogs in the Control Panel.

As an administrator, you may need to set up users like "Lotti Stein" having the permissions **Access in Control panel** and **View** on the Blogs portlet in the Control Panel. This means that you need to add the permissions **Access in Control panel** and **View** on the portlet Blogs in the Control Panel for them. How to achieve this? The following is an example using the role "MB Topic Admin", as shown in the following screenshot.

1. Log in as an administrator, say "Palm Tree".
2. Click on **Roles** under the category **Portal** of **Control Panel** first.

3. Then locate a role, say **MB Topic Admin**.

4. Click on the **Define Permissions** icon from the **Actions** button next to the right of the role.

5. Click on the **Applications | Blogs** link, check the checkboxes **Access in Control Panel** and **View**.

6. Click on the **Save** button when you are ready.

Try to log in as "Lotti Stein", and go to the **Manage | Control Panel** under the dock bar menu. You would see **Blogs** under the category **Content** of **Control Panel**.

Of course, you would like to assign the permissions **View** and **Configuration** to different users on the portlet Blogs in the page "Blogs". To do so, click on **More | Configuration.|.Permissions** of the portlet Blogs and assign the permissions **View** and **Configuration** to different roles.

Permissions on Blogs entries

The following table shows permissions on Blogs entries. The role Community Member may set up permissions (marked as 'X') such as **Add Entry**. On the other hand, the role Guest can't set up the permission **Add Entry**. By default, the role Community Member doesn't have the permission **Add Entry**.

Action	Description	Community	Guest
Add Entry	Ability to add Blogs entry	X	

Apparently, as a member of the Guest community, "Lotti Stein" doesn't have the permission **Add Entry** on the portlet Blogs, by default. Note that the permission **Add Entry** isn't used for individual content. Instead, it is used for a group of content. By default, you could assign the permission **Add Entry** either in a group or in the current portal instance.

For the permission **Add Entry** in a group, you would be able to assign permissions in the Control Panel via the custom community role (or Community Member) for community pages or the custom organization role (or Organization Member) for organization pages. For the permission **Add Entry** in the current portal instance, you would be able to assign this permission in the Control Panel via custom regular roles within the scope of the current portal instance.

Permissions on Blogs entry

The following table shows permissions on Blogs entries. The role Community Member may set up all permissions (marked as 'X') such as **View**, **Update**, **Delete**, **Permissions**, **Add Discussion**, **Delete Discussion**, and **Update Discussion**. On the other hand, the role Guest may set up the permission **View**. By default, the role Community Member has the permission actions **View** and **Add Discussion** (marked as '*'), whereas the role Guest only has the permission action **View**.

Action	Description	Community	Guest
View	Ability to view blog entries	X, *	X, *
Update	Ability to update blog entries	X	
Delete	Ability to delete blog entries	X	
Permissions	Ability to assign permissions on blog entries	X	
Add Discussion	Ability to add a discussion on blog entries	X, *	
Delete Discussion	Ability to delete a discussion on blog entries	X	
Update Discussion	Ability to update a discussion on blog entries	X	

Obviously, as a member of the Guest community, "Lotti Stein" has the permissions **View** and **Add Discussion** on the entry, by default. As the role Guest doesn't have the permissions **Update**, **Delete**, **Permissions**, **Delete Discussion**, and **Update Discussion**, "Lotti Stein" also doesn't have these permissions. Therefore, "Lotti Stein" can't see the action icons (edit, permission, and delete) on the entries. Moreover, "Lotti Stein" doesn't have the actions icons (for example, **Delete Discussion** and **Update Discussion**) on the comments.

As an administrator, you may need to reset users having permissions **Update Discussion** and **Delete Discussion** on the entry "How to write a computer book". This means that you need to add permissions (**Update Discussion** and **Delete Discussion**) on the entry "How to write a computer book". The following is a sample.

1. Locate the entry "How to write a computer book".

2. Click on the **Permissions** icon under the entry title.

3. Select permissions under the role Community Member, such as **Delete Discussion** and **Update Discussion**.

4. Click on the **Submit** button if you are ready.

Try to log in as "Lotti Stein". You would be able to view entries only without the actions (update, delete, and permissions). However, now you can also view, add, delete, and update discussions (that is, comments).

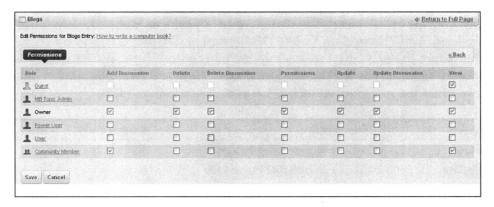

Similarly, as an administrator, you can set up the community users to have permissions (that is, update, delete, and permissions) on the entry "How to write a computer book". Then try to log in as "Lotti Stein"—you can view the entry "How to write a computer book" with the actions icons (that is, edit, permissions, and delete).

As you can see, we have assigned permissions on individual entries. Besides this, you would find permissions on entries in the following scopes:

- A set of entries in a group, for example the Guest community.

- All entries in a group, for example the Guest community

- All entries in a portal instance.

There isn't a solution yet for a set of entries in a group. For all entries in a group, you would be able to assign permissions in the **Control Panel** via the custom community role (or Community Member) for community pages or the custom organization role (or Organization Member) for organization pages. For all entries in a portal instance, you'll be able to assign permissions in the **Control Panel** via custom regular roles in the scope of the portal instance. The following is an example of assigning the permission **Update** on all entries of the current portal instance.

1. Log in as an admin, say "Palm Tree".
2. Click on **Roles** under the category **Portal** of the **Control Panel** first.
3. Then locate a role, say "MB Topic Admin".
4. Click on the **Define Permissions** icon from the **Actions** next to the right of the role.
5. Click on the **Content | Blogs** link, check the checkbox **Update**
6. Click on the **Save** button when you are ready.

As the role "MB Topic Admin" is a regular one, the permission **Update** was assigned in the scope of the current portal instance.

Using blogs effectively

Generally speaking, a **blog** (short for web-log) is personal online content, which is frequently updated for general public consumption. Blogs are a series of entries posted to a single page in reverse-chronological order. Generally, they represent the author personality or reflect the purpose to host the blog on the website. Topics of blogs could be brief philosophical musings, links to other sites that the author favors, commentary on Internet and other social issues, and so on. Blog content could include: what is happening in a person's life and what is happening on the Web, a kind of hybrid diary or guide site, and so on.

The author of a blog is called a Blogger. Bloggers can syndicate their blog content to subscribers using RSS. In general, blogs are frequent, chronological publications of personal thoughts and web links.

Blogs types

There are various types of blogs such as v-log, link-log, photo log, and so on. Each of them is different in the way that content is delivered and written.

Blogs can be classified by media type such as a v-log (one comprising videos), a link-log (one comprising links), a sketch-blog (a site containing a portfolio of sketches), a photo-blog (one comprising photos), tumble-logs, art-log (a form of art sharing and publishing), and so on.

In addition, blogs can be classified by device, for example, a mo-blog (written by a mobile device like a mobile phone or PDA).

The Blogs portlet

The Blogs portlet can help you publish information on the Web easily. It helps in the rapid development of your community and furthermore gives your enterprise a platform to easily share information among different departments.

The Blogs portlet allows users of the enterprise to manage web-log entries in a portal page. You can create, edit, and delete web-log entries, and change permissions on entries. In addition, it provides a simplified interface for creating web-logs and publishing them as RSS feeds.

The Blogs portlet has the following features:

- Highly configurable
- RSS feed capability for each blog and all blogs combined
- Ability to view a list of all available blogs
- Calendar view for blog entries
- Ability to navigate directly to "My Blog"
- Comments capability
- A direct link for each blog entry and each user blog
- Ability to add Tags and labels (categories)
- An entry rating system

The following figure depicts Blogs structure overview. Blogs is made up of a set of entries. Each entry may have many comments. In turn, each entry may have many ratings. Of course, users can rate an entry only once. Moreover, each entry enables flags—allowing users to flag content as inappropriate and enables the capability of trackbacks. In addition, an entry may have many tags and / or categories.

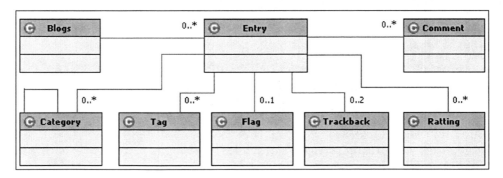

Setup

As you can see, the portlet Blogs is highly configurable. To configure Blogs, including RSS feeds, click on the **More | Configuration** icon on the top-right of the Blogs portlet. With the **Setup | Current** tab selected, there are a set of sub-areas: regular Page and RSS.

As shown in the following screenshot, you can set the display styles used to display Blogs when viewed as a regular page or as an RSS. For regular pages, you can set the following items:

- **Maximum Items to Display**: The number of displayed blog entries; the attributes of **Display Style** include **Full Content**, **Abstract**, or **Title**.
- **Enable Flags**: A checkbox to enable flags on blog entries.
- **Enable Ratings**: A checkbox to enable ratings on blog entries.
- **Enable Comments**: A checkbox to enable comments on blog entries.
- **Enable Comment Ratings**: A checkbox to enable ratings on comments.
- **Format**: **Atom 1.0**, **RSS 1.0**, and **RSS 2.0**.

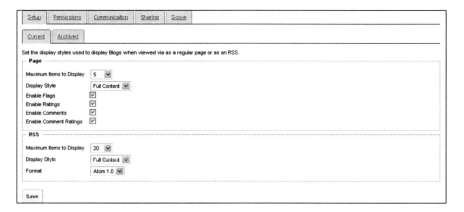

Additionally if comments have been added to a blog entry, the author of the blog entry would be able to get an e-mail notification. Let's look at how this is done.

What's happening?

The portal sets the following properties in `portal.properties` by default.

```
blogs.email.comments.added.enabled=true
blogs.page.abstract.length=400
blogs.rss.abstract.length=200
blogs.trackback.enabled=true
blogs.trackback.excerpt.length=50
blogs.trackback.verifier.job.interval=5
blogs.ping.google.enabled=true
blogs.entry.comments.enabled=true
```

As shown in the preceding code, you could configure e-mail notification settings via the property `blogs.email.comments.added.enabled`. The default abstract length of page is set as `400` and the default abstract length of RSS is set as `200`. The portal sets the property `blogs.trackback.enabled` to `true` to enable trackbacks. The excerpt length for trackbacks was set as 50, whereas the interval on which the `Trackback-Verifier-Job` will run was set as 5 for one-minute increments.

You can set the property `blogs.ping.google.enabled` to `true` in order to enable pinging Google on new and updated blog entries. You can also set the property `blogs.entry.comments.enabled` to `true` to enable comments for blog entries. Of course, you could override these properties according to your own requirements in `portal-ext.properties`.

Asset render framework, search, indexing, and social activity

The framework via the tag `asset-renderer-factory` called **Asset Render Framework** will allow registering custom asset types so that generic portlets, such as the Asset Publisher portlet, can be used to publish them. This is the reason that we can publish blog entries through the Asset Publisher portlet. In fact, the portlet Blogs supports asset render framework as follows in `$PORTAL_ROOT_HOME/WEB-INF/liferay-portlet.xml`.

```xml
<indexer-class>com.liferay.portlet.blogs.util.Indexer</indexer-class>
<open-search-class>
  com.liferay.portlet.blogs.util.BlogsOpenSearchImpl
</open-search-class>
<social-activity-interpreter-class>
  com.liferay.portlet.blogs.social.BlogsActivityInterpreter
</social-activity-interpreter-class>
<asset-renderer-factory>
  com.liferay.portlet.blogs.asset.BlogsEntryAssetRendererFactory
</asset-renderer-factory>
```

As shown in the preceding code, besides the tag `asset-renderer-factory`, the portlet also specifies tags `indexer-class`, `open-search-class`, and `social-activity-interpreter-class`. The tag `social-activity-interpreter-class` adds social activity tracking to a portlet, and recorded social activities will appear on the **Activities** portlet.

Meanwhile, the tag `indexer-class` value is called to create or update a search index for the portlet Blogs, whereas the tag `open-search-class` is called to get search results in the **Open-Search** standard.

Tags and categories

As you can see, when displaying an entry, a set of categories and tags of the current entry are also displayed next to the flag. Why? There are taglibs called `<liferay-ui:asset-categories-summary>` and `<liferay-ui:asset-tags-summary>` that allow us to tag any type of content or pages in any portlet. Of course, you could find UI taglibs `<liferay-ui:asset-categories-summary>` and `<liferay-ui:asset-tags-summary>` in $PORTAL_ROOT_HOME/html/portlet/blogs/view_entry_content.jspf. All you will need is `Class-Name`, `Primary-Key`, and `portlet-URL` of any object to associate it with tags and categories as follows:

```
<span class="entry-categories">
  <liferay-ui:asset-categories-summary
    className="<%= BlogsEntry.class.getName() %>"
    classPK="<%= entry.getEntryId() %>"
    portletURL="<%= renderResponse.createRenderURL() %>"
  />
</span>
<span class="entry-tags">
  <liferay-ui:asset-tags-summary
    className="<%= BlogsEntry.class.getName() %>"
    classPK="<%= entry.getEntryId() %>"
    portletURL="<%= renderResponse.createRenderURL() %>"
  />
</span>
```

As you can see, you can tag blog entries with tags and categories. The portal has specified the following code in $PORTAL_ROOT_HOME/html/portlet/blogs/edit_entry.jsp:

```
<aui:input name="categories" type="assetCategories" />
<aui:input name="tags" type="assetTags" />
```

As shown in the preceding code, it uses tag `<aui:input>` with types `assetTags` and `assetCategories`. Of course, you could find similar code for Message Boards messages, Wiki articles, and so on.

Blogs in scope

Considering the pattern `Portal-Group-Page-Content`, entries of the portlet Blogs could be scoped into a group, for example, all pages including both private and public pages, by default. In addition, blog entries could be scoped into an individual page—a set of data isolated from the other data of the same portlet.

For instance, when the portlet Blogs is added to a page, for example, "Blogs" of the group Guest, it will use the default scope to the group Guest. If you add the portlet Blogs to a second page, say "Welcome", it will show the same data as that of the previous page. This means that the portlet Blogs is scoped into the group Guest when it is added to any page of the group Guest. Fortunately, you are able to switch the content of the portlet Blogs to different groups. How can you achieve this? The following is an example:

1. Go to **Settings | Control Panel**.
2. Locate Blogs under the category **Content** of **Control Panel**, and click on **Blogs**.
3. Switch groups by selecting different groups from the drop-down menu **Content for**.

The portlet Blogs could be scoped into a page. How do we scope the Blogs portlet to a page? The following is a sample:

1. Locate a page, say "Blogs", and go to the portlet Blogs in the current page.
2. Go to **More | Configuration** of the portlet Blogs.
3. Click on the tab **Scope**.
4. Choose "Current page (Blogs)" from the select menu **Scope**, and click on the **Save** button.

How to customize the scope feature? The portal has default settings for the portlet Blogs as follows in `$PORTAL_ROOT_HOME/WEB-INF/liferay-portlet.xml`.

```
<control-panel-entry-category>content</control-panel-entry-category>
<control-panel-entry-weight>7.0</control-panel-entry-weight>
<scopeable>true</scopeable>
```

The preceding code shows that the portlet Blogs will appear in the category **Content** of **Control Panel**, at position 7, and it is scopeable—giving it the capability to use the tab **More | Configuration | Scope** and change the scope from default to the current page.

Friendly URL

As you can see, when you view blog entries, you will see URLs like `/web/guest/blogs/-/blogs/11201` and `/web/guest/blogs/-/blogs/11214`. Similarly, when you view RSS feeds, you would see URL like `/web/guest/blogs/-/blogs/rss`. This is short, friendly URL. In fact, the portlet Blogs supports friendly URL mapping as follows in `$PORTAL_ROOT_HOME/WEB-INF/liferay-portlet.xml`.

```
<friendly-url-mapper-class>
   com.liferay.portlet.blogs.BlogsFriendlyURLMapper
</friendly-url-mapper-class>
```

As shown in the preceding code, the content inside a portlet will use a friendly URL via the tag `friendly-url-mapper-class`.

Blogs in communication

There is a tab called **Communication** under **More | Configuration** in the Blogs portlet, and shared parameters could be mapped into `categoryId` and `tag` because the portlet has the following configuration in `$PORTAL_ROOT_HOME/WEB-INF/portlet-custom.xml`.

```
<supported-public-render-parameter>categoryId</supported-public-
render-parameter><supported-public-render-parameter>tag</supported-
public-render-parameter>
```

As shown in the preceding code, there are two parameters, namely, `categoryId` and `tag`. Of course, you can set mapping between these parameters, or even ignore some or all of them in the tab **More | Configuration | Communication**. You simply change the mapping and/or ignorance, and click on the **Save** button when you are ready.

Enhancement

As you can see, we can either assign permissions on all blog entries of a given group or assign permissions on individual blog entries. However, we can't assign permissions on a set of blog entries of a given group, and it would be nice if we could do so. This can be implemented by adding categories (similar to folders) on the Blogs portlet, that is, blog entries are grouped. In this case, we can assign different permissions based on both blog categories and blog entries. This feature isn't ready yet, but is expected in version 6. In addition, blog entries could be grouped with tag categories, and then permissions on blog entries having "book" category, for example, can be assigned.

Publishing blogs

As stated above, we have discussed how to create entries in order to let small teams work on specific projects and share files and Blogs about the project process. As a user at the enterprise "Palm Tree Publication", you may have created a lot of entries, which will be needed to show a list of the latest users from a given department and the latest posts for a given department too.

The Recent Bloggers portlet

The portlet Recent Bloggers (portlet ID 114) shows a list of the latest users who posted a blog entry. In practice, you may ask the question "Do you want to show a list of the last users from the Editorial department in the Guest community?" The portlet Recent Bloggers would be useful, showing a list of the latest users who posted a blog entry. Let's do it by following these steps:

1. Navigate to the page "Blogs".
2. Go to **Add | More...** under the dock bar menu.
3. Add the **Recent Bloggers** portlet to the page "Blogs".
4. Click on **More | Configuration | Setup** of the portlet.
5. Choose **Select Method** from **Users** and **Scope**, using the default value **Users**.
6. Select an organization, for example, "Editorial Department", using the default value in this example.
7. Select display style, for example, **User Name and Image** using the default settings.
8. Select **Maximum Bloggers** to **Display**, in this case, 20.
9. Click on the **Save** button when you are ready.

Of course, you can select other organizations, for example, "Engineering Department". The recent Bloggers portlet will show a list of the latest users from the "Engineering Department" in the Guest community. You can also remove the organization, if required. In this case, the portlet will show a list of the latest users from any of the departments in the Guest community.

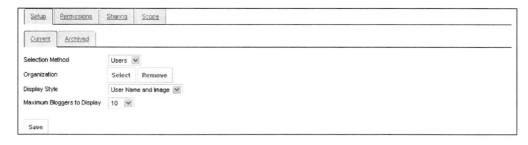

As you can see, the portlet Recent Bloggers grabs blog entries from the current portal instance or by specific organizations. As shown in the previous screenshot, the portlet Recent Bloggers is configurable. You can configure it with the following items:

- **Selection Method**: Users or scope
- **Organization**: Select or remove organizations when users were selected
- **Display Style**: **User Name and Image** and **User Name**
- **Maximum Bloggers to Display**: Number of bloggers

In a word, the Recent Bloggers portlet allows us to show a list of the latest users of the portal instance that have written a blog entry.

What's happening?

As you can see, the portlet Recent Bloggers is configurable and scopeable. Why? The portal has default settings for the portlet Recent Bloggers as follows in $PORTAL_ ROOT_HOME/WEB-INF/liferay-portlet.xml:

```
<configuration-action-class>
  com.liferay.portlet.recentbloggers.action.ConfigurationActionImpl
</configuration-action-class>
<scopeable>true</scopeable>
```

The preceding code shows that the portlet Recent Bloggers is **scopeable** — it has the capability to use the tab **More | Configuration | Scope** and the ability to change the scope from default (current group) to the current page. The portlet Recent Bloggers is configurable with the tag `configuration-action-class`, which allows users to configure the portlet at runtime.

In addition, all the look and feel of the portlet can be changed in the theme. Therefore, you can change the theme as you want to. Furthermore, you can change the view of the portlet directly at $PORTAL_ROOT_HOME/html/portlet/recent_ bloggers/view.jsp.

For example, you can configure the portlet by selecting a display style from either of the two options — **User Name and Image** or **User Name**. In the previous file, you only have the permission to update and set the display style as **Image**.

Enhancement

It would be useful if the portlet had the ability to configure which information is displayed about a user and which users are displayed. Of course, you may have your own requirements on the portlet Recent Bloggers. Additionally, it would be useful if the portlet could publish recent bloggers from more than one group, for example, the current group Guest and the group shared Global, or from multiple groups—both communities and organizations.

The Blogs Aggregator portlet

The portlet Blogs Aggregator (portlet ID 115) grabs blog entries from the entire portal or by specific organizations. Do you want to show the latest posts from the Editorial department in the Guest community? Let's do it by following these steps:

1. Navigate to the page "Blogs".
2. Go to **Add | More ...** under the dock bar menu.
3. Add the **Blogs Aggregator** portlet to the page "Blogs".
4. Click on the link **More | Configuration | Setup**.
5. From the **Select Method** menu, choose from options **Users** and **Scope**—use the default value **Users**.
6. Select an organization, for example, "Editorial Department", using default settings.
7. Select display style like **Abstract**. Other display styles are available such as **Body and Image, Body, Abstract without Title, Quote, Quote without Title**, and **Title**. Use the default settings.
8. Choose **Maximum Items to Display**, say "20".
9. Select the checkbox **Enable RSS Subscription**.
10. Click on the **Save** button when you are ready.

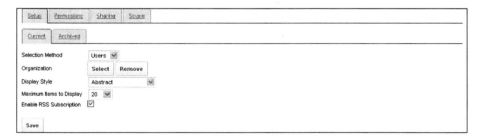

Of course, you can select other organizations, for example, "Engineering Department". The Blogs Aggregator portlet will show the latest entries from all the entries of the Engineering Department in the Guest community. Also, you can remove the organization if required and select **Scope** as the value of **Select Method**. In this case, the portlet Blogs Aggregator will show the latest entries from all the entries of any department in a group such as the Guest community.

As you can see, the portlet Blogs Aggregator grabs blog entries from the current portal instance or from a specific organization. As shown in the preceding screenshot, the portlet Blogs Aggregator is configurable. You can configure it using following items:

- **Selection Method**: Users or Scope
- **Organization**: Select or remove organizations when users were selected; aggregate blogs from only specific organizations
- **Display Style**: Body and Image, Body, Abstract, Abstract without Title, Quote, Quote without Title, and Title
- **Maximum Items to Display**: Number of blogs
- **Enable RSS Subscription**: A checkbox on RSS subscription, allowing the users to subscribe using RSS

In general, the Blogs Aggregator portlet shows the latest posts from all the entries of any departments in a group, such as the Guest community, which specifies the blogs that should be aggregated. It specifies a set of display styles, and moreover, it has the ability to expose an aggregated RSS feed.

What's happening?

Similar to the portlet Recent Bloggers, the portlet Blogs Aggregator is configurable and scopeable. Why? The portal has the default settings for the portlet Blogs Aggregator as follows in `$PORTAL_ROOT_HOME/WEB-INF/liferay-portlet.xml`.

```
<configuration-action-class>com.liferay.portlet.blogsaggregator.
action.ConfigurationActionImpl</configuration-action-class>
<scopeable>true</scopeable>
```

As shown in the preceding code, the portlet Blogs Aggregator is scopeable, that is, it has the capability to use the tab **More | Configuration | Scope** and the ability to change the scope from default (current group) to the current page. The portlet Blogs Aggregator is also configurable—the tag `configuration-action-class` allows users to configure the portlet at runtime.

In fact, all the look and feel of the portlet Blogs Aggregator could be changed in the theme. Therefore, you can change the theme asper your requirements. Furthermore, you can change the view of the portlet Blogs Aggregator directly in $PORTAL_ROOT_HOME/html/portlet/blogs_aggregator/view_entry_content.jspf.

For instance, using configuration, you may select the display style. In the previous view file, you can update and/or set the display style as desired.

Enhancement

As you can see, the configuration view of the portlet Blogs Aggregator portlet allows us to change the default behavior of the portlet— for example to set the maximum number of messages shown; allowing the users to subscribe using RSS, aggregating blog posts regarding users/scopes, aggregating blogs from only specific organizations. It would be nice if we could aggregate blogs from multiple groups—either communities or organizations. This feature isn't ready yet, but is expected soon.

WYSIWYG editors

As stated above, we have discussed how to create an entry, for example, "How to write a computer book?". The content of the entry is simple, but it contains image and text with center alignment. How do we align text, insert image, and so on? These functions are related to WYSIWYG editors.

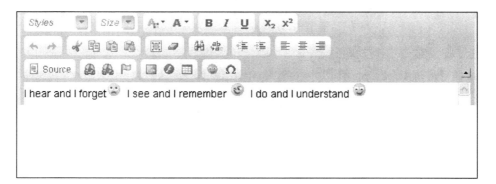

As shown in the preceding screenshot, the portal integrates FCKEditor as the default HTML text editor. Of course, it is possible that, as an administrator, you can integrate other WSYIWYG editors with the portal. Here, we will first use FCKEditor as an example in order to build the contents of Blogs' entries.

FCKEditor is web-based HTML text editor with powerful formatting capabilities. It brings to the web much of the power of desktop editors like MS Word. Moreover, it is the most used rich HTML editor on the Web. It's also lightweight and doesn't require any kind of installation on the client's computer. In the year 2009, this product was renamed into **CKEditor**. Refer to http://ckeditor.com for more details.

Let's consider the following use cases about the usage of the WYSIWYG editor:

- Upgrade FCKEditor to the latest version.
- Use general functions on text, namely, font, size, alignment, color, background color, copy, paste, list, and so on. You would be able to use them easily.
- Insert images.
- Insert links.
- Insert flash, tables, smileys, and special characters.
- Edit a source directly.
- Customize WYSIWYG editors.

Upgrading FCKeditor

First of all, let's upgrade the WYSIWYG text editor, FCKeditor, to the latest version. By default, the portal has bundled FCKeditor with a specific version. This may not be the latest version. Let's upgrade the FCKeditor to the latest version by following these steps:

1. Download the latest version of FCKeditor from http://ckeditor.com.
2. Rename the folder fckeditor under the folder $PORTAL_ROOT_HOME/html/js/editor to fckeditor.backup.
3. Unzip the ZIP file to the folder $PORTAL_ROOT_HOME/html/js/editor.

Then, let's add a customized configuration to the JSP file fckconfig.jsp. To do so, you can simply copy the JSP file fckconfig.jsp from the folder $PORTAL_ROOT_HOME/html/js/editor/fckeditor.backup to the $PORTAL_ROOT_HOME/html/js/editor/fckeditor folder.

4. Finally, we need to generate the portal browser folder $PORTAL_ROOT_HOME/html/js/editor/fckeditor/editor/filemanager/browser/liferay in the following manner:

- ° Locate the folder `$PORTAL_ROOT_HOME/html/js/editor/`
  `fckeditor.backup/editor/filemanager/browser`

- ° Copy the folder `liferay` (including all subfolders and files)
  from `$PORTAL_ROOT_HOME/html/js/editor/fckeditor.`
  `backup/editor/filemanager/browser` to `$PORTAL_ROOT_`
  `HOME/html/js/editor/fckeditor/editor/filemanager/`
  `browser`.

That's it! From now on, you can enjoy the latest version of FCKeditor.

Note that you can use SDK plugins and do this in the ext plugin. This tutorial works only for FCKEditor 2, but it doesn't work with CKEditor 3 or higher. Configurations and folder structures have changed too much in CKEditor 3.x and other newer versions. Integration with CKEditor 3 will come out soon.

End user features

FCKeditor isn't only functional, flexible, and fast, but it's also innovative, smart, and user friendly. The following are end-user features, but it's not limited to them.

- The formatting features include:
  - ° **Basic** and **Advanced Styling**: Rich styles under the **Control** tab
  - ° Real Block-quoting: Properly quote text using the appropriate and semantics aware `<blockquote>` tag.
  - ° Colors: Applying colors to text is a matter of a few clicks with the color selector.
  - ° Advanced **Paste from Word**: This makes it easy to convert these texts using the powerful **Past from Word** feature.
  - ° Advanced Linking: Build advanced links that can open pop ups, links to anchors, e-mails, or any kind of web resource.
  - ° E-mail Linking: inserting the desired e-mail address, even the message subject and text.
- The User Interface features include:
  - ° Visual link anchors: You can use this feature by inserting page "anchors", so that other pages (or even the same page) can link to them, thus positioning the reader in the right place.

- ° Maximize: With a single click, you can fill the entire space available in the page, and with another click, it returns to its original size.

- ° Visible Blocks: Outlining every single block of text, making it easy to control the semantics and the quality of the edited content.

- ° Resizable: Through a simple drag operation, this makes it possible to have the perfect fit.

- ° Right-to-left interface: Renders from right to left, making end users feel at home.

- ° Elements Selector: By showing the hierarchy of HTML tags around the current cursor position, this making it easy to manage them.

- ° Find and Replace: Finding words in the text is simple and effective using this feature, and replacing words is also as easy, including massive replacement operations.

- Rich Content

  - ° Images: It helps to insert images into the content and is easily configurable.

  - ° Flash Content: It enables inserting flashes on their pages, and easily controlling the playback features of Flash movies.

  - ° Easy Tables: Creation of tables that play well with accessibility, as well as designing them to present their contents in a better way.

  - ° Smiles: This feature comes with a set of exclusively designed smiley graphics that can be freely and easily used for displaying smiles.

  - ° Print Breaks: Precisely controls the printing breakpoints inside the contents.

  - ° Templates: It makes pieces of HTML reusable again and again.

  - ° Form Creation Tools: It enables bringing all necessary tools to proper "create and manage" forms and fields.

- The usability features include:

  - ° Interface usability: Making it intuitive to be understood and used; bringing the best editing experience to the hands of our end users.

- ° Strong accessibility: Compliance with worldwide accessibility standards such as the W3C WCAG and the US Section 508.

- ° Spell Check as You Type: Bringing a "zero installation" spell check based on the quality spell checking services provided by `SpellChecker.net`.

- ° Keyboard navigable: The keyboard is "totally" keyboard navigable, meaning that you don't need a mouse to use its features, and you will never be limited as a result of it.

- ° *Tab*-key friendly: Using the *Tab* key to navigate through pages, special forms, is quite common and intuitive. CKEditor respects it. It does not interfere in the way users would expect pages to behave. It makes navigation so natural.

- ° Intuitive context menu: Context menus are easy and intuitive ways to add functionality to applications.

- ° Safely undo: Every single action can be safely reverted, guaranteeing that you'll never break things or lose your text.

Inserting images

You can insert an image as an internal image (from Image Gallery) or an external image (a URL outside of the portal). For example, imagine that you need to insert an image using the URL `http://liferay.cignex.com/palm_tree/book/0387/chapter06/muppets.png` in the entry "How to write a computer book". Let's do it by following these steps:

1. Click on the **Edit** icon below the title "**How to write a computer book**".

2. Locate the position where you want to insert an image.

3. Click on the **Insert Image / Edit Image** icon in FCKeditor.

4. Enter a URL for the external image by entering the URL `http://liferay.cignex.com/palm_tree/book/0387/chapter06/muppets.png`, and then properties, for example.

5. Click on the **OK** button.

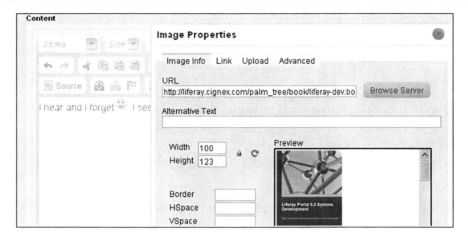

As shown in the preceding screenshot, you can configure the following items related to **Image Info**:

- **URL**: The URL of images
- **Alternative Text**: Using the `alt` setting
- **Width**: The dimensions in terms of the width of the image
- **Height**: The dimensions in terms of the height of the image
- **Border**: Removing the visible border around images
- **HSpace**: The horizontal space between the image and surrounding text
- **VSpace**: the vertical space between the image and surrounding text
- **Align**: Left, Abs Bottom, Abs Middle, Baseline, Bottom, Middle, Right, Text Top, and Top

The size of the dimensions (**Height** and **Width**) of the image could be reset, and the ratio of these dimensions of the image could be locked. You can find the two icons next to **Width** and **Height**—namely, **Lock Ratio** and **Reset Size**. The functions from the tabs **Link** and **Advanced** are not involved in the current integration.

Of course, you can insert an image as an internal image (from Image Gallery). You can do it by following these steps:

1. Click on the **Edit** icon below the title "**How to write a computer bo**ok".
2. Select the position where you want to insert an image.
3. Click on the Insert/Edit Image button in the WYSIWYG editor.
4. Click on the **Browse Server** (internal image) button.

5. Click on a folder, say "Guest".

6. Click on **Create New Folder** to add a folder "Images" under the current folder.

 Any folder and image added here will be placed in the Image Gallery. The Image Gallery provides a centralized repository for images to be stored and given a unique URL.

7. Type the name of the new folder **Images**, and click on the **OK** button.

8. Navigate to the folder **Images**.

9. Click on the **Choose File** button to select an image `muppets.png` from your local machine.

10. Click on the **Upload** button to add the image to the folder.

11. Click on the image `muppets.png`, and click on the **OK** button to add the image to the document.

12. Click on the **Save** button to save the updates.

 In addition, you can insert an image, flash, or document link from the Alfresco repository. It is called full RESTful integration between Liferay and Alfresco. In this case, Alfresco is used as a repository of Liferay.

As you can see, you can select an existing image from Image Gallery, or create a folder, upload an image, and select the newly uploaded images.

What's happening?

As stated earlier, we have copied the JSP file `fckconfig.jsp` from the folder `$PORTAL_ROOT_HOME/html/js/editor/fckeditor.backup` to the folder `$PORTAL_ROOT_HOME/html/js/editor/fckeditor`. The JSP file `fckconfig.jsp` provides integration of FCKeditor and the portal.

First, it customizes tool bar sets "liferay" (for wiki pages, blog entries, and so on), "liferay-article" (for Web Content), "edit-in-place", and "e-mail" at `$PORTAL_ROOT_HOME/html/js/editor/fckeditor/fckconfig.jsp`. For example, the tool bar set "`liferay`" has been specified as follows:

```
FCKConfig.ToolbarSets["liferay"] = [
    ['Style','FontSize','-','TextColor','BGColor'],
    ['Bold','Italic','Underline','StrikeThrough'],
    ['Subscript','Superscript'], '/',
```

```
    ['Undo','Redo','-','Cut','Copy','Paste',
    'PasteText','PasteWord','-','SelectAll','RemoveFormat'],
    ['Find','Replace','SpellCheck'],
    ['OrderedList','UnorderedList','-','Outdent','Indent'],
    ['JustifyLeft','JustifyCenter','JustifyRight','JustifyFull'],
    '/',
    ['Source'],['Link','Unlink','Anchor'],
    ['Image','Flash','Table','-','Smiley','SpecialChar']
] ;
```

As shown in the preceding code, the style and font size are grouped as one tab, and the Image, Flash, and Table are grouped as another tab.

Then it sets the CSS and makes links it to the themes. The following is some sample code:

```
String cssPath = ParamUtil.getString(request, "cssPath");
String cssClasses = ParamUtil.getString(request, "cssClasses");
FCKConfig.BodyClass = 'html-editor <%= cssClasses %>' ;
FCKConfig.CustomStyles = {};
FCKConfig.StylesXmlPath = FCKConfig.EditorPath + 'fckstyles.xml' ;
FCKConfig.EditorAreaCSS = '<%= HtmlUtil.escape(cssPath) %>/main.css';
```

Most importantly, it specifies the image browser URL as follows:

```
long plid = ParamUtil.getLong(request, "p_l_id");
String mainPath = ParamUtil.getString(request, "p_main_path");
String doAsUserId = ParamUtil.getString(request, "doAsUserId"); String
connectorURL = HttpUtil.encodeURL(mainPath + "/portal/fckeditor?p_l_
id=" + plid + "&doAsUserId=" + HttpUtil.encodeURL(doAsUserId));
FCKConfig.ImageBrowserURL = FCKConfig.BasePath + "filemanager/browser/
liferay/browser.html?Type=Image&Connector=<%= connectorURL %>";
```

Inserting links

You can also insert internal links and external links into content like blog entries. For example, you are going to insert a link with the URL http://liferay.cignex.com/ palm_tree/book/0387/chapter06/4701_01_3rdDraft.pdf in the entry **How to write a computer book**. Let's do it by following these steps:

1. Click on the **Edit** icon below the title "How to write a computer book".

2. Locate the position where you want to insert a link.

3. Input some text, for example **Liferay Portal 5.2 System Development, Chapter 1**, and then select the text that you want to become a link.

4. Click on the **Insert/Edit Link** button in the WYSIWYG editor.

5. You can add a URL directly for external links, that is, `http://liferay.cignex.com/palm_tree/book/0387/chapter06/4701_01_3rdDraft.pdf`

6. Click on the **OK** button.

As shown in the preceding screenshot, you can configure the following items related to **Link Info**:

- Link Type: **URL**, **Link to anchor** in this page, **E-Mail**
- Protocol: `http://`, `https://`, `ftp://`, `news://`, and `<other>`
- URL: The URL of links

As you can see, the external links refer to any links outside of the portal, where link types would be **URL**, **Link to anchor in the text**, and **E-Mail**. Protocols would be `http`, `https`, `news`, `ftp`, and `<other>`. For example, the value of URL would be `liferay.cignex.com/palm_tree/book/0387/chapter06/4701_01_3rdDraft.pdf` if the link type is URL. Besides the tab **Link Info**, you can also use the functions from the tabs **Target** and **Advanced**.

The internal links refer to any links in the portal; for example, links to images in the Image Gallery, links to documents in the Document Library, and links to pages of the current group. In short, there are three types of resources related to internal links: **Document**, **Image**, and **Page**.

Link to documents

As previously mentioned, you may need to link to a document, as mentioned. To link text to a document, follow these steps:

1. Click on the **Edit** icon below the title **How to write a computer book**.

2. Locate the position where you want to insert a link.

3. Select a text like "**Liferay Portal 5.2 System Development, Chapter 1**".

4. Click on the **Insert/Edit Link** button in the WYSIWYG editor.

5. Click on the **Browse Server** button, that is, **Internal Link**.

6. In the **Resource Type** menu, select **Document**—note that the default value of resource type is **Document**.

7. Click on a folder like "Guest"

8. Click on **Create New Folder** to add the folder **Documents** under the current folder.

9. Type the name of the new folder **Documents**, and click on the **OK** button.

10. Navigate to the folder **Documents**.

11. Click on the **Choose File** button to select a document `4701_01_3rdDraft.pdf` from your local machine.

12. Click on the **Upload** button to add the document to the folder.

13. Click on the document, and then click on the **OK** button to add the document to the content of the Blogs entry.

14. Click on the **Save** button to save the updates.

As you can see, the value that links a text to a document would be something like `/c/document_library/get_file?uuid=0abb3b7d-1a3a-446e-b192-03e739c6b919&groupId=10143` if the link type is URL.

 Any folders and documents that are added here will be placed in the Document Library. The Document Library provides a centralized repository where documents can be stored and given a unique URL.

Link to pages

We have discussed how to link text to documents. However, you may need to link text to a page, for example, `web/guest/home`. We can do it by following these steps:

1. Click on the **Edit** icon below the title **How to write a computer book**.

2. Select the position where you want to insert a link.

3. Select the text, like **Liferay Portal 5.2 System Development, Chapter 1**.

4. Click on the **Insert/Edit Link** button in the WYSIWYG ditor.

5. From the **Resource Type** menu select **Page**.

6. Select group, say "Guest", in which the page is located.

7. Click on the page that you want to link the selected text to, for example, /web/guest/home.

8. Click on **OK** to link the page with the selected text.

As you can see, the value which links text to a page would be something like /web/guest/home, if link type is **URL**.

Link to images

We have discussed how to link a text to documents and / or pages. You may need to link a text to an image. You can do it as follows.

1. Click on the **Edit** icon below the title **How to write a computer book**.

2. Locate the position where you want to insert a link.

3. Select the text, like **Liferay Portal 5.2 System Development, Chapter** 1".

4. Click on **Insert/Edit Link** button in WYSIWYG editor

5. In the **Resource Type** menu, select **Image**.

6. Select a group, like "Guest", in which the image is located; we should upload an image here, just as with the document link tutorial.

7. Navigate to the folder **Images**.

8. Select the image, for example muppets.png.

9. Click on the **OK** button to link the image with the selected text.

As you can see, the value that links text to a page would be something like /image/image_gallery?uuid=045f0c99-0fa4-4b4b-9c59-751a84b83af3&groupId=10143&t=1254186548453, if the link type is **URL**.

What's happening?

As mentioned previously, there are three resource types for links—**Document**, **Image**, and **Page**. The default resource type is **Document**. How so? When we had upgraded the FCKEditor, we had copied the folder liferay (including all of its subfolders and files) from $PORTAL_ROOT_HOME/html/js/editor/fckeditor.backup/editor/filemanager/browser to $PORTAL_ROOT_HOME/html/js/editor/fckeditor/editor/filemanager/browser.

In the file $PORTAL_ROOT_HOME/html/js/editor/fckeditor/editor/filemanager/browser/liferay/frmresourcetype.html, we had overridden the value of resource types as follows:

```
aTypes = [
    ['Document','Document'],
    ['Image','Image'],
    ['Page','Page']
] ;
```

The preceding code shows that there would be three resource types, namely, Document, Image, and Page. Similarly, in the file $PORTAL_ROOT_HOME/html/js/ editor/fckeditor/editor/filemanager/browser/liferay/browser.html, we have overridden the value of default resource type as follows:

```
if ( oConnector.ShowAllTypes )
    oConnector.ResourceType = 'Document' ;
```

The preceding code sets the default resource type as Document.

Most importantly, the configuration file $PORTAL_ROOT_HOME/html/js/editor/ fckeditor/fckconfig.jsp specifies the link browser URL as follows:

```
FCKConfig.LinkBrowserURL = FCKConfig.BasePath + "filemanager/browser/
liferay/browser.html?Connector=<%= connectorURL %>";
```

The preceding code specifies the link browser URL.

 Note that the preceding tutorial works only for FCKEditor 2. Integration with CKEditor 3 or higher isn't available yet.

Insert flashes, tables, smileys, and special characters

We have discussed how to link text to documents and/or pages and/or images. You may need to "insert" and/or "edit" flash in the content like blogs entries by following these steps:

1. Click on the **Edit** icon below the title **How to write a computer book**.

2. Select the position where the flash will be inserted.

3. Click on **Insert/Edit Flash** in the WYSIWYG editor.

4. Enter a URL for flash, by entering a URL like http://liferay.cignex.com/ palm_tree/book/0387/chapter06/AroundTheWorld.swf and properties in the **Info** tab. Optionally, enter details in the **Advanced** tab.

5. Click on the **OK** button to insert the flash content with the selected text.

6. To edit flash content, locate the flash content first, and then right-click to open **Flash Properties**.

As shown in the preceding screenshot, you can configure the following items related to **Info**.

*   **URL**: The URL of flashes
*   **Width**: The dimensions of the width of the flash content
*   **Height**: The dimensions of the height of the flash content
*   **Preview**: Preview the selected flash content

Besides the tab **Info**, you can also use the functions from the tab **Advanced**. As you can see, the URL of flash would be something like `http://liferay.cignex.com/` `palm_tree/book/0387/chapter06/AroundTheWorld.swf`.

Similarly, you can insert/edit a table as follows:

1. Locate the position where the table is to be inserted.
2. Click on **Insert/Edit Table** in the WYSIWYG editor.
3. To edit a table, locate the table first. Then right-click on the table name to open the table properties.

In addition, you can insert/edit smileys, that is, a set of icons, as follows:

1. Locate the position where the smiley will be inserted.
2. Click on **Insert/Edit Smiley** in the WYSIWYG editor.
3. To edit a smiley, locate the smiley icon first. Then right-click on this icon to open image properties.

In particular, you can insert/edit special characters as follows:

1. Locate the position where the special character will be inserted.

2. Click on **Insert Special Character** in the WYSIWYG editor.

3. To edit the special character, locate the table first. Then cut or copy and paste the character.

What is Flash?
Flash here refers to SWF, which is a proprietary vector graphics file format, in addition to rich user interface, animations, and video streaming.

What's happening?

As you can see, there are only external flash files available. Additionally, there are only external link upload, image upload, and flash upload. The reason is that in the configuration file $PORTAL_ROOT_HOME/html/js/editor/fckeditor/fckconfig. jsp, we specified the following settings.

```
FCKConfig.FlashBrowser = false ;
FCKConfig.LinkUpload = false ;
FCKConfig.ImageUpload = false ;
FCKConfig.FlashUpload = false ;
```

The preceding code shows that internal flashes, link upload, image upload, and flash upload are not specified by default. Of course, you can customize these if necessary. For more details, you may refer to *Chapter 6, Customizing the WYSIWYG Editor, Liferay portal 5.2 System Development, Packt Publishing.*

Editing source

As advanced users, you would like to edit the HTML source directly and manually. To edit the source directly, you simply need to click on the **Source** button. The following table shows the possible HTML tags and examples for editing the source manually.

Action	HTML tag	Example
Insert image	`<img>`	`<img src=" http://liferay.cignex.com/ palm_tree/book/0387/chapter06/muppets. png"/>`
Link to a document	`<a>`	`<a href=" /c/document_library/get_ file?uuid=0abb3b7d-1a3a-446e-b192- 03e739c6b919&groupId=10143" />`
Link to an image	`<a>`	`<a href=" /image/image_ gallery?uuid=045f0c99-0fa4-4b4b-9c59- 751a84b83af3&amp;groupId=10143&amp ;t=1254185037171" />`
Link to a page	`<a>`	`<a href ="/web/guest/home" />`
Insert Flash	`<embed>`	`<embed width="600" height="400" type="application/x-shockwave-flash" pluginspage="http://www.macromedia.com/ go/getflashplayer" src=" http://liferay. cignex.com/palm_tree/book/0387/chapter06/ AroundTheWorld.swf " play="true" loop="true" menu="true"></embed>`
Insert smiley	`<img>`	`<img src="/html/js/editor/fckeditor/ editor/images/smiley/msn/regular_smile. gif" />`

Insert table	`<table>`	`<table width="200" cellspacing="1" cellpadding="1" border="1">`
		
		`<tbody> <tr><td> </td>`
		`<td> </td>`
		`</tr>`
		`</tbody>`
		
		`</table>`

Insert special character	none	@, $, and so on

Customization

The WYSIWYG editor of the portal is highly configurable. In general, you can configure individual JSP pages to use a specific implementation of the available WYSIWYG editors: `liferay`, `fckeditor`, `simple`, `tinymce`, or `tinymcesimple`. Moreover, you can include the WYSIWYG editor in the edit page of blog entries, web content, wiki pages, mail configuration, and so on.

What's happening?

The portal has specified the following settings related to the WYSIWYG editor in `portal.properties`:

```
editor.wysiwyg.default=fckeditor
editor.wysiwyg.portal-web.docroot.html.portlet.blogs.edit_entry.
jsp=fckeditor
editor.wysiwyg.portal-web.docroot.html.portlet.calendar.edit_
configuration.jsp=fckeditor
editor.wysiwyg.portal-web.docroot.html.portlet.enterprise_admin.view.
jsp=fckeditor
editor.wysiwyg.portal-web.docroot.html.portlet.invitation.edit_
configuration.jsp=fckeditor
editor.wysiwyg.portal-web.docroot.html.portlet.journal.edit_article_
content.jsp=fckeditor
editor.wysiwyg.portal-web.docroot.html.portlet.journal.edit_article_
content_xsd_el.jsp=fckeditor
editor.wysiwyg.portal-web.docroot.html.portlet.journal.edit_
configuration.jsp=fckeditor
editor.wysiwyg.portal-web.docroot.html.portlet.login.configuration.
jsp=fckeditor
editor.wysiwyg.portal-web.docroot.html.portlet.mail.edit.jsp=fckeditor
editor.wysiwyg.portal-web.docroot.html.portlet.mail.edit_message.
jsp=fckeditor
editor.wysiwyg.portal-web.docroot.html.portlet.message_boards.edit_
configuration.jsp=fckeditor
editor.wysiwyg.portal-web.docroot.html.portlet.shopping.edit_
configuration.jsp=fckeditor
editor.wysiwyg.portal-web.docroot.html.portlet.wiki.edit.html.
jsp=fckeditor
```

As shown in the preceding code, the default WYSIWYG editor is `fckeditor`. This WYSIWYG editor is included in the edit page of blog entries, web content, wiki pages, mail configuration, and so on.

Adding more plugins in FCKEditor

FCKEditor is totally plugin-based, including many of its core features. Plugins live in separate files, making them easy to organize and maintain. Here we're going to add more plugins to FCKEditor.

Firstly, a token like `@page_break@` will be translated to its applicable runtime value (that is, page break) at processing time. The token `@page_break@` was added to eliminate the need for page break in code. How to add page breaks in FCKEditor? The following is a sample:

1. Copy the folder `liferaypagebreak` (including all subfolders and files) from `$PORTAL_ROOT_HOME/html/js/editor/fckeditor.backup/editor/ / plugins` to `$PORTAL_ROOT_HOME/html/js/editor/fckeditor/editor/ plugins`.

2. Set up the page break in the configuration file `$PORTAL_ROOT_HOME/html/ js/editor/fckeditor/fckconfig.jsp`

In the preceding configure file, we have set the page break as follows.

```
var sOtherPluginPath = FCKConfig.BasePath.substr(0,
FCKConfig.BasePath.length - 7) + 'editor/plugins/' ;
var _TOKEN_PAGE_BREAK = '<%= _TOKEN_PAGE_BREAK %>';
FCKConfig.Plugins.Add('liferaypagebreak', null, sOtherPluginPath );
```

The preceding code adds `liferaypagebreak` as a plugin in FCKEditor. An example is given in the toolbar set "liferay-article". When editing Web Content, you would see the icon to "Insert page break" next to the icon to "Insert Special Character".

Secondly, as shown in the preceding screenshot, FCKEditor offers a "zero installation" spell check-as-you-type solution. Nothing in your server is needed for it because it's based on the quality spell checking services provided by `www.spellChecker.net`. How can we set this up?

In the configuration file, find the line:

```
$PORTAL_ROOT_HOME/html/js/editor/fckeditor/fckconfig.jsp
FCKConfig.SpellChecker = 'SCAYT' ;
```

At the end of the preceding line, add:

```
FCKConfig.Plugins.Add('liferaypagebreak', null, sOtherPluginPath ) ;
```

As shown in the preceding code, it sets the value of FCKConfig.SpellChecker as SCAYT (short for Spell Check As You Type).

Thirdly, you may be interested in integrating the **YouTube** plugin for FCKEditor with the portal. Use the following simple steps to implement it:

1. Download the latest version of the YouTube plugin—a ZIP file found at http://sourceforge.net/project/showfiles.php?group_id=215257&package_id=260057&release_id=651317

2. Unzip the ZIP file into $PORTAL_ROOT_HOME/html/js/editor/fckeditor/editor/plugins

3. Add the following line after the line FCKConfig.SpellChecker = 'SCAYT' ; in the configuration file $PORTAL_ROOT_HOME/html/js/editor/fckeditor/fckconfig.jsp:

   ```
   FCKConfig.Plugins.Add( 'youtube', 'en,ja' ) ;
   ```

4. Update the toolbar set "liferay" in the configuration file $PORTAL_ROOT_HOME/html/js/editor/fckeditor/fckconfig.jsp as follows:

```
FCKConfig.ToolbarSets["liferay"] = [
  <!-- ignore details -->
  ['Image','Flash','YouTube','Table','-','Smiley','SpecialChar']

] ;
```

As shown in the preceding code, the YouTube plugin has been added between "Flash" and "Table". After refreshing the page, you would see the icon **Insert/Edit YouTube** next to the icon **Insert/Edit Flash**, as shown in the preceding screenshot.

From now on, you would be able to insert YouTube into any content. The following are sample steps to insert YouTube into blog entries.

1. Click on the **Edit** icon below the title "**How to write a computer book**".

2. Locate the position where you want to insert YouTube.

3. Click on the **Insert/Edit YouTube** icon in FCKEditor.

4. Enter a URL for an external image by entering URL and properties (that is, **Width, Height,** and **Qualify High**). For example, http://liferay.cignex.com/palm_tree/book/0387/chapter06/HereIAmToWorship.flv.

5. Click on the **OK** button.

Of course, you can add other plugins to FCKEditor smoothly by following this pattern.

Using different WYSIWYG editors

As you can see, FCKEditor is used as the default editor in the portal. In general, you can configure individual JSP pages to use a specific implementation of available WYSIWYG editors: **Liferay, FCKEditor, Simple, TinyMCE, TinyMCESimple**. The **Liferay** editor is a WYSIWYG editor provided by Liferay, the **Simple** editor is a simple blank HTML text editor. On the other hand, the **TinyMCE** editor is a JavaScript HTML WYSIWYG editor and the **TinyMCESimple** editor is simple version of the **TinyMCE** editor.

 TinyMCE is a platform-independent web-based JavaScript HTML WYSIWYG editor. For more details, refer to http://tinymce.moxiecode.com.

The following screenshot depicts the TinyMCE editor. Let's say that you're going to use TinyMCE as the default WYSIWYG editor.

You can configure the default WYSIWYG editor in portal-ext.properties as follows:

```
editor.wysiwyg.default=tinymce
editor.wysiwyg.portal-web.docroot.html.portlet.blogs.edit_entry.
jsp=tinymce
editor.wysiwyg.portal-web.docroot.html.portlet.journal.edit_article_
content.jsp=tinymce
editor.wysiwyg.portal-web.docroot.html.portlet.journal.edit_article_
content_xsd_el.jsp=tinymce
editor.wysiwyg.portal-web.docroot.html.portlet.journal.edit_
configuration.jsp=tinymce
editor.wysiwyg.portal-web.docroot.html.portlet.message_boards.edit_
configuration.jsp=tinymce
editor.wysiwyg.portal-web.docroot.html.portlet.wiki.edit.html.
jsp=tinymce
```

The preceding code sets the default editor (editor.wysiwyg.default) to tinymce. It also sets the editor of blog entries, wiki pages, web content, and others to tinymce.

The WYSIWYG editor in portlets

As mentioned earlier, the portlet Blogs integrated the WYSIWYG editor just like the portlets Wiki, Web Content, and so on. The portlet Blogs uses the following tags in `$PORTAL_ROOT_HOME/html/portlet/blogs/edit_entry.jsp`.

```
<aui:field-wrapper label="content">
  <liferay-ui:input-editor editorImpl=
    "<%= EDITOR_WYSIWYG_IMPL_KEY %>" />
  <aui:input name="content" type="hidden" />
</aui:field-wrapper>
```

The preceding code shows that the portlet Blogs uses taglibs `<aui:field-wrapper>`, `<aui:input>`, and `<liferay-ui:input-editor>` to include the default WYSIWYG editor.

As you can see, the taglib `liferay-ui:input-editor` is the key to include the default WYSIWYG editor. In fact, the taglib `liferay-ui:input-editor` implements the WYSIWYG editor via the HTML tag `iframe`. You can view the details, as follows, in `$PORTAL_ROOT_HOME/html/taglib/ui/input_editor/page.jsp`.

```
<iframe frameborder="0" height="<%= height %>" id="<%= name %>"
   name="<%= name %>" scrolling="no" src="<%= editorURL %>"
   width="<%= width %>"></iframe>
```

The WYSIWYG portlet

In some cases, you may simply need a portlet that allows you to enter content with the WYSIWYG editor and then publish the content in the same portlet. Therefore, you could use the WYSIWYG portlet. By using this portlet, you could type content in the configuration mode with the default WYSIWYG editor, and then the portlet will publish your content in the **View** mode.

How does it work? The following is a sample that could bring the portlet WYSIWYG into the portal.

1. Download the WAR file `${wysiwyg.portlet.war}` from `http://liferay.cignex.com/palm_tree/book/0387/chapter06/wysiwyg-portlet-5.3.0.1.war`

2. Drop the WAR file `${wysiwyg.portlet.war}` to the folder `$LIFERAY_HOME/deploy` when the portal is running.

Enhancement

CKEditor 3 or above inherits the quality and strong features people were used to finding in FCKeditor 2 or below, in a much more modern product, added with dozens of new benefits like accessibility and ultimate performance. Web accessibility is a reality, and CKEditor is for everybody. CKEditor supports the standards WAI-AA (The Web Accessibility Initiative of the World Wide Web Consortium), WCAG (Web Content Accessibility Guidelines) 1.0, and Section 508. Refer to `http://ckeditor.com/`.

CKFinder is a powerful and easy-to-use Ajax file manager for web browsers. Its simple interface makes it intuitive and quick to learn for all kinds of users—from advanced professionals to Internet beginners. Refer to `http://ckfinder.com/` for more details.

These two tools are very helpful, and they should be integrated with the portal.

RSS

As an administrator, you may need to include formatted data (news) from external **Really Simple Syndication (RSS)** feeds. For example, you're going to add CNN news feeds (for example, `http://rss.cnn.com/rss/cnn_world.rss`), BBC news feeds (for example, `http://newsrss.bbc.co.uk/rss/newsonline_world_edition/front_page/rss.xml`), and Yahoo! news feeds (`http://rss.news.yahoo.com/rss/tech`) in the page "RSS" of the Guest community. Whenever an RSS XML file is updated on the remote site, the page will reflect those updates on the next portal page reload, as shown in the following screenshot:

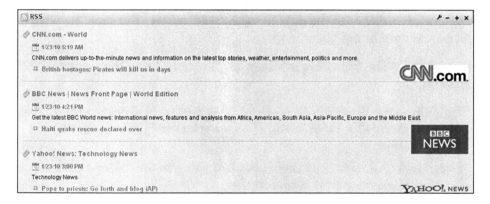

Let's add the RSS portlet at the page "RSS" first by following these steps:

1. Add a page called **RSS** in the Guest community public pages by clicking on **Add | Page** under the dock bar menu.

2. Add the **RSS** portlet in the page **RSS** of the Guest community, where you want to manage RSS news by clicking on **Add | More...** under the dock bar menu.

The RSS portlet

How do we get RSS news? You need to configure the RSS portlet (portlet ID 39) by following these steps:

1. To set the feeds that you want to display, click on the **More | Configuration** icon first at the top-right of the RSS portlet.

2. By default, the tab **Setup | Current** is selected.

3. To add a feed, first click on the **Add** icon, then enter a title, say **CNN** and a URL like `http://rss.cnn.com/rss/cnn_world.rss`.

4. To add another feed, click on the **Add** icon first, then enter a title, for example, **BBC** and a URL like `http://newsrss.bbc.co.uk/rss/ newsonline_world_edition/front_page/rss.xml`.

5. To delete a feed, locate the feed first, and click on the **Delete** icon at the right of the feed.

6. To edit a feed, locate the feed, and click on the title and/or URL, and then change the title and URL to what you want.

7. Configure the following items as expected. Here we use the default settings, as shown in the next screenshot:

   ```
   Show Feed Title: a checkbox
   Show Feed Published Date: a checkbox
   Show Feed Description: a checkbox
   Show Feed Image: a checkbox
   Show Feed Item Author: a checkbox
   Number of Entries Per Feed: number of entries per feed;
   Number of Expanded Entries Per Feed: a number of entries;
   Feed Image Alignment: Right, Left;
   Header Web Content: including web content as header;
   Footer Web Content: including web content as footer.
   ```

8. Click on the **Save** button to save the changes, and then click on the **Return to Full Page** arrow to return to the page.

Of course, you can use other news feeds. In short, to add a feed, simply click on the **Add** icon first, then input the title and the URL. In order to remove a feed, first locate the feed, and then click on the **Delete** icon.

As you can see, there are three news feed URLs by default, two items per channel, and there are two entries per feed. Moreover, the portlet RSS is configurable and instanceable—you can add multiple RSS portlets in a page.

What's happening?

The portlet RSS was specified as being instanceable and configurable, as follows, in `$PORTAL_ROOT_HOME/WEB-INF/liferay-portlet.xml`.

```
<configuration-action-class>
  com.liferay.portlet.rss.action.ConfigurationActionImpl
</configuration-action-class>
<instanceable>true</instanceable>
```

The preceding code shows that the portlet RSS is configurable via the tag `configuration-action-class` and instanceable via the tag `instanceable`.

In addition, the portlet RSS has a set of preferences specified in `$PORTAL_ROOT_HOME/WEB-INF/portlet-custom.xml` as follows:

```
<portlet-preferences>
  <preference>
```

```
        <name>urls</name>
        <value>http://rss.news.yahoo.com/rss/tech</value>
        <value>http://csmonitor.com/rss/scitech.rss</value>
        <value>http://partners.userland.com/nytRss/technology.xml</value>
    </preference>
    <preference>
        <name>items-per-channel</name>
        <value>2</value>
    </preference>
    <preferences-validator>
        com.liferay.portlet.rss.RSSPreferencesValidator
    </preferences-validator>
</portlet-preferences>
```

As shown in the preceding code, the portlet preference `urls` has three values—
`http://rss.news.yahoo.com/rss/tech`, `http://csmonitor.com/rss/scitech.`
`rss`, and `http://partners.userland.com/nytRss/technology.xml`. On the
other hand, the portlet preference `items-per-channel` has value 2. This is the
main reason that there are three news feeds URL, by default, in the portlet
RSS—two items per channel.

The Weather portlet

As an administrator at the enterprise "Palm Publications", you may be interested
in the latest weather message in the page **RSS**. As the enterprise has two locations,
that is, US (San Jose city) and Germany (Frankfurt/main city), the latest weather
messages about both US (San Jose city) and Germany (Frankfurt/main city) are
required in the page **RSS**. At the same time, you may be interested in the latest
weather message about other cities, such as Rome (Italy), Zurich (Switzerland), and
Beijing (China), as shown in the following screenshot:

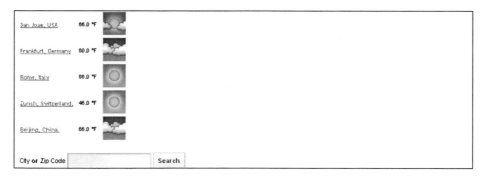

First of all, you need to deploy the portlet **Weather**. The following is an example on how to deploy it. We will discuss other options for deployment in the next chapter.

1. Download the Weather portlet WAR file at `http://liferay.cignex.com/palm_tree/book/0387/chapter06/weather-portlet-5.3.0.1.war`

2. Drop the WAR file into the folder `$LIFERAY_HOME/deploy` when the portal is running.

3. You would see that the portal will deploy the portlet Weather automatically. When the portlet Weather is available for use, you can configure it according to the requirements mentioned previously. Let's do it by following these steps:

    ° Add the Weather portlet in the page RSS of the Guest community where you want to receive the latest weather messages by clicking on **Add | More...** under the dock bar menu.

    ° To set a city or zip code that you want displayed in the portlet, first click on the **More | Preferences** icon at the top-right of the Weather portlet.

    ° Enter one city or zip code per line, for example: San Jose, USA; Frankfurt/Mainz, Germany; Rome, Italy; or Zurich, Switzerland; or Beijing, China.

    ° Select the temperature format, that is, **Fahrenheit** or **Celsius**. Here we select **Fahrenheit** as the default value.

    ° Click on the **Save** button to save the changes and then click on **Return to Full Page** arrow to return.

Of course, you can show the latest weather message about other cities around the world. The Weather portlet provides the ability to display the temperature and weather on a portal page. It displays the temperature and weather information for a given zip code or city. Users may also be interested in querying temperatures and weather for alternate zip codes or cities without any customization.

What's happening?

By default, the **Weather Channel** is used as a weather message provider to bring the latest weather to its viewers and users.

 The **Weather Channel** (also known as **TWC**) is a U.S. cable and satellite television network that broadcasts weather forecasts and weather-related news 24 hours a day. Refer to `http://weather.com.` for more details.

As you can see, the portlet Weather can't be instanced. In other words, in a page, you can't have more than one portlet. The main reason is that the portlet Weather doesn't specify the tag `instanceable` with a value `true` in $AS_WEB_APP_HOME/weather-portlet/WEB-INF/liferay-portlet.xml.

In addition, the portlet Weather has a set of preferences specified in $AS_WEB_APP_HOME/weather-portlet/WEB-INF/portlet.xml as follows.

```
<portlet-preferences>
  <preference>
    <name>zips</name>
    <value>90210</value>
    <value>Chicago</value>
    <value>Frankfurt, Germany</value>
    <value>Rome, Italy</value>
  </preference>
  <preference>
    <name>fahrenheit</name>
    <value>true</value>
  </preference>
  <preferences-validator>
    com.liferay.weather.portlet.WeatherPreferencesValidator
  </preferences-validator>
</portlet-preferences>
```

As shown in the preceding code, the portlet preference `zips` has four values: `90210`, `Chicago`, `Frankfurt, Germany`, and `Rome, Italy`. The portlet preference `fahrenheit` has the value `true`. This is main reason that, in the portlet Weather, there are four cities by default, and the default temperature format is `fahrenheit`.

Announcements and Alerts

Announcements and **Alerts** are two separate portlets, which are responsible for broadcasting messages to a list of users within a scope. Essentially, these portlets provide a mass messaging engine and one-way messaging. All Announcement and / or Alert entries are tracked so that they can be "read" by each individual user and each user can individually hide an entry.

Managing entries

In both the **Announcements** and **Alerts** portlets, entries are manageable. If you are going to add an entry in the portlet **Announcements** in the page **RSS** of the Guest community, you would be able to do it as shown in the following steps and the screenshot:

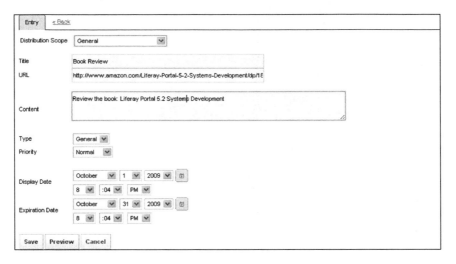

1. Add the **Announcements** portlet in the page "RSS" of the Guest community where you want to manage entries by clicking on **Add | More...** under the dock bar menu.

2. Select the tab **Manage Entries**, and click on the button **Add Entry**.

3. Select **Distribution Scope**—the scope would be portal, community, or role like the following items:

    ○ **General**: Portal instance

    ○ **Communities**: Guest and other communities

    ○ **Roles**: Regular, organization, and community roles

4. Type a title like "Book Review", a URL like `http://www.amazon.com/ Liferay-Portal-5-2-Systems-Development/dp/1847194702`, and enter content like "Review the book: Liferay Portal 5.2 Systems Development".

5. Select the **Type** from the drop-down list: **General, News, Test**. We use the default value **General**.

6. Select the **Priority** from the drop-down list: **Normal, Important**. We use the default value **Normal**.

7. Enter the display date and expiration date—note that the display date and the expiration date should be different.

8. Click on the **Save** button when you are ready.

9. You can preview the entry before saving by clicking on the button **Preview**.

Of course, you would be able to add more entries if you have proper permissions. After adding the entry "Test Social Office", you are able to view and manage entries, as shown in the following screenshot. You can update an entry by clicking on the icon **Edit** next to the entry, or you can delete an entry by clicking on the icon **Delete** next to the entry. In addition, you could mark an entry as "read" by clicking on the link **Mark as Read** next to the entry. Afterwards, the link **Mark as Read** will be changed to **Show**.

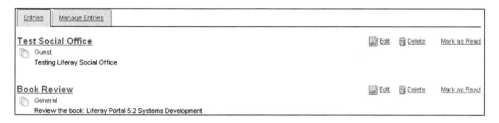

In addition, you would able to configure remote delivery of alerts and announcements. As shown in the next screenshot, remote delivery would be enabled through e-mail and SMS. Each user will have an opportunity to individually configure delivery in the user profile for each configured "type" of announcement entry. Normally, by going to **My Account | Miscellaneous | Announcements**, you would be able to configure your own remote delivery of alerts and announcements.

As a normal user, if you have the proper permission, you would be able to configure other users' remote delivery of alerts and announcements. The following are simple steps to show you how it's done:

1. Go to **Manage | Control Panel** under the dock bar menu.
2. Select **Users** under the category **Portal** of Control Panel.
3. Locate a user, say "Lotti Stein", and click on the icon **Edit** of the **Actions** menu next to the user.
4. Go to **Miscellaneous | Announcements**, you would be able to configure the user's remote delivery of Alerts and Announcements.

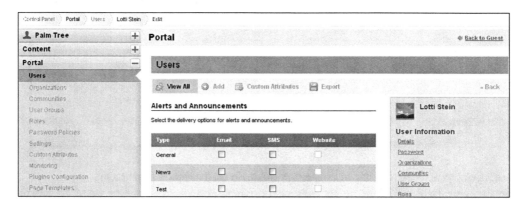

Why Announcements portlet?

The following are the main features of the portlet **Announcements**.

- Being configurable and supporting unlimited number of announcement types.
- Delivery to scopes including general (that is, portal instance), communities, and roles.
- Delivery mechanisms include **Email**, **SMS**, and **Website**. Note that **Website** delivery is achieved simply by adding the portlet to any page accessible to the user.
- Scheduled delivery—each entry has a display date and an expiration date.
- Readable tracking, website delivery tracks time-stamped read status per user, per entry on.
- Subscription control per user and per announcement type.
- Broadcast control of announcements.

What's happening?

The portal sets the following items for e-mail notification announcements by default in `portal.properties`.

- `announcements.email.from.name=Joe Bloggs`
- `announcements.email.from.address=test@liferay.com`
- `announcements.email.to.name=`
- `announcements.email.to.address=noreply@liferay.com`

As shown in the preceding code, e-mail notification settings are configured. The e-mail **FROM** name is **Joe Bloggs** and the e-mail **FROM** Address is `test@liferay.com`. The e-mail **TO** name is **empty** and the e-mail **TO** Address is `noreply@liferay.com`. You will definitely be able to override these settings in `portal-ext.properties`.

In addition, the portal has some specified types of announcements as default settings, as shown in the following lines in `portal.properties`:

```
announcements.entry.types=general,news,test
announcements.entry.check.interval=15
```

As shown in the preceding code, the default types of announcement entries are `general`, `news`, and `test`. The property `announcements.entry.types` sets the list of announcement types, while the property `announcements.entry.check.interval` sets the interval on which the `Check-Entry-Job` will run. The value 15 is set in one minute increments.

Note that the display text of each announcement type, especially custom announcement type, could be set in `$PORTAL_WEB_INF_HOME/classes/content/Language-ext.properties`. How do we achieve it? The following is just an example.

Let's say that you are required to set the announcement types as `general`, `news` and `updates`. You can first override the property `announcements.entry.types` in `portal-ext.properties` as follows.

```
announcements.entry.types=general,news,updates
```

Then create a folder named `content` under the folder `$PORTAL_WEB_INF_HOME/classes`, and create a file named `Language-ext.properties` in the folder `$PORTAL_WEB_INF_HOME/classes/content`. Last but not least, add the following line at the end of the file `Language-ext.properties`.

```
updates=Updates
```

After restarting the application server, you would see the preceding changes on the portlet Announcements.

Assigning permissions

There are two kinds of permissions that you can assign; namely, permissions on portlets and permissions on entries.

The following table shows permissions on the portlets Announcements and Alerts. The role Community Member may set up all permissions (marked as 'X'): **View**, **Configuration**, and **Add Entry**. On the other hand, the role Guest may set up the permission **View**. By default, the role Community Member has the permission action **View** (marked as '*') just like the role Guest.

Action	Description	Community	Guest
View	Ability to view the portlet	X, *	X, *
Configuration	Ability to configure the portlet	X	
Add Entry	Ability to add entry	X	

As you can see, "Lotti Stein", a member of the Guest community, doesn't have the permission **Add Entry**. This means that the tab "Manage Entries" is invisible for "Lotti Stein". If we want "Lotti Stein" to have the ability to add entry, it can be achieved by following these steps:

1. Locate the portlet **Announcements** in the page **RSS**.
2. Go to **More | Configuration | Permissions** on the top-right of the portlet.
3. Check the permission **Add Entry** under the role Community Member.
4. Click on the **Submit** button when you are ready.

The following table shows permissions on entries. The role Community Member may set up all permissions (marked as 'X'): **View**, **Update**, and **Delete**, whereas the role Guest may set up the permission **View**. By default, the role Community Member has the permission action **View** (marked as '*'). On the other hand, the role Guest can have the permission **View** only on entries that have been scoped to general (that is, current portal instance).

Action	Description	Community	Guest
View	Ability to view the entry	X, *	X
Update	Ability to update the entry	X	
Delete	Ability to delete the entry	X	

Obviously, "Lotti Stein", a member of the role "MB Topic Admin", doesn't have the permissions Update and Delete. This means that the icons Edit and Delete next to the entries are invisible for "Lotti Stein". Let's say that "Lotti Stein" should be able to update or delete entries, how do we accomplish it? We can do it by following these steps:

1. Log in as an admin, like "Palm Tree", and go to **Manage | Control Panel** in the dock bar menu.

2. Click on **Roles** under the category **Portal** of **Control Panel**.

3. Locate the role "MB Topic Admin", and click on the icon **Define Permissions** under the **Actions** menu next to the role.

4. Navigate to **Content | Announcements**, and check the permissions **View**, **Update**, and **Delete** under the title **Announcement**.

5. Click on the **Save** button when you are ready.

As shown in the preceding processes, permissions are assigned on all entries related to the announcements through the regular role. Of course, you can assign these permissions through the organization role or the community role. Don't forget that the scopes of the regular role, the organization role, and the community role are different. Note that permission on an individual entry isn't supported yet.

What's different between two portlets?

As you can see, alerts and announcements are similar. Both of them can be used to broadcast some messages to a list of users within a scope, thus providing a one-way messaging engine. Moreover, each type of alert or announcement can be styled to whatever purpose it might serve. However, in fact, they are slightly different.

Announcements are the day-to-day type occurrences, where users can view the history of the announcements they received. However, there is no history view for alerts. More importantly, alerts are hidden by default—that is, the portlet **Alerts** is invisible to the end user unless an alert is published.

Enhancement

As you can see, the portlets **Announcements** and **Alerts** are similar. Both of them even share the same database table AnnouncementsEntry, distinguished only by the column alert (0 represents announcements, whereas 1 represents alerts). Thus, it would be better to merge these two portlets into one. How can we do this?

We can simply add the portlet configuration **type** with values: **Announcement** or **Alert**. If the type has the value **Announcement**, then the portlet would have the same look and feel as that of the portlet Announcements. Otherwise, the portlet would have the same look and feel as that of the portlet Alerts. When you navigate to **More** | **Configuration** | **Setup** | **Current** of the portlet, it will provide you with the capability to select the value of **type** of setup: **Announcement** or **Alert**. Of course, the portlet would be able to archive the setup under **More** | **Configuration** | **Setup** | **Archived** as well.

These two portlets are not localizable. It would be useful to have the text content as a link to an existing journal article. Then we could get the benefits of localization, workflow, versioning, templating, and so on. With such a design, these portlets would be appropriate for Newsletter usage.

Using RSS effectively

Generally speaking, a **web feed** is an XML-based document containing content items with web links to longer versions. For example, common sources for web feeds may include news websites, blogs, and structured information such as weather data, "top ten" lists of hit tunes to search results, and so on. **RSS** and **Atom** are two main web-feed formats.

The Atom applies to two standards. The **Atom Syndication Format (ASF)** is an XML language used for web feeds, and the **Atom Publishing Protocol (APP)** is an HTTP-based protocol for creating and updating web resources.

In general, RSS is used to refer to the following formats:

- Really Simple Syndication (RSS 2.0)
- RDF Site Summary (RSS 1.0 and RSS 0.90)
- Rich Site Summary (RSS 0.91)

Three formats of syndication have emerged: RSS 2.0, RSS 1.0, and Atom. Which feed format do we choose? In general, these three formats are for three goals:

1. The simplest format (although extensible) — RSS 2.0: To display links to articles of a site
2. RSS 1.0: To get information on the feed.
3. Atom: Requires special software to process and has more requirements regarding the format of data.

In short, **RSS** is an XML-based web content syndication format, in compliance with the XML 1.0 specification.

RSS specification

RSS is not a perfect format but is very popular and widely supported. Here, we briefly introduce the RSS 2.0 specification.

 For more details related to RSS specification, refer to http://www.rss-specifications.com/rss-specifications.htm.

An RSS document has an element <rss> with an attribute version at the top level. The attribute version specifies the version of RSS that the document conforms to. Subordinate to the <rss> element is a single element <channel>, which contains information about the channel and its contents.

The following table depicts a list of the required channel elements, each with a brief description:

Element	Description
Title	The name of the channel.
Link	The URL link to the website corresponding to the channel.
Description	Phrase or sentence describing the channel.
Item	One item tag, at least for the content.

For example,

```
<rss version="2.0">
  <channel>
    <title>Integration</title>
    <link>http://liferay.cignex.com/</link>
    <description>LDAP, SSO, Liferay and Alfresco full integration
    </description>
    <item></item>
  </channel>
</rss>
```

A channel may contain any number of items. An item represents content. The description is a synopsis of the content while the link points to the full content.

For example:

```
<item>
    <title>Liferay and Alfresco - RESTFul Integration</title>
    <link>http://liferay.cignex.com/sesame</link>
    <description>Integration based on REST</description>
</item>
```

How does it work?

Suppose there are web pages that we want to display on other websites. The set of web pages is the RSS feed. The RSS system, which publishes articles and news over the web, works as follows:

- An XML file defines the RSS feed that holds the URL, title, and summary of each page to be displayed.

- A user, who wants to read the feed on his/her computer, uses an RSS reader or their browser and just adds the feed with the proper command of its software.

- Alternatively, a user displays the feed on a website—loading the RSS file from the provider by extracting URLs of pages and displaying titles and summaries. The user can also read them with the News Reader software or on the iGoogle page.

- When visiting the website of the receiver, the script is launched first. It recalls the RSS file from the provider's website and displays a list of news from the extracted data.

- Visitors display a page from the provider by clicking on the title of the list.

Summary

This chapter introduced us to adding entries to Blogs, managing (that is, to view, update, and delete) entries of Blogs, and adding comments to a given entry of Blogs first. Then it discussed how to assign permissions on the Blogs portlet and entries of Blogs. It also introduced the ways to publish blogs through the Recent Bloggers portlet and the Blogs Aggregator portlet, and also introduced us to building Blogs with the WYSIWYG editor FCKEditor. Finally, it discussed RSS and other related portlets such as the RSS portlet, Weather portlet, Announcements portlet, and Alerts portlet.

In this chapter, we have learned how to:

- Create blog entries
- View, update, and delete blog entries
- Add comments and rating on blog entries
- Assign permissions on the Blogs portlet and blog entries
- Publish blog entries through the Recent Bloggers portlet and the Blogs Aggregator portlet
- Build blog entries with WYSIWYG editors

- Configure WYSIWYG editors
- Use RSS including the RSS portlet, the Alert portlet, the Announcement portlet, and the Weather portlet.

In the next chapter, we're going to roll out to others teams, while discussing details about their communities and relationships with organizations.

7
Roll Out to Other Teams

In the intranet website "bookpub.com" of the enterprise "Palm Tree Publications", it would be nice to have the ability to build websites with communities, where employees can share interests about the communities Book Street and Book Workshop, and roll out to other teams. The communities provide teams with the ability to create and manage communities and enable their members to build different websites. The community has its own pages, which includes public pages and private pages, content management system, membership management, and permissions management.

Meanwhile it would be nice if we could stage, schedule, and publish web content in our website "bookpub.com" locally or remotely through workflow. As a content creator, you may update what you've created and publish it in a staging area. Then other users could review and modify it in the staging area. Moreover, content editors could make a decision whether to publish web content from the staging to live. Before going live, you may schedule web content as well. For publishing features, you might choose either local publishing or remote publishing; you may publish either the entire website or just a subset of pages.

This chapter will discuss how to manage communities. It will include a discussion of how to create and manage communities, as well as how to create and manage the pages, teams, and members within a community. It will also introduce staging and publishing, workflow, scheduling, virtual hosting, and a set of community tools.

By the end of this chapter, you will have learned how to:

- Manage communities, pages, teams, and memberships of a community
- Apply site templates and page templates
- Employ virtual hosting
- Stage, preview, and publish websites
- Manage staging workflow

- Schedule and publish remotely
- Use community tools

What's a community?

As an administrator at the Enterprise "Palm Tree Publication", you would be required to provide an environment to roll out to other teams. Thus you may provide an environment for users to manage communities, which includes managing pages (both public pages and private pages), managing teams, assigning members, assigning user roles, and so on.

What's community? Loosely speaking, a community is a special group that users in this group would share same of similar interest. In general, a community is a collection of users who have a common interest. Both roles and users can be assigned to a community, as shown in following screenshot:

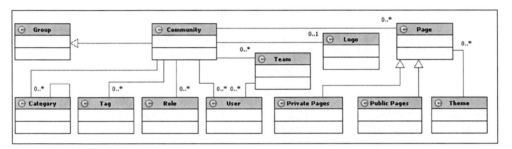

As mentioned earlier, an organization is a special group too. So, you may ask: What's the difference between a community and an organization? When should you use communities instead of organizations? Organizations are hierarchical in nature while communities are flat. But communities give us the ability to join and invite members; organizations don't have this ability. Therefore, if you are planning to build a website and to provide the ability to join and invite members and no hierarchical structure is in need, then use communities. If you are planning to build a website and hierarchical structure is required, then use organization.

In general, communities can be created and managed in two portlets. The first portlet is Enterprise Admin Communities (portlet ID 134) in the **Control Panel**, the second is My Communities (portlet ID 29). Why two portlets? The portlet My Communities provides a way to navigate from community to community, which could be added to any page in current portal instance. We're going to describe the portlet Enterprise Admin Communities first, the portlet My Communities will be introduced in the coming section.

Adding a community

The portlet Enterprise Admin Communities provides the ability to manage communities. Note that this portlet is hidden in the normal access path **Add | More** under the dock bar menu, but it is available in the **Control Panel**.

Supposed that you're going to use the portlet Enterprise Admin Communities as well as to add the communities named "Book Street" and "Book Workshop". First of all, you need to access the portlet Enterprise Admin Communities in the **Control Panel**. Let's do it by following these steps:

1. Log in as an administrator, say Palm Tree.
2. Go to **Manage | Control Panel** under the dock bar menu.
3. Locate **Communities** under the category **Portal** of **Control Panel**.
4. Click on **Communities** under the category **Portal** of **Control Panel**, you would be able to use the portlet Enterprise Admin Communities.

Once you are in the **Control Panel**, you would be able to add the community "Book Street" if you have the proper access right, as shown in following screenshot. Let's do it by following these steps:

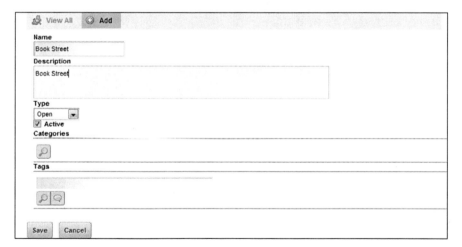

1. Click on **Communities** under the category **Portal** of **Control Panel**, you would be able to see the existing communities like **Guest** and the icons **View All** and **Add** below the title **Communities** if you have proper access rights.
2. Click on the icon **Add** next to the icon **View All**.
3. Type a name like **Book Street** and a description like **Book Street**.

4. Select the type value **Open** if you want users to be able to join and leave this community on their own. There are other type values such as **Restricted** and **Private**. The default type value is **Open**.

   ◦ **Open**: Allows users to join and leave a Community whenever they want to.

   ◦ **Restricted**: Requires a community administrator or owner to add users to the community or to remove users from the community; users don't have ability to join the community. Instead, they could request membership; of course, users have the ability to leave the community.

   ◦ **Private**: The process of adding users doesn't show up at all; neither do users have the ability to join the community, nor do they have the ability to request membership.

5. Enable the checkbox **Active** if you want to activate this community directly.

6. Select proper categories by clicking on the **Select Categories** button.

7. Press the button **Select Tags** or input tag, and then press button **Add Tags** if you need to add tags, or search tags by clicking on the **Suggestions** button.

8. Click on the **Save** button if you want to save the inputs, or click on the **Cancel** button to discard the inputs.

Of course, you can create other communities. After adding the community, say "Book Workshop", with the type **Restricted**, you can view all communities, as shown in the following screenshot:

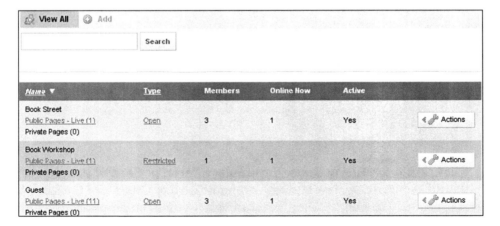

- **Name**: The name of the community plus Public Pages–Live (#number) (if there are any), Private Pages–Live (#number) (if there are any), an orderable column.

- **Type**: Open, Restricted, and Private.
- **Members**: Number of members.
- **Online Now**: Number of members who are online now.
- **Active**: Yes or No.
- **Actions**: A set of icons such as **Edit, Manage Pages, Manage Teams Assign User Roles, Assign Members, Leave** (if the current user is a member already) or **Join** (if the current user isn't a member yet), **Delete.**

 Note that the portal would generate a default system group called the **Guest** community when the portal starts the first time. The group **Guest** can't be deleted because it is a required system group.

Managing communities

After adding a set of communities, you can manage them easily. You can view communities, search, edit, and delete communities as well.

Viewing communities

To view available communities, you need to have proper access rights. You could simply click on **Communities** under the category **Portal** of **Control Panel**. Note that you can only see **Communities** when you are a member of any communities in the current portal instance.

As shown in following screenshot, communities will appear with **Name, Type, Members, Online Now**, and **Actions** button with a set of icons such as **Edit, Manage Pages, Manage Teams, Assign Members, Assign User Roles, Leave, Delete**, and so on.

- **Edit**: Update current community.
- **Permissions**: Assign permissions on individual community.
- **Manage Pages**: Manage public pages and private pages of current community.
- **Manage Teams**: Manage teams for current community, like adding a new team, updating existing teams, assigning users and deleting existing teams.
- **Assign User Roles**: Assign community-scoped roles to users.
- **Assign Member**: Assign users to the community as members.
- **Request Membership**: Users would be able to request membership on a given restricted community.

- **View Membership Requests**: The community owner would be able to view membership requests of a restricted community and also be able to approve or deny membership requests.

- **Join/Leave**: Join the community if the current user isn't a member of the community, or leave the community if the current user is a member of the community.

- **Delete**: Delete the current community from the current portal instance.

We can see the columns in communities. Note that you can only see the communities of which you are a member. In other words, if you aren't a member of a community, you wouldn't be able to view that community.

Searching communities

To search communities, you could simply type the search criteria in a search input field first. Then click on the **Search** button. The portlet will list the search results, that is, a list of communities, while each community has columns like **Name**, **Type**, **number of Members**, **number of Online Now**, and **Actions** button with a set of icons, for example, **Edit**, **Manage Pages**, **Manage Teams**, **Assign Members**, **Assign User Role**, **Leave**, **Delete**, and so on.

Note that you would be able to only search a set of communities of which you are a member. In other words, if you aren't a member of one community, you wouldn't be able to find that community by search.

Editing a community

Suppose that you want to update the description of the community "Book Street" from "Book Street" to "A community for Book Street", the following are the steps we will follow:

1. Log in as an administrator, say "Palm Tree".

2. Go to **Manage | Control Panel** under the dock bar menu.

3. Locate **Communities** under the category **Portal** of **Control Panel**.

4. Click on **Communities** under the category **Portal** of **Control Panel**.

5. Locate a community, let's say "Book Street", you want to delete.

6. Click on the **Edit** icon from the **Actions** button next to the community "Book Street".

7. Type the changes like "A community for Book Street" in the **Description** field, as shown in the previous screenshot.

8. Click on the **Save** button if you want to save the changes, or click on the **Cancel** button if you want to cancel these actions.

 Note that when editing a community, you would see **Group ID** for the current community. In this example, you would see the **Group ID** with value **10262**. Make a note on the **Group ID**, as you will require this ID later in remote publishing.

Deleting a community

Suppose that the community "Book Workshop" doesn't exist anymore, you're going to delete it. The following are the simple steps to delete the community "Book Workshop".

1. Click on **Communities** under the category **Portal** of **Control Panel**.

2. Locate a community, let's say **Book Workshop**, you want to edit.

3. Click on the **Delete** icon from the **Actions** button on the right of the community **Book Workshop**.

4. A screen will appear asking if you want to delete the selected community. Click on the **OK** button to delete, or click on the **Cancel** button if you don't want to delete the selected community.

Note that deleting a community will delete all pages that belong to the community. At the same time, the links of all users and roles assigned to the community will get released immediately

Managing pages

A community is just a shell that can contain a set of pages, both public pages and private pages. Via the portlet Enterprise Admin Communities, you would be able to manage the pages of a given community if you have the proper access right.

Viewing pages

To view pages of a community, first locate a community, for example, "Book Street" community in the **Control Panel**. Then click on the **Manage Pages** icon from the **Actions** tab next to the right of the community. The pages that belong to the "Book Street" community are displayed in a tree structure on the left. Every page can have child pages, as shown in the following screenshot. To actually view these pages in the portal, use the **View Pages** button.

To view all pages in the tree structure, simply click on the **Expand All** button. While to view only top-level pages and the root node, that is, community name in the tree structure, simply click on the **Collapse All** button.

To view all pages in public pages, simply click on the **Public Pages** tab. Similarly, to view all pages in private pages, simply click on the **Private Pages** tab.

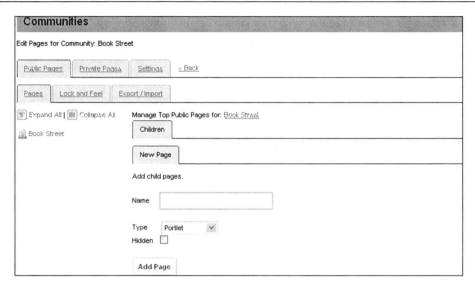

In brief, you can add, edit, and delete the pages and assign permissions on individual page. You may use following functional items, but you are not limited to do so. By the way, you can re-order pages by dragging and dropping pages, thus you can change the parent/children relation between pages. In addition, you should have the ability to search pages through the advanced options for pages, keywords, title, description, languages, and so on.

- **Public Pages**: Managing public pages of the current community.
- **Private Pages**: Managing private pages of the current community.
- **Settings**: Changing settings of the current community.
- **Pages**: Managing pages and their child pages of either public pages or private pages.
- **Look and Feel**: Changing themes of either public pages or private pages.
- **Export/Import**: Exporting all pages, either public pages or private pages, of the current community to LAR files, importing LAR files to the current community, either public pages or private pages.

Importing and exporting pages

Data export and import generally revolve around the concept of storing data outside the portal permanently or temporarily. The portal does this by handling the creation and interpretation of the LAR files. The functions of data export and import are portlet-wise. In the portlet Enterprise Admin Communities, you would be able to export all pages, either public pages or private pages, of a given community to a LAR file. What would you like to export? The following are possible items you may include, but not limited.

- **Pages**: By default.
- **Portlets**: By default including Setup, Archived Setup, User preferences, Data, and so on.
- **Permissions**: The permissions assigned for the exported pages and individual portlet windows will be included if this option is checked.
- **Theme**: When selected on export, the top-level theme and all of its files will be included in the resulting LAR files. When selected on import, the theme will be installed and all the pages will be configured to use it.
- **Categories**: When selected, all categories will be exported or imported, keeping their hierarchy. During import, duplicate categories will not be created if a category with the same name already exists.

We have discussed what you would like to export. Now, let's export pages in a given community, for example, "Book Street" by following these steps:

1. Click on **Communities** under the category **Portal** of **Control Panel**.
2. Locate a community, let's say "Book Street", that you want to export and/or import.
3. Click on the **Manage Pages** icon from the **Actions** button on the right of the community "Book Street".
4. Select pages, either public pages or private pages. Let's say that you're going to export public pages, click on the **Public Pages** tab.
5. Click on the **Export/Import** tab. As you can see, the tab **Export** would be selected by default.
6. If you click on the **Export** tab, it will export all pages (public pages in this example), their layouts, their configurations, their look and feel, and their permissions to a LAR file (Liferay Archive). After clicking on the Export tab, you would be asked to export the selected data to the given LAR filename and to select what you would like to export.
7. Click on the **Export** button. The portal will generate a LAR file and asks you to save it locally.

Of course, you could be able to export private pages too. To do so, first click on the **Private Pages** tab, and go to the **Export/Import** tab. The tab **Export** would be selected by default.

If necessary, you can import a LAR file into the current community by following these steps:

1. Select pages (either public pages or private pages). Let's say that you're going to import into public pages. Click on the **Public Pages** tab.

2. Click on the **Export/Import** tab.

3. After clicking on the **Import** tab, you would be asked to import (upload) a LAR file to overwrite the selected data and to select what you would like to import.

4. Click on the **Import** button. The portal will overwrite the selected data of the current community.

Of course, you could be able to import into private pages too. To do so, first click on the **Private Pages** tab, and go to the **Export/Import** tab. Then click on the **Import** tab. Moreover, you would have the ability to merge data and to manage the ID of resources. A warning about the fact that you can export permissions on resources but not on users (not even roles). Therefore, roles and users have to be the same, on source and target.

 Note that LAR is short for Liferay Archive. It includes all of the pages, their layouts, their configurations, their look and feel, their permissions, and so on. Importing a LAR file will overwrite any existing pages of a given community configured in the LAR file.

Updating look and feel of pages

Besides the ability to export and/or import either private pages or public pages, you would have ability to changing themes, that is, the look and feel of these pages as well. In general, each page must have a theme associated, all pages, from either public pages or private pages, could share the same theme.

Let's say that you are going to apply the theme **so-theme** on the public pages of the community "Book Street". There are two tasks you have to accomplish: Firstly, deploy the theme so-theme. Secondly, apply the theme so-theme on public pages. How to implement it? The following are the steps:

1. Download the theme ${so-theme-war} from http://liferay.cignex. com/palm_tree/book/0387/chapter07/so-theme-6.0.0.1.war.

2. Drop WAR file ${so-theme-war} to the folder $LIFERAY_HOME/deploy. The portal will deploy it automatically, when the portal is running.

3. Click on **Communities** under the category **Portal** of **Control Panel**.

4. Locate a community, let's say "Book Street", where you want to update the theme.

5. Click on the **Manage Pages** icon from the **Actions** button on the right of the community "Book Street".

6. Select pages, either public pages or private pages. Let's say that you're going to apply a theme on a public page. Click on the **Public Pages** tab.

7. Click on the **Look and Feel** tab, you would see the available themes like **Classic**, **Social Office**, and so on.

8. Click on the theme **so-theme**.

As shown in this processes, themes can be applied to either public or private pages, as the default value of "Use the general look and feel for the public pages?" is **Yes**. Of course, you would be able to apply a theme on an individual page. How you may ask? Locate a page say "Home" and click on it. You would see the tab **Look and Feel**. By selecting the tab **Look and Feel**, you would be able to apply themes to the current page individually.

Uploading a logo

As mentioned earlier, each community can have a logo as its enterprise logo. Thus we could upload a logo as the enterprise logo of a community. If no logo has been uploaded, then the community would use the default enterprise logo for public and private pages.

Let's say that you are going to upload a logo called `BookStreet_logo.png` on the pages of the community "Book Street". You may be wondering how to upload the logo? The following are the steps that you may take. It is shown in the following screenshot:

1. Click on **Communities** under the category **Portal** of **Control Panel**.

2. Locate a community, say "Book Street", that you want to export and/or import.

3. Click on the **Manage Pages** icon from the **Actions** button on the right of the community "Book Street".

4. Click on the tab **Settings**. You would then see a sub tab **Logo** that has been selected by default. You can upload a logo for all pages that will be used instead of the default enterprise logo.

5. Upload the file BookStreet_logo.png by clicking on the button **Choose File**.

6. In order to make the logo active, you need to enable the checkbox **Use Logo**. By default, the checkbox **Use Logo** is checked.

7. Click on the **Save** button whenever you are ready.

Note that some themes will support uploading logo, but others may not. For example, the default theme **Classic** will support uploading logo, but the theme **so-theme** doesn't, as the theme **so-theme** overrides the company logo. In the theme **Classic**, we have the following code in $PORTAL_ROOT_HOME/html/themes/classic/templates/portal_normal.vm

```
<h1 class="logo">
<a class="png" href="$company_url">$the_title - $company_name</a>
<span class="current-community">$community_name</span>
</h1>
```

But in the theme **so-theme**, we have following code in $AS_WEB_APP_HOME/so-theme/templates/portal_normal.vm.

```
<h1 class="logo">
#if ($is_signed_in)
<a class="png" href="$themeDisplay.getPathFriendlyURLPublic()/$user.
getScreenName()">
#else
<a class="png" href="$company_url">
#end
<span>$company_name</span>
</a>
</h1>
```

As you can see, there are a set of sub tabs under the tab **Settings**. The following is a list of some of them.

- **Logo**: Uploading a logo for both public and private pages
- **Virtual Hosting**: Setting public and private virtual hosts and a friendly URL for the current community
- **Sitemap**: Setting sitemap protocol for the current community
- **Monitoring**: Tracking all the pages of the current community
- **Merge Pages**: Merging pages of the Guest community
- **Staging**: Setting staging and workflow

Merging pages

More interestingly, you would be able to configure the top-level public pages of the current community (any communities except the default one **Guest**) to merge with the top level pages of the public pages of the Guest community. Therefore, users can then navigate between the two sites more seamlessly.

Let's say that you need to merge the top level public pages of the Guest community into the public pages of the community "Book Street", you may ask how are we going to achieve it? The following are the steps:

1. Click on **Communities** under the category **Portal** of **Control Panel**.
2. Locate a community, let's say "Book Street", you want to merge.
3. Click on **Manage Pages** icon from the **Actions** button on the right of the community "Book Street".
4. Click on the tab **Settings**. You would see a list of tabs including the **Merge Pages** tab.
5. Click on the tab **Merge Pages**.
6. Enable the checkbox **Merge Guest Public Pages**.
7. Click on the **Save** button.

Note that you can merge only the top-level public pages of the Guest community into the public pages of a community, except the Guest community. In other words, non-top pages of the public pages of the Guest community shouldn't be involved, only public pages of communities, including Guest, are included, not private pages.

In fact, the pages of the public pages of the **Guest** community aren't copied to a target community. Only a link called `mergeGuestPublicPages=true` in the column `typeSettings` of the table `Group_` was generated. When the link is set as `mergeGuestPublicPages=false`, the feature `mergeGuestPublicPages` would be disabled.

Monitoring pages

Let's say that you're going to use **Google Analytics** (GA) to generate detailed statistics about the visitors to a website. Let's do it by following these steps:

1. Click on **Communities** under the category **Portal** of **Control Panel**.
2. Locate a community, let's say "Book Street", you want to monitor.
3. Click on the **Manage Pages** icon from the **Actions** button on the right of the community "Book Street".

4. Click on the tab **Settings**. You would see a list of tabs including the **Merge Pages** tab.

5. Click on the **Monitoring** tab. Set the **Google Analytics ID** that will be used for this set of pages.

6. Set the **Google Analytics ID** to something like **UA-5808951-1**.

7. Click on the **Save** button to save the inputs.

 Google Analytics generates detailed statistics about the visitors to a website. Refer to http://www.google.com/analytics.

These processes set the **Google Analytics ID** that will be used to track this set of pages. What's happening? In the file $PORTAL_ROOT_HOME/html/portlet/communities/edit_pages_settings.jsp, it sets the value UA-5808951-1 of the group property googleAnalyticsId as follows.

```
<table class="lfr-table"> <tr> <td>
<liferay-ui:message key="google-analytics-id" />
</td> <td> <%
String googleAnalyticsId = PropertiesParamUtil.
getString(groupTypeSettings, request, "googleAnalyticsId");
%>
<input name="<portlet:namespace />googleAnalyticsId" size="30"
type="text" value="<%= HtmlUtil.escape(googleAnalyticsId) %>" />
</td> </tr> </table>
```

In the file $PORTAL_ROOT_HOME/html/common/themes/bottom.jsp, it checks the group property googleAnalyticsId and consumes this property to generate the following pages:

```
<%
UnicodeProperties groupTypeSettings = layout.getGroup().
getTypeSettingsProperties();
String googleAnalyticsId = groupTypeSettings.getProperty("googleAnaly
ticsId");
if (Validator.isNotNull(googleAnalyticsId)) {
%>
<script type="text/javascript">
var gaJsHost = (("https:" == document.location.protocol) ? "https://
ssl." : "http://www.");
document.write(unescape("%3Cscript src='" + gaJsHost + "google-
analytics.com/ga.js' type='text/javascript'%3E%3C/script%3E"));
</script>
<script type="text/javascript">
```

```
var pageTracker = _gat._getTracker("<%= googleAnalyticsId %>");
pageTracker._trackPageview();
</script>
<% } %>
```

This process sets **Google Analytics ID** to trace all pages of a given community. How can we track all pages of the entire portal? Here we give a sample:

1. First, get an account from Google Analytics. Your account ID will be a string of letters and numbers, for example **UA-5808951-1**. You should use your own account number in the code.

2. Then, locate the JSP file `bottom-ext.jsp` under the folder `$PORTAL_ROOT_HOME/html/common/themes`. Add the following lines at the end of the JSP file and save it.

    ```
    <script type="text/javascript">
    var gaJsHost = (("https:" == document.location.protocol) ?
    "https://ssl." : "http://www.");
    document.write(unescape("%3Cscript src='" + gaJsHost +
    "googleanalytics.
    com/ga.js' type='text/javascript'%3E%3C/script%3E"));
    </script>
    <script type="text/javascript">
    var pageTracker = _gat._getTracker("UA-5808951-1");
    pageTracker._trackPageview();
    </script>
    ```

As shown in the preceding code, it uses a single Google Analytics account **UA-5808951-1** to track all pages of the entire portal. Or you can use `portal-ext.properties` to store this ID and call it here with `PropsUtils`. In addition, you would be able to integrate other web analytics like **WebTrends Analytics** in the same pattern.

> Webtrends Analytics is a Web analytics tool that collects and presents information about user behavior on web sites. Refer to `http://www.webtrends.com`.

Sitemap

What is a Sitemap? A Sitemap is protocol to help search engines crawl the website and make sure that all the relevant stuff gets indexed. The sitemap protocol notifies search engines of the structure (sitemap) of the website. In brief, sitemaps are an easy way for webmasters to inform search engines about pages on their sites that are available for crawling. For more details, refer to *Chapter 10, Search, WAP, CRM, Widgets, Reporting and Auditing.*

How to use it? It's actually pretty simple since the portal generates the sitemap XML automatically for all public websites. The following are the steps to configure sitemaps in our example.

1. Click on **Communities** under the category **Portal** of **Control Panel**.
2. Locate a community, say "Book Street", you want to set a Sitemap to.
3. Click on the **Manage Pages** icon from the **Actions** button on the right of the community "Book Street".
4. Click on the tab **Settings**. You would see a list of tabs including the **Merge Pages** tab.
5. Click on the **Sitemap** tab. You would be able to send sitemap information to preview or to configure sitemaps like Google or Yahoo!.

By default, the portal supports sitemaps Google and Yahoo!. The sitemap Yahoo! requires login though. Note that the sitemap protocol notifies search engines of the structure (that is, sitemap) of the website, as well as the pages of the current community (public and private pages).

How to customize the sitemap? The sitemap protocol allows us to set the following parameters for each page of the website.

- **Change Frequency**: Always, Hourly, Daily, Weekly, Monthly, Yearly, Never.
- **Page Priority**: A number from 0.0 to 1.0 indicating the priority of the page relative to other pages of the website.
- **Include**: Yes, No.

To set up a sitemap for a community go to **Manage Pages** of a community. Under the tab **Public Pages** and the sub tab **Pages**, locate a page, for example "Home". Then select the tab **Page**, and expand **Meta Robots** of current page, where you can set up the sitemap protocol. Similarly you can manage teams of a specific community. In general, you can have many teams for a given community. You can then manage these teams by clicking on the **Manage Teams** icon from **Actions** to the right of the community and assign members to teams.

Bringing users into the communities

As mentioned earlier, you would have the ability to assign users to communities if you have proper access control. You are also able to assign users to community roles for a given community. And moreover, users would have the ability to join or leave an open community. More interestingly, you would be able to request membership in a given community as a member, or you would be able to approve or deny membership request as an owner of a given community. This section will bring users into communities.

Assigning users

A community can have a set of users as its members, for instance, the user "Lotti Stein" isn't a member of the community "Book Street" yet. Now as an administrator, you want to assign the user "Lotti Stein" to the community "Book Street", as shown in following screenshot. How do we implement it? Just follow these steps:

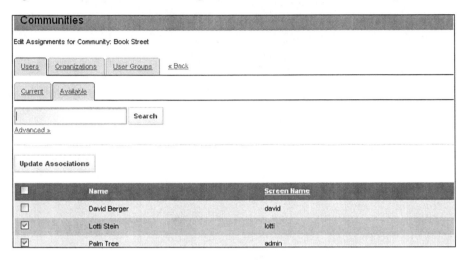

1. Log in as an administrator, let's say "Palm Tree".
2. Go to **Manage | Control Panel** under the dock bar menu.
3. Click on **Communities** under the category **Portal** of **Control Panel**, you would see a list of communities.
4. Locate a community say "Book Street", and click on the icon **Assign Members** from the **Actions** button next to the right of the community. By default, the tab **Users** and the sub tab **Users | Current** are selected.
5. Click on the tab **Users | Available**, and locate the user "Lotti Stein". By the way, you could find the user by search.
6. Enable the checkbox next to the left of the user "Lotti Stein", and click on the **Update Associations** button.

Similarly, you would be able to assign users of organizations and/or user groups into a community indirectly.

- `Users`: assigning selected users into a community
- `Organizations`: assigning users of selected organizations into a community
- `User Groups`: assigning users of selected user groups into a community

Note that if a user says "Lotti Stein" has been assigned into a community via both Users and Organizations, only one record would be saved in the database. As you can see, this is a more flexible approach to assign users to a community.

Assign User Roles

As stated earlier, **Assign User Roles** allows us to assign community-scoped roles to users. By default, communities are created with three community-scoped roles: Community Administrator, Community Member, and Community Owner, as shown in following screenshot. In general, you can assign one or more of these roles to users in a community if you have proper access rights. Note that all members of a community will get the role Community Member.

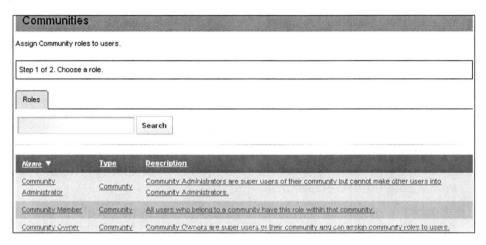

- `Community Administrator`: They are super users of their community but cannot make other users into Community Administrators
- `Community Member`: All users who belong to a community have this role within that community
- `Community Owner`: These are super users of their community and can assign community roles to users

Generally speaking, there are two steps to assign community roles to users: to choose a role and to assign community roles to users. For example, the user "Lotti Stein" is a member of the community "Book Street". Now as an administrator, you want to assign the user "Lotti Stein" to the community role **Community Owner**. How can we implement it? The following are sample steps:

1. Log in as an administrator, say "Palm Tree".
2. Go to **Manage | Control Panel** under the dock bar menu.

3. Click on **Communities** under the category **Portal** of **Control Panel**, you would see a list of communities.

4. Locate a community say "Book Street", and click on the icon **Assign User Roles** from the **Actions** button next to the right of the community.

5. Choose a community role says "Community Owner". By default, the tab **Users** and the sub tab **Users | Current** are selected.

6. Click on the tab **Users | Available**, and locate the user "Lotti Stein". By the way, you could find the user by search.

7. Enable the checkbox next to the left of the user "Lotti Stein", and click on the **Update Associations** button.

Join

As mentioned earlier, the portal provides the ability to allow users to join an open community and become members of the community. For example, as a user say "Lotti Stein" of the enterprise "Palm Tree Publication", you're going to join the community "Book Street". Let's simply do it in a sequence by following these steps:

1. Log in as a user, say "Lotti Stein".

2. Go to **Manage | Control Panel** under the dock bar menu.

3. Click on **Communities** under the category **Portal** of **Control Panel**, you would see a list of communities.

4. Locate a community, say "Book Street", and click on the icon **Join** next to the right of the community, you would see that the icon **Join** would now become the icon **Leave**.

Leave

As mentioned earlier, the portal provides the ability to allow a member of the community to leave the community. For example, as a user, say "Lotti Stein", of the enterprise "Palm Tree Publication", you are a member of the community "Book Street". For some reasons, you may want to leave this community. How do we achieve it? Let's do it in sequence by following these steps:

1. Log in as a user, say "Lotti Stein".

2. Go to **Manage | Control Panel** under the dock bar menu.

3. Click on **Communities** under the category **Portal** of **Control Panel**, you would see a list of communities.

4. Locate a community says "Book Street", and click on the icon **Leave** next to the right of the community, you would see that the icon **Leave** would now become the icon **Join** for an open community. From now on, you would have a chance to join the community later.

Requesting membership

As mentioned earlier, users could request membership on restricted communities, and the community owners of a given restricted community could be able to view membership requests of restricted communities and then approve or deny membership requests. Of course, these membership request processes are only available for **Restricted** communities. How does it work?

For example, as a user, "Lotti Stein" of the enterprise "Palm Tree Publication" wants to be a member of a restricted community like "Book Workshop". How can we set this up? Let's do it by following these steps:

1. Log in as a user, say "Lotti Stein".

2. Go to **Manage | Control Panel** under the dock bar menu.

3. Click on **Communities** under the category **Portal** of **Control Panel**, you would see a list of communities.

4. Locate a community, let's say "Book Workshop", and click on the icon **Request Membership** next to the right of the community.

5. Then input comments like "my favorite website" and click on the **Save** button to save the changes. Your membership request is pending and you would see the icon **Request Membership** next to the right of the community.

Note that once this membership request gets approved, the user "Lotti Stein" would see the icon **Request Membership** becoming the icon **Leave**. From now on, the user "Lotti Stein" would have the ability to leave the community, that is, the restricted community.

Of course, any users could send membership requests on any restricted communities. The community owner would handle these membership requests. For instance, the community owner, like "Palm Tree", is going to handle membership requests on the restricted community like "Book Workshop". How do we accomplish it? Let's do it by following these steps:

1. Log in as a community owner, say "Palm Tree".

2. Go to **Manage | Control Panel** under the dock bar menu.

3. Click on **Communities** under the category **Portal** of **Control Panel**, you would see a list of communities.

4. Locate a community, for example "Book Workshop", and click on the icon **View Membership Requests** on the right of the community, you would see a list of pending membership requests, as shown in the following screenshot:

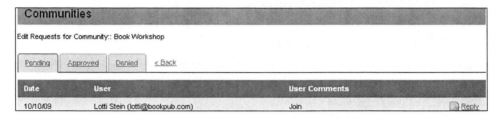

5. Locate a request, for example "Lotti Stein", and click on the icon **Reply** next to the right of the membership request.

6. Choose the status, **Approve** or **Deny**. Let's say you selected **Approve**, and input comments like "Welcome" optionally.

7. Click on the **Save** button to save the inputs, or click on the **Cancel** button to discard inputs. You would be able to view the approved membership request or denied membership request, and you can go back to **Communities** by clicking on the link **Back**.

Note that only community owners would have the ability to view membership requests in a given restricted community.

- **Pending**: A set of pending membership requests with Date, user, User Comments, and an icon Reply. The community owner would be able to approve or to deny membership request.

- **Approved**: A set of approved membership requests with Date, user, User Comments, Reply Date, Replier, and Reply Comments.

- **Denied**: A set of denied membership requests with Date, user, User Comments, Reply Date, Replier, and Reply Comments.

As shown in the preceding code, all membership requests of a given restricted community will go to the **Pending** tab first. Once the request has been approved, it will go to the **Approval** tab, and the user will be a member of the restricted community. Otherwise, once the request got denied, it will go to the **Denied** tab, and the user will not be a member of the currently restricted community.

Assigning permissions

As mentioned earlier, the portlet Enterprise Admin Communities is available only in the **Control Panel**. If a user like "Lotti Stein" was a member of a community like "Guest" in the current portal instance, then the user would be able to access the portlet Enterprise Admin Communities in the **Control Panel**, and she would have the ability to manage the pages of the current community by going to **Manage | Page** and **Add | Page** under the dock bar menu. This is convenient to access the portlet Enterprise Admin Communities and to manage pages of the community. This is not a standard approach. Normally the portlet Enterprise Admin Communities should be accessed through permission action **Access in Control Panel**, and the ability to manage pages of a community via permission **Manage Pages**. In this section, we're going to discuss permissions on a portlet, permission in a community, and the differences between community and organization.

Permissions on the portlet Enterprise Admin Communities

The following table shows permissions on the portlet Enterprise Admin Communities. The role Community Member may set up all permissions (marked as 'X'): **View**, **Configuration**, and **Access in Control Panel**, while the role Guest may set up the permission **View**. The by default action of the roles Community Member and Guest are **View** (marked as '*') **permission**.

Action	Description	Community	Guest
View	Ability to view the portlet	X, *	X, *
Configuration	Ability to configure the portlet	X	
Access in Control Panel	Ability to access the portlet in the Control Panel	X	

Let's say the user "David Berger", a member of the role "MB Topic Admin", was not a member of any communitiy. As an administrator, like "Palm Tree", you are required to grant the permission **Access in Control Panel** on the portlet Enterprise Admin Communities for the user "Lotti Stein", and also grant permission **Add Community** too. How do we accomplish this? We do it by following these steps:

1. Log in as an admin, say "Palm Tree".

2. Click on **Roles** under the category **Portal** of **Control Panel** first.

3. Then locate a role, say "MB Topic Admin".

4. Click on the **Define Permissions** icon from the **Actions** next to the right of the role.
5. Click on the **Portal | General** link, enable the checkbox **Add Community**.
6. Click on the **Save** button.
7. Click on **Applications | Communities** link, enable the checkboxes: **Access in Control Panel** and **View**.
8. Click on the **Save** button.

From now on, users and the members of the role "MB Topic Admin", will have access on the portlet Enterprise Admin Communities in the **Control Panel**. Moreover, they would have the ability to add new communities, seeing an **Add** icon next to the right of the icon **View All** under the title **Communities**.

Permissions on communities

The following table shows permissions on a community. The role Community Member may set up all permissions (marked as 'X'): **Approve Proposal**, **Assign Members**, **Assign Reviewer**, **Assign User Roles**, **Delete**, **Manage Announcements**, **Manage Archived Setups**, **Manage Pages**, **Manage Teams**, **Manage Staging**, **Permissions**, **Publish Staging**, **Update**, and **View**. All permission actions are unsupported for the role Guest.

Action	Description	Community	Guest
Approve Proposal	Ability to approve proposals	X	
Assign Members	Ability to assign members	X	
Assign Reviewer	Ability to assign reviewers	X	
Assign User Roles	Ability to assign users to community roles	X	
Delete	Ability to delete the community	X	
Manage Announcements	Ability to manage announcements	X	
Manage Archived Setups	Ability to manage archived setups	X	
Manage Pages	Ability to manage pages	X	
Manage Teams	Ability to manage teams	X	
Manage Staging	Ability to manage staging pages	X	
Permissions	Ability to assign permissions on the community	X	
Publish Staging	Ability to publish staging pages	X	
Update	Ability to update the community	X	
View	Ability to view the community	X	

As mentioned, the user "David Berger", a member of the role "MB Topic Admin", was not a member of any community, as an administrator like "Palm Tree", he wants to have the ability to manage pages of any community, How do we accomplish it? We can do it by following these steps:

1. Log in as an admin, say "Palm Tree".
2. Click on **Roles** under the category **Portal** of **Control Panel** first.
3. Then locate a role, say "MB Topic Admin".
4. Click on the **Define Permissions** icon from the **Actions** tab next to the role.
5. Click on the **Portal | Communities** link, enable the checkbox **Manage Pages**.
6. Click on the **Save** button.
7. As shown in the preceding processes, it grants permission **Manage Pages** for the role "MB Topic Admin" on all communities in the current portal instance. As a member of the role "MB Topic admin", "David Berger" would see **Manage | Page** and **Add | Page** under the dock bar menu in any community.

Of course, you can grant the permission **Manage Pages** on an individual community. Let's say that you roll back the preceding processes and you're going to assign the permission **Manage Pages** on the community "Book Workshop" for the user "David Berger". How do we implement it? The following is an option:

1. Log in as an admin, say "Palm Tree".
2. Click on **Communities** under the category **Portal** of **Control Panel** first.
3. Then locate the icon **Permissions of the actions** button next to the community "Book Workshop".
4. Enable the checkbox **Manage Pages** under the role "MB Topic Admin".
5. Click on the **Submit** button.

As shown in the preceding processes, it grants the permission **Manage Pages** on the community "Book Workshop" for the role "MB Topic Admin" only.

What's the difference between community and organization?

As mentioned earlier, community and organization are similar. Both of them are special groups, as shown in following image. Both of them may have a logo, their pages may be either public or private. Both of them can have a set of users as members, who are associated with different roles. Moreover, you can tag both community and organization with tags and categories.

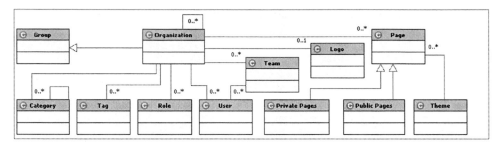

Although community and organization look similar in many aspects, they are different in several ways. Of course, it would be nice that community and organization could be merged into one in a future release.

First of all, community has a flat structure, while organization has a hierarchical structure. Thus a community can't have parent or children, while organization can have a parent organization and many child organizations. The leaves of a hierarchy are called locations. Some of their leaves can be locations.

Secondly, only community has ability to join and invite members, while an organization can't. However, an organization could have identification like Addresses, Phone Numbers, Additional E-mail Addresses, Websites, Services, miscellaneous like Comments and Reminder Queries, and so on.

Thirdly, permission actions on both community and organization are a little bit different. The following table shows permissions on organizations. The role Organization Member may set up all permissions (marked as 'X'): **Approve Proposal, Assign Members, Assign Reviewer, Assign User Roles, Delete, Manage Announcements, Manage Archived Setups, Manage Pages, Manage Teams, Manage Staging, Manage Sub-Organizations, Manage Users, Permissions, Publish Staging, Update,** and **View**. All permission actions are unsupported for the role Guest. Moreover, the permission actions **Manage Sub-Organizations** and **Manage Users** are available on organization, not community.

Action	Description	Organization	Guest
Approve Proposal	Ability to approve proposals	X	
Assign Members	Ability to assign members	X	
Assign Reviewer	Ability to assign reviewers	X	
Assign User Roles	Ability to assign users to organization roles	X	
Delete	Ability to delete the organization	X	
Manage Announcements	Ability to manage announcement	X	
Manage Archived Setups	Ability to manage archived setups	X	
Manage Pages	Ability to manage pages	X	
Manage Teams	Ability to manage teams	X	
Manage Staging	Ability to manage staging pages	X	
Manage Sub-organizations	Ability to manage sub-organizations of organizations	X	
Manage Users	Ability to manage users of organizations	X	
Permissions	Ability to assign permissions on the organization	X	
Publish Staging	Ability to publish staging pages	X	
Update	Ability to update the organization	X	
View	Ability to view the organization	X	

Last but not least, both community and organization have their own roles. Community roles are scoped into communities. Therefore, users of communities would be available to both community roles and regular roles. While organization roles are scoped into organizations. Thus, users of organizations would be available to both organization roles and regular roles.

- **Organization Administrator**: Super users of their organization, but cannot make other users into Organization Administrators.

- **Organization Member**: All users who belong to an organization have this role within that organization.

- **Organization Owner**: Super users of their organization and can assign organization roles to users.

When assigning users to organization roles, only the tab Users is available. This means that you can't assign users of user groups or communities into organization roles. But for community roles, you could assign users and users of organizations or user groups. For regular roles, you could assign users and users of organizations, communities, or user groups.

As you can see, community and organization are almost same. Why not merge these two terminologies into one? Of course, communities and organizations could be merged into one, providing there is some hierarchical structure and the ability to join and invite members. This feature isn't ready yet, but highly expected. Hopefully, it will be ready in future version.

What's happening?

As stated earlier, the portlet Enterprise Admin Communities is available in the **Control Panel**. What's happening? When membership requests have been approved or denied, e-mails would be sent to requestors. How to set it up you ask?

Settings

The portal sets the following properties in `portal.properties` by default.

```
communities.email.from.name=Joe Bloggs
communities.email.from.address=test@liferay.com
communities.email.membership.reply.subject=com/liferay/portlet/
communities/dependencies/email_membership_reply_subject.tmpl
communities.email.membership.reply.body=com/liferay/portlet/
communities/dependencies/email_membership_reply_body.tmpl
communities.email.membership.request.subject=com/liferay/portlet/
communities/dependencies/email_membership_request_subject.tmpl
communities.email.membership.request.body=com/liferay/portlet/
communities/dependencies/email_membership_request_body.tmpl
```

This code sets the e-mail FROM name via the property `communities.email.from.name` and the e-mail FROM address via the property `communities.email.from.address`. Of course, you can override them in `portal-ext.properties`.

Email notification settings for membership reply and request are configurable too. Thus the subject and body of membership reply and request are specified as TMPL files. Obviously, you could customize these setting through overriding TMPL files in `portal-ext.properties`. These settings should be configurable through web UI too. Unfortunately, this feature isn't available at the time of writing, but it is highly expected.

In addition, the portal has the following settings to add the ability to configure the portlet Enterprise Admin Communities in the **Control Panel**.

```
communities.control.panel.members.visible=true
```

This code sets the property to `true` to allow community members to see the Communities portlet and the communities he/she is a member of in the **Control Panel**. Of course, you can set the property to `false` in `portal-ext.properties`, and it will only allow administrators to see the portlet in the **Control Panel**.

Configuration

The portal has default settings for the portlet Enterprise Admin Communities as follows in `$PORTAL_ROOT_HOME/WEB-INF/liferay-portlet.xml`.

```
<control-panel-entry-category>portal</control-panel-entry-category>
<control-panel-entry-weight>3.0</control-panel-entry-weight>
<control-panel-entry-class>com.liferay.portlet.enterpriseadmin.
CommunitiesControlPanelEntry</control-panel-entry-class>
```

This code shows that the portlet Enterprise Admin Communities will appear in the category **Content** of the **Control Panel**, position 3, and the tag `control-panel-entry-class` has been set as CommunitiesControlPanelEntry.

Enhancement

It would be better to add permission control to the `Save`, `Permissions`, and `Delete` buttons of **Manage Pages** (portlet ID 88). Why is it important? There are use cases requiring flexibility to control permissions on **Save**, **Permissions**, and **Delete** buttons of **Manage Pages** via **Roles**. For example, the user "Lotti Stein" can view a page say "Home"; the user "David Berger" can view, update, and delete the page, say "Home". Currently this flexibility is missing in `$PORTAL_ROOT_HOME/html/portlet/communities/edit_pages_page.jsp`.

```
<br />
<input type="submit" value="<liferay-ui:message key="save" />" />
<liferay-security:permissionsURL
modelResource="<%= Layout.class.getName() %>"
modelResourceDescription="<%= selLayout.getName(locale) %>"
resourcePrimKey="<%= String.valueOf(selLayout.getPlid()) %>"
var="permissionURL"
/>
<c:if test="<%= !group.isLayoutPrototype() %>">
<input type="button" value="<liferay-ui:message key="permissions" />"
onClick="location.href = '<%= permissionURL %>';" />
<input type="button" value="<liferay-ui:message key="delete" />"
```

```
onClick="<portlet:namespace />deletePage();" />
</c:if>
```

As shown in the previous code, there is no access control on the `Save`, `Permissions`, and `Delete` buttons. How to implement it? First add permission action keys `PERMISSIONS` and `DELETE` in the model resource `Layout`. Then update the preceding code by adding permission control in the `Save`, `Permissions`, and `Delete` buttons of `Manage Pages`. For more details, refer *Chapter 5*, *Managing Pages* of the book *Liferay Portal 5.2 Systems Development*.

Site templates and page templates

As shown in previous chapters, the portal has a lot of powerful features. However, it is difficult for users who want to just create a community and start collaborating. They have to first create layouts, add portlets, and then update portlets. The portlet **Site Templates** would be a good tool in this case when creating websites with preconfigured pages, which include layouts, portlets, and themes. The portlet **Site Templates** allows the portal administrator to define a set of site templates as predefined websites that the users will be able to choose from for creating new websites.

As you have seen, you don't need to create new pages as blank, instead you would be able to apply the layout and portlets of preconfigured pages on newly created pages. The portlet **Page Templates** allows the portal administrator to define a set of page templates as predefined pages that the users will be able to choose from for creating new pages.

Page templates

A page template is a preconfigured page with page layout and a set of portlets. By default, new pages are always created blank. Fortunately page templates would change this scenario and reduce page creation time; new pages can be created from preconfigured pages. Page templates allow the portal administrator to define a set of page templates that the users will be able to choose from to create preconfigured pages.

Managing page templates

Page templates are manageable that is, you are able to add, delete, update page templates and also assign permissions, if you have the proper access right. Note that page templates are specified as a database table `LayoutPrototype` with columns: `layoutPrototypeId`, `companyId`, `name`, `description`, `settings_`, and `active_`. Let's have a deep look at management of page templates.

First of all, let's create a page template called "Editorial Page Template", as shown in the following screenshot.

1. Log in as an admin, for example "Palm Tree".
2. Go to **Manage | Control Panel** under the dock bar menu.
3. Select **Page Templates** under the category **Portal** of **Control Panel**.
4. Click on the icon **Add**.
5. Type a name like "Editorial Page Template", note that you would be able to type the name in other languages as well.
6. Type a description like "Editorial Page Template".
7. Enable the checkbox **Active**. Note that the checkbox **Active** is checked by default and the page template must be active in order to be selected.
8. Click on the **Save** button to save your changes, or click on the **Cancel** button to discard the changes.

Of course, you can add other page templates as you expected. After adding the page template "Engineering Page Template", you are able to view page templates, as shown in the following screenshot:

As you can see, you can edit and delete page templates, and also assign permissions on page templates. When updating a page template, you would have a chance to update the name and description. More interestingly, you would be able to uncheck the checkbox **Active**, making the page template invisible to end users. Therefore, we can say that only active page templates would be enabled for end users.

When editing a page template, you would be able to see a link called **Open Page Template** under the title **Configuration**. On clicking the link, a new window will open with a URL like `/group/template-id/layout`, where you would be able to add portlets, update portlets, update page layout, and so on. Note that `template-id` is a pattern, that is, it is a keyword `template-` plus id, where the `id` would be the value of column `layoutPrototypeId`.

Assigning permissions

As you have seen, the portlet Page Templates is available only via the **Control Panel**. Therefore, in order to view the portlet Page Templates, you need to have permission **Access in Control Panel** first.

The following table shows permissions on the portlet Page Templates. The role Community Member is set up with all the permissions (marked as 'X'): **Access in Control Panel**, **Configuration**, and **View**. While the role Guest only has the possibility to set up permission **View** (marked as 'X'). The by default Action for the roles Community Member and Guest is the **View** (marked as '*') permission.

Action	Description	Community	Guest
View	Ability to view the portlet	X,*	X,*
Configuration	Ability to configure the portlet	X	
Access in Control panel	Ability to access the portlet in Control Panel	X	

The user "Lotti Stein", as a member of the role "MB Topic Admin", doesn't have access on the portlet **Page Template** in **Control Panel**. Suppose that you have a request–granting permission **Access in Control Panel** to the user "Lotti Stein", how do you implement it? The following is an example, but you would have other options as well.

1. Log in as an admin, say "Palm Tree", and go to **Manage** | **Control Panel** under the dock bar menu.
2. Click on **Roles** under the category **Portal** of **Control Panel** first.
3. Then locate a role, say "MB Topic Admin".
4. Click on the **Define Permissions** icon from the **Actions** next to the role.

5. Click on **Applications | Page Templates** link, enable the **Access** checkboxes in the **Control Panel** and **View**.

6. Click on the **Save** button.

As shown in the preceding implementation, the user "Lotti Stein" would be able to access the portlet Page Templates under the category **Portal** of **Control Panel**.

After assigning permissions on the portlet Page Templates, you could go deeper and assign permissions on page templates. The following table shows permissions on page templates. The role Community Member is set up with all permissions (marked as 'X'): **Delete**, **Update**, **Permissions**, and **View**. While the role Guest only has the possibility to set up permission **View** (marked as 'X'). The by default action for the roles Community Member and Guest is the View (marked as '*') permission.

Action	Description	Community	Guest
View	Ability to view the page template	X, *	X, *
Update	Ability to update the page template	X	
Delete	Ability to delete the page template	X	
Permissions	Ability to assign the permissions on page templates	X	

Obviously, the user "Lotti Stein" doesn't have permissions **View**, **Update**, **Delete**, and **Permissions** on any page templates. Suppose that you have a request–granting permissions **View**, **Update**, **Delete**, and **Permissions** on any page templates to the user "Lotti Stein", how do you implement it? The following are sample processes:

1. Log in as an admin, say "Palm Tree", and go to **Manage | Control Panel** under the dock bar menu.

2. Click on **Roles** under the category **Portal** of **Control Panel**.

3. Then locate a role, say "MB Topic Admin".

4. Click on the **Define Permissions** icon from the **Actions** next to the role.

5. Click on the **Portal | Communities** link, enable the checkboxes **View**, **Delete**, **Update**, and **Permissions** under the title "Page Template".

6. Click on the **Save** button.

As shown in the preceding implementation, the user "Lotti Stein" would be able to edit and delete a Page Template, and also assign permissions on individual page templates.

Of course, you would also have an ability to assign permissions on individual Page Templates if you have the proper access rights. The icon **Permissions** of the **Actions** button next to an individual page template is designed for this purpose.

Applying page templates

Once page templates are available, you would be able to apply them when adding a new page, either a private page or a public page. When a page template has been applied, the page will have same page layout and portlets as that of the page template. Note that you wouldn't see the title "Template" and a drop-down list of page templates if page templates are empty. How to apply page templates? As shown in following screenshot, when you add a new page, page templates are available. The following is just an example:

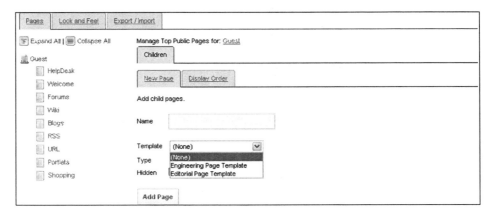

1. Go to **Manage Pages** under the dock bar menu.

2. In the **Manage Pages** view, click on the root **Guest**.

3. Under **Children** | **New Page** | **Template**, you would see a list of page templates.

4. You would be able to select either a page template or none.

Obviously, you can only apply page templates on new pages. In other words, page templates are unavailable for existing pages, neither public nor private pages.

What's happening?

When adding a new page, you would have the ability to select a page template. How? The portal has specified this logic at $PORTAT_ROOT_HOME/html/portlet/ communities/edit_pages_children.jsp as follows:

```
<%
List<LayoutPrototype> layoutPrototypes = LayoutPrototypeServiceUtil.
search(company.getCompanyId(), Boolean.TRUE, null);
%>
<c:if test="<%= !layoutPrototypes.isEmpty() %>">
<tr><td>
<liferay-ui:message key="template" />
</td>
<td colspan="2">
<select id="<portlet:namespace />layoutPrototypeId"
name="<portlet:namespace />layoutPrototypeId">
<option selected value="">(<liferay-ui:message key="none" />)</option>
<%
for (LayoutPrototype layoutPrototype : layoutPrototypes) {
%>
<option value="<%= layoutPrototype.getLayoutPrototypeId() %>"><%=
layoutPrototype.getName(user.getLanguageId()) %></option>
<% } %>
</select></td></tr>
</c:if>
```

As shown in the preceding code, it first searches page templates, then it displays page templates as a list for selection. Note that there is a value `Boolean.TRUE` on the function of search on page templates. This means that only active page templates would be available.

As you have seen that the portlet Page Templates (portlet ID 146) resides in the category **Portal** of **Control Panel**, position 11. Why you may ask? The portal has default settings for the portlet Page Templates can be seen in $PORTAL_ROOT_HOME/ WEB-INF/liferay-portlet.xml.

```
<control-panel-entry-category>portal</control-panel-entry-category>
<control-panel-entry-weight>11.0</control-panel-entry-weight>
<scopeable>true</scopeable>
```

The preceding code shows that the portlet Page Templates will appear in the category **Portal** of **Control Panel**, position 11, and it is scopeable, too. That is, you would be able to use the tab **More | Configuration | Scope** to change the scope from the default to the current page. As you can see, there is no use for changing scope for page templates.

Site templates

Site templates are preconfigured websites, either public pages or private pages, with page layouts, a set of portlets, and themes. By default, new websites are always created as blank. Fortunately site templates would change this scenario and reduce website creation time. New websites would be created from preconfigured websites. In a word, the portlet Site Templates allows the portal administrator to define a set of site templates so that the users will be able to choose from preconfigured websites to build a new website, both public pages and private pages.

Managing site templates

Site templates are manageable. That is, you are able to add, delete, and update site templates, to manage pages of site templates, and furthermore, to assign permissions if you have proper access right. Similar to page templates, site templates are specified as a database table LayoutSetPrototype with columns: layoutSetPrototypeId, companyId, name, description, settings_, and active_. How does it work? Let's have a deep look at the management of site templates.

First, let's create a site template called "Street Site Template", as shown in the following screenshot:

1. Log in as an admin, say "Palm Tree".
2. Go to **Manage | Control Panel** under the dock bar menu.
3. Select Site Templates under the category **Portal of Control Panel**.
4. Click on the icon **Add**.
5. Type a name, say "Street Site Template", note that you would be able to type name in other languages as well.

6. Type a description, say "Street Site Template".

7. Enable checkbox **Active**, note that the checkbox **Active** is checked by default and the site template should be active in order to be selected.

8. Click on the **Save** button to save the changes, or click on the **Cancel** button to discard the changes.

Definitely, you can add other site templates according to your requirements. After adding a site template named "Workshop Site Template", you would be able to view the site templates.

As shown in the previous screenshot, you would be able to edit and delete site templates, and also assign permissions on site templates. When updating a site template, you would have a chance to update the name and description. Moreover, you would also be able to disable the checkbox **Active**, making the site template invisible to end users. Note that only active site templates would be enabled for end users.

When editing a site template, you would see a link called **Open Site Template** under the title Configuration. On clicking the link, a new window will open with a URL like /group/template-id/home, where you are able to add portlets, update portlets, update page layout, and so on. Note that template-id is a pattern, that is, keyword template- plus id, where the id would be the value of column layoutSetPrototypeId.

Building site templates

The tasks to building site templates would involve two processes: Managing pages and updating layout templates and portlets for each page.

The process of managing pages of a site template would be simple: clicking on the **Manage Pages** icon next to the site templates, adding new pages from scratch or from page templates, and updating the look and feel with different themes if applicable.

The process of updating layout template and portlets for each page of a site template would look like this: click on the link of a site template first and then click on the link "Open site template", you would see that a new window will be opened with a page selected. Finally you could just update the layout template and portlets for each page.

Suppose that you're going to use a custom layout template called **3-2-3 Columns** on pages of site templates, how do you implement it? The following are samples:

1. Download the layout template `${3-2-3-column-layouttpl-war}` from `http://liferay.cignex.com/palm_tree/book/0387/chapter07/3-2-3-columns-layouttpl-6.0.0.1.war`.

2. Drop the WAR file `${3-2-3-column-layouttpl-war}` to the folder `$LIFERAY_HOME/deploy`. The portal will deploy it automatically, if the portal is running.

3. Go to **Manage** | **Page Layout** under the dock bar menu, and you would see the layout template `3-2-3 Columns`. It can be applied on pages.

You could absolutely deploy more layout templates like `1-2-1 Columns`, `2-1-2 Columns`, `1-3-1 Columns`, and so on.

Permissions on site templates

Similar to the portlet Page Templates, the portlet Site Templates is only available in the **Control Panel**. Thus, in order to view the portlet Site Templates, you have to get the permission **Access in Control Panel** first.

The following table shows permissions on the portlet Page Templates. The role Community Member is set up with all permissions (marked as 'X'): Delete, Update, Permissions, and View. While the role Guest only has the possibility to set up permission View (marked as 'X'). The by default action for the roles Community Member and Guest is the View (marked as '*') permission.

Action	Description	Community	Guest
View	Ability to view the portlet	X,*	X,*
Configuration	Ability to configure the portlet	X	
Access in Control panel	Ability to access the portlet in Control Panel	X	

Similar to that of the portlet Page Templates, you can assign the permission **View** and **Access in Control Panel** to a user via a regular role like "MB Topic Admin".

After assigning permissions on the portlet Site Templates, you would like to go deeper and to assign permissions on site templates. The following table shows permissions on site templates. The role Community Member is set up with all permissions (marked as 'X'): **Delete**, **Update**, **Permissions**, and **View**. While the role Guest has the possibility to set up permission **View** (marked as 'X') only. The by default permission action of the role Community Member and Guest is (marked as '*') **View**.

Action	Description	Community	Guest
View	Ability to view site template	X, *	X,*
Update	Ability to update site template	X	
Delete	Ability to delete site template	X	
Permissions	Ability to assign permissions on page templates	X	

The user "Lotti Stein" doesn't have the permissions **View**, **Update**, **Delete**, and **Permissions** on the site template "Street Site Template". Let's say that you are going to grant permissions **View**, **Update**, **Delete**, and **Permissions** on the site template "Street Site Template" to the user "Lotti Stein", how do we implement it? The following is an option.

1. Log in as an admin, say "Palm Tree", and go to **Manage | Control Panel** under the dock bar menu.
2. Click on Site Templates under the category **Portal** of **Control Panel** first.
3. Then locate the site template, say "Street Site Template".
4. Click on the **Permissions** icon from the **Actions** next to the site template.
5. Enable the checkboxes **View**, **Delete**, **Update**, and **Permissions** next to the role "MB Topic Admin".
6. Click on the **Submit** button.

As shown in preceding implementation, the user "Lotti Stein" would be able to edit and to delete the site template "Street Site template", and also assign permissions on the site template "Street Site Template". Thus, you would see **Actions** button next to the site template "Street Site Template" with icons **Edit, Manage Pages, Permissions,** and **Delete**. But there is no **Actions** button next to the site template "Workshop Site Template", since you don't have the permissions **Edit, Permissions**, and **Delete** on the site template "Workshop Site Template".

Note that the permission **Manage Pages** is associated to the permission **Update**. If you grant permission **Update**, they would get both permissions **Update** and **Manage Pages**. If you revoke permission **Update**, then they would lose both permissions **Update** and **Manage Pages**.

Of course, you would be able to assign permissions on any site templates via **Define Permissions** to a regular role, like "MB Topic Admin", in the **Control Panel**, if you do have proper access rights.

Applying site templates

Essentially, site templates are predefined websites, a set of pages, layout templates, portlets, and themes working together. Normally, there are three kinds of websites: user's public and private pages, organization's private and public pages, and community's private and public pages. The public pages could be a website available to the public and no sign-in is required, while the private pages would be a website too, available on the intranet with access right or sign-in required.

As stated in the previous chapter, each organization would have its own public pages and private pages. When building pages of an organization, we could be able to apply site templates on both public and private pages, as shown in the following screenshot:

How do you get it, you may ask? The following is an example:

1. Go to **Organizations** under the category **Portal** of **Control Panel**.

2. Click on the **Add** icon to add a new organization. By default, the menu item **Organization Information | Details** is selected.

3. Click on **Organization Information | Pages**, you would be able to see a screenshot like the preceding one, where you are able to select site templates and apply them to current organization's private and/or public pages.

In the same way, you could apply site templates to user's public and/or private pages. To do so, you go to **Users** under the category **Portal** of **Control Panel**, click on the **Add** icon to add a new user, and then click on **User Information | Pages**. You would be able to the select site templates for the current user's private and/or public pages.

Likewise, you would also be able to apply site templates on community's public and private pages. To achieve this, go to **Communities** under the category **Portal** of **Control Panel**, click on the **Add** icon to add a new community, and then you would be able to select site templates for the current community's private and/or public pages.

What's happening?

When adding a new community, you would have the ability to select site templates for both private pages and public pages. How does it work? The portal has specified the logic at $PORTAT_ROOT_HOME/html/portlet/communities/edit_community. jsp as follows:

```
<%
List<LayoutSetPrototype> layoutSetPrototypes =
LayoutSetPrototypeServiceUtil.search(company.getCompanyId(), Boolean.
TRUE, null);
%>
<c:if test="<%= (group != null) || !layoutSetPrototypes.isEmpty() %>">
<c:choose>
<c:when test="<%= ((group == null) || (group.
getPublicLayoutsPageCount() == 0)) && !layoutSetPrototypes.isEmpty()
%>">
<aui:select label="public-pages" name="publicLayoutSetPrototypeId">
<aui:option label="none" selected="<%= true %>" value="" />
<%
for (LayoutSetPrototype layoutSetPrototype : layoutSetPrototypes) {
%>
<aui:option value="<%= layoutSetPrototype.getLayoutSetPrototypeId()
%>"><%= layoutSetPrototype.getName(user.getLanguageId()) %></
aui:option>
<% } %>
</aui:select>
</c:when>
```

As shown in the previous code, it first searches sites templates, and then it displays site templates as a list for selection. Note that there is a value `Boolean.TRUE` on the search function on site templates, this means that only active site templates would be available for usage.

Similarly, the portal has specified the logic applying site templates on user's private pages and public pages at `$PORTAT_ROOT_HOME/html/portlet/enterprise_admin/user/pages.jsp`. In the same way, the portal has specified the logic–applying site templates on organization's private and public pages at `$PORTAT_ROOT_HOME/html/portlet/enterprise_admin/organization/pages.jsp`.

As you have seen, the portlet Site Templates (portlet ID `149`) resides in the category **Portal** of **Control Panel**, position `12`. How does it work? This portal has the default settings for the portlet Site Templates as follows in `$PORTAL_ROOT_HOME/WEB-INF/liferay-portlet.xml`.

```
<control-panel-entry-category>portal</control-panel-entry-category>
<control-panel-entry-weight>12.0</control-panel-entry-weight>
<scopeable>true</scopeable>
```

The preceding code shows that the portlet Page Templates will appear in the category **Portal** of **Control Panel**, position `12`, and it is scopeable too. Obviously, there is no use of being scoped to a page for a site template.

Virtual hosting

Generally speaking, virtual hosting is a method that servers like web servers use to host more than one domain name on the same computer, sometimes on the same IP address.

For example, the community "Book Street" has both public and private pages. For public pages, to access a page say "Home", you need to type the URL `http://localhost:8080/web/book-street/home`. In most cases, you would like to remove "`/web/book-street/`" and to expect "`/home`" only with a friendly domain name like `street.bookpub.com`. That is, for the public pages of community "Book Street", the URL becomes "`http://street.bookpub.com:8080/`". This would be a nice feature.

Setting up virtual hosting

Suppose that you have a domain name: street.bookpub.com and you want to set up virtual hosting for the public pages of the community "Book Street" on this domain, that is, end users can visit the public pages of community "Book Street" in the domain name. How do we accomplish it? The following is an example:

1. Set virtual hosts in the local host file, yours should look similar to the following note that `127.0.0.1 localhost` is the default setting in most cases.

   127.0.0.1 localhost

   127.0.0.1 street.bookpub.com

2. Log in as an admin, say "Palm Tree", and go to **Manage | Control Panel** under the dock bar menu.

3. Click on **Communities** under the category **Portal** of **Control Panel**.

4. Locate a community, say "Book Street".

5. Click on the **Manage Pages** icon from the **Actions** button on the right of the community "Book Street".

6. Click on the **Setting | Virtual Host** tab.

7. In the **Virtual Host** tab, enter the public virtual host, for example "street.bookpub.com" that will map to the public-friendly URL.

8. Optionally, enter the friendly URL, "book-street", that will be used by the public pages, as shown in the following image.

9. Click on the **Save** button to save the changes.

   ° **Public Virtual Host**: Entering a public virtual host that will map to public-friendly URL.

   ° **Private Virtual Host**: Entering a private virtual host that will map to private-friendly URL.

   ° **Friendly URL**: Entering the friendly URL for both public and private pages. The friendly URL is appended to `/web for public pages` and `/group for private pages`.

   ° **Staging Public Virtual Host**: Entering public virtual host that will map to staging public pages friendly URL when the staging group is activated.

- ° **Staging Private Virtual Host**: Entering private virtual that will map to staging private pages friendly URL when the staging group is activated.

- ° **Staging Friendly URL**: Entering the friendly URL such as "book-street-staging" for both public pages and private pages of staging group when the staging group is activated. The friendly URL is appended to `/web for public pages` and `/group for private pages`.

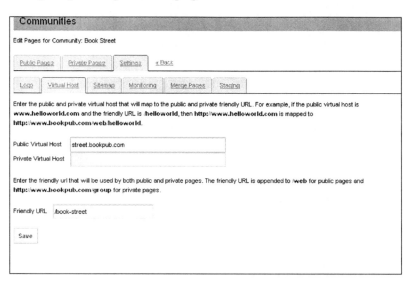

Using virtual hosting effectively

Virtual hosting means to host more than one domain name on the same computer, usually on the same IP address. There are two basic methods to fulfill virtual hosting: name-based, and IP address/IP-based. Name based virtual hosts are used with multiple host names in order to share the same web server IP address. While in IP-based virtual hosting, each site will point to a unique IP address. You can configure the web server with multiple physical network interfaces, virtual network interfaces on the same physical interface, or multiple IP addresses on one interface.

Virtual Hosting is an extension of the friendly URL functionality. It allows one or more communities in a single portal instance, identified by separate and unique host names. End users only input the name of the host they expect to visit into the address bar in the browser, and while it appears to the users that they are visiting different websites, they are in fact being directed to a single web server. In fact, based on the host name, the server determines the community present to the user.

What's happening?

There are two steps to set up the virtual hosting. The first step is to ensure that a **Domain Name Server** (DNS) entry exists for each virtual host you want, and the second is to see that every one of them point to the IP address of the server. For example, you need to set the following in the local host file.

```
127.0.0.1 street.bookpub.com
127.0.0.1 workshop.bookpub.com
```

The preceding code sets virtual hosts `street.bookpub.com` and `workshop.bookpub.com` to the same IP `127.0.0.1`. In the same way, you would be able to set up your virtual hosts.

Next, the portal sets up a virtual host filter at `portal.properties` as follows.

```
com.liferay.portal.servlet.filters.virtualhost.
VirtualHostFilter=true
```

As shown in preceding code, the virtual hosting filter maps hosts to public and private pages. For example, if the public virtual host is `street.bookpub.com` and the friendly URL is `/book-street`, then `http://street.bookpub.com` is mapped to `http://localhost:8080/web/book-street`.

Of course, you would be able to turn off virtual host filter by setting the property `com.liferay.portal.servlet.filters.virtualhost.VirtualHostFilter` to `false` in `portal-ext.properties`.

> Note that the virtual host filter maps hosts both public and private pages of a group, community or organization, or user personal site.

Setup

As you have seen, some extensions, hosts, and paths got ignored when you set up virtual hosts. In fact, the portal has specified the following properties for virtual hosts in `portal.properties`.

```
virtual.hosts.ignore.extensions
virtual.hosts.ignore.hosts
virtual.hosts.ignore.paths
virtual.hosts.default.community.name=Guest
```

As you can see, you can set the extensions that will be ignored for virtual hosts via the property `virtual.hosts.ignore.extensions`, set the hosts that will be ignored for virtual hosts via the property `virtual.hosts.ignore.hosts`, and also set the paths that will be ignored for virtual hosts via the property `virtual.hosts.ignore.paths`.

In particular, you could specify the community name that will default to the company's virtual host via the property `virtual.hosts.default.community.name`. If the specified community has a virtual host, then that will take precedence. If it doesn't, then it will use the company's virtual host. This property is useful to remove "/web/guest" or any other community from the default URL. For example, if this property isn't set, then the default URL would be `http://localhost:8080/web/guest/home`. If this property is set, then the default URL would be `http://localhost:8080/home`.

Staging, workflow, and publishing

It is normal for users to need the capability to stage their work. That is, they need the ability to work on a working copy of the website first. At the same time, they need to manipulate this working copy and preview it as if it were the website. Moreover, they need the capability to have many "working copies" in progress at any one time. More interesting, users should be able to preview a working copy at any time without disrupting the live pages.

Meanwhile, it is required to manage staging properly. Let's consider one scenario. Here we have a content creator who can create the pages in the staging, a content producer who can approve the pages or reject the pages and return it to the content creator, a content reviewer who can approve the pages or reject the pages to the content producer, and a content editor who can either reject the pages to the content producer or publish the pages. Let's implement these requirement as follows.

Staging

The purpose of the staging feature is to deploy a new version of the website in a fully functional form, which can be tested and reviewed by content producers or content editors. Content producers or content editors, who are evaluating the web content changes, are able to navigate the site without having to choose which version to see.

Activating staging

First of all, let's activate staging on a community, for example, Book Street. Note that the staging is activated in a group, either organization or community. Before taking a deep look at staging, we use the Book Street community as an example. Here are the steps you should follow to create a community named Book Street, as shown in the following screenshot:

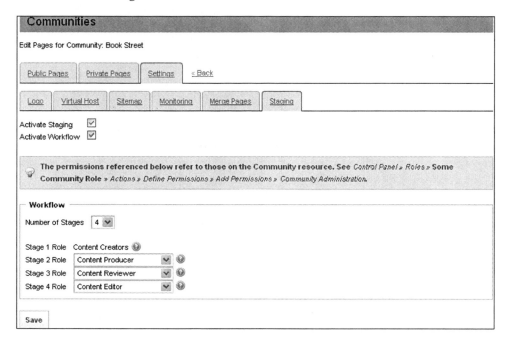

1. Log in as an admin, for example, Palm Tree.

2. Go to **Manage | Control Panel**, and go to **Communities** in the category **Portal** of **Control Panel**.

3. Locate a community, say "Book Street" first. Then click on the **Manage Pages** icon from the **Actions** next to the right of the community.

4. Go to **Settings | Staging** and you would see a checkbox **Activate Staging**.

5. To activate staging, just select the **Activate Staging** checkbox. You will receive a message when the staging environment for the Book Street community has been created properly.

To deactivate staging, just disable the **Activate Staging** checkbox. You will receive a message when the staging environment for the Book Street community has been removed properly.

Note that when deactivating staging, all pages in the staging group would get deleted, and moreover, current workflow settings and task proposals in current staging would get disabled too. Note the red background indicates you are in the staging environment, where you would see the new Staging menu on the dock bar with a drop-down list, the yellow background indicates that you are in the live environment, where you would see the Staging menu too on the dock bar with a different drop-down list.

What's happening?

When activating staging, the portal will create a staging group. When deactivating the staging environment, the portal will remove the staging group. It first gets a staging group ID and a flag. If the current group is a staging group and has a value `false`, it removes the current staging group. Otherwise, it creates a group for the staging environment. As you can see, the name of staging group is the name of the current community name and (Staging).

The live group ID of the staging group is the current community group ID. For instance, the current community group has the name Book Street with a group ID as `10401`. Thus, the staging group has the name Book Street (Staging) with a live group ID as `10401` and a group ID as `10501`. Note that the group ID value is showed as an example. During runtime, these values will be different. At the same time, all of the layouts (either private pages or public pages) have been populated from the current Book Street community to the Book Street (Staging) staging group.

Publishing locally

Once the staging environment is set, you would be able to copy pages from the live group to the staging group and to publish selected pages or an entire website from the staging group to the live group. When the staging environment is activated, the changes have to be published to make them available to end users.

Publishing pages

Publishing is an ability to push one or more assets from staging to a live environment. Publishing should include the following features:

1. Publishing should include the capability to publish to local and remote systems.

2. Publishing should be as simple as a push of a button or be included as a step in a workflow.

3. Publishing should not disrupt the production environment except to effect the published change.

To publish the pages in the staging group, simply click on the **Publish to Live** button next to the button **View Pages**. The portal will copy the staging group into the live group.

 Note that the pages in the live group will be overwritten by the pages in the staging group.

To copy from the live group to the staging group, simply click on the button **Copy from Live** next to the buttons **View Pages** and **Publish to Live**. The following figure depicts how to activate staging, to copy from live to staging, and to publish from staging to live.

 Note that the pages in the staging group will be overwritten by the pages in the live group.

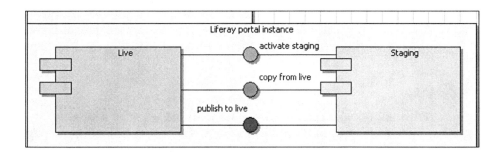

- `Activate Staging`: Create a staging group and copy pages, both public and private pages, from the live group to the staging group.

- `Copy from live`: Copy pages from the live group to the staging group.

- `Publish to live`: Publish the selected pages or an entire website from the staging group to the live group.

What's happening?

Once the staging group is created, you can update the staging group any time. This feature is called **Copy from Live**. That is, copy all pages from the live group to the staging. For instance, the Book Street (Staging) staging group was created based on the `Book Street` live group. Then we just work on the Book Street (Staging) staging group. In the middle of updating the staging group, we may need to roll back to the live group. In such a case, we can use the **Copy from Live** feature — copying all pages from the live group to the staging group. Thus, we can make the Book Street (Staging) staging group synchronized with the `Book Street` live group.

Once the staging group updates are ready, you can publish all the pages of the staging to the live group. This feature is called **Publish to Live**. That is, copy all pages from the staging group to the live group. For instance, the Book Street (Staging) staging group is ready and we want to apply all changes of the staging group to the Book Street live group. In this case, we can use the **Publish to Live** feature — copying all pages from the staging group to the live group. Thus, we can make the Book Street live group synchronized with the Book Street (Staging) staging group.

In short, the approach of staging and publishing web content locally would be a good idea when the website is small and the loading traffic is a minor concern — the processes of content management and publishing can share the same portal instance. A feature, called `local staging and publishing`, would be useful for intranets. As a content creator, you can manipulate a working copy and preview it as if it was the website to work on a working copy at any time without disrupting the live pages.

Workflow

In a staging environment, users can work on the working copy by a staging workflow. For instance, a proposal applies to any web content (for example pages) that enters the workflow, whereas a review exists when a proposal is assigned to a reviewer. In the staging environment, we discussed that an actor, Staging Manager, has the power to create or break a staging environment. This actor is either the community owner, super user, or someone who has been granted the MANAGE_ STAGING permission action key.

In the staging workflow, we can specify other actors, namely, content creator, content producer, content reviewer, and content editor. Note that these four roles are not mandatory—one can only have two or three roles instead of four. A content creator represents anyone having the permission MANAGE_LAYOUTS. A content creator can create content and edit pages in which he/she can then propose a change into the workflow. He/she can edit the web content of a proposal and add comments on a proposal.

The content producer can reject a proposal, assign reviewers to the proposal, and delete a proposal outright. Moreover, just like the content creator, he/she can edit the content of a proposal, and add comments to a proposal. A content reviewer is a knowledge expert and represents the Q&A element in the workflow. Any number of different reviewers can be assigned to a given proposal. The reviewers can't edit the content of a proposal, they can reject or approve a proposal, or add comments to a proposal. A content editor participates in the final act of a proposal. He/she can publish a proposal from staging to live, reject a proposal, edit the content of a proposal, or add comment on a proposal.

This is called a role-based staging workflow. In the following section, we will discuss how to use staging workflow and how to customize it.

Activating workflow

Let's say that you have created community roles, that is, Content Producer, Content Reviewer, and Content Editor, you're going to activate staging workflow. To activate staging workflow, just enable the checkbox **Activate Workflow**. After activating the workflow, you have the ability to set up the workflow. Of course, to disable the staging workflow, you just have to disable the checkbox **Activate Workflow**.

As an admin, you can choose **Number of Stages** and the stage role for each stage in order to set up a workflow. Considering the previous scenario, we will set the **Number of Stages** as **4**. The default value of **Stage 1 Role** is for content creators. Set the value of **Stage 2 Role** to content producer, the value of **Stage 3 Role** to content reviewer, and the value of **Stage 4 Role** to content editor.

- **Stage 1 Role-Content Creators**: This is an implied stage comprised of the entire set of users who have the **Manage Pages** permission. Any users with this permission can submit Content-Change Proposals to the workflow.

- **Stage 2 Role-Content Producer**: The role at **Stage 2** should grant, at least, **Approve Proposal**, **Assign Reviewer**, and **Manage Pages** permissions to its members, and add more permissions as individually required.

- **Stage 3 Role–Content Reviewer**: The role in a **Review Stage** should grant, at least, the **Approve Proposal** permission to its members. Add more permissions if individually required.

- **Stage 4 Role–Content Editor**: The role in the **Last Stage** should grant, at least, **Approve Proposal**, **Manage Pages**, and publish staging permissions to its members. Add more permissions if individually required.

Of course, you could set up workflow as you expected. Once the workflow is activated, the portal will save data in the column `typeSetting` of the database table `Group_` like:

```
workflowEnabled=true workflowStages=3 workflowRoleNames=Content
Producer, Content Reviewer, Content Editor
```

Creating task proposals

We have activated staging workflow. Now let's experience it. As a content creator, log in as "Lotti Stein" first. Go to the **Book Street** community, and then select **Staging | View Staged Page** under the dock bar menu. You will be in the **Home** page. Go further to update the **Home** page by adding the Reports portlet in the **Home** page, for instance. Then select **Staging | Proposals Publication** under the dock bar menu, and enter a name for a proposal, for example, "How about this page and web content" and select a reviewer from a list. Then click on the **Proceed** button.

You have successfully submitted a proposal in the workflow as a content creator. As shown in the following screenshot, you can go further to view the proposal, including **Name**, **Type**, **ID**, **User**, **Due Date**, **Status**, and the **Actions** button with a set of icons like **Edit** and **Delete**. To do so, just select **Staging | View Proposals**, and you would see the tab **Proposals** next to the tab **Export/Import** in the **Manage Pages** portlet.

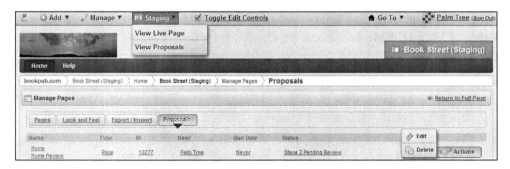

Once you have located a task proposal and clicked on the task proposal, you would be able to handle the following:

- **Proposal information**: User, Name, Type, ID and status, Description
- **Due Date**: Due date of the proposals
- **Activities**: Show or hide activities
- **Assign Reviewers**: Show or hide assign reviewers
- **Actions**: Save, Preview, Publish to Live, Approve or Reject, and Cancel
- **Reviewers**: Review history like User, Stage, Status, and Reviewer Date
- **Comments**: Add or update or delete comments on task proposals

Assigning permissions

The following table shows permissions on task proposals. The role Community Member may set up all permissions (marked as 'X'): **View**, **Update**, **Delete**, **Add Discussion**, **Update Discussion**, and **Delete Discussion**, while these permissions are unsupported for the role Guest. The 'by default' permission actions of the role Community Member are **View** and **Add Discussion** (marked as '*').

Action	Description	Community	Guest
View	Ability to view task proposals	X,*	
Update	Ability to update task proposals	X	
Add Discussion	Ability to add comments to task proposals	X,*	
Update Discussion	Ability to update comments on task proposals	X	
Delete Discussion	Ability to delete comments on task proposals	X	
Delete	Ability to delete task proposals	X	

Enhancement

As you can see, the current workflow is associated with the staging group only. That is, the workflow is available in a staging environment. It is possible to associate workflow with the live group, thus we could use the live group in one box as a staging box, and at the end of the workflow, we could publish the live group in the current box to that of a live group in a remote box. This feature has not yet been released, but should be available soon.

Most importantly, there is no way to delete a root page on live when a workflow is activated. Moreover, we should be able to apply all this workflow system to journal articles as well–this was implemented as Assets Workflow.

Scheduling and remote publishing

The portal provides remote staging and publishing capability through which the users can select subsets of pages and data, and transfer them to the live site, that is, the remote portal instance. Using this, we can export the selected data to the group of a remote portal instance or to another group in the same portal instance.

First, let's consider the scenario: Export the selected pages and data to another group in the same portal instance. In the website www.bookpub.com, we already have a default community named Guest with a group ID as 10148. In the public pages of the Guest community, create a page named **Remote Publishing** and add the **Hello World** and **Asset Publisher** portlets in this page. Next, we will create a community named **Book Workshop** with a group ID as 11307. We're going to publish the **Remote Publishing** page from the public pages of the Guest community to the public pages of the **Book Workshop** community.

How to publish?

How to publish this page you ask? We can use the publishing feature as follows:

1. Log in as an admin, for example "Palm Tree", and go to **Manage | Control Panel**.

2. Click on **Communities** under the category **Portal** of **Control Panel**.

3. Locate the **Guest** community, and click on the **Manage Pages** action.

4. Click on the **Publish to Remote** button, and you will see following screenshot:

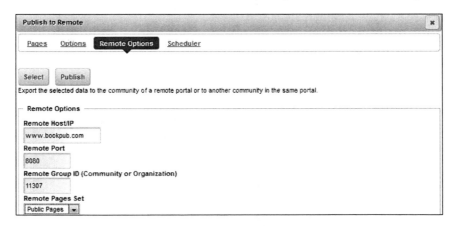

Now let's set up the publishing feature as follows:

1. Under the **Pages** tab, choose **Scope** as **Selected Pages**.

2. Select the **Remote Publishing** page.

3. Under the **Remote Option** tab, enter the values for remote options, as shown in the preceding screenshot—**Remote Host/IP** as **www.bookpub.com** (for example, external IP: 64.71.191.145), **Remote Port** as **8080**, **Remote Group ID** as **11307**, and **Remote Pages Set** as **Public Pages**.

4. When you are ready, click on the **Pages** tab, and then click on the **Publish** button. The **Remote Publishing** page will be published from the public pages of the **Guest** community to the public pages of the **Book Workshop** community.

 Now we're going to consider another scenario: publish the selected data to the community of a remote portal instance. We're going to publish the **Remote Publishing** page from the public pages of the **Guest** community to the public pages of the **Guest** community of a remote portal instance. Let's suppose the remote portal has the external IP 69.198.171.104 (domain name http://liferay.cignex.com), port number 8080, and group ID 11383 of the **Guest** community.

How can you publish this page to a remote portal instance? Under the **Pages** tab, choose **Scope** as **Selected Pages**, and select the **Remote Publishing** page. Under the **Remote Option** tab, input values for remote options, for example, **Remote Host/IP** as **liferay.cignex.com** (or for example an external IP 69.198.171.104. Of course, you can have different remote portal instances), **Remote Port** as **8080**, **Remote Group ID** as **11383**, and **Remote Pages Set** as **Public Pages**.

When you are ready, click on the **Pages** tab, and then click on the **Publish** button. The **Remote Publishing** page will be published from the public pages of the **Guest** community of the current portal instance, for example, www.bookpub.com, to the public pages of the **Guest** community of the remote portal instance, for example http://liferay.cignex.com.

Options

What do you want to publish? The portal provides options for publishing. This is similar to that of export settings.

- **Pages**: Default settings.
- **Portlets**: Default settings, including **Setup**, **User Preferences** and **Data**, and so on.
- **Permissions**: The permissions assigned for the exported pages and individual portlet windows will be included if this option is checked.
- **Categories**: When selected, all categories will be exported or imported, while keeping their hierarchy. During import, duplicate categories will not be created if a category with the same name already exists.

Scheduler

At the end of staging workflow, we may need to schedule jobs in order to transfer pages from the staging to the live. That is, the scheduling capability is very useful. We can select data and subsets of pages, or all of the pages of a given community, and transfer them to the live site, which can be a separate, remote portal instance — that is, remote staging and publishing.

Data for publishing to live can be scheduled in advance. This means that you would be able to schedule the publishing as events.

- **Schedule Event**: Description, Start Date, and End Date
- **Repeat**: Never, Daily, Weekly, Monthly, Yearly
- **Add Event**: Adding as many events as needed
- **Scheduled Events**: A list of events with Description, Start Date, and End Date

The portal has specified the scheduler in `portal.properties` as follows.

```
scheduler.enabled=true
scheduler.classes=
```

You can set the property `scheduler.enabled` to `false` in `portal-ext.properties` to disable all scheduler classes defined in `$PORTAL_ROOT_HOME/WEB-INF/liferay-portlet.xml` and in the property `scheduler.classes`.

What's happening?

We have introduced local staging and publishing in the previous section. Local staging and publishing means that we have only one box and only one portal instance. For a given group, for example Book Street, we created a staging group Book Street (Staging) — a working copy of the Book Street group. Now users can work on the staging group only. When they are ready, they can publish pages of the Book Street (Staging) staging group to the pages of the Book Street group.

As the staging and publishing happen in one box, and the Book Street (Staging) staging group and the Book Street live group belongs to the same portal instance, it is called local staging and publishing. This would be useful when the website is small with less traffic and a small group of end users.

But when the website is huge — heavy traffic, big groups of end users — we have to consider the remote staging and publishing feature. As shown in the following figure, there is one staging box and two production boxes. All of the boxes have live groups only. For instance, the Book Street live group in the staging box will be mapped into the Book Street live group in the production boxes. Thus, the Book Street live group in the staging box could be called as a staging group of the Book Street live group in the production boxes.

All of the internal content management users are working in the staging box only. They can use CMS and WCM tools to manage the content and web content, for example, building a live website. They can also apply workflow to approve or reject the content and web content. That is, the staging box is used only for the internal content management team. Once the pages are approved, the content management team can publish these pages into the production boxes.

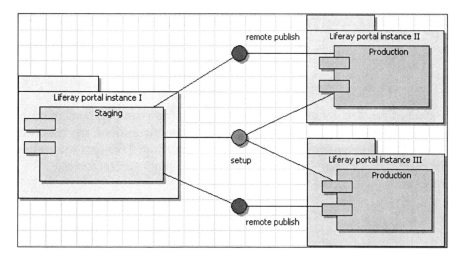

The production boxes are used only for end users (either public users or private customers). These boxes are set up with the same content and web content from the staging box at the beginning. Afterwards, they will accept updates via remote staging and publishing. They also save specific data in the production boxes, such as users' ratings, comments, preferences, and so on.

In addition, you can have a set of production boxes — more than two boxes as stated in the preceding figure. These production boxes can be organized as clustering environment. Furthermore, these production boxes can be distributed geographically. For instance, it is possible that you can put one box in California, USA, and another box in Zurich, Switzerland. In order to show remote staging and publishing, we use the external IP `64.71.191.145` for the staging box I, and external IPs `69.198.171.104` and `69.198.171.105` for the production boxes II and III respectively.

Setup

In order to communicate with the remote server, and moreover, to protect HTTP connection, we need to set up a tunnel web in `portal-ext.properties`. This means that we need to add the following lines at the end of `portal-ext.properties`.

```
tunnel.servlet.hosts.allowed=127.0.0.1,SERVER_IP,69.198.171.104,69.198
.171.105,64.71.191.145
tunnel.servlet.https.required=false
```

This code shows a `tunnel.servlet.hosts.allowed` property with a list of allowed hosts, for example, `69.198.171.104`, `69.198.171.105`, and `64.71.191.145`. As stated earlier, we used these hosts as examples only. You can have your own real hosts. Meanwhile, it specifies the `tunnel.servlet.https.required` property. By default, it is set to `false`. You can set it to `true` if you want to use HTTPS.

Employing community tools

There are a set of portlets related to the community, for example, bookmarks, directory, enterprise announcements, community announcement, my communities, invitation, communities, page comments, and page rating. This section mainly introduces portlets including my communities, bookmarks, directories, and invitations.

My Communities portlet

As mentioned earlier, the portlet My Communities (portlet ID 29) provides a way to navigate from community to community, which could be added to any page in the current portal instance. Generally speaking, the portlet My Communities has similar features as that of the portlet Enterprise Admin Communities–they are same codebase. But functions of My Communities are different from that of the portlet Enterprise Admin Communities in the following aspects:

- My Communities can be added to any page, while Enterprise Admin Communities is available only in the **Control Panel**.

- My Communities provides a way to navigate from community to community: **Communities I Own**, **Communities I Have Joined**, and **Available Communities**, while Enterprise Admin Communities provides one view: **All Communities**.

The portlet will display related communities in different ways as follows:

- **Communities I Own**: Communities that the current user is an owner on

- **Communities I Have Joined**: Communities that the current user has joined

- **Available Communities**: All communities in the current portal instance, except private communities

- **All Communities**: All communities in the current portal instance,

Obviously, you can view the communities that you own by clicking on the tab **Communities I Own**, view the communities that you have joined by clicking on the tab **Communities I Have Joined**, and view the open available communities by clicking on the tab **Available Communities**.

As you can see, the tab **All Communities** is invisible. How do you make it visible? The following is an option to implement this feature:

- Locate the JSP file `view.jsp` in the folder `$PORTAL_ROOT_HOME/html/ portlet/communities` and open it.

- Find the string `names="communities-owned,communities- joined,available-communities"`, and replace it with the string `names="communities-owned,communities-joined,available- communities,all-communities"`.

- Save the JSP file `view.jsp`.

Refreshing the page, you would see that the tab **All Communities** is appended next to the tab **Available Communities**.

Bookmarks portlet

Bookmarks are retrievable names and URLs (that is, web page locations). Their primary purpose is to catalog and access web pages that users have visited easily either by name or by URL. The Bookmarks portlet (portlet ID 28) provides the ability for users to keep track of URLs in the portal. An administrator can use bookmarks to publish relevant links to a group of users.

The portlet Bookmarks is available both in the **Control Panel** and in a specific page. To add a bookmark to the Bookmarks portlet, simply follow these steps in sequence:

1. Locate a page "Home" of the Guest community, and go to **Add | More** under the dock bar menu.

2. Add the Bookmarks portlet to the page "Home" of the Guest community to which you want to show bookmarks, if the portlet is not there. To add a bookmark (or called an entry) to an empty Bookmarks portlet, you should first add a folder.

3. Click on the **Add Folder** button, and type a name, say "My Home", and a description like "This is a bookmark for My Home" for the folder.

4. The permissions for the folder determine what users can do. To change the permissions, simply click on the **Configuration** link. To change all permissions, click on the **More** link.

5. Click on the **Save button.**

Then you can view the folder. The folders will appear with the folder name, the number of sub folders, a number of entries, and the **Actions** button with a set of actions, for example, **Edit**, **Permissions**, and **Delete**.

1. To add a **Bookmark** to the folder "My Home", click on the folder name which says "My Home".

2. You can either add more folders to divide your bookmarks further into more specific categories or you can add a bookmark to the current folder. Click on the **Add Bookmark button.**

3. The **Type** name says "SSO, LDAP, Liferay and Alfresco", the **URL** says "http://liferay.cignex.com", and **Comments** says "Full integration of SSO, LDAP, Liferay and Alfresco" to the bookmark.

4. The permissions for the entry determine what users can do. To change the permissions, simply click on the **Configuration** link. To change all permissions, click on the **More** link.

5. Select the proper categories by clicking on the **Select Categories** button.

6. Press the **Select Tags** button or `input tag` and press the **Add Tags** button if you need to add tags. Alternatively, you can search tags by clicking on the **Suggestions** button.

7. Click on the **Save button**.

Then you can view the bookmarks under the folder with the entry name, URL, a number of visits, priority, and the **Actions** button with a set of actions such as **Edit**, **Permissions**, and **Delete**.

Note that when editing an entry, you would be able to change the folder, either by selecting another folder or by removing the current folder.

Configuration

In short, the Bookmarks portlet provides a way for users to store the names and URLs of websites. After a bookmark is created, you can click on the link to open the site in a new browser window.

To view recent entries, you can simply click on the **Recent Entries** tab. Similarly, to view entries that you have created, simply click on the **My Entries** tab. The bookmarks will appear with the entry name, URL, number of visits, number of priority, modified date, and the **Actions** button with a set of action icons such as **Edit**, **Permissions**, and **Delete**. More interestingly, the number of visits will be updated dynamically when the site has been visited through the URL link in the Bookmarks portlet.

Assigning permissions

There are four levels of permission actions in the portlet Bookmarks: Permissions on the portlet, permissions on bookmarks, permission on folders, and permissions on entries.

The following table shows permissions on the portlet Bookmarks. The role Community Member is set up with all the permissions (marked as 'X'): **View**, **Configuration**, and **Access in Control Panel**, while the role Guest is set up with the permission action **View**. By default, the roles Community Member has the permission action **View** (marked as '*') as well as those of the role Guest.

Action	Description	Community	Guest
View	Ability to view the portlet	X, *	X, *
Configuration	Ability to configure the portlet	X	
Access in Control panel	Ability to access the portlet in the Control Panel	X	

The following table shows permissions on bookmarks. The role Community Member has the ability to set up the permission (marked as 'X'): **Add Entry** and **Add Folder**. These permission actions are unsupported for the role Guest.

Action	Description	Community	Guest
Add Entry	Ability to add Bookmark entry	X	
Add Folder	Ability to add Bookmark folder	X	

The following table shows permissions on folders. The role Community Member has the ability to set up permissions (marked as 'X'): **Access**, **Add Entry**, **Add Sub Folder**, **View**, **Permissions**, **Update**, and **Delete**. The permissions actions **Add Entry**, **Add Sub Folder**, and **Update** are unsupported for the role Guest. By default, the roles Community Member has the permission actions **View** and **Add Entry** (marked as '*'), while the role Guest only has the permission action **View**.

Action	Description	Community	Guest
Access	Ability to access bookmarks folders	X	X
Add Entry	Ability to add a Bookmark entry	X,*	
Add Sub Folder	Ability to add a Bookmark sub folder	X	
View	Ability to add Bookmark folders	X,*	X,*
Permissions	Ability to assign permissions on Bookmark folders	X	X
Update	Ability to update the Bookmarks folders	X	
Delete	Ability to delete the Bookmarks folders	X	X

The following table shows permissions on entries. The role Community Member may set up all permissions (marked as 'X'): **View**, **Update**, **Permissions**, and **Delete**, while the role Guest may set up the permission **View**. By default, the roles Community Member and Guest have the permission action **View** (marked as '*').

Action	Description	Community	Guest
View	Ability to add Bookmark entries	X,*	X,*
Permissions	Ability to assign permissions on Bookmark entries	X	
Update	Ability to update Bookmarks entries	X	
Delete	Ability to delete Bookmarks entries	X	

Note that you would able to assign permissions on an individual entry or on all entries scoped into the portal instance and groups. Definitely, permissions would be assigned via the roles–regular roles, community roles, or organization roles.

What's happening?

As you can see, the portlet Bookmarks defines a set of folders to hold entries, as shown in following figure. Each folder can have many sub folders. Thus the folders form a hierarchy. Each folder can have many entries. Each entry can have one URL and zero to one comment. More interestingly, entries can be classified by categories, entries can have many tags associated–thus end users can group entries in their own way.

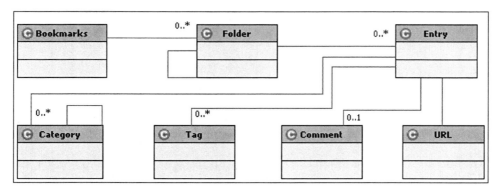

The portal has default settings for the portlet Bookmarks in the following file `$PORTAL_ROOT_HOME/WEB-INF/liferay-portlet.xml` which is as shown next:

```
<indexer-class>com.liferay.portlet.bookmarks.util.BookmarksIndexer</
indexer-class>
<open-search-class>com.liferay.portlet.bookmarks.util.
BookmarksOpenSearchImpl</open-search-class>
<portlet-data-handler-class>com.liferay.portlet.bookmarks.lar.
BookmarksPortletDataHandlerImpl</portlet-data-handler-class>
<control-panel-entry-category>content</control-panel-entry-category>
<control-panel-entry-weight>4.0</control-panel-entry-weight>
<asset-renderer-factory>com.liferay.portlet.bookmarks.asset.
BookmarksEntryAssetRendererFactory</asset-renderer-factory>
```

The preceding code shows that the portlet Bookmarks will appear in the category **Content** of the **Control Panel**, position 4. The framework via the `tag asset-renderer-factory` allows registering custom asset types so that generic portlets like **Asset Publisher** can be used to publish them. Thus we could publish bookmark entries through the **Asset Publisher** portlet. Meanwhile, the tag `indexer-class` value is called to create or update a search index for the portlet Bookmarks, while the tag `open-search-class` is called to get search results in the **Open-Search** standard. The `tag portlet-data-handler-class` specifies export and import capabilities on bookmarks.

Note that bookmarks content folders and entries are scoped into a group. This means that when portlets are added to a group, either public or private pages, they act as completely the same portlets. For instance, when the portlet Bookmarks is added to a page for example, "Home", of the **Guest** community, it will use the default scope. If you add the portlet Bookmarks to a second page, say "Welcome", it will show the same data as that of the first page. When the portlet Bookmarks is added to a page, it will get scoped immediately into the group that the current page belongs to. You don't have the flexibility to switch groups in this case. But this limitation could be solved through the **Control Panel**. In the **Control Panel**, you are able to switch the content of the portlet Bookmarks to different groups.

Directory portlet

The directory portlet provides the ability to display a list of users registered on the portal. The directory portlet displays personal information for individual users and also gives listings of available organizations and user groups.

You can find users by basic search. You just input the search criteria and click on the **Search** button. Similarly, you can find users by an advanced search, for example, **First Name**, **Middle Name**, **Last Name**, **Screen Name**, and **Email Address**. You just click on the **Advanced** link first, and then input search criteria for the advanced search, and then click on the **Search** button. Moreover, you can find users by available organizations as well as that of user groups.

- **Users**: Finding users by basic search and advanced search.
- **Organizations**: Viewing users who are members of organizations; finding organizations by basic search and advanced search. The inputs for advanced search include Name, Street, City, Zip, Type (Any, Regular Organization, Location), Country, and Region.
- **User Groups**: Viewing users who are members of user groups, finding User Groups by basic search.

Setup

As you can see, the **Directory** portlet (portlet ID 11) allows us to view a list of users registered on the portal.

Note that there are two permission actions **Configuration** and **View** on the portlet **Directory** being unsupported for the role Guest. It means the Guest user would be unable to view the portlet **Directory**. Therefore, make sure that the **Directory** portlet would be used by non-guest users.

Invitation portlet

The **Invitation** portlet allows us to invite friends to come and see our websites or portal pages. The following is a simple set of steps to invite friends by the **Invitation** portlet.

1. Locate a page "Home" of Guest community and go to **Add | More** under the dock bar menu.

2. Add the **Invitation** portlet in the page "Home" of the Guest community where you want to invite friends, if the portlet is not there.

3. Click on the **Invite Friends** link.

4. Enter up to 20 e-mail addresses of friends you would like to invite; enter one e-mail address per line.

5. Click on the **Invite Friends** button.

Setup

As you can see, the **Invitation** portlet (portlet ID 100) allows us to invite friends to come and see our websites or portal pages. To change the e-mail setup, simply click on the **More | Configuration | Setup | Current** icon at the top-right of the portlet. To manage setup archives, simply click on the **More | Configuration | Setup | Archived** icon at the top-right of the portlet.

Of course, you would be able to set permissions to what users can access. To do so, simply click on the **More | Configuration | Permissions** icon at the top-right of the portlet. To share the portlet, simply click on the **More | Configuration | Sharing** icon at the top-right of the portlet.

Note that there are two permission actions (**Configuration** and **View**) on the portlet **Invitation**, which are supported for the role Guest, and the permission **View** was assigned to both the role Community Member and Guest. Therefore, the Guest user could be able to view the portlet **Invitation**.

What's happening?

The number of e-mail addresses of friends you would like to invite is configurable, since the portal has set the following property in portal.properties.

```
invitation.email.max.recipients=20
invitation.email.message.body=com/liferay/portlet/invitation/
dependencies/email_message_body.tmpl
invitation.email.message.subject=com/liferay/portlet/invitation/
dependencies/email_message_subject.tmpl
```

Of course, you can change the number of recipient and override this property in `portal-ext.properties`. E-mail notification settings for invitation are configurable. As you can see, the subject and body of the message are specified as TMPL files. Obviously, you could customize these setting via overriding TMPL files in `portal-ext.properties`. By the way, you can configure the same via the web UI at **More | Configuration | Setup | Current**.

Summary

This chapter first introduced communities portlet, mentioned how to add a community, and how to manage (edit, delete, search, join, leave) communities and teams. Then it discussed how to add and manage the pages and users within a community, how to assign permissions on communities, and how to show what's different between an organization and a community. How to employ community virtual hosting is also introduced. Furthermore, it discussed how to use stage, preview, and publish websites, and managed staging workflow. Scheduling and remote publishing were also addressed in detail. Finally, it introduced how to use community tools; for example, my communities, bookmarks, invitations, directories, and so on.

In the next chapter, we're going to introduce CMS and WCM.

8
CMS and WCM

In the intranet website "bookpub.com" of the enterprise "Palm Tree Publications", we have to manage a huge number of images and documents, a lot of web content called Journal articles, and much more, to publish web content. This task can be made easier with a **Content Management System (CMS)** and **Web Content Management (WCM)**. In fact, WCM is a kind of CMS.

A CMS includes a set of portlets — Document Library and Image Gallery — to aggregate and manage images and documents. WCM includes the Web Content Management portlet to create and publish articles, as well as article templates and structures; the **Web Content Display** portlet to publish an article, the **Web Content List** portlet to display a dynamic list of all the journal articles for a given community, the **Asset Publisher** portlet to publish any piece of content, the **Nested Portlets** to drag-and-drop portlets into other portlets, XSL content portlet, and much more.

This chapter will first introduce you to managing and publishing images. Then it will discuss how to manage and publish documents. Finally, it will focus on web content called articles creation, management, and publishing.

By the end of this chapter, you will have learned how to:

- Manage folders and images in Image Gallery
- Assign permissions on folders and images
- Manage folders and documents in Document Library
- Assign permissions on folders and documents
- Publish documents
- Manage structures, templates, feeds, and web content in Web Content Management
- Assign permissions on articles, templates, structures, and feeds
- Publish web content
- Employ other WCM tools

The Image Gallery portlet

In order to let small teams manage web content and publish web content easily, we should first use web content. Before creating web content, we have to prepare a set of images and documents. Let's take a look at managing images first.

The portlet Image Gallery provides the ability to manage your images and organize them in folders. The images can also be accessed and uploaded using **WebDAV**. The portlet can be found in the **Control Panel** under the section **Content** or also placed in a page.

First of all, let's use the Image Gallery portlet in a page. As an administrator of the enterprise "Palm Tree Publications", you may create a page called **CMS** at the Guest Community and then add the Image Gallery portlet in the page **CMS**. Furthermore, you may create folders such as "Home" and "Liferay" and sub-folders, for example, "Book", in order to hold a set of images. At the same time, you need to group all images into different folders to make your task easy-to-use and easy-to-manage.

Managing folders

First of all, we need to create a folder called "Home", which contains a number of images. Let's do it as follows:

1. Log in as an Admin first, then go to **Go To | liferay.com** under the dock bar menu.

2. Go to **Add | Page** under the dock bar menu, and add a page called **CMS** at the Guest community private pages if the page is not there.

3. Go to **Add | More...**, and add the Image Gallery portlet in the page **CMS** of the Guest community where you want to manage images, if the Image Gallery portlet is not there.

4. Click on the **Add Folder** button.

5. Enter the name "Home" and the description "Images folder for Guest community".

6. Set **Permissions** by clicking on the **Configure** link. To configure additional permissions, click the **More** link. Here we just use default settings. By default, the checkbox **Public** is disabled.

7. Click on the **Save** button to save the inputs, or click on the **Cancel** button to discard the inputs.

Adding sub-folders

Let's say that we need to create a sub-folder named "Book" under the folder "Home", where it will contain a set of images for "Liferay Books". Let's do it by following these steps:

1. Locate the folder "Home", click on the link of the folder "Home", for example, the name.

2. Click on the **Add Subfolder** button.

3. Enter the name for example, "Book" and the description for example, "Images folder for books".

4. Set **Permissions** by clicking on the **Configure** link. To configure additional permissions, click on the **More** link. Here we just use default settings. By default, the checkbox **Public** is disabled.

5. Click on the **Save** button to save the inputs.

Of course, you can create other folders as siblings of the folder "Home". After adding a folder "Liferay", you would be able to view folders, as shown in following screenshot. First, go back to the root by clicking on the **CMS** link located in the breadcrumbs. The folders are displayed with the columns: **Folder, Number of Folders, Number of Images** and the **Actions** button with a set of icons: **Edit, Permissions, Delete, Add Subfolder, Add Image,** and **Access from my desktop**.

Obviously all folders' or sub-folders' names form a folder tree. The names of folders or sub-folders must be unique at the same level in the folder tree. However, the names can be the same at different levels.

As you can see, the right-side box shows the current folder, that is, the root in this case, with the name **Image Home** plus the presentation icon `folder_empty.png` if the folder is empty or `folder_full_image.png` if the folder isn't empty, and a set of action icons, for example, **Permissions**, **Add Folder**, **Add Image**, and **Access from My Desktop**.

> Note that you would be able to find the icons `folder_empty.png` and `folder_full_image.png` at `$PORTAL_ROOT_HOME/html/themes/${theme.name}/images/file_system/large`; where `${theme.name}` should be `classic`, `control_panel`, and any custom themes.

Updating folders

Folders and sub-folders are editable. For example, you may need to change the description of the folder "Liferay" from "Images Folder for Liferay" to "Images Folder for Integration". Let's do it by following these steps:

1. Locate the folder, for example "Liferay", that you want to edit.

2. Click on **Edit** icon from the **Actions** button located next to the folder.

3. Maintain the value of the name and update the description of the selected folder "Images Folder for Liferay" with the value "Images Folder for Integration".

4. Click on the **Save** button to save the changes.

Of course, you can update the name as well. For example, you can update the name "Liferay" with the value "Liferay-Integration".

Optionally, you can change the parent folder by selecting a folder as the parent folder of the folder or sub-folder, merging with the parent folder, or removing the parent folder. If you remove the parent folder, the current folder will become a folder at the root level. Merging with the parent folder means that all images in the parent folder will be copied into the current folder.

Folders or sub-folders are removable. For example, the folder "Liferay-Integration" doesn't exist anymore, and you can remove it. Let's do it as follows:

1. Locate the folder, say "Liferay-Integration", that you want to delete.

2. Click on the **Delete** icon from the **Actions** button located next to the folder.

3. A screen will appear asking if you want to delete this. Click on **OK** to confirm deletion.

> Note that deleting a folder will delete all related sub-folders and images that belong to this folder.

Managing images

Finally, we can add an image to a given folder. Let's say that we need to add a logo of "Palm Tree Publications" in the folder "Home". Let's do it by following these steps:

1. Locate the "Home" folder, and click on it's name.

2. Click on the **Add Image** button.

3. Click on the **Browse** icon to find an image `PalmTree_logo.png` in the local machine. You can browse multiple files like `PalmTree_logo.png`, `United_States.png`, and `Germany.png`.

4. Click on the **Upload Files** icon to upload files. Optionally, you can cancel all uploads by clicking on the link **Cancel All Uploads**.

As you can see, you can import images as a bulk by clicking on the icon **Browse**, where you can select multiple files. You can use the classic uploader to upload images one-by-one.

- **Folder**: Selecting a folder or removing a folder.

- **File**: Uploading an image file.

- **Name**: A title of the current image.

- **Description**: Image description.

- **Categories**: Selecting categories.

- **Tags**: Adding a tag, selecting a tag, or search tags.

- **Permissions**: Either public or configured by specific permissions.

- **Save/Cancel**: Saving or discarding inputs.

- **Use the new uploader**: A link to the previous view.

Of course, you can add other images. After adding images `"zhangjiajie-*.png"` under the folder `root`, you can view all images under the folder `root`, as shown in the preceding screenshot. Eventually they are default thumbnails of images generated from original images. The Image Gallery has been re-skinned to display images in a grid format; in other words, when viewing a given folder, you are shown a grid of thumbnails instead of a list of images.

After adding folders and images, you can manage images easily. You would be able to view images one-by-one, view images as a slideshow, search images, edit images, and delete images.

Viewing images as a slideshow

Images are viewable. To view an image, simply click on the default thumbnail of an image. For example, if you want to view the image `"PalmTree_logo.png"` under the folder "Home", then you can just click on the link of the folder "Home" first, and then locate the default thumbnail of the image `PalmTree_logo.png`. Finally, click on the default thumbnail of the image. A new window will appear showing a full-size image of `PalmTree_logo.png`, with a set of icons, that is, **Edit**, **Permissions**, and **Delete**.

Optionally you can view your own images by clicking on the tab **My Images** of the Image Gallery portlet and can view the recent images by clicking on the tab **Recent Images** of the Image Gallery portlet.

All images from a folder could be viewed as a slideshow. For example, you want to view all images under the folder "Home" as a slideshow. First click on the folder "Home", and then click on the **View Slide Show** button. A new window will appear showing a full-size image and a set of buttons `previous`, `play`, `pause`, `next`, `speed` selection, and so on.

Searching images

Images are searchable. There are three options to search images. You can search images from the root, search images from the current folder only, or search images both in the current folder and its sub-folders.

Suppose that there is an image "Book Street Logo" under the folder "Book", which is sub-folder of the folder "Home". And furthermore, there is an image "Book Workshop Logo" under the folder "Liferay-Integration".

First, let's search for the images from the root. In the Image Gallery portlet, simply input the keyword, for example, "logo", and click on the **Search Folders** button for all folders of the current folder. A list of images will appear including the previous two images, with a thumbnail image, title, and relevance rated as five stars.

Then, let's search for the image from the folder "Home" and its sub-folders. In Image Gallery, locate the folder "Home", and click the link of the folder "Home". Simply input the keyword, let's say, "logo", and click on the **Search Folders** button for all folders of the current folder. A list of images will appear, except the image "Book Workshop Logo".

Finally, let's search for the image from the folder "Home" only. Simply input the keyword, let's say "logo", and click on the **Search this Folder** button for the current folder under the tab **Images**. A list of images will appear, except the images "Book Workshop Logo" and "Book Street Logo".

Editing images

Images are editable. For example, you may need to change the description of the image `PalmTree_logo.png` under the folder "Home" from `PalmTree_logo.png` to "Palm Tree Publications Logo". Let's do it by following these steps:

1. Click the folder, say "Home".
2. Locate the image default thumbnail `PalmTree_logo.png` that you want to edit, and click on the default thumbnail.
3. Click on the **Edit** icon under the original image. Optionally, you would see the icons **Download**, **View**, **Edit**, **Permissions**, and **Delete**.

4. Update the description of the selected image, say `PalmTree_logo.png`, with the value "Palm Tree Publications Logo".

5. Click on the **Save** button to save the changes.

Optionally, you can change the description as well, and you can also change the folder by selecting a folder. At the same time, you can change the content of the image by uploading another image file. Furthermore, you can find a URL for the image when viewing an image. You can reference the image by this URL. For instance, you can refer to an image in an article. We'll see how to work with URLs later.

In addition, you would see the default thumbnail image, dimensions (weight and height), size of the current image, and WebDAV URL of current image when viewing the image. You would be able to reference the image by this URL. Moreover, you would be able to select categories on this image, and add or select tags on this image when editing the image. Later, you would be able to search images by categories and/or tags, and furthermore, re-group images by categories and/or tags.

Deleting images

Images are removable. For example, the image `PalmTree_logo.png` doesn't exist anymore, so you need to remove it. Let's do it as follows:

1. Locate the default thumbnail of the image `PalmTree_logo.png` that you want to delete.

2. Click on the default thumbnail of the image `PalmTree_logo.png`.

3. Then click on the **Delete** icon under the image **PalmTree_logo.png**.

4. A screen will appear asking if you want to delete this. Click on **OK** to confirm deletion.

Export and Import

More interestingly, you can easily export and then import images to another server. How do we do it? Simply click on the **More | Export/Import** icon of the portlet. Following the processes, you can export and import contents smoothly. What would you like to export? The following are items you can export:

- **Export the selected data to the given LAR filename**: Specifying the LAR name.
- **What would you like to export?**: Data—Folders and Images, Tags, Data Range, Permissions—permissions assigned for exported portlet will be included if this option is checked.
- **Export**: Export this data.

What would you like to import? The following are items you can import.

- **Import a LAR file to overwrite the selected data**: Choose the LAR file.
- **What would you like to import?**: Delete portlet data before importing; Data — Folders and Images, Tags, Data Strategy, and User ID Strategy; Permissions — assigned for imported portlet window will be included if this option is checked.
- **Import**: Import this data.

Assigning permissions

We have used the default settings for the Image Gallery portlet in the page **CMS** under the **Guest** community private pages. As an administrator, say "Palm Tree", logged in, you will see the button **Add Folder**. As we know that the user "Lotti Stein" is also a member of the Guest community, try to log in as "Lotti Stein", and you will see that there is no **Add Folder** button. Furthermore, you see the folders "Home" and "Liferay-Integration" without the **Actions** button.

Why so? Due to permissions, different users will have different permission actions in the Image Gallery portlet. Normally, there are four levels of permissions: permissions on portlet, permissions on Image Gallery, permissions on folders, and permissions on images.

Permissions on portlet

The following table shows permissions on the Image Gallery portlet. The role Community Member is set up with all the permissions (marked as 'X'): **View**, **Configuration**, and **Access in Control Panel**, while the role Guest user is set up with permissions **View** and **Configuration**. The 'by default' action for the roles Community Member and Guest is the **View** (marked as '*') permission.

Action	Description	Community	Guest
View	Ability to view the portlet	X, *	X, *
Configuration	Ability to configure the portlet	X	X
Access in Control Panel	Ability to access the portlet in the Control Panel	X	

Obviously, as a member of the Guest community, "Lotti Stein" has the permission **View** only on the portlet Image Gallery by default. Since the role Community Member of the Guest community has no **Access in Control Panel** permission, "Lotti Stein" has no **Access in Control Panel** permission too. This means that "Lotti Stein" doesn't have access on the portlet **Image Gallery** in **Control Panel**.

Permissions on Image Gallery

The following table shows permissions on Image Gallery, that is, the root of all folders and images. The role Community Member is set up with all the permissions (marked as 'X') **Add Folder**, **Permissions**, **View**, and **Add Image**, unsupported for the role Guest, except the permission action **View**.

Action	Description	Community	Guest
Add Folder	Ability to add folders to the root	X	
Add Image	Ability to add images to the root	X	
Permissions	Ability to assign permissions in the root	X	
View	Ability to view images in the root	X	X

As you can see, users can get permissions on the root via the roles, like **Add Folder** and **Add Image**. But they have no chance to assign these permissions. Thus the permission action key **PERMISSIONS** should be added on Image Gallery as well as that of **Add Folder** and **Add Image**. This feature is missing at present but is highly expected.

Permissions on folders

The following table shows permissions on folders. All permission actions (marked as 'X') are supported for the role Community Member: **Access**, **View**, **Add Image**, **Add Subfolder**, **Delete**, **Permissions**, and **Update**, while permission actions **Add Image**, **Add Subfolder**, and **Update** are unsupported for the role Guest. By default, the role Community Member got permission actions **View** and **Add Image** (marked as '*'), while the role Guest got the permission **View** only.

Action	Description	Community	Guest
Access	Ability to access the folder	X	X
View	Ability to view this folder	X, *	X, *
Add Image	Ability to add images to the folder	X, *	
Add Subfolder	Ability to add sub-folders to the folder	X	
Delete	Ability to delete the folder	X	X
Permissions	Ability to assign permissions on the folder	X	X
Update	Ability to update the folder	X	

Obviously, as a member of the Guest community, "Lotti Stein" has the permissions **View** and **Add Image** on folders, by default.

Permissions on images

Similarly, the following table depicts permissions on images. The role Community Member is set up with all the permissions on images (marked as 'X'): **View**, **Delete**, **Permissions**, and **Update**, while the role Guest is set up with permissions: **View**, **Delete**, and **Permissions**. The 'by default' Action for the roles Community Member and Guest is the **View** (marked as '*') permission.

Action	Description	Community	Guest
View	Ability to view the image	X, *	X, *
Delete	Ability to delete the image	X	X
Permissions	Ability to assign permissions on the image	X	X
Update	Ability to update the image	X	

Apparently, as a member of the Guest community, "Lotti Stein" has the permission action **View** on images by default. As you can see, you would be able to assign permissions on images in the following scopes:

- Individual image.
- A set of images belonging to a folder like "Home".
- All images in a group like the Guest community.
- All images in a portal instance like the current portal instance.

How to implement the preceding use cases? For an individual image, you could be able to assign permissions in the portlet Image Gallery via custom regular roles, custom community roles (or Community Member) for community pages, or custom organization roles (or Organization Member) for organization pages.

For all images in a group, you can assign permissions in the **Control Panel** via custom community roles (or Community Member) for community pages or custom organization roles (or Organization Member) for organization pages.

For all images in a portal instance, you can assign permission in the **Control Panel** via custom regular roles. For a set of images belonging to a folder, you could use a folder hierarchy structure.

What's happening?

Image Gallery provides the ability to manage images. Generally speaking, Image Gallery is a central repository of images used via a unique URL.

The sequent diagram depicts an overview of Image Gallery conceptually. Image Gallery has a set of folders associated. Each folder may have many sub-folders associated. Thus folders form a hierarchy structure. Each folder (or sub-folder) may have a set of images. And each image has a unique URL to be referred. More interestingly, each image can have a thumbnail and two custom thumbnails optionally.

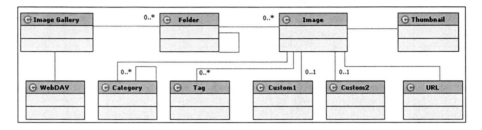

Setup

Thumbnails are reduced-size versions of pictures, used to help in recognizing and organizing them, serving the same role for images as a normal text index does for words. The portal automatically creates thumbnails for images when they are uploaded. How, you ask? The portal has specified the following properties in `portal.properties`.

```
ig.image.max.size=10240000
ig.image.extensions=.bmp,.gif,.jpeg,.jpg,.png,.tif,.tiff
ig.image.thumbnail.max.dimension=150
```

As shown in the preceding code, the property `ig.image.max.size` sets the maximum file size and valid file extensions for images. A value of 0 for the maximum file size can be used to indicate unlimited file size. Note that the maximum file size (for any uploaded image and document) allowed is set in the property `com.liferay.portal.upload.UploadServletRequestImpl.max.size`, default value `104857600=1024*1024*100`.

The property `ig.image.extensions` sets image file extensions. A file extension of `*` will permit all file extensions. The property `ig.image.thumbnail.max.dimension` sets the maximum thumbnail height and width in pixels.

Of course, you can override the preceding properties in `portal-ext.properties`. In addition, another two thumbnail images with different custom sizes can be created, namely, `custom1` and `custom2`. That is, you would be able to specify different thumbnail images—creating a scaled image of that size—in `portal-ext.properties` as follows:

```
ig.image.custom1.max.dimension=100
ig.image.custom2.max.dimension=50
```

As shown in the preceding code, you could set dimension of the custom images to `0` in order to disable creating a scaled image of that size.

Images in scope

One of the most powerful characteristics of Image Gallery (portlet ID `31`) is the fact that when they are added to different groups they act as completely independent portlets, each with their own data. For instance, when the portlet Image Gallery is added to a page for example, "CMS", of the Guest community, it will use the default scope. If you add the portlet Image Gallery to a second page, for example "Welcome", it will show the same data as that of the first page. When the portlet Image Gallery was added to a page, it will get scoped immediately into the group that the current page belongs to.

As you can see, the portlet Image Gallery is scoped into the group Guest when it was added into any pages in the group Guest. It seems that you don't have the flexibility to switch groups in this case. Fortunately, you can do it through the **Control Panel** by following these steps:

1. Go to **Manage | Control Panel** under the dock bar menu.
2. Locate Image Gallery under the category **Content**, and click on **Image Gallery**, you would see same folders and images as that of the page **CMS** because, by default, the content of the portlet Image Gallery is scoped to the group Guest.
3. Switch groups by selecting different groups from the drop-down menu **Content for**.
4. The portlet Image Gallery could get scoped into a page. How, you ask? To make the portlet Image Gallery use a different data scope, you would follow these simple steps:
5. Locate a page, say **CMS**, and the portlet Image Gallery in the current page.
6. Go to **More | Configuration** of the portlet Image Gallery.
7. Click on the tab **Scope**.
8. Choose **Current page (CMS)** from the select menu **Scope**, and click on the **Save** button.

Considering the pattern `Portal-Group-Page-Content`, the content of the portlet Image Gallery could be scoped into a group, for example, all pages including both private and public pages, by default. It could also be scoped into an individual page. This means that a set of data, for example, folders and images, is isolated from other data of the same portlet.

How to customize the scope feature? The portal has default settings for the portlet Image Gallery as follows in `$PORTAL_ROOT_HOME/WEB-INF/liferay-portlet.xml`.

```
<control-panel-entry-category>content</control-panel-entry-category>
<control-panel-entry-weight>3.0</control-panel-entry-weight>
<asset-renderer-factory>com.liferay.portlet.imagegallery.asset.
IGImageAssetRendererFactory</asset-renderer-factory>
<scopeable>true</scopeable>
```

The preceding code shows that the portlet Image Gallery will appear in the category **Content** and position 3 and it is scopeable, that is, you are able to use the tab **Scope** and change the scope from default to the current page. In addition, asset renderer framework is supported via the tag `asset-renderer-factory`. Thus you could publish images via the Asset Publisher portlet.

Customization

More interestingly, you could customize the portlet Image Gallery in JSP files. For example, the portal has specified a default implementation of slideshow. You may want to employ your own implementation of slideshow on the portlet Image Gallery.

The default slideshow is specified at `$PORATL_ROOT_HOME/html/portlet/image_gallery/view_slide_show.jsp` as follows.

```
<table class="lfr-table"> <!-- ignore details -->
<% if (images.size() > 0) {
IGImage image = (IGImage)images.get(0);
%>
<img border="0" name="<portlet:namespace />slideShow" src="<%=
themeDisplay.getPathImage() %>/image_gallery?img_id=<%= image.
getLargeImageId() %>&t=<%= ImageServletTokenUtil.getToken(image.
getLargeImageId()) %>" />
<% } <!-- ignore details -->
</table>
```

As shown in the preceding code, you would be able to override the JSP file directly.

Persist for images

As you have seen, the portlet Image Gallery stores metadata of images in the database, and it also stores the content of images in the database. Why you ask? The portal has used Database Hook by default in `portal.properties`.

```
image.hook.impl=com.liferay.portal.image.DatabaseHook
```

The preceding code shows that the content of images would be hooked via the database. The portal will use this to persist for images.

Besides Database Hook, there are another two hooks available to persisting for images, namely, Document Library (DL) Hook and File System Hook. If you're going to use DL Hook, you could add the following line at the end of `portal-ext.properties`.

```
image.hook.impl=com.liferay.portal.image.DLHook
```

However, if you think that File System Hook is much better, you could add the following line at the end of `portal-ext.properties`.

```
image.hook.impl=com.liferay.portal.image.FileSystemHook
```

When using File System Hook, the default file system root directory was set as follows in `portal.properties`.

```
image.hook.file.system.root.dir=${liferay.home}/data/images
```

Of course, you can override this property at the end of `portal-ext.properties`.

Setting up the image size in database

As you can see, the content of images is stored in the database, for example, MySQL. The server's default `max_allowed_packet` value is 1MB. You can increase this if the server needs to handle big queries. For example, to set the variable to 16MB, start the server like this:

shell> mysqld --max_allowed_packet=16M

You can also use the option files to set `max_allowed_packet`. For example, to set the size of the server to `16M`, add the following lines in the options file.

```
[mysqld]
max_allowed_packet=16M
```

Customizing default images

By the way, there are a set of default images you may want to override. Of course, you would be able to customize the portal in many ways without involving any Java code.

```
image.default.spacer=com/liferay/portal/dependencies/spacer.gif
image.default.company.logo=com/liferay/portal/dependencies/company_
logo.png
image.default.organization.logo=com/liferay/portal/dependencies/
organization_logo.png
image.default.user.female.portrait=com/liferay/portal/dependencies/
user_female_portrait.png
image.default.user.male.portrait=com/liferay/portal/dependencies/user_
male_portrait.png
```

As shown in the preceding code, the property `image.default.spacer` sets the location of the default spacer image, which is used for missing images. The property `image.default.company.logo` sets the location of the default company logo image, which is used for missing company logo images. The property `image.default.organization.logo` sets the location of the default organization logo image, which is used for missing organization logo images. Both `image.default.user.female.portrait` and `image.default.user.male.portrait` set the locations of the default user portrait images that are used for missing user portrait images. Note that these images must be available in the class path.

How to customize default images? There are two options to override default images:

- Create a class path `${class.path}` equal to `/com/liferay/portal/dependencies` under the folder `$PORTAL_ROOT_HOME/WEB_INF/classes` first, and then put customized images as the same image filename in the class path `${class.path}`.

- Override properties with a class path `${class.path}` plus customized image file names in `portal-ext.properties` first, and then create the class path `${class.path}` under the folder `$PORTAL_ROOT_HOME/WEB_INF/classes` and put customized images in it.

For example, let's say that you have your own company logo named "`PalmTree_logo.png`" and you're going to override the default company logo with your company's logo. For the first option, you can create a class path `${class.path}` equal to `/com/liferay/portal/dependencies` under the folder `$PORTAL_ROOT_HOME/WEB_INF/classes`, copy `PalmTree_logo.png` to `${class.path}`, and rename `PalmTree_logo.png` to `company_logo.png`.

For the second option, let's say that the class path ${class.path} is equal to com/ ext/dependencies/, you could add the following line at the end of portal-ext. properties, create the class path ${class.path} under the folder $PORTAL_ROOT_ HOME/WEB_INF/classes, and copy PalmTree_logo.png to ${class.path}.

```
image.default.company.logo=com/ext/dependencies/PalmTree_logo.png
```

In the same pattern, you would be able to customize other default images as well.

Enhancement

The Image Gallery portlet provides capabilities to manage your images and to organize them in folders, to link to My Images (images uploaded by you), to link to Recent Images, nice JavaScript pop up functionality to see images one at a time, slideshow, to access and to upload image using WebDAV, and to create multiple thumbnail images.

As you can see, the Image Gallery portlet defines the maximum dimension of the thumbnail. Optionally, another two thumbnail images with different custom sizes can be created, namely, custom1 and custom2. You can access thumbnail images when showing images as a list. But custom1 and custom2 are accessible only programmatically. It would be nice that the portlet Image Gallery could provide URLs for custom1 and custom2 if they are configured as well as that of the image URL, thus they would be accessible through a URL directly. In addition, it would be nice if the Editor could allow attaching any thumbnail images, including custom1 and custom2, to Web Content. This feature is not ready yet, but it is expected to be added soon.

Why WebDAV?

As you have seen, WebDAV URLs are available for Image Gallery folders and images. Why WebDAV? WebDAV provides capabilities to create, change, and move documents and images on a remote server, typically a web server. WebDAV is supported by all major Operating Systems and Desktop Environments including Windows, MacOS X, and Linux such as KDE, GNOME, and so on.

The portlets Image Gallery, Document Library, and Web Content Management provide support for the WebDAV protocol so that users can upload and organize resources from both a web interface and the file explorer of their desktop operating system.

- **Image Gallery**: Navigate to a specific folder or an image and edit it. You would see the direct WebDAV URL for that location or that image.

- **Document Library**: Navigate to a specific folder or a document and edit it. You will see the direct WebDAV URL for that location or that document.

- **Web Content**: Navigate to the specific template or structure and edit it. You would see the direct WebDAV URL for that template or that structure.

 WebDAV, short for **Web-based Distributed Authoring and Versioning**refers to the set of extensions to the Hypertext Transfer Protocol (HTTP). It allows users to collaboratively edit and manage files on remote World Wide Web servers, functionality to create, change, and move documents on a remote server. Refer to `http://www.webdav.org`, `http://en.wikipedia.org/wiki/WebDAV`

Each WebDAV-accessible resource of the portal has an associated URL. Copy that URL and use it to configure the file or WebDAV browser that you prefer. You will be asked to authenticate with a username and password.

You can log in using the login credentials you use to access the portal. In fact, you can use the e-mail address, user ID, or screen name—all three should work well.

Setup

In general, the portal allows WebDAV URL connections from any server using HTTP by default in `portal.properties`.

```
webdav.litmus=false
webdav.ignore//ignore details   webdav.servlet.hosts.allowed=
webdav.servlet.https.required=false
```

As shown in the preceding code, you may set the property `webdav.litmus` to `true` to enable programmatic configuration to let the WebDAV be configured for litmus testing. Note that litmus is a testing tool. The property `webdav.ignore` sets a list of files for the WebDAV servlet to ignore processing. The property `webdav.servlet.hosts.allowed` lists the allowed hosts, while empty means any hosts are allowed. The property `webdav.servlet.https.required` shows whether it requires HTTPS or not.

Of course, you can have a more secure configuration through the properties in `portal-ext.properties`, for example, setting a list of allowed hosts and making HTTPS required.

```
webdav.servlet.hosts.allowed=127.0.0.1,SERVER_IP
webdav.servlet.https.required=true
```

What's happening?

As mentioned earlier, Web Content Management, Document Library, and Image Gallery portlets make content available on WebDAV via their implementations. All WebDAV calls are translated to methods through tokens such as `image_gallery` for Image Gallery, `document_library` for Document Library, and `journal` for Web Content Management.

In general, there are two tags related to WebDAV: `webdav-storage-token` and `webdav-storage-class`. For example, the portlet Image Gallery (portlet ID `31`) has specified `$PORTAL_ROOT_HOME/WEB-INF/liferay-portlet.xml` WebDAV-related tags as follows:

```
<webdav-storage-token>image_gallery</webdav-storage-token>
<webdav-storage-class>com.liferay.portlet.imagegallery.webdav.
IGWebDAVStorageImpl</webdav-storage-class>
```

Similarly, the portlet Web Content (portlet ID `20`) has specified WebDAV-related tags in `$PORTAL_ROOT_HOME/WEB-INF/liferay-portlet.xml` as follows:

```
<webdav-storage-token>document_library</webdav-storage-token>
<webdav-storage-class>com.liferay.portlet.documentlibrary.webdav.
DLWebDAVStorageImpl</webdav-storage-class>
```

The portlet Web Content Management (portlet ID `15`) has specified WebDAV-related tags in `$PORTAL_ROOT_HOME/WEB-INF/liferay-portlet.xml` as follows:

```
<webdav-storage-token>journal</webdav-storage-token>
<webdav-storage-class>com.liferay.portlet.journal.webdav.
JournalWebDAVStorageImpl</webdav-storage-class>
```

As you can see, only two attributes `webdav-storage-token` and `webdav-storage-class` are required to enable WebDAV capability. Therefore WebDAV interfaces would be available in plugins SDK. For more details, you may refer to *Chapter 3, ServiceBuilder and Development Environments* of the book *Liferay Portal 5.2 Systems Development*.

The Document Library portlet

CMS provides one central place to aggregate and manage all your content. Each community or organization gets its own separate Document Library, equipped with customizable folders and act as a web-based shared drive for all your team members, no matter where they are. Each individual document is as open or as secure as you need it to be, since content is accessible only by permissions.

In order to let small teams manage web content and publish web content, you don't only need a set of images, but you also need a set of documents. The Document Library portlet provides document management that can be backed by different persistence systems. Similar to that of the portlet Image Gallery, the Document Library portlet is accessible both in the Control Panel and in a page. Here we're going to introduce the Document Library portlet in a page first.

As an administrator of the enterprise "Palm Tree Publications", you may want to add the Document Library portlet in the page **CMS** of the Guest community private pages. Furthermore, you need to create the folders "Books" and "Integration" and sub-folder "Chapters" in order to hold a set of documents. As well as that of the Image Gallery portlet, you would like to group all documents into different folders to make things easy-to-use and easy-to-manage.

Managing folders

Before adding a document, we need to create a folder called "Books", which contains a lot of documents. Let's do it by following these steps:

1. First, log in as an admin. Then go to **Go To | bookpub.com** under the dock bar menu. You would see a default domain like bookpub.com instead of Guest, if you have set **Settings | Main Configuration | Name** as bookpub. com under **Control Panel**.

2. Locate the page called **CMS** and go to **Add | More...** under the dock bar menu.

3. Add the Document Library portlet in the page **CMS** of the Guest community private pages where you want to manage documents, if the Document Library portlet is not there.

4. Click on the **Add Folder** icon.

5. Enter the name "Books" and the description "Documents Folder for Books".

6. Set **Permissions** by clicking on the **Configure** link. To configure additional permissions, click on the **More** link. Here we just use the default settings. By default, the checkbox **Public** is unchecked.

7. Click on the **Save** button to save the inputs, or click on the **Cancel** button to discard the inputs.

Adding sub-folders

Let's say that we need to create a sub-folder named "Chapters" under the folder "Books", where it will contain a set of documents for "Liferay Book". Let's do it as follows:

1. Locate the folder "Books", click on the link of the folder "Books", for example, the name.

2. Click on the **Add Subfolder** icon

3. Enter a name say "Chapters" and a description say "Documents Folder for Chapters".

4. Set **Permissions** by clicking on the **Configure** link. To configure additional permissions, click on the **More** link. Here we just use the default settings. By default, the checkbox **Public** is unchecked.

5. Click on the **Save** button to save the inputs, or click on the **Cancel** button to discard the inputs.

Similarly, you can create other folders as siblings of the folder "Books". After adding a folder "Integrations", we can view folders. The folders are displayed with columns: **Folders, Number of Folders, Number of Documents**, and the **Actions** button with a set of icons, for example, **Edit, Permissions, Delete, Add Subfolder, Add Document, Add Shortcut**, and **Access from My Desktop**. In particular, WebDAV URL is available for the root of Document Library and for all folders of Document Library.

As you can see, the right-side box shows the current folder, that is, the root in this case, with the name "Document Home" plus a presentation `folder_empty.png` icon if the folder is empty or `folder_full_document.png` if the folder isn't empty, and a set of action icons, for example **Permissions, Add Folder, Add Document, Add Shortcut**, and **Access from My Desktop**.

Note that you would be able to find the icons `folder_empty.png` and `folder_full_document.png` at `$PORTAL_ROOT_HOME/html/themes/${theme.name}/images/file_system/large`, where `${theme.name}` should be `classic`, `control_panel`, or any custom themes.

Similarly, you could find the icons `bookmark.png`, `folder_empty.png`, and `folder_full_bookmark.png` at `$PORTAL_ROOT_HOME/html/themes/${theme.name}/images/file_system/large` for the Bookmarks portlet entries and folders, where `${theme.name}` should be `classic`, `control_panel`, and any custom themes. This means that the current folder is presented with the name "Bookmarks Home" and the presentation `folder_empty.png` icon if the folder is empty or the presentation `folder_full_bookmark.png` icon if the folder isn't empty, and each entry is presented as the entry name plus the presentation icon `bookmark.png`.

Updating folders

Folders and sub-folders are editable. For example, you may need to change the description of the folder "Integrations" from "Documents Folder for Integration" to "Documents Folder for Liferay Integrations". Let's do it by following these steps:

1. Locate the folder, say "Integrations", that you want to edit.

2. Click on the **Edit** icon from the **Actions** button located next to the folder.

3. Maintain the value of the name and update the description of the selected folder "Documents Folder for Integrations" with the value "Documents Folder for Liferay Integrations".

4. Click on the **Save** button to save the changes.

Of course, you can update the name as well. For example, you can update the name "Integrations" to change it to "Liferay-Integrations".

If you have proper access rights, you can change the parent folder by selecting a folder as the parent folder of the folder or sub-folder, by merging with the parent folder, or by removing the parent folder. Eventually, if you remove the parent folder, the current folder will become a folder at the root level.

Folders or sub-folders are removable. For example, the folder "Integrations" doesn't exist anymore, so you can remove it. Let's do it by following these steps:

1. Locate the folder, say "Integrations", that you want to delete.

2. Click on the **Delete** icon from the **Actions** button located next to the folder.

3. A screen will appear asking if you want to delete this. Click on **OK** to confirm deletion.

 Note that deleting a folder will delete all related sub-folders and documents that belong to this folder.

In brief, the functions of managing folders in the **Document Library** are the same as that of managing folders in **Image Gallery** and **Bookmarks**. The folders and sub-folders are editable and removable.

Managing documents

Each document has its original name, but it is possible to change it in the portlet Document Library. You can also update the document and get the version history for it. Each document can have a title and a description, additional tags, and categories as well. Users can rate and comment on documents. You can see both your own personal rating and average rating for the document. Each document can have a WebDAV URL and HTTP URL in the same way as that of folders.

Adding documents in bulk

Once folders are created, you can add documents in bulk for a given folder as well as that of images. Let's say that you are going to add documents "4701_01_3rdDraft. pdf" and "4701_01_3rdDraft.doc" under the folder "Books". Let's do it by following these steps:

1. Locate the folder "Books", click on the link of the folder "Books",that is, the name.
2. Click on the **Add Document** icon.
3. Click on the **Browse** icon to find files `4701_01_3rdDraft.pdf` and `4701_01_3rdDraft.doc`.
4. Click on the **Upload Files** icon to upload files, optionally you can cancel all uploads by clicking on the link **Cancel All Uploads**.

Note that the filename plus extension will be used as the title and description of documents when documents get imported in bulk. For example, document "4701_01_3rdDraft.pdf" will have both its title and description as "4701_01_3rdDraft.pdf".

As you can see, you can import documents in bulk by clicking on the icon **Browse**, where you can select multiple files. You would be able to use the classic uploader to upload documents one at a time.

- **Folder**: Selecting a folder or removing a folder.
- **File**: Uploading a document file.
- **Title**: A title of the current document.
- **Description**: Document description.

- **Categories**: Selecting categories.
- **Tags**: Adding a tag, selecting a tag, or search tags.
- **Permissions**: Either public or configured by specific permissions.
- **Save/Cancel**: Saving or discarding inputs.
- **Use the new uploader**: A link to the previous view.

Adding shortcuts

You are able to create a shortcut to any document that you have read access for. The permissions set on the shortcut enable others to access the original document through the shortcut. You can create a shortcut to any document that you have read access for by clicking on the **Add Shortcut** icon, where you can select a specific community and a specific document. The permissions set on the shortcut enable others to access the original document through the shortcut. Let's say that you're going to add a shortcut under the folder "Books" for the document "4701_01_3rdDraft.doc". Let's do it by following these steps:

1. Locate a folder, for example "Books", and click on it's name.
2. Click on the **Add Shortcut** icon.
3. Select the community, for example Guest, as shown in the following screenshot.
4. Select a document, say `4701_01_3rdDraft.doc`.
5. Set **Permissions** by clicking on the **Configure** link. To configure additional permissions, click on the **More** link. By default, the checkbox **Public** is unchecked. Here we just use the default settings.
6. Click on the **Save** button to save the inputs, or click on the **Cancel** button to discard the inputs.

As you can see, shortcuts are scoped into any group such as communities, organizations, and the current user's community called My Community. This means that user groups aren't involved.

Note that shortcuts aren't real documents, just the name of a target file that the shortcut represents. Thus shortcuts are presented as original documents plus additional image icon `overlay_link.png`. You would be able to find this icon `overlay_link.png` at `$PORTAL_ROOT_HOME/html/themes/${theme.name}/images/file_system/large`, where `${theme.name}` should be `classic`, `control_panel`, and any custom themes.

Viewing documents

Documents are viewable. Let's say that you want to view the document "4701_01_3rdDraft.doc" under the folder "Books". Let's do it by following these steps:

1. Click the folder "Books", you would see a set of documents displayed with the columns **Name, Size, Downloads, Locked**, and the **Actions** button plus a set of icons, namely, **Download** (#KB), **Edit**, **Permissions**, and **Delete**.

2. Locate the document, say 4701_01_3rdDraft.doc, that you want to view.

3. Click on any link, such as **Name, Size, Downloads**, and **Locked**, and you would view the document, as shown in the following screenshot:

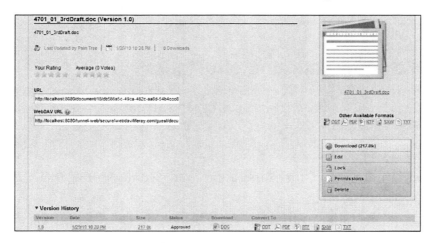

You would be able to view the details on documents or shortcuts.

-   **Title**: Title plus version information.
-   **Basic info**: Updated by, update date, and number of downloads.
-   **Rank**: Your rating, average ratings.
-   **URL**: Document or shortcut URL.
-   **WebDAV URL**: For document only.
-   **Community**: For shortcut only.
-   **Version History**: A list of versions.
-   **Comments**: Comments on document.
-   **Presentation info**: Group icon, a link like **Title** to download, plus "overlay_link.png" for a shortcut.

- **Other Available Formats**: OpenOffice based conversion.
- **Action Icons: Edit, Permissions, Delete, View Original File** for shortcut only.

Optionally, you can view your own documents by clicking on the **My Documents** tab of the Document Library portlet. You can also view the recent documents by clicking on the tab **Recent Documents** of the Document Library portlet.

Searching documents and shortcuts

Documents are searchable as well as that of images. There are three options to search documents. You can search documents from the root, search documents from the current folder only, or search documents both in the current folder and its sub-folders.

Editing documents and shortcuts

Documents are editable as well as that of images. For example, you may need to change the description of the document "4701_01_3rdDraft.doc" under the folder "Books" to the value "Book Chapter 1". Let's do it as follows:

1. Click on the folder, say "Books".
2. Locate a document, for example `4701_01_3rdDraft.doc`, that you want to edit.
3. Click on the **Edit** icon from the **Actions** button located next to the document.
4. Update the description of the selected document `4701_01_3rdDraft.doc` with the value "Book Chapter 1".
5. Click on the **Save** button.

Optionally, you can change the folder by selecting another folder. At the same time, you can change the content of the document by uploading another file. As shown in the preceding screenshot, updating the content of the document will create a new version of the document. Furthermore, you can find a URL for the document. You can reference the document by this URL in an article (called web content).

In addition, you can find a WebDAV URL for the document. You can reference the document by this URL from the file explorer. In brief, documents and folders can be managed directly from the file explorer of your desktop operating system.

Deleting documents and shortcuts

Documents are removable, just like images. For example, imagine that the document "4701_01_3rdDraft.pdf" doesn't exist anymore, so you need to remove it. Let's do it by following these steps:

1. Locate the document, say `4701_01_3rdDraft.pdf`, that you want to delete.

2. Then click on the **Delete** icon from the **Actions** button located next to the document.

3. A screen will appear asking if you want to delete this. Click on **OK** to confirm deletion.

Note that deleting a shortcut will delete the shortcut only, but deleting a document will delete the original document plus its associated versions, shortcuts, ratings, and comments.

Viewing version history

Whenever the content of the document changes, a new version of the document generates. To view versions, first view the original document, and then click on the **Version History** tab. For example, we want to view the version history of the document "`4701_01_3rdDraft.doc`". Let's do it by following these steps:

1. Locate the document, say `4701_01_3rdDraft.doc`, that you want to view.

2. Then click on any link such as **Name**, **Size**, **Downloads**, **Locked**.

3. By default, the **Version History** tab was selected. The versions are displayed as columns: **Version**, **Date**, **Size**, **Status**, **Delete** for shortcuts, **Download**, and **Convert To** for documents. All versions of the document will appear below the button **Compare Versions**.

4. Check the checkbox at the right of the version, for example, "1.0", "1.1", and then click on the button **Compare Versions**. A comparing result will appear, for example, "There are no differences between 1.0 and 1.1". How does it work? Refer to the section *What's happening?*

Giving your rating

As well as rating a blog entry, you can give your own rating for any document or shortcut. For example, as an administrator, you can read the document "4701_01_3rdDraft.pdf". If you want to give a document rating of two stars, then you simply click on the second star under "Your Rating" of the document.

Try logging in as "Lotti Stein", then reading the document "4701_01_3rdDraft.pdf". Then, if you want to give a rating of four stars, you simply click on the fourth star under "Your Rating" of the document. Now you will find the average is three stars with the message "2 Votes".

Note that each user can rate only once for a given document or shortcut. However, users can update their ratings for a given document or shortcut whenever they want.

Adding comments

As stated, the administrator has created a document called "4701_01_3rdDraft.pdf". As a user of the enterprise "Palm Tree Publications", "Lotti Stein" wants to review the document and add comments, say "Need more details". As well as adding comments on an entry of Blogs, "Lotti Stein" can add comments on documents similarly.

Export and Import

More interestingly, you can easily export and then import documents to another server. How to do it? Simply click on the **More | Export/Import** icon of the portlet first. Then following the processes, you can export and import documents and shortcuts smoothly.

Assigning permissions

Similar to the permissions on Image Gallery, there are five-group permissions for the portlet Document Library, namely, permissions on the portlet, permissions on Document Library, permissions on folders, permissions on documents, and permissions on shortcuts. Permissions on the portlet Documents Library are the same as that of `Image Gallery`.

Permissions on the portlet

The following table shows permissions on the Document Library portlet. The role Community Member is set up with all the permissions (marked as 'X'), namely, **View**, **Configuration**, and **Access in Control Panel**, while the role Guest user is set up with permissions **View** and **Configuration**. The 'by default' Action for the roles Community Member and Guest is the **View** (marked as '*') permission.

Action	Description	Community	Guest
View	Ability to view the portlet	X, *	X, *
Configuration	Ability to configure the portlet	X	X
Access in Control Panel	Ability to access the portlet in Control Panel	X	

Obviously, as a member of the Guest community, "Lotti Stein" has the permission **View** only on the portlet Document Library by default. Since the role Community Member of the Guest community has no permission **Access in Control Panel**, "Lotti Stein" doesn't have the permission **Access in Control Panel** too. This means that "Lotti Stein" doesn't have access on the Document Library portlet in **Control Panel**.

Permissions on Document Library

The following table shows the permissions on Document Library, that is, the root of all folders and documents. The role Community Member is set up with all the permissions (marked as 'X') **Add Folder**, **Add Document**, and **Add Shortcut**, unsupported for the role Guest.

Action	Description	Community	Guest
Add Folder	Ability to add folders to the root	X	
Add Document	Ability to add documents to the root	X	
Add Shortcut	Ability to add shortcut to the root	X	
Permissions	Ability to assign permissions at the root	X	
View	Ability to view documents at the root	X	X

As you can see, users can get permissions on the root via the roles, that is, **Add Folder**, **Add Document**, and **Add Shortcut**. But they have no chance to assign these permissions to other users. Thus the permission action key **PERMISSIONS** should be added on the Document Library as well as that of **Add Folder**, **Add Document**, and **Add Shortcut**. This feature is missing at present but it is expected to be added soon.

Permissions on folders

The following table shows the permissions on folders. All permission actions (marked as 'X') are supported by the Community Member role: **Access, View, Add Document, Add Shortcut, Add Subfolder, Delete, Permissions**, and **Update**, while permission actions **Add Document, Add Shortcut, Add Subfolder**, and **Update** are unsupported for the Guest role. By default, the Community Member role has the permission actions **View, Add Shortcut,** and **Add Document** (marked as '*'), while the Guest role only has the permission **View**.

Action	Description	Community	Guest
Access	Ability to access the folder	X	X
View	Ability to view the folder	X, *	X, *
Add Document	Ability to add Documents to the folder	X, *	
Add Shortcut	Ability to add Shortcuts to the folder	X,*	
Add Subfolder	Ability to add sub-folders to the folder	X	
Delete	Ability to delete the folder	X	X
Permissions	Ability to assign permissions on the folder	X	X
Update	Ability to update the folder	X	

Obviously, as a member of the Guest community, "Lotti Stein" has the permissions **View, Add Shortcut,** and **Add Document** on the folders by default.

Permissions on documents

Similarly, the following table shows permissions on documents. The Community Member role has all the permissions (marked as 'X'), namely, **View, Add Discussion, Delete, Permissions, Delete Discussion, Update Discussion,** and **Update** supported, while the Guest role only has the permissions **View, Delete,** and **Permissions** supported. The 'by default' Action for the Community Member role are the permissions **View** and **Add Discussion** (marked as '*'), while the Guest role only has the permission **View**.

Action	Description	Community	Guest
View	Ability to view the document	X, *	X, *
Add Discussion	Ability to add discussion on the document	X, *	
Delete Discussion	Ability to delete discussion on the document	X	
Update Discussion	Ability to update discussion on the document	X	
Delete	Ability to delete the document	X	X
Permissions	Ability to assign permissions on the document	X	X
Update	Ability to update the document	X	

Obviously, as a member of the Guest community, "Lotti Stein" has the permission actions **View** and **Add Discussion** on documents by default. Of course, you would be able to assign permissions on documents (and shortcuts) in the following scopes:

- Individual document or shortcut.
- A set of documents (and shortcuts) belonging to a folder like "Books".
- All documents (and shortcuts) in a group like the Guest community.
- All documents (and shortcuts) in a portal instance like the current portal instance.

How to implement them? For individual documents or shortcuts, you could be able to assign permissions in the portlet Document Library via custom regular roles, custom community roles (or Community Member) for community pages, or custom organization roles (or Organization Member) for organization pages.

For all documents in a group, you are able to assign permissions in the **Control Panel** via custom community roles (or Community Member) for community pages or custom organization roles (or Organization Member) for organization pages.

For all documents in a portal instance, you are able to assign permissions in the **Control Panel** via custom regular roles. For a set of documents (and shortcuts) belonging to a folder, you could use a folder hierarchy structure.

Permissions on shortcuts

Just like permissions on documents, the following table shows permissions on shortcuts. The Community Member role has all permissions (marked as 'X'), namely, **View**, **Add Discussion**, **Delete**, **Permissions**, **Delete Discussion**, **Update Discussion**, and **Update** supported, while the Guest role has only the permissions **View**, **Delete**, and **Permissions** supported. By default, the Community Member role has the permissions **View** and **Add Discussion** (marked as '*'), while the Guest role has only the permission **View**.

Action	Description	Community	Guest
View	Ability to view the shortcut	X, *	X, *
Add Discussion	Ability to add discussions on the shortcut	X, *	
Delete Discussion	Ability to delete discussions on the shortcut	X	
Update Discussion	Ability to update discussions on the shortcut	X	
Delete	Ability to delete the shortcut	X	X
Permissions	Ability to assign permissions on the shortcut	X	X
Update	Ability to update the shortcut	X	

Publishing documents

There are two portlets, namely, Document Library Display (portlet ID 101) and Recent Documents (portlet ID 64) that can be used to publish documents.

Document Library Display

The Document Library Display portlet could be used to show a specific folder of the Document Library portlet. It looks and works like the Document Library portlet, but it doesn't contain any actions or other modification features. The main idea of the portlet is to function as a read-only view for a selected document library.

The Document Library Display portlet could be used to view folders and files in a document library, with no modification features. The configuration is pretty much the same as that of the Document Library portlet.

Note that the Document Library Display portlet is instanceable. This means that in a page, you could be able to add more than one Document Library Display portlet.

Recent Documents

The Recent Documents portlet displays the documents most recently accessed from the Document Library. A set of recent documents will appear in this portlet. Note that the Recent Documents portlet is non-instanceable. That is, in a page you would be able to add only one Recent Document portlet.

What's happening?

Document Library acts as a centralized repository with versioning and library services for example, check-in, check-out, metadata, versioning, and so on.

The following diagram depicts an overview of the Document Library conceptually. The Document Library has a set of folders. Each folder may have many sub-folders associated. Therefore, a hierarchy structure is supported in folders. Each folder (or sub-folder) may have a set of documents. Each document is referred to by an unique URL. In particular, each document may have a number of comments (that is, posts and replies) and ratings associated with it. Each document may also have a list of versions.

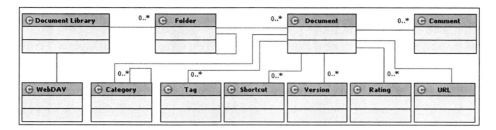

Setup

As you have seen, you are able to add comments and ranks on documents by default. Why? The portal has specified the following properties in portal.properties.

```
dl.file.max.size=3072000
dl.file.extensions=//ignore details
dl.comparable.file.extensions=.css,.js,.htm,.html,.txt,.xml
dl.layouts.sync.enabled=false
dl.layouts.sync.private.folder=Pages - Private
dl.layouts.sync.public.folder=Pages - Public
dl.file.entry.comments.enabled=true
dl.file.rank.enabled=true
```

As shown in the preceding code, the property `dl.file.max.size` sets the maximum file size for documents. A value of `0` for the maximum file size can be used to indicate unlimited file size. The property `dl.file.extensions` sets the file extensions allowed. A file extension of `*` will permit all file extensions.

The property `dl.comparable.file.extensions` sets which file extensions are comparable by the `diff` tool. If OpenOffice integration is enabled, then it is also possible to compare some binary files that are convertible to text. By default, you can compare files with the extensions `.css`, `.js`, `.htm`, `.html`, `.txt`, and `.xml`. But you can customize this according to your own requirements in `portal-ext.properties` as follows:

```
dl.comparable.file.extensions=.css,.doc,.js,.htm,.html,.odt,.rtf,.
sxw,.txt,.xml
```

Properties (`dl.layouts.sync.*`) set the folder names that will be used to synchronize with a community's set of private and public layouts, allowing users to manage layouts using the Document Library portlet, and ultimately, via WebDAV. Meanwhile the portal sets the property `dl.file.entry.comments.enabled` to `true` to enable comments for document library files, the portal sets the property `dl.file.rank.enabled` to `true`, to enable file rank for document library files.

Of course, you can override these properties in `portal-ext.properties`. In particular, you may want to add file extensions like `.wav`, `.mov`, and `.m4v`. To do this, there are two things you need to take into account:

- Add customized file extensions in `portal-ext.properties` such as `dl.file.extensions=.bmp,.css,.doc,.docx,.dot,.gif,.gz,.htm,.html,.jpg,.js,.lar,.odb,.odf,.odg,.odp,.ods,.odt,.pdf,.png,.ppt,.pptx,.rtf,.swf,.sxc,.sxi,.sxw,.tar,.tiff,.tgz,.txt,.vsd,.xls,.xlsx,.xml,.zip,.jrxml,.wav,.mov,` and `.m4v`.
- Copy media files like `wav.png`, `mov.png`, `m4v.png` to all `$PORTAL_ROOT_HOME/html/themes/${theme.name}/images/file_system/small`, where `${theme.name}` should be `classic`, `control_panel`, and any custom themes.

That's it. From now on, you will be able to upload files with custom extensions, such as `.wav`, `.mov`, and `.m4v` and view files with custom icons like `wav.png`, `mov.png`, and `m4v.png`.

Configuration

Besides the features of **Export/Import** and **Look and Feel**, the configuration of the portlet Document Library portlet consists of four different parts: **Setup, Permissions, Sharing**, and **Scope. Parts Permissions** and **Sharing** are exactly the same as that of other portlets.

Setup contains three categories: **Folders Listing, Documents Listing,** and **Ratings.** **Folders Listing** has the setting for the **Root Folder** as a starting point for the portlet Document Library. You can select a folder as the root folder or remove the current root folder. Then you can select whether or not to show breadcrumbs, search, and sub-folders. **Folders for Page** determine the number of folders to show on one page. You can also select which columns are shown for folders, where the **Current list** contains the columns that are currently shown and the **Available list** contains the columns that are still available.

The **Document Listing** configuration can be used for documents contained in folders. You can choose whether or not to show the search bar, and you can set how many documents to list on one page. Of course, you would be able to set up which columns to show for documents, where the **Current list** contains the columns that are currently shown and the **Available list** contains the columns that are still available.

In the **Ratings** configuration, you can turn on and off comment ratings.

In addition, you would be able to save current settings as archives, and also manage archives of the portlet Document Library.

Document presentation

You may have noticed that all documents are grouped when they are presented in download mode through file extensions. These groups involve compressed, document, flash, image, music, pdf, presentation, spreadsheet, and video. The following table shows the grouping feature. Note that the display images reside at `$PORTAL_ROOT_HOME/html/themes/${theme.name}/images/file_system/large`

Groups	File Extensions	Display Images
compressed	lar, rar, zip	compresses.png
default	unknown	default.png
document	doc, docx, rtf, odt	document.png
flash	flv, swf	flash.png
image	bmp, gif, jpeg, jpg, odg, png, svg	image.png
music	acc, mid, mp3, wav, wma	music.png
pdf	pdf	pdf.png
presentation	odp, ppt, pptx	presentation.png
spreadsheet	csv, ods, xls, xlsx	spreadsheet.png
video	avi, mov, mp4, mpg, qt, rm, wmv	video.png

At the time of writing, the mappings between file extensions and grouping aren't configurable. In fact, the mappings are hardcoded. For example, if you need to add the file extension `m4v` in the group `video`, then you have to change the code like `map.put("m4v", "video")`.

It would be nice that these mappings are configurable through `properties` in both `portal.properties` and `portal-ext.properties`. This feature is not yet available but is highly expected.

In addition, you can use following property to present a file with extension like GIF as an icon like gif in `portal-ext.properties`.

```
dl.file.icons=.bmp,.css,.doc,.docx,.dot,.gif,.gz,.htm,.html,.jpg,.js,.
lar,.odb,.odf,.odg,.odp,.ods,.odt,.pdf,.png,.ppt,.pptx,.rtf,.swf,.
sxc,.sxi,.sxw,.tar,.tiff,.tgz,.txt,.vsd,.xls,.xlsx,.xml,.zip,.jrxml
```

As you can see, you can present a file the extension like `GIF` as an icon like gif by adding the image to the theme's image display and document library folder. The wildcard extension of `*` will be ignored. For example, the default image for the `DOC` extension would be found in `$PORTAL_ROOT_HOME/html/themes/_unstyled/images/file_system/small/doc.gif`.

Check-in and check-out lockable documents

As you have noticed, you would check-in or check-out documents. Behind the scenes, a locking function is applied. When clicking on the `Lock` button, you would see a message saying "You now have a lock on this document. No one else can edit this document until you unlock it. This lock will automatically expire in 1 day".

The portal introduced a new locking mechanism — persistence locking mechanism — starting from version 6. Before 6, the portal used the singleton instance `LockPool` to hold locking information, and this flag was only available when the portal was running. You would lose the locking information when restarting the portal.

The new locking mechanism is database persistence. A table called `Lock_` is introduced with the columns `uuid_`, `lockId`, `companyId`, `userId`, `userName`, `createDate`, `className`, `key_`, `owner`, `inheritable`, and `expirationDate`. In particular, the column `Key_` stores the locked object information such as `fileEntryId#FolderId#fileName - 10144#10403#DLFE-1`.

Why will the lock automatically expire in one day? The portal has the default settings for the lock function in `portal.properties`.

```
lock.expiration.time.com.liferay.portlet.documentlibrary.model.
DLFolder=86400000
lock.expiration.time.com.liferay.portlet.documentlibrary.model.
```

```
DLFileEntry=86400000
```

The preceding code sets the lock expiration time (the default value is one day: `86400000=1000*60*60*24`) for folders and document of Document Library. Of course, you would be able to override these properties in `portal-ext.properties`. By the way, you can set this property to `0` to disable auto-expiration. That is, you could create a lock that never expires, using `0` (zero) for the expiration time.

Documents in scope

Similar to that of Image Gallery, when the Document Library portlets are added to different groups, they act as completely independent portlets, each with its own data. For instance, when the Document Library portlet is added to a page, let's say **CMS**, of the Guest community, it will use the default scope. If you add the Document Library portlet to a second page, say "Welcome", it will show the same data as that of the first page. When the Document Library portlet was added to a page, it will get scoped immediately into the group that the current page belongs to.

Considering the pattern `Portal-Group-Page-Content`, the content of the Document Library portlet could be scoped into a group, for example, all pages including both private and public pages, by default. Alternatively, it could be scoped into an individual page, it means that a set of data, for example, folders and documents, is isolated from other data of the same portlet.

How to customize the scope feature? The portal has default settings for the Document Library portlet, as follows, in `$PORTAL_ROOT_HOME/WEB-INF/liferay-portlet.xml`.

```
<control-panel-entry-category>content</control-panel-entry-category>
<control-panel-entry-weight>2.0</control-panel-entry-weight>
<asset-renderer-factory>com.liferay.portlet.imagegallery.asset.
IGImageAssetRendererFactory</asset-renderer-factory>
<scopeable>true</scopeable>
```

This code shows that the Document Library portlet will appear in the category **Content** and position 2, and it is scopeable, that is, you are able to use the tab **Scope** and change the scope from **default** to the current page. In addition, the asset renderer framework is supported via the tag `asset-renderer-factory`. Thus, you could publish documents via the Asset Publisher portlet.

Document persistence

The portal provides hooks into various persistence systems, which are configurable. The hooks include File System Hook, Advanced File System Hook, CMIS Hook, S3 Hook, and JCR Hook. A new hook to allow Document Library to use Documentum as a repository will come out shortly.

- **File System Hook** and **Advanced File System Hook**: saves directly to the server's file system and doesn't use any database or translation layer.

- **CMIS Hook**: Content Management Interoperability Services (CMIS) — a standard proposal consisting of a set of Web services for sharing information among disparate content repositories that seeks to ensure interoperability for people and applications using multiple content repositories. Alfresco, Day Software, Dennis Hamilton, EMC, FatWire, IBM, Microsoft, Open Text, Oracle, and SAP have joined forces to propose CMIS.

- **S3 Hook**: Amazon S3 (Simple Storage Service) is an online storage web service offered by Amazon Web Services. Amazon S3 provides unlimited storage through a simple web services interface.

- **JCR Hook**: Content Repository API for Java (JCR) — a specification for a Java platform API for accessing content repositories in a uniform manner. It provides hooks to a JCR (JSR-170) using Jackrabbit.

Setup

As you have seen, the File System Hook is used by default. Why? This is because the portal has the following default settings in `portal.properties`.

```
dl.hook.impl=com.liferay.documentlibrary.util.FileSystemHook
dl.hook.file.system.root.dir=${liferay.home}/data/document_library
```

As shown in the preceding code, the default hook is set as File System Hook and the root directory is `${liferay.home}/data/document_library`. Of course, you would able to use other hooks like CMIS Hook, S3 Hook, and JCR Hook in `portal-ext.properties`.

Amazon S3 is storage for the Internet. It is designed to make web-scale computing easier for developers. If you were interested in this feature, you could set up S3 hook in `portal-ext.properties` as follows:

```
dl.hook.impl=com.liferay.documentlibrary.util.S3Hook
dl.hook.s3.access.key=
dl.hook.s3.secret.key=
dl.hook.s3.bucket.name=
```

As shown in the preceding code, you need to have an Amazon S3 account first and need to specify your bucket name.

CMIS allows for different CMS systems to interchange information. It is basically JSR-170 with two differences: not Java-specific and document-management-centric. If you are interested in this feature, then you could have a CMIS producer setup, and in `portal-ext.properties`, configure the following:

```
dl.hook.impl=com.liferay.documentlibrary.util.CMISHook
cmis.credentials.username=none
cmis.credentials.password=none
```

Depending on which CMIS producer you are using, you may need to change the repository URL.

When do we use Advanced File System Hook?

As you can see, both File System Hook and Advanced File System Hook save directly into the server's filesystem and they don't use any database or translation layer. What's the difference between File System Hook and Advanced File System Hook? You would see the difference with examples: uploading two documents (PDF and WORD) under the folder "Home"; once, using File System Hook, and the next time, using Advanced File System Hook.

The left-side shows documents stored via File System Hook, using the following folder structure.

```
data->document_library->companyID->folderID->DLFE-${number.
extension}
```

The right-side shows documents stored through Advanced File System Hook, using the following folder structure.

```
data->document_library->companyID->folderID->DLFE->${number.
extension}
```

Advanced File System Hook extends the File System Hook by distributing the files in multiple directories and thus avoiding filesystem limits on a number of files per directory. It divides the data into smaller groups. If you expect to have a significant number of files, and as a result, you may fear hitting the filesystem limit for the number of files in a given folder, you should use the Advanced File System Hook.

Why JCR Jackrabbit?

As already mentioned, the portal provides hooks to a JCR (JSR-170) using Jackrabbit. The portal has specified JCR as follows:

```
jcr.jackrabbit.repository.root=${liferay.home}/data/jackrabbit
jcr.jackrabbit.config.file.path=${jcr.jackrabbit.repository.root}/
repository.xml
jcr.jackrabbit.repository.home=${jcr.jackrabbit.repository.root}/home
jcr.jackrabbit.credentials.username=none
jcr.jackrabbit.credentials.password=none
```

If in need, you could override these settings at the end of `portal-ext.properties`. In general, the Document Library portlet could be backed by a `JCR-170` compliant Java Content Repository (Jackrabbit). JCR 2.0 is ongoing in `JSR 283`, being available shortly.

> Apache Jackrabbit is a fully conforming implementation of the Content Repository for Java Technology API (JCR). URL `http://jackrabbit.apache.org/`

If you were interested in using JCR Hook, you could set the following line at the end of `portal-ext.properties`.

```
dl.hook.jcr.fetch.delay=500
dl.hook.jcr.fetch.max.failures=5
dl.hook.impl=com.liferay.documentlibrary.util.JCRHook
```

The preceding code shows that the Document Library portlet will use JCR Hook on documents persistence. The fetch delay would be 500 ms and the fetch max failures would be 5 times.

The Jackrabbit repository configuration file, typically called `repository.xml` under `${jcr.jackrabbit.repository.root}`, specifies global options like security, versioning, and clustering settings. Persistence mechanism is highlighted with Local File System mapping abstract filesystem accesses to the specified directory within the native filesystem or Database File System mapping abstract filesystem accesses to the database.

By default, **Local File System** is used as persistence mechanism as follows:

```
<?xml version="1.0"?>
<Repository>
    <!-- ignore details, refer to code repository-fs.xml -->
  <Workspaces rootPath="${rep.home}/workspaces"
defaultWorkspace="liferay" />
    <!-- ignore details, refer to code repository-fs.xml -->
```

As shown in the preceding code, it shows configuration about **FileSystem**, **Security**, **Workspaces**, **Workspace**, and **Versioning**. Of course, you could switch it from **Local File System** to **Database File System**. Let's say that you were using MySQL database lportal with an account username/password lportal/lportal, you can configure the Jackrabbit repository as follows:

```xml
<?xml version="1.0"?>
<Repository>
  <FileSystem class="org.apache.jackrabbit.core.fs.db.DbFileSystem">
    <!-- ignore details, refer to code repository-db.xml -->
  </FileSystem>
      <!-- ignore details, refer to code repository-db.xml -->
</Repository>
```

The preceding code is a sample configuration for MySQL persistence. For other databases, change the connection, credentials, and schema settings correspondingly. For clustering settings, refer to *Chapter 11, Ongoing Admin Tasks*.

Enhancement

In short, the portlet Document Library provides document management that can be backed by different persistence systems, including check-in, checkout, metadata, and versioning features. Document file formats could be converted at the time of uploading, if needed. This means that when uploading a document, you convert it into other formats and save them. You can add as many sub-folders as possible under any folder if you have the proper access rights, and each folder and file has individual WebDAV URL.

More interestingly, you would be able to add lots of custom metadata as you want through Custom Fields (also called Custom Attributes). However, only basic data types are supported in Custom Fields, custom data types like Image Gallery image and Document Library document aren't supported yet. This means that you couldn't add reference objects (like Image Gallery Image and Document Library Document) in Document Library Document metadata. This feature is highly expected.

As you can see, there is only one content type with the default metadata in addition to custom metadata through the Custom Attributes. The custom content types of Document Library Document aren't supported yet. For example, for the type Video, you may have a set of metadata; for the type Game, you may have another set of metadata. Now you expect to manage documents with different content types in the Document Library. This feature too is not yet supported, but it is highly expected.

In addition, metadata of documents and images like **Title**, **Name**, and **Description** is not localizable. A link to web content articles with a structure would fix everything: image or document metadata, aspects, localization, and so on.

Web Content Management portlet

Last but not least, we are ready to create journal articles, that is, web content, based on preceding images and documents. For example, we're planning to create web content called "About Us" with texts, images, and links to documents, as shown in following image (named as Original Required View). Obviously, the Web Content Management portlet would be useful for this purpose.

The Web Content Management portlet (portlet ID 15) is accessible only through the **Control Panel**, and it offers a full suite of tools to manage structured and unstructured content to be published on a website. There are many options to know the features of the Web Content Management portlet in depth. Here we adopt the approach **driving-by-examples**. Let's build this article using the Web Content Management portlet.

Managing structures

First of all, we need to create a structure for the previous article. A structure, named "Structure About Us", defines the dynamic parts of the article "About Us". Let's create the structure by following these steps:

1. Log in as an Admin, and then go to **Manage | Control Panel** under the dock bar menu.

2. Click on **Web Content** in the category **Content** of the **Control Panel**. By default, you would see **Content for Guest**. If not, select **Guest**.

3. Click on the **Structures** tab.

4. Click on the **Add Structures** button.

5. Enable the checkbox **Auto Generate ID**, input the name "Structure About us" and the description "Structure for About us".

6. Select the parent structure by clicking on the **Select** button. To remove current parent structure, click on the button **Remove**. Here we keep it as it is.

7. Set **Permissions** by clicking on the **Configure** link. To configure additional permissions, click on the **More** link. Here we just use the default settings. By default, the checkbox **Public** is unchecked.

8. Add a row, for example "title", by clicking on the **Add Row** button, and select the type of the row, for example, **Text**.

9. Add more rows like "caption", "image_caption", and so on.

10. Optionally, you can click on the **Up** and **Down** icons next to the row to change the order of rows. Alternatively, you can click on the **Add** icon next to the row to add a sub row, or click on the **Remove** icon next to the row to delete the current row.

11. Click on the **Save** button.

Note that only rows can be moved up and down in the same level. This means that you can't move a row from the child level to parent level, or vice verse. In addition, you would be able to add a child row by clicking on the **Add** icon next to the checkbox **Repeatable** or delete a row by clicking on the **Remove** icon next to the **Add** icon of the row.

As you can see, a structure consists of row elements. You can build a structure by web UI or through the Launching Editor. When using web UI, each row will be specified by name, type, index-type, repeatable, and so on.

- **Launch Editor**: Building structure with the help of editor, Editor types—Plain or Rich.

- **Download**: When editing a structure, you would be able to download the current structure in an XML format.

- **Name**: Element name.

- **Type: Text, Text Box, Text Area (HTML), Image, Image Gallery, Boolean Flag, Selection List, Multi-Selection List, Link to Page**.

- **Index-type**: Not Searchable, Searchable—Keyword, Searchable—Text.

- **Repeatable**: Whether element is repeated or not.

Of course, you can add other structures as well. After adding a structure "one image", we can view structures. When structures are created, it is simple to manage them. You can either edit a structure or delete a structure. Each structure has a unique URL and a WebDAV URL which can be used to refer to it.

Viewing structures

By clicking on the **Structures** tab in the Web Content Management portlet, you can view structures with paginations. You can view templates for a given structure by clicking on the **Views Templates** icon. Alternatively, you can add templates for a given structure by clicking on the **Add Templates** icon. Furthermore, you can view articles related to a given structure by clicking on the **Views Web Content** icon. Alternatively, you can add articles associated to a given structure by clicking on the **Add Article** icon.

More interestingly, you can download the structure and back it up on a local machine. For example, we need to download the structure "one image". Let's do it by following these steps:

1. Locate the structure, say "one image", that you want to update.

2. Then click on the **Edit** icon from the **Actions** button located next to the structure.

3. Click on the **Download** button. The structure in the XML schema will appear in your browse. Just save it as an XML schema in your local machine if needed. Actually, the unique URL of the structure is used for reference.

Of course, you can copy the content of the structure from one to another. For example, we need to copy the structure "one image" to a new ID "ONE_IMAGE_COPY". Let's do it by following these steps:

1. Locate the structure, say "one image", that you want to update.

2. Then click on the **Copy** icon from the **Actions** button located next to the structure.

3. Input **New ID**, say "ONE_IMAGE_COPY".

4. Click on the **Copy** button.

Note that **New ID** must be unique in structure. The copied structure will have the same content as that of the original one, except the ID. For example, the structure "ONE_IMAGE_COPY" (ID `one_image_copy`) has the same content as that of the structure "one image" (ID `10306`), except for the IDs.

In addition, you can find structures through either basic search or advanced search. To search structures, simple click on the **Search** button for both basic search and advanced search. You can switch a basic search interface into an advanced search interface by clicking on the **Advanced** link, or you can switch an advanced search interface into a basic search interface by clicking on the **Basic** link.

Editing structures

Structures of documents and images are editable. For example, you may need to add a row of the structure "one image" with the name "title". Let's do it by following these steps:

1. Locate the structure, say "one image", that you want to update.

2. Then click on the **Edit** icon from the **Actions** buttons located next to the structure.

3. Add a row, say "title", by clicking on the **Add Row** button, and select the type of the row, say **Text**.

4. Optionally, you can launch an editor to update the rows directly. If you know the XML schema by clicking on the **Launch Editor** button first, then you can use the editor types, either **Plain** or **Rich**, to update the XML schema. Finally, click on the **Update** button and click on the **Save** button or the **Save and Continue** button.

 Note that the buttons **Save** and **Save and Continue** are slight different. When clicking on the **Save** button, it will save the current input and then return to the parent page. When clicking on the **Save and Continue** button, it will save the current input and then stay in the current page.

Deleting structures

Structures of documents and images are removable as well. Let's say that the structure "one image" doesn't exist anymore. Let's delete it by following these steps:

1. Locate the structure, say "one image", that you want to delete.

2. Then click on the **Delete** icon from the **Actions** button located next to the structure.

3. A message will appear asking if you want to delete this. Click on the **OK** button to confirm deletion.

> Note that you can't delete a structure that is used by templates. In order to delete this structure, you need to edit the templates and remove the structure association first. Then you can delete the structure.

What's happening?

A structure is an XML (Extensible Mark-up Language) definition of the dynamic parts of journal articles (called web content). These parts may be a text, a text box, a text area (HTML), an image, an Image Gallery image, a Document Library document, a Boolean flag (true or false), a selection list, a multiple selection list, or a link to a page. Actually, the structure is a specific XML schema.

A structure defines the fields of web content. This can be done in the following ways:

- Through a web UI in the Control Panel
- Using an integrated web editor
- By uploading an XML file
- By editing the XML file with a desktop application through WebDAV

As you have seen, you are asked to input a structure ID or enable the checkbox **Autogenerate ID**—in order to auto-generate structure ID. Why? How can we generate a structure ID in force? The portal has specified the following property in `portal.properties`.

```
journal.structure.force.autogenerate.id=false
```

Of course, you can override this and set this to true in `portal-ext.properties` if structure IDs should be auto-generated in force.

Repeatable structure fields are supported. While creating a structure, you can't predict how many fields of a certain type of Web Content entry will be needed. Fortunately, for each row in a structure, there is a **Repeatable** checkbox. For instance, the element named "image" is repeatable, as shown in the following code:

```
<root>
  <dynamic-element name='image' type='image' index-type=''
repeatable='true'>
    <dynamic-element name='document' type='document_library' index-
type='' repeatable='false'></dynamic-element>
  </dynamic-element>
</root>
```

The structure has the ability to support searchable fields. When adding a row, you would have the ability to set searchable features: **Not Searchable, Searchable-Keyword, Searchable-Text**. Once structure fields are set as searchable, either keyword-based or text-based, the portal would index structure fields separately.

Hierarchy structure fields are supported too. When adding a row, you would be able to specify it as a first-level element or a child of a given element.

```
<root>
  <dynamic-element name='caption' type='text' index-type='text'
repeatable='false'>
    <dynamic-element name='section' type='text' index-type='text'
repeatable='false'></dynamic-element>
  </dynamic-element>
</root>
```

As shown in the preceding code, there are only two XML tags: `root` and `dynamic-element`. The tag `root` appears only once; while the tag `dynamic-element` could be repeatable and hierarchic. There are four attributes for the tag `dynamic-element` as shown in following table: **Name, type, index-type**, and **repeatable**.

Attribute name	Attribute values
Name	custom inputs, like 'caption', 'section', and so on.
type	'text', 'text_box', 'text_area', 'image', 'image_gallery', 'document_library', 'boolean', 'list', 'multi-list', 'link_to_layout'
index-type	'','text', 'keyword'
repeatable	'true', 'false'

Fortunately, you would find details in the JSP file $PORTAL_ROOT_HOME/html/ portlet/journal/edit_structure_xsd_el.jsp. As you can see, there are a set of types. How do types work? The following table depicts name, display text, and runtime HTML tags.

Type name	Display text	Description
text	Text	`<input type="text" />`
text_box	Text Box	`<textarea />`
text_area	Text Area (HTML)	`<liferay-ui:input-editor />`
image	Image	Upload image; `<input type="file" />`
image_gallery	Image Gallery	Select image from Image Gallery
document_ library	Document Library	Select document from Document Library
boolean	Boolean Flag	`<input type="checkbox" />`
list	Selection List	`<select> <option /> </select>`
multi-list	Multi-Selection List	`<select> <option /> </select>`
link_to_ layout	Link to Page	A link to page

Of course, you could find details in the JSP file $PORTAL_ROOT_HOME/html/portlet/ journal/edit_article_content_xsd_el.jsp.

Last, but not least, the structure has the ability to support metadata on Structure XSD. For example, the following code specifies the element "TextField" with the metadata name "displayAsToolTip" and the value "true".

```
<dynamic-element name='TextField' type='text_box' index-type=''
repeatable='false'>
    <meta-data>
        <entry name="displayAsToolTip">
            <![CDATA[true]]>
        </entry>
    </meta-data>
</dynamic-element>
```

Managing templates

Then, we need to create a template for the previous article—web content. A template, named "Template About Us", is a pattern to rapidly generate the web content "About Us". Let's create the template as follows:

1. Click on the **Templates** tab.

2. Click on the **Add Templates** button.

3. Enable the checkbox **Auto Generate ID**, input the name "Template About us" and the description "Template for About us".

4. Select a structure, say "Structure About us", by clicking on the **Select** button next to the **Structure**.

5. Select **Language Type**, say "VM", (that is, Velocity Macro) as default.

6. Upload a template script file say "template-about-us.vm" from the local machine by clicking on the **Browse...** button next to the **Script**.

7. Upload a small image, say "template-about-us.png", from local machine by clicking on the **Browse...** button next to the **Small Image**.

8. Enable the checkbox **Use Small Image**.

9. Set **Permissions** by clicking on the **Configure** link. To configure additional permissions, click on the **More** link. Here we just use the default settings. By default, the checkbox **Public** is disabled.

10. Click on the **Save** button.

When adding a new template, you would have a chance to configure the following items:

- **Cacheable**: Only uncheck it when developing templates that use request handling dynamic features

- **Structure**: Select a structure or remove a structure

- **Language Type**: VM, FTL, XSL, CSS

- **Script**: Upload script file

- **Format Script**: Whether using a script file or not

- **Small Image URL**: External URL for a small image

- **Small Image**: Upload image file

- **Use Small Image**: Whether using a small image to replace a description or not

- **Permissions**: Sets the default permissions for the roles Community Member and Guest

You can add other templates as you wish. After adding a template "Template one image" associated with the structure "one image", we can view templates.

Similar to that of structures, you can either edit a template or delete a template. Each template may have a structure associated, and it has a unique URL and WebDAV URL which can be used to reference it.

Viewing templates

By clicking on the **Templates** tab in the Web Content Management portlet, you can view templates with paginations, as shown in the following image. You can edit the structure associated to a given template by clicking on the **Edit Structure** icon. Furthermore, you can view articles related to a given template by clicking on the **View Web Content** icon. Alternatively, you can add an article associated to a given template by clicking on the **Add Web Content** icon.

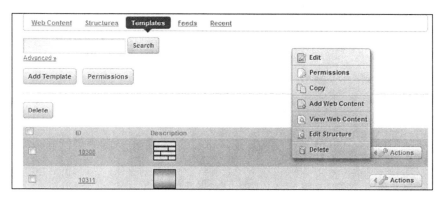

As you can see, the description of templates is replaced by icons. What's the icon in description of templates for? The icon (small image) could be used to show the look of the template. For example, "Template one image" has a simple look, while "Template About Us" has a different and complex look. It is a good idea using a small image to present templates with an icon, isn't it? Moreover, why is the description of templates replaced by icons? When building templates, we had uploaded **Small Image**, and enabled the checkbox **Use Small Image**.

Similarly, you can download the template via the unique URL and back it up in the local machine as well as that of the structure. For example, we need to download the template "Template one image". Let's do it by following these steps:

1. Locate the template, say "Template one image", that you want to update.
2. Then click on the **Edit** icon from the **Actions** located next to the template.

3. Click on the **Download** button. The template in the script file will appear in your browser. Just save it as a script file in your local machine if needed. Actually, the unique URL of the template is used for reference.

Of course, you can copy the content of the template from one to another. For example, we're going to copy the template "Template one image" to a new ID "ONE_IMAGE". Let's do it by following these steps:

1. Locate the template, say "Template one image", that you want to update.

2. Then click on the **Copy** icon from the **Actions** button located next to the template.

3. Input **New ID**, say "ONE_IMAGE".

4. Click on the **Copy** button.

Note that **New ID** must be unique in templates. The targeted template would have the same content as that of the original one, except for the ID. For example, the template "ONE_IMAGE" (ID ONE_IMAGE) has the same content as that of the template "Template one image" (ID 10311), except for the IDs.

In addition, you can query templates through either basic search or advanced search as well as through structures.

Editing templates

Templates are editable too. For example, you may need to change the expression of the template "Template one image" with the new item "title" according to the structure "one image". Let's do it by following these steps:

1. Locate the template "Template one image" that you want to update.

2. Then click on the **Edit** icon from the **Actions** button located next to the template.

3. Launch an editor to update the content of the template by clicking on the **Launch Editor** button first. Then you can use the editor types, either **Plain** or **Rich,** to update the content such as adding the new item according to the structure "one image". Finally, click on the **Update** button.

4. Click on the **Save** button.

Deleting templates

Templates are removable. Let's say that the template "Template one image" doesn't exist anymore. Let's delete it by following these steps:

1. Locate the template, say "Template one image", that you want to delete.
2. Then click on the **Delete** icon from the **Actions** button located next to the template.
3. A message will appear asking if you want to delete this. Click on the **OK** button to confirm deletion.

> Note that you can't delete a template which is being used by articles. In order to delete this template, you need to edit the articles and remove the template association first.

What's happening?

A template defines the look of the custom structures by using Velocity, FreeMarker, or XSL templates. This can be done in the following ways:

- Using an integrated web editor
- By uploading the template file once finished
- Editing the template file with a desktop application through WebDAV

As you have seen, when creating templates, you are asked to input a template ID or enable the checkbox **Autogenerate ID**—in order to auto-generate a template ID. Why? How to avoid this? The portal has specified the following property in `portal.properties`.

```
journal.template.force.autogenerate.id=false
journal.template.velocity.restricted.variables=serviceLocator
journal.error.template.velocity=com/liferay/portlet/journal/
dependencies/error.vm
journal.error.template.xsl=com/liferay/portlet/journal/dependencies/
error.xsl
```

Of course, you can override this and set this to `true` in `portal-ext.properties` if template IDs should always be auto-generated. Moreover, the template variable `serviceSelector` is restricted from access by templates by default in `portal.properties`. You can input a comma delimited list of variables, which are restricted from the context in Velocity-based templates. If you really need this variable, then you need to override the property `journal.template.velocity.restricted.variables` in `portal-ext.properties`. In addition, you may specify the path to the template used for providing error messages on the Journal template in `portal-ext.properties`.

As mentioned earlier, you would be able to build templates via VM (Velocity Macro), FTL (FreeMarker Template Language), XSL (EXtensible Stylesheet Language), and CSS (Cascading Style Sheets). The portal uses VM as the default template language type.

> Velocity is a Java-based template engine. It permits web page designers to reference methods defined in Java code. Refer to `http://velocity.apache.org`.
>
> The FreeMarker template engine is a generic tool to generate text output (anything from HTML to auto-generated source code) based on templates. Refer to `http://freemarker.org`

VM variables are used in template script file by default. The following is sample code abstracted from the template "Template one image" script file.

```
<html>
  <head>
    <title>$reserved-article-id.getData()</title>
  </head>
</html>
```

As shown in the preceding code, the VM variable `$reserved-article-id.getData()` is in use. The rest are HTML tags. Of course, you can include CSS in template script. The following is some sample code:

```
<style>
  .bar-title {
    background: #D3DADD;
  }
</style>
```

You just put this code at the beginning of the template script file. The CSS code starts with the tag `<style>` and ends with the tag `</style>`.

More interestingly, you would be able to add JavaScript in template script. The following lines are pieces of code:

```
<script>
  AUI().ready(function(){
   jQuery('.bar-title'){
    alert('You've clicked on the link BAR TITLE!');
    jQuery(this).remove();
   }
  }
  );
</script>
```

You just put the preceding code at the beginning of the template script. The JavaScript code is starting with the tag `<script>` and ending with the tag `</script>`.

Managing Web Content

When structures and templates are ready, we can create the article "About Us" now. An article (called Web Content) is the actual content of the web page, which may be associated with a template and a structure. Let's create the article by following these steps:

1. Click on the **Web Content** tab.
2. Click on the **Add Web Content** button.
3. Use **Auto Generate ID**, input a name, say "About Us", and a description, say "Article for About us".
4. Select a structure, say "Structure About Us", first by clicking on the **Select** link under **Structure**. Then select a template, say "Template About Us".
5. Or select the template, say "Template About us", by clicking on the **Select** button under **Template**. The content pieces will change following the structure and template.
6. Set **Permissions** by clicking on the **Configure** link. To configure additional permissions, click on the **More** link. Here we just use the default settings.
7. Optionally, you can input an abstract for this article. Input a description, say "Article About Us for a page", upload a small image, say "article.png", from the local machine by clicking on the **Browse...** button next to the **Small Image**. Enable the checkbox **Use Small Image**.
8. In addition, you can set up the **Schedule** such as **Display Date**, **Expiration Date,** and **Review Date.**
9. Or click on the **Select Tags** button if you want to select any existing tags, click on the **Add Tags** button if you need to add tags, or select categories by clicking on the **Select Categories** button.
10. Click on the **Save** button when you just want to save your changes, click on the **Save and Continue** button if you want to save your changes and continue with the current work, or click on the **Save and Approve** button when you want to save changes and approve them. Here we use **Save and Approve.**

 Note that an article can be approved or not approved. Only approved articles can be used in the pages.

When adding or editing articles, you would see following features.

- **Name**: Web content name—it can be duplicated.
- **Language**: Multi-language supports—each article can be entered in as many languages as desired.
- **Abstract**: Summary and small images to present web content.
- **Permissions**: Set default permissions for the roles Community Member and Guest.
- **Structure**: Define the fields of the web content by creating structures.
- **Template**: Define the look of the custom structures by using Velocity or XSL templates.
- **Workflow**: Simple approval workflow (supports versioning).
- **Categorization**: type-Announcements, Blogs, News, General, Press Release and test; tags; categories; searchable tags and categories.
- **Schedule**: Scheduled publishing—display date, expiration date, Never Auto Expire, Review Date, Never Review.

Of course, you can add other articles as desired. After adding an article, like "Article one image" which is associated with the template "Template one image", we can view articles.

Each article may have a template and a structure associated. After adding a set of articles, you can edit, delete, preview, search, and approve articles. Moreover, you can make articles expired, restore an expired article, or create new versions of articles.

As you can see, the Web Content portlet allows defining a structure on the fly with nice toolbars and drag-and-drop capabilities, seeing the edit button of structure panel. In addition, Multiple languages get supported as well—web content can be entered in as many languages as desired.

Viewing articles

By clicking on the **Web Content** tab in the Web Content Management portlet, you can view Articles with paginations if there are a lot of articles. You can edit the article by clicking on the **Edit** icon from the **Actions** button next to the article.

To view recent articles, structures, and templates that you can access, simply click on the **Recent** tab. The portal will display the last **20** web content, structures, and templates that you accessed.

Meanwhile, you can preview an article. Let's say that you want to preview the article "About Us". Let's do it by following these steps:

1. Locate the article "About Us" that you want to update.
2. Then click on the **Preview** icon from the **Actions** button located next to the article.

In addition, you can query articles by either basic search or advanced search just like structures and templates. In particular, you can search by **Version**, **Content**, **Type**, and **Status** in advanced search.

Of course, you can copy the content of the article from one to another. For example, we need to copy the article "Article One Image" to a new ID "COPY_ONE_IMAGE". Let's do it by following these steps:

1. Locate the article, say "Article One Image", that you want to update.
2. Then click on the **Copy** icon from the **Actions** button located next to the article.
3. Input **New ID**, for example "COPY_ONE_IMAGE".
4. Click on the **Copy** button.

Note that **New ID** must be unique in articles. The target article will have the same content as that of the original one, except for the ID. So remember that if you copy content that has been approved, the copy will be immediately be approved as well.

Editing articles

Articles are editable just like structures and templates. For example, you may need to change the content pieces of the article "Article one image" with another image "PalmTree_logo.png" according to the structure of "one image". Let's do it by following these steps:

1. Locate some web content, say "Article one image", that you want to edit.

2. Then click on the **Edit** icon from the **Actions** button located next to the article, the content piece **Image**.

3. Upload the image, say "PalmTree_logo.png", by clicking on the **Select** button above **Update**.

4. Click on the **Save** button.

5. An article may have a list of versions. Let's say that the article "Article one image" abstract description is updated with value "Palm Tree Logo" in a new version. Let's do it by following these steps:

6. Locate the article "Article one image" that you want to update.

7. Then click on the **Edit** icon from the **Actions** button located next to the article.

8. Update **Abstract | Description** with the value "Palm Tree Logo".

9. Select the checkbox **Increment Version on Save** under the **Workflow**.

10. Click on the **Save and Approve** button.

In addition, you can make an article expired and restore an expired article. Let's say that the article "Article one image" has expired. Let's do it by following these steps:

1. Locate an article, say "Article One Image", that you want to update.

2. Then click on the **Edit** icon from the **Actions button** located next to the article.

3. Click on the **Expire** button under the **Workflow**.

Later, we may want to restore the article "Article One Image" and then we may want to update it for other purposes. Let's do it by following these steps:

1. Locate the article, say "Article One Image", that you want to update.

2. Then click on the **Edit** icon from the **Actions** button located next to the article.

3. Click on the **Save and Approve** button.

Deleting articles

Articles are removable just like structures and templates. Let's say that the article "Article One Image" isn't needed anymore. Let's delete it by following these steps:

1. Locate the article "Article One Image" that you want to delete.
2. Then click on the **Delete** icon from the **Actions** button located next to the article.
3. A message will appear asking if you want to delete this. Click on the **OK** button to confirm deletion.

 Note that after an article is deleted, you can't restore it. If you don't want to delete it actually, you can just make it expired. Sooner or later, when you want to reuse this article, you can restore it easily

Managing feeds

More interestingly, the portal provides the ability to create an RSS feed using Journal Articles—Web content. If you have proper access rights, you would be able to add the feeds RSS and manage feeds. RSS types, such as Atom 1.0, RSS 1.0, and RSS 2.0, are supported as well.

When adding a feed, you would be asked to input the following items:

- **ID**: custom ID, auto-generated ID.
- **Name**: feed name.
- **Description**: feed description.
- **Target Page Friendly URL**: Enter the friendly URL of a page to where the feed will target currently unlisted feed items. The feed will only target pages within the community to which this URL belongs.
- **Target Portlet ID**: Optionally, specify the portlet ID of a Web Content Display portlet on the target page in which unlisted items will be displayed. The portlet must exist or content will not display.
- **Permissions**: Set default permissions for the roles Community Member and Guest.
- **Web Content Constraints**: Web Content Type selection: Structure and Template.
- **Presentation settings**: Feed Item Content—Web Content Description, Render Web Content such as User Default Template, feed Type—RSS 2.0, RSS 1.0, Atom 1.0, Maximum Items to Display, Order by Column—Modified Date, Display Date, Order By Type—Ascending, Descending.
- **Save / Cancel**: Save the feed or cancel inputs.

After adding a set of feeds, you would be able to view feeds. Feeds are displayed with the columns **ID**, **Description**, and the **Actions** button plus a set of icons, that is, **Edit**, **Permissions**, and **Delete**.

As you can see, feeds are searchable too. You can search feeds by either basic search or advanced search.

As you have seen, you are asked to input a feed ID or enable the checkbox **Autogenerate ID**—in order to auto-generate the feed ID. Why? How can we automatically generate a feed ID? The portal has specified the following property in `portal.properties`.

```
Journal.feed.force.autogenerate.id=false
```

Of course, you can override this and set this to `true` in `portal-ext.properties` if feed IDs should always be auto-generated.

Setup

As an administrator of the enterprise "Palm Tree Publications", you would be able to set up the Web Content Management portlet. For example, you can configure **Email From**.

To configure **Email From**, click on the **More | Configuration** icon on the Web Content Management portlet. With the **Setup** tab selected, there are five sub-tabs that appear: **Email From, Article Denied Email, Article Granted Email, Article Requested Email**, and **Article Review Email**.

With the **Email From** tab selected, you can change the name and address of the automatically sent e-mails.

The **Article Denied Email** tab allows the Administrator to edit the e-mail that is sent whenever an article is denied. To disable e-mail notification, uncheck the **Enabled** checkbox, and click on the **Save** button after making any changes.

Similarly, as an administrator, you can set up **Article Granted Email, Article Requested Email**, and **Article Review Email** as you desire.

Assigning permissions

Let's say that "David Berger" is a content designer who can create structures and templates, "Lotti Stein" is a content writer who can write articles, and "Rolf Hess" is a content editor who can edit and approve articles. How do we implement this? Let's see what permissions in the Web Content Management portlet are by default.

In general, there are four-group permissions, namely, permissions on portlet, permissions on Web Content Management, permissions on Web Content, and permissions on structures, templates, and feeds.

Permissions on portlet

The following table shows the permissions on the Web Content Management portlet. The role Community Member is set up with all the permissions (marked as 'X'): **View**, **Configuration**, and **Access in Control Panel**, while the user with the Guest role is set up with the permissions **View** and **Configuration**. The default action for the roles Community Member and Guest is the **View** (marked as '*') permission.

Action	Description	Community	Guest
View	Ability to view the portlet	X, *	X, *
Configuration	Ability to configure the portlet	X	X
Access in Control Panel	Ability to access the portlet in Control Panel	X	

Obviously, as a member of the Guest community, "Lotti Stein" has the permission **View** only on the Web Content Management portlet by default. Since the role Community Member of the Guest community has no **Access in Control Panel** permission, "Lotti Stein" has no **Access in Control Panel** permission too. This means that "Lotti Stein" doesn't have access on the portlet Web Content Management in the Control Panel.

As mentioned earlier, the Web Content Management portlet is accessible in the Control Panel only. Thus, in order to use Web Content Management, a user like "Lotti Stein" must get the permissions **Access in Control Panel** first. How? The following is an option.

1. Log in as an admin, say "Palm Tree".
2. Click on **Roles** under the category **Portal of Control Panel** first.
3. Then locate a role, say "MB Topic Admin".
4. Click on the **Define Permissions** icon from the **Actions** button next to the role.
5. Click on the **Applications | Web Content** link, enable the checkboxes: **Access in Control Panel** and **View**.
6. Click on the **Save** button.

Permissions on Web Content Management

The following table shows the permissions on Web Content Management. The role Community Member is set up with all the permissions (marked as 'X'): **Add Content, Add Feed, Add Structure, Add Template, Approve Content**, and none of them are supported by the role Guest.

Action	Description	Community	Guest
Add Content	Ability to add articles	X	
Add Feed	Ability to add feeds	X	
Add Structure	Ability to add structures	X	
Add Template	Ability to add templates	X	
Approve Content	Ability to approve article on the portlet	X	

As members of the Guest community, "David Berger", "Lotti Stein", and "Rolf Hess" can only have the View permission on a portlet, by default. How to implement the preceding requirements? The following is an option, and you may have different but functionally similar implementations.

1. Create a regular role named **Content Designer,** and assign "David Berger" as its member.

2. Create a regular role named **Content Writer,** and assign "Lotti Stein" as its member.

3. Create a regular role named **Content Editor,** and assign "Rolf Hess" as its member.

4. Update permissions on **Content Designer** with **Add Content, Add Feed, Add Structure, Add Template**, and **Approve Content** by clicking on **Roles | Content Designer | Define Permissions | Content | Web Content |** Web Content Management.

5. Update permissions on **Content Writer** with **Add Content** by clicking on **Roles | Content Writer | Define Permissions | Content | Web Content |** Web Content Management.

6. Update permissions on **Content Editor** with **Add Content** and **Approve Content** by clicking on **Roles | Content Editor | Define Permissions | Content | Web Content |** Web Content Management.

Thus, as a content designer, "David Berger" can create structures and templates. As a content writer, "Lotti Stein" can write articles only. As a content editor, "Rolf Hess" can edit and approve articles. Try to log in as "David Berger", "Lotti Stein", or "Rolf Hess". You will have different permission actions on the **Web Content Management** portlet.

Note that permissions on the Web Content Management could be scoped into a group or portal instance. They are unavailable to individual objects such as articles, templates, structures, feeds, and so on.

Permissions on Web Content

We can set up permissions based on individual articles or based on a group or portal instance. The following table shows permissions on articles. The Community Member role is set up with all the permissions (marked as 'X'): **View**, **Add Discussion**, **Delete**, **Expire**, **Permissions**, **Update Discussion**, **Delete Discussion**, and **Update**, while the Guest role is set up with permissions: **View**, **Add Discussion**, **Delete**, and **Permissions**. By default, the Community Member role has the permissions **View** and **Add Discussion** (marked as '*'), while the Guest role only has the permission **View**.

Action	Description	Community	Guest
View	Ability to view an article	X, *	X, *
Add Discussion	Ability to add comments on the article	X, *	X
Delete	Ability to delete an article	X	X
Expire	Ability to make an article expired	X	
Permissions	Ability to assign permission on an article	X	X
Update	Ability Edit this article	X	
Update Discussion	Ability to update comments on the article	X	
Delete Discussion	Ability to delete comments on the article	X	X

As you can see, it would be nice if we could assign permissions in the following scopes:

- Individual articles
- A set of articles
- All articles in a group like the Guest community
- All articles in the current portal instance

For an individual article, we could go to the **Permissions** icon of the **Actions** button next to the article and assign permissions based on roles.

For all articles in a group, you could be able to assign permissions in the **Control Panel** via the custom community role (or Community Member) or the custom organization role (or Organization Member).

For articles in a portal instance, you could be able to assign permission in the **Control Panel** through custom regular roles. For a set of articles, there is no direct solution at the time of writing, but you may have to assign permissions individually.

Permissions on structures, templates, and feeds

We can set up permissions based on individual structures, templates, or feeds, or based on a group or portal instance. Since permissions on structures, templates, and feeds are the same, we discuss them together. Eventually, different model-resources (such as **JournalStructure**, **JournalTemplate**, and **JournalFeed**) of structure, template, and feed are different and separated. However, each model resource has the same permission specification.

The following table shows permissions on structures, templates, and feeds. The role Community Member user is set up with all permissions (marked as 'X'): **View**, **Delete**, **Permissions**, and **Update**, while the role Guest is set up with the permissions: **View**, **Delete**, and **Permissions**. By default, the role Community Member has the permission action **View** (marked as '*') as well as that of the role Guest.

Action	Description	Community	Guest
View	Ability to view structure, template, or feed	X, *	X, *
Delete	Ability to delete structure, template, or feed	X	X
Permissions	Assign permission on structure or template	X	X
Update	Edit this structure or template	X	

Similar to that of articles, you can assign permissions in the following scopes:

- Individual structures, templates, or feeds
- All structures, templates, or feeds in a group like the Guest community
- All structures, templates, or feeds in the current portal instance

Enhancement

As stated, it is possible to assign permissions on individual web content, on all web content in a scope of a group, and on all web content in the current portal instance. Assigning permissions on a set of web content is missing, that is, Journal Articles. Thus, it would be better to provide folders to group web content, than to provide the ability to assign permissions based on folders. This feature is unavailable, but highly expected.

In addition, the summary, that is, the abstract of web content, should be localizable. Moreover, the feature for adding the opportunity to mark Web Content Structure fields as required is also highly expected.

What's happening?

The following diagram depicts the relationships conceptually among article, template, and structure. Normally, an article may have one template associated with it. It is possible that an article may not use any template, while a template may serve many articles. This is the reason why we can view articles by a given template. In particular, each article may have a number of comments (that is, posts and replies) and ratings associated. Moreover, each article may have a list of versions, and each article may also have many tags and categories associated — thus you would be able to classify articles via categories or organize articles in your own way by tags. More interestingly, each article has a different status: approved or not approved, expired, or review.

As you can see, you can set the review status on articles, for example, someone creates an article, and another group of people can review the same article. Similarly, you can set the expired status on articles. Once an article is expired, it can't be displayed anymore. It should be archived as well.

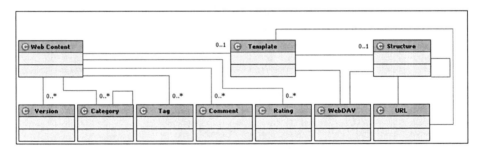

Similarly, a template may have one structure associated with it or it does not employ any structure. Meanwhile, a structure may serve many templates. Thus, on one hand, we can edit a structure by a given template. On the other hand, we can view templates and articles by a given structure. In particular, each template and/or structure has a unique URL and a WebDAV URL which can be used to reference it. By the way, a structure has hierarchy, that is, each structure can have another structure as its parent in order to share common fields among structures.

Building structures

A structure is an XML (Extensible Mark-up Language) definition of the dynamic parts of the article. These parts may be text, a text box, a text Area (HTML), an image, Image Gallery, Document Library, a Boolean flag (true or false), a selection list, a multiple selection list, and so on. Actually, the structure is a specific XML schema.

By structures, we can unify articles with the same numbers and types of items. For example, the page "About Us" of "Palm Tree Publications" might have five articles, each requiring a title, a caption, and an image for the headquarters, an image and a text area for the US office, and a text area and an image for the Germany office. A structure would be created with three images, two texts, and two text areas, each named accordingly. This allows writers to create the individual articles and other texts without needing to recreate the page structure for each article.

Based on the example (Original Required View), the structure lists out the eight content pieces:

- One text element named "title" (**1**).

- One text box element named "caption" (**2**).

- Two text area elements named "text_us" (**5**) and "text_de" (**6**), in particular, a link to a document from Document Library "Open Source project" (**8**).

- Three image elements named "image_caption" (**3**), "image_us" (**4**), and "image_de" (**7**).

The following is the real code of the structure "Structure About Us".

```
<root>
  <dynamic-element name='title' type='text' index-type='text'
repeatable='false'></dynamic-element><!-- ignore details -->
</root>
```

Creating templates

Template (Web Template) is a pattern to rapidly generate and mass-produce web pages, associated to a structure. A template defines the layout of the article and determines how content items will be arranged.

Templates used for creating articles can be created in XSL, Velocity (VM), CSS, Free-Marker, and so on. You can create many templates for one structure, or you can give writers discretion in deciding the best layout.

The following is the real code of the template "Template About Us" in VM.

```html
<html>
  <head>
    <title>$reserved-article-id.getData()</title>
  </head> <!-- ignore details -->
</html>
```

Constructing articles

An article is the actual content of the web page, which is associated with a structure and a template. Each content piece is populated with actual text and images. Each article is integrated with two statuses of workflow, either approved or not approved. Meanwhile, each article may have a set of dates associated such as display date, expiration date, review date, and so on.

There are three kinds of users involved in an article's lifecycle: designers, writers, and editors. Typically, designers create structures and templates first, then articles are written normally by writers, and editors edit and approve articles. Finally, articles are displayed or made expired by designers.

By default, article types include **Announcements**, **Blogs**, **News**, **General**, **Press Release**, and **Test**. The following table depicts default type names and descriptions.

Type name	Description
Announcements	Publications made known publicly
Blogs	Frequent and chronological publications of personal thoughts and Web links
News	Information about recent events or happenings
General	General publications / information
Press release	News that is sent out or released by the company making the news.s
Test	Testing information

It is important to note that these article types are configurable. For example, you can configure articles types in `portal-ext.properties` by removing `Test` as follows:

```
journal.article.types=announcements,blogs,general,news,press-release
```

The preceding code sets the list of article types. Note that the display text of each of the article types is set in `content/Language.properties`.

Setup

As you have seen, when setting up e-mail notification, there are default settings. Why? The portal has specified the following properties to configure e-mail notification settings in `portal.properties`.

```
journal.email.from.name=Joe Bloggs
journal.email.from.address=test@liferay.com
journal.email.article.approval.denied.enabled=false
## ignore details journal.email.article.review.body=com/liferay/
portlet/journal/dependencies/email_article_review_body.tmpl
```

Of course, you would be able to override these settings in web UI under **More | Configuration | Setup | Current** of the portlet Web Content Management. Alternatively, you may override the preceding settings in `portal-ext.properties`.

When adding web content, you would see that the ID is generated automatically and is different from that of structure, template, and feed. Why so? The portal has set the following properties in `portal.properties`.

```
journal.article.force.autogenerate.id=true
journal.article.force.increment.version=false
journal.article.check.interval=15
journal.article.view.permission.check.enabled=false
journal.article.comments.enabled=true
```

As shown in the preceding code, the property `journal.article.force.autogenerate.id` is set to `true` if the article IDs should always be auto-generated. You may set the property `journal.article.force.increment.version` to `true` so that only the latest version of an article, which is also not approved, can be saved without incrementing version. The property `journal.article.check.interval` sets the interval on which the `Check-Article-Job` will run in one minute increments. You may set `journal.article.view.permission.check.enabled` to `true` to check that a user has the **VIEW** permission on a Journal article (web content) when its content is rendered.

When adding web content, you would be able to specify the abstract of web content called summary, especially small image on web content. Sometimes, you may see a message saying—wrong file extension or too big file. Why does this happen? The portal has set the following properties for small images in `portal.properties`.

```
journal.image.small.max.size=51200
journal.image.extensions=.gif,.jpeg,.jpg,.png
```

As shown in the preceding code, the property `journal.image.small.max.size` sets the maximum file size and valid file extensions for images. A value of 0 for the maximum file size can be used to indicate unlimited file size. However, the maximum file size allowed is set in the property `com.liferay.portal.upload.UploadServletRequestImpl.max.size`. The property `journal.image.extensions` sets permission on all file extensions. A file extension of * will permit all file extensions.

In short, you would be able to override the preceding properties in `portal-ext.properties`.

Configuration

The Web Content Management portlet is the main management interface for integrated web publishing system, allowing users to create, edit, and publish articles, as well as article templates for one-click changes in layout, built in workflow, article versioning, search, and metadata.

Considering the pattern `Portal-Group-Page-Content`, the content of the Web Content Management portlet could be scoped into a group, for example, all pages including both private and public pages, by default. Alternatively, it could be scoped into an individual page. This means that a set of data, for example, web contents, structures, templates, and feeds, is isolated from other data of the same portlet.

How can we customize scope features? The portal has default settings for the Web Content Management portlet, as follows, in `$PORTAL_ROOT_HOME/WEB-INF/liferay-portlet.xml`.

```
<configuration-action-class>com.liferay.portlet.journal.action.
ConfigurationActionImpl</configuration-action-class>
<indexer-class>com.liferay.portlet.journal.util.JournalIndexer</
indexer-class>
<open-search-class>com.liferay.portlet.journal.util.
JournalOpenSearchImpl</open-search-class>
<scheduler-class>com.liferay.portlet.journal.job.JournalScheduler</
scheduler-class>
<friendly-url-mapper-class>com.liferay.portlet.journal.
JournalFriendlyURLMapper</friendly-url-mapper-class>
<portlet-data-handler-class>com.liferay.portlet.journal.lar.
JournalPortletDataHandlerImpl</portlet-data-handler-class>
<webdav-storage-token>journal</webdav-storage-token>
<webdav-storage-class>com.liferay.portlet.journal.webdav.
JournalWebDAVStorageImpl</webdav-storage-class>
<control-panel-entry-category>content</control-panel-entry-category>
<control-panel-entry-weight>1.0</control-panel-entry-weight>
```

```
<asset-renderer-factory>com.liferay.portlet.journal.asset.
JournalArticleAssetRendererFactory</asset-renderer-factory>
<workflow-handler>com.liferay.portlet.journal.workflow.
JournalArticleWorkflowHandler</workflow-handler>
<scopeable>true</scopeable>
```

The preceding code shows that the message boards portlet will appear in the **Content** category in position **1,** and it is scope-able, that is, you are able to use the tab **Scope** and change the scope from default to the current page. There are also two tags related to WebDAV, namely, `webdav-storage-token` and `webdav-storage-class`.

In addition, you would see the following tags:

- `configuration-action-class`: For setup at **More** | **Configuration** | **Setup** | **Current.**

- `indexer-class`: Search indexing.

- `open-search-class`: Open-search implementation.

- `scheduler-class`: Scheduling and publishing.

- `friendly-url-mapper-class`: Friendly URL mapping.

- `workflow-handler`: Pluggable workflow implementations — it will appear automatically in the workflow admin portlet (portlet ID 151) so users can associate workflow entities with available permissions. Of course, you can register your own workflow handler implementation for any entity you build like Document Library documents.

- `asset-renderer-factory`: Asset renderer framework; thus you could publish web content via the Asset Publisher portlet.

As mentioned earlier, the portlets Image Gallery (Portlet ID 31) and Document Library (Portlet ID 20) are available in a page and not in the Web Content Management portlet. Why, you ask? In the `$PORTAL_ROOT_HOME/WEB-INF/liferay-display.xml`, the portal has the following specification:

```
<display>
 <category name="category.cms">
   <portlet id="20" />
   <portlet id="31" />
   <!-- ignore details -->
 </category>
 <!-- ignore details -->
 <category name="category.hidden">
  <portlet id="9" />
  <portlet id="15" />
  <!-- ignore details -->
```

```
  </category>
  <!-- ignore details -->
</display>
```

As shown in the preceding code, the portlets Image Gallery and Document Library are available at `category.cms` (display text Content Management), while the Web Content Management portlet can be found in `category.hidden`.

Customization

As stated earlier, we have discussed how to remove `Test` from the web content (article) types. But how do we add a new type in the journal article types? Let's say that you are going to add an article type **article-content** with display text **Article Content**, How do we implement this? The following is an option:

- Add the following line at the end of `portal-ext.properties`. Of course, you can change the order of article types.

  ```
  journal.article.types=announcements,blogs,general,news,press-release,article-content
  ```

- Create a folder `content` under the folder `$PORTAL_ROOT_HOME/WEB-INF/classes` if the folder `content` doesn't exist.

- Create a file `Language-ext.properties` under the folder `$PORTAL_ROOT_HOME/WEB-INF/classes/content` if the file `Language-ext.properties` doesn't exist.

- Add the following line at the end of `Language-ext.properties`. Obviously, you could have different display text.

  ```
  article-content=Article Content
  ```

In short, to add a new article type, put a new type name as part of the value of the property `journal.article.types` in `$PORTAL_ROOT_HOME/WEB-INF/classes/portal-ext.properties`, and then set the display text in `$PORTAL_ROOT_HOME/WEB-INF/classes/content/Language-ext.properties`.

Default tokens

The token `@view_counter@` will be automatically translated to the logic of the view counter increment. It means that you would be able to add the views counter through the journal articles token. To do so, you can simply add `@view_counter@` anywhere in the text and save it. If you are interested in inserting simple page breaks in articles, then you can simply add token `@page_break@`. How, you ask? The portal has specified the following property in `portal.properties`.

```
journal.article.token.page.break=@page_break@
```

As shown in the preceding code, the property `journal.article.token.page.break` sets the token `@page_break@`, which is used when inserting simple page breaks in articles.

Besides the tokens `@view_counter@` and `@page_break@`, there is a set of tokens you can use at runtime, translating to their applicable runtime value at processing time. The following is a complete list of tokens and their runtime values.

```
@cdn_host@: themeDisplay.getCDNHost()
@company_id@: themeDisplay.getCompanyId()
@group_id@: groupId
@cms_url@: themeDisplay.getPathContext() + "/cms/servlet"
@image_path@: themeDisplay.getPathImage()
@friendly_url_private_group@: themeDisplay.
getPathFriendlyURLPrivateGroup()
@friendly_url_private_user@: themeDisplay.
getPathFriendlyURLPrivateUser()
@friendly_url_public@: themeDisplay.getPathFriendlyURLPublic()
@main_path@: themeDisplay.getPathMain()
@portal_ctx@: themeDisplay.getPathContext()
@portal_url@: Http.removeProtocol(themeDisplay.getURLPortal())
@root_path@: themeDisplay.getPathContext()
@theme_image_path@: themeDisplay.getPathThemeImages()
@language_id@: the language_id of the current request
```

Custom tokens

A new property has been added for custom tokens in the portal. You would be able to set up a list of custom tokens and values of custom tokens as follows.

- `journal.article.custom.tokens=custom_token_1,custom_token_2`
- `journal.article.custom.token.value[custom_token_1]`=This is the first custom token.
- `journal.article.custom.token.value[custom_token_2]`=This is the second custom token.

The portal provides capability to set a list of custom tokens that will be replaced when article content is rendered. For example, if the property `journal.article.custom.tokens` is set to "custom_token_1", then "@custom_token_1@" will be replaced with its token value This is the first custom token before an article is displayed; and if the property `journal.article.custom.tokens` is set to "custom_token_2", then "@custom_token_2@" will be replaced with its token value This is the second custom token before an article is displayed.

Default templates

There are various types of fields available in structured content, which allows velocity macros to be used to display structured content. The following is a list of velocity macros used for Journal Articles—web contents.

```
reserved-article-id, reserved-article-version, reserved-article-
title, reserved-article-create-date, reserved-article-modified-
date, reserved-article-display-date, reserved-article-author-id,
reserved-article-author-name, reserved-article-author-email-
address, reserved-article-author-comments, reserved-article-
author-organization, reserved-article-author-location,reserved-
article-author-job-title.
```

Moreover, you can use velocity macros in `JournalVmUtil` and `VelocityVariables`, `request` (e.g., `request.attributes.USER_ID`), `company`, `companyId`, `groupId`, `journalTemplatesPath`, `locale`, and `randomNamespace`.

Of course, you can also use customized velocity macros in your article templates. In addition, you can get the list of available variables in `VelocityVariables` by referring to the *Chapter 7, Customizing CMS and WCM* of the book *Liferay Portal 5.2 Systems Development*.

Publishing Web Content

We have used the Web Content Management portlet to create web content (called articles) stored in WMS. Now we are ready to publish content in websites.

Suppose that there are two pages, namely, "Articles" and "About Us" under the "Home" page on the Guest community public pages. The "Articles" page will display all articles, and users can navigate these articles, while the "About Us" page will display the article "About Us" only. The portlets **Web Content Display** and **Web Content List** would be very useful for these two scenarios.

The Web Content Display portlet

As an administrator of the enterprise "Palm Tree Publications", you need to create a page called "About Us" under the page "Home" at the Guest community and then add the portlet Web Content Display (portlet ID 56) in the page "About Us". Finally, publish the article "About Us" in the page "About Us". Let's do it by following these steps:

1. Add a page called "About Us" under the page "Home" at the Guest community public pages, if the page is not there.

2. Change the layout with the value say "1-Column" by clicking on the link **Manage-Page Layout** under the dock bar menu.

3. Add the portlet Web Content Display in the page "About Us" of the Book Lovers community where you want to publish the article by clicking on **Add | Web Content Display** under the dock bar menu.

4. Select an article by clicking on the **Select Web Content** icon in the portlet Web Content Display.

5. Locate the article "About Us", and select the article by clicking on the link **Name**.

6. Optionally, enable the checkbox **Enable Ratings** to enable ratings, and enable the checkbox **Enable Comments** to enable comments. Here we just use the default settings.

7. Click on the **Return to Full Page** arrow.

8. Optionally, remove the border of the portlet by clicking on the **More | Look and Feel** icon and then disable the checkbox **Show Border**, click on the **Save** button, and click on the **Remove** icon on the top-right to return.

9. Open a new browser, and input a URL with the value "`http://localhost:8080/web/guest/aboutus`". You will see the page "About Us".

Do you find any difference between this page and the Original Required View? Of course, all content pieces are the same as that of the Original Required View such as images, texts, and links. However, the look and feel is slightly different. As stated, the content designer can update the template "Template About Us" with CSS to provide the best layout. In short, you can provide the best layout as you can imagine through templates and CSS.

When going to **More | Configuration | Setup | Current**, you would see a set of options to display an article.

- **Override Default Template**: Update the template of the selected article.
- **Show Available Locales**: Multi-language display.
- **Convert To**: DOC, ODT, PDF, RTF, SXW, TXT.
- **Enable Print**: Whether or not to display the icon **Print**.
- **Enable Ratings**: Whether or not to enable ratings.
- **Enable Comments**: Whether or not to enable comments on the article.
- **Enable Comments Ratings**: Whether or not to enable comments on ratings.

When displaying an article in the Web Content Display portlet, you would see a list of icons at the bottom if you have proper permissions.

- **Edit Web Content**: Update the current article.
- **Edit Template**: Update the template of the current article.
- **Select Web Content**: Select an article.
- **Add Web Content**: Add a new article and display it.

How can we configure the preceding settings? You can find a JSP file at $PORTAL_ROOT_HOME/html/portlet/journal_content/view.jsp. You may override this JSP file according to your requirements.

By the way, the Web Content Display portlet is instanceable—you can add more than one portlet to a page because the Web Content Display portlet has been specified in $PORTAL_ROOT_HOME/WEB-INF/liferay-portlet.xml as follows:

```
<instanceable>true</instanceable>
```

The Web Content List portlet

As an administrator of the enterprise "Palm Tree Publications", you may create a page called "Articles" under the page "Home" at the Guest community and then add the portlet (portlet ID 62) in the page "Articles". Finally, publish the articles in the page "Articles". Let's do it by following these steps:

1. Add a page called "Articles" under the page "Home" at the Guest community public pages if the page is not there by clicking on **Manage | Page** under the dock bar menu.

2. Change the layout with the value say "1-Column" by clicking on the link **Manage | Page Layout**.

3. Add the Web Content List portlet to the "Articles" page of the Guest community where you want to publish articles, if the Web Content List portlet isn't there.

4. Click on the **More | Configuration** link to modify the properties of the portlet.

5. Choose a **Community**, say "Guest", **Web Content Type**, say "General", **Display URL**, **Display per Page**, **Order by Column**, and **Order by Type** as well.

6. Optionally, select a structure to filter the web content list by a structure.

7. Click on the **Return to Full Page** arrow.

Do you find a list of articles in the page "Articles"? One of them should be the article "About Us".

 Note that only approved articles will appear in the portlet Web Content List. You can't see the articles that are either not approved or expired.

- **Community**: Groups like the Guest community and My Community in the organization Palm Tree Enterprise.
- **Web Content Type**: Article types like General.
- **Display URL**: Maximized, Normal, Pop up.
- **Display per Page**: A number.
- **Order By Column**: Display Date, Created Date, Modified Date, Web Content Title, ID.
- **Order By Type**: Ascending, Descending.
- **Structure**: Select a structure to filter the web content list by a structure.

As you can see, a list of web content (articles) is displayed with the **Name, Display Date**, and **Author**. How do we add more columns like `description`? You can find the look of the Web Content List portlet at `$PORTAL_ROOT_HOME/html/portlet/ journal_articles/view.jsp`, and add more columns or override the display in this JSP file—you can do whatever you want.

In addition, you would see a list of numbers in **Display per Page: 5, 10, 25, 50, 100**. How do we customize this? The portal has specified the following items in `portal.properties`.

```
journal.articles.page.delta.values=5,10,25,50,100
```

As shown in the preceding code, the property `journal.articles.page.delta. values` sets the available values for the number of articles to display per page. You would definitely be able to override this property in `portal-ext.properties`.

By the way, the Web Content List portlet is instanceable—just like the Web Content List portlet, since the Web Content List portlet has been specified in `$PORTAL_ROOT_ HOME/WEB-INF/liferay-portlet.xml` as follows:

```
<instanceable>true</instanceable>
```

Other WCM tools

There are some other WCM tools, which are useful for web content publishing. Here we just list some of them as follows:

- XSL Content portlet: Provides the ability to publish XML-based content.
- Asset Publisher portlet: Provides ability to publish a generic frontend to several content types and sources, for example, Blogs Entries, Bookmark Entries, Document Library Documents, Image Gallery Images, Web Content, and last but not least, custom portlets like the Knowledge base portlet. For more details, refer to *Chapter 4 Forums, Categorization, and Asset Publishing*.
- Nested Portlets portlet: Holds one or more portlets inside. It provides a nested portlets layout, that is, portlets within portlets.

Nested Portlets

The Nested Portlets portlet provides capabilities where users can drag-and-drop portlets into other portlets, making complex page layouts possible. This portlet is like a portlet container.

The Nested Portlets portlet is configurable. By going to **More | Configuration | Setup** on the portlet Nested Portlets, you would see following settings:

- **Layout Template**: Available default layout templates and custom layout templates — you are asked to choose one of them.
- **Show Borders**: Show borders or not.

Once the Nested Portlets portlet gets configured, you would be able to drag portlets to nest them. Of course, you would be able to change configuration at any time. Note that the Nested Portlets portlet is instanceable, which means that you can add multiple portlets to a page.

As you can see, the default layout template in the Nested Portlets portlet (portlet ID 118) is **2_columns_i**, named as **2 Columns (50/50)**. Moreover, there are two unsupported layout templates: **freeform** and **1_column** named as **1 Column**. Why, you ask? The portal has specified the following properties in portal.properties.

```
nested.portlets.layout.template.default=2_columns_i
nested.portlets.layout.template.unsupported=freeform,1_column
```

As shown in the preceding code, the property nested.portlets.layout.template.default sets the default layout template in the Nested Portlets portlet, while the property nested.portlets.layout.template.unsupported adds a comma separated list of layout template IDs that shouldn't be allowed in the Nested Portlets portlet.

Where are layout templates? Default layout templates are specified in `$PORTAL_ROOT_HOME/WEB-INF/liferay-layout-templates.xml`, where you would be able to find layout templates like **freeform, 1_column, 2_columns_i,** and so on.

These default layout templates may not satisfy your requirements. Let's say that you were interested in a custom layout template, say **2_1_2_columns**, named as **2-1-2 Columns,** you're planning to use the layout template **2_1_2_columns** as the default layout template in the Nested Portlets portlet. How do we implement this? The following is an option:

1. Download the WAR file `${layouttpl.war}` from `http://liferay.cignex.com/palm_tree/book/0387/chapter08/2-1-2-columns-layouttpl-6.0.0.1.war`

2. Drop the WAR file `${layouttpl.war}` to the folder `$LIFERAY_HOME/deploy` when the portal is running.

3. Add the following line at the end of `portal-ext.proporties`.

   `nested.portlets.layout.template.default=2_1_2_columns`

4. Stop the portal and restart it.

That's it. When going to **More | Configuration** on the Nested Portlets portlet, you would see the custom layout template **2-1-2 Columns** selected as default.

The XSL Content portlet

The portlet XSL Content allows publishing remote XML content by applying an XSL style sheet that converts it to HTML. Both the XML content and the XSL files are configurable using URLs.

The XSL Content portlet (portlet ID `102`) is configurable. By going to **More | Configuration | Setup** on the XSL Content portlet, you would see following settings:

- **XML URL**: A URL for XML—providing data like `@portal_url@/html/portlet/xsl_content/example.xml`.

- **XSL URL**: A URL for XSL—providing an XSL style sheet that converts it to HTML like `@portal_url@/html/portlet/xsl_content/example.xsl`.

As you can see, the examples `example.xml` and `example.xsl` are located at `$PORTAL_ROOT_HOME/html/portlet/xsl_content`, where the variable `$PORTAL_ROOT_HOME` and the token `@portal_url@` points to the same location. Therefore, you can override these files according to your own requirements. Of course, you would need to provide your own remote XML content and an XSL style sheet to publish your own content in the XSL Content portlet. Note that the XML file and the XSL file must be accessible through URLs.

More interestingly, you could upload `example.xml` and `example.xsl` to the document library and use the URL it provides. The following is an option:

1. Upload files `example.xml` and `example.xsl` into the portlet Document Library, under a folder say "Integrations".

2. Make a note on the URL of `example.xml` and `example.xsl`: `${xml.url}` and `${xsl.url}` respectively.

3. After going to **More | Configuration | Setup** on the portlet XSL Content, just enter `${xml.url}` for the XML URL and `${xsl.url}` for the XSL URL.

4. Click on the **Save** button.

Summary

This chapter first introduced us to adding folders and sub-folders for images, managing folders and sub-folders, adding images in folders and managing images, setting up permission on folders and images. Then we discussed how to add folders and sub-folders for documents, how to manage documents, how to add comments, how to give your rating, how to view versions, how to set up permission on folders and documents, and how to publish documents. It then introduced structures management, templates management, and articles management.

We emphasised on how to build articles based on structures and templates, and how to set up permissions on Web Content Management, articles, templates, structures, and feeds. Finally, we introduced how to publish articles and to employ other WCM tools. In short, WCM doesn't only provide high availability to publish, manage, and maintain web contents and documents, but it also does separate content from the layout.

In the next chapter, we're going to introduce Social Office, hooks and custom fields.

9
Social Office, Hooks, and Custom Fields

In the intranet website 'Palm Tree Publications', it would be nice to provide an environment for employees to enjoy chatting, instant messaging, mailing, and SMS text messaging. Most importantly, it should provide a Social Office environment that users can start collaborating on.

Social Office is a social collaboration on top of the portal — a full virtual workspace that streamlines communication and builds up group cohesion. All components are tied together seamlessly, which gets everyone on the same page by sharing the same look and feel. The dynamic activity tracking gives us a birds-eye view of who has been doing what and when, within each individual site. Note that Social Office isn't another separate portal, but a specific instance of the portal. Many portlets are involved in Social Office such as `Chat`, `Mail`, `Contacts`, `Tasks Management Systems`, and so on.

This chapter will introduce you to chatting and instant messaging It will discuss how to manage e-mails and how to use the `SMS Text Messenger` portlet. It will show you how to build social office and how to apply hooks on the portal — the name hook implies hooking into Liferay, allowing us to hook into the events system, model listeners, JSPs, services, and portal properties. Finally, it will introduce Custom Attributes (also called Custom Fields) and how to apply them to any asset.

In this chapter, you will learn about:

- Checking online friends and chat
- Setting up the portlet chat
- Setting up e-mail accounts
- Managing (check, delete, forward, reply, search) e-mails

- Managing the SMS Text Messenger portlet
- Building Social Office with themes, portlets, and hooks
- Enjoying hooks
- Applying custom fields on any assets

The Chat portlet

The chat portlet is an AJAX Enterprise Instant Messaging client that allows users to automatically chat with other logged-in portal users. Chat sessions are persisted across portal pages and are as secure as other portal functionalities.

In order to let employees enjoy chatting and instant messaging with others, we should use the Chat portlet. In addition, Social Office is a social collaboration on top of the portal, consisting of the generic portal and set of portlets such as Chat, Mail, so theme, so-portlet, and so on. Let's see how to enjoy chatting and instant messaging first.

Sample of a Chat portlet

The following is a sample which could bring the chat portlet into the portal of Social Office:

- Download the WAR file ${chat.portlet.war} from http://liferay. cignex.com/palm_tree/book/0387/chapter10/chat-portlet- 6.0.0.1.war.
- Drop the file into the folder $LIFERAY_HOME/deploy when the portal is running.

Checking for online friends

When you sign in, you ould see a chat bar at the bottom of the portal, in which you can see online friends and can change chat settings. Normally, the number of online friends shows up at the bottom-right corner of the screen. Click it to pull up a list of these friends and click on a specific person to open a chat box with that friend.

As shown in the following screenshot, you could be able to enjoy AJAX Enterprise Instant Messaging in the portal.

The following screenshot shows the `Chat` portlet in **Social Office**. You would see that the number of online friends shows up in the bottom-right corner of the screen. As a user of **Social Office, Lotti Stein** can update her chat settings anytime.

Clicking on the **Settings**, you would be able to configure your chat settings as follows:

- "**${user.full.name} is**": Input your status (for example, **Busy**), which will be seen by your friends under your name.

- **Show me as online**: A checkbox that can either show you as online or offline.

- **Play a sound when I receive a new message in a hidden window**: A checkbox to play a sound upon receiving a message.

- **Save**: A button to save the chat.

Beginning with chatting

Once your friends are online, you can chat with them. Let's imagine that your friend is online and you want to ct with him. Perform the following to chat with him:

- Click on the chat list to display the list of online friends.

- Click on a specific person with whom you want to chat. A chat box opens up, in which you can type and send messages to your friend.

The chat box contains a user's name and logo at the upper-left corner. You can close the current chat box by clicking on the **X** mark at the upper-right corner. To minimize it, you can click on the – mark at the upper-right corner.

You can also chat with multiple users. To do this, simply click on the user's name link; a chat box for each user opens up.

To send messages, input your messages at the message input box and press *Enter*. Your messages will appear starting with the keyword `${user.full.name}` in the message box, and the messages sent by another user will appear starting with the username.

The `Chat` portlet is an AJAX Enterprise Instant Messaging client that allows users to automatically chat with other users logged onto the portal. Chat sessions persist across portal pages and are as secure as other portal functionalities.

Folder structure

The `Chat` portlet has the following folder structure at `$AS_WEB_APP_HOME/chat-portlet`.

- Images: This folder contains the image files
- META-INF: Contains the `context.xml` file
- WEB-INF: Web info specification includes the sub-folders `classes`, `lib`, `service`, `sql`, `src`, and `tld`

As you can see, all JSP files, flash files, and JavaScript files reside in `$AS_WEB_APP_HOME/chat-portlet`. The flash file `alert.swf` is used to play a sound when a chat message ived.coming.

Employing AJAX

AJAX stands for Asynchronous JavaScript and XML. In short, AJAX makes portal pages feel more responsive by exchanging the amounts of data as less as possible with the server. Thus the entire portal page does not have to be reloaded when the user requests a change. You can use AJAX to increase the portal page's interactivity, usability, functionality, and speed.

In other word, AJAX acts as asynchronous data transfer, that is, HTTP requests between the browser and the portal server, allowing portal pages to request a few bits of information from the server instead of whole portal pages. The AJAX makes portal applications smaller, faster, and more user-friendly, as shown in the following figure.

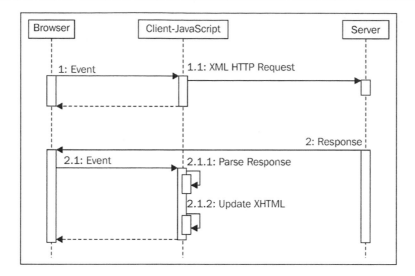

In general, AJAX is based on the following standards:

- JavaScript—Scripting language of the web
- XML—Extensible Markup Language
- XHTML—Extensible Hypertext Markup Language
- HTTP protocol
- CSS—Cascading Style Sheets

AJAX follows web standards supported by all major browsers. As a result, AJAX applications are browser and platform independent. The main advantage of AJAX is the separation of data, format, style, and function.

Setting up a Chat portlet

The `Chat` portlet has specified the default set of portlets as follows at `$AS_WEB_APP_HOME/chat-portlet/WEB-INF/classes/portlet.properties`:

```
buddy.list.strategy=all
```

As shown in the previous code snippet, the chat buddy list strategies would be `all`, `communities`, and `friends`. The default setting for the property `chat.buddy.list.strategy` is `all`. Of course, you would be able to override these properties any time at `$AS_WEB_APP_HOME/chat-portlet/WEB-INF/classes/portlet.properties`.

Access on the portlet

As you may have noticed, the Chat portlet is invisible if you didn't sign in. It has the following specifications at $AS_WEB_APP_HOME/mail-portlet/view.jsp.

```
<%@ include file="/init.jsp" %>
<c:if test="<%= themeDisplay.isSignedIn() %>">
<!-- ignore details -->
</c:if>
```

The preceding code shows that the portlet checks whether the current user signed-in or not. If the user has signed-in, then shows the content of the portlet.

Configuration of a Chat portlet

The Chat portlet has the following configuration at $AS_WEB_APP_HOME/chat-portlet/WEB-INF/liferay-portlet.xml.

```
<portlet>
  <portlet-name>1</portlet-name>
  <friendly-url-mapper-class>com.liferay.chat.portlet.
ChatFriendlyURLMapper</friendly-url-mapper-class>
  <poller-processor-class>com.liferay.chat.poller.
ChatPollerProcessor</poller-processor-class>
  <use-default-template>false</use-default-template>
  <css-class-wrapper>chat-portlet</css-class-wrapper>
  <system>true</system>
</portlet>
```

As shown in the preceding code, the portlet sets the <system> value to true, that is, the portlet is a system portlet that a user can't manually add to their page. The default value of <system> is false. The value of <poller-processor-class> is triggered by Liferay.Poller, a JavaScript class. It allows a portlet to use polling to be notified of data changes. The portlet sets the <use-default-template> value to false—that is, the portlet doesn't use the default template to decorate and wrap content. The default value is true. The most common use of <use-default-template> is if you want the portlet to look different from the other portlets, or if you want the portlet to not have borders around the outputted content.

In addition, the portlet specified tags <friendly-url-mapper-class>, <portlet-name>, and <css-class-wrapper>. The <portlet-name> element contains the unique name of the portlet. This name must match the portlet-name specified in $AS_WEB_APP_HOME/chat-portlet/WEB-INF/portlet.xml.

Service model

As you hed, the Chat portlet has specified service model with a package com. liferay.chat. You would be able to find details at $AS_WEB_APP_HOME/ chat-portlet/WEB-INF/service.xml. The Service-Builder in SDK plugins will automatically generate services against service.xml, plus XML file like portlet-hbm.xml, portlet-model-hints.xml, portlet-spring.xml, base-spring.xml, dynamic-data-source-spring.xml, hibernate-spring.xml, and infrastructure-spring.xml at $AS_WEB_APP_HOME/chat-portlet/WEB-INF/ classes/META-INF. More details, base-spring.xml, dynamic-data-source-spring.xml, hibernate-spring.xml, and infrastructure-spring.xml are the generic specifications for the Hibernate-Spring framework, but portlet-hbm.xml, portlet-model-hints.xml, and portlet-spring.xml are specific declarations to service models for the Hibernate-Spring framework. Therefore, if you're going to merge service models, you only need to merge these specific declarations.

The service.xml specified chat info as two tables Chat Entry and Chat Status. Each Chat Entry includes the columns: entry Id (as the Primary key), create Date, from User Id, to User Id, and content. Each Chat Status includes the columns: status Id (as Primary key), user Id, modified Date, online, awake, active Panel Id, message, and play Sound.

By the way, the custom SQL scripts were provided at $AS_WEB_APP_HOME/chat-portlet/WEB-INF/classes/custom-sql/default.xml. Both Service-Builder and service.xml will take care of most basic needs in querying the database; custom queries are one of them, separating queries from code, easy-to-find and easy-to-edit.

Enhancement

As you can see, only two users can chat with each other currently. Multi-user (more than two users) chat isn't supported, though it's a helpful feature.

In addition, all JSP files, flash files, and JavaScript files reside in $AS_WEB_APP_HOME/ chat-portlet. It would be better to re-organize JSP files into the folder $AS_WEB_APP_HOME/chat-portlet/chat, flash files into the folder $AS_WEB_APP_HOME/ chat-portlet/flash, and JavaScript files into the folder $AS_WEB_APP_HOME/chat-portlet/javascript.

The Mail portlet

The `Mail` portlet is a full AJAX-based webmail client that can be configured to interface with many popular IMAP email servers. Thise portlet allows users to send and check their e-mail directly through the portal, and also allows them to visualize all e-mails of a given account from several e-mail accounts.

In order to let employees manage their e-mails, we should bring the `Mail` portlet into the portal. As an administrator of Palm Tree Publications, you need to create a page called `Mail` at the `Guest` community public pages to add the `Mail` portlet in the page. In Social Office, the `Mail` portlet has been added in the **Mail** page next to the **Home** and **Profile** pages of the user's public pages with a friendly URL like `/web/${user. screen.name}/mail`.

Working of a Mail portlet

The following is a sample which could bring the `Mail` portlet into the portal or Social Office:

- Download the WAR file `${mail.portlet.war}` from `http://liferay. cignex.com/palm_tree/book/0387/chapter10/mail-portlet- 6.0.0.1.war`.

- Drop the file into the folder `$LIFERAY_HOME/deploy` when the portal is running.

Managing e-mails

First of all, log in as **Palm Tree,** and create a page called `Mail` at the `Guest` community public pages, and then add the `Mail` portlet in the **Mail** page. Let's do it by following these steps:

1. Add a page called `Mail` at the **Guest** community public pages (if it isn't there).

2. Add the `Mail` portlet in the **Mail** page. The portlet can be seen in the next screenshot.

3. If you signed in successfully, you would see the message **Configure email account**. After clicking on this link, you would be able to configure the e-mail account.

Configuring e-mail accounts

As shown in the following screenshot, there are two onfiguringto configure an e-mail account, namely, **Add a Mail Account** or **Add a Gmail Account**.

As an editor from the Editorial Department, you may want to manage your mails in the bookpub.com mail domain. Let's add a mail account by following these steps:

1. Log in as **Lotti Stein**.
2. Go to the **Mail** page on the **Guest** community public pages.
3. Locate the Mail portlet, and then click on **Add a Mail Account**.
4. Input values for **Email Address, User Name** (should be the same as **Email Address), Password, Incoming Port, Use Secure Incoming Connection, Outgoing SMTP Server, Outgoing Port,** and **Use Secure Outgoing Connection**.
5. Click on the **Save** button when you are ready. Note that a validator will warn you if you can't connect to the IMAP server you specified.

You can click on the link **Return to Full Page** after the e-mail account has been saved. You can add your Gmail account, if you have one. For a Gmail account, only an e-mail ID and password are required. The rest of the configuration has been set in the portlet properties.

Once the mail acc is saved, you willould be able to check your e-mail or configure the e-mail account again. You can now check for new messages in your inbox by clicking on the link **Check your email** first. Then you can view unread messages and either check your mail or create a new mail.

Checking e-mail

You can go to the **Email Management** page by clicking on any link of **Unread Messages**, the **Compose** button, or the **New** button. Furthermore, you can manage e-mails using the `Mail` portlet for your current account. E-mail management includes creating, checking, replying to, replying to all, forwarding, deleting, marking as read/unread, and searching for an e-mail.

As you can see, e-mails are grouped into different folders: **INBOX, Calendar, Contacts, Delete Items, Drafts, Journal, Junk E-mail, Notes, Sent Items, Tasks,** and so on.

 Note that the first e-mail with the subject **Test-SMS Text Messenger test!** was sent by the `SMS Text Messenger` portlet. For more details, refer to the forthcoming section.

Sending e-mail

Suppose that you want to send an e-mail to a person named David Berger, you can do it by following these steps:

- Locate the `Mail` portlet, and click on **Check your email**.
- Click on **Compose Email**.
- Input `david@bookpub.com` in the **To** e-mail address field.
- Input values for **CC** and **BCC**, if applicable.
- Input values for **Subject** and **Attachments** if possible.
- Use the default WYSIWYG editor and input the e-mail message.
- Click on the **Send** button when you are ready or the **Discard** button to discard inputs.
- Of course, this e-mail will be sent and a copy of this e-mail will be saved in the folder **Sent Items**.

Assigning permissions

The following table shows permissions for the `Mail` portlet. The roles may set up all permissions (marked as X) as well as thoseat of the role `Guest` role, namely, **View**, **Configuration**, and **Preferences**. By default, both the roles have the **View** permission action (marked as *).

Action	Description	Community	Guest
View	Ability to view the portlet	X, *	X, *
Configuration	Ability to configure the portlet	X	X
Preferences	Ability to configure e-mail accounts	X	X

A `Community` member does not have the **Preferences** permission action.

As an administrator, you may need to set up the `Community Member` role having both the **Preferences** and **View** permissions on the `Mail` portlet. Thus, users in that role can configure e-mail accounts. Permissions can be added on the role by carrying out the following steps:

1. Locate the `Mail` portlet.
2. Click on the **Configuration** icon at the top-right of the `Mail` portlet.
3. Click on the **Permissions** tab.
4. Check the checkbox of the permission **Preferences** under the role **Community Member**.
5. Click on the **Submit** button if you are ready.

As you can see, the portlet allows us to visualize all e-mails from several e-mail accounts. It aggregates several e-mail accounts, filters e-mails using tags, and sends e-mails from any account. In short, the `Mail` portlet provides a full AJAX-based webmail client that can be configured to interface with many popular IMAP e-mail servers, allowing users to send and check e-mail directly through the portal.

Setup

The `Mail` portlet has specified the default set of portlets as follows at `$AS_WEB_APP_HOME/mail-portlet/WEB-INF/classes/portlet.properties`.

```
disk.root.dir=${liferay.home}/data/mail
javamail.debug=false
messages.to.prefetch=25
messages.per.page=25
synchronize.interval.minutes=3
```

```
preconfigured.mail.accounts = \
  { // ignore details
  }
```

As shown in the preceding code, the property `disk.root.dir` sets the default mail repository. By default, the property `javamail.debug` has been specified as `false`. TsIt means that Java Mail Debug got disabled. The `messages.to.prefetch` property and the `messages.per.page` properties are set as `25`. You can change these values later, if you wish to.

The property `synchronize.interval.minutes` is set to 3 minutes — that is, a synchronizing interval will happen in 3 minutes. Pre-configured mail accounts are set by the property `preconfigured.mail.accounts`. This is the reason why we could add either a mail account or a Gmail account.

Mail Engine settings

In order to make the `Mail` portlet work, we have to set up a mail server with IMAP and SMTP protocol. As mentioned, there are two pre-configured email accounts, namely, a mail account and a Gmail account. For a mail account, you need to configure the following items:

```
Email Address: like administrator@cignex.com
User Name: like administrator@cignex.com
Password: ${password}
Incoming IMAP Server: like exg3.exghost.com
Incoming Port: 143
Use Secure Incoming Connection: false;
Outgoing SMTP Server: like exg3.exghost.com;
Outgoing Port: 2525;
Use Secure Outgoing Connection: false;
```

For a Gmail account, only the e-mail address and password are required for input, and the username would be the same as that of the e-mail address. The following items are pre-configured.

```
Incoming IMAP Server: imap.gmail.com;
Incoming Port: 993;
Use Secure Incoming Connection: true;
Outgoing SMTP Server: smtp.gmail.com;
Outgoing Port: 456;
Use Secure Outgoing Connection: true;
```

In short, the `Mail` portlet is an AJAX web-mail client. We can configure it to work with any mail server. It reduces page refreshes, since it displays message previews and message lists in a dual pane window.

The mail repository

The mail repository root directory has been set using the property `disk.root.dir`. Under the `${disk.root.dir}`, e-mails are grouped as `${user.id}/${email.address}`. By default, the mails have the following folders under `${user.id}/${email.address}`.

```
Calendar: calendar info;
Contacts: contacts info;
Delete Items: deleted emails;
Drafts: drafts emails;
INBOX: email inbox;
Journal: Journal info;
Junk+E-Mail: junk emails;
Notes: notes info;
Outbox: email outbox;
Sent+Items: sent emails;
Tasks: tasks info.
```

Configuration

The `Mail` portlet has specified the following configuration at `$AS_WEB_APP_HOME/mail-portlet/WEB-INF/life ray-portlet.xml`.

```xml
<portlet>
  <portlet-name>1</portlet-name>
  <icon>/icon.png</icon>
  <indexer-class>com.liferay.mail.util.Indexer</indexer-class>
  <friendly-url-mapper-class>com.liferay.mail.portlet.
MailFriendlyURLMapper</friendly-url-mapper-class>
  <render-weight>1</render-weight>
  <ajaxable>false</ajaxable>
  <header-portlet-css>/css.jsp</header-portlet-css>
  <footer-portlet-javascript>/javascript.js</footer-portlet-
javascript>
  <css-class-wrapper>mail-portlet</css-class-wrapper>
</portlet>
```

As shown in the preceding code, the `Mail` portlet sets `<ajaxable>` to `fal`. ThisIt means that the portlet can never be displayed using Ajax. The portlet also sets the name of the CSS class as `mail-portlet` that will be injected in the `DIV` that wraps the portlet. In addition, `<header-portlet-css>` sets the path of CSS that will be referenced in the page's header, relative to the portlet context path. While `<footer-portlet-javascript>` sets the path of JavaScript that will be referenced in the page's footer relative to the portlet context path.

The `<indexer-class>` is called to create or update a search index for the portlet. The `Mail` portlet uses `<friendly-url-mapper-class>`, since content inside the portlet needs to have a friendly URL. In addition, the default value of `<render-weight>` is 1. If it is set to a value of less than 1, then the portlet is rendered in parallel. If set to a value of 1 or greater, then the portlet is rendered serially. Portlets with a greater render weight have greater priority and will be rendered before portlets with a lower render weight. If the `<ajaxable>` value is set to `false`, then the `<render-weight>` is always set to 1 if it is set to a value less than 1. This means `<ajaxable>` can override render weight if `<ajaxable>` is set to `false`.

Access on the portlet

As you have noticed, you would receive amessagsayingike **"you must be authenticated to use this portlet"** if you are not lg in yet. In fact, the `Mail` portlet has the following specification at `$AS_WEB_APP_HOME/mail-portlet/view.jsp`.

```
<%@ include file="/init.jsp" %>
<c:choose>
 <c:when test="<%= themeDisplay.isSignedIn() %>">
<!--- ignore details -->
 </c:when>
 <c:otherwise>
    <liferay-ui:message key="you-must-be-authenticated-to-use-this-
portlet" />
 </c:otherwise>
</c:choose>
```

This code shows that the `Mail` portlet checks whether the current user signed-in or not. If the user has been signed-in, then shows the content of the portlet. Otherwise, it shows the message **"You must be authenticated to use this portlet"**.

Enhancement

The `Mail` portlet aggregates several e-mail accounts in the portlet, filters e-mails using tags, and sends e-mails from any of your accounts. But there is no wizard for configuring the e-mail settings. It would be nice to configure the `Mail` portlet using a wizard.

Moreover, it would be nice to have an automatic Ajax alert when a new message comes (to check a `POP` server, if it's not already possible, and so on).

Using the Mail portlet effectively

The portal can integrate with Washington IMAP + Sendmail, Cyrus IMAP + Postfix, and Dovecot + Postfix, as well as integrate with Microsoft Exchange and other IMAP servers. As stated above, the mail servuh aslike `"exg3.xghost.com"`, is a Microsoft Exchange server.

You can access e-mail through an IMAP server. If the access is on IMAP, the portal doesn't have to know where to persist the mail.

IMAP stands for **Internet Message Access Protocol**.
`http://www.imap.org/`

One popular protocol used for e-mail is IMAP, an application layer Internet protocol. It operateson port `143`, by default, allowing a local client to access e-mail on a remote server.

IMAP supports both connected and disconnected modes of operation. Until the user explicitly deletes them, IMAP e-mail clients generally leave messages on the server. Moreover, it offers access to the mail store.

IMAP has a lot of advantages. Here we just list some of them.

- The use of connected and disconnected modes of operation
- Users can connect to the same mailbox simultaneously
- Users can access MIME message parts and partial fetch
- Having message state information
- Supporting multiple mailboxes on the server
- Provide ability to perform server-side searches
- Having built-in extension mechanism

SMS Text Messenger

In order to let employees send text message to others anytime, we should use the SMS Text Messenger portlet (portlet ID 24). As an administrator of Palm Tree Publications, you need to create a pagealled SMS inof the **Guest** community public pages, and then add SMS Text Messenger portlet on the page. The portlet can be added to any page.

SMS Text Messenger portlet

First of all, log in as **Palm Tree** and create a page called SMS at the **Guest** community and then add the SMS Text Messenger portlet on the page. Let's do it as follows:

1. Log in as **Palm Tree**.
2. Navigate to **Go To | bookpub.com Public** under the dock bar menu.
3. Go to **Add | Page** under the dock bar menu.
4. Add a page called SMS at the **Guest** community public page, if the page isn't there.
5. Go to **Add | More...** under the dock bar menu.
6. Add the SMS Text Messenger portlet in the SMS page of the **Guest** community where you want to set it up, if it isn't there.

As an editor of the Editorial Department (consider **Lotti Stein**), you want to send a message, **Test—SMS Text Messenger test!** to a user, say **David Berger**, with the e-mail address david@bookpub.com. Let's do it by following these steps.

1. Log in as **Lotti Stein**.
2. Go to the page SMS under the **Guest** community public page.
3. Locate the portlet SMS Text Messenger.
4. Input the value david@bookpub.com for **To** and **Test—SMS Text Messenger test!** for both, **Subject** and **Message**.
5. Click on the **Send Text Message** button.

The user will receive this e-mail sooner or later, if the mail engine has been configured properly.

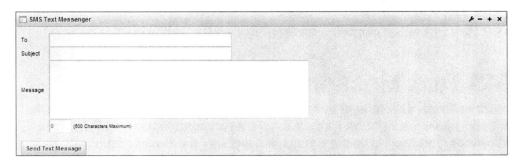

As shown in the previous screenshot, you should be asked to input the following items.

- **To** — To an e-mail address
- **Subject** — subject of the e-mail
- **Message** — text message of the e-mail
- **Send Text Message** — send the text message via the mail engine

Obviously, only one **To** e-mail address isgot supported. This means that at one time, you could input one and only one **To** e-mail address. It would be nice if multiple **To** e-mail addresses could get supported.

What's happening?

As you can see, the content of the SMS Text Messenger portlet is visible only to the users who have signed in. At the same time, the portlet provides the capability to send text messages using a configured mail engine.

Accessing the portlet

As you may have noticed, you would receive the message, **you-must-be-authenticated-to-use-this-portlet**, if you didn't log in yet. Why? The portlet has the following specifications at $PORTAL_ROOT_HOME/html/portlet/sms/view.jsp.

```
<%@ include file="/html/portlet/sms/init.jsp" %>
<c:choose>
  <c:when test="<%= themeDisplay.isSignedIn() %>">
<!-- ignore details -->
  </c:when>
  <c:otherwise>
    <liferay-ui:message key="you-must-be-authenticated-to-use-this-
portlet" />
  </c:otherwise>
</c:choose>
```

As shown in the preceding code, the portlet checks whether the current user signed-in or not. If the user was signed-in, the portlet will show the content of the SMS portlet. Otherwise, the portlet will show the message **you-must-be-authenticated-to-use-this-portlet**.

Mail Engine

In order to make SMS T Messenger working well, we have to set up a mail server with SMTP protocol. Normally, there are two options to set up a mail engine in the portal, namely, by JNDI name `mail/MailSession` and by `JavaMail`. If one of them was set properly, then the portlet SMS would send SMS Text messages via the configured mailengine (refer to *Chapter 2, Setting Up a Home Page and Navigation Structure for the Intranet*).

In short, the `SMS Text Messenger` portlet allows you to send SMS text messages in your portal page any`SMS Text Messenger` portlet could be used as a tester to verify mail engine settings in the portal. If the mail engine was set properly, then you should be able to send message as e-mail through the `SMS Text Messenger` portlet. If you use a mobile phone, you would be able to receive these messages.

Enhancement

As you can see, the lgth of a message subject and body—should be less than `${max.message.length}`, like `500`. The maximum length of a message is hardcoded in the `SMS` portlet. It would be nice if the maximum length of a message `${max.message.length}` is configurable at `portal.properties`. Thus users could override the maximum length of the message `${max.message.length}` later.

How to fully install Social Office

Social Office is a social collaboration solution for the enterprise. It allows people to collaborate effectively and efficiently. One of the handy features of Social Office is its usage of Microsoft Office integration. Definitely, it isn't another separate portal package, but a specific instance of the portal.

In general, all of the features of Social Office are available in the portal as well. In fact, the portal is the framework and Social Office is a customization of this framework (for example, custom portlets, themes, properties, and so on). The core functionality is identical between the portal and Social Office. What differs is the user experience—Social Office is for a specific use case, whereas the portal is for a more generic use case.

In short, Social Office is built on top of the portal, a special theme called `so theme`, and a specil portlet called `so-portlet`, together with hooks. Some additional portlets are involved such as the `Task Management System` portlet, `Contacts` portlet, and so on.

The SO theme

The SO theme uses CSS, images, JavaScript, and Velocity templates to control the whole look and feel of the Social Office pages. In the following screenshot, you can see how the SO theme looks:

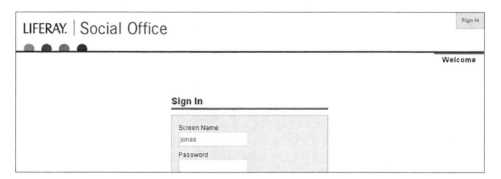

Structure

The theme SO theme has the following folder structure at $AS_WEB_APP_HOME/so-theme.

> css: Cascading Style Sheets; all CSS files set the look and feel of social office; includes application.css, bas.css, custom.css, dockbar.css, form.css, layout.css, main.css, navigation.css, portlet.css,
> images: all images files for the look and feel of social office with sub-folders structure; the logo image logo.png is stayed in the sub-folder /custom.
> javascript: JavaScript file for the look and feel of social office.
> templates: contains the Velocity templates that control the HTML generated by the theme;
> WEB-INF: web info specification; includes sub-folders classes, lib and tld.

The following CSS file main.css in the /css folder is the main CSS that includes other CSS files.

```
@import url(base.css);
@import url(application.css);
@import url(layout.css);
@import url(dockbar.css);
@import url(navigation.css);
@import url(portlet.css);
@import url(forms.css);
@import url(custom.css);
```

As shown in the preceding code, the CSS files will be loaded by order. The previous CSS files like `application.css`, `bas.css`, `dockbar.css`, `form.css`, `layout.css`, `navigation.css`, and `portlet.css` would be overridden in last CSS file like `custom.css`.

By default, many of the templates in the `/templates` directory have been consolidated. The `portal_normal.vm` file contains the overall site structure, from the opening HTML tag to the closing. It includes the header and footer, two templates (`navigation_top.vm` and `navigation.vm`), and also the system files. This file is the main index file that contains the base HTML. The `navigation_top.vm` file contains the entire HTML for the top navigation, the file `navigation.vm` contains the entire HTML for the navigation, and the file `portal_pop_up.vm` contains the entire HTML structure for pop-up windows. It is similar to the file `portal_normal.vm`, except for the fact that it is shown in pop-up windows. By the way, the file `portlet.vm` contains the HTML that wraps every portlet, including the portlet title and portlet icons. The file `init_custom.vm` allows us to override and define new velocity variables.

Configuration

In general, the properties of the theme are specified at `/WEB-INF/liferay-plugin-package.properties`. The theme `so-theme` has the following properties at `/WEB-INF/liferay-plugin-package.properties`.

```
name=Social Office
module-group-id=liferay
module-incremental-version=1
// ignore details
author=Liferay, Inc.
licenses=AGPL
```

The preceding code shows the plugin package name as `Social Office`, the module group ID as `liferay`, the module incremental version as `1`, the author as `Liferay, Inc.`, and so on.

The look and feel of the theme has been specified at `/WEB-INF/liferay-look-and-feel.xml`. The SO theme has the following definition at `/WEB-INF/liferay-look-and-feel.xml`.

```
<?xml version="1.0"?>
<!DOCTYPE look-and-feel PUBLIC "-//Liferay//DTD Look and Feel 6.0.0//
EN" "http://www.liferay.com/dtd/liferay-look-and-feel_6_0_0.dtd">
<look-and-feel>
  <compatibility>
    <version>6.0.0+</version>
  </compatibility>
  <theme id="so" name="Social Office" />
</look-and-feel>
```

The previous code shows the registration of the theme so-theme, with the ID as so, the name as Social Office, and a compatibility version like 6.0.0+.

In addition, you would be able to find DTD of look and feel at $PORTAL_ROOT_HOME/ dtd/liferay-look-and-feel_6_0_0.dtd. For example, you would be able to find the following DTD definition at $PORTAL_ROOT_HOME/dtd/liferay-look-and-feel_6_0_0.dtd.

```
<!ELEMENT look-and-feel (compatibility, company-limit?, group-limit?,
themorking
```

How does it work?

The following example could bring the so-theme into Social Office.

- Download the WAR file ${so.theme.war} from http://liferay.cignex. com/palm_tree/book/0387/chapter10/so-theme-6.0.0.1.war

- Drop the file to the folder $LIFERAY_HOME/deploy when the portal is running

The theme uses CSS Sprites for multiple images in the themes. CSS Sprites are used to group multiple images into one composite image and to display it using a CSS background positioning. This means that it should combine the background images into a single image and use the CSS background-image and background-position properties to display the desired image segment.

For example, let's say that the portal combines the background images into a single image and two versions (gif and png) in /images/custom are generated, namely, .sprite.gif and .sprite.png. Then the portal uses the CSS background-image and background-position properties to display the desired image segment. You could find CSS background-image and background-position properties in .sprite.properties.

```
/custom/bullet.png=64,3,3
/custom/folder_small.png=83,16,16
/custom/lock.png=44,16,16
/custom/menu_arrow.png=60,4,7
/custom/priority_important.png=28,16,16
/custom/priority_normal.png=99,16,16
/custom/tag_small.png=16,12,12
/custom/unlock.png=0,16,16
/custom/user.png=67,16,16
```

You would be able to find CSS Sprites in folders and sub-folders that contain at least one image file, either gif or png.

The logo of the theme could be overridden anytime. By default, you could find the logo image file `logo.png` at `/images/custom`.

The theme shortcut icon and thumbnail image can also be overridden. Normally, you can find the shortcut icon `liferay.ico` and thumbnail image `thumbnail.png` at `/imaes`.

As you can see, only thea page called `/home` is updatable. This happens because the theme has specified the following code in `/templates/portal_normal.vm`.

```
#if (!$layout.getFriendlyURL().equals("/home"))
  <script type="text/javascript">
    Liferay.Layout = null;
  </script>
#end
```

By the way, the file `portlet.vm` contains the HTML that wraps every portlet, including the portlet title and icons. The `so` theme doesn't want to show portlet icons; it just comments on the portlet title and portlet icons in `/templates/portlet.vm` as follows:

```
<div class="portlet" id="portlet-wrapper-$portlet_id">
  <div class="portlet-topper">
    <span class="portlet-title not-editable">
    $portlet_title
    </span>
  <div class="portlet-icons" id="portlet-small-icon-bar_$portlet_id">
    <!-- ignore details -->
  </div>
  </div>
  <div class="portlet-content">
  $portlet_content
  </div>
</div>
```

As you have noticed, in normal pages navigation, you can't remove a page or add a new page in the Social Office. This is because the `so` theme has removed the `class` attribute `class="sort-pages modify-pages"` in `/templates/navogation.vm` as follows:

```
<div id="navigation">
  <ul>
    #foreach ($nav_item in $nav_items)
    <!-- ignore details -->
    #end
  </ul>
</div>
```

The theme included top navigation links such as **My Home, My Profile, Add Application, Control Panel, My Site,** and **Sign Out**. This navigation was specified at /templates/navigation_top.vm. For example, applications (portlets) could be added in the page /home only, and only administrators can access the **Control Panel** page. The so theme has specified the following conditions at /templates/navigation_top.vm:

```
#set ($show_add_content = ($show_add_content && ($layout.
getFriendlyURL().equals("/home"))))
#set ($show_control_panel = $permissionChecker.isOmniadmin())
```

Setup

The portal has specified the following properties for themes in portal.properties:

```
theme.css.fast.load=true
theme.images.fast.load=true
theme.shortcut.icon=liferay.ico
theme.virtual.path=
theme.loader.storage.path=
theme.loader.new.theme.id.on.import=false
theme.portlet.decorate.default=true
theme.portlet.sharing.default=false
```

As shown in the preceding code, the portal sets the property theme.css.fast.load to true to load the theme's merged CSS files for faster loading and production. You can set the property to false for easier debugging for development. You can also disable fast loading by setting the URL parameter css_fast_load to 0.

Similarly, the portal set the property theme.images.fast.load to true to load the theme-merged image files for faster loading for production. You could set this property to false for easier debugging for development. You can also disable fast loading by setting the URL parameter images_fast_load to 0.

The portal sets the theme's shortcut icon by using the theme.shortcut.icon property. This property can be overridden in portal-ext.properties.

In addition, you could set the property theme.virtual.path to set the default virtual path for all hot deployed themes. Themes can be imported using LAR files. You can set the property theme.loader.storage.path to true if imported themes should use a new theme ID on every import. This will ensure that a copy of the old theme is preserved in the theme loader storage path. However, this also means that a lot of themes that are no longer used remain in the filesystem. It is recommended that you set this to false.

By default, the portal sets the property `theme.portlet.decorate.default` to `true` to decorate portlets and the portal sets the property `theme.portlet.sharing.default` to `true` to exposing sharing icons for portlets.

Most importantly, you uld speed up the portal by using the setting `theme.css.fast.load` and `theme.images.fast.load` as `true` in `portal-ext.properties`.

The SO portlet

Te `so-portlet` provides a general process — four portlets for Social Office, namely, `activities`, `members`, `profiles`, and `invite-members`. It also provides hooks to override JSPs with custom JSPs, portal properties hooks, language properties hooks, and portal services hooks.

The following is a sample, which could bring te `so -portlet` into Social Office:

- Download the WAR file `${so.portlet.war}` from `http://liferay.cignex.com/palm_tree/book/0387/chapter10/so-portlet-6.0.0.1.war`.

- Drop the file into the folder `$LIFERAY_HOME/deploy` when the portal is running

The following screenshot shows the user's home page, **My Home**. The left side of the user's home page lists the communities (called sites in this case) and a button to add sites if the user has an admin role. The right side of the page has three view activity options — **My Sites, My Friends,** and **Me**. The **My Sites** option lists all of the recent activities for the sites that the user belongs to, the **My Friends** option lists the recent activities for user's friends, and the **Me** option lists all of the activities of the logged-in user. For the management purpose of sites, we can reusetlet communities portlet. The **Activities** portlet of Social Office shows the users' activities and their friends' activities.

As shown in the following screenshot, the **Members** page lists all the members of that particular community on the right. You can click on a specific person to see more information, that is, **Profile**. Moreover, Social Office should have the ability to let users send a request to join or to leave a site. For example, Lotti Stein has joined `bookpubstreet.com`. She will have a choice to leave the website. In other words, the portlet so-portlet provides three portlets in Social Office, namely, members, profiles, and invite-members.

The **Calendar** page allows us to see all of the events, appointments, and meetings, associated with that particular community. As an admin, you can automatically add and edit events in the calendar. While the **Documents** page shows Document Library documents.

The **Forums** page displays the site's `Message Boards`. A list of quick links is displayed on the left side of the page. This allows us to quickly navigating right to the content you want to see. Once on the **Blog** page, you can navigate through all the blogs created by users within the site. The **Wiki** page is the perfect place to create documentation or post information for the site.

As shown in the following screenshot, the portlet **Activities** from the `so-portlet` displays friends' activities. The activities are grouped into three categories: **My Sites**, **My Friends**, and **Me**. **My Sites** lists all the recent activities for the sites that you belong to, **My Friends** lists the recent activities for your friends, and **Me** lists all of your (the signed-in user's) activities.

The goal of Social Office was to allow people to collaborate effectively and efficiently. The `so-portlet` provides the capability to create communities easily. Once signed-in, you could start by creating communities. These are essentially mini-sites that are used to collaborate on. You can create sites for any grouping of people who want to collaborate together. Once a community is created, you can start adding content to that site.

Note that the site could be either open community or private comty The restricted communities don't get supported, as shown in the following screenshot:

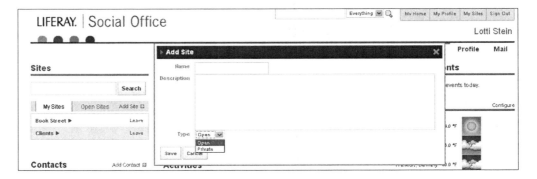

Structure

The `so-portlet` has the following folder structure at `$AS_WEB_APP_HOME/so-portlet`.

- activities: JSP files for the `Activities` portlet of Social Office
- invite_members: JSP files for the `Invite Members` portlet of Social Office

- members: JSP files for the Members portlet of Social Office
- META-INF: Contains custom JSP folders and files and `context.xml`
- profiles: JSP files for the `Profiles` portlet of Social Office
- WEB-INF: Web info specification—includes sub-folders classes, `lib`, services, `sql`, `src`,and `tld`

The `so-portlet` has the following folder structure at `$AS_WEB_APP_HOME/so-portlet/WEB-INF`:

classes: Properties such as `service.properties`, `portal.properties`, `portlet.properties`, and Java classes, which contain language properties at the subfolder `/content`

lib: Dependent JAR files, including `so-portlet-service.jar`

service: Source code of services.

sql: SQL scripts such as `indexes.sql`, `sequences.sql`, and `tables.sql`, and properties files like `indexes.properties`.

src: Source code of the portlet implementation, which contains language properties at the subfolder `/content`.

tld: **Tag Library Descriptor** files such as `c-rt.tld`, `liferay-au.tld`, `liferay-portlet-ext.tld`, `liferay-portlet.tld`, `liferay-security.tld`, `liferay-theme.tld`, `liferay-ui.tld`, and `util.tld`.

The `portlet so-portlet` has been defined by a few XML files like `liferay-display.xml`, `liferay-portlet.xml`, `portlet.xml`, and `liferay-plugin-package.xml` at `$AS_WEB_APP_HOME/so-portlet/WEB-INF`. In `liferay-plugn-package.xml`, the so- portlet has been specified as a plugin.

```
name=Social Office
module-group-id=liferay
module-incremental-version=1
//ignore details
author=Liferay, Inc.
  //ignore details
```

The preceding code shows the plugin package name as `Social Office`, the module group ID as `liferay`, the module incremental version as `1`, the author as `Liferay, Inc.` and so on.

The XML file `portlet.xml` defines the portlet `2.0` deployment descriptor for portlets such as `Activities`, `Invite Members`, `Members`, and `Profiles` with the following public render parameter. The `public-render-parameter` defines a render parameter, which is allowed to be public and thus be shared with other portlets. The identifier must be used for referencing this public render parameter in the portlet code.

```
<public-render-parameter>
  <identifier>invitedMembersCount</identifier>
  <qname xmlns:x="http://www.liferay.com/public-render-
  parameters">x:invitedMembersCount</qname>
</public-render-parameter>
```

The XML Schema for the Portlet `2.0` deployment descriptor can be found at `$PORTAL_ROOT_HOME/dtd/portlet-app_2_0.xsd`.

The XML file `liferay-portlet.xml` defines four portlets, namely, `Activities`, `Invite Members`, `Members`, and `Profiles` with the tag `<liferay-portlet-app>`. You would be able to find DTD of portlets at `$PORTAL_ROOT_HOME/dtd/liferay-portlet-app_6_0_0.dtd`. For instance, you would be able to find the following DTD definition at `$PORTAL_ROOT_HOME/dtd/liferay-portlet-app_6_0_0.dtd`.

```
<!ELEMENT liferay-portlet-app (portlet*, role-mapper*, custom-user-
attribute*)>
<!ELEMENT portlet (portlet-name, icon?, virtual-path?, struts-path?,
// ignore details add-default-resource?, system?, active?, include?)>
```

The XML file `liferay-display.xml` defines display categories of four portlets, namely, `Activities`, `Invite Members`, `Members`, and `Profiles` with the tag `<liferay-display>`. The use of this file is to make portlets available in `Add Applications`. You would be able to find DTD of portlet display at `$PORTAL_ROOT_HOME/dtd/liferay-display_6_0_0.dtd` as follows:

```
<!ELEMENT display (category*)>
<!ELEMENT category (category*, portlet*)>
```

As shown in the preceding code, the category element organizes a set of portlets. A portlet can exist in more than one category.

Last but not least, you would be able to see the `<hook>` definition at `liferay-hook.xml`. The so-portlet has the following hooks specification.

```
<?xml version="1.0" encoding="UTF-8"?>
<!DOCTYPE hook PUBLIC "-//Liferay//DTD Hook 6.0.0//EN" "http://www.
liferay.com/dtd/liferay-hook_6_0_0.dtd">
<hook>
  <portal-properties>portal.properties</portal-properties>
```

```
    <language-properties>content/Language_en.properties</language-
properties>
    <custom-jsp-dir>/META-INF/custom_jsps</custom-jsp-dir>
</hook>
```

As shown in the preceding code, it sets portlet properties hook as `portal.
properties`, language properties hook as `content/Language_en.properties`,
and custom JSPs hook as `/META-INF/custom_jsps`. Note thwe're going to exploreain
hooks in details in the next section of this chapter.

Setup

The `so-portlet` has specified a set of properties at `$AS_WEB_APP_HOME/so-
portlet/WEB-INF/classes/portlet.properties`.

```
    applications.allowed=6,16,23,25,26,27,29,30,39,64,84,101,114
    control.panel.items=2,125,127,128,129,130,131,135,137
```

As shown in the preceding code, the portlet so-portlet sets the IDs of core portlets
that can be added to a customizable page through the property `applications.
allowed`. The involved portlets are `Reverend Fun (6)`, `Dictionary (23)`, `Polls
(25)`, `Translators (26)`, `Unit Converter (27)`, `Bookmarks (28)`, `Communities
(29)`, `Network (30)`, `RSS (39)`, `Recent Documents (64)`, `Announcements (84)`,
`Asset Publisher (101)`, and `Recent Bloggers (114)`.

The `so-portlet` also sets the IDs of core portlets that can appear in the Control
Panel via the property `control.panel.items`. Involved portlets are `My Account
(2)`, `Enterprise Admin User (125)`, `Enterprise Admin User Group (127)`,
`Enterprise Admin Roles (128)`, `Enterprise Admin Password Policies (129)`,
`Enterprise Admin Settings (130)`, `Enterprise Admin Monitoring (131)`,
`Admin Instances (135)`, and `Admin Server (137)`. The better way to know
the relation between an ID and the application name is to open the `Language.
properties` file.

Furthermore, the `so-portlet` has specified a set of properties related to the default
home page as follows at `$AS_WEB_APP_HOME/so-portlet/WEB-INF/classes/
portlet.properties`.

```
    site.layout.template=3_columns
    user.layout.template=3_columns
```

The preceding code shows the default layout template `3_columns` that will be used
on the site's and user's home page.

In addition, the `so-portlet` has specified the default set of portlets as follows at `$AS_WEB_APP_HOME/so-portlet/WEB-INF/classes/portlet.properties`.

```
site.layout.portlets.column-1=1_WAR_wysiwygportlet,28,39_INSTANCE_abcd
site.layout.portlets.column-2=84,1_WAR_soportlet
site.layout.portlets.column-3=64,1_WAR_todayseventsportlet
user.layout.portlets.column-1=29,1_WAR_contactsportlet
user.layout.portlets.column-2=84,1_WAR_soportlet,1_WAR_tmsportlet
user.layout.portlets.column-3=1_WAR_todayseventsportlet,1_WAR_
weatherportlet
```

The preceding code sets the default set of portlets that will be placed on the site's and user's home page. If you don't install absolutely all of this portlet, the entire page won't be available at all. Of course, you could input a list of comma delimited portlet IDs to specify more than one portlet. If the portlet was instanceable, you need to add the suffix `_INSTANCE_abcd` to the portlet ID, where `abcd` is any random alphanumeric string.

The involved portlets are `Bookmarks (28)`, `My Communities (29)`, `RSS (39)`, `Recent Documents (64)`, `Announcements (84)`, and plugins such as `WYSIWYG`, `Today's Event`, `Contacts`, `TMS (Tasks Management Systems)`, `Weather`, `Activities` of `so- portlet`.

How does it work?

The `so-portlet` removed users account and created a new user account as the default administrator. All message related to this newly created user account are hardcoded in the Start-up action.

The `so-portlet` also specified the default theme as `so-theme` in Layout Set Listener. In addition, it adds a user's default pages such as `Home`, `Profile`, and `Mail` and the site's default pages such as `Home`, `Calendar`, `Documents`, `Forums`, `Blog`, `Wiki`, and `Members`.

The `so-portlet` removed the default portal page `/web/guest/home` and set the redirect as `/web/${user.screen.name}/home` for the **Home** page and `/web/${user.screen.name}/profile` for the **Profile** page at **Service Pre Action**.

More interestingly, the `so-portlet` overrode the login post action and set the redirect as `/web/${user.screen.name}/home` at **Login Post Action**.gned-in to the Social Office, the user will get redirected to his/her **Home** page, instead of the Guest Home page, when they ign in to the Social Office..

What's happening?

The `so-portlet` used hooks at three areas, namely, portal-properties (called portal properties hooks), language-properties (called language properties hooks), and custom-jsp-dir (called custom JSPs hooks).

In `$AS_WEB_APP_HOME/so-portlet/WEB-INF/classes/portal.properties`, the `so-portlet` overrode the following portal properties:

```
release.info.build.number=151
release.info.previous.build.number=150
upgrade.processes=\
    com.liferay.so.hook.upgrade.UpgradeProcess_1_5_1
terms.of.use.required=false
## ignore details
my.places.show.organization.public.sites.with.no.layouts=false
my.places.show.organization.private.sites.with.no.layouts=false
my.places.show.community.public.sites.with.no.layouts=false
my.places.show.community.private.sites.with.no.layouts=false
```

In `$AS_WEB_APP_HOME/so-portlet/WEB-INF/classes/content/language_en.properties`, the `so-portlet` overrode or added the following language properties:

```
## Portlet titles
javax.portlet.title.8=Events
javax.portlet.title.29=Sites
javax.portlet.title.39=Feeds
javax.portlet.title.101=Related Content
javax.portlet.title.134=Sites
## Messages
## Ignore details
view-file-entry=View File Entry
```

For example, the `Calendar (8)` portlet, the `Communities (29)` portlet, the `RSS (39)` portlet, and the `Asset Published (101)` portlet have all been re-titled as `Events, Sites, Feeds,` and `Related Content`.

The `so-portlet` modified JSP files of the portals `portlets` and `taglib` at `$AS_WEB_APP_HOME/so-portlet/META-INF/custom_jsps/html`. More specifically, it overrode the default `portlets` portal at `/portlet` and the tal `taglib` UI at `/taglib/ui`.

In /taglib/ui, the so-portlet modified the following taglib UI:

- calendar: page.jsp
- page_iterator: showingresult.jspf
- search: start.jsp

In /portlet, the so-portlet overrode the following portlets portal JSP files:

- announcements: view.jsp, init-ext.jsp, tabs1.jsp, entry_select_scope.jspf, entry_scope.jspf, entry_action.jspf, edit_entry.jsp, and css.jsp
- asset_publisher: add_asset.jspf, asset_actions.jsp, init-ext.jsp, view_dynamic_list.jspf, and /display/title_list.jsp
- blogs: edit_entry.jsp, init-ext.jsp, search.jsp, sidebar_with_form.jsp, sidebar.jsp, tabs1.jsp, view_entries.jspf, view_entry_content.jspf, view_entry.jsp, view.jsp
- bookmarks: view.jsp
- calendar: edit_event.jsp, events.jspf, export_import_action.jsp, init-ext.jsp, mini_calendar.jsp, sidebar.jsp, tabs1.jsp, view_event.jsp, view.jsp
- communities: community_action.jsp, community_iterator.jspf, edit_community.jsp, group_search.jsp, view.jsp
- directory: view.jsp and /user/search_columns.jspf
- document_library: edit_file_entry.jsp, edit_folder.jsp, file_entry_columns.jspf, folder_columns.jspf, init-ext.jsp, search.jsp, sidebar_file_entries.jspf, sidebar.jsp, tabs1.jsp, and view.jsp
- login: login.jsp
- message_boards: edit_category.jsp, edit_message.jsp, init-ext.jsp, move_thread.jsp, search.jsp, sidebar.jsp, tabs1.jsp, view_message.jsp, and view.jsp
- recent_documents: view.jsp
- requests: view.jsp
- search: init-ext.jsp and search.jsp
- wiki: edit_node.jsp, sidebar.jsp, top_links.jsp, view_nodes.jsp, and view_page_details.jsp

Note that the folder $AS_WEB_APP_HOME/so-portlet/META-INF/custom_jsps/html should map to the folder $PORTAL_ROOT_HOME/html. Moreover, JSP files under the folder $AS_WEB_APP_HOME/so-portlet/META-INF/custom_jsps/html must have the same names as those in the $PORTAL_ROOT_HOME/html folder.

Enhancement

The so-portlet removes default user account and creates a new user account for default administrator. All messages related to this newly created user account are hardcoded in the Start-up action. It would be convenient that all messages related to this newly-created user account could be configurable. For example, set all messages related to this newly created user account as values of properties at $AS_WEB_APP_HOME/so-portlet/WEB-INF/classes/portlet.properties first. Then the portlet consumes these properties in the Start-up action.

Similarly, the default theme has been hardcoded as so-theme in Layout Set Listener. It would be nice if the default theme could also be configurable. For example, you can set the default theme as a value of the property portlet.default.theme at $AS_WEB_APP_HOME/so-portlet/WEB-INF/classes/portlet.properties first. Then the portlet consumes the property portlet.default.theme in Layout Set Listener. Moreover, if we want to undeploy the so-portlet, it would be nice to get our previous users back.

The Extending Calendar portlet

As you can see, the portlet Calendar (portlet ID 8) has provided a lot of features. But in some use cases, only some minor features are required. In general, there are many different ways to extend the Calendar portlet. In the next sections, we have TMS and Today's Events as examples.

Task Management System

The Tasks portlet is a **Task Management System (TMS)** that provides the ability to manage tasks and track the tasks and their completion status. You can create and assign tasks to yourself or your contacts, and you can also track tasks and their completion status.

The following steps could bring the portlet into a page:

- Download the WAR file ${tms.war} from http://liferay.cignex.com/palm_tree/book/0387/chapter10/tms-portlet-6.0.0.1.war

- Drop the file into the folder $LIFERAY_HOME/deploy when the portal is running

- Go to **Add|More...** under the dock bar menu and add the portlet TMS on the page

When adding a new task, you would be able to add the following items:

- Description: Description of a task
- Assignee: The user to whom a task has been assigned
- Priority: High, Normal, or Low
- Due Date: Due date of the task
- Never Due: Whether a task is due or not
- Tags: Adding, selecting, or searching tags
- Save/Cancel: Save current task or cancel inputs

Each task is editable. For example, let's assume that you had input a task Review Book. Now you're going to update the complete status. All tasks are displayed in two tabs—**Assigned To Me** and **I've Assigned**—plus an icon **Add Task**. Each task is displayed with the columns **Description** and **Due**. In additio would have the ability to show completed tasks if needed. You could locate the task Review Book and click on the link for description.

You would view the task Review Book first with the following items.

- Tasks: Description of tasks
- Reporter: Full name of reporter
- Assignee: Full name of assignee
- Priority: The value of task priority
- Status: Task status (default is open)
- Tags: Tags on current task
- Comments: Ability to add comments on current task
- Edit/Cancel: Updating current task or canceling inputs

When editing a task, you would be able to update all items for adding a task plus one more column, Status. You could update the status with the following values: Open, 20% complete, 40% complete, 60% complete, 80% complete, 100% complete, Resolved, Reopened. The details of these values are stored in $AS_WEB_APP_HOME/tms-portlet/tasks/edit_task.jsp. Moreover, able to find the display text at $AS_WEB_APP_HOME/tms-portlet/WEB-INF/classes/content/Language.properties. Of course, you could customize the status by overriding the previous two files.

Note that the TMS portlet depends on the environment settings of Social Office — that is, so-portlet and hooking functions. If you need the TMS portlet in the generic portal, you could add so-portlet-related hooks first, and then use the TMS portlet in the portal.

Today's Event

The Today's Event portlet provides users with the ability to view all calendar events from all of their websites at one place on a page. Another usage is in Social Office, which will be discussed in the next chapter (where users can view all calendar events from all of their websites in a single place on their **Home** page).

The following is an option which could bring the portlet into a page:

- Download the WAR file ${today.event.war} from http://liferay.cignex.com/palm_tree/book/0387/chapter10/todays-events-portlet-6.0.0.1.war
- Drop the file to the folder $LIFERAY_HOME/deploy when the portal is running
- Go to **Add | More...** under the dock bar menu, and add the portlet Today's Event in a page

As you may havicedhe portlet Toay's Event portlet cannot be instantiated. This means that you can add only one portlet on one page. Moreover, the portlet Today's Event appears in the category Collaboration. The portlet has specified the following in $AS_WEB_APP_HOME/todays-events-portlet/WEB-INF/liferay-display.xml:

```
<?xml version="1.0" encoding="UTF-8"?>
<!DOCTYPE display PUBLIC "-//Liferay//DTD Display 6.0.0//EN" "http://
www.liferay.com/dtd/liferay-display_6_0_0.dtd">
<display>
  <category name="category.collaboration">
    <portlet id="1"></portlet>
  </category>
</display>
```

As shown in the preceding code, the portlet with the ID 1 in the plugin ${today.event.war} will appear in the category category.collaboration and display the text Collaboration.

The Contacts portlet

As mentioned earlier, Social Office was based on a set of portlets and themes. Besides the portlets Chat, Mail, and so-portlet, and the theme so-theme, Social Office involved more portal-default portlets such as Requests (portlet ID 121), Calendar (portlet ID 8), Document Library (portlet ID 20), Message Boards (portlet ID 19), Blogs (portlet ID 33), Wiki (portlet ID 36), Asset Publisher (portlet ID 101), RSS (portlet ID 39), My Communities (portlet ID 29), and so on. Moreover, Social Ofice includesd plugins such as the Weather portlet, the WYSIWYG portlet, the TMS (Task Management Systems) portlet, the Today's Event portlet, and the Contacts portlet. You'll be introduced to the Contacts portlet, as we've already seen the others previously.

The Contacts portlet enables users to manage customers and friends, including phone, address, birthday, company, e-mail, and so on. The contact list shows all the people on various sites, as well as friends, and provides a quick way to message them and to find their information.

Setup

As shown in the following screenshot, the Contacts portlet appears in a user's **Home** page under the My Communities portlet (renamed as Sites). As stated earlier, the Contacts portlet has been set in the so-portlet using portlet properties at $AS_WEB_APP_HOME/so-portlet/WEB-INF/classes/portlet.properties.

Generally, you can search users by inputting keywords such as first name, last name, screen name, and so on. The a set of users will be displayed under the Search button. As you can see, search results are displayed as user logo, last login date, **Contacts** icon, send-email icon, and online icon.

You can add contacts with following items:

> **Name**: Contact's full name;
>
> **Email**: contact's email address;
>
> **Comments**: contact's comments
>
> **Add Contacts/Cancel**: either to save inputs or to discard;

One could be able to add more contact information for a given user. By simply clicking on the icon **Contacts** next to a user, say "Lotti Stein", you hnwould be able to update the folowing items:.

> **Phone Numbers**: Extendible
>
> **Number**: Phone number
>
> **Extension**: Phone extension
>
> **Type**: Business, Business Fax, Mobile, Other, pager, Personal, personal Fax, TTY
>
> **Address**: extendible;
>
> **Street1**: street line 1
>
> **Street2**: street line 2
>
> **Street3**: street line 3
>
> **Country**: countries
>
> **Region**: regions or states of selected country
>
> **Type**: Business, Business Fax, Mobile, Other, pager, Personal, personal Fax, TTY
>
> **Zip**: zip code
>
> **City**: city
>
> **Comments**: contact comments
>
> **Save/Cancel**: either to save inputs or to discard

In addition, you would be able to send e-mails with contact information for a given user. By simply clicking on the icon **Send Email** next to a user, you would be able to update the following items.

TO: TO email address;

CC: carbon copy;

BCC: Blind carbon copy;

Subject: email subject;

Body: email body;

Send Email / Cancel: either to send email or to discard;

Configuration

The `portlet Contacts` portlet has the following portlet description at `$AS_WEB_APP_HOME/contacts-portlet/WEB-INF/liferay-portlet.xml`.

```
<portlet>
  <portlet-name>1</portlet-name>
  <icon>/icon.png</icon>
  <ajaxable>false</ajaxable>
  <header-portlet-css>/css.jsp</header-portlet-css>
  <header-portlet-javascript>/javascript.js</header-portlet-
javascript>
  <css-class-wrapper>contacts-portlet</css-class-wrapper>
</portlet>
```

As shown in the preceding code, the default value of `<ajaxable>` is `false`. The portlet Contacts sets `<ajaxableto false`. ThisIthat the portlet Contacts portlet can never be displayed via Ajax. The portlet also sets the name of the CSS class as `contacts-portlet` that will be injected in the DIV that wraps the portlet. In addition, `<header-portlet-css>` sets the path of CSS that will be referenced in the page's header relative to the portlet context path, while `<header-portlet-javascript>` sets the path of the JavaScript that will be referenced in the page's header relative to the portlet context path. By the way, the portlet doesn't specify the tab `<instanceable>`. `<instanceable>` sets the instanceable value to `true` if the portlet can appear multiple times on a page. If it is set to `false`, the portlet can only appear once on a page. The default value of `<instanceable>` is false, the portlet Contacts portlet instanceable. It can only appear once on a page.

In addition, the portlet Contacts added the following hooks in `$AS_WEB_APP_HOME/contacts-portlet/WEB-INF/liferay-hook.xml`.

```xml
<?xml version="1.0" encoding="UTF-8"?>
<!DOCTYPE hook PUBLIC "-//Liferay//DTD Hook 6.0.0//EN" "http://www.
liferay.com/dtd/liferay-hook_6_0_0.dtd">
<hook>
 <portal-properties>portal.properties</portal-properties>
</hook>
```

How does it work?

The following is a sample that could be uring theportlet `Contacts` portlet into the Social Office.

- Download the WAR file `${contacts.portlet.war}` from `http://liferay.cignex.com/palm_tree/book/0387/chapter10/contacts-portlet-6.0.0.1.war`

- Drop the WAR file `${contacts.portlet.war}` to the folder `$LIFERAY_HOME/deploy` when the portal (Social Office, in this case) is running.

What's happening?

The portlet `Contacts` portlet has specified the defaul set of portlets, as follows, at `$AS_WEB_APP_HOME/contacts-portlet/WEB-INF/classes/portlet.properties`.

```
contact.list.strategy=communities,friends
```

As shown in the preceding code, the contacts list strategies would be `all`, `communities`, and `friends`. The default setting for the property `contact.list.strategy` is `communities,friends`. Of course, you would be able to override these properties anytime at `$AS_WEB_APP_HOME/contacts-portlet/WEB-INF/classes/portlet.properties`.

The portlet `Contacts` used hooks at three areas, namely, portal-properties (called portal properties hooks), and language-properties (called language properties hooks).

In `$AS_WEB_APP_HOME/contacts-portlet/WEB-INF/classes/portal.properties`, the portlet contacts overrode the following portal properties.

```
application.shutdown.events=com.liferay.contacts.hook.events.
ShutdownAction
application.startup.events=com.liferay.contacts.hook.events.
StartupAction
value.object.listener.com.liferay.portal.model.Group=com.liferay.
contacts.hook.listeners.GroupListener
```

Service model

As you have noticed, the portlet `Contacts` has specified the service model with a package `com.liferay.contacts`. You would be able to find details at `$AS_WEB_APP_HOME/contacts-portlet/WEB-INF/service.xml`. Service-Builder in plugins SDK will automatically generate services against `service.xml`, plus XML files like `portlet-hbm.xml`, `portlet-model-hints.xml`, `portlet-spring.xml`, `base-spring.xml`, `dynamic-data-source-spring.xml`, `hibernate-spring.xml`, and `infrastructure-spring.xml` at `$AS_WEB_APP_HOME/contacts-portlet/WEB-INF/classes/META-INF`.

The `service.xml` specified contact info as Entry. Each entry included columns, namely, entry ID as the primary key, group ID, company ID, user ID, user Name, create Date, modified Date, entry User ID, e-mail Address, full Name and comments.

By the way, the custom SQL scripts were provided at `$AS_WEB_APP_HOME/contacts-portlet/WEB-INF/classes/custom-sql/default.xml`.

Enhancement

As you can see, all JSP files and JavaScript files reside in `$AS_WEB_APP_HOME/contacts-portlet`. It would be better to re-organize JSP files into the folder `$AS_WEB_APP_HOME/contacts-portlet/contacts` and JavaScript files into the folder `$AS_WEB_APP_HOME/contacts-portlet/javascript`.

By the way, the link Add Contact doesn't work due to a JavaScript problem related to the AUI update. This issue should get fixed shortly.

Hooks

Hooks is a feature to catch hold of the properties and JSP files into an instance of the portal as if catching them with a hook. Hook plugins are more powerful plugins that come to complement portlets, themes, layout templates, and web modules. A hook plugin is always combined with a portlet pluginstance, the portlet `so-portlet` is a portlet plugin for Social Office with hooks. In general, hooks would be very helpful tools to customize the portal without touching the code part of the portal. In addition, you would use hooks to provide patches for the portal systems or Social Office products.

Setup

In general, there are four kinds of hook parameters. They are portal-properties (called portal properties hooks), language-properties (called language properties hooks), custom-jsp-dir (called custom JSPs hooks), and service (called portal service hooks), as specified in $PORTAL_ROOT_HOME/dtd/liferay-hook_6_0_0.dtd.

```
<!ELEMENT hook (portal-properties?, language-properties*, custom-jsp-
dir?, service*)>
<!ELEMENT portal-properties (#PCDATA)>
<!ELEMENT language-properties (#PCDATA)>
<!ELEMENT custom-jsp-dir (#PCDATA)>
<!ELEMENT service (service-type, service-impl)>
<!ELEMENT service-type (#PCDATA)>
<!ELEMENT service-impl (#PCDATA)>
```

As shown in the preceding code, the ordering of elements is significant in the **DTD (Document Type Definition)** — you need to have your portal properties (only one marked by ?), language properties (could be many marked by *), custom-jsp-dir (only one marked by ?) and service (could be many marked by *) declared in the same order.

Language properties hooks allow us to install new translations or override a few words in existing translations. JSP hooks provide a way to easily modify JSP files without having to alter the core of the portal, whereas portal properties hooks allow runtime re-configuration of the portal. Portal service hooks provide a way to easily override portal services. The portal configuration properties can be altered by specifying an override file, where the properties will immediately take effect when deployed.

Note that not all portal properties can be overridden via a hook. The supported properties are:

```
auth.forward.by.last.path
auto.deploy.listeners
application.startup.events
auth.failure
auth.max.failures
auth.pipeline.post
auth.pipeline.pre
auto.login.hooks
captcha.check.portal.create_account
control.panel.entry.class.default
default.landing.page.path
dl.hook.impl
field.enable.com.liferay.portal.model.Contact.birthday
```

```
field.enable.com.liferay.portal.model.Contact.male
field.enable.com.liferay.portal.model.Organization.status
hot.deploy.listeners
image.hook.impl
javascript.fast.load
layout.static.portlets.all
layout.template.cache.enabled
layout.user.private.layouts.auto.create
layout.user.private.layouts.enabled
layout.user.private.layouts.modifiable
layout.user.public.layouts.auto.create
layout.user.public.layouts.enabled
layout.user.public.layouts.modifiable
ldap.attrs.transformer.impl
login.create.account.allow.custom.password
login.events.post
login.events.pre
logout.events.post
logout.events.pre
mail.hook.impl
my.places.show.community.private.sites.with.no.layouts
my.places.show.community.public.sites.with.no.layouts
my.places.show.organization.private.sites.with.no.layouts
my.places.show.organization.public.sites.with.no.layouts
my.places.show.user.private.sites.with.no.layouts
my.places.show.user.public.sites.with.no.layouts
passwords.passwordpolicytoolkit.generator
passwords.passwordpolicytoolkit.static
servlet.session.create.events
servlet.session.destroy.events
servlet.service.events.post
servlet.service.events.pre
session.phishing.protected.attributes
terms.of.use.required
theme.css.fast.load
theme.images.fast.load
upgrade.processes
users.email.address.generator
users.email.address.required
users.full.name.validator
users.screen.name.always.autogenerate
users.screen.name.generator
users.screen.name.validator
value.object.listener.*
```

What's happening?

As you can see, hooks can be standalone plugins, where one XML file is required — `liferay-hook.xml`. Alternatively, hooks can work together with portlets, where we simply add one XML file — `liferay-hook.xml`.

```xml
<?xml version="1.0" encoding="UTF-8"?>
<!DOCTYPE hook PUBLIC "-//Liferay//DTD Hook 6.0.0//EN" "http://www.
liferay.com/dtd/liferay-hook_6_0_0.dtd">
<hook>
    <portal-properties>portal.properties</portal-properties>
    <language-properties>content/Language_en.properties</language-
properties>
    <custom-jsp-dir>/META-INF/custom_jsps</custom-jsp-dir>
</hook>
```

Portal Properties Hooks

Through Portal Properties Hooks, we could change certain configuration properties dynamically and inject behavior into the hooks defined in the `portal.properties` file. All of the hooks that we have discussed in this chapter will revert, and their targeted functionality will be disabled immediately as soon as they are un-deployed from the portal. Moreover, each type of hook can easily be disabled via the `portal.properties` file.

Note that a `portal.properties` file must exist in the plugin hook's `WEB-INF/classes` folder if the portal properties hooks are enabled. Plugin hooks can override the properties like `dl.hook.impl`, `mail.hook.impl`, `image.hook.impl`, and so on. To override these properties, add these properties to a `portal.properties` file in the plugin hook's `WEB-INF/classes` folder.

Language Properties Hooks

Language Properties Hooks allow us to install new translations or override few words in existing translations. For example, you're going to rename "Custom Attributes" as "Custom Fields" in the user editing mode or the organization editing mode. You can create a folder `content` under plugin hook's `WEB-INF/classes`, and then you could create a properties file `Language_en.properties` under the plugin hook's `WEB-INF/classes/content`. Finally, add the following line at `Language_en.properties`.

```
custom-attributes=Custom Fields
```

The preceding code shows that the message key `custom-attributes` will have the display text **Custom Fields**.

Note that a `Language_en.properties` file must exist in the plugin hook's `WEB-INF/classes/content` folder if the language properties hooks got enabled.

More interestingly, language properties hooks allow us to install new translations or override few words in existing translations in both a single language and multiple languages. You can specify multiple language properties files at `liferay-hook.xml`. Therefore, multiple language properties files are supported via hooks, and this is a nice feature.

Custom JSP Hooks

Custom JSP Hooks provide a way to easily modify JSP files of the portal without having to alter the core of the portal. A folder `/META-INF/custom_jsps` must exist in the plugin hook's `Root` folder, if language properties hooks are enabled.

Under the folder `/META-INF/custom_jsps`, the same folder structure, like `html`, as that of `$PORTAL_ROOT_HOME/html` will be used to override portal JSP files with custom JSP files. In runtime, the original JSP like `${name}.jsp` or `${name}.jspf` will be renamed as `${name}.portal.jsp` or `${name}.portal.jspf` under `$PORTAL_ROOT_HOME/html`; while custom JSP files `${name}.jsp` or `${name}.jspf` will get copied to the folder `$PORTAL_ROOT_HOME/html`.

For example, you're going to override the view of the login portlet. You can put the custom JSP file `login.jsp` of the hook plugin at `/META-INF/custom_jsps/html/portlet/login`. During runtime, the portal will rename the original JSP `login.jsp` as `login.portal.jsp` under `$PORTAL_ROOT_HOME/html/portlet/login` first, and then the portal will copy the custom JSP file `login.jsp` of the hook plugin at `/META-INF/custom_jsps/html/portlet/login` to the folder `$PORTAL_ROOT_HOME/html/portlet/login`. More interestingly, you can include renamed original JSP as follows in the custom JSP file `login.jsp` of the hook plugin at `/META-INF/custom_jsps/html/portlet/login` again.

```
<liferay-util:include page="/html/portlet/login/login.portal.jsp" />
```

Therefore, after deploying the hook plugin, you would see both `login.jsp` and `login.portal.jsp` under the folder `$PORTAL_ROOT_HOME/html/portlet/login`.

Portal Service Hooks

Portal service hooks allow us to customize portal services and models. This means that plugin hooks can override services and models. For example, to override `UserLocalService`, you can add the followg toin `liferay-hook.xml`.

```
<hook>
 <service>
  <service-type>com.liferay.portal.service.UserLocalService</service-
type>
  <service-impl>com.ext.hook.service.impl.ExtUserLocalServiceImpl</
service-impl>
 </service>
</hook>
```

As shown in the preceding code, the service was specified by the tags `<service-type>` and `<service-impl>`. The tag `<service-type>` provides the original service or model in the portal, and the tag `<service-impl>` provides customized portal service or model, which will override the original service or model in the portal. More interestingly, yle to specify many tags `<service>`, if needed.

> Note that portal service hooks, portal properties hooks, and language properties hooks will get inactive when Hook plugins were un-deployed.

Enhancement

Custom JSP hooks provide a way to easily modify the JSP files of the portal without having to alter the core of the portal. In runtime, the original JSP like `${name}.jsp` or `${name}.jspf` will be renamed as `${name}.portal.jsp` or `${name}.portal.jspf` under `$PORTAL_ROOT_HOME/html`. When the hook plugin got un-deployed, the original JSPs should get rolled back. For example, let's look at the custom JSP on the logon view. When the hook plugin got un-deployed, the portal should delete the JSP `login.jsp` under `$PORTAL_ROOT_HOME/html/portlet/login` and rename `login.portal.jsp` as `login.jsp` under `$PORTAL_ROOT_HOME/html/portlet/login`. This is a nice feature that allows us to restore the original JSPs of the portal when the hook plugin is un-deployed.

What happens when you deploy two hooks that override the same JSP file? Changing the same JSP file with more than one hook is not currently supP file. You need to check the hooks for collision (you can use a separate repository for handling this). If you have a collision, then the last deployed JSP will be used, but it should be done with care as the order of deployment is not guaranteed. The hooks should be smart enough to have it—this feature is expected to be added soon.

As you can see, there are five different kinds of plugins, namely, portlet, theme, layout template, web, and ext. For more details, refer to *Chapter 10, Search, WAP, CRM, Widgets, Reporting and Auditing*. Ideally, one plugin should contain only one kind of plugin like web, ext, theme, hook, and layout template. But the plugin portlet can contain many portlets plus hooks optionally. For example, the plugin `so-portlet` included several portlets and a hook.

Custom Fields

The portal also provides a framework to add custom attributes or called custom fields to any Service Builder-generated entities at runtime, where indexed values, text boxes, and selection lists for input and dynamic UI are available. For example, you could add custom fields on any entity like a wiki page, Message Boards category, Message Boards message, Calendar event, page, organization, user, Web Content, Document Library document, Document Library folder, Bookmarks entry, Bookmarks folder, Image Gallery image, Image Gallery folder, Blogs entry, and so on. able to add custom felds ton custom entities in plugins.

Managing custom fields

As you would have noticed, the entity `User` has a set of attributes such as the first name, last name, and description. In most cases, these attributes would satisfy our requirements. But in some cases, you may need to extend these attributes by adding new attributes dynamically. For example, you're going to add the attributes `Ext Name` and `Ext Desc` on the entity `User`. The portal provides a `Custom Fields` framework. Thud be able add attrbutes ton the entities, including `User` and `Organization`, without writing any code.

Adding custom fields

We'll need to add the attributes `Ext Name` and `Ext Description` through custom fields to the entity `User`, without writing any Java code. As shown in the following screenshot, you could do it in the **Control Panel** with the `Expando` portlet.

You could simply click on **Users** in the category **Portal** of **Control Panel** first, and then click on the icon **Custom Fields** next to the icon **Add**.

In the same pattern, you would be able to use Custom Fields against Organizations. You could simply click on **Organizations** in the category **Portal** of **Control Panel** first, and then click on the icon **Custom Fields** next to the icon **Add**.

When adding a custom fielbe able to input a key and select a type as follows:

- **Key**: The custom field key is used to access the field programmatically through the tag `<liferay-ui:custom-attribute>`

- **Type**: Choose the field type carefully, as once it is defined it cannot be changed

- **Presets**: selection of integer value, selection of decimal values, selection of text values, textbox, textbox indexed, text field secret, text field indexed

- **Primitives**: Boolean, Date, Double, Float, Integer, Long, Short, String

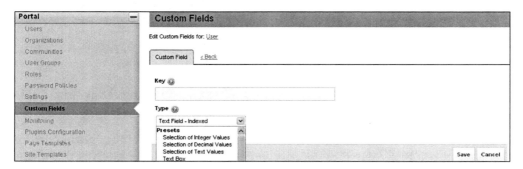

Let us add the custom fields `Ext Name` and `xt Desc` ton a user by following these steps:

- Log in as an administrator (for example, Palm Tree)
- Go to **Manage | Control Panel** under the dock bar menu
- Go to **Users** at the category **Portal** of **Control Panel**
- Click on the icon **Custom Fields**. You will see the title **Custom Field** message **Edit Custom Fields** for **User**, a tab **Custom Fields**, a button **Add Custom Field**, and a **Back** link
- Click on the button **Add Custom Field**, and input **Ext_Name** for `Key` and select the value **Text Field—Indexed** for `Type`
- Click on the **Save** button when you are ready
- Click on the button **Add Custom Field** again and input **Ext_Desc** for `Key` and select the value **Text Field—Indexed** for `Type`
- Click on the **Save** button when you are ready

Viewing custom fields

After adding at least one custom field, you can view it, as shown in the following screenshot:

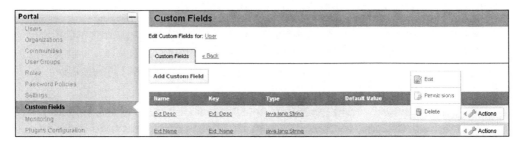

Each custom field is displayed with the **Name**, **Key**, **Type**, **Default Value** columns, and an **Actions** button with a set of icons, namely, **Edit**, **Permissions**, and **Delete**.

A link can be edited by clicking on any of the column entries. Alternatively, you can click on the icon **Edit** of the **Actions** button next to the custom field.

When editing a custom fi be able to view or update the following items (in addition to columns mentioned above):

- `Hidden`: Value is either false or true. Setting a custom field to hidden means that the field's value is never shown in any user interface besides this one. This allows the field to be used for some more obscure and advanced purposes like acting as a placeholder for custom permissions

- `Searchable`: Value is either true or false. Setting a custom field to searchable means that the value of the field will be indexed when the entity is modified. Only the `java.lang.String` fields can be made searchable. Note that when a field is newly made searchable, the indexes must be updated before the data is available to search

- `Secret`: The value could be either false or true. Setting a custom field to `Secret` means that the value of the field will be displayed as a dot or a * in place of the characters that you type in

- `Height`: The height of the input box

- `Width`: The width of the input box

Adding/updating values for custom fields

Once a few custom fielave been are added on a resol be able to add values to custom fields when editing that particular resource. For example, you have added `Ext Desc` and `Ext Name` on the resource `User` previously. When you edit an instance of that resource, you would be able to add values for the custom fields `Ext Desc` and `Ext Name`. The following is an example to add values for custom fields.

- Log in as an administrator
- Go to **Manage | Control Panel** under the dock bar menu
- Go to **Users** at the category **Portal** of **Control Panel**
- Locate a user, and click on the **Edit** icon of the **Actions** button next to the user
- Click on the **Miscellaneous | Custom Fields** link on the right-side box
- Input **My Desc** for the custom field `Ext Desc` and **My Name** for `Ext name`
- Click on the **Save** button when you are ready

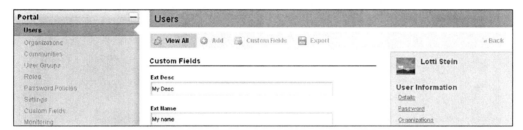

In the same way, you could add values for the custom fields on **Organization** by clicking on the **Miscellaneous | Custom Fields** of a given organization. Note that it will say **No custom fields are defined for Organization**, if no custom fields were specified on the resource.

You could use the same pattern to add values to custom fields on Message Boards category, Message Boards message, Calendar event, page, Web Content, Document Library document, Document Library folder, Bookmarks entry, Bookmarks folder, Image Gallery image, Image Gallery folder, Blogs entry, and so on.

Most interestild be able to use the same processes to update values for custom fields when you edit a resource. For instance, after adding a custom field `Keyword` on Image Gallery images, you would be able to add a value for it, when editing it.

Applying custom fields on any resources

The portlet Expando provides the ability to add custom fields on any resources. Logically, you are able to apply custom fields on any resources. The following screenshot shows resources with the custom field framework. For applying custom fields on any resource, complete the following sequence of steps:

- Log in as an administrator
- Go to **Manage | Control Panel** under the dock bar menu
- Go to **Custom Fields** under the category **Portal** of **Control Panel**

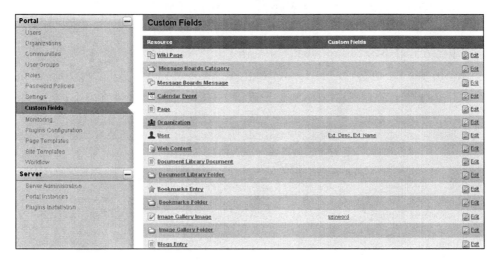

The portlet Expando will display resources that have the **Custom Fields** framework with the columns **Resource, Custom Fields,** and the icon **Edit**. As you can see, the function of the icon **Edit** next to the resource **User** is the same as that of **Users | Custom Fields** in the **Control Panel**. Similarly, the function of the icon **Edit** next to the resource **Organization** would be the same as that of **Organizations | Custom Fields** in the **Control Panel**.

Assigning permissions

As you can see, the portlet Expando is available only in the **Control Panel**. Moreover, there are two levels of permissions, namely, permissions on portlet and permissions on Expando columns.

Permissions on portlet

The following table shows permissions on the portlet Expando. The role **Community** member may set up all permissions (marked as **X**), namely, VIEW, CONFIGURATION, and ADD_EXPANDO, while the role **Guest** may set up the permission VIEW. By default, the role **Community** member and the role **Guest** have the permission action key VIEW (marked as *).

Action	Description	Community	Guest
VIEW	Ability to view the portlet	X, *	X, *
CONFIGURATION	Ability to configure the portlet	X	
ADD_EXPANDO	Ability to add Expando columns on resources	X	

A member of the role **Community** Member doesn't have the permissions action ADD_EXPANDO. Thus a user can't add Expando columns on any resource.

Permissions on Expando columns

The following table shows permissions on Expando columns. The role **Community** member may set up permissions (marked as X): VIEW, UPDATE, PERMISSIONS, and DELETE, while the role **Guest** could set up permissions VIEW and UPDATE. By default, the roless **Community** member and **Guest** do not have any permission.

Action	Description	Community	Guest
VIEW	Ability to view Expando columns	X	X
UPDATE	Ability to update Expando columns	X	X
PERMISSIONS	Ability to assign permissions Expando columns	X	
DELETE	Ability to delete Expando column	X	

A member of the **Guest** community doesn't have the permissions VIEW, UPDATE, PERMISSIONS, and DELETE on Expando columns by default. Note that these permissions could be used for either individual or groups of columns. By default, you could assign permissions individually, in a group, or in the current portal instance.

For these permissions in a group, you could be able to assign permissions in the **Control Panel** by way of a custom community role (or **Community** member) or a custom organization role (or **Organization** member). For these permissions in current portal instance, you could be able to assign these permissions in the **Control Panel** by way of custom regular roles in the scope of the current portal instance.

Enhancement

As you can see, no permission is available to apply custom fields on resources. The icon **Custom Fields** icon under **User** and **Organization** of **Control Panel** is controlled by the role Administrator only. You could find the following code in both `$PORRAL_ROOT_HOME/html/portlet/enterprise_admin/user/toolbar.jsp` and `$PORRAL_ROOT_HOME/html/portlet/enterprise_admin/organization/toolbar.jsp`.

```
<c:if test="<%= RoleLocalServiceUtil.hasUserRole(user.getUserId(),
user.getCompanyId(), RoleConstants.ADMINISTRATOR, true) %>">
```

The icon **Edit** next to resources under the **Custom Fields** of **Control Panel** is controlled by the role Administrator role too. You could find the following code in `$PORRAL_ROOT_HOME/html/portlet/expando/resource_action.jsp`.

```
<c:if test="<%= permissionChecker.isCompanyAdmin() %>">
```

It would be better to have the permission action `CUSTOM_FIELDS_IN_RESOURCE`. In addition, there is no permission action key `ACCESS_IN_CONTROL_PANEL` in the portlet `Expando`. Thus only the role Administrator role would be able to access the portlet `Expando` in the **Control Panel**. It would be nice to have the permission action key `ACCESS_IN_CONTROL_PANEL` in the portlet `Expando`.

To do that, we need to add permission action keys `ACCESS_IN_CONTROL_PANEL` and `CUSTOM_FIELDS_IN_RESOURSE`. Then we need to add permission controls tn the preceding JSP files.

What's happening?

The portlet `Expando` (portlet ID `139`) provides the capability to manage custom attributes, applied to any entity generated by Service Builder, whereas the portlet can be used to manage them. No changes are required to the portlet; just create the portlet URL, as we can find it in the **User** and **Organization** management or any entities generated by Service Builder.

Configuration

As stated earlier, the portlet `Expando` is available only in the `Control Panel`. The portal has default settings for the portlet `Expando` as follows in `$PORTAL_ROOT_HOME/WEB-INF/liferay-portlet.xml`:

```
<control-panel-entry-category>portal</control-panel-entry-category>
<control-panel-entry-weight>8.0</control-panel-entry-weight>
<system>true</system>
```

The preceding code shows that the portlet Expando will appear in the category Portal and position 8, and it is systemable — that is, the portlet Expando is available only in a system called **Control Panel**.

Customization

As mentioned earlier, the icon **Custom Fields** under **User** and **Organization** of the **Control Panel** is the entry point for applying Expando columns on entities. You could find the following code in both $PORTAL_ROOT_HOME/html/portlet/ enterprise_admin/user/toolbar.jsp and $PORTAL_ROOT_HOME/html/portlet/ enterprise_admin/organization/toolbar.jsp.

```
<liferay-portlet:renderURL windowState="<%= WindowState.MAXIMIZED.
toString() %>" var="expandoURL" portletName="<%= PortletKeys.EXPANDO
%>">
  <portlet:param name="struts_action" value="/expando/view_attributes"
/>
  <portlet:param name="redirect" value="<%= currentURL %>" />
  <portlet:param name="modelResource" value="<%= ${resource}.class.
getName() %>" />
</liferay-portlet:renderURL>
```

The preceding code specifies an entry to view custom fields and to add custom fields, where ${resource} could be the entities User or Organization.

In general, the icon **Edit** next to resources under the **Custom Fields** of the **Control Panel** is an entry point for applying Expando columns on any entities that have the Custom Fields framework. What's happening? You could find the following code in $PORTAL_ROOT_HOME/html/portlet/expando/view.jsp.

```
<portlet:renderURL windowState="<%= WindowState.MAXIMIZED.toString()
%>" var="rowURL">
  <portlet:param name="struts_action" value="/expando/view_attributes"
/>
  <portlet:param name="redirect" value="<%= currentURL %>" />
  <portlet:param name="modelResource" value="<%=
customAttributesDisplay.getClassName() %>" />
</portlet:renderURL>
```

The preceding code specifies the entry for viewing and adding custom fields. customAttributesDisplay could be any entities with the Custom Fields framework. Obviously, customAttributesDisplay could be custom entities with the Custom Fields framework.

In addition, you would be able to customize the behavior to add custom fields on resources in `$PORTAL_ROOT_HOME/html/portlet/expando/edit-expando.jsp`.

Custom attribute display

The `Custom Fields` framework allows us to use custom attributes (called custom fields) for our own entities (even for plugins). Firstly, create a `CustomAttributeDisplay` subclass and register it through `$PORTAL_ROOT_HOME/WEB-INF/liferay-portlet.xml`. For example, the resource wiki portage is available for adding custom fields, since the portlet Wiki has the following specification.

```
<custom-attributes-display>
  com.liferay.portlet.wiki.WikiPageCustomAttributesDisplay
</custom-attributes-display>
```

Then, use JSP tags `liferay-ui:custom-attributes-available` and `liferay-ui:custom-attribute-list` to show the custom field values of form fields in the portlet's JSPs. For instance, the Wiki portlet uses the following code to show the custom field values of form fields in `$PORTAL_ROOT_HOME/html/portlet/wiki/view.jsp`.

```
<liferay-ui:custom-attributes-available className="<%=
            WikiPage.class.getName() %>">
  <div class="custom-attributes">
    <liferay-ui:custom-attribute-list
      className="<%= WikiPage.class.getName() %>"
      classPK="<%= (wikiPage != null) ?
              wikiPage.getResourcePrimKey() : 0 %>"
      editable="<%= false %>"
      label="<%= true %>"
    />
  </div>
</liferay-ui:custom-attributes-available>
```

Of courses, you would find the same pattern in the Message Boards category, Message Boards messages, Calendar event, page, organization, user, organization, Web Content, Document Library documents, Document Library folders, Bookmarks entiesy, Bookmarks folders, Image Gallery images, Image Gallery folders, Blogs entiesy, and so on.

Enhancement

It is nice that custom attributes support types, both primitives (such as Boolean, Integer, String, Short, and so on) and presets (such as textbox, selection, and so on). But it would be better to extend the preceding types and let custom attributes support custom types, that is, Image Gallery images and Document Library documents. Thus, the target objects such as **User** and **Organization** can have references or called associations with Image Gallery images and Document Library documents via custom attributes. Moreover, the target objects such as Document Library documents can have special references like other Document Library documents via custom attributes.

It would be much better if custom attributes were localizable. A web content structure would be a better system and custom attributes could use it; including all types, image gallery values, inheritance, and so on.

Summary

In this chapter, we were introduced to adding a participant for chatting, managing (viewing and deleting) participants in the Chat portlet, starting the chat, and setting up the Chat portlet. Then we moved on to discussing how to manage (checking, deleting, adding, replying, forwarding, and searching) e-mails and further, setting up the Mail portlet properly. We also saw how to manage the SMS Text Messenger portlet and to send SMS text messages. Then, we discussed how to build Social Office with `so-theme`, `so-portlet` together with hooks and other portlets. Finally, we learned how to apply custom fields on any asset.

In this chapter, we have learned how to:

- Check online friends and chat
- Set up the portlet Chat
- Set up e-mail accounts
- Manage (check, delete, forward, reply, search) e-mails
- Manage the SMS Text Messenger portlet
- Build Social Office with themes, portlets, and hooks
- Use hooks
- Apply custom fields on any assets

In the next chapter, we're going to see how to set up search, search engine optimization (SEO), Open-Search, WAP, CRM, reporting and auditing.

10
Search, WAP, CRM, Widgets, Reporting and Auditing

In the intranet website "bookpub.com" of the enterprise "Palm Tree Publications", it is necessary to query assets like Message Boards entries, Blogs posts, Wikis articles, users in Directory, Document Library documents, bookmark entries, Image Gallery images, and so on. Furthermore, a lot of content is stored and managed in third-party repositories. Thus, it is also necessary to search contents from these repositories in the intranet websites. Meanwhile, it would be helpful to have maps' search, CSZ search, Web Content search, WAP, widgets, reporting, and auditing.

This chapter will introduce you to federated search, CSZ search, maps search, and OpenSearch concepts first. The Web Content search portlet is also discussed in detail. Accordingly, it will discuss how to use the sitemap for search engines, how to set up pluggable enterprise search, and how to manage plugins. Finally, it will address WAP sites, CRM integration, widgets, and reporting and auditing in detail.

In this chapter, you will learn how to:

- Employ federated search, OpenSearch, CSZ search, and maps search
- Employ Web Content search
- Configure sitemap for search engines and pluggable enterprise search
- Manage plugins
- Build WAP sites
- Report and audit
- Integrate with CRM and Netvibes widgets

Federated search

Federated search is the simultaneous searching of multiple online databases or web resources, and it is an emerging feature of automated web-based library and information retrieval systems. Here, federated search refers to the portal.

It is very useful to provide federated search abilities, such as searches for blog entries, users, organizations, Calendar entries, Bookmarks entries, Document Library documents, Image Gallery images, Message Boards messages, Wiki articles, Web Content articles, Directory, and so on. The portal provides a set of search portlets. In this section, we're going to take an in-depth look at these portlets.

The Search portlet

The Search portlet (portlet ID 3) is a JSR-286-compliant portlet that can be used for federated search. By default, the portal itself is the search provider.

As shown in following screenshot, Search Portlet provides a federated search against Blogs entries, users, organizations, Calendar entries, Bookmarks entries, Document Library documents, Image Gallery images, Message Boards message, Wiki articles, Web Content articles, Directory, and so on. In addition, the Search Portlet provides a federated search against plugin portlets like the Alfresco Content portlet.

The following is an example of how to use the Search portlet:

- Add the Search portlet to the page **Home** of the community Guest where you want to carry out a search, if the Search portlet isn't already present
- Enter the search criterion, for example **My**
- Click on the **Search** icon

Note that when searching for assets, you will have the ability to specify the scope of the search results: **Everything** or **This Community**. **Everything** would generate search results that will come from any group in the current portal instance such as communities, organizations, and my community. **This Community** will generate search results that come from the current group in the portal instance such as community Guest, organization "Palm Tree Enterprise", and My Community.

The search results would cover Blogs entries, users, organizations, Calendar entries, Bookmarks entries, Document Library documents, Image Gallery images, Message Boards messages, Wiki articles, Web Content articles, Directory, and so on. Additionally, search results will include assets from plugin portlets like Alfresco Content portlet.

As you can see, search results would be displayed as a title with a link. If you have the proper permission on an asset, you could click on the title of the asset (which is a link to it) and view the asset as well. But if you don't have proper permission on an asset, clicking on the title would bring up a permission error message.

What's happening?

The portal provides many portlets to support OpenSearch framework such as Message Boards, Blogs, Wikis, Directory and Document Library, Users, Organizations, and so on. In addition, plugins like the Alfresco Content portlet also support the OpenSearch framework. Normally, these portlets have the following OpenSearch framework configuration.

```
<open-search-class>class-name</open-search-class>
```

The Search portlet obtains an OpenSearch instance from each portlet that has the tag `<open-search-class>` definition. For example, the portlet Directory (portlet ID 11) allows users to search for other users, organizations, or user groups. OpenSearch has been specified for the portlet Directory in `$PORTAL_ROOT_HOME/WEB-INF/liferay-portlet.xml` as follows:

```
<open-search-class>
   com.liferay.portlet.directory.util.DirectoryOpenSearchImpl
</open-search-class>
```

As shown in the preceding code, the `open-search-class` value must be a class that implements `com.liferay.portal.kernel.search.OpenSearch`, which is called to get search results in the OpenSearch standard.

Besides the OpenSearch framework, the portal provides UI taglib to display search results. In `$PORTAL_ROOT_HOME/html/portlet/search/view.jsp`, you could find the following code.

```
<liferay-ui:search />
```

For more details on UI taglib `<liferay-ui:search>`, you can check JSP files `start.jsp` and `end.jsp` under the folder `$PORTAL_ROOT_HOME/html/taglib/ui/search`. In addition, the portal scopes OpenSearch results through the UI taglib `<liferay-ui:search>`. For example, the scope of search results, namely, **Everything** or **This Community** has been specified in `$PORTAL_ROOT_HOME/html/taglib/ui/search/start.jsp` as follows:

```
<select name="<%= namespace %>groupId">
  <!—ignore details -->
  <option value="<%= group.getGroupId() %>" <%= (groupId != 0) ?
    "selected" : "" %>><liferay-ui:message key='<%= "this-" +
    (group.isOrganization() ? "organization" : "community") %>' />
  </option>
</select>
```

As you can see, the value of **This Community** would be an organization or community.

By default, the OpenSearch implementation in the portal supports both formats: **ATOM** and **RSS**. The default format would be **ATOM**. Therefore, the search results from plugin portlets must be returned in the format ATOM. For example, in the portlet Alfresco Content, the format of search results must be ATOM. Why? The portlet Search has specified the following code in $PORTAL_ROOT_HOME/html/ portlet/search/open_search_description.jsp.

```
<OpenSearchDescription xmlns="http://a9.com/-/spec/OpenSearch/1.1/">
 <!—ignore details --><Url type="application/rss+xml" template="<%=
themeDisplay.getPortalURL() %><%= PortalUtil.getPathMain() %>/
search/open_search?keywords={searchTerms}&amp p={startPage?}&amp
c={count?}&amp format=rss" />
</OpenSearchDescription>
```

In addition, the search results are displayed in pagination through the search container. Fortunately, search container is configurable. The portal has specified the following properties in portal.properties.

```
search.container.page.delta.values=5,10,20,30,50,75
search.container.page.iterator.max.pages=25
```

As shown in the preceding code, the property search.container.page.delta. values sets the available values for the number of entries to be displayed per page. An empty value, or commenting out the value, will disable delta resizing. The default of 20 will apply in all cases. Note that you need to always include 20 because it is the default page size when no delta is specified. The absolute maximum allowed delta value is 200.

The property search.container.page.iterator.max.pages sets the maximum number of pages, which are available before and / or after the currently displayed page. Of course, you could override these properties anytime in portal-ext.properties.

Configuration

As mentioned previously, OpenSearch in the Search portlet covers the in-and-out of Blogs, Calendar, Bookmarks, Document Library, Image Gallery, Message Boards, Wiki, Web Content, Directory, and so on. Fortunately, the portal adds the ability to remove these portlets from the list of portlets searched by the portlet Search as follows:

```
com.liferay.portlet.blogs.util.BlogsOpenSearchImpl=true
## ignore details
com.liferay.portlet.wiki.util.WikiOpenSearchImpl=true
```

As shown in the preceding code, you can set any of these properties to `false` to disable the portlet from being searched by the Search portlet in `portal-ext.properties`.

Customization

In real cases, you may be required to use the portlet Search in different ways. You would be able to customize the portlet Search. Here we're going to discuss how to use the Search portlet in Social Office and how to use the Search portlet in themes.

The Social Office overrides the UI taglib `<liferay-ui:search>` in the portlet `so-portlet` through JSP file hooks in `$AS_WEB_APP_HOME/so-portlet/META-INF/custom_jsps/html/taglib/ui/search/start.jsp` as follows:

```
<liferay-util:include page="/html/taglib/ui/search/start.portal.jsp"
/>
<c:if test="<%= group.isUser() %>">
  <script type="text/javascript">
    var searchOptions = jQuery('select[name=<%= namespace %>
                                      groupId] option')
    searchOptions.each( //ignore details  )
  </script>
</c:if>
```

As shown in the preceding code, the Social Office overrides the look and feel of the portlet Search. For example, it will remove search options.

Of course, you can add the portlet Search as a runtime portlet in themes. You could add the Velocity template `$theme.search()` in the theme, specifically in the VM file `portal_normal.vm` or the VM file included in `portal_normal.vm`. For example, Social Office specifies the following lines in the theme `so-theme` such as `$AS_WEB_APP_HOME/so-theme/templates/navigation_top.vm`.

```
#if ($is_signed_in)
  <div class="my-search">$theme.search()</div>
#end
```

As shown in the preceding code, when the user signs in, the Social Office will show the customized portlet Search in "my-search" style.

OpenSearch in plugins

In general, the portal provides an OpenSearch framework, so that a user can create an OpenSearch implementation in the plugin environment. The portal will try to call this OpenSearch implementation when you hit the Search portlet. The Search portlet goes through all registered implementations and tries to create an instance.

We could search content from the Alfresco repository, just as we did for Blogs, Bookmarks, Calendar, Directory, and so on via the OpenSearch framework of the portlet Search. How does it work?

How does it work?

First of all, we need to install the Alfresco Web Client, and then we need to deploy the portlet Alfresco Content. By following these three steps, you would bring the Alfresco Web Client into Tomcat as well:

1. Download the latest Alfresco-Tomcat bundle from `http://www.alfresco.com`, and install it to the folder `$ALFRESCO_HOME`.

2. Locate the Alfresco Web Client application `alfresco.war` under the folder `$ALFRESCO_HOME`, and drop it to the folder `$TOMCAT_AS_DIR/webapps`.

3. Create a database `alfresco` in MySQL and restart Tomcat.

```
drop database if exists alfresco
create database alfresco character set utf8
grant all on alfresco.* to 'alfresco'@'localhost' identified by
'alfresco' with grant option
grant all on alfresco.* to 'alfresco'@'localhost.localdomain'
identified by 'alfresco' with grant option
```

Then we could deploy the plugin Alfresco Content portlet. The following is an example of how to bring the portlet Alfresco Content into the portal.

1. Download the WAR file `${alfresco.content.portlet.war}` from `http://liferay.cignex.com/palm_tree/book/0387/chapter12/alfresco-content-portlet-6.0.0.1.war`.

2. Drop the WAR file `${alfresco.content.portlet.war}` to the folder `$LIFERAY_HOME/deploy` when the portal is running.

That's it! When you search for content again in the portlet Search, you will be able to see assets coming from the Alfresco Web Client. In addition, you would see a message like "**Searched Alfresco Content, Blogs ...**" in the portlet Search.

Web services

As you can see, the Alfresco Content plugin displays content from the Alfresco repository. Two kinds of services are involved — web services and RESTful services. A **web service** is a software system designed to support interoperable machine-to-machine interaction over a network. With the portlet Alfresco Content, you could search or navigate content of the Alfresco repository via web services.

You have to simply go to **More** | **Configuration** | **Setup** | **Current** of the portlet Alfresco Content first. Then you should enter a User ID like "admin" and a password like "admin", and click on the **Save** button. Now, you will be able to see the root folder "Company Home".

The following property is specified in the portlet Alfresco Content:

```
$AS_WEB_APP_HOME/alfresco-content-portlet/WEB-INF/classes/portlet.
properties
content.server.url=http://localhost:8080
```

As shown in the preceding code, the property `content.server.url` sets the location of the Alfresco server URL.

RESTful services

Representational State Transfer (REST) is a style of software architecture for distributed hypermedia systems. Alfresco not only provides the ability to expose its search engines via OpenSearch, but it also provides an aggregate OpenSearch feature in the Alfresco Web Client through RESTful services. To summarize, Alfresco RESTful services-based keyword search mimics the keyword search of the Alfresco Web Client.

The following search URL template is used for OpenSearch in the plugin Alfresco Content.

```
http://<host>:<port>/alfresco/service/api/search/keyword.atom?q={searc
hTerms}&p={startPage?}&c={count?}&l={language?}
```

In the preceding code, the URL will have the following values:

- `searchTerms`: The keyword or keywords to search
- `startPage` (optional): The page number of search results desired by the client

- count (optional): The number of search results per page (the default is 10)
- language (optional): The locale to search with (XML 1.0 Language ID, for example en-GB)

Besides RESTful APIs for OpenSearch, Alfresco provides the following RESTful APIs built as Web Scripts:

- **Repository API Reference**: Remote services for interacting with the Alfresco Repository
- **CMIS API Reference**: Content Management Interoperability Services
- Portlets such as My Inbox and My Checked-Out for hosting in any portal
- Office Integration for hosting in Microsoft Office

Moreover, in order to allow the Alfresco Content portlet to support OpenSearch, the portlet has set the value open-search-class at $AS_WEB_APP_HOME/alfresco-content-portlet/WEB-INF/liferay-portlet.xml as follows:

```
<open-search-class>
  com.liferay.portlet.alfrescocontent.util.AlfrescoOpenSearchImpl
</open-search-class>
```

Finally, the portlet has set the following values in $AS_WEB_APP_HOME/alfresco-content-portlet/WEB-INF/classes/portlet.properties, which will be used to query Alfresco via OpenSearch.

```
open.search.enabled=true
## ignore details open.search.path=/alfresco/service/api/search/
keyword.atom
```

Of course, you could override the preceding properties according to your own environment, for example, server domain name, port number, search user name, search password, and so on.

CMIS

Besides web services and OpenSearch, Alfresco supports CMIS as well. **Content Management Interoperability Services (CMIS)** is a specification that defines how **Enterprise Content Management (ECM)** systems exchange content, defining a domain model and a set of bindings, such as Web Service and RESTful Atom-Pub that can be used by applications to work with one or more content management repositories. Alfresco supports the CMIS REST API Binding, the CMIS web services API Binding, and Web Service WSDL.

The portal has specified the following properties for CMIS in portal.properties:

```
cmis.credentials.username=none
```

```
mis.credentials.password=none
cmis.repository.url=http://localhost:8080/alfresco/service/api/cmis
cmis.repository.version=1.0
cmis.system.root.dir=Liferay Home
```

As mentioned earlier, we could use CMIS hook to configure a repository. In addition, we could use these properties in the Alfresco Content portlet and provide OpenSearch capabilities based on CMIS.

CSZ Search

Let's say that we know the city name "Mountain View" and the state name "California" in USA, and we want to find the related zip code. The CSZ search portlet would be useful for this requirement. Let's do it as follows.

1. Install the portlet CSZ, and then add the CSZ Search portlet in the page "Home" of the community Guest where you want to search based on CSZ, if the CSZ Search portlet isn't there.
2. First enter the city name as "Mountain View" and the state name as "California".
3. Then click on the **Search** button, and the zip code associated with the preceding given city and state will appear.
4. Optionally, you may enter the zip code first, then click on the **Search** button, and the city and state pairs, associated with the given zip code, will appear.

The following screenshot depicts the CSZ Search example and the respective search results. It shows all related zip code values for the city name **Mountain View** and the state name **California** in **USA**.

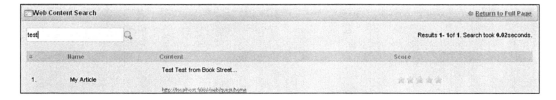

How does it work?

The following is an example of how to bring the portlet CSZ Search into the portal.

- Download the WAR file ${csz.search.portlet.war} from http://liferay.cignex.com/palm_tree/book/0387/chapter12/csz-search-portlet-6.0.0.1.war
- Drop the WAR file ${csz.search.portlet.war} to the folder $LIFERAY_HOME/deploy when the portal is running

What's happening?

In general, the **CSZ** (city, state, and zip) **Search** portlet provides a way to search for the zip code using the address, city, and state. Conversely, it also allows you to search for a city and state by zip code. A USPS ZIP code lookup is used as a web service provider.

 USPS (U.S. Postal Service) provides services for zip code lookup. Check the following link for more information: http://www.usps.com/zip4/

Maps search

If we know the city name **Mountain View** and state name **California** in USA and we want to find related maps, the Maps Search portlet would be useful for this purpose. To use it, follow these steps:

1. Install the portal Maps Search and then add the **Maps Search** portlet in the page **Home** of the community Guest where you want to search for maps, if the Maps portlet isn't already there.

2. First enter the address city name **Mountain View**, state **California**, zip code, and country name **USA**.

3. Then click on the **Search** button.

A map associated with the given address, city, state, zip code, and country will appear, as shown in the following screenshot:

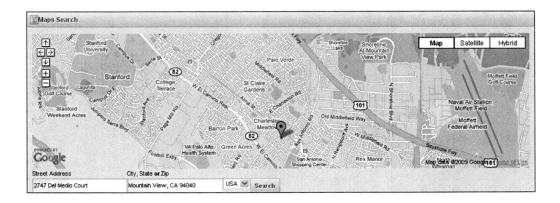

How does it work?

The following is an example of how to bring the portlet Maps Search into the portal.

- Download the WAR file ${maps.search.portlet.war} from: http://liferay.cignex.com/palm_tree/book/0387/chapter12/maps-search-portlet-6.0.0.1.war.

- Drop the WAR file ${maps.search.portlet.war} to the folder $LIFERAY_HOME/deploy when the portal is running.

What's happening?

The following properties are specified in the portlet Maps Search in $AS_WEB_APP_HOME/maps-search-portlet/WEB-INF/classes/portlet.properties:

```
map.google.maps.api.key=ABQIAAAAVUlXDwsmwMn1hOVRL9PRThTWJHub0YR0Jk5J
LS-JSo2KSqAp1BS26tv54N3FLvxz-mCy-TtY-iQwQg
map.google.maps.height=250
map.input.enabled=false
map.directions.input.enabled=false
map.default.address=Mountain View, CA 94040
map.default.directions.address=Mountain View, CA 94040
```

As shown in the preceding code, you can configure the properties map.google.maps.api.key, map.google.maps.height, map.input.enabled, map.directions.input.enabled, map.default.address, and map.default.directions.address and override the preceding properties as well.

Additionally, the portlet Maps Search is configurable. You can navigate to the JSP file $AS_WEB_APP_HOME/maps-search-portlet/view.jsp with JavaScript code, and go further by updating the JSP file and JavaScript code inside.

In short, the Maps portlet provides the ability to find maps by address, city, state, zip code, and country. Google Maps is used as a web service provider.

 Google Maps is a basic web-mapping service application. Refer to http://maps.google.com/ for more information.

What's OpenSearch?

As previously stated, we use OpenSearch to integrate Alfresco content in the Alfresco Content portlet. We will now see what's OpenSearch and why OpenSearch.

OpenSearch is a collection of simple formats in order to share search results. Generally speaking, OpenSearch allows publishing of search results in a format for syndication and aggregation. It is a useful way for both websites and search engines to publish search results in a standard and accessible format.

Design principles

OpenSearch consists of the following elements:

- **Description**: XML files that identify and describe a search engine.
- **Query Syntax**: This describes from where to retrieve the search results.
- **RSS** or **Response**: Format for providing OpenSearch results.
- **Aggregators**: Sites that can display OpenSearch results.
- **Auto-discovery**: This will signal the presence of a search plugin link to the user and the link embedded in the header of the HTML pages.

OpenSearch description lists search results or responses for the given website. It provides support for multiple responses in any format. General speaking, RSS and Atom are the only elements formally supported by OpenSearch aggregators, however, other types, such as HTML, are perfectly acceptable.

OpenSearch specification

The OpenSearch description document defines three kinds of elements in general — the OpenSearch Query element, the OpenSearch URL template syntax, and the OpenSearch Response element.

OpenSearch description documents are referred to through the type: `application/ OpenSearchdescription+xml`. The XML Namespaces URI for the XML data formats described in this specification, by default, is `http://a9.com/-/spec/ OpenSearch/1.1/`.

An example of a simple OpenSearch description document is shown as follows:

```
<?xml version="1.0" encoding="UTF-8"?>
<OpenSearchDescription
  xmlns="http://a9.com/-/spec/OpenSearch/1.1/">
  <ShortName>Web Search</ShortName>
  <!-- ignore details -->
  <Url type="application/rss+xml" template="http://bookpub.com/?
        q={searchTerms}&amp pw={startPage?}&amp format=rss"/>
```

```
</OpenSearchDescription>
```

As shown in the following table, the root node of the OpenSearch description document is `OpenSearchDescription`. We can use this table as a reference for OpenSearch specification, by referring to `$PORTAL_ROOT_HOME/html/portlet/search/open_search_description.jsp`.

Element name	Description
OpenSearchDescription	The root node of the OpenSearch description document
ShortName	Contains a brief human-readable title that identifies this search
Description	Contains a human-readable text description of the search engine
URL	Describes an interface by which a search client can make search requests to the search engine
Contact	Contains an e-mail address at which the maintainer of the description document can be reached
Tags	Contains a set of words that are used as keywords to identify and categorize this search content
LongName	Contains an extended human-readable title that identifies this search engine
Image	Contains an image that identifies this search engine
Query	Defines a search query that can be performed by search clients
Developer	Contains the human-readable name or identifier of the creator or maintainer of the description document
Attribution	Contains a list of all sources or entities that should be credited for the content contained in the search feed
SyndicationRight	Contains a value that indicates the degree to which the search results provided by this search engine can be queried, displayed, and redistributed
AdultContent	Contains a Boolean value that should be set to true if the search results contain material intended only for adults
Language	Contains a string that indicates that the search engine supports search results in the specified language
InputEncoding	Contains a string that indicates that the search engine supports search requests encoded with the specified character encoding
OutputEncoding	Contains a string that indicates that the search engine supports search responses encoded with the specified character encoding

Web Content Search

The portlet Web Content Search (portlet ID 77) displays a textbox, which allows end users to search for all the Web Content of a website. Note that the portlet doesn't search for any other content types such as blogs, message board entries, wiki, and so on. So this portlet should mainly be used for a website, where the main content is web content.

In the intranet bookpub.com, you will have a lot of web content sooner or later. In order to manage this web content easily, search functionalities become very important. Fortunately, the portlet Web Content Search provides the ability to search for web content by types in a website. Let's have a deep look at the portlet Web Content Search by following these steps:

1. Add the Web Content Search portlet to the page "Home" of the community Guest, where you want to search for web content, if the Web Content Search portlet isn't already there.

2. First enter keywords as search criterion, for example, "test".

3. Then click on the **Search** icon, as shown in the following screenshot.

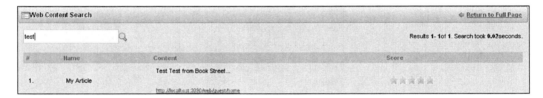

The portlet Web Content Search will search for web content published by the portlet Web Content Display (portlet ID 56) in the current group, say the community Guest. The search results will be displayed with columns such as number (marked as **#**), **Name** (the title of web content), **Content** (the web content and a link to the page where the web content got published through the Web Content Display portlet), and **Score** (relevance in five-star style). As you can see, pagination of the search container is also supported.

Setup

It is simple to configure the Web Content Search portlet. If we need to search for web content against the type **General**, then we could do it by following these steps:

1. Click on the **More | Configuration | Setup | Current** icon on the upper-right of the portlet.

2. With the **Setup** and the **Current** tabs selected, there is the Web Content type list. You can select the Web Content type, say **General**, which you would like to limit the search to.

3. Select the checkbox, that is, "**Only show results for web content listed in a Web Content Display portlet**", if you want to show only search results for web content listed in the portlet Web Content Display.

4. Input a value for **Target Portlet ID**, if required.

5. Then click on the **Save** button to save the changes.

6. If required, click on the arrow icon **Return to Full Page** to return.

There are several web content types by default—announcements, blogs, news, general, press release, and test. As mentioned earlier, these web content types are configurable through the property `journal.article.types` in `portal.properties` as follows:

```
journal.article.types=announcements,blogs,general,news,
press-release,test
```

Note that if there is no type selected, the portlet Web Content Search will search any articles (that is, web content) against any type.

You can also change permissions of the Web Content Search portlet. You can simply click on the **More | Configuration | Permissions** tab. You could update permission actions such as **View**, **Add to Page**, and **Configuration** by roles. Optionally, you can set up features of exporting and importing.

What's happening?

As you can see, the portal only shows search results for web content listed in a Web Content Display portlet. In general, the portlet Web Content Search searches for web content in the current community or organization and filters content searched by type of web content. Moreover, it specifies a target portlet, the location where the web content will be displayed, and when its link will be clicked in a search results list.

Configuration

The portal has specified the following property for the portlet Web Content Search in `portal.properties`.

```
journal.content.search.show.listed=true
```

As shown in the preceding code, the property `journal.content.search.show.listed` sets whether unlisted articles are excluded from search results. By default, unlisted articles are excluded from search results.

In real cases, you may need to apply the portlet Web Content Search to all pages of a website. Therefore, you could add the portlet Web Content Search for themes. To achieve this, you simply need to add the Velocity template `$theme.journalContentSearch()` in the theme, specifically in the VM file `portal_normal.vm` or the VM file included in `portal_normal.vm`. For example, you can replace the portlet Search with the portlet Web Content Search in Social Office, the theme `so-theme` such as `$AS_WEB_APP_HOME/so-theme/templates/navigation_top.vm`.

```
#if ($is_signed_in)
  <div class="my-search">$theme.journalContentSearch()</div>
#end
```

As shown in the preceding code, when the user signs in, the Social Office will show the customized portlet Web Content Search in the "my-search" style instead of the portlet Search.

Lucene search engine

This portal provides search capabilities to search for web content in any website. The portlet Web Content Search, by default, is powered by the Apache Lucene search engine.

> Apache Lucene acts as a high-performance and full-featured text search engine. It is suitable for almost any application that requires full-text search, especially cross-platform applications. Refer to `http://lucene.apache.org/` to know more about it.

In general, the Apache Lucene search engine has many useful features such as Ranked searching—here, best results are returned first. This includes many powerful query types—phrase queries, wildcard queries, proximity queries, range queries, and more.

It also allows fielded searching (for example, title, author, contents), date-range searching, sorting by any field, multiple-index searching with merged results, and simultaneous update and searching.

Search Engine Optimization

Search Engine Optimization (**SEO**) is the process of improving the volume or quality of traffic to websites from search engines via natural or unpaid search results as opposed to **search engine marketing** (**SEM**), which deals with paid inclusion. Refer to `http://en.wikipedia.org/wiki/Search_engine_optimization` for details.

The portal is used to build public websites, and for this reason, it provides a wide range of features to help make websites show up at the top of the search results. Note that it is more concerned with Internets than intranets. In general, the portal implements the Sitemap Protocol to notify Google or Yahoo! of the sitemap of a website. Generally speaking, search engines read the words present in the URL of a given portal page and give them higher relevance than those words found in the body of the document. For this reason, the portal uses URLs called friendly URLs to reflect the contents of a page, which will increase the chances of having that page on the top of the search results when the users look for such words. Besides the URL, search engines also read certain HTML tags to find specific information about the contents of the page such as title, description, and keywords.

The portal provides the ability to generate the sitemap XML automatically for all public websites. Using sitemaps, we can easily inform search engines about pages on the sites that are available for crawling.

Sitemaps are an easy way for webmasters to inform search engines about pages on their sites that are available for crawling. In its simplest form, a **sitemap** is an XML file that lists URLs for a site along with additional metadata about each URL (when it was last updated, how often it usually changes, and how important it is, relative to other URLs in the site) so that search engines can more intelligently crawl the site. Refer to `http://www.sitemaps.org` for more information.

Sitemap

As an administrator of the enterprise **Palm Tree Publications**, imagine that you need to apply the sitemap for a website like the Guest community's public page. You can do it by following these steps:

1. Log in as an administrator, for example **Palm Tree**.
2. Go to **Manage | Control Panel** under the dock bar menu.
3. Click on **Portal | Communities**, and locate the Guest community's public pages.
4. Click on the **Manage Pages** icon from the **Actions** next to the right of the Guest community's where you want to apply the sitemap.

5. Locate the **Settings** tab, and click on it.

6. Click on the **Sitemap** tab, and you would see the sitemap settings.

As you can see, the sitemap protocol notifies search engines of the structure (sitemap) of the website. You can send sitemap information to preview through Google or Yahoo!. By clicking on the **Search Engine** links, the sitemap will be sent to them.

 Note that it's only necessary to do this once per site. The search engine crawler will automatically ask for the sitemap again, ever so often.

If you want to see the generated XML, you can click on the **Preview** link. Using this link, you may view what is being sent to the search engines. The following is an example of the sitemap XML for the community Guest.

```
<urlset>
  <url>
    <loc>http://localhost:8080/c/portal/layout?p_l_id=10157</loc>
  </url>
  <!--ignore details -->
</urlset>
```

As shown in the preceding processes, you have applied sitemaps on a website, that is, to all pages of the website. In addition to this, you will be able to customize a sitemap on a page individually.

Customizing sitemaps for pages

Let's say that, as an administrator of the enterprise "Palm Tree Publications", you want to customize the sitemap for the page "Welcome" of the community Guest public pages. You can do it by following these steps:

1. Log in as an admin, say **Palm Tree**.

2. Go to **Manage | Control Panel** under the dock bar menu.

3. Click on **Portal | Communities**, and locate the community Guest public pages.

4. Click on the **Manage Pages** icon from the **Actions** next to the right of the community Guest where you want to apply the sitemap.

5. Click on the tab **Public Pages**, and going further, click on the tab **Pages**.

6. Select a page say "Welcome", and click on the tab **Page**.

7. Expand **Meta Robots**.

8. Set the value of **Change Frequency** as, say, **daily** from a list of options: **always, hourly, daily, weekly, monthly, yearly, never,** and so forth.

9. Set **Page Priority** as **0.3** for example. A number from **0.0** to **1.0** indicates the priority of the page relative to other pages of the website.

10. Set the value of **Include** to **Yes** for example from a list of **Yes** or **No**. Selecting **No** means that this page won't be considered by a search engine.

11. Click on the **Save** button.

What's happening?

The Sitemap Protocol notifies search engines of the structure (that is, sitemap) of the website. In a word, a sitemap provides the ability to make newly added pages searchable by major search engines without additional configuration.

It also provides the ability to inform search engines about pages scrawling on their sites. We can benefit from sitemaps in the following situations:

- Access all areas of a website through a browseable interface: Thus search engines can't find these pages with content such as "Achieves" and "Database" easily.

- Use rich AJAX or Flash: Thus search engines can't navigate through to get to the content.

We can first generate a sitemap containing all accessible URLs on the site. We can then submit it to search engines. As search engines, such as Google, MSN, and Yahoo! support the same protocol, by using a sitemap, we could update the search engines with the latest pages' information.

The portal Sitemap protocol makes any new pages searchable by the major search engines, supporting the feature of automatically updating sitemap information, which is available for web-crawling.

XML sitemap format

You may be interested in the XML sitemap format. Here we list some of the XML sitemap formats for reference. You can leave it as future requirements and proceed to the next section.

The Sitemap protocol format consists of XML tags. All data values in a sitemap must be entity-escaped. The file itself must be UTF-8 encoded. Note that the sitemap must comply with the following rules:

- Begin with an opening `<urlset>` tag and end with a closing `</urlset>` tag.

- Specify the namespace (protocol standard) within the `<urlset>` tag.
- Include a `<url>` entry for each URL as a parent XML tag.
- Include a `<loc>` child entry for each `<url>` parent tag.

As shown in the following table, other tags are optional. Note that support for these optional tags may vary among search engines.

Attribute	Required	Description
urlset	Yes	Encapsulates the file and references the current protocol standard.
url	Yes	Parent tag for each URL entry. The remaining tags are children of this tag.
loc	Yes	URL of the page.
lastmod	No	The date of the last modification of the file. This date should be in W3C Date-Time format. This format allows you to omit the time portion, if desired, use YYYY-MM-DD.
changefreq	No	How frequently the page is likely to change. This value provides general information to search engines and may not correlate exactly to how often the page was crawled.
priority	No	The priority of this URL relative to other URLs on your site. Valid values range from 0.0 to 1.0.

The following is a sample sitemap that contains just one URL and uses all optional tags, as mentioned previously.

```
<urlset xmlns:xsi="http://www.w3.org/2001/XMLSchema-instance"
  xsi:schemaLocation="http://www.sitemaps.org/schemas/sitemap/0.9
  http://www.sitemaps.org/schemas/sitemap/0.9/sitemap.xsd">
  <url>
    <loc>http://www.bookpub.com</loc>
    <!-- ignore details -->
  </url>
</urlset>
```

Pluggable Enterprise Search

As an alternative to using Lucene, the portal supports pluggable search engines. The first implementation of this uses the open source search engine Solr, but in the future, there will be many such plugins for search engine of your choice, such as **FAST**, **GSA**, **Coveo**, and so on. In this section, we're going to discuss caching, indexing, and using **Solr** for search.

Caching settings

EHCache is a widely-used cache implemented in Java, which the portal uses to provide distributed caching in a clustered environment. **EHCache** is also used in a non-clustered environment to speed up repeated data retrievals. The portal uses EHCache caching by default. At the same time, the portal uses Hibernate caching as well. The portal provides the capability to configure EHCache caching and Hibernate caching.

The portal has specified Hibernate as default **ORM (Object-Relational Mapping)** persistence in `portal.properties`.

```
persistence.provider=hibernate
```

The preceding code sets the provider `hibernate` used for ORM persistence. Of course, you can set this property to `jpa` **(Java Persistence API)**, thus the properties with the prefix `jpa.*` will be read. Similarly, if this property is set to `hibernate`, then the properties with the prefix `hibernate.*` will be read. Note that this property affects the loading of `hibernate-spring.xml` or `jpa-spring.xml` in the property `spring.configs`. For example, the portal has the following JPA configuration specified in `portal.properties`:

```
jpa.configs=\
META-INF/mail-orm.xml,\
META-INF/portal-orm.xml
jpa.provider=eclipselink
jpa.provider.property.eclipselink.allow-zero-id=true
jpa.load.time.weaver=org.springframework.instrument.
classloading.ReflectiveLoadTimeWeaver
```

As shown in the preceding code, the property `jpa.configs` sets a list of comma-delimited JPA configurations. The default JPA provider is set as `eclipselink` via the property `jpa.provider`. You can set it to other values such as `hibernate`, `openjpa`, and `toplink`. The property `jpa.provider.property.eclipselink. allow-zero-id` specifies provider-specific properties prefixed with `jpa.provider. property.*`.On the other hand, `LoadTimeWeaver` interface specified via the property `jpa.load.time.weaver` is a Spring class that allows JPA `ClassTransformer` instances to be plugged in a specific manner depending on the environment. Note that not all JPA providers require a JVM agent. If your provider doesn't require an agent or you have other alternatives, the loadtime weaver shouldn't be used.

Configure Hibernate caching

First of all, let's consider Hibernate caching settings. The portal will automatically detect the Hibernate dialect. However, you can set the property in `portal-ext.properties` to manually override the automatically detected dialect.

```
hibernate.dialect=
```

The portal also specified the following properties related to Hibernate caching in `portal.properties`.

```
hibernate.configs=\//ignore details

 META-INF/ext-hbm.xml
hibernate.cache.provider_class=com.liferay.portal.dao.orm.hibernate.
EhCacheProvider
net.sf.ehcache.configurationResourceName=/ehcache/hibernate.xml
hibernate.cache.use_query_cache=true
hibernate.cache.use_second_level_cache=true
hibernate.cache.use_minimal_puts=true
hibernate.cache.use_structured_entries=false
hibernate.jdbc.batch_size=20
hibernate.jdbc.use_scrollable_resultset=true
hibernate.bytecode.use_reflection_optimizer=true
hibernate.query.factory_class=org.hibernate.hql.classic.
ClassicQueryTranslatorFactory
hibernate.generate_statistics=false
```

As shown in the preceding code, the property `hibernate.configs` sets Hibernate configurations. You may input a list of comma-delimited Hibernate configurations in `portal-ext.properties`. The property `hibernate.cache.provider_class` sets the Hibernate cache provider. On the other hand, the property `net.sf.ehcache.configurationResourceName` is used if Hibernate is configured to use Ehcache's cache provider, where Ehcache is recommended in a clustered environment. In a clustered environment, you need to set the property in `portal-ext.properties` as follows:

```
net.sf.ehcache.configurationResourceName=
   /ehcache/hibernate-clustered.xml
```

The portal has specified other Hibernate cache settings with properties starting with `hibernate.cache.use_*`. The property `hibernate.jdbc.batch_size` sets the JDBC batch size to improve performance. Note that if you're using Hypersonic databases or Oracle 9i, you should set the batch size to 0 as a workaround for a logging bug in the Hypersonic database driver or Oracle 9i driver.

In addition, the property `hibernate.query.factory_class` sets the classic query factory, whereas the portal sets the property `hibernate.generate_statistics` to `false`. Of course, you could set the property `hibernate.generate_statistics` to `true` to enable Hibernate cache monitoring in `portal-ext.properties`.

Setting up EHCache caching

The portal has specified the following EHCache caching settings in `portal.properties`.

```
ehcache.single.vm.config.location=/ehcache/liferay-single-vm.xml
ehcache.multi.vm.config.location=/ehcache/liferay-multi-vm.xml
ehcache.portal.cache.manager.jmx.enabled=true
ehcache.blocking.cache.allowed=true
```

As shown in the preceding code, the property `ehcache.single.vm.config.location` sets the classpath to the location of the Ehcache configuration file `/ehcache/liferay-single-vm.xml` for internal caches of a single VM, whereas the property `ehcache.multi.vm.config.location` sets the classpath to the location of the Ehcache configuration file `/ehcache/liferay-multi-vm.xml` for internal caches of multiple VMs. In a clustered environment, you need to set the following in `portal-ext.properties`:

```
ehcache.multi.vm.config.location=/ehcache/
liferay-multi-vm-clustered.xml
```

In addition, the portal sets the property `ehcache.portal.cache.manager.jmx.enabled` to `true` to enable JMX integration in `com.liferay.portal.cache.EhcachePortalCacheManager`. Moreover, the portal sets the property `ehcache.blocking.cache.allowed` to `true` to allow Ehcache to use blocking caches. This improves performance significantly by locking on keys instead of the entire cache. The drawback is that threads can hang if the cache isn't used properly. Therefore, make sure that all queries that return a miss also immediately populate the cache, or else other threads that are blocked on a query of that same key will continue to hang.

Of course, you can override the preceding properties in `portal-ext.properties`.

Customization

As you can see, the property `net.sf.ehcache.configurationResourceName` can have the value `/ehcache/hibernate.xml` for a non-clustered environment and `/ehcache/hibernate-clustered.xml` for a clustered environment. The property `net.sf.ehcache.configurationResourceName` can have the value `/ehcache/hibernate.xml` for a non-clustered environment and `/ehcache/hibernate-clustered.xml` for a clustered environment.

In the same pattern, the property `ehcache.single.vm.config.location` can have the value `/ehcache/liferay-single-vm.xml` and the property `ehcache.multi.vm.config.location` can have the value `/ehcache/liferay-multi-vm.xml` for a non-clustered environment.

`ehcache.multi.vm.config.location` has a value `/ehcache/liferay-multi-vm-clustered.xml` for a clustered environment.

In real cases, you may need to update both Hibernate caching settings and Ehcache caching settings, either in a non-clustered environment or in a clustered environment. The following is an example of how to do this:

1. Create a folder named `ext-ehcache` under the folder `$PORTAL_ROOT_HOME/WEB-INF/classes/`. Obviously, you can have different names for the folder `${ehcache.folder.name}`. Here we use the folder `ext-ehcache` of `${ehcache.folder.name}` as an example.

2. Locate the JAR file `portal-impl.jar` under the folder `$PORTAL_ROOT_HOME/WEB-INF/lib` and unzip all the files under the folder `ehcache` into the folder `$PORTAL_ROOT_HOME/WEB-INF/classes/ext-ehcache`.

3. Update following files according to your requirements for both a non-clustered environment and a clustered environment.

   `hibernate.xml`

   `hibernate-clustered.xml`

   `liferay-single-vm.xml`

   `liferay-multi-vm.xml`

   `liferay-multi-vm-clustered.xml`

4. Set the following for a non-clustered environment in `portal-ext.properties`:

   `net.sf.ehcache.configurationResourceName=/ext-ehcache/hibernate.xml`

   `ehcache.single.vm.config.location=/ext-ehcache/liferay-single-vm.xml`

   `ehcache.multi.vm.config.location=/ext-ehcache/liferay-multi-vm.xml`

5. Otherwise, set the following for a clustered environment in `portal-ext.properties`:

   `net.sf.ehcache.configurationResourceName=/ext-ehcache/hibernate-clustered.xml`

   `ehcache.multi.vm.config.location=/ext-ehcache/liferay-multi-vm-clustered.xml`

That's it! You have customized both the both Hibernate caching settings and Ehcache caching settings.

Indexing settings

Search engine indexing collects, parses, and stores data to facilitate fast and accurate information retrieval. Apache Lucene is a high-performance, full-featured text search engine library written entirely in Java-based indexing. It is a technology suitable for nearly any application that requires full-text search, especially cross-platform. Refer to http://lucene.apache.org for more information. By default, the portal uses Lucene search and indexing.

Lucene search

The portal sets the default Lucene index on start-up to false for faster performance, as follows, in portal.properties:

```
index.read.only=false
index.on.startup=false
index.on.startup.delay=60
index.with.thread=true
```

As you can see, the portal sets the property index.read.only to false to allow any writes to the index. You should set it to true if you want to avoid any writes to the index. This is useful in some clustering environments where there is a shared index, and only one node of the cluster updates it.

The portal sets the property index.on.startup to false in order to avoid indexing on every startup. You could set this property to true if you want to index your entire library of files on startup. This property is available so that automated test environments index the files on startup.

 Don't set this to true on production systems, or else your index data will be indexed on every startup.

The property index.on.startup.delay adds a delay before indexing on startup. A delay may be necessary if a lot of plugins need to be loaded and re-indexed. Note that this property is only valid if the property index.on.startup is set to true.

In addition, the portal sets the property index.with.thread to true to allow indexing on startup to be executed on a separate thread to speed up execution.

Of course, you could re-index either all resources or an individual resource through web UI. For example, for re-indexing all search indexing, you can go to **Control Panel | Server | Server Administration | Resources | Actions**, and click on the button **Execute** next to the "**Reindex all search indexes**" option.

Suppose that you're going to re-index individual resource like Users, you can use the Plugin Installation portlet in the Control Panel. Go to **Control Panel | Server | Plugin Installation | Portlet Plugins**, and click on the button **Reindex** next to the portlet **Users**.

Index storage

Lucene stores could be in the filesystem, the database, or in RAM. Anyway, the portal provides a set of properties to configure index storage as follows in `portal.properties`.

```
lucene.store.type=file
lucene.store.jdbc.auto.clean.up=false
lucene.store.jdbc.dialect.*
lucene.dir=${liferay.home}/data/lucene/
lucene.file.extractor=com.liferay.portal.search
.lucene.LuceneFileExtractor
lucene.file.extractor.regexp.strip=
lucene.analyzer=org.apache.lucene.analysis.standard
.StandardAnalyzer
lucene.commit.batch.size=0
lucene.commit.time.interval=0
lucene.buffer.size=16
lucene.merge.factor=10
lucene.optimize.interval=100
```

As shown in the preceding code, the property `lucene.store.type` designates whether Lucene stores indexes in a database via JDBC, filesystem, or in RAM. The default setting is filesystem. When using Lucene's storage of indexes via JDBC, temporary files don't get removed properly. This can eat up disk space over time. Thus set the property `lucene.store.jdbc.auto.clean.up` to `true` to automatically clean up the temporary files once a day.

The property `lucene.store.jdbc.dialect.*` sets the JDBC dialect so that Lucene can use it to store indexes in the database. This property is referenced only when Lucene stores indexes in the database. The portal will attempt to load the proper dialect based on the URL of the JDBC connection.

The property `lucene.dir` sets the directory where Lucene indexes are stored. This is referenced only when Lucene stores indexes in the filesystem. In a clustered environment, you could point the property `lucene.dir` to a shared folder, which is accessible for all nodes. More interestingly, you could set one node to allow any writes to the indexes via the property `index.read.only` and set the rest of nodes to allow read only.

The property `lucene.file.extractor` specifies a class, called by Lucene to extract text from complex files so that they can be properly indexed. The file extractor can sometimes return text that isn't valid for Lucene. The property `lucene.file.extractor.regexp.strip` expects a regular expression. Any character that doesn't match the regular expression will be replaced with a blank space. You can set an empty regular expression to disable this feature. The property `lucene.analyzer` sets the default analyzer used for indexing and retrieval.

In addition, the property `lucene.commit.batch.size` sets how often index updates will be committed. Set the batch size to configure how many consecutive updates will trigger a commit. If the value is 0, then the index will be committed on every update. The property `lucene.commit.time.interval` sets the time interval in milliseconds to configure how often to commit the index. The time interval isn't read unless the batch size is greater than 0 because the time interval works in conjunction with the batch size to guarantee that the index is committed after a specified time interval. The portal sets the time interval to 0 to disable committing the index by a time interval.

The property `lucene.buffer.size` sets Lucene's buffer size in megabytes and the property `lucene.merge.factor` sets Lucene's merge factor. For both of these properties, higher numbers mean that indexing goes faster but uses more memory. The default value from Lucene is 10. Note that this should never be set to a number less than 2. The property `lucene.optimize.interval` sets how often to run Lucene's `optimize` method. Optimization speeds up searching but slows down writing. You can set this property to 0 to always optimize.

Indexer framework

As mentioned earlier, you could re-index either all resources or an individual resource through web UI. For example, you could re-index out-of-the-box portlets like Users (Portlet ID 125) and plugins like the Mail portlet. This is because, in `$PORTAL_ROOT_HOME/WEB-INF/liferay-portlet.xml`, the portlet Users (named as `enterprise_admin_users`) has specified the following line:

```
<indexer-class>
   com.liferay.portlet.enterpriseadmin.util.UserIndexer
</indexer-class>
```

As shown in the preceding code, the `indexer-class` value, which is the specified indexer framework, must be a class that implements `com.liferay.portal.kernel.search.Indexer` and is called to create or update a search index for the portlet Users. Additionally, you could find the indexer framework in out-of-the-box portlets such as Organizations (portlet ID 126, called `enterprise_admin_organizations`), Web Content (portlet ID 15), Image Gallery (Portlet ID 31), Document Library (Portlet ID 20), and so on.

Similarly the `indexer-class` value, which is the specified indexer framework, is also available in plugins. For example, the portlet Mail has specified the following line in `$AS_WEB_APP_HOME/mail-portlet/WEB-INF/liferay-portlet.xml`.

```
<indexer-class>com.liferay.mail.search.Indexer</indexer-class>
```

In the same pattern, you may add the indexer framework in other plugins, like the Knowledge base portlet `KBIndexer`, which supports keyword search against titles, descriptions, content, tags, categories and category hierarchy, and "San Francisco" as one word, and 'San Francisco' as multiple words ("San" or "Francisco") at `http://liferay.cignex.com/palm_tree/book/0387/chapter11/knowledge-base-portlet-6.0.0.1.war`.

Solr search

Solr is the fast open source enterprise search platform, providing powerful full-text search, hit highlighting, faceted search, dynamic clustering, database integration, and rich document (for example, Word, PDF, and so on) handling. Solr is highly scalable, providing distributed search and index replication. Refer to `http://lucene.apache.org/solr`. In this section, we're going to show how to integrate Solr within the portal.

Install Solr instance

In five steps, you can install the Solr example as an instance under Tomcat. Of course, you can find similar installation processes for JBoss, Jetty, Resin, WebSphere, Weblogic, and so on.

1. Download the latest version of Solr from `http://lucene.apache.org/solr`, install it, and mark the root of installation folder as the variable `$SOLR_HOME`.

2. Copy the WAR file `$SOLR_HOME/dist/apache-solr-${solr.version}.war` into `$SOLR_HOME/example` where `${solr.version}` represents the Solr version number, that is, `1.4.0`.

3. Create a Tomcat Context fragment called `solr.xml` with the following lines:

   ```xml
   <?xml version="1.0" encoding="utf-8"?>
   <Context docBase="$SOLR_HOME/example/apache-solr-${solr.version}.war" debug="0" crossContext="true">
     <Environment name="solr/home" type="java.lang.String" value="$SOLR_HOME/example" override="true"/>
   </Context>
   ```

4. Drop the file `solr.xml` into the folder `$TOMCAT_AS_DIR/conf/Catalina/localhost`

5. Add the following line at the end of `$TOMCAT_AS_DIR/bin/setenv.sh` for Linux or MacOS as follows:

```
JAVA_OPTS="$JAVA_OPTS -Dsolr.solr.home=$SOLR_HOME/example/solr/data"
```

Or add the following line at the end of `$TOMCAT_AS_DIR/bin/setenv.bat` for Windows as follows:

```
set JAVA_OPTS=%JAVA_OPTS% -Dsolr.solr.home=$SOLR_HOME/example/solr/data
```

Repeat the preceding steps with different installation directories to run multiple instances of Solr side-by-side. Starting Tomcat, the Solr admin should be available at `http://${solr.host.domain}:${solr.port.number}/solr/admin`, where `${solr.host.domain}` represents the Solr instance domain name, such as `locahost`, and `${solr.port.number}` represents the Solr instance port number such as `8080`.

Configuring the Solr plugin

Once the Solr instance is set, you can install the Solr plugin in the portal. How does it work?

The following is an example of how you can bring the plugin `solr-web` into the portal. The plugin `solr-web` is the Solr Search Engine implementation.

1. Download the WAR file `${solr.web.war}` from `http://liferay.cignex.com/palm_tree/book/0387/chapter12/solr-web-6.0.0.1.war`

2. Drop the WAR file `${solr.web.war}` to the folder `$LIFERAY_HOME/deploy` when the portal is running.

After having deployed it successfully, you should shut down the portal and Solr instance and also configure the Solr instance with the Solr plugin as follows:

1. Open the XML configuration file `$AS_WEB_APP_HOME/solr-web/WEB-INF/classes/META-INF/solr-spring.xml` and update the Solr instance settings as follows:

```xml
<bean id="solrServer"
  class="com.liferay.portal.search.solr.
  server.BasicAuthSolrServer">
  <constructor-arg type="java.lang.String"
  value=" http://${solr.host.domain}:${solr.port.number}/solr"
/>
</bean>
```

2. Drop the schema file `schema.xml` from `$AS_WEB_APP_HOME/solr-web/WEB-INF/conf` to `$SOLR_HOME/example/solr/conf` in the domain `${solr.host.domain}` — replacing the existing schema file `schema.xml`, and restart the Solr instance and the portal.

What's happening?

The XML file `solr-spring.xml` under the folder `$AS_WEB_APP_HOME/solr-web/WEB-INF/classes/META-INF` describes how to integrate Solr in the portal via the plugin web. The following is a piece of code.

```
<bean id="indexSearcher.solr" class="com.liferay.portal.search.solr.
SolrIndexSearcherImpl">
  <property name="solrServer" ref="solrServer" />
</bean>
```

As shown in the preceding code, the XML file `solr-spring.xml` describes the index searcher, index writer, search engine, and so on.

The XML file `schema.xml` under the folder `$AS_WEB_APP_HOME/solr-web/WEB-INF/conf` describes how the fields will be indexed to the Solr index. The following is a piece of code:

```
<schema>
  <types>
    <fieldType name="string" class="solr.StrField"
      sortMissingLast="true" omitNorms="true" />
<!-- ignore details -->
  </types>
  <fields>
    <field name="comments" type="text"
      indexed="true" stored="true" />
<!-- ignore details -->
  </fields>
  <uniqueKey>uid</uniqueKey>
  <defaultSearchField>content</defaultSearchField>
  <solrQueryParser defaultOperator="OR" />
</schema>
```

As shown in the preceding code, the XML file `schema.xml` uniquely describes types, fields, default search field, and Solr query parser.

In addition, there are a lot of the benefits to Solr in clustered environments. Solr can be installed in a separated Tomcat, and that is its main benefit.

Thus you can deal with stop words, localization, synonyms, along with other great features including:

- Advanced full-text search capabilities optimized for high-volume web traffic
- Standards-based open interfaces — XML, JSON, and HTTP, comprehensive HTML administration interfaces, server statistics exposed over JMX for monitoring
- Scalability — efficient replication to other Solr search servers, flexible and adaptable with XML configuration, extensible Plugin architecture

Plugins management

The portal supports six different types of plugins out of the box — Portlets, Themes, Layout Templates, Webs, Hooks, and Ext. Note that a single plugin can contain multiple portlets, themes, and hook packages in a single WAR file logically:

- Portlets: Web applications that run in a portion of a web page
- Themes: Look and feel of pages
- Layout Templates: Ways of choosing how the portlets will be arranged on a page
- Hooks: Allow hooking into the portal's core functionality — for example, the plugin Asset Importer, a portlet with hook, which reads a file and converts it into web content and uses hook service
- Webs: Regular Java EE web modules designed to work with the portal, such as ESB (Enterprise Service Bus), SSO (Single Sign-On), and so on
- Ext: Ext environment as a plugin

Plugins installation

The use of plugins is one of the primary ways to extend the functionality of the portal. The portlet Plugins Installation (portlet ID 136) shows a list of the plugins installed and allows us to install new ones.

The Plugin Installer portlet

The portlet Plugin Installer (portlet ID 111) gives us access to the Liferay public repository. The portlet allows us to search and browse for different types of plugins such as **Portlets**, **Themes**, **Layout Templates**, **Hooks**, and **Web Plugins**.

To install a plugin, choose the plugin from Liferay's public repository from under the tab **Browse Repository** by clicking on its name. You can search and browse for different types of plugins. As you can see, you can search plugins with the following items. First log in as an administrator, then go to **Control Panel | Server | Plugins Installation**, and then click on the **Install more portlets** button.

- **Keywords**: Keywords of plugins
- **Tag**: All and others
- **Repository**: All, `http://plugins.liferay.com/official`, `http://plugins.liferay.com/community`
- **Install Status: All, Out of Date, Not Installed, Out of Date**, or **Not Installed**
- **Refresh**: Refresh plugins from `http://plugins.liferay.com/official` and `http://plugins.liferay.com/community`.

Similarly, you can upload or download WAR files via the Plugin Installer portlet. You can also set up the configuration for hot deployment. You can then enable the hot deploy, set up display directory and destination directory, set the interval as, say `10` seconds, and blacklist threshold to something like `10`. You can unpack WAR, Custom `portlet.xml`, Tomcat Configuration Directory, Tomcat Library Directory, Trusted Plugin Repositories, Un-trusted Plugin Repositories, Plugin Notification Enabled, Plugin Package with Updates Ignored, and so on.

How to make the Plugins Installer appear? You could simply navigate to **Control Panel**, then go to **Server | Plugins Installation**, and click on the button **Install More Portlets**.

Plugins administration

In order to get Plugins Installation to appear, you could navigate to **Control Panel** first, and then go to **Server | Plugins Installation**. As shown in the following screenshot, installed plugins would be displayed with a set of columns: Plugins (like Portlet, Theme, layout Template, Hook, and Web), Active, Roles, and Search Index (for portlets only). For example, the portlet Software catalog has the value Yes for Active, the values Power User and User for Roles, and a button `Reindex` for Search Index.

Auto Deploy

As mentioned earlier, you could install plugins manually via downloading a WAR file or by uploading a WAR file in the portlet Plugin Installer. This process is called Hot Deploy.

In addition, you could also deploy a WAR file to the portal automatically, called Auto Deploy. To do so, download the WAR file `${name.version.war}` first, then drop the WAR file `${name.version.war}` to the folder `$LIFERAY_HOME/deploy` when the portal is running. That's it!

What's happening?

The portal has specified auto deploy as follows, but not limited, in `portal.properties`.

```
auto.deploy.listeners=\
  com.liferay.portal.deploy.auto.ExtAutoDeployListener,\
  com.liferay.portal.deploy.auto.HookAutoDeployListener,\
  com.liferay.portal.deploy.auto.LayoutTemplateAutoDeployListener,\
  com.liferay.portal.deploy.auto.PortletAutoDeployListener,\
  com.liferay.portal.deploy.auto.ThemeAutoDeployListener,\
  com.liferay.portal.deploy.auto.WebAutoDeployListener,\ auto.deploy.
enabled=true
auto.deploy.deploy.dir=${liferay.home}/deploy
auto.deploy.interval=10000
auto.deploy.blacklist.threshold=10
auto.deploy.unpack.war=true
auto.deploy.custom.portlet.xml=false
```

As shown in the preceding code, the property `auto.deploy.listeners` takes a list of comma-delimited class names as input, which are used to process the auto-deployment of WARs. The auto-deployable plugins include Ext, Hook, Layout Template, Portlet, Theme, and Web.

The portal first sets the property `auto.deploy.enabled` to `true` to enable auto-deployment of layout templates, portlets. It then sets the directory to scan for layout templates, portlets, and finally, themes to auto deploy. This the main reason that you can drop the WAR file `${name.version.war}` to the folder `$LIFERAY_HOME/deploy` for auto-deploy. The property `auto.deploy.interval` sets the interval in milliseconds, that is, how often to scan the resource directory for updates.

The property `auto.deploy.blacklist.threshold` sets the number of attempts to deploy a file before blacklisting it. Moreover, the portal sets the property `auto.deploy.unpack.war` to `true` to unpack deployed WARs. However, you should set this property to `false` if your application server has concurrency issues with deploying large WARs. The property `auto.deploy.custom.portlet.xml` is set to `false`, that is, you don't want your application server to rename `portlet.xml` to `portlet-custom.xml`. This is only needed when deploying the portal on WebSphere 6.1.x because WebSphere's portlet container will try to process a portlet at the same time at which Liferay is trying to process a portlet.

Furthermore, the portal has specified hot deploy and hot un-deploy in `portal. properties` as follows, but its features are not limited to them.

```
hot.deploy.listeners=\
   com.liferay.portal.deploy.hot.PluginPackageHotDeployListener,\
   ## ignore details
hot.undeploy.enabled=true
hot.undeploy.interval=0
hot.undeploy.on.redeploy=false
```

As shown in the preceding code, the property `hot.deploy.listeners` takes a list of comma-delimited class names as input, used to process the deployment and un-deployment of WARs at runtime. The hot-deployable plugins include Ext, Hook, Layout Template, Portlet, and Theme. Note that `PluginPackageHotDeployListener` must always be the first to be deployed.

The portal has set the property `hot.undeploy.enabled` to `true` to enable the un-deploying plugins. The property `hot.undeploy.interval` sets the un-deploy interval in milliseconds, depending on how long to wait for the un-deploy process to finish. On the other hand, the property `hot.undeploy.on.redeploy` sets the re-deploy function. You can set this to `true` to un-deploy a plugin before deploying its new version. This property will only be used if the property `hot.undeploy.enabled` is set to `true`.

Plugins configuration

The portlet Plugins Configuration (portlet ID `132`) provides the capability to configure each kind of plugin installed in the portal. You can use this portlet to configure which portal roles have access to the plugins.

For example, if you want to limit the use of the portlet Sitemap to just power users, then you can use the tab **Portlets** and remove the Users role and leave only the Power Users role in the field. To do this, simply click on the portlet you want, and enter the role names in the field provided. Any role names that you enter here will be able to use this portlet.

How to get Plugins Configuration displayed? Firstly, you can simply navigate to the **Control Panel**, and then go to **Portal | Plugins Configuration**.

What's happening?

The portal has specified the following properties for plugins in `portal.properties`.

```
plugin.types=portlet,theme,layout-template,hook,web
plugin.repositories.trusted=http://plugins.liferay.com/official
plugin.repositories.untrusted=http://plugins.liferay.com/community
plugin.notifications.enabled=true
```

As shown in the preceding code, the property `plugin.types` takes a list of comma-delimited supported plugin types as input, such as `portlet`, `theme`, `layout-template`, `hook`, and `web`. Of course, you could add custom plugin types, for example `ext` in `portal-ext.properties`. The properties `plugin.repositories.trusted` and `plugin.repositories.untrusted` take a list of Liferay plugin repositories separated by characters as input. In addition, the property `plugin.notifications.enabled` is set to `true`, by default, to receive on-screen notifications whenever there is a new version of an installed plugin. You can set this property to `false` to avoid receiving on-screen notifications. How to develop your plugins? You may refer to the book *Liferay Portal 5.2 System Development, Packt Publishing* for details.

WAP

Liferay goes mobile! As smart-phones continue to impede the space between dialing a number, taking a picture, or discovering new music, mobile browsers offer us the next frontier in the previously desktop-exclusive market of web design. A **mobile browser** is a web browser designed for use on a mobile device such as a mobile phone, PDA, iPhone, which is optimized to display web content most effectively for small screens on portable devices. A WAPbrowser provides all of the basic services of a web browser, but is simplified to operate within the restrictions of a mobile phone, such as its smaller view screen. The websites generated by the portal go with mobile browsers, or any WAP browsers. Thus you can browse portal websites, called WAP sites, through mobile devices.

Themes (look and feel of websites or WAP sites) in the portal will detect mobile devices dynamically. As mentioned earlier, each site may have its own look and feel and each page could have its own look and feel. Under the tab **Look and Feel**, you would see **Regular Browsers** and **Mobile Devices**, where available themes will appear.

Of course, you can develop your mobile themes or WAP themes depending on your own requirements. Here we're going to discuss several existing mobile themes or WAP themes, and going further, see what themes are and how they work.

Jedi Mobile theme

The theme Jedi Mobile has been applied on the home page of the community Guest. As you can see, the theme Jedi Mobile takes the original Jedi theme and packs it into a bite-sized, smart-phone punch.

Structure

The theme Jedi Mobile has the following folder structure at `$AS_WEB_APP_HOME/jedi-mobile-theme`.

- `css`: CSS files
- `images`: Image files
- `javascripts`: JavaScript files
- `templates`: Velocity template files
- `WEB-INF`: Web info specification includes sub-folders classes, lib, and tld

As you can see, web-info specification covers `liferay-look-and-feel.xml`, `liferay-plugin-package.properties`, `liferay-plugin-package.xml`, and `web.xml`. Knowing the structure of the theme would be helpful to customize that theme.

How does it work?

You could bring the theme **Jedi Mobile Theme** into the portal by following these steps:

- Download the WAR file `${jedi.mobile.theme.war}` from `http://liferay.cignex.com/palm_tree/book/0387/chapter12/jedi-mobile-theme-6.0.0.1.war`
- Drop the WAR file `${jedi.mobile.theme.war}` to the folder `$LIFERAY_HOME/deploy` when the portal is running

Then apply the theme as the current look and feel of pages. You may refer to *Chapter 2, Setting Up a Home Page and Navigation Structure for the Intranet*.

What's happening?

The theme Jedi Mobile has specified the following script at `$AS_WEB_APP_HOME/jedi-mobile-theme/templates/portal_normal.vm`.

```
<script type="text/javascript">
  iPhone = function() {
    setTimeout("window.scrollTo(0,1) ", 100)
  }
  if (navigator.userAgent.indexOf('iPhone') != -1) {
```

```
      addEventListener("load", iPhone, false)
      addEventListener("onorientationchange", iPhone, false)
   }
</script>
```

As shown in the preceding code, it detects the navigator, whether it is an iPhone or not.

iPhone theme

The theme **iPhone** takes a much more direct approach to web applications. With its indigenous appearance and feel, the WAP site starts to feel like a playlist, user experience appears native, and navigation comes naturally.

How does it work?

You can bring the iPhone Theme into the portal by following these steps:

1. Download the WAR file `${iphone.theme.war}` from `http://liferay. cignex.com/palm_tree/book/0387/chapter12/iphone-theme- 6.0.0.1.war`.

2. Drop the WAR file `${iphone.theme.war}` to the folder `$LIFERAY_HOME/ deploy` when the portal is running.

Then apply the theme as the current look and feel of pages.

What's happening?

The theme iPhone introduces a new browser detection mechanism for specialized mobile functionality. If you visit the site on an iPhone, you get the bare minimum — JavaScript, HTML, and CSS. If you visit the site on a regular browser, you get all the more advanced UI features.

The theme iPhone has specified the following script at `$AS_WEB_APP_HOME/iphone- theme/templates/portal_normal.vm`.

```
#set ($isIphone = $request.getHeader("User-Agent").toLowerCase().
indexOf("iphone") != -1)
<!-- ignore details -->
#if ($isIphone)
<!-- ignore details -->
#else
  $theme.include($top_head_include)
#end
</head>
<!-- ignore details -->
```

iPhone Redirect theme

The theme iPhone Redirect takes the browser detection mechanism and takes intelligent redirection. The theme iPhone Redirect is an unstyled theme, coming with a custom initialization feature—that is, it can detect an iPhone browser visiting the page, check for a Mobile community, and automatically redirect the iPhone user to that community if found. Moreover, it will work with a virtual host.

How does it work?

You could bring the theme iPhone Redirect Theme into the portal by following these steps:

1. Download the WAR file `${iphone.redirect.theme.war}` from `http://liferay.cignex.com/palm_tree/book/0387/chapter12/iphone-redirect-theme-6.0.0.1.war`.

2. Drop the WAR file `${iphone.redirect.theme.war}` to the folder `$LIFERAY_HOME/deploy` when the portal is running.

Then apply the theme as the current look and feel of pages.

What's happening?

The theme **iPhone Redirect** has the following code specified at `$AS_WEB_APP_HOME/iphone-detect-theme/templates/init_custom.vm`.

```
//ignore details
#set ($isIphone = $request.getHeader("User-Agent").toLowerCase().
indexOf("iphone") != -1)
#if ($isIphone && $mobileGroup && $group_id != $mobileGroup.groupId)
 <script type="text/javascript">
   window.location.href = '${layoutSet.virtualHost}' ? 'http://' +
'${layoutSet.virtualHost}' + ((window.location.port) ? ':' + window.
location.port : '') : '/web${mobileGroup.friendlyURL}'
 </script>
#end
```

Of course, you could customize the preceding themes according to your own requirements. For more details, you may refer to *Chapter 9, Developing Layout Templates and Themes* of the book *Liferay Portal 5.2 Systems Development, Packt Publishing*.

Reporting

JasperReports is an open source Java reporting tool that can write to screen, a printer, or to PDF, HTML, Microsoft Excel, RTF, ODT, CSV (Comma Separated Value) formats, and XML files. It can be used in Java-enabled applications, including Java EE or Web applications to generate dynamic content. It reads its instructions from an XML or .jasper file. Refer to `http://www.jasperforge.org/jasperreports` for more information.

The portal provides full integration of JasperReports with the reporting framework — a web called `reporting-jasper-web` and a portlet called `reports-console-portlet`. The portal provides the ability to schedule reports and deliver them via Document Library and e-mail. In addition, the portal has added support for Jasper XLS data source to a reporting framework.

JasperReports Engine

The Liferay JasperReports Report Engine provides implementation of Liferay BI using Jasper. You can bring the web Reporting Jasper into the portal by following these steps:

- Download the WAR file `${reporting.jasper.web.war}` from `http://liferay.cignex.com/palm_tree/book/0387/chapter12/reporting-jasper-web-6.0.0.1.war`.

- Drop the WAR file `${reporting.jasper.web.war}` to the folder `$LIFERAY_HOME/deploy` when the portal is running.

Note that the current integration of JasperReports version is 3.6.2. You will be able to upgrade it to the latest version of JasperReports anytime.

The Reports portlets

The plugin Reports Console defines two portlets: **Reports Console** at **Control Panel** and **Reports Display**. The portlet **Reports Display** is instanceable — that is, you can add more than one instance of the portlet on a page.

You could bring the plugin **Reports Console** into the portal by following these steps:

1. Download the WAR file `${reports.console.portlet.war}` from `http://liferay.cignex.com/palm_tree/book/0387/chapter12/reports-console-portlet-6.0.0.1.war`.

2. Drop the WAR file `${reports.console.portlet.war}` to the folder `$LIFERAY_HOME/deploy` when the portal is running.

As shown in the following screenshot, the portlet Reports Display provides the ability to search for reports and display search results with pagination. Search results will be displayed with a set of columns: **Report Definition Name**, **Report Format**, **Requested Date**, and **Reporting Date**.

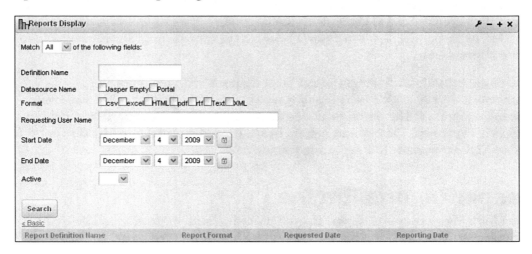

As you can see, you can search for reports via basic search or advanced search. The advanced search would cover the following items:

- **Match All of the following fields**: **All** or **Any**
- **Definition Name**: User's input
- **Datasource Name**: **Jasper Empty**, **Portal**
- **Format**: **csv**, **excel**, **HTML**, **pdf**, **rtf**, **Text**, and **XML**
- **Requesting User Name**: User's input
- **Start date**: A date
- **End date**: A date
- **Active**: **Yes** or **No**

The portlet Reports Console provides the abilities to manage reports in the Control Panel. By going to **Content | Reports Console** under the **Control Panel**, you can search for generated reports under the tab **Generated Reports**. You can also create report definitions under the tab **Report Definitions**.

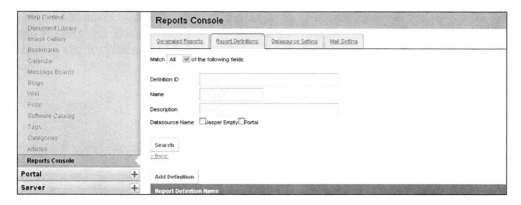

Under the tab **Report Definition**, you would be able to search report definitions via basic search or advanced search. The advanced search would cover the following items:

- **Match All of the following fields**: **All** or **Any**
- **Definition ID**: User's input
- **Name**: User's input
- **Description**: User's input
- **Datasource Name**: Multiple checkboxes, **Jasper Empty** or **Portal**

Of course, you could add definitions with the following items:

- **Definition Name**: Input required
- **Description**: User's input
- **Datasource Name**: Empty or Portal
- **Template**: Uploading template file (required)
- **Report Parameters**: Multiple pair (key, value)
- **Key**: User's input; optionally, it is bound to Report parameters
- **Value**: User's input
- **Permissions**: A checkbox—Public permissions configuration.

Setup

The Data Source Setting and Mail Setting of the portlet Reports Console are configurable. Clicking on **Content | Report Console** under the **Control Panel**, you would be able to configure the Data Source setting and Mail Setting. You would be able to configure following items under the Data Source setting.

- **Datasource Name**: Company or community selecting the scope to search for knowledge base articles when selecting Community, it will list groups like organizations and communities – where you could choose multiple groups
- **Datasource Type**: csv, jdbc, xls, xml
- **Datasource File**: Uploading data source file
- **Column Names**: Columns
- **Charset Name**: Character set name
- **Permissions**: A checkbox Public permissions configuration. Note that you may use button Test to test database connection.

Obviously, you would be able to search the data source by basic search or advanced search. Data source search results will appear with a set of columns like Data Source ID, Data Source Name, and Data Source Type. In addition, you would be able to configure the following items on Mail Setting.

- **Mail From Name**: David Berger, for example
- **Mail From Address**: david@bookpub.com, for example
- **Notification Subject**: Subject of e-mail notification
- **Notification By**: Body of e-mail notification
- **Delivery Subject**: Subject of e-mail delivery
- **Delivery By**: Body of e-mail delivery

Structure

The plugin Reports Console has the following folder structure at $AS_WEB_APP_ HOME/reports-console-portlet:

- css: CSS files
- datasource: JSP files for data source
- definition: JSP files for reporting definition
- js: JavaScript files
- mail: JSP files for mail settings
- META-INF: context.xml
- request: JSP files for requests
- WEB-INF: web-info specification, includes sub-folders, classes, lib, service, sql, src, and tld

As you can see, web-info specification covers liferay-display.xml, liferay-plugin-package.properties, liferay-plugin-package.xml, portlet.xml, service.xml and web.xml. Knowing the structure of the portlet would be helpful to customize the portlet.

Assign permissions

There are two portlets in the plugin Reports Console: Reports Console and Reports **Display**. Generally speaking, there are five-levels of permissions—permissions on portlets, permissions on Reports Data Source, permissions on Reports Definition, permissions on Requested Report, and permissions on Reports Date Source.

The following table shows permissions on the portlet Reports Console. The role Community Member may set up all permissions (marked as 'X'): **View, Configuration, Add Data Source, Add Definition, Edit mail Setting, Permissions,** and **Access in Control Panel**. On the other hand, the role Guest will only have the permission **View**. By default, the role Community Member has the permission actions (marked as '*') **View, Add Data Source, Add Definition, Edit mail Setting,** and **Permissions,** whereas the role Guest only has the permission action **View**.

Action	Description	Community	Guest
View	Ability to view the portlet	X, *	X, *
Configuration	Ability to configure the portlet	X	
Access in Control Panel	Ability to access the portlet in Control Panel	X	
Add Data Source	Ability to add data source	X, *	
Add Definition	Ability to add definition	X, *	
Edit Mail Setting	Ability to edit e-mail setting	X. *	
Permissions	Ability to assign permissions on all the mentioned actions	X, *	

There are permission actions **View, Configuration, Add to Page** set in the portlet Report Display. The role Community Member has the permission action **View,** by default, just as that of the role Guest.

The following table shows permissions on Report Data Source. The role Community Member may set up permissions (marked as 'X'): **View, Delete, Permissions,** and **Update**. On the other hand, the role Guest may set up the permission **View**. By default, the role Community Member has the permission action (marked as '*') **View**.

Action	Description	Community	Guest
View	Ability to view data source	X, *	X
Delete	Ability to delete data source	X	
Permissions	Ability to assign permissions on data source	X	
Update	Ability to update data source	X	

The following table shows permissions on Report Definition. The role Community Member may set up permissions (marked as 'X'), namely, **View**, **Delete Definition**, **Permissions**, **Generate Report**, and **Update**, whereas the role Guest may set up the permission **View**. By default, the role Community Member has the permission action (marked as '*') **View** just like the role Guest.

Action	Description	Community	Guest
View	Ability to view a definition	X, *	X,*
Delete Definition	Ability to delete a definition	X	
Permissions	Ability to assign permissions on a definition	X	
Update	Ability to update a definition	X	
Generate Report	Ability to generate a report	X	

The following table shows permissions on Requested Report. The role Community Member may set up permissions (marked as 'X'): **View**, **Delete Definition**, **Permissions**, **Archive Request**, **Delete Report**, **Download Report**, **Un-schedule**, and **Update**. On the other hand, the role Guest may set up the permission **View**. By default, the role Community Member has the permission actions (marked as '*') **View** and **Download Report**, whereas the role Guest only has permission action **View**.

Action	Description	Community	Guest
View	Ability to view a requested report	X, *	X,*
Delete	Ability to delete a requested report	X	
Permissions	Ability to assign permissions on a requested report	X	
Update	Ability to update a requested report	X	
Archive Request	Ability to archive a requested report	X	
Delete Report	Ability to delete a report	X	
Download Report	Ability to download a report	X, *	
Un-schedule	Ability to un-schedule a report	X	

The following table shows permissions on Report Date Source. The role Community Member may set up permissions (marked as 'X'), namely, **View** and **Update**, whereas the role Guest may set up the permission **View**. By default, the role Community Member has the permission action (marked as '*') **View**.

Action	Description	Community	Guest
View	Ability to view date source	X, *	X
Update	Ability to update date source	X	

What's happening?

The portlet Reports Console has the following portlet specification at `$AS_WEB_APP_HOME/reports-console-portlet/WEB-INF/liferay-portlet.xml`.

```
<control-panel-entry-category>content</control-panel-entry-category>
<control-panel-entry-weight>14.0</control-panel-entry-weight>
```

As shown in the preceding code, the portlet Reports Console will appear in the category Content of the Control Panel at the position 14.

The portlet Reports Console also defined permission resources or actions in `$AS_WEB_APP_HOME/reports-console-portlet/WEB-INF/classes/resource-actions/default.xml`. These permission resources or actions get registered at `$AS_WEB_APP_HOME/reports-console-portlet/WEB-INF/classes/portlet.properties` as follows:

```
resource.actions.configs=resource-actions/default.xml
```

The preceding code sets resource actions in plugins. Moreover, the portlet Reports Console specified custom SQL in `$AS_WEB_APP_HOME/reports-console-portlet/WEB-INF/classes/custom-sql/default.xml`.

In addition, the portlet has specified e-mail notification settings as follows. These permission resources or actions get registered at `$AS_WEB_APP_HOME/reports-console-portlet/WEB-INF/classes/portlet.properties`.

```
email.from.name=David Berger
email.from.address=david@bookpub.com
delivery.email.message.body=../dependencies/delivery_email_message_
body.tmpl
delivery.email.message.subject=../dependencies/delivery_email_message_
subject.tmpl
notifications.email.message.body=../dependencies/notifications_email_
message_body.tmpl
notifications.email.message.subject=../dependencies/notifications_
email_message_subject.tmpl
```

As shown in the preceding code, the property `email.from.name` was set as David Berger and `email.from.address` was set as *david@bookpub.com*. The delivery e-mail message and notification e-mail message are specified in a `.tmpl` file. This is the reason that when configuring e-mails, you would see the values of the e-mail subject and the e-mail body coming from these `.tmpl` file. You will be able to modify these `.tmpl` files according to your requirements.

Audit service

An audit trail of user actions is required by many organizations. Fortunately, the portal provides **audit service**: a pluggable way of storing the audit trail from the portal and plugins. Then the information processed by the audit service plugin can be stored into a log file or database. Note that audit services employ Liferay Lightweight Message Bus and Plugin architecture. The audit service itself is a plugin, handling the processing and logging of the audit messages sent through the Message Bus. Therefore, any plugin can then produce audit messages to the audit message bus destination.

Audit hook

An auditing framework has been added to the portal. The auditing framework will allow the system administrator to track a user's action in the portal. The portal has the following settings for the auditing framework in `portal.properties`.

```
com.liferay.portal.servlet.filters.audit.AuditFilter=false
```

As you can see, the auditing framework has been disabled by default. This is helpful to speed up the portal. To enable the auditing framework, you need to set the following in `portal-ext.properties`.

```
com.liferay.portal.servlet.filters.audit.AuditFilter=true
```

As shown in the preceding code, the audit filter populates the `AuditRequestThreadLocal` with the appropriate request values to generate audit requests. Note that if an administrator is impersonating another user, the audit records look as if the actions are performed by the impersonated user. The records should record the real user that performs an action.

How does it work?

You could bring the hook **Audit** into the portal with the following steps:

1. Download the WAR file `${audit.hook.war}` from `http://liferay.cignex.com/palm_tree/book/0387/chapter12/audit-hook-6.0.0.1.war`

2. Drop the WAR file `${audit.hook.war}` to the folder `$LIFERAY_HOME/deploy` when the portal is running

What's happening?

The following events got audited:

- **Login, Logout, Login failure,** and **Impersonation**
- **Role create, remove,** and **update**
- **Role grant** and **revoke**
- **User create, remove,** and **update**
- **User Group create, remove,** and **update**
- **User Group assign,** and **revoke**

The hook Audit added the following hooks in `$AS_WEB_APP_HOME/audit-hook/WEB-INF/liferay-hook.xml`.

```
<hook>
  <portal-properties>portal.properties</portal-properties>
</hook>
```

Furthermore, the hook Audit provided a hook in `$AS_WEB_APP_HOME/audit-hook/WEB-INF/classes/portal.properties` as follows:

```
auth.failure=com.liferay.portal.audit.events.authentication.
LoginFailureAudit
login.events.post=com.liferay.portal.audit.events.authentication.
LoginAudit
logout.events.post=com.liferay.portal.audit.events.authentication.
LogoutAudit
// ignore details value.object.listener.com.liferay.portal.
model.UserGroupRole=com.liferay.portal.audit.events.user.
UserGroupRoleModificationAudit
```

When deploying the hook Audit, you would see a message saying, "**The plugin Audit hook can not be deployed before audit portlet gets deployed.**". Why? The hook has specified the following in `$AS_WEB_APP_HOME/audit-hook/WEB-INF/liferay-plugin-package.properties`.

```
required-deployment-contexts=\
  audit-portlet
```

The Audit portlet

The portlet Audit provides the ability to manage audit reports. The portlet Audit will appear under the category **Portal** of the Control Panel. As shown in the following screenshot, you could search for audit events by **Type, User Name, User ID, Resource Name, Resource ID, Session ID, Client IP, Server IP, Begin Date,** and **End Date**.

As you can see, the search results would be displayed with a set of columns such as **User Name, Resource Name, Resource ID, Type, Client IP,** and **Timestamp**.

How does it work?

You could bring the portlet **Audit** into the portal by following these steps:

- Download the WAR file ${audit.portlet.war} from http://liferay. cignex.com/palm_tree/book/0387/chapter12/audit-portlet-6.0.0.1.war.

- Drop the WAR file ${audit.portlet.war} to the folder $LIFERAY_HOME/ deploy when the portal is running.

The Service model

The portlet stores the information processed by the audit service—a model called AuditEvent, with a package named com.liferay. portal.audit. The model is specified at $AS_WEB_APP_HOME/audit-portlet/WEB-INF/service.xml in detail.

As you can see, in `service.xml`, the entry `AuditEvent` covered the columns: `event Id` as primary key, `additional Info`, `class Name`, `class PK`, `client Host`, `client IP`, `company Id`, `message`, `server Name`, `server Port`, `session Id`, `timestamp`, `user Id`, `user Name`, and the original `Message`. You can customize this service model and use Service Builder in plugins SDK to regenerate services.

What's happening?

The portlet Audit has the following portlet specification at `$AS_WEB_APP_HOME/audit-portlet/WEB-INF/liferay-portlet.xml`.

```
<control-panel-entry-category>portal</control-panel-entry-category>
<control-panel-entry-weight>15.0</control-panel-entry-weight>
```

As shown in the preceding code, the portlet Audit will appear in the category **Portal** of the Control Panel and at the position `15`.

As mentioned earlier, the information processed by the audit service plugin can be stored into a log file or database. How? The information has been installed in the database via the data model `AuditEvent`. In addition, the Audit log CSV (comma-separated values) is configurable. The portlet Audit provided a property to configure the Audit log in `$AS_WEB_APP_HOME/audit-portlet/WEB-INF/classes/portlet.properties` as follows.

```
audit.log.csv.columns=companyId,userId,
userName,classPK,className,type,sessionID,
clientIP,serverIP,timestamp,additionalInfo
```

Of course, you can override the Audit log CSV directly.

Document Library Record

The plugin Document Library Record hook to audit who downloaded the special resources such as Document Library documents, Image Gallery images, and so on. The original purpose of the plugin is to audit who downloaded Document Library documents.

The portlet Document Library Record appeared in the category **Content** of the **Control Panel**. There are two tabs: **Resource** and **Trace Definition**, where you can view all records.

How does it work?

The following is an option that can bring the portlet **Document Library Record** into the portal.

1. Download the WAR file `${document.library.record.portlet.war}` from `http://liferay.cignex.com/palm_tree/book/0387/chapter12/document-library-record-portlet-6.0.0.1.war`.

2. Drop the WAR file `${document.library.record.portlet.war}` to the folder `$LIFERAY_HOME/deploy` when the portal is running.

The Service model portlet

This portlet uses a set of models: `DLRecordDifinition` and `DLRecordLog`. As you can see, the portlet Document Library Record has specified services and models with a package named `com.liferay.dlrecord`. You will be able to find details at `$AS_WEB_APP_HOME/document-library-record-portlet/WEB-INF/service.xml`.

The `service.xml` contains certain records specified as entries: `DLRecordDifinition` and `DLRecordLog`. The entry `DLRecordDifinition` includes columns `definition Id` as primary key, and other columns such as `folder Id`, `group Id`, `company Id`, `user Id`, `create Date`, `modified By`, `modified Date`, `name`, `title`, and `sign-in Required`. On the other hand, the entry `DLRecordLog` includes the columns: `Log Id` as the primary key, `group Id`, `company Id`, `user Id`, and `create Date`.

More interestingly, you could use Service Builder in plugins SDK to generate services against `service.xml`, plus XML files such as `portlet-hbm.xml`, `portlet-model-hints.xml`, `portlet-spring.xml`, `base-spring.xml`, `dynamic-data-source-spring.xml`, `hibernate-spring.xml`, and `infrastructure-spring.xml` under the folder `$AS_WEB_APP_HOME/ document-library-record-portlet/WEB-INF/classes/META-INF`.

Of course, you could customize this service model and use Service Builder in the plugins SDK to regenerate services.

What's happening?

The portlet Document Library Record has the following portlet specification at `$AS_WEB_APP_HOME/document-library-record-portlet/WEB-INF/liferay-portlet.xml`.

```
<control-panel-entry-category>content</control-panel-entry-category>
<control-panel-entry-weight>15.0</control-panel-entry-weight>
```

As shown in the preceding code, the portlet Document Library Record will appear in the category Content of the Control Panel and at the position 15.

The portlet Document Library Record has added the following hooks in $AS_WEB_ APP_HOME/document-library-record-portlet/WEB-INF/liferay-hook.xml.

```
<hook>
  <portal-properties>portal.properties</portal-properties>
</hook>
```

Furthermore, the portlet Document Library Record provides a hook in $AS_WEB_ APP_HOME/document-library-record-portlet/WEB-INF/classes/portal. properties as follows:

```
servlet.service.events.pre=com.liferay.
portal.events.DocumentLiraryRecordAction
```

In addition, the resource that got traced is configurable. The portlet Document Library Record provided a property to configure the traced resource's URI (Uniform Resource Identifier) in $AS_WEB_APP_HOME/document-library-record-portlet/WEB-INF/classes/portlet.properties as follows:

```
traceingURI=/c/document_library/get_file
```

As you can see, the property traceingURI has been specified with the value /c/ document_library/get_file — that is, Document Library documents downloading URI.

Of course, you can trace other resources such as Image Gallery images. If you're going to trace who downloaded images, you can set the property in $AS_WEB_ APP_HOME/document-library-record-portlet/WEB-INF/classes/portlet. properties as follows:

```
traceingURI=/image/image_gallery
```

Everything in the portal should be audited by the audit-hook, for example, adding a listener to Document Library. The Document Library Record portlet is a special usage of the audit-hook.

CRM

The portal provides the ability to integrate third-party systems smoothly. In this section, we're going to introduce you to integration of CRM.

CRM—Salesforce.com

Customer Relationship Management (CRM) can be described as methods that companies use to interact with customers, including employee training and special-purpose CRM software, and handling incoming customer phone calls and e-mail, although the information collected by CRM software may also be used for promotion and surveys such as polling customer satisfaction.

Salesforce.com is one of the pioneers of the **Software as a Service (SaaS)** model of distributing business software, in which access to business software is purchased on a subscription basis and hosted offsite. Refer to http://www.salesforce.com for more information.

The included portlets should be Accounts, Opportunities, Contacts, Leads, Events, Tasks, and so on.

How does it work?

The following is an option that could bring the portlet salesforce into the portal.

1. Download the WAR file ${salesforce.portlet.war} from http://liferay.cignex.com/palm_tree/book/0387/chapter12/salesforce-portlet-6.0.0.1.war .

2. Drop the WAR file ${salesforce.portlet.war} to the folder $LIFERAY_HOME/deploy when the portal is running.

>
> Note that the main functions of the portlet salesforce are incomplete. You can use it as a framework to integrate the main features of salesforce in depth. In the same or a similar way, you will be able to integrate the portal with **SugarCRM**, by referring to http://www.sugarcrm.com/crm/, with MicroStrategy, by referring to http://www.microstrategy.com/, and so on.

Widgets and gadgets

In general, a **widget** is a piece of reusable code, pluggable into virtually any website. On the other hand, a **gadget** acts just like a widget, it's a small technological object that has a particular function.

Widgets—Netvibes

The plugin Netvibes Widget provides the capability to show any widget from Netvibes in websites. A widget is an element of a graphical user interface (GUI) that displays an information arrangement changeable by the user. **Netvibes** is a multi-lingual Ajax-based personalized start page or personal web portal. You could find an ecosystem at `http://eco.netvibes.com/widgets`, the largest widget directory.

Also, you can publish the widget `Astrofiles.net`, for example, in any page through the plugin Netvibes Widget. Here the widget `Astrofiles.net` in French: "Ayez toujours avec vous les dernières photos de la NASA (apod), le phénomène astronomique du jour, ainsi qu'un quiz d'astronomie !".

That is, it always provides you with the latest photographs of NASA (apod), the astronomic phenomenon of day, as well as a quiz on astronomy! As you can see, you can choose any widget, for example, "Bible Quotes".

How does it work?

The following is an option that could bring the portlet Netvibes Widgets into the portal.

- Download the WAR file `${netvibes.widget.portlet.war}` from `http://liferay.cignex.com/palm_tree/book/0387/chapter12/netvibes-widget-portlet-6.0.0.1.war`
- Drop the WAR file `${netvibes.widget.portlet.war}` to the folder `$LIFERAY_HOME/deploy` when the portal is running.

The following is a sample: first, add the portlet Netvibes Widget to a page. Then go to **More | Configuration | Setup | Current**, search with the keyword "`Astrofiles.net`", and locate the widget "`Astrofiles.net`". Click on the button **Choose** next to the widget "`Astrofiles.net`". Finally, click on the icon "**Return to Full Page**". That's it!

Setup

As you can see, the portlet Netvibes Widget is configurable. Before using it, you are required to configure this portlet to make it visible to all users—electing a widget from the widget repository. By going to **More | Configuration | Setup | Current**, you will be able to configure the following items:

- **Search**
- **Sort: Most Recent, Most Popular**
- **Category: All, News**, and so on

- **Region**: **All, Canada, Germany,** and so on.
- **Search Keyword Input Box**: An input box
- **Search**: A button to search widgets — search results are displayed with pagination
- **Choose**: A button to select the widget and to attach the selected widget
- **Netvibes** Widget URL
- **URL Input Box**: An input box
- **Netvibes Widget URL**: A button to attach the URL

Once a widget is selected, you will have a chance to update the following IFrame properties: `alt`, `frameborder`, `height-maximized`, `height-normal`, `hspace`, `scrolling`, `vspace`, and `width`.

What's happening?

The portlet has specified the following portlet parameters at `$AS_WEB_APP_HOME/netvibes-widget-portlet/WEB-INF/liferay-portlet.xml`.

```
<configuration-action-class>com.liferay.netvibeswidget.action.
ConfigurationActionImpl</configuration-action-class>
<instanceable>true</instanceable>
<ajaxable>false</ajaxable>
```

As shown in the preceding code, in the portlet Netvibes Widget, `ajaxable` is set to `false`, that is, the portlet can never be displayed via Ajax. The portlet sets the `instanceable` value to `true`, so that the portlet can appear multiple times on a page. In addition, the portlet sets the `configuration-action-class` to `com.liferay.netvibeswidget.action.ConfigurationActionImpl`, called to allow users to configure the portlet at runtime. This is the main reason that you can go to **More | Configuration | Setup | Current**, and configure the portlet at runtime.

Netvibes regions have been hardcoded at the API `NetvibesWidgetUtil`. Netvibes categories are retrieved dynamically from the `NetvibesCategoriesWebCacheItem` service in the API:

```
http://api.eco.netvibes.com/categories?format=json
```

The search results of widgets are coming from the `NetvibesWidgetsWebCacheItem` service at the API:

```
http://api.eco.netvibes.com/search?category=...
```

You will be interested in customizing the portlet Netvibes Widget by modifying the view JSP file and configuration JSP file. You can find the view JSP file `view.jsp` and the configuration JSP file `configuration.jsp` in the folder `$AS_WEB_APP_HOME/netvibes-widget-portlet`.

Mash-ups

A **mash-up** is a web page or application, combining data or functionality from two or more external sources to create a new service. In fact, the application `Astrofiles.net`, a widget, could be shared through a piece of JavaScript code. In order to share the application `Astrofiles.net` on any website, you have to just copy the code (that is, piece of JavaScript) as follows and paste it into the web page, and the application `Astrofiles.net` will show up:

```
<script type="text/javascript"
        src="http://cdn.widgetserver.com/syndication/
                        subscriber/InsertWidget.js">
</script>
<script>
  if (WIDGETBOX) WIDGETBOX.
    renderWidget('9ed9b0f2-a417-4ed6-aec6-e8abbd558c44')
</script>
<noscript>Get the
  <a href="http://www.widgetbox.com/widget/biblequotes">Bible Quotes</
a> widget and many other
  <a href="http://www.widgetbox.com/">great free widgets</a> at
  <a href="http://www.widgetbox.com">Widgetbox</a>!
    Not seeing a widget? (<a href="http://docs.widgetbox.com
    /using-widgets/installing-widgets/why-cant-i-see-my-widget/">
    More info</a>)
</noscript>
```

In addition, you can first create web content, and then paste the preceding code into content source, and finally publish it in the portlet Web Content Display. The application `Astrofiles.net` will show up in the portlet Web Content Display in a given page.

In general, the portal includes two portlets to mash-up content from `iGoogle` (`google-gadget-portlet`) and `Netvibes` (`netvibes-widget-portlet`). If you want to mash-up content from other sites, you only need to choose the proper widget type and paste the URL.

As mentioned earlier, the portal allows for external mash-ups, capabilities to share portlets in any websites via widgets. Under the tab **More | Configuration | Sharing** of any portlet, you could find the widget, a piece of JavaScript code. To share the portlet on any website, you have to just copy the widget code and paste it into a web page, and the portlet will show up in that web page. To share the portlet on Google Gadget, you can use the Google Gadget URL to create a Google Gadget such as the URL for the portlet Sign in (portlet ID) on the **home** page `http://localhost:8080/google_gadget/web/guest/home/-/58` to share the portlet on Netvibes, you could use the Netvibes Widget URL to create a Netvibes Widget such as a URL for the portlet Sign in on the **home** page `http://localhost:8080/netvibes/web/guest/home/-/58`.

Eventually, when publishing a portlet as a widget or gadget, you aren't publishing a copy, but pointing to the portlet, so that you always get the latest version. Note that if you select iGoogle, then you need to configure everything to run on port `80`, as Google removes the port information in URLs when adding widgets or gadgets.

The Widget Consumer portlet

The portlet Widget Consumer provides the ability to publish any widget code in the portal. For example, if you're going to publish **World Clock** widget in a page, you simply have to add the portlet Widget Consumer in the page first, then go to **More | Configuration | Setup Current**, paste in the widget code as follows, and click on the **Save** button.

```
<script src="http://www.gmodules.com/ig/ifr?url=http://www.cheap-
parking.net/world-clocks.xml&up_myTimeZone0=-5~EST-%20Eastern%20
Standard%20Time&up_myTimeZone1=-8~PST-%20Pacific%20Standard%20Time&syn
d=open&w=250&h=170&title=World+Clocks&border=%23ffffff%7C3px%2C1px+sol
id+%23999999&output=js"></script>
```

Of course, you could publish any kind of widget code. The only thing you need is to find the widget code and paste it into the portlet Widget Consumer.

How does it work?

The following is an option that could bring the portlet Widget Consumer into the portal:

1. Download the WAR file `${widget.consumer.portlet.war}` from `http://liferay.cignex.com/palm_tree/book/0387/chapter12/widget-consumer-portlet-6.0.0.1.war`

2. Drop the WAR file `${widget.consumer.portlet.war}` to the folder `$LIFERAY_HOME/deploy` when the portal is running.

Summary

This chapter introduced us to employing federated search and integrating search against content from plugins first. Then it discussed how to use the CSZ search and Map Search portlets. In particular, it discussed the OpenSearch concept. It also introduced us to Web Content search and how to configure sitemap and pluggable enterprise search. Finally, it discussed plugins management, WAP sites, reporting, auditing, CRM, and widgets.

In this chapter, we have learned how to:

- Employ federated search, OpenSearch, CSZ search, and Maps search
- Employ Web Content search
- Configure sitemap for search engines and pluggable enterprise search
- Manage plugins
- Build WAP sites
- Report and Audit
- Integrate with CRM and Netvibes widgets

In the next chapter, we're going to address ongoing admin tasks such as system administration, portal administration, dynamic data source settings (read-write data), database sharding, clustering, performance tuning, and full integration of Alfresco, OpenX, SSO, and LDAP with the portal.

11
Ongoing Admin Tasks

In the intranet website "bookpub.com" of the enterprise "Palm Tree Publications", it would be nice to have capabilities to manage servers and instances in order to employ password policies, update website settings, and monitor users' activities. Moreover, it may need to publish contents stored in third party systems such as Alfresco and OpenX. The portal provides system administration to manage servers and instances, and portal administration to manage password policies and enterprise information settings, and to monitor users' activities.

This chapter will introduce how to manage server and instances via system administration first. It will also discuss how to monitor portal and portlet operations, and how to set up dynamic data source called database read-writer and database sharding Then it will discuss how to use password policies, how to update portal settings, and how to monitor users' activities in portal administration It will address in details the clustering environment, data backup and migration, and performance tuning. It will also explain how to integrate with Alfresco, LDAP and CAS SSO. Finally, it will introduce Ad Server OpenX integration.

By the end of this chapter you will have learned how to:

- Manage servers and portal instances
- Use dynamic data source called database read-writer and database sharding
- Use password policies
- Update portal settings
- Monitor users' activities
- Build the clustering environment and run the portal in a cloud computing environment
- Backup data and migrate data
- Speed up the portal performance tuning

- Integrate with Alfresco, SSO CAS, and LDAP
- Integrate with ad server OpenX

Systems administration

The portlet Admin Server and Admin Instances provide abilities to view server information to administer resources, to create and manage instances, and so on. This section will introduce server management and instances management in depth.

Server management

The portlet Admin Server shows the portal version information, logging information, current live sessions, and so on. And it allows us to perform administratve tasks such as re-indexing, clearing caches, and so on. In brief, server administration involves many aspects such as **Resources, Log Levels, Properties, Data Migration, File Uploads, Mail, OpenOffice, Script**, and **Shutdown**.

Resources

As shown in the following screenshot, you're immediately presented with a graph showing the resources available in the JVM when going to **Server | Server Administration** in **Control Panel**.

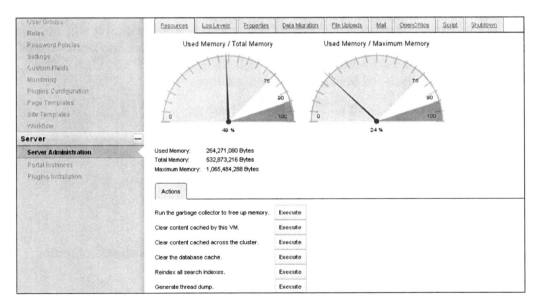

By the portlet Admin Server, you can manage resources of the server by clicking on the **Resources** tab and then click on the **Execute** button for following tasks:

- **Run the garbage collector to free up memory**: Begin the garbage collection task
- **Clear content cached by this VM**: Clear a single VM (Virtual Machine) cache
- **Clear content cached across the cluster**: Clear the cluster cache
- **Clear the database cache**: Clear the database cache
- **Re-index all search indexes**: Regenerate all search indexes
- **Generate thread dump**: Generate a thread dump for performance tuning

Note that re-indexing all search indexes will impact the portal performance if you are using Lucene indexing other than an enterprise engine like a Solr search server. So, we have a golden rule: don't re-index all search indexes except at non-peak times.

Shutdown

With the portlet Admin Server, you can also shutdown the server as follows:

1. Click on the **Shutdown** tab under **Server | Server Administration** of the Control Panel.
2. Input the number of minutes such as **5** before the server will be shutdown in the **Number of Minutes** box.
3. Add notes saying "shutdown server in 5 minutes" in the **Custom Message** box.
4. Click on the **Shutdown** button.
5. Optionally, you can cancel shutdown action. Enter a value such as **0** in the **Number of Minutes** box and click on the **Shutdown** button.

Log levels

You would be able to update the categories of log levels for any class hierarchy in the portal by changing the log levels, such as **OFF, FATAL, ERROR, WARN, INFO, DEBUG, ALL** under the **Log Levels** tab.

You can not only modify the log levels for any class hierarchy in the portal, but you can also modify the log levels for any class hierarchy for custom code. Suppose that you're going to debug CAS SSO integration; you could use the **Add Category** tab to add it like "org.jasig.cas.client".

Properties

You can view system properties under the **Properties | System Properties** tab, and survey portal properties under the **Properties | Portal Properties** tab. As mentioned earlier, the portal has provided system properties in `system.properties` and portal properties in `portal.properties`. And you may also have custom system properties in `system-ext.properties` and custom portal properties in `portal-ext.properties`. Therefore, you are able to verify both system properties and portal properties during runtime.

File upload

We have discussed how to configure file upload settings for many portlets through properties in `portal-ext.properties`. Fortunately, the portlet Admin Server provides capability to configure file upload settings through the web UI. By default, you would be able to configure file upload settings with the following items. Note that everything saved through the Admin UI is stored in the database and always override configurations in `portal.properties` and `portal-ext.properties`. So, even if you change configuration in `portal-ext.properties` after a modification here, it won't be considered.

```
General
Overall Maximum File Size:
Temporary Storage Directory:
Document Library
Maximum File Size:
Allowed File Extensions:
Image Gallery
Maximum File Size:
Allowed File Extensions:
Maximum Thumbnail Dimensions:
Web Content Images
Maximum File Size:
Allowed File Extensions:
Shopping Cart Images
Maximum File Size (Large Image):
Maximum File Size (Medium Image):
Maximum File Size (Small Image):
Allowed File Extensions:
Software Catalogue Images
Maximum File Size:
Maximum Thumbnail Height:
Maximum Thumbnail Width:
User Images
Maximum File Size:
```

As you can see, you would be able to update file size and add more allowed file extensions during runtime.

Mail

As mentioned in *Chapter 2, Setting Up a Home Page and Navigation Structure for the Intranet*, mail configuration could be specified in `portal-ext.properties`. In addition, the portlet Admin Server provides capability to configure mail through web UI. By default, you would be able to configure the mail server settings with the following items:

```
Incoming POP Server:
Incoming Port:
Use a Secure Network Connection:
User Name:
Password:
Outgoing SMTP Server:
Outgoing Port:
Use a Secure Network Connection:
User Name:
Password:
```

It seems that the preceding settings have limitations on mail configuration. Fortunately, the portlet Admin Server provides the capability to add advanced properties. Through advanced properties, you can manually specify additional Java Mail properties to override the above configuration by inputting custom advanced properties. That is, you would be able to configure mail engine with multiple properties.

As you can see, there are more tabs available in the Admin Server such as **Script, Data Migration,** and **OpenOffice**. We have discussed the tabs **Script** and **OpenOffice**, while the tab **Data Migration** will be addressed later in the next section.

What's happening?

The portlet Admin Server (Portlet ID 137) was displayed at the category **Server** of **Control Panel**. How does it work? The portal has specified default settings as follows in `$PORTAL_ROOT_HOME/WEB-INF/liferay-portlet.xml`.

```
<portlet-url-class>com.liferay.portal.struts.StrutsActionPortletURL</
portlet-url-class>
<control-panel-entry-category>server</control-panel-entry-category>
<control-panel-entry-weight>1.0</control-panel-entry-weight>
<control-panel-entry-class>com.liferay.portlet.admin.
OmniadminControlPanelEntry</control-panel-entry-class>
```

The preceding code shows that the portlet Admin Server will appear in the category **Server** and position **1**. And the `control-panel-entry-class` value is called by the Control Panel to decide whether the portlet should be shown to a specific user in a specific context.

Instances management

The portal provides capabilities to run multiple portal instances from one server installation. This allows you to run two or more completely separate portals on different domain names. Data for one portal instance is kept separate from every other portal instance. However, all portal data from different portal instances is kept in the same database by default. This scenario will change when using }database sharding.

Updating portal instances

As mentioned previously, the portal allows us to run more than one portal instance on a single server. That is, the portal may have many portal instances. Fortunately the portlet Admin Instance (portlet ID `135`) provides the ability to manage portal instances easily.

As shown in following screenshot, the portlet Admin Instances is located at the category **Server** of **Control Panel**. Log in as an admin say "Palm Tree" and go to the section **Server | Portal Instances**, and you will be able to see current existing portal instances.

As you can see, portal instances are displayed as a set of columns like **Instance ID**, **Web ID**, **Virtual Host**, **Mail Domain**, and **Number of users**. That is, each portal instance requires its own virtual host, web ID, and mail domain. The portal will direct users to the proper portal instance based on this domain name. Therefore, before you configure an instance, configure its domain name in your network first:

- **Instance ID**: System-generated ID for the portal instance.
- `Web ID`: Use domain name for the portal instance as a general convention; it's a user-generated ID for the portal instance.

- **Virtual Host**: Domain name configured in the network. When users are directed to your portal server via this domain name, the portal will then be able to send them to the proper portal instance.

- **Mail Domain**: Domain name for the mail hosted for this instance. The portal will use this to send email notifications from the portal.

Portal instances are editable. Suppose that you want to edit the instance with Web ID "liferay.com" and reset the main domain with a value, say "mail.bookpub.com". Let's do this as follows:

1. Locate the instance with Web ID say, "liferay.com".

2. Click on instance link such as **Instance ID**, **Web ID**, **Virtual Host**, **Mail Domain**, and **Number of Users.**

3. Change the item **Main Domain** with a value "mail.bookpub.com".

4. Click on the **Save** button if you want to save to your input, or click on the **Cancel** button if you want to cancel your input.

Adding portal instances

You can easily add a new instance. Suppose you want to add a new instance with web ID "bookpubstreet.com", virtual host `www.bookpubstreet.com` and mail domain "bookpubstreet.com". The following are options to create a new instance:

- Preparation: Use DNS configuration to assign a new domain to the server where the portal is installed, like "www.bookpubstreet.com", make sure all the necessary changes to external software, like web servers, load balancers, and firewalls, have also been made. Assume that the domain, `www.bookpubstreet.com`, has been set up.

- Access the portal as an administrator like "Palm Tree" and go to the section **Server | Portal Instances** under **Control Panel**.

- Click on the **Add** button.

- Fill fields: **Web ID**—"bookpubstreet.com", **Virtual Host**—"www.bookpubstreet.com", **Mail Domain**—"bookpubstreet.com".

- Click on the **Save** button if you want to save to your inputs, or click on the **Cancel** button if you want to cancel your inputs.

Now you can access the newly created instance in a different browser window. In this example, you could do it through the URL `http://www.bookpubstreet.com`, if the port number "80" was applied, or `http://www.bookpubstreet.com:8080`, if you are accessing Tomcat directly and is running in its default port.

Of course, you could create other portal instance as well. For example, you could create an instance with a web ID "bookpubworkshop.com", virtual host `www.bookpubworkshop.com` and mail domain "bookpubworkshop.com".

As you can see, the portal supports multiple portal instances in a single installation in order to obtain a complete isolation of the users, organizations, communities, and any other data created through portlets. Users in one portal instance have no information about the other portal instance. The portal instances are separated by domains and each portal instance exists in its own space identified by ID, such as portal instance ID.

By the way, the portal provides ability to create new portal instances directly from the web UI with no need to restart the application server. More interestingly, this method works well with any application server. In a word, the creation and administration of portal instances can be done through the portlet Admin Instances at Control Panel.

What's happening?

As you have seen, the portlet Admin Instances (portlet ID 135) gets displayed at the category **Server** of **Control Panel**. Why? The portal has default settings for the portlet Admin Instances as follows in `$PORTAL_ROOT_HOME/WEB-INF/liferay-portlet.xml`.

```
<portlet-url-class>com.liferay.portal.struts.StrutsActionPortletURL</
portlet-url-class>
<control-panel-entry-category>server</control-panel-entry-category>
<control-panel-entry-weight>2.0</control-panel-entry-weight>
<control-panel-entry-class>com.liferay.portlet.admin.
OmniadminControlPanelEntry</control-panel-entry-class>
```

The preceding code shows that the portlet Admin Instances will appear in the Category **Server** and position **2**. And the `control-panel-entry-class` value implemented `com.liferay.portlet.ControlPanelEntry`, called by the Control Panel to decide whether the portlet should be shown to a specific user in a specific context.

By the way, the default portal instance has Web ID "liferay.com". Why? The portal has specified following line by default in `portal.properties`.

```
company.default.web.id=liferay.com
```

As shown in the preceding code, the property `company.default.web.id` sets the default Web ID. Omni-admin users must belong to the company, that is, portal instance, with this Web ID. Of course, you would be able to override default Web ID in `portal-ext.properties`.

Considering the pattern `Portal-Group-Page-Content`, the portal is implemented by portal instances. That is, the portal can manage multiple portal instances in one installation. And each portal instance can have many groups, which are implemented as organizations, communities, user groups, and users.

Monitoring portal and portlets operations

The portal provides abilities to monitor portlet and portal transactions. These abilities include, but not limited:

- Average transaction times per portlet for each phase of the portlet life cycle
- Minimum and maximum transaction times for each portlet transaction
- Average times for portal requests, inclusive of all portlets
- Minimum and maximum times for each portal request

By the way, statistics were exposed via **JMX MBeans**. The portal also enables users to register MBeans from their own portlets. What is JMX ? JMX provides tools for managing and monitoring any Java applications network. Refer to `http://java.sun.com/javase/technologies/core/mntr-mgmt/javamanagement`.

Setup

The portal has specified the following properties for monitoring portal and portlet operations in `portal.properties`:

```
monitoring.level.com.liferay.monitoring.Portal=HIGH
monitoring.level.com.liferay.monitoring.Portlet=HIGH
monitoring.portal.request=false
monitoring.portlet.action.request=false
monitoring.portlet.event.request=false
monitoring.portlet.render.request=false
monitoring.portlet.resource.request=false
```

As shown in the preceding code, you can configure the appropriate level for monitoring Liferay. Valid values are: **HIGH**, **LOW**, **MEDIUM**, **OFF**. By default, monitoring on portal request and portlet action/event/render/resource request is disabled. Of course, you would be able to enable monitoring on portal request and portlet action/event/render/resource request by setting related properties to **true** in `portal-ext.properties`.

Database read-writer

The portal provides capability to use one database cluster for read calls and another database cluster for write calls, called dynamic data source or database read-writer. The portal allows us to use two different data sources for reading and writing, enabling us to split database infrastructure into two sets: one optimized for reading and another optimized for writing.

Setup

Suppose there are two database servers, `${database.reader}` and `${database.writer}`, and both of them are clustered. Here we're going to use these two different data sources for reading and writing, that is, `${database.reader}` for reading and `${database.writer}` for writing. How do we achieve this? The following is an option to set up database read-writer connections:

1. First, configure two different dynamic data sources in `portal-ext.properties`, one for reading, and one for writing:

   ```
   jdbc.read.driverClassName=com.mysql.jdbc.Driver
   jdbc.read.url=jdbc:mysql://${database.reader}:3306/lfso?useUnicode
   =true&characterEncoding=UTF-8&useFastDateParsing=false
   jdbc.read.username=lportal
   jdbc.read.password=lportal
   jdbc.write.driverClassName=com.mysql.jdbc.Driver
   jdbc.write.url=jdbc:mysql://${database.write}:3306/lfso?useUnicode
   =true&characterEncoding=UTF-8&useFastDateParsing=false
   jdbc.write.username=lportal
   jdbc.write.password=lportal
   ```

   As shown in the preceding code, MySQL was used as an example only. You would definitely be able to use another database. The database name, port number, user name, and password should be adjusted to real values too. Obviously, you should use real database domain names or IPs for both `${database.reader}` and `${database.writer}`.

2. Then, enable dynamic data source configuration for the property `spring.configs` as follows in `portal-ext.properties`.

   ```
   spring.configs=\
     # ignore details
     META-INF/audit-spring.xml,\
     META-INF/dynamic-data-source-spring.xml,\
     #META-INF/shard-data-source-spring.xml,\
     META-INF/monitoring-spring.xml,\
   ```

```
\
META-INF/ext-spring.xml
```

What's happening?

As you can see, you can configure the portal to use one database cluster for read calls and another database cluster for write calls. The convention is to create a set of properties prefixed with `jdbc.read.*` to handle read calls and another set of properties prefixed with `jdbc.write.*` to handle write calls. These data sources can also be created via JNDI by setting the properties `jdbc.read.jndi.name` and `jdbc.write.jndi.name`.

In fact, the portal has specified JDBC data sources, available for database read-writer in the `dynamic-data-source-spring.xml` file as follows:

```
<bean id="liferayDataSource" class="org.springframework.jdbc.
datasource.LazyConnectionDataSourceProxy">
 <property name="targetDataSource">
  <bean class="org.springframework.aop.framework.ProxyFactoryBean">
   <property name="targetSource" ref="dynamicDataSourceTargetSource"
/>
  </bean>
 </property>
</bean>
<!--ignore details -->
```

As shown in the preceding code, JDBC data sources like "read" and "write" have been configured as "jdbc.read." and "jdbc.write." in the `dynamic-data-source-spring.xml` file.

Database sharding

As mentioned above, we have discussed database read-writer—dynamic data source. And moreover, all portal data from different portal instances is kept in the same database by default. In real cases, portal data from different portal instances should be kept in different databases. That's the reason we need database sharding in portal instances. What's database sharding? Let's have a look at a shared-nothing partitioning scheme—**Database Sharding**.

Database Sharding is a shared-nothing partitioning scheme for large databases across a number of servers, enabling new levels of database performance and scalability. It provides a method for scalability across independent servers, each with their own CPU, memory, and disk. Refer to `http://www.codefutures.com/database-sharding`.

In general, database sharding is a way of scaling your database horizontally. For a set of tables, you could split up the data, stored and fetched based on a given hash. In database sharding, one database doesn't get overloaded; there are smaller queries, as each table has less data now. You will get better overall throughput under load as all your IO isn't going through one database server. The portal supports database sharding for handling data across multiple portal instances.

Setup

Suppose there are three intranet websites such as Bookpub, BookpubStreet, and Bookpubworkshop in the enterprise "Palm Tree Publications". These are named as "bookpub.com", "bookpubstreet.com", and "bookpubworkshop.com" in a single server; where "bookpub.com" would be the web ID for default portal instance. These three websites should have their data set in three separated databases; there are no data shared among these websites. How do we achieve this? One approach is setting these websites as different portal instances with database sharding in a single server. The following is an option to achieve it:

1. First, set the default web ID as follows in `portal-ext.properties`.

   ```
   company.default.web.id=bookpub.com
   ```

   The default value of the property `company.default.web.id` was set as `liferay.com` in `portal.properties`. Note that Omni-admin users must belong to the company with this web ID; and your default admin account will become "test@bookpub.com/test".

2. Second, prepare databases like `book`, `bookstreet`, and `bookworkshop` in `portal-ext.properties`. Note that you would have different database names, user names, and passwords with different database server IPs.

   ```
   jdbc.default.driverClassName=com.mysql.jdbc.Driver
   jdbc.default.url=jdbc:mysql://localhost/book?useUnicode=true&chara
   cterEncoding=UTF-8&useFastDateParsing=false
   jdbc.default.username=lportal
   jdbc.default.password=lportal
   jdbc.one.driverClassName=com.mysql.jdbc.Driver
   jdbc.one.url=jdbc:mysql://localhost:3306/bookstreet?useUnicode=tru
   e&characterEncoding=UTF-8&useFastDateParsing=false
   jdbc.one.username=lportal
   jdbc.one.password=lportal
   jdbc.two.driverClassName=com.mysql.jdbc.Driver
   jdbc.two.url=jdbc:mysql://localhost:3306/bookworkshop?useUnicode=t
   rue&characterEncoding=UTF-8&useFastDateParsing=false
   jdbc.two.username=lportal
   jdbc.two.password=lportal
   ```

3. Then enable database sharding by adding following lines in `portal-ext.properties`.

```
shard.available.names=default,one,two
shard.default.name=default
shard.selector=com.liferay.portal.dao.shard.
RoundRobinShardSelector
```

The property `shard.available.names` specifies JDBC data sources, available for database sharding. These must be configured in the `jdbc.*` section above as well as in the `shard-data-source-spring.xml` file. The property `shard.default.name` sets the database that is to be used for the default company and globally used tables in a sharded environment. The property `shard.selector` specifies an algorithm for selecting a new shard on portal instance creation. Using the algorithm `com.liferay.portal.dao.shard.RoundRobinShardSelector`, the portal will select from several different portal instances and evenly distribute the data across them. Note that you can use `com.liferay.portal.dao.shard.ManualShardSelector` for shard selection via the web UI.

4. Finally, make sure the spring configuration is included in the `portal-ext.properties` as follows, which by default is commented out:

```
spring.configs=\
  # ignore details
    #META-INF/dynamic-data-source-spring.xml,\
  META-INF/shard-data-source-spring.xml,\
  # ignore details
  META-INF/ext-spring.xml
```

The property `spring.configs` sets a list of comma delimited Spring configurations. These will be loaded after the bean definitions specified in the `contextConfigLocation` parameter in `$PORTAL_ROOT_HOME/WEB-INF/web.xml`.

What's happening?

Database Sharding is splitting up your database by various types of data that may be in it. It is a technique used for high scalability scenarios. When users log in, they are directed to the instance of the application that has their data in it.

In fact, the portal has specified JDBC data sources that are available for database sharding in the `shard-data-source-spring.xml` file as follows:

```
<bean id="liferayDataSource" class="org.springframework.jdbc.
datasource.LazyConnectionDataSourceProxy">
 <property name="targetDataSource">
```

```
<bean class="org.springframework.aop.framework.ProxyFactoryBean">
  <property name="targetSource" ref="shardDataSourceTargetSource" />
</bean>
</property>
</bean>
<!--ignore details -->
```

As shown in the preceding code, JDBC data sources such as "default", "one", and "two" have been configured as "jdbc.default.", "jdbc.one.", and "jdbc.two." in the `shard-data-source-spring.xml` file.

Of course, you would be able to customize it according to your requirements. Suppose you want four shard data sources: default, one, two, and three. You're going to build four portal instances, where each portal instance has its own database. How do we implement it? The following is one option:

1. Create a folder named `META-INF` under the folder `$PORTAL_ROOT_HOME/WEB-INF/classes/`.

2. Locate the JAR `portal-impl.jar` under the folder `$PORTAL_ROOT_HOME/WEB-INF/lib`; and unzip all files under the folder `META-INF` to the folder `$PORTAL_ROOT_HOME/WEB-INF/classes/META-INF`.

3. Update following file according to your requirements for both non-clustered environment and clustered environment.

   `shard-data-source-spring.xml`

4. And finally do the related changes in the `jdbc.*` section and in the property `shard.available.names`.

Portal administration

The portal provides portal administrative functions. Thus we can not only access all organizations, roles, user groups, and users, but we can also manage portal version information and enterprise information such as organization name, ticker symbol, address, logo, current live sessions, authentication preferences, LDAP configuration and SSO integration, new user preferences, mail configuration, password policies, and more. We have discussed authentications in *Chapter 3, Bringing in Users*. In this section we're going to discuss password policies, enterprise information settings, and current live sessions.

Password policies

The portal implements enterprise password policies and user account lockout. As shown in the following screenshot, you can go to **Portal | Password Policies** under **Control Panel** and manage password policies.

You can either search the password policies by inputting search keyword and clicking on the **Search** button, or add the password policies by clicking on the **Add** icon next to the icon **View All**.

You can also either update permissions by clicking on the **Permissions** icon from the **Actions** button, or change members by clicking on the **Assign Members** icon from the **Actions** button.

You can edit password policies by clicking on the **Edit** icon from the **Actions** button first, and then you can change the settings of password policies as follows:

You can use **Changeable Settings** as follows:

- **Changeable**: Allow user to change his/her own password
- **Change Required**: Require the user to change his password when the user first logs in
- **Minimum Age**: Determines how long a user must wait before changing their password again

You can change **Password Syntax Checking** by enabling the checkbox **Syntax Checking Enabled** first, and then configuring the following items:

- **Syntax Checking Enabled**: Enable portal to check for certain words and length requirements
- **Allow Dictionary Words**: Allow a dictionary word to be used as the password
- **Minimum Length**: The minimum length of a password

You can also change **Password History** by enabling the checkbox **History Enabled** first and then configuring the following items:

- **History Enabled**: Enable tracking of password history, to prevent reuse of old passwords
- **History Count**: The number of passwords to keep in the history

Similarly, you can update **Password Expiration** by enabling the checkbox **Expiration Enabled** and configuring the following items:

- **Expiration Enabled**: Enable passwords to expire after a specified time
- **Maximum Age**: The maximum time that a password is valid, before it needs to be changed again
- **Warning Time**: The time before a password expires, in which to warn the user of the upcoming password expiration
- **Grace Limit**: The number of logins allowed after the password has already expired.

To update **User Account Lockout,** you can click on the checkbox **Lockout Enabled** and then configure following items.

- **Lockout Enabled**: Enable user accounts to get locked out after a specified number of failed logins
- **Maximum Failure**: The maximum number of failed login attempts before the account is locked out
- **Reset Failure Count**: The time before the "failed login count" is reset
- **Lockout Duration**: The time that a user is locked out, preventing them from logging back in

In a word, the portal provides ability to implement enterprise password policies and user account lockout. Password policies are managed internally from the portlet Enterprise Admin Password Policies (portlet ID `129`). Note that everything here can be configured in `portal-ext.properties` as well.

Assigning permissions

There are two-level permissions related to Password Policies: permission on portlet and permissions on password policies.

The following table shows permissions on the portlet. The role Community Member is set up with all the permissions (marked as 'X'): **View**, **Configuration** and **Access in Control Panel**, while the role Guest is set up with the permission action **View**. By default, the roles Community Member & Guest have permission action View (marked as '*').

Action	Description	Community	Guest
View	Ability to view the portlet	X, *	X, *
Configuration	Ability to configure the portlet	X	
Access in Control panel	Ability to access the portlet in Control Panel	X	

The following table shows permissions on password policies. The role Community Member is set up with the permissions (marked as 'X'): **View, Delete, Permissions, Assign Members,** and **Update.**

Action	Description	Community	Guest
View	Ability to view password policies	X	
Delete	Ability to delete password policies	X	
Permissions	Ability to assign permissions on password policies	X	
Update	Ability to update password policies	X	
Assign Members	Ability to assign members on password policies	X	

What's happening?

As you have seen, the Enterprise Password Policies portlet (portlet ID 129) gets displayed at the category **Portal** of **Control Panel**. Why? The portal has default settings for the Enterprise Admin Password Policies portlet as follows in $PORTAL_ ROOT_HOME/WEB-INF/liferay-portlet.xml.

```
<portlet-url-class>com.liferay.portal.struts.StrutsActionPortletURL</
portlet-url-class>
<control-panel-entry-category>portal</control-panel-entry-category>
<control-panel-entry-weight>6.0</control-panel-entry-weight>
```

The preceding code shows that the portlet Enterprise Password Policies will appear in the category **Portal** and position **6**. And moreover, the portlet-url-class value extends com.liferay.portlet.PortletURLImplWrapper.

Portal settings

You can update enterprise information under the **Portal** | **Settings** of **Control Panel** like general configuration, authentication, default user associations, reversed screen names, mail host names, email notifications, addresses, phone numbers, additional email addresses, websites, display settings, and Google Apps. The following figure depicts the main tabs which can be used to change the enterprise information in details.

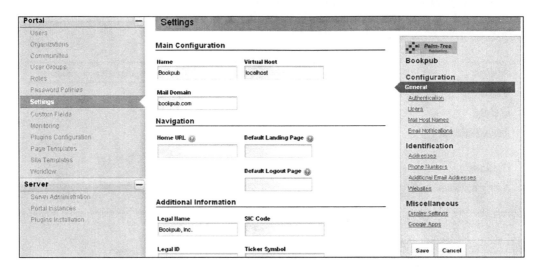

As you can see, the portlet Enterprise Admin Settings provides capabilities to update enterprise information under the **Portal** | **Settings** of the **Control Panel**. Portal settings have been grouped into three sections at the right-side menu under the portal logo and portal name: **Configuration**, **Identification**, and **Miscellaneous**. Each section has a set of items as follows:

The set of items within the Configuration section are as follows:

- **General**: Including main configuration, navigation and additional information

- **Authentication**: Including general authentication information, LDAP. CAS, NTLM, OpenID, Open SSO, Siteminder

- **Users**: Covering Fields, Reserved Credentials and Default User Associations

- **Mail Host Names**: Enter one mail host name per line for all additional mail host names

- **Email Notifications**: Covering Sender, Account Created Notification, and Password Changed Notification

The set of items within the Identification section are as follows:

- **Addresses**: Supporting multiple addresses for the portal instance
- **Phone Numbers**: Supporting multiple phone numbers for the portal instance
- **Websites**: Supporting multiple websites for the portal instance

The set of items within the Miscellaneous section are as follows:

- **Display Settings**: Covering language and time zone, logo, look and feel
- **Google Apps**: The default user name and password for Google Apps integration

General information

Under the **Configuration | General** tab selected, you can change the enterprise's information as follows:

The **Main Configuration**:

- **Name**: Default value comes from the value of the property `company.default.web.id`, the value will be the name of Guest community in navigation breadcrumb.
- **Virtual Host**: Default value is localhost.
- **Mail Domain**: Default value comes from the value of the property `company.default.web.id`; set the property `mail.mx.update` to **false** if the administrator should not be allowed to change the mail domain.

The **Navigation**:

- **Home URL**: This is the home page of the portal. For example, if you want the home page to be `http://localhost:8080/web/guest/home`, then set this to `/web/guest/home`; the default value comes from the value of the property `company.default.home.url`.
- **Default Landing Page**: This is the page that users are automatically redirected to after logging in. For example, if you want the default landing page to be `http://localhost:8080/web/guest/login`, then set this to `/web/guest/login`; the default value comes from the value of the property `default.landing.page.path`.
- **Default Logout Page**: This is the page that users are automatically redirected to after logging out. For example, if you want the default logout page to be `http://localhost:8080/web/guest/logout`, then set this to `/web/guest/logout`; the default value comes from the value of the property `default.logout.page.path`.

- **Additional Information**: Additional Information such as **Legal Name**, **Legal ID, Legal Type, SIC Code, Ticker Symbol, Industry Type**.

Users

As mentioned above, the item Users covers the tabs such as **Fields**, **Reserved Credentials**, and **Default User Associations**. Under the tab **Fields**, you can change the default user settings as follows:

- **Terms of Use Required**: Checked by default.
- **Auto-generate User Screen Names**: Un-checked by default.
- **Enable Birthday**: Checked by default.
- **Enable Gender**: Checked by default.

Under the **Reserved Credentials** tab, you can change the default **Reserved Credentials** with newly created users as follows:

- **Screen Names**: Enter one screen name per line to reserve the screen name.
- **Email Addresses**: Enter one user email address per line to reserve the user email address.

Under the **Default User Associations** tab, you can change the default associations with newly created users as follows:

- **Apply to Existing Users**: Check to apply the changes to existing users. Changes take effect the next time a user signs in.
- **Communities**: Enter the default community names per line that are associated with newly created users.
- **Roles**: Enter the default role names per line that are associated with newly created users. Note that these are roles of the type regular.
- **User Groups**: Enter the default user group names per line that are associated with newly created users.

Email notifications

As mentioned above, the item **Email Notifications** covers the tabs such as **Sender**, **Account Created Notifications**, and **Password Changed Notifications**. Under the tab **Sender**, you can change the configuration of email notifications of the sender as follows:

- **Name**: Sender's name
- **Address**: Sender's email address

Under the tabs **Account Created Notifications** or **Password Changed Notifications**, you can change the configuration of email account created notifications or password changed notifications as follows:

- **Enabled**: Checked by default for both email account created notifications and password changed notifications
- **Subject**: The subject of email account created notifications or password changed notifications
- **Body**: The body of email account created notifications or password changed notifications

Display settings

Fortunately you are able to update display settings of the portal instance, such as **Language** and **Time Zone**, **Logo**, **Look and Feel**.

The various settings within **Language and Time Zone** are as follows:

- **Default Language**: Default value is English (United States)
- **Available Languages**: Default value comes from the property `locales`
- **Time Zone**: Default value is UTC

The various settings within **Logo** are as follows:

- **Allow community administrators to use their own logo**: Checked by default
- **Change/Delete**: Uploading or deleting logo icon

The various settings within **Look and Feel** are as follows:

- **Default Regular Theme**: Default value is**Classic**
- **Default Mobile Theme**: Default value is**Mobile**
- **Default Control Panel Theme**: Default value is **Control Panel**

How does it work?

As you have seen, the Enterprise Admin Settings portlet (portlet ID `130`) got displayed at the category **Portal** of **Control Panel**. Why? The portal has default settings for the Enterprise Admin Settings portlet as follows in `$PORTAL_ROOT_HOME/WEB-INF/liferay-portlet.xml`.

```
<control-panel-entry-category>portal</control-panel-entry-category>
<control-panel-entry-weight>7.0</control-panel-entry-weight>
```

The above code shows that the Enterprise Admin Setting portlet will appear in the category **Portal** and position **7**.

What's happening?

As you can see, there are three sections in portal settings, **Configuration**, **Identification**, and **Miscellaneous**, and each section has a different set of items. What's happening? The portal has the following settings for the company settings form in `portal.properties`:

```
company.settings.form.configuration=general,authentication,users,mail-
host-names,email-notifications
company.settings.form.identification=addresses,phone-
numbers,additional-email-addresses,websites
company.settings.form.miscellaneous=display-settings,google-apps
```

As shown in the preceding code, you could input a list of sections that will be included as part of the company settings form. Of course, you would be able to customize this setting form by updating the above properties in `portal-ext.properties`. For example, adding a new item, or removing an existing item.

The portal has specified the following properties for general information about the portal settings.

```
company.default.web.id=liferay.com
mail.mx.update=true
company.default.home.url=/web/guest
default.landing.page.path=
default.logout.page.path=
```

As shown in the preceding code, the property `company.default.web.id` sets the default web ID. The property `mail.mx.update` is set to true so that the administrator is allowed to change the mail domain, while the property `company.default.home.url` sets the default home URL of the portal.

The property `default.landing.page.path` sets the default landing page path for logged in users relative to the server path. This is the page that users are automatically redirected to after logging in. For example, if you want the default landing page to be `http://localhost:8080/web/guest/login`, set this to `/web/guest/login`. To activate this feature, set the property `auth.forward.by.last.path` to true.

The property `default.logout.page.path` sets the default logout page path for users relative to the server path. This is the page that users are automatically redirected to after logging out. For example, if you want the default logout page to be `http://localhost:8080/web/guest/logout`, set this to `/web/guest/logout`. To activate this feature, set the property `auth.forward.by.last.path` to true.

The portal has specified the following properties related to Users at the portal settings:

```
terms.of.use.required=true
users.screen.name.always.autogenerate=false
field.enable.com.liferay.portal.model.Contact.male=true
field.enable.com.liferay.portal.model.Contact.birthday=true
admin.reserved.screen.names=
admin.reserved.email.addresses=
admin.default.group.names=
admin.default.role.names=Power User\nUser
admin.default.user.group.names=
admin.sync.default.associations=false
```

As shown in the preceding code, the property `terms.of.use.required` is set to true if all users are required to agree to the terms of use. As mentioned earlier, you would be able to modify this feature via Web UI. The property `users.screen.name.always.autogenerate` is set to true to always auto-generate user screen names even if the user gives a specific user screen name.

The properties `field.enable.com.liferay.portal.model.Contact.male` and `field.enable.com.liferay.portal.model.Contact.birthday` set policies when requiring gender and birthday information. Of course, you should set these properties to `false` in the `portal-ext.properties` so users can't see them, if your company policies require gender and birthday information to always be hidden.

The properties `admin.reserved.screen.names` and `admin.reserved.email.addresses` set reserved screen names and reserved email addresses. You should be able to input a list of reserved screen names separated by \n characters, as well as a list of reserved email addresses separated by \n characters.

The properties `admin.default.group.names`, `admin.default.role.names` and `admin.default.user.group.names` set default group names, role names, and user group names that are associated with newly created users. You should be able to input a list of group names or role names or user group names separated by \n characters. The property `admin.sync.default.associations` is set to false, so default associations should only be applied to a user when a user is created. You should be able to set this property to true in `portal-ext.properties` to ensure that a user is synchronized with the default associations of groups, roles, and user groups upon every login.

By the way, the portal has specified the following properties related to both Users and Organizations when they are created:

```
field.enable.com.liferay.portal.model.Organization.status=false
field.editable.com.liferay.portal.model.User.screenName=user
field.editable.com.liferay.portal.model.User.emailAddress=user
```

As shown in the preceding code, you should be able to enable Organization status by setting `field.enable.com.liferay.portal.model.Organization.status` to true in `portal-ext.properties`. The portal sets properties `field.editable.com.liferay.portal.model.User.screenName` and `field.editable.com.liferay.portal.model.User.emailAddress` to user, so a user can edit his/her own field. You would be able to set these to `administrator` if only an administrator can edit that field. For example, some installations will allow users to change their own screen names. Other installations may only allow administrators to change screen names. As you can see, an administrator is anyone who has the Administrator role.

Moreover, the portal has specified the following default setting on mail host names of the portal instance:

```
admin.mail.host.names=
```

As shown in above code, the property `admin.mail.host.names` sets mail host names. Of course, you could input a list of mail host names separated by \n characters in `portal-ext.properties`.

The portal has specified the following default settings on email notifications of the portal instance:

```
admin.email.from.name=Joe Bloggs
admin.email.from.address=test@liferay.com
admin.email.user.added.enabled=true
admin.email.user.added.subject=com/liferay/portlet/admin/dependencies/
email_user_added_subject.tmpl
admin.email.user.added.body=com/liferay/portlet/admin/dependencies/
email_user_added_body.tmpl
admin.email.password.sent.enabled=true
admin.email.password.sent.subject=com/liferay/portlet/admin/
dependencies/email_password_sent_subject.tmpl
admin.email.password.sent.body=com/liferay/portlet/admin/dependencies/
email_password_sent_body.tmpl
```

As shown in the preceding code, the property `admin.email.from.*` sets email from name and address, and the property `admin.email.user.added.*` sets email body and subject when email account is created, while the property `admin.email.password.sent.*` sets email body and subject when password is changed.

The portal has specified the following properties for display settings of the portal instance in `portal-ext.properties`.

```
locales=ar_SA,eu_ES,bg_BG,ca_AD,ca_ES,zh_CN,zh_TW,cs_CZ,nl_NL,en_
US,fi_FI,fr_FR,gl_ES,de_DE,el_GR,hu_HU,it_IT,ja_JP,ko_KR,nb_NO,fa_
IR,pl_PL,pt_BR,pt_PT,ru_RU,sk_SK,es_ES,sv_SE,tr_TR,vi_VN
time.zones=Pacific/Midway,Pacific/Honolulu,America/Anchorage,America/
Los_Angeles,America/Denver,America/Chicago,America/New_York,America/
Puerto_Rico,America/St_Johns,America/Sao_Paulo,America/
Noronha,Atlantic/Azores,UTC,Europe/Lisbon,Europe/Paris,Europe/
Istanbul,Asia/Jerusalem,Asia/Baghdad,Asia/Tehran,Asia/Dubai,Asia/
Kabul,Asia/Karachi,Asia/Calcutta,Asia/Katmandu,Asia/Dhaka,Asia/
Rangoon,Asia/Saigon,Asia/Shanghai,Asia/Tokyo,Asia/Seoul,Australia/
Darwin,Australia/Sydney,Pacific/Guadalcanal,Pacific/Auckland,Pacific/
Enderbury,Pacific/Kiritimati
company.security.community.logo=true
default.regular.theme.id=classic
default.wap.theme.id=mobile
control.panel.layout.regular.theme.id=controlpanel
```

As shown in the above code, the portal specifies the available locales and time zones. The property `company.security.community.logo` is set to true to allow community administrators to use their own logo instead of the enterprise logo. The default regular theme is set to **Classic** via the property `default.regular.theme.id`, the default WAP theme is set to **Mobile** via the property `default.wap.theme.id`, and the Control Panel layout regular theme is set to **controlpanel** via the property `control.panel.layout.regular.theme.id`.

By the way, the default language, country and time zone are set in `system.properties` with the following properties:

```
user.country=US
user.language=en
user.timezone=UTC
```

As shown in above code, the portal sets the default locale like country as `US` and language as `en`. The portal also sets the default time zone as `UTC`. Of course, you can override the above properties in `system-ext.properties`.

In addition, the portal has configured following properties in `portal.properties`:

```
google.apps.username=
google.apps.password=
```

As shown in the above code, the portal sets the default user name and password for Google Apps integration. Note that the domain used by Google Apps is retrieved from the portal's mail domain.

Fortunately you will be able to customize portal settings by modifying JSP files at `$PORTAL_ROOT_HOME/html/portlet/enterprise_admin/settings`.

Monitoring live users' activities

As an administrator say "Palm Tree" at the enterprise "Palm Tree Publications", you may need to monitor users' activities. Suppose that the users "Lotti Stein" and "David Berger" are online now. Let's monitor their activities as follows:

1. Log into the portal as an administrator say "Palm Tree".
2. Go to **Manage** | **Control Panel** under the dock bar menu.
3. Click the tab **Portal** | **Monitoring** under Control Panel.
4. A set of live sessions will appear with **Session ID**, **User ID**, **Name**, **Screen Name**, **Last Request**, and **Number of Hits**. For example, "David Berger" has **6** hits and "Lotti Stein" has **5** hits.

Of course, you can display details of a user's session. To do so, select a session by clicking on the user name such as "Lotti Stein" as a link. Then you would see details of a user's session as follows:

- **Session ID**: such as D73CEB992A3BC5D77D4B181A670EA808
- **User ID**: such as 10303
- **Name**: such as Lotti Stein
- **Email Address**: such as lotti@bookpub.com
- **Last Request**: such as 12/20/09 3:06 PM
- **# of Hits**: such as 5
- **Browser/OS Type**: such as Mozilla/5.0 (Windows; U; Windows NT 5.1; en-US; rv:1.9.1.6) Gecko/20091201 Firefox/3.5.6 GTB6
- **Remote Host/IP**: 127.0.0.1 / 127.0.0.1
- **Accessed URLs**: such as /portal/layout?p_l_id=10147?, and so on
- **Session Attributes**: such as HTTPS_INITIAL, LAST_PATH, and so on

In addition, you can terminate a user's session. To end a user's session, select a session by clicking on the user name say "Lotti Stein" as a link first. Then in **Live Session** click on the **Kill Session** button. Note that you can't kill your own session.

How does it work?

By default, display of live session data is disabled, as the portal has the following setting for displaying live session data in `portal.properties`:

```
live.users.enabled=false
```

To enable tracking via live users, you should set the following portal property in `portal-ext.properties`:

```
live.users.enabled=true
```

What's happening?

As you have seen, the portlet Enterprise Admin Monitoring (portlet ID 131) was displayed at the category **Portal** of **Control Panel**. Why? The portal has default settings for the portlet Enterprise Admin Monitoring as follows in `$PORTAL_ROOT_HOME/WEB-INF/liferay-portlet.xml`:

```
<portlet-url-class>com.liferay.portal.struts.StrutsActionPortletURL</
portlet-url-class>
<control-panel-entry-category>portal</control-panel-entry-category>
<control-panel-entry-weight>9.0</control-panel-entry-weight>
```

The above code shows that the portlet Enterprise Admin Monitoring will appear in the category **Portal** and position **9**. The `portlet-url-class` value extends `com.liferay.portlet.PortletURLImplWrapper`.

Clustering - high availability

Clustering allows us to run portal instances on several parallel servers, called cluster nodes. The load is distributed across different servers, and even if any of the servers fail, the portal is still accessible via other cluster nodes. Clustering is crucial for scalable portal enterprise, as you can improve performance by simply adding more nodes to the cluster.

For larger installations, you would likely need a clustered configuration in order to handle the traffic of a popular website. A cluster allows us to distribute the traffic coming in to a website to several machines. It allows websites to handle more web traffic at a faster pace than would be possible with a single machine. The portal definitely works well in a clustered environment.

A cluster is a set of nodes. Suppose that there are two nodes: **Node1** and **Node2**. We're going to use Apache HTTP server and database MySQL as shown in the following screenshot. In real cases, you may have more than two nodes, but the process of clustering configuration should be the same.

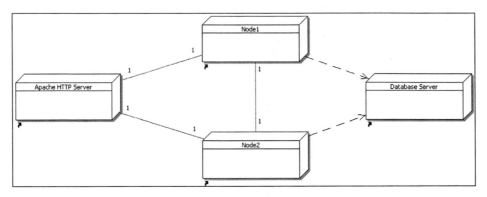

Before starting, you need to set four environment variables: $JAVA_HOME, $TOMCAT_AS_DIR, $JBOSS_AS_DIR and $APACHE_HTTPD_DIR. $JAVA_HOME should point to JDK installation directory, $TOMCAT_AS_DIR should point to the installation directory for Tomcat, $JBOSS_AS_DIR should point to the installation directory for JBoss and $APACHE_HTTPD_DIR should point to the installation directory for Apache HTTPD.

And moreover, Apache HTTP Server has been installed at the $APACHE_DIR directory.

Apache HTTP Server has the following settings:

```
IP: 192.168.2.170
Apache Tomcat Connector mod_jk 1.2 or above
Apache JServ Protocol AJP 1.3 or above
JDK 1.6 or above
Apache HTTP Server 2.2 or above
```

Node1 has the following settings:

```
IP: 192.168.2.171;
Portal with Tomcat 6.x or JBoss 5.x.GA (or JBoss 4.2.3.GA)
```

Node2 has the following settings:

```
IP: 192.168.2.172;
Portal with Tomcat 6.x or JBoss 5.x.GA (or JBoss 4.2.3.GA)
```

Database server has the following settings

```
IP: 192.168.2.173;
Database MySQL 5.0 or above
```

HTTP services

HTTP session replication is used to replicate the state associated with portals on other nodes of a cluster. Thus, in the event that one node crashes, another node in the cluster will be able to recover. There are two ways of clustering portals on Tomcat or JBoss. Here we use **Sticky Session** as an example:

- **Sticky Session**: User request will always go to the same portal instance.
- **Session Replication**: Users requests can go to any tomcat or JBoss in cluster and their session is copied on entire cluster.

Configuring mod_jk

First of all, we need to install mode_jk, which is the connector used to connect Tomcat JSP container with web servers such as Apache. Simply download the latest version from http://apache.tradebit.com/pub/tomcat/tomcat-connectors/jk/binaries. Depending on the physical box of Apache HTTP server, you need to choose OS and furthermore choose either 32-bit or 64-bit. The terms 32-bit and 64-bit refer to the way a computer's processor handles information.

After downloading, rename it to mod_jk.so before putting it in $APACHE_HTTPD_DIR/ modules directory. With mod_jk installed, we must now configure Apache to load the module by editing $APACHE_HTTPD_DIR/conf/httpd.conf. Configuring Apache to load mod_jk is a simple two-line step—add the following lines at the end of $APACHE_HTTPD_DIR/conf/httpd.conf:

```
#Load the mod_jk connector
LoadModule jk_module modules/mod_jk.so
```

Then we need to configure worker properties. A Tomcat worker is a Tomcat instance that is waiting to execute servlets or any other content on behalf of some web server. For example, we can have a web server such as Apache forwarding servlet requests to a Tomcat process (the worker) running behind it. To do so, we should create a file named workers.properties at $APACHE_HTTPD_DIR/conf with the following settings:

```
# Define list of workers that will be used
# for mapping requests
worker.list=loadbalancer,status
# Define Node1
# modify the host as your host IP or DNS name.
worker.node1.port=8009
worker.node1.host=192.168.2.171
worker.node1.type=ajp13
worker.node1.lbfactor=1
```

```
# Define Node2
# modify the host as your host IP or DNS name.
worker.node2.port=8009
worker.node2.host=192.168.2.172
worker.node2.type=ajp13
worker.node2.lbfactor=1
# Load-balancing behaviour
worker.loadbalancer.type=lb
worker.loadbalancer.balance_workers=node1,node2
worker.loadbalancer.sticky_session=1
# Status worker for managing load balancer
worker.status.type=status
```

As shown in the preceding code, mod_jk uses a file named workers.properties, defining where Apache looks for the Tomcat instances. worker.list is a comma-separated list of worker names. Each worker needs to define the port on which the connector is configured to work; for example, 8009 for both **Node1** and **Node2**.

Finally, to get all of this started, we need to tell Apache where to find the workers.properties file and where to log mod_jk requests. We also need to specify the format of the log files and the options specific to mod_jk. To do so, simply add the following line at the end of $APACHE_HTTPD_DIR/conf/httpd.conf:

```
JkWorkersFile conf/workers.properties
JkLogFile logs/mod_jk.log
JkLogLevel error
JkLogStampFormat "[%a %b %d %H:%M:%S %Y]"
JkMount /* loadbalancer
```

The preceding code tells Apache to use $APACHE_HTTPD_DIR/conf/workers.properties for the worker definitions and to use the $APACHE_HTTPD_DIR/logs/mod_jk.log log file.

In addition, it would be better to serve all images and CSS from Apache htdocs directly. How do we achieve this? The following is one option:

1. Copy $PORTAL_ROOT_HOME/html to $APACHE_HTTPD_DIR/htdocs.

2. Copy $AS_WEB_APP_HOME/${plugin.name} to $APACHE_HTTPD_DIR/htdocs, where ${plugin.name} represents custom themes, portlets, webs, and so on.

3. Add the following lines at the end of $APACHE_HTTPD_DIR/conf/httpd.conf:

```
Jkunmount /*.jpg loadbalancer
Jkunmount /*.gif loadbalancer
Jkunmount /*.png loadbalancer
```

```
Jkunmount /*.ico loadbalancer
Jkunmount /*.css loadbalancer
```

Note we have to repeat this process each time we want to upgrade the portal.

Configuring Tomcat

In the `$TOMCAT_AS_DIR/conf/server.xml` file, find the line that reads:

```
<Engine name="Catalina" defaultHost="localhost">
```

Change it for each VM so that it includes the appropriate worker name. For `node1`, it would look like the following line:

```
<Engine name="Catalina" defaultHost="localhost" jvmRoute="node1">
```

For `node2`, it would look like the following line:

```
<Engine name="Catalina" defaultHost="localhost" jvmRoute="node2">
```

In order to enable Tomcat clustering, add the following code in `$TOMCAT_AS_DIR/conf/server.xml`:

```
<Cluster className="org.apache.catalina.ha.tcp.SimpleTcpCluster"
channelSendOptions="6">
  <Manager className="org.apache.catalina.ha.session.BackupManager"
expireSessionsOnShutdown="false"
notifyListenersOnReplication="true"
mapSendOptions="6"/> <!-- ignore details -->
</Cluster>
```

In order to enable session replication, edit `$TOMCAT_AS_DIR/conf/context.xml`, and update `<Context>` with `<Context distributable="true">`.

Configuring JBoss

In the `$JBOSS_AS_DIR/server/default/deploy/jbossweb.sar/server.xml` file (for JBoss `4.2.3.GA`, the web folder is `/jboss-web.deployer` instead of `/jbossweb.sar`), find the line that reads:

```
<Engine name="jboss.web" defaultHost="localhost">
```

Change it for each VM so that it includes the appropriate worker name. For `node1`, it would look like the following line:

```
<Engine name="jboss.web" defaultHost="localhost" jvmRoute="node1">
```

For `node2`, it would look like the following line:

```
<Engine name="jboss.web" defaultHost="localhost" jvmRoute="node2">
```

To enable replication of your web application sessions, you need to tag the portal as distributable in the `$PORTAL_ROOT_HOME/WEB_INF/web.xml` descriptor. The following is an example:

```
<?xml version="1.0" encoding="UTF-8"?>
<web-app xmlns="http://java.sun.com/xml/ns/j2ee" xmlns:xsi="http://
www.w3.org/2001/XMLSchema-instance" xsi:schemaLocation="http://java.
sun.com/xml/ns/j2ee http://java.sun.com/xml/ns/j2ee/web-app_2_4.xsd"
version="2.4">
    <!-- ignore details -->
    <distributable/>
</web-app>
```

Configuring portal

For each node, add the following lines at the end of `portal-ext.properties`:

```
net.sf.ehcache.configurationResourceName=/ehcache/hibernate-
clustered.xml
ehcache.multi.vm.config.location=/ehcache/liferay-multi-vm-
clustered.xml
```

Database replication and clustering

There are two options to cluster databases: database replication and database clustering.

Database replication is the frequent copying of data from a database in one server to a database in another. The result is a distributed database in which the portals can access data relevant to their tasks without interfering with the work of others.

When using MySQL database and spreading the load across multiple servers, you can setup database replication. Almost in real-time, copying all commands from the master server to the slave server, the database will keep the data the same on both servers, so that both servers can serve requests simultaneously, sharing the load. The following is an example:

- Create a user on the Master server that allows replication:
  ```
  # mysql -u root -p
  mysql> grant replication slave on *.* TO repl@"%" identified by
  '${repl.password}';
  mysql> quit
  ```

- Edit the file `my.cnf` to start binary logging of the Master server. Under the `[mysqld]` heading add the following lines:
  ```
  log-bin=mysql-bin
  server-id=1
  binlog-ignore-db="mysql"
  ```

- Restart the MySQL Master server service.

- Copy the databases to Slave server.

- Edit the Slave server's MySQL configuration file `my.cnf` to identify its server number, master host and user. Under the `[mysqld]` heading add the following lines:
  ```
  server-id=2
  master-host = ${ip.master.server}
  master-user = repl
  master-password = ${repl.password}
  master-port = 3306
  ```

  Note that you should replace `${repl.password}` with the actual `repl` user password, and `${ip.master.server}` with the IP address of the Master server.

- Restart the MySQL Slave server service.

Database clustering offers load balancing and transparent failover. Databases are replicated over multiple nodes in the clustering environment.

Sequoia is a database clustering middleware offering load balancing and transparent failover. Within Sequoia, databases are replicated over multiple nodes; Sequoia balances the queries between them, supporting online maintenance and recovery operations. Refer to `http://sequoiadb.sourceforge.net`.

Repository clustering

Jackrabbit clustering works: content is shared between all cluster nodes. That means all Jackrabbit cluster nodes need access to the same persistent storage (persistence manager and data store). The cluster nodes store information identifying items they modified in a journal. This journal must again be globally available to all nodes in the cluster. This can be either a folder in the file system (called file journal) or a standalone database (called database journal).

First, use a file-based journal implementation, where the journal files are created in a shared folder exported by NFS, for example, /nfs/server/journal:

```
<Cluster id="node1" syncDelay="5">
  <Journal class="org.apache.jackrabbit.core.journal.FileJournal">
    <param name="revision" value="${rep.home}/revision.log" />
    <param name="directory" value="/nfs/server/journal" />
  </Journal>
</Cluster>
```

As shown in the preceding code, the file journal is configured for node1 through the following properties: revision — location of the cluster node's revision file, directory — location of the journal folder. Do the same in node2 with the value id="node2".

```
<Cluster id="node1" syncDelay="5">
  <Journal class="org.apache.jackrabbit.core.journal.DatabaseJournal">
    <param name="revision" value="${rep.home}/revision"/>
    <param name="driver" value="com.mysql.jdbc.Driver"/>
    <param name="url" value="jdbc:mysql://192.168.2.173:3306/
lportal"/>
    <param name="user" value="lportal"/>
    <param name="password" value="lportal"/>
    <param name="schema" value="mysql"/>
    <param name="schemaObjectPrefix" value="J_C_"/>
  </Journal>
</Cluster>
```

As shown in the preceding code, the database journal is configured through the following properties: revision — location of the cluster node's revision file, driver — JDBC driver class name, url — JDBC URL, user — user name of default account, password — password of default account.

We have set clustering of Jackrabbit for Node1. Do the same in Node2 with the value id="node2".

By the way, if you have a Storage Area Network (SAN) and a shared folder, you can configure the portal to store documents there to take advantage of the extra redundancy. In this case, you could use **File System Hook** and **Advanced File System Hook**, besides **JCR Hook** with **File System**.

To configure the location where your documents are stored, you would be able to use following properties in portal-ext.properties:

```
dl.hook.impl=com.liferay.documentlibrary.util.AdvancedFileSystemHook
dl.hook.file.system.root.dir=//bookpub.com/liferay-portal/data/
document_library
```

As shown in the preceding code, you would be able to use **Advanced File System Hook**. There are no differences between **File System Hook** and **Advanced File System Hook**, if you are using exFAT (Extended File Allocation Table) — format size limits and files per directory limits are practically eliminated.

 Note that when using **File System Hook** or **Advanced File System Hook**, you would be able to get better performance on repository clustering than with **JCR Hook** with **File System**.

UrlRewrite filter

In addition, the portal is integrated with **UrlRewrite filter**. Based on the mod_rewrite for apache, UrlRewrite filter is a Java Web Filter for any J2EE compliant web application server, such as Resin, Orion, or Tomcat, which allows us to rewrite URLs before they get to the code. Refer to http://tuckey.org/urlrewrite/.

Performance on the UrlRewrite filter is very good and the UrlRewrite filter allows for convenient configuration of URLs where JkMount is pointing to /* or the web server isn't running behind Apache.

Configuration

The portal has specified the following to $PORTAL_ROOT_HOME/WEB-INF/web.xml. Note that you need to add it near the top above other filter mappings if you have any:

```
<filter>
  <filter-name>URL Rewrite Filter</filter-name>
  <filter-class>org.tuckey.web.filters.urlrewrite.UrlRewriteFilter</filter-class>
    <!-- ignore details -->
</filter>
<filter-mapping>
  <filter-name>URL Rewrite Filter</filter-name>
 <url-pattern>/*</url-pattern>
</filter-mapping>
```

Then, the portal created `urlrewrite.xml` under the folder `$PORTAL_ROOT_HOME/WEB-INF` and added default configuration to the `$PORTAL_ROOT_HOME/WEB-INF/urlrewrite.xml` as follows:

```
<urlrewrite>
 <rule>
  <from>(.*)/blog/blogs/rss(.*)</from>
  <to type="permanent-redirect">$1/blog/-/blogs/rss$2</to>
 </rule>
<!-- ignore details -->
</urlrewrite>
```

The preceding code shows how automatically rewrite blog RSS URLs with an ampersand right after a question mark. Of course, you could add your own configuration to the `$PORTAL_ROOT_HOME/WEB-INF/urlrewrite.xml`.

In addition, you can set allowed redirect IPs for the portal as follows in portal-ext.properties:

```
redirect.url.ips.allowed=127.0.0.1,SERVER_IP
```

As you can see, you can input a list of comma delimited IPs which the portal is allowed to redirect to. Input a blank list to allow any `IP`. `SERVER_IP` will be replaced with the IP of the host server.

Cloud Computing

Cloud Computing refers to both the applications delivered as services over the Internet (**SaaS Software as a Service**) and the hardware and systems software in the virtual data centre that provide those services `http://en.wikipedia.org/wiki/Cloud_computing`.

There are different types of public cloud computing service providers. **Amazon EC2** is the most widely used web service that allows subscribers to run applications with resizable compute capacity in an Amazon cloud computing environment. An EC2 instance can serve as a practically unlimited set of virtual machines but looks much like a physical hardware with a running operation systems such as Windows, Linux, or Unix. Generally speaking, an EC2 subscriber has control over nearly the entire software stack including the kernel. More specifically, a subscriber can run Liferay Portal in EC2 instance as follows:

- Sign up for Amazon EC2.
- Create an **Amazon Machine Image (AMI)** containing the operating system, applications, libraries, data, and associated configuration settings.
- Configure security and network access on the Amazon EC2 instance.

- Install Liferay Portal including a database server such as MySQL or Oracle, application server, Liferay Portal, and web server, and so on(just as you would normally do on a typical server). Login to Liferay Portal from the browser to verify the installation.
- Use Amazon command line tools to re-bundle the AMI image and upload it to the **Amazon Simple Storage Service (Amazon S3)**.
- Register with Amazon EC2 to create an AMI identifier as a new image template.
- Use online AWS Management Console to launch a new EC2 instance from the AMI image template.
- Choose an instance type to be launched, then start, terminate, and monitor as many instances of your AMI as needed.

In addition, a subscriber can also select a pre-configured templated image to launch a new instance and get up and running immediately if such an image is available. Once an AMI with Liferay Portal has been created, the subscriber can expand the virtual machines on an as-needed basis. Capacity can be expanded or shrunk in real time from as few as one to over 1000 virtual machines simultaneously. Billing takes place according to the computing and network resources consumed. The main advantages include following, but are not limited to:

- Separation of IT infrastructure from application development
- Usage-based pricing model for computing resources
- No or very low upfront investment for infrastructure
- Ability to scale to meet peak demand quickly
- Separate security for each cloud instance

In brief, an enterprise can deploy Liferay Portal in Amazon EC2 so that the security settings for this portal server can be separated from the security of the enterprise's own network. This is particularly useful when the enterprise doesn't want to expose its own network to its partners or portal users. Also, the Liferay Portal EC2 instances can be launched or terminated within minutes and the subscriber gets billed only for the actual hours used.

Data backup and migration

A backup or the process of backing up refers to making copies of data so that these additional copies may be used to restore the original data after a data loss event. The portal needs to be backed up properly. Once you have an installation of portal running, you need to have proper backup procedures in place in case of a catastrophic failure.

You may have setup an entire project first, and then wonder why you were using the default demo DB Hypersonic; and then you want to move to another database. That is, you want to migrate from existing database to a new one. Fortunately the portal provides the ability to migrate data from one database to another database.

More interestingly, you may start out storing documents using Jackrabbit hooked to a database by default. As time goes by and you use more portlets deployments, the number of database connections reserved for Jackrabbit alone will get close to the maximum number of database connections. Thus you want to switch from using **JCRHook** over to using **FileSystemHook** to store documents on a SAN. Fortunately the portal provides the ability to migrate data from one repository hook to another repository hook.

Data backup

Once the websites (and WAP sites) are running, you will have proper backup procedures in place in case of catastrophe. Generally speaking, the portal isn't much different from any other applications running in an application server. There are three specific components that need to be backed up on a regular basis.

- Source code repository — custom ext code, custom plugins code, and so on.
- File systems — the portal stores configuration files, search indexes, the default Jackrabbit repository, and optionally files in its home folder `$LIFERAY_HOME/ data`. In the `$AS_WEB_APP_HOME/WEB-INF/classes` folder, it includes custom property files, cluster and cache configuration files, and other custom code.
- Databases — if database vendor supports database backup, you can back it up live. Otherwise, you can do a dump of the database to a text file and then back up the exported file.

In brief, you need to back up your source code repository, `$AS_WEB_APP_HOME/ WEB-INF/classes` folder, `$LIFERAY_HOME/data` folder, portal database, and Jackrabbit database.

Data migration

As shown in the following screenshot, the portal provides capabilities for database migration from an existing database to another database, and repository migration from one repository hook to another repository hook called Document Library hooks migration. How do we get it? By going to **Server** | **Server Administration** | **Data Migration** under **Control Panel**, you will see **Database Migration** and **Repository Migration**.

By the way, if you are currently using permission algorithm 1-5, instead of permission algorithm 6, you would see one more data migration—a message "Convert legacy permission algorithm" and a button **Execute**. With this capability, you could convert legacy permission algorithm 1-5 to 6.

Database migration

When doing data migration from one database to another, you need to enter the following JDBC information for a new database.

```
JDBC Driver Class Name: like oracle.jdbc.driver.OracleDriver
JDBC URL: like jdbc:oracle:thin:@localhost:1521:xe
JDBC User Name: like lportal;
JDBC Password: like lportal
```

When starting migrating, you would see this message: "The system is currently undergoing maintenance. Please try again later". When migration is done, you will see this message "The system is shutdown. Please try again later".

Note that if the target JDBC driver such as `ojdbc6.jar` (Oracle database 11 JDBC driver) wasn't included by default at `/lib/ext`, for example in Tomcat `$TOMCAT_AS_DIR/lib/ext`, you should add the target JDBC driver at `/lib/ext`. By default, the portal has included a few JDBC drivers like `hsql.jar`, `mysql.jar`, `jtds.jar` and `postgresql.jar`.

Repository migration

By default, the portal used the following **File System Hook** called **FS Hook** in `portal.properties`. The Document Library repository will use these hook persist documents:

```
dl.hook.impl=com.liferay.documentlibrary.util.FileSystemHook
```

After a while, you may want to convert repository from **File System Hook** to **Advanced File System Hook** called **AFS Hook**. You could do it as follows:

1. Go to **Server | Server Administration | Data Migration** under **Control Panel**.
2. Select **com.liferay.documentlibrary.util.AdvancedFileSystemHook** from the drop-down list next to the text **dl.hook.impl**.
3. Click on the button **Execute** under the text **dl.hook.impl**.

When starting migrating, you would see message like "… Please set dl.hook.impl in your portal-ext.properties to use com.liferay.documentlibrary.util.AdvancedFileSystemHook. …". When migration was done, you would see message "The system is shutdown. Please try again later".

Before restarting the portal, set following line in `portal-ext.properties`:

```
dl.hook.impl=com.liferay.documentlibrary.util.AdvancedFileSystemHook
```

Of course, you would be able to do repository migration from one hook to another. In a word, every combination is possible.

What's happening?

As you can see, the convert processes include database migration, document library hook migration and legacy permission algorithm migration. What's happening? The portal has specified the following property for convert processes:

```
convert.processes=\
  com.liferay.portal.convert.ConvertDatabase,\
  ## ignore details
  com.liferay.portal.convert.ConvertWikiCreole
```

As shown in the preceding code, you could input a list of comma delimited class names that implement `com.liferay.portal.convert.ConvertProcess`. The classes such as `ConvertDatabase`, `ConvertDocumentLibrary`, `ConvertPermissionAlgorithm`, `ConvertPermissionTuner` and `ConvertWikiCreole` can be run from within the portlet Admin Server to convert older data to match a new configuration of the portal.

Performance tuning

As an infrastructure portal, the portal can support over `3300` concurrent users on a single server with mean login times under `0.5` a second and maximum throughput of `79+` logins per second. In collaboration and social networking scenarios, each physical server supports over `1300` concurrent users at an average transaction times of under `800` ms. Note that this benchmark was generated based on the application server: 2 x Intel Core 2 Quad E5430 2.66GHz CPU, 12MB L2 cache (8 cores total), 8GB memory, 2 x 146GB 10k RPM SCSI, CentOS 5.2 64-bit Linux.

The portal's CMS/WCM scales to beyond `150,000` concurrent users on a single Portal server with average transaction times under `50ms` and `35%` CPU utilization. Given sufficient database resources and efficient load balancing, the portal can scale linearly as one adds additional servers to a cluster. How do we achieve this? Here we list `TEN` golden rules:

- Adjust the server's thread pool and JDBC connection pool:. By default, the portal is configured for a maximum of 100 database connections. For Tomcat and JBoss, a good number is between 200 and 400 threads in the thread pool.

- Turn off unused servlet filters: Servlet filters dynamically intercept requests and transform them. The portal contains more than 20 servlet filters, so turn off the ones you aren't using.

For example, you could turn off the following servlet filters by overriding them in `portal-ext.properties`:

```
com.liferay.portal.servlet.filters.audit.AuditFilter=false
com.liferay.portal.servlet.filters.sso.cas.CASFilter=false
com.liferay.portal.servlet.filters.sso.ntlm.NtlmFilter=false
com.liferay.portal.sharepoint.SharepointFilter=false
com.liferay.portal.servlet.filters.virtualhost.VirtualHostFilter=false
com.liferay.portal.servlet.filters.sso.opensso.OpenSSOFilter=false
```

As shown in the preceding code, Audit Filer, SSO CAS Filter, SSO NTLM Filter, SSO OpenSSO Filter, Virtual Host Filter, and SharePoint Filter got turned off.

- Tune JVM parameters: This is the most efficient rule.

You can set `setenv.bat` as follows (suppose that there is more than 4GB memory available) in Tomcat for Windows:

```
set JAVA_OPTS=%JAVA_OPTS% -Xms2048m –Xmx2048m -XX:MaxPermSize=1024m
-Dfile.encoding=UTF8 -Duser.timezone=GMT -Djava.security.auth.login.
config="%CATALINA_HOME%/conf/jaas.config" -Dorg.apache.catalina.
loader.WebappClassLoader.ENABLE_CLEAR_REFERENCES=false
```

You can set `setenv.sh` as follows (supposed that there is more than 4GB memory available) in Tomcat for Linux and MacOS:

```
JAVA_OPTS="$JAVA_OPTS -Xms2048m –Xmx2048m -XX:MaxPermSize=1024m
-Dfile.encoding=UTF8 -Duser.timezone=GMT -Djava.security.auth.login.
config=$CATALINA_HOME/conf/jaas.config -Dorg.apache.catalina.loader.
WebappClassLoader.ENABLE_CLEAR_REFERENCES=false"
```

Note that `XX:MaxPermSize` is really important to tune for Java applications as Perm Gen Memory space is widely used. For other application servers, you would have similar settings for JVM parameters. Depending on available memory (that is, more than 8 GB), you could increase JVM parameters settings like this:

```
-Xms4096m –Xmx4096m -XX:MaxPermSize=1024m
-Xms6144m –Xmx6144m -XX:MaxPermSize=1024m
```

In addition, garbage collection can become a bottleneck depending on the requirements of the portals. By understanding the requirements of the portal and the garbage collection options, it is possible to minimize the impact of garbage collection. The following is one option:

```
-XX:+UseConcMarkSweepGC
-XX:+CMSIncrementalMode
```

```
-XX:+CMSIncrementalPacing
-XX:CMSIncrementalDutyCycleMin=0
-XX:+CMSIncrementalDutyCycle=10
-XX:+PrintGCDetails
-XX:+PrintGCTimeStamps
-XX:-TraceClassUnloading
```

As shown in the preceding code, the first three options enable the concurrent collector, concurrent marking phase, and concurrent marking phase automatic pacing. The next two set the minimum duty cycle to `0` and the initial duty cycle to `10`, as the default values (`10` and `50`, respectively) are too large for a number of portals. The last three options relate to diagnostic information on the collection, so that the behavior of concurrent marking phase can be seen and later analyzed.

 Note that `-XX:+UseParallelGC` shouldn't be used with `-XX:+UseConcMarkSweepGC`.

Of course, you could reset the following performance options:

```
-XX:MaxNewSize=1024m
-XX:NewRatio=2
-XX:NewSize=3m
-XX:SurvivorRatio=8
-XX:TargetSurvivorRatio=50
```

The first option sets the maximum size of new the generation in bytes and the second option sets the ratio of new/old generation sizes. `-XX:NewSize` specifies the default size of the new generation; `-XX:SurvivorRatio` sets the ratio of survivor space size; `-XX:TargetSurvivorRatio` sets the desired percentage of survivor space used after scavenge.

- Tune Ehcache — the portal uses Ehcache, a cluster-aware, tunable cache. Caching greatly speeds up performance by reducing the number of times the application has to go grab something from the database. If you have a heavily trafficked message board, you may want to consider adjusting the cache for the message board.
- For example replace Lucene with Solr, which allows you to abstract out of the portal installation everything that has to do with search, and run search from a completely separate environment.
- Optimize Counter Increment. You could set this to a higher number to reduce the number of database calls for primary keys within the portal.
- Use **Content Delivery Network (CDN)** wherever possible. CDN serves up static content from a location that is geographically close to the end user.
  ```
  cdn.host.http=
  cdn.host.https=
  ```

As shown in the preceding code, the property `cdn.host.http` sets the hostname that will be used to serve static content through a CDN for requests made over the HTTP protocol; the property `cdn.host.https` sets the hostname that will be used to serve static content through a CDN for requests made over the HTTPS protocol.

- Use a web server to serve static resources. All static content, such as images, CSS, JavaScript, and so on is served by a web server instead of by an application server.

- Use dynamic data source and/or database sharding. Sharding is splitting up database by the various types of data that may be in it. When users log in, they are directed to the instance of the application that has their data in it. The dynamic data source configures the portal to use one database cluster for read calls and another database cluster for write calls.

- CSS/JS Sprites. Instead of standard `<img src>` tag, use the `<liferay-ui:icon>` tag. Note that this is hard to maintain.

Integrating with Alfresco, SSO CAS, and LDAP

The portal provides ability for full integration with Alfresco to take care of users, communities, and permissions synchronization so that users can see Alfresco as direct repository and use it through portlets. These portlets include `Alfresco Client` and `Alfresco Content`.

Alfresco is the leading open source for enterprise content management. The open source model allows Alfresco to employ best-of-breed open source technologies and contributions from the open source. The URL is: `http://www.alfresco.com/`

In brief, you can integrate Alfresco in the portal in the following ways:

- Web services, referring to the portlet **Alfresco Content** in *Chapter 10, Search, WAP, CRM, Widgets, Reporting and Auditing*.

- RESTful services OpenSearch, referring to the portlet **Alfresco Content** in *Chapter 10, Search, WAP, CRM, Widgets, Reporting and Auditing*.

- RESTful services web scripts, using Alfresco as direct repository of Liferay, referring to *Chapter 6, Customizing the WYSIWYG Editor of the book Liferay Portal 5.2 Systems Development*.

- CMIS using CMIS document library hook, referring to *Chapter 8, CMS and WCM*.

- Portlets using Alfresco web client as a set of portlets, and maybe WebDAV.

In this section, we're going to discuss how to integrate Alfresco with LDAP and SSO CAS? How do we integrate an Alfresco web client as a set of portlets? How do we integrate Liferay, Alfresco, LDAP and SSO CAS fully? and, How do we migrate content from Liferay CMS and WCM to an Alfresco repository?

Alfresco, LDAP and SSO CAS

Alfresco can be integrated with SSO CAS and LDAP seamlessly. Let's take a detailed look at this integration. In the following steps, you will be able to integrate Alfresco with SSO CAS and LDAP. You could use Alfresco 3.1.1 or above, (either the community edition or the enterprise edition). Suppose that the default LDAP (Lightweight Directory Access Protocol) is `ldap://docs.cignex.com:10389`, the default SSO CAS (Central Authentication Service) version 3.3 or above is `http://docs.cignex.com/cas-web`, and the default database is MySQL database. You can find downloaded files at `http://liferay.cignex.com/palm_tree/book/0387/chapter13/alfresco-sso-ldap`.

1. Get Alfresco web client application WAR file `alfresco.war`. Suppose that you have installed Alfresco-Tomcat bundle at `$ALFRESCO_INSTALL`, you would find `alfresco.war` in the folder `$ALFRESCO_INSTALL/tomcat/webapps`.

2. Unzip `alfresco.war` to a folder called `$ALFRESCO_HOME`, any folder in your local machine, for example, new folder `/alfresco-sso-ldap`.

3. Copy the SSO configuration file `sso-ldap-authentication-context.xml` to `$ALFRESCO_HOME/WEB-INF/classes`, and copy the LDAP configuration files `ldap-authentication.properties` and `ldap-authentication-context.xml` to `$ALFRESCO_HOME/WEB-INF/classes/alfresco/extension`. Note that you can configure any LDAP other than `ldap://docs.cignex.com:10389`.

4. Copy the SSO CAS support API `bookpub-sso-ldap.jar` to `$ALFRESCO_HOME/WEB-INF/lib`.

5. Add the following lines before the first `<filter>` in `$ALFRESCO_HOME/WEB-INF/web.xml`.

```
<filter>
<filter-name>CAS Filter</filter-name>
<filter-class>com.bookpub.portal.servlet.filters.sso.cas.
CASFilter</filter-class>
<init-param>
 <param-name>cas_server_url</param-name>
 <param-value>http://docs.cignex.com/cas-web</param-value>
</init-param>
```

```
<init-param>
 <param-name>service_path</param-name>
 <param-value>/index.jsp</param-value>
</init-param>
<init-param>
 <param-name>application_type</param-name>
 <param-value>Alfresco</param-value>
</init-param>
</filter>
```

Note that you can update SSO CAS other than `http://docs.cignex.com/cas-web`, then add the following lines after the last `</filter>` in `$ALFRESCO_HOME/WEB-INF/web.xml`:

```
<filter-mapping>
  <filter-name>CAS Filter</filter-name>
  <url-pattern>/index.jsp</url-pattern>
</filter-mapping>
<filter-mapping>
  <filter-name>CAS Filter</filter-name>
  <url-pattern>/logout</url-pattern>
</filter-mapping>
```

And add the following line after the line `<import resource="classpath:alfresco/web-services-application-context.xml" />` in `$ALFRESCO_HOME/WEB-INF/web-application-context.xml`;

```
<import resource="classpath:sso-ldap-authentication-context.xml" />
```

As shown in the preceding code, the SSO CAS configuration is registered.

1. Add the following lines after the first `--%>` in `$ALFRESCO_HOME /jsp/parts/titlebar.jsp`

    ```
    <%
    String protocol = request.getProtocol();
    protocol = protocol.substring( 0 , protocol.indexOf("/")).
    toLowerCase();
    String address = request.getServerName();
    String port = request.getServerPort() + "";
    String path = request.getContextPath();
    if(port.endsWith("443")) protocol += "s";
    String currentURL = protocol + "://" + address + ":" + port + path
    + "/logout";
    %>
    ```

You have the following line:

```
<a:actionLink id="logout" image="/images/icons/logout.gif"
value="#{msg.logout} (#{NavigationBean.currentUser.userName})"
rendered="#{!NavigationBean.isGuest}" action="#{LoginBean.logout}"
immediate="true" />
```

Replace it with this line:

```
<a:actionLink id="logout" image="/images/icons/logout.gif"
value="#{msg.logout} (#{NavigationBean.currentUser.userName})"
rendered="#{!NavigationBean.isGuest}" action="#{LoginBean.
logout}" showLink="false" target="_parent" href="<%= currentURL
%>" immediate="true" /> <a href="<%= currentURL %>" target="_
parent"><h:outputText value="#{msg.logout} (#{NavigationBean.
currentUser.userName})" /></a>
```

2. Update `dir.root` in `$ALFRESCO_HOME/WEB-INF/classes/alfresco/
   repository.properties` such as

   ```
   dir.root=$ALFRESCO_REPOSITORY/alf_data
   ```

   where `$ALFRESCO_REPOSITORY` could be any folder in your server.

3. Copy `mysql.jar` to `$ALFRESCO_HOME/WEB-INF/lib` and create a database
   Alfresco in MySQL as follows:

   ```
   drop database if exists alfresco;

   create database alfresco character set utf8;

   grant all on alfresco.* to 'alfresco'@'localhost' identified by
   'alfresco' with grant option;

   grant all on alfresco.* to 'alfresco'@'localhost.localdomain'
   identified by 'alfresco' with grant option;
   ```

4. For enterprise edition only, create a folder license under `$ALFRESCO_HOME/
   WEB-INF/classes/alfresco/extension` and add your license file to
   `$ALFRESCO_HOME/WEB-INF/classes/alfresco/extension/license`

5. Package all files as a WAR file `alfresco.war`, and drop the WAR file to
   `$TOMCAT_AS_DIR/webapps`.

Optionally you can use the result directly: simply download WAR file from `http://
liferay.cignex.com/palm_tree/book/0387/chapter13/alfresco-sso-ldap/
alfresco.war` and deploy it in the folder `$TOMCAT_AS_DIR/webapps`. Note that JAR
file is compliant with JDK 1.6 (that is, `1.6.0_18`).

How does it work?

As you can see, if the Alfresco-SSO-LDAP bundle was deployed successfully, you will be able to see the CAS SSO server login page. Typing your credential which is coming from the LDAP server, you would be able to login to CAS SSO and then Alfresco directly. Note that the Net ID and password are coming from LDAP `cn` and `userpassword`. How do we map the user ID entered by the user to that passed through to LDAP? At `$ALFRESCO_HOME/WEB-INF/classes/alfresco/extension`, the properties file `ldap-authentication.properties` specifies the following line.

```
ldap.authentication.userNameFormat=cn=%s,ou=users,ou=system
```

Depending on which LDAP server you are using, you would be able to configure it smoothly.

Alfresco web client as a set of portlets

Alfresco could be integrated as a set of portlets in the portal seamlessly. Let's have a deep look on this integration. In the following steps, you would be able to integrate Alfresco as a set of portlets. You could use Alfresco 3.1.1 or above, either community edition or enterprise edition. By the way, default database is MySQL database. You could find downloaded files at `http://liferay.cignex.com/palm_tree/book/0387/chapter13/alfresco-portlets`.

1. Get Alfresco web client application WAR file `alfresco.war`, suppose that you have installed Alfresco-Tomcat bundle at `$ALFRESCO_INSTALL`, you would find `alfresco.war` at the folder `$ALFRESCO_INSTALL/tomcat/webapps`.

2. Unzip `alfresco.war` to a folder called `$ALFRESCO_HOME`, any folder in your local machine, for example, new folder `/alfresco-portlets`.

3. Update `dir.root` in `$ALFRESCO_HOME/WEB-INF/classes/alfresco/repository.properties` with

   `dir.root=$ALFRESCO_REPOSITORY/alf_data`.

   Where `$ALFRESCO_REPOSITORY` could be any folder in your server.

4. Create a database `alfresco` and username/password as `alfresco/alfresco` in MySQL.

5. Remove the JAR file `$ALFRESCO_HOME/WEB-INF/lib/portlet-api-lib.jar`.

6. Add `/WEB-INF/faces-config.xml` to the faces configure files list at `$ALFRESCO_HOME/WEB-INF/web.xml` like:

```
<context-param>
  <param-name>javax.faces.CONFIG_FILES</param-name>
  <param-value>/WEB-INF/faces-config.xml,/WEB-INF/faces-config-
app.xml,/WEB-INF/faces-config-beans.xml,
/WEB-INF/faces-config-navigation.xml,/WEB-INF/faces-config-
common.xml,
/WEB-INF/faces-config-repo.xml,/WEB-INF/faces-config-wcm.xml,/WEB-
INF/faces-config-custom.xml</param-value>
</context-param>
```

7. Download and add files: `faces-config.xml`, `liferay-display.xml`, `liferay-portlet.xml`, `portlet.xml` to `$ALFRESCO_HOME/WEB-INF`.

8. For enterprise edition only, create a folder `license` under `$ALFRESCO_HOME/WEB-INF/classes/alfresco/extension` and add your license file to `$ALFRESCO_HOME/WEB-INF/classes/alfresco/extension/license`.

9. Package all files as a WAR file `alfresco.war`.

10. Drop the WAR file to `$LIFERAY_HOME/deploy`.

Optionally you can use the result WAR directly. Download WAR from `http://liferay.cignex.com/palm_tree/book/0387/chapter13/alfresco-portlet/alfresco.war` and deploy it to `$LIFERAY_HOME/deploy`.

How does it work?

As you can see, if Alfresco portlets bundle got deployed successfully, you would be able to see portlets under the category Alfresco: **Alfresco Client Portlet, Document List, My Spaces, My Tasks, My Web Files** and **My Web Forms**. Why? We have specified the following lines at `$ALFRESCO_HOME/WEB-INF/liferay-display.xml`.

```
<display>
  <category name="category.alfresco">
    <portlet id="AlfrescoClient"/>
<!-- ignore details -->
  </category>
</display>
```

Note that you may not be able to add alfresco portlets like **Document List, My Spaces** and **My Tasks** in the portal pages properly, as alfresco portlets requires to be signed in first. Fortunately, there is simple solution—you can create an account "admin/admin", that is, default account in alfresco, in the portal, and assign this account to role "Administrator". Then login as "admin/admin" in the portal, and add alfresco portlets in the portal pages, again.

Full Integration—Liferay, Alfresco, LDAP, and SSO CAS

Of course, you can integrate Alfresco as a set of portlets plus LDAP and SSO CAS seamlessly. Let's have a deep look on this integration. In the following steps, you would be able to integrate Alfresco as a set of portlets. You could use Alfresco 3.1.1 or above, either community edition or enterprise edition. Set the default LDAP as `ldap://docs.cignex.com:10389`, set default SSO CAS (version 3.3 or above) as `http://docs.cignex.com/cas-web`, and set default database as MySQL database. You could find downloaded files at `http://liferay.cignex.com/palm_tree/book/0387/chapter13/alfresco-portlets`.

1. Get Alfresco web client application WAR file `alfresco.war`, suppose that you have installed Alfresco-Tomcat bundle at `$ALFRESCO_INSTALL`, you would find `alfresco.war` at the folder `$ALFRESCO_INSTALL/tomcat/webapps`.

2. Unzip `alfresco.war` to a folder called `$ALFRESCO_HOME`, any folder in your local machine, for example, new folder `/alfresco`.

3. Copy SSO configuration file `sso-ldap-authentication-context.xml` to `$ALFRESCO_HOME/WEB-INF/classes`, and copy LDAP configuration files `ldap-authentication.properties` and `ldap-authentication-context.xml` to `$ALFRESCO_HOME/WEB-INF/classes/alfresco/extension`, note that you can configure any LDAP other than `ldap://docs.cignex.com:10389`.

4. Copy SSO CAS support API `bookpub-sso-ldap.jar` to `$ALFRESCO_HOME/WEB-INF/lib`, and remove the JAR file `$ALFRESCO_HOME/WEB-INF/lib/portlet-api-lib.jar`.

5. And add following line after the line `<import resource="classpath:alfresco/web-services-application-context.xml" />` in `$ALFRESCO_HOME/WEB-INF/web-application-context.xm`.

   `<import resource="classpath:sso-ldap-authentication-context.xml" />`

6. Update `dir.root` in `$ALFRESCO_HOME/WEB-INF/classes/alfresco/repository.properties` like

   `dir.root=$ALFRESCO_REPOSITORY/alf_data`

   Where `$ALFRESCO_REPOSITORY` could be any folder in your server.

7. Download and add files: `faces-config.xml`, `liferay-display.xml`, `liferay-portlet.xml`, `portlet.xml` to, and add `/WEB-INF/faces-config.xml` to the faces configure files list at `$ALFRESCO_HOME/WEB-INF/web.xml` like:

```
<context-param>
  <param-name>javax.faces.CONFIG_FILES</param-name>
  <param-value>/WEB-INF/faces-config.xml,/WEB-INF/faces-config-
app.xml,/WEB-INF/faces-config-beans.xml,
/WEB-INF/faces-config-navigation.xml,/WEB-INF/faces-config-
common.xml,
/WEB-INF/faces-config-repo.xml,/WEB-INF/faces-config-wcm.xml,/WEB-
INF/faces-config-custom.xml</param-value>
</context-param>
```

8. Create a database `alfresco` and username/password as `alfresco/alfresco` in MySQL.

9. For enterprise edition only, create a folder license under `$ALFRESCO_HOME/WEB-INF/classes/alfresco/extension` and add your license file to `$ALFRESCO_HOME/WEB-INF/classes/alfresco/extension/license`

10. Package all files as a WAR file `alfresco.war`, and drop the WAR file to `$LIFERAY_HOME/deploy`.

Optionally you can use the result WAR directly download WAR from `http://liferay.cignex.com/palm_tree/book/0387/chapter13/full-integration/alfresco.war` and deploy it to `$LIFERAY_HOME/deploy`.

How does it work?

As you can see, Alfresco portlets have been integrated with LDAP and SSO CAS. It is time to integrate the portal with LDAP and SSO CAS. You should take following items on LDAP server, that is, **Apache Directory Server**, by default. Of course, you can use any LDAP server like OpenLDAP, OpenDS, and so on. Note that first login as an admin, then go to **Control Panel | Server | Server Administration**.

- **How do users authenticate**: By Screen Name
- **Enabled**: Checked
- **Required**:Un-checked
- **Base Provider URL**: `ldap://docs.cignex.com:10389`
- **Base DN**: ou=users,ou=system
- **Principal**: uid=admin,ou=system
- **Credentials**: secret

- **Authentication Search Filter**: (cn=@screen_name@)
- **Import Search Filter**: (objectClass=inetOrgPerson)
- **User Mapping**: Using default settings
- **Group Mapping**: Using default settings

In addition, you should take following items on SSO server, that is, CAS, by default. Of course, you could be able to use your own SSO CAS server.

- **Enabled**: Checked;
- **Import from LDAP**: Checked
- **Login URL**: `http://docs.cignex.com/cas-web/login`
- **Logout URL**: `http://docs.cignex.com/cas-web/logout`
- **Server Name**: `localhost:8080`
- **Server URL**: `http://docs.cignex.com/cas-web`
- **Service URL**: (empty)

As you can see, you would be able to see CAS SSO server login page when typing URL `http://localhost:8080/c/portal/login`. Typing your credential from the LDAP server, you would be able to login to CAS SSO and then Alfresco directly. Note that Net ID and password are coming from LDAP server `cn` and `userpassword`. When signing in to the portal, you would see that you would be signed in automatically to the portlet Alfresco Client, too.

What's happening?

The following diagram shows full integration of Liferay, Alfresco, LDAP, and SSO CAS. A generic solution (full integration) has been developed for SSO CAS plus LDAP against Liferay portal and Alfresco portlets. Here it is a generic solution of SSO CAS plus LDAP against following applications.

```
Alfresco Standalone Application - shown as SSO 1;
Liferay Portal and, furthermore, Alfresco Portlets - shown as SSO 2,
SSO 3, and SSO 4";
```

To integrate SSO CAS plus LDAP with Liferay Portal and Alfresco Portlets such as Alfresco client portlet and Alfresco content portlet, simply come in sequence the following steps:

1. First configure Liferay portal authenticating with LDAP.
2. Then configure SSO CAS server authenticating with LDAP.

3. Finally configure Alfresco portlets (Alfresco client and Alfresco content) authenticating with SSO.

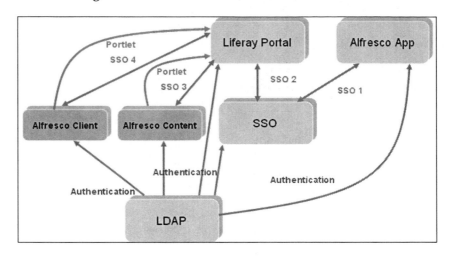

For example, you can first login in to Alfresco standalone application `http://liferay.cignex.com:8090/alfesco` by a user account. You are asked to input authentication information first. Then you will see alfresco web client standalone application. Afterwards click Liferay portal `http://liferay.cignex.com:8080/c/portal/login`, you will see that you don't have to log in the Liferay portal. You have logged in the alfresco web client portlet automatically. That is, web applications like Alfresco standalone application, Liferay portal and portlets share same access ticket to defer all authentications to a trusted central server like SSO and LDAP.

The full integration involves two main functionalities: filters in action for the portal and Alfresco applications, and portlets in action for any portlets in the portal. The following are general instructions to implement these two main functionalities: filters in action and portlets in action.

 Filters in action involve the following: enhanced SSO Filter, authenticating SSO CAS Server with LDAP, enhanced validating URL in SSO CAS Server, authenticating with LDAP, and log-in automatically. While portlets in action which involved following: loading portlet, tracing current user from Filter, authenticating portlet with LDAP, and log-in automatically.

Integrating with Ad server OpenX

As the world's leading open source portal platform, the portal provides a unified web interface to data and tools scattered across many sources. Within the portal, a portal interface is composed of a number of portlets self contained interactive elements that are written to a particular standard. As portlets are developed independently of the portal itself, and loosely coupled with the portal, they are apparently **SOA (Service-Oriented Architecture)**. This section will discuss how to use SOA to integrate other systems, focusing on Ad Server OpenX.

The OpenX community has grown rapidly to become the web's largest ad space community, since then tens of thousands of people are making their websites pay. OpenX Ad server gives site owners everything they need to generate revenue from their websites. Publishers can get complete control of banners and campaigns along with a tracking system. Obviously, OpenX would be better for internets other than intranets.

OpenX integration

How do you integrate it in the portal? The following is an option to integrate OpenX in the portal.

- Consume web services from Ad Server in OpenX.
- Prepare a portlet called Ad Manager to manage ads in the portal, where an ad is set of banners with display rules.
- Prepare a portlet called Ad Viewer to publish ads in any portal pages.
- Deploy these two portlets Ad Manager and Ad Viewer in the portal.
- The features setting up the banners of the content of Ads portlet should include:
    - Displaying ads, that is, a set of banners, based on a specific day, for example, in Christmas, showing banner of GUND.
    - Displaying ads based on general day, for example, on Monday, display the banner of Fisher-Price, on Tuesday, display the banner of GUND.
    - Displaying ads based on percentage for a given day, for example, on Tuesday, display GUND 40% and Fisher-price 60%.
- Use ads server OpenX to manage companies' information including banners called Ads repository as well as that of Alfresco server for content repository. At the same time, get complete control of banners and campaigns along with a tracking system.

- Provide version feature for Ads in the portal. Thus, you could see which one it was in the past.

- Separate `Ad Viewer` from `Ad` management in the portal. In ads, administrators will manage all possible ads with rules as mentioned above, similar to portlet Web Content. The portlet `Ad Viewer` provides a way to display ads, similar to that of display articles in `Web Content Display`, in any pages.

- Schedule ads, that is, a set of banners, in the portlet `Ad Manager`, same as that of articles in `Web Content`. You can preview pages on a specific date like July 14th including all updated pages, home page, and all scheduled articles and ads in the portal `Ad Viewer`.

 OpenX is a hugely popular, free ad server for web publishers. It takes control, manages your advertising and makes more money from online advertising. URL: `http://www.openx.org/`

Ad Manager

First of all, install the Ad portlet. Like the portlet Web Content, the portlet Ad Manager provides capability to build ads and to manage ads You can use the portlet Ad Manager to do reporting ads tracking reporting, search ads, and add an ad.

You would be able to search ads by **Short Name**, **Title**, **Description**, **Keywords**, and **Version**. The search results, that is, ads, will appears with columns **Short Name**, **Version**, Title, Description, the button **Actions** with a set of icons, such as **Preview**, **Copy**, **Edit**, **Delete** and **Permissions**. Note that you need first login as an admin, then go to **Control Panel | Content | Manage Ads**.

When adding an ad, you would be able to input ad features: **Short Name**, **Title**, **Type**, **Description**, **Dimensions**, and so on. And you can search banners by fields: **Content Type**, **Description**, **Keywords**, **Parameters**, **Comments**, **File Name**, **Dimensions**, **Target**, and URL. The search results would be displayed with columns: **Select**, **Thumbnail**, **File Name**, **Size**, the button **Actions** with icons **Preview**. And moreover, you would be able to select multiple banners with rules like by percentage, by specific date, or by specific day of week. Of course, you would be able to add more rules by customizing the portlet Ad Manager.

How does it work?

How does it work? The following is an option which you could bring the portlet Ad into the portal.

1. Download WAR file ${ad.portlet.war} from `http://liferay.cignex.com/palm_tree/book/0387/chapter13/add-portlet-6.0.0.1.war`.

2. Drop the WAR file ${add.portlet.war} to the folder `$LIFERAY_HOME/deploy` when the portal is running.

Of course, you would be able to use the portlet Portal Installation to install the portlet Ad through web UI.

What's happening?

The portlet Ad (Ad Manager in details) has following portlet specification at `$AS_WEB_APP_HOME/ad-portlet/WEB-INF/liferay-portlet.xml`.

```
<control-panel-entry-category>content</control-panel-entry-category>
<control-panel-entry-weight>16.0</control-panel-entry-weight>
```

As shown in above code, the portlet Ad will appear in the category **Content** of **Control Panel** and position **16**.

The portlet Add added following service in `$AS_WEB_APP_HOME/ad-portlet/WEB-INF/context/admanager-portlet.xml`.

```
<bean id="bannerService" class="com.book.portlet.admanagerportlet.service.impl.BannerServiceImpl">
 <property name="serviceURL" value="http://docs.cignex.com/ad_services/services"/>
</bean>
```

As shown in the preceding code, you would be able to use your own Ads service other than this `http://docs.cignex.com/ad_services/services`.

Enhancement

The portlet Ad used its own service model like Spring-Hibernate mapping, DAO and service managers in `$AS_WEB_APP_HOME/ad-portlet/WEB-INF/classes/data-source.xml`. Obviously it should use `service.xml` and `Service-Builder` to generate services and models.

By default, the portlet uses a lot of jQuery. Thus it should be upgraded to Alloy UI. In addition, the portlet Ad uses Spring MVC framework, for example, the portlet class `org.springframework.web.portlet.DispatcherPortlet`. It would be good to use JSP portlet `com.liferay.util.bridges.mvc.MVCPortlet`, as JSP portlet is simple MVC portlet.

Ad Viewer

Similar to that of the portlet Web Content Display, the portlet Ad Viewer is instance-able. The portlet Ad Viewer allows displaying one ad in any portal pages. You would be able to edit current ad, to select an ad from ads repository, or to add a new ad. In brief, the portlet Ad Viewer provides a way to publish ads in portal pages smoothly.

As you can see, each banner in an ad has a target URL. If users click on a banner in an ad, it will bring users to the target URL. At the same time, users' activities on the ad got tracked: where the user comes from, which ad and/or banner is involved, when the user clicked on the ad, etc. That is, it prepares ad tracking data for reporting.

What's happening?

The portlet Ad (Ad Viewer in details) has following portlet specification at `$AS_WEB_APP_HOME/ad-portlet/WEB-INF/liferay-portlet.xml`.

```
<portlet> <!-- ignore details -->
 <restore-current-view>false</restore-current-view>
 <layout-cacheable>true</layout-cacheable>
 <instanceable>true</instanceable>
 <private-request-attributes>true</private-request-attributes>
 <private-session-attributes>true</private-session-attributes>
<render-weight>1</render-weight>
</portlet>
```

As show in the preceding code, the `portlet-name` element contains the unique name of the portlet. This name must match the `portlet-name` specified in `$AS_WEB_APP_HOME/ad-portlet/WEB-INF/portlet.xml` like `adviewer`. It sets the `use-default-template` value to true if the portlet uses the default template to decorate and wrap content. Setting this to `false` allows the developer to own and maintain the portlet entire outputted content. Note that the default value is `true`.

It sets the `restore-current-view` value to `false`, thus the portlet will reset the current view when toggling between maximized and normal states. You can set it to `true`, so that the portlet restores to the current view when toggling between maximized and normal states. If it sets to `false`, By the way, the default value is `true`. It sets the `layout-cacheable flag` to `true`, so that the data contained in this portlet will never change unless the layout or Ads entry is changed.

In addition, it sets the `instanceable` value to `true` therefore the portlet can appear multiple times on a page. It sets the `private-request-attributes` value to `true`, so the portlet doesn't share request attributes with the portal. The default value is `true`. The property `request.shared.attributes` in `portal.properties` specifies which request attributes are shared even when the `private-request-attributes` value is `true`. And moreover it sets the `private-session-attributes` value to `true` thus the portlet doesn't share session attributes with the portal. The default value is `true`. The property `session.shared.attributes` in `portal.properties` specifies which session attributes are shared even when the `private-session-attributes` value is `true`.

Last but not the least, the default value of `render-weight` is `1`. If set to a value less than `1`, the portlet is rendered in parallel. If set to a value of `1` or greater, then the portlet is rendered serially. Portlets with a greater render weight have greater priority and will be rendered before portlets with a lower render weight. If the `ajaxable` value is set to `false`, then `render-weight` is always set to `1` if it is set to a value less than `1`. This means `ajaxable` can override `render-weight`, if it is set to `false`.

Enhancement

It would be nice that the portlet Ad Viewer could add more features like: ability to show the list of available locales, ability to show links for automatic conversion of the ads to PDF, DOC, ODT, ability to add ratings on ads, ability to add comments on ads, ability to add tags and categories on ads. These features are unavailable but highly expected.

Ad Services

As you can see, an advertiser is the owner of the advertising you display on a website. Advertisers run campaigns containing banners. A campaign contains a set of banners sharing delivery settings.

A banner is any creative content, displayed as an ad. Banners can be in many file formats, including `gif`, `jpg`, `png`, `swf`, JavaScript, `text`, and HTML. Zones are spaces on your website used for displaying advertisements. A zone can be a single space on a specific page or a space which is used on multiple pages which shows the same collection of banners.

As you have seen, ad services were provided as RESTful services, that is, OpenX got integrated into the portal via RESTful services. The ad service provides the following services, but not limited.

- **Basic Search**: action=search like `http://docs.cignex.com/ad_services/ services?action=search`

- **Advanced Search**: action=advancedSearch like `http://docs.cignex.com/ ad_services/services?action=advancedSearch&filename=gif`

- **Reporting**: action=report like `http://docs.cignex.com/ad_services/ services?action=report`

- **Download**: action=download for instance `http://docs.cignex.com/ad_ services/services?action=download&uid=6`

- **Tracking**: action=tracker for example `http://docs.cignex.com/ad_ services/services?action=tracker&uid=5&url=http://liferay. cignex.com&source=http://liferay.cignex.com`

How does it work?

Suppose that you have installed OpenX in the server with port `81`, it is using MySQL database, as the integrating service `ad_services` supports MySQL only at the time of writing. Database name, user name, password are same as `openx`, and this is configurable. If different database name/user name/password are used, configure same information in integrating service. Integrating service `ad_services` with Tomcat must be installed in the same box with OpenX server. For example, integrating service `ad_services` is using the port `80` in the same domain of OpenX such as `docs.cignex.com`.

To install ad services, you can just drop `ad_services.war` to the folder `$TOMCAT_ AS_DIR/webapps`. Of course, you can download the WAR from `http://liferay. cignex.com/palm_tree/book/0387/chapter13/ad_services.war`.

Enhancement

As you can see, ad services are implemented as RESTful services. In real cases, more OpenX integration services are expected as well. The following are possible options:

- Web services: Calling advertisers, banners, campaigns, zones through web services.

- RESTful services: Getting advertisers, banners, campaigns, zones through OpenSearch.

- AMIS: Ad Management Interoperability Services, similar to that of CMIS, use OpenX as an ad repository compliant with AMIS, and build AMIS hook in the portal to get advertisers, banners, campaigns, zones, and so on. This is highly expected.

More integration

It would be nice that we could integrate other applications like **Pentaho** and **Intalio**, and so on. Here we just have brief discussions.

By Pentaho, we can add **ETL(Extract, Transform, Load**, a data warehousing process) capabilities for **Business Intelligence (BI)** inside the portal.

 Pentaho is an Open Source application software for reporting, analysis, dashboard, data mining, and workflow and Business Intelligence. URL: http://www.pentaho.com

By Intalio | BPMS, we can integrate the BPMN and BELP inside the portal.

Intalio | BPMS is the BPMS to natively support the BPMN and BPEL industry standards. URL: http://www.intalio.com/

These integrations aren't available at the moment, but highly expected. In real cases, you would have different requirements on integrating with third party applications. Of course, you could leverage the portal framework and architecture, and going further, you could integrate these third party applications as well.

Summary

This chapter first introduced system administration which provides ability to view system information, to create and manage instances. Moreover, it discussed monitoring portal and portlets operations, dynamic data source (database read-writer), and database sharding. Then it introduced portal administration which doesn't only allow users with permissions to manage users, organizations, user groups, and roles, but also does it show portal settings information, password policies, and monitors users' activities. It also addressed how to build clustering environment, how to backup data and to migrate data, and how to speed up the portal. In addition, it discussed full integration with Alfresco by web services, RESTful services like OpenSearch, and moreover, CMIS. Furthermore, it introduced full integration of LDAP, SSO CAS, Liferay and Alfresco. Finally, it discussed Ad server OpenX integration. In this chapter, we have learned how to:

- Manage servers and portal instances.
- Use dynamic data source called database read-writer and database sharding.
- Use password policies, update portal settings, and monitor users' activities.
- Build clustering environment and run the portal in a cloud computing environment.
- Backup data and migrate data, and speed up the portal — performance tuning.
- Integrate with Alfresco, SSO CAS, and LDAP, and ad server OpenX.

As you can see, Liferay is a good solution especially for intranet usage. The main roadmap will cover more third party integrations and more powerful frameworks available in plugins SDK.

Index

home URL 605
Nested Portlets portlet 470
Netvibes, widget
  about 581
  mash-up 583
  setup 581, 582
  working 581
nodes, Wikis
  adding 212-214
  deleting 214
  editing 214
  managing 212
  pages, importing 215
  RSS feeds, viewing 214
  subscribing 224
ntlm.auth.enabled property 137

O

ontology
  about 185
  using, for tag merge 199
OpenOffice
  configuring 241, 242
  documents, converting 241, 242
  integrating 241
  settings 242, 243
openoffice.cache.enabled property 242
openoffice.server.enabled property 242
OpenSearch
  about 540
  elements 540
  specifications 540, 541
OpenSearch, in plugins
  about 534
  CMIS 536
  RESTful services 535, 536
  web services 535
  working 534
Open-Search standard 285
OpenX 640
OpenX integration
  about 639, 640
  Ad Manager, installing 640
  Ad Services 643
  Ad Viewer portlet 642
  AMIS 645

options 639, 640
  RESTful services 645
  web services 645
Orbeon Forms
  about 250
  creating 251
  working 251
  XForm 250
organization
  about 33, 94
  child organization, adding 97, 98
  deleting 100
  editing 99, 100
  effective use 102
  managing 97-102
  community, differentiating 354-356
  searching 98
  settings 107
  shared global 111
  top-level organization, adding 96
  user, assigning 101
  viewing 98
organization administration tool 107
organization settings
  about 107
  assignment related properties, overriding
    109
  membership related properties, overriding
    109
  organization forms 108
  organization types 107, 108
ORM (Object-Relational Mapping) 549

P

pages
  adding 40
  building 40
  Dock bar menu, items 39, 40
  layout templates, changing 43
  portal pages, setting up 44
  portlets, adding 42
  portlets, removing 42
  private page 40
  public page 40
  removing 41

Thank you for buying
Liferay Portal 6 Enterprise Intranets

About Packt Publishing

Packt, pronounced 'packed', published its first book "*Mastering phpMyAdmin for Effective MySQL Management*" in April 2004 and subsequently continued to specialize in publishing highly focused books on specific technologies and solutions.

Our books and publications share the experiences of your fellow IT professionals in adapting and customizing today's systems, applications, and frameworks. Our solution based books give you the knowledge and power to customize the software and technologies you're using to get the job done. Packt books are more specific and less general than the IT books you have seen in the past. Our unique business model allows us to bring you more focused information, giving you more of what you need to know, and less of what you don't.

Packt is a modern, yet unique publishing company, which focuses on producing quality, cutting-edge books for communities of developers, administrators, and newbies alike. For more information, please visit our website: www.packtpub.com.

About Packt Open Source

In 2010, Packt launched two new brands, Packt Open Source and Packt Enterprise, in order to continue its focus on specialization. This book is part of the Packt Open Source brand, home to books published on software built around Open Source licences, and offering information to anybody from advanced developers to budding web designers. The Open Source brand also runs Packt's Open Source Royalty Scheme, by which Packt gives a royalty to each Open Source project about whose software a book is sold.

Writing for Packt

We welcome all inquiries from people who are interested in authoring. Book proposals should be sent to author@packtpub.com. If your book idea is still at an early stage and you would like to discuss it first before writing a formal book proposal, contact us; one of our commissioning editors will get in touch with you.

We're not just looking for published authors; if you have strong technical skills but no writing experience, our experienced editors can help you develop a writing career, or simply get some additional reward for your expertise.

Liferay Portal Enterprise Intranets

ISBN: 978-1-847192-72-1   Paperback: 408 pages

A practical guide to building a complete corporate intranet with Liferay

1. Install, set up, and use a corporate intranet with Liferay—a complete guide

2. Discussions, document management, collaboration, blogs, and more

3. Clear, step-by-step instructions, practical examples, and straightforward explanation

Drupal: Creating Blogs, Forums, Portals, and Community Websites

ISBN: 978-1-904811-80-0   Paperback: 284 pages

How to setup, configure and customise this powerful PHP/MySQL based Open Source CMS

1. Install, configure, administer, maintain and extend Drupal.

2. Control access with users, roles and permissions

3. Structure your content using Drupal's powerful CMS features

4. Includes coverage of release 4.7

Please check **www.PacktPub.com** for information on our titles

LaVergne, TN USA
16 August 2010
193497LV00003B/65/P